Introduction to Networking with Network+

Timothy Pintello

WILEY

Credits

VP & PUBLISHER	Don Fowley
EXECUTIVE EDITOR	John Kane
EDITOR	Bryan Gambrel
DIRECTOR OF SALES	Mitchell Beaton
EXECUTIVE MARKETING MANAGER	Chris Ruel
EDITORIAL PROGRAM ASSISTANT	Jennifer Lartz
SENIOR PRODUCTION & MANUFACTURING MANAGER	Janis Soo
ASSOCIATE PRODUCTION MANAGER	Joel Balbin
ASSISTANT MARKETING MANAGER	Debbie Martin
CREATIVE DIRECTOR	Harry Nolan
COVER DESIGNER	Jim O'Shea
TECHNOLOGY AND MEDIA	Tom Kulesa/Wendy Ashenberg
COVER PHOTO	Arthur Kwiatkowski /Getty Images, Inc

This book was set in Garamond by Aptara®, Inc. and printed and bound by Bind-Rite Robbinsville. The cover was printed by Bind-Rite Robbinsville.

ISBN 9780470487327

Printed in the United States of America

10 9 8 7 6 5 4 3 2 1

Welcome to *Introduction to Networking with Network+*. Wiley aims produce a series of textbooks that deliver compelling and innovative teaching solutions to instructors and superior learning experiences for students. Crafted by a publisher known worldwide for the pedagogical quality of its products, these textbooks maximize skills transfer in minimum time. Students are challenged to reach their potential by using their new technical skills as highly productive members of the workforce.

■ The Wiley Program

Introduction to Networking with Network+ includes a complete program for instructors and institutions to prepare and deliver a fundamentals of networking course and prepare students for CompTIA's Network+ certification exam. We recognize that, because of the rapid pace of change in networking technology and changes in the CompTIA Network+ curriculum, there is an ongoing set of needs beyond classroom instruction tools for an instructor to be ready to teach the course. Our program endeavors to provide solutions for all these needs in a systematic manner in order to ensure a successful and rewarding course experience for both instructor and student—technical and curriculum training for instructor readiness with new software releases; the software itself for student use at home for building hands-on skills, assessment, and validation of skill development; and a great set of tools for delivering instruction in the classroom and lab. All are important to the smooth delivery of an interesting introduction to networking course, and all are provided with the Wiley technology program. We think about the model below as a gauge for ensuring that we completely support you in your goal of teaching a great course. As you evaluate your instructional materials options, you may wish to use the model for comparison purposes with available products.

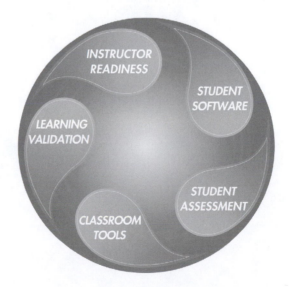

■ Pedagogical Features

Introduction to Networking with Network+ is designed to cover all the learning objectives for the Network+ exam, which is referred to as its "exam objectives." The Network+ exam objectives are highlighted throughout the textbook. Many pedagogical features have been developed specifically for our Wiley information technology titles.

Presenting the extensive procedural information and technical concepts woven throughout the textbook raises challenges for the student and instructor alike. The Illustrated Book Tour that follows provides a guide to the rich features available with Introduction to Networking with Network+. Following is a list of key features in each lesson designed to prepare students for success on the certification exams and in the workplace:

- Each lesson begins with an **Exam Objective Matrix**. More than a standard list of learning objectives, the Exam Objective Matrix correlates each software skill covered in the lesson to the specific Network+ exam objective.

- **Illustrations:** Screen images provide visual feedback as students work through the exercises. The images reinforce key concepts, provide visual clues about the steps, and allow students to check their progress.

- **Key Terms:** Important technical vocabulary is listed at the beginning of the lesson. When these terms are first used later in the lesson, they appear in bold italic type and are defined.

- Engaging point-of-use **Reader aids**, located throughout the lessons, tell students why this topic is relevant (*The Bottom Line*), provide students with helpful hints (*Take Note*), or show alternate ways to accomplish tasks (*Another Way*). Reader aids also provide additional relevant or background information that adds value to the lesson.

- **Certification Ready** features throughout the text signal students where a specific certification objective is covered. They provide students with a chance to check their understanding of that particular Network+ exam objective and, if necessary, review the section of the lesson where it is covered.

- **Knowledge Assessments** provide progressively more challenging lesson-ending activities, including practice exercises and case scenarios.

- A **Lab Manual** is integrated with this textbook. The Lab Manual contains hands-on lab work corresponding to each of the lessons within the textbook. Numbered steps give detailed, step-by-step instructions to help students learn networking. The labs are constructed using real-world scenarios to mimic the tasks students will see in the workplace.

■ Lesson Features

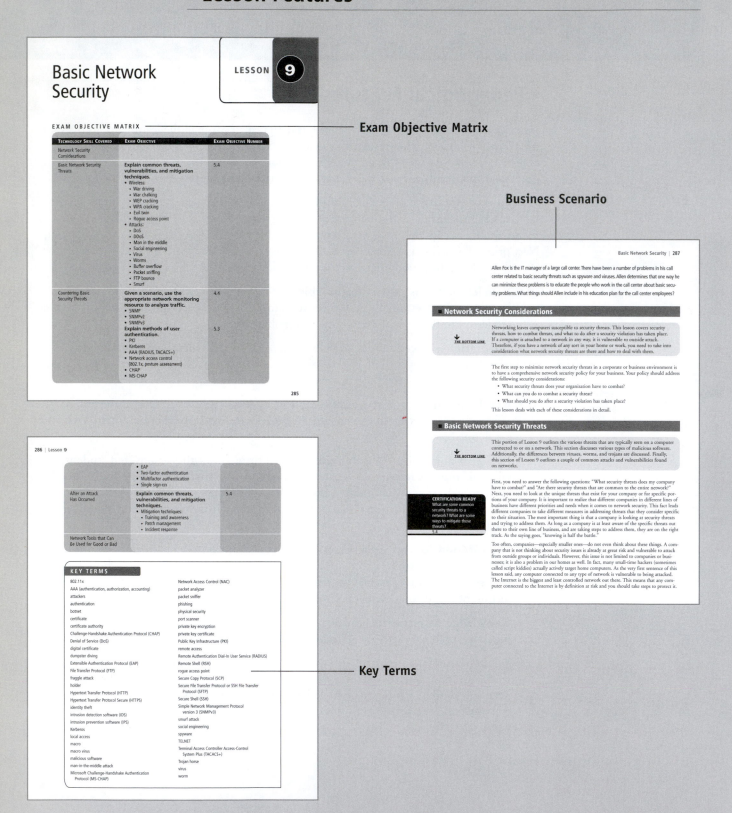

Exam Objective Matrix

Business Scenario

Key Terms

228 | Lesson 7

also has to be replaced. This has resulted in a slow adoption of this technology. In order for 10GBase-T to be used effectively with a range of up to 100 meters in a LAN environment, CAT 6A wiring needs to be in place. Standard CAT 6 can work in some situations, but it is not able to achieve the full 100-meter range that CAT 6A can achieve.

40/100 GIGABIT ETHERNET

40 Gigabit and 100 Gigabit Ethernet are the latest Ethernet standards available. Both are defined under the IEEE 802.3ba standard that was released in June 2010. 40/100 Gigabit Ethernet is full-duplex just like 10 Gigabit Ethernet and is intended to be used with multi-mode fiber, single-mode fiber, and copper cabling. 100 Gigabit Ethernet is also intended to have a range of up to 40 km using single-mode fiber. 40/100 Gigabit Ethernet also does not support CSMA/CD just like the previously discussed 10 Gigabit Ethernet. Finally 40/100 Gigabit Ethernet is intended as a bridge technology between current Ethernet standards and an eventual Terabit Ethernet standard that has not been developed yet.

■ **Other LAN Concepts**

↓ **THE BOTTOM LINE**

In this portion of Lesson 7, the basic LAN concepts of broadcasting, collision, bonding, speed, and distance are discussed. This section of Lesson 7 also explains how distance needs to be taken into account when designing a new network. Additionally, a few concepts related to networking and particularly to LANs are discussed.

— **Bottom Line**

Broadcast

CERTIFICATION READY
What are broadcasts? How are they used in networking? How does this relate to Ethernet?
3.7

In its simplest terms, a ***broadcast*** is where a computer sends data across a network by sending the data frame containing the data to all computers directly connected to it on a local network. In ***broadcast networking***, broadcasts, as described here, are used to send data across a local network. Ethernet is a broadcast-based network technology.

In the case of Ethernet, when a computer on a local network wishes to send data to another computer on the local network, it creates a data frame. This data frame contains the data that a computer needs to send across the network as well as its own physical address and the physical address of the computer for which the data frame is intended. The sending computer then releases the prepared data frame to all the computers on the local network. The computers on the local network listen to every data frame that comes by and read their physical destination addresses. If the physical destination is the same as that of the computer looking at it, the computer retrieves the data frame and processes it. If the destination physical address does not match that of the computer looking at it, the data frame is ignored and not opened.

COLLISION

CERTIFICATION READY
What is a collision? When do collisions occur?
3.7

A ***collision*** is where two different data frames from two different computers interfere with each other because they were released onto the network at the same time. The previously discussed broadcast-based networking technologies create the circumstances that allow collisions to take place. Because a data frame is sent to all the computers on a local network segment, if any two computers on that segment send data at the same time, a collision is inevitable.

Collisions are inevitable because every data frame sent out by one computer is going to every other computer on the network. Sooner or later the two data frames that were released at the same time will collide. CSMA/CD and CSMA/CA were developed so that a network would be able to do two things: (1) limit the number of collisions that take place on a network and (2) so the network and the computers on it would know how to recover when a collision did take place.

— **Screen Images**

442 | Lesson 12

Figure 12-22
Cable certifier

TIME-DOMAIN REFLECTOMETER (TDR)

The main use for ***Time-Domain Reflectometers (TDRs)*** is to test cables that are in place. A TDR is not only sonar for copper cables and other connections. When you connect a TDR to a metal cable it will send an electrical pulse down the wire. The response back tells the TDR if there is a fault in the wiring somewhere and exactly how far down the cable the fault is located if there is one. TDRs can also be used in metal circuit boards and can tell where faults may be in the circuit board. Some cable certifiers like the one shown in Figure 12-22 have TDR capabilities built into them. Figure 12-23 shows a TDR.

Figure 12-23
Time-Domain Reflectometer (TDR)

CERTIFICATION READY
What are TDRs and OTDRs? How are they related? How are they different?
4.2

OPTICAL TIME-DOMAIN REFLECTOMETER (OTDR)

An ***Optical Time-Domain Reflectometer (OTDR)*** is basically a TDR for fiber-optic cables. It works the same way as a TDR, except that it is designed for fiber-optic cable instead of copper cables. The cable certifier shown in Figure 12-22 also has OTDR capabilities.

Media | 57

Figure 3-9
Shielded twisted-pair cable showing its shielding

CERTIFICATION READY
What are STP cables? How do they differ from UTP cables?
3.1

CERTIFICATION READY
What is coaxial cable? What applications was it used in during the past? Where are you most likely to find coaxial cable today? What are the two most commonly used types of coaxial cable?
3.1

Coaxial

Coaxial cable, referred to as *coax*, contains a center conductor made of copper that is surrounded by a plastic jacket. The plastic jacket then has a braided shield over it. A plastic such as PVC or Teflon covers this metal shield. The Teflon-type covering is frequently referred to as a plenum-rated coating. This coating is expensive; however, it is often mandated by local or municipal fire code when cable is hidden in walls and ceilings. Many municipalities require these coatings because if ***plenum-rated cable*** is used in a building that catches fire, it will not release toxic gases. Non-plenum-rated cables *do* release toxic gases when they are burned. Plenum rating applies to all types of cabling, including UTP and STP cables, and is an approved replacement for all other compositions of cable sheathing and insulation. There is more about plenum and non-plenum cabling later in this lesson.

— **Take Note Reader Aid**

Table 3-1 lists some specifications for the different types of coaxial cables. You should note, however, that we tend to use only RG-59 and RG-6 in modern day situations.

RG Rating	Popular Name	Ethernet Implementation	Type of Cable
RG-58 U	N/A	None	Solid copper
RG-58 A/U	Thinnet	10Base-2	Stranded copper
RG-8	Thicknet	10Base-5	Solid copper
RG-59	Cable television Low cost, short distance	N/A	Solid copper
RG-6	Cable television, cable modems Longer distances than RG-59; some power implementations	N/A	Solid copper
RG-62	ARCnet (obsolete)	N/A	Solid/stranded copper

Table 3-1
Coaxial Cable Specifications

**Certification
Ready Alert**

**Cross Reference
Reader Aid**

**More Information
Reader Aid**

**Easy-to-Read
Tables**

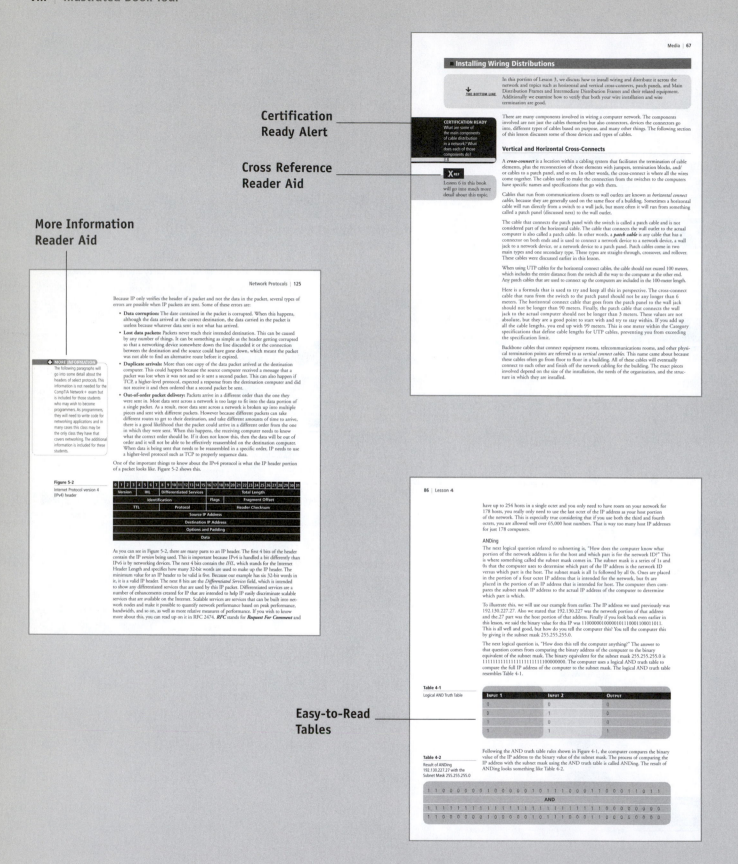

Summary Skill Matrix

Knowledge Assessment Questions

Lab Exercises

Case Scenarios

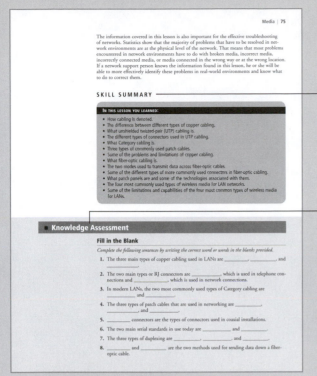

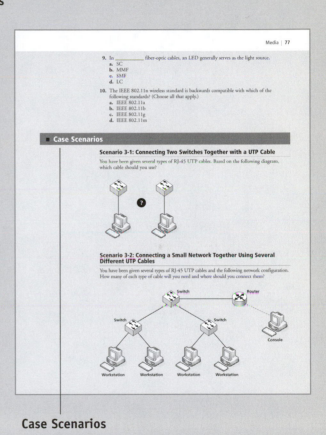

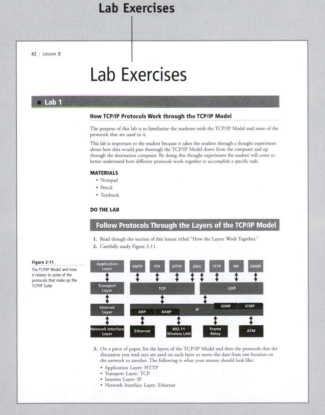

www.wiley.com/college/ or
call the Toll-Free Number: 1+(888) 764-7001 (U.S. & Canada only)

Conventions and Features Used in This Book

This book uses particular fonts, symbols, and heading conventions to highlight important information or to call your attention to special steps. For more information about the features in each lesson, refer to the Illustrated Book Tour section.

CONVENTION	MEANING
↓ **THE BOTTOM LINE**	This feature provides a brief summary of the material to be covered in the section that follows.
CERTIFICATION READY	This feature signals the point in the text where a specific certification objective is covered. It provides you with a chance to check your understanding of that particular exam objective and, if necessary, review the section of the lesson where it is covered.
TAKE NOTE*	Reader aids appear in shaded boxes found in your text. *Take Note* provides helpful hints related to particular tasks or topics.
X REF	These notes provide pointers to information discussed elsewhere in the textbook or describe interesting features of networking that are not directly addressed in the current topic or exercise.
A ***shared printer*** can be used by many individuals on a network.	Key terms appear in bold italic on first appearance.

Instructor Support Program

Introduction to Networking with Network+ is accompanied by a rich array of resources to form a pedagogically cohesive package. These resources provide all the materials instructors need to deploy and deliver their courses:

- Perhaps the most valuable resource for teaching this course is the software used in the course lab work. **DreamSpark Premium** is designed to provide the easiest and most inexpensive developer tools, products, and technologies available to faculty and students in labs, classrooms, and on student PCs. A free 3-year membership to the DreamSpark Premium is available to qualified textbook adopters.

  Resources available online for download include:

- The **Instructor's Guide** contains solutions to all the textbook exercises as well as chapter summaries and lecture notes. The Instructor's Guide and Syllabi for various term lengths are available from the Book Companion site (www.wiley.com/college/).

- The **Test Bank** contains hundreds of questions organized by lesson in multiple-choice, true-false, short answer, and essay formats and is available to download from the Instructor's Book Companion site (www.wiley.com/college/). A complete answer key is provided.

- Complete **PowerPoint Presentations and Images** are available on the Instructor's Book Companion site (www.wiley.com/college/) to enhance classroom presentations. Tailored to the text's topical coverage and Skills Matrix, these presentations are designed to convey key networking concepts addressed in the text.

  All figures from the text are on the Instructor's Book Companion site (www.wiley.com/ college/). You can incorporate them into your PowerPoint presentations or create your own overhead transparencies and handouts.

  By using these visuals in class discussions, you can help focus students' attention on key elements of the products being used and help them understand how to use them effectively in the workplace.

- When it comes to improving the classroom experience, there is no better source of ideas and inspiration than your fellow colleagues. The **Wiley Faculty Network** connects teachers with technology, facilitates the exchange of best practices, and helps to enhance instructional efficiency and effectiveness. Faculty Network activities include technology training and tutorials, virtual seminars, peer-to-peer exchanges of experiences and ideas, personal consulting, and sharing of resources. For details visit www.WhereFacultyConnect.com.

DREAMSPARK PREMIUM—FREE 3-YEAR MEMBERSHIP AVAILABLE TO QUALIFIED ADOPTERS!

DreamSpark Premium is designed to provide the easiest and most inexpensive way for universities to make the latest Microsoft developer tools, products, and technologies available in labs, classrooms, and on student PCs. DreamSpark Premium is an annual membership program for departments teaching Science, Technology, Engineering, and Mathematics (STEM) courses. The membership provides a complete solution to keep academic labs, faculty, and students on the leading edge of technology.

Software available in the DreamSpark Premium program is provided at no charge to adopting departments through the Wiley and Microsoft publishing partnership.

Contact your Wiley rep for details.

For more information about the DreamSpark Premium program, go to:

www.dreamspark.com

■ Important Web Addresses and Phone Numbers

To locate the Wiley Higher Education Rep in your area, go to the following Web address and click on the "*Who's My Rep?*" link at the top of the page.

www.wiley.com/college

Or call the toll-free number: 1 + (888) 764-7001 (U.S. & Canada only).

Student Support Program

Book Companion Web Site (www.wiley.com/college/)

The students' book companion site includes any resources, exercise files, and Web links that will be used in conjunction with this course.

Wiley Desktop Editions

Wiley Desktop Editions are innovative, electronic versions of printed textbooks. Students buy the desktop version for 40% off the U.S. price of the printed text and get the added value of permanence and portability. Wiley Desktop Editions provide students with numerous additional benefits that are not available with other e-text solutions.

Wiley Desktop Editions are NOT subscriptions; students download the Wiley Desktop Edition to their computer desktops. Students own the content they buy to keep for as long as they want. Once a Wiley Desktop Edition is downloaded to the computer desktop, students have instant access to all of the content without being online. Students can also print the sections they prefer to read in hard copy. Students also have access to fully integrated resources within their Wiley Desktop Edition. From highlighting their e-text to taking and sharing notes, students can easily personalize their Wiley Desktop Edition as they are reading or following along in class.

Microsoft Software

As an adopter of this textbook, your school's department is eligible for a free three-year membership to the DreamSpark Premium program. Through DreamSpark Premium, students gain access to the full-version of various Microsoft software. See your Wiley rep for details.

Acknowledgments

We thank Jeff Riley and Box Twelve Communications for their diligent review and for providing invaluable feedback in the service of quality instructional materials.

Focus Group and Survey Participants

Finally, we thank the hundreds of instructors who participated in our focus groups and surveys to ensure that our Wiley information technology curriculum and textbook designs best met the needs of our customers.

Jean Aguilar, Mt. Hood Community College

Konrad Akens, Zane State College

Michael Albers, University of Memphis

Diana Anderson, Big Sandy Community & Technical College

Phyllis Anderson, Delaware County Community College

Judith Andrews, Feather River College

Damon Antos, American River College

Bridget Archer, Oakton Community College

Linda Arnold, Harrisburg Area Community College–Lebanon Campus

Neha Arya, Fullerton College

Mohammad Bajwa, Katharine Gibbs School–New York

Virginia Baker, University of Alaska Fairbanks

Carla Bannick, Pima Community College

Rita Barkley, Northeast Alabama Community College

Elsa Barr, Central Community College–Hastings

Ronald W. Barry, Ventura County Community College District

Elizabeth Bastedo, Central Carolina Technical College

Karen Baston, Waubonsee Community College

Karen Bean, Blinn College

Scott Beckstrand, Community College of Southern Nevada

Paulette Bell, Santa Rosa Junior College

Liz Bennett, Southeast Technical Institute

Nancy Bermea, Olympic College

Lucy Betz, Milwaukee Area Technical College

Meral Binbasioglu, Hofstra University

Catherine Binder, Strayer University & Katharine Gibbs School–Philadelphia

Terrel Blair, El Centro College

Ruth Blalock, Alamance Community College

Beverly Bohner, Reading Area Community College

Henry Bojack, Farmingdale State University

Matthew Bowie, Luna Community College

Julie Boyles, Portland Community College

Karen Brandt, College of the Albemarle

Stephen Brown, College of San Mateo

Jared Bruckner, Southern Adventist University

Pam Brune, Chattanooga State Technical Community College

Sue Buchholz, Georgia Perimeter College

Roberta Buczyna, Edison College

Angela Butler, Mississippi Gulf Coast Community College

Rebecca Byrd, Augusta Technical College

Kristen Callahan, Mercer County Community College

Judy Cameron, Spokane Community College

Dianne Campbell, Athens Technical College

Gena Casas, Florida Community College at Jacksonville

Jesus Castrejon, Latin Technologies

Gail Chambers, Southwest Tennessee Community College

Jacques Chansavang, Indiana University–Purdue University Fort Wayne

Nancy Chapko, Milwaukee Area Technical College

Rebecca Chavez, Yavapai College

Sanjiv Chopra, Thomas Nelson Community College

Greg Clements, Midland Lutheran College

Dayna Coker, Southwestern Oklahoma State University–Sayre Campus

Tamra Collins, Otero Junior College

Janet Conrey, Gavilan Community College

Carol Cornforth, West Virginia Northern Community College

Gary Cotton, American River College

Edie Cox, Chattahoochee Technical College

Rollie Cox, Madison Area Technical College

David Crawford, Northwestern Michigan College

J.K. Crowley, Victor Valley College

Rosalyn Culver, Washtenaw Community College

Sharon Custer, Huntington University

Sandra Daniels, New River Community College

Anila Das, Cedar Valley College

Brad Davis, Santa Rosa Junior College

Susan Davis, Green River Community College

Mark Dawdy, Lincoln Land Community College

Jennifer Day, Sinclair Community College

Carol Deane, Eastern Idaho Technical College

Julie DeBuhr, Lewis-Clark State College

Janis DeHaven, Central Community College

Drew Dekreon, University of Alaska–Anchorage

Joy DePover, Central Lakes College

Salli DiBartolo, Brevard Community College

Melissa Diegnau, Riverland Community College

Al Dillard, Lansdale School of Business

Marjorie Duffy, Cosumnes River College

Sarah Dunn, Southwest Tennessee Community College

Shahla Durany, Tarrant County College–South Campus

Kay Durden, University of Tennessee at Martin

Dineen Ebert, St. Louis Community College–Meramec

Donna Ehrhart, State University of New York–Brockport

Larry Elias, Montgomery County Community College

Glenda Elser, New Mexico State University at Alamogordo

Angela Evangelinos, Monroe County Community College

Angie Evans, Ivy Tech Community College of Indiana

Linda Farrington, Indian Hills Community College

Dana Fladhammer, Phoenix College

Richard Flores, Citrus College

Connie Fox, Community and Technical College at Institute of Technology West Virginia University

Wanda Freeman, Okefenokee Technical College

Brenda Freeman, Augusta Technical College

Susan Fry, Boise State University

Roger Fulk, Wright State University–Lake Campus

Sue Furnas, Collin County Community College District

Sandy Gabel, Vernon College

Laura Galvan, Fayetteville Technical Community College

Candace Garrod, Red Rocks Community College

Sherrie Geitgey, Northwest State Community College

Chris Gerig, Chattahoochee Technical College

Barb Gillespie, Cuyamaca College

Jessica Gilmore, Highline Community College

Pamela Gilmore, Reedley College

Debbie Glinert, Queensborough Community College

Steven Goldman, Polk Community College

Bettie Goodman, C.S. Mott Community College

Mike Grabill, Katharine Gibbs School–Philadelphia

Francis Green, Penn State University

Walter Griffin, Blinn College

Fillmore Guinn, Odessa College

Helen Haasch, Milwaukee Area Technical College

John Habal, Ventura College

Joy Haerens, Chaffey College

Norman Hahn, Thomas Nelson Community College

Kathy Hall, Alamance Community College

Teri Harbacheck, Boise State University

Linda Harper, Richland Community College

Maureen Harper, Indian Hills Community College

Steve Harris, Katharine Gibbs School–New York

Robyn Hart, Fresno City College

Darien Hartman, Boise State University

Gina Hatcher, Tacoma Community College

Winona T. Hatcher, Aiken Technical College

BJ Hathaway, Northeast Wisconsin Tech College

Cynthia Hauki, West Hills College–Coalinga

Mary L. Haynes, Wayne County Community College

Marcie Hawkins, Zane State College

Steve Hebrock, Ohio State University Agricultural Technical Institute

Sue Heistand, Iowa Central Community College

Heith Hennel, Valencia Community College

Donna Hendricks, South Arkansas Community College

Judy Hendrix, Dyersburg State Community College

Gloria Hensel, Matanuska-Susitna College University of Alaska Anchorage

Gwendolyn Hester, Richland College

Tammarra Holmes, Laramie County Community College

Dee Hobson, Richland College

Keith Hoell, Katharine Gibbs School–New York

Pashia Hogan, Northeast State Technical Community College

Susan Hoggard, Tulsa Community College

Kathleen Holliman, Wallace Community College Selma

Chastity Honchul, Brown Mackie College/Wright State University

Christie Hovey, Lincoln Land Community College

Peggy Hughes, Allegany College of Maryland

Sandra Hume, Chippewa Valley Technical College

John Hutson, Aims Community College

Celia Ing, Sacramento City College

Joan Ivey, Lanier Technical College

Barbara Jaffari, College of the Redwoods

Penny Jakes, University of Montana College of Technology

Eduardo Jaramillo, Peninsula College

Barbara Jauken, Southeast Community College

Susan Jennings, Stephen F. Austin State University

Leslie Jernberg, Eastern Idaho Technical College

Linda Johns, Georgia Perimeter College

Brent Johnson, Okefenokee Technical College

Mary Johnson, Mt. San Antonio College

Shirley Johnson, Trinidad State Junior College–Valley Campus

Sandra M. Jolley, Tarrant County College

Teresa Jolly, South Georgia Technical College

Dr. Deborah Jones, South Georgia Technical College

Margie Jones, Central Virginia Community College

Randall Jones, Marshall Community and Technical College

Diane Karlsbraaten, Lake Region State College

Teresa Keller, Ivy Tech Community College of Indiana

Charles Kemnitz, Pennsylvania College of Technology

Sandra Kinghorn, Ventura College

Bill Klein, Katharine Gibbs School–Philadelphia

Bea Knaapen, Fresno City College

Kit Kofoed, Western Wyoming Community College

Maria Kolatis, County College of Morris

Barry Kolb, Ocean County College

Karen Kuralt, University of Arkansas at Little Rock

Belva-Carole Lamb, Rogue Community College

Betty Lambert, Des Moines Area Community College

Anita Lande, Cabrillo College

Junnae Landry, Pratt Community College

Karen Lankisch, UC Clermont

David Lanzilla, Central Florida Community College

Nora Laredo, Cerritos Community College

Jennifer Larrabee, Chippewa Valley Technical College

Debra Larson, Idaho State University

Barb Lave, Portland Community College

Audrey Lawrence, Tidewater Community College

Deborah Layton, Eastern Oklahoma State College

Larry LeBlanc, Owen Graduate School–Vanderbilt University

Philip Lee, Nashville State Community College

Michael Lehrfeld, Brevard Community College

Vasant Limaye, Southwest Collegiate Institute for the Deaf – Howard College

Anne C. Lewis, Edgecombe Community College

Stephen Linkin, Houston Community College

Peggy Linston, Athens Technical College

Hugh Lofton, Moultrie Technical College

Donna Lohn, Lakeland Community College

Jackie Lou, Lake Tahoe Community College

Donna Love, Gaston College

Curt Lynch, Ozarks Technical Community College

Sheilah Lynn, Florida Community College–Jacksonville

Pat R. Lyon, Tomball College

Bill Madden, Bergen Community College

Heather Madden, Delaware Technical & Community College

Donna Madsen, Kirkwood Community College

Jane Maringer-Cantu, Gavilan College

Suzanne Marks, Bellevue Community College

Carol Martin, Louisiana State University–Alexandria

Cheryl Martucci, Diablo Valley College

Roberta Marvel, Eastern Wyoming College

Tom Mason, Brookdale Community College

Mindy Mass, Santa Barbara City College

Dixie Massaro, Irvine Valley College

Rebekah May, Ashland Community & Technical College

Emma Mays-Reynolds, Dyersburg State Community College

Timothy Mayes, Metropolitan State College of Denver

Reggie McCarthy, Central Lakes College

Matt McCaskill, Brevard Community College

Kevin McFarlane, Front Range Community College

Donna McGill, Yuba Community College

Terri McKeever, Ozarks Technical Community College

Patricia McMahon, South Suburban College

Sally McMillin, Katharine Gibbs School–Philadelphia

Charles McNerney, Bergen Community College

Lisa Mears, Palm Beach Community College

Imran Mehmood, ITT Technical Institute–King of Prussia Campus

Virginia Melvin, Southwest Tennessee Community College

Jeanne Mercer, Texas State Technical College

Denise Merrell, Jefferson Community & Technical College

Catherine Merrikin, Pearl River Community College

Diane D. Mickey, Northern Virginia Community College

Darrelyn Miller, Grays Harbor College

Sue Mitchell, Calhoun Community College

Jacquie Moldenhauer, Front Range Community College

Linda Motonaga, Los Angeles City College

Sam Mryyan, Allen County Community College

Cindy Murphy, Southeastern Community College

Ryan Murphy, Sinclair Community College

Sharon E. Nastav, Johnson County Community College

Christine Naylor, Kent State University Ashtabula

Haji Nazarian, Seattle Central Community College

Nancy Noe, Linn-Benton Community College

Jennie Noriega, San Joaquin Delta College

Linda Nutter, Peninsula College

Thomas Omerza, Middle Bucks Institute of Technology

Edith Orozco, St. Philip's College

Dona Orr, Boise State University

Joanne Osgood, Chaffey College

Janice Owens, Kishwaukee College

Tatyana Pashnyak, Bainbridge College

John Partacz, College of DuPage

Tim Paul, Montana State University–Great Falls

Joseph Perez, South Texas College

Mike Peterson, Chemeketa Community College

Dr. Karen R. Petitto, West Virginia Wesleyan College

Terry Pierce, Onandaga Community College

Ashlee Pieris, Raritan Valley Community College

Jamie Pinchot, Thiel College

Michelle Poertner, Northwestern Michigan College

Betty Posta, University of Toledo

Deborah Powell, West Central Technical College

Mark Pranger, Rogers State University

Carolyn Rainey, Southeast Missouri State University

Linda Raskovich, Hibbing Community College

Leslie Ratliff, Griffin Technical College

Mar-Sue Ratzke, Rio Hondo Community College

Roxy Reissen, Southeastern Community College

Silvio Reyes, Technical Career Institutes

Patricia Rishavy, Anoka Technical College

Jean Robbins, Southeast Technical Institute

Carol Roberts, Eastern Maine Community College and University of Maine

Teresa Roberts, Wilson Technical Community College

Vicki Robertson, Southwest Tennessee Community College

Betty Rogge, Ohio State Agricultural Technical Institute

Lynne Rusley, Missouri Southern State University

Claude Russo, Brevard Community College

Ginger Sabine, Northwestern Technical College

Steven Sachs, Los Angeles Valley College

Joanne Salas, Olympic College

Lloyd Sandmann, Pima Community College–Desert Vista Campus

Beverly Santillo, Georgia Perimeter College

Theresa Savarese, San Diego City College

Sharolyn Sayers, Milwaukee Area Technical College

Judith Scheeren, Westmoreland County Community College

Adolph Scheiwe, Joliet Junior College

Marilyn Schmid, Asheville-Buncombe Technical Community College

Janet Sebesy, Cuyahoga Community College

Phyllis T. Shafer, Brookdale Community College

Ralph Shafer, Truckee Meadows Community College

Anne Marie Shanley, County College of Morris

Shelia Shelton, Surry Community College

Merilyn Shepherd, Danville Area Community College

Susan Sinele, Aims Community College

Beth Sindt, Hawkeye Community College

Andrew Smith, Marian College

Brenda Smith, Southwest Tennessee Community College

Lynne Smith, State University of New York–Delhi

Rob Smith, Katharine Gibbs School–Philadelphia

Tonya Smith, Arkansas State University–Mountain Home

Del Spencer–Trinity Valley Community College

Jeri Spinner, Idaho State University

Eric Stadnik, Santa Rosa Junior College

Karen Stanton, Los Medanos College

Meg Stoner, Santa Rosa Junior College

Beverly Stowers, Ivy Tech Community College of Indiana

Marcia Stranix, Yuba College

Kim Styles, Tri-County Technical College

Sylvia Summers, Tacoma Community College

Beverly Swann, Delaware Technical & Community College

Ann Taff, Tulsa Community College

Mike Theiss, University of Wisconsin–Marathon Campus

Romy Thiele, Cañada College

Sharron Thompson, Portland Community College

Ingrid Thompson-Sellers, Georgia Perimeter College

Barbara Tietsort, University of Cincinnati–Raymond Walters College

Janine Tiffany, Reading Area Community College

Denise Tillery, University of Nevada Las Vegas

Susan Trebelhorn, Normandale Community College

Noel Trout, Santiago Canyon College

Cheryl Turgeon, Asnuntuck Community College

www.wiley.com/college/ *or*
call the Toll-Free Number: 1+(888) 764-7001 (U.S. & Canada only)

Steve Turner, Ventura College

Sylvia Unwin, Bellevue Community College

Lilly Vigil, Colorado Mountain College

Sabrina Vincent, College of the Mainland

Mary Vitrano, Palm Beach Community College

Brad Vogt, Northeast Community College

Cozell Wagner, Southeastern Community College

Carolyn Walker, Tri-County Technical College

Sherry Walker, Tulsa Community College

Qi Wang, Tacoma Community College

Betty Wanielista, Valencia Community College

Marge Warber, Lanier Technical College–Forsyth Campus

Marjorie Webster, Bergen Community College

Linda Wenn, Central Community College

Mark Westlund, Olympic College

Carolyn Whited, Roane State Community College

Winona Whited, Richland College

Jerry Wilkerson, Scott Community College

Joel Willenbring, Fullerton College

Barbara Williams, WITC Superior

Charlotte Williams, Jones County Junior College

Bonnie Willy, Ivy Tech Community College of Indiana

Diane Wilson, J. Sargeant Reynolds Community College

James Wolfe, Metropolitan Community College

Marjory Wooten, Lanier Technical College

Mark Yanko, Hocking College

Alexis Yusov, Pace University

Naeem Zaman, San Joaquin Delta College

Kathleen Zimmerman, Des Moines Area Community College

www.wiley.com/college/ *or*
call the Toll-Free Number: 1+(888) 764-7001 (U.S. & Canada only)

Brief Contents

Contents

www.wiley.com/college/ or
call the Toll-Free Number: 1+(888) 764-7001 (U.S. & Canada only)

Introduction to Networks

EXAM OBJECTIVE MATRIX

Technology Skill Covered	Exam Objective	Exam Objective Number
Basic Definitions	**Describe different network topologies.** • Peer-to-peer • Client-server	3.5
Basic Network Topologies	**Describe different network topologies.** • Point-to-point • Point-to-multipoint • Ring • Star • Mesh • Bus • Hybrid	3.5
Basic Network Configuration in Windows		

KEY TERMS

bus network topology

client/server network

Enterprise network

hybrid network topology

Internet

Internet Service Provider (ISP)

local area network (LAN)

logical topology

Media Access Unit (MAU)

mesh network topology

Metropolitan Area Network (MAN)

network topology

partial mesh network topology

peer-to-peer network

physical topology

point-to-multipoint network topology

point-to-point network topology

ring network topology

star network topology

User Account Control (UAC)

wide area network (WAN)

World Wide Web (WWW)

You work for the consulting firm Key's Computer Consulting, Ltd. The publishing firm Harbor Publishing, Inc. has contracted the consulting firm you work for and the assignment has been given to you to determine the best type of network to build for Harbor Publishing, Inc. What do you do? Where do you start? How do you go about determining the answers to these questions and many more? This lesson will get you started on finding some of those answers.

■ Basic Definitions

THE BOTTOM LINE

This section of Lesson 1 explains what a network is, looks at a brief history of computer networking, and defines some basic network terms.

The purpose of this lesson is to introduce you to some of the basic concepts related to computer networking. To do this, the first thing that needs to be discussed is what a network of computers is exactly. In the simplest terms, a computer network is a group of computers that are connected to each other and can communicate information back and forth between them.

A Brief History of Networking

The very first networks were humorously called sneaker nets. This term was used because the person who wanted to move data from one computer to another had to first copy the data to be moved to some sort of movable storage such as a floppy disk and then had to "put on his sneakers" and carry it over to the intended destination computer. As you can imagine, this was not the most efficient way to move data from one computer to another. This method also created some problems of its own, not the least of which was how to make sure all computers had the most recent copy of a set of data on it instead of an older copy. Obviously a different solution had to be worked out.

The first solution people thought of was to place all the information on a large central computer called a mainframe computer and connect different terminals, called dumb terminals, to this large mainframe computer. The dumb terminal was essentially a screen and a keyboard connected to the mainframe computer. The user accessed the data on the mainframe from one of the dumb terminals.

In parallel to this, academia and the military were working together to develop some method to connect these various mainframe computers to each other across the country and around the world. This work was spearheaded by an organization called ARPA, which stands for Advanced Research Projects Agency. This organization has now come to be known as DARPA or Defense Advanced Research Projects Agency. Work by this agency resulted in what we know of today as the *Internet*. That is right; the Internet was invented by the military.

For a long time, ARPANet, The network created by ARPA, and the mainframe computer connected to dumb terminals were the only networking game in town. However, advancements were taking place in other parts of the computer industry—the biggest of which was the development of the personal computer. By the mid 1980s, personal computers (PCs) had finally begun to make a significant impression on how work was done. Businesses realized it would be very useful to be able to connect PCs together in networks much like mainframes linked to dumb terminals. Novell and a few other companies spearheaded this effort. By the late 1980s, it was not unusual to find companies with a network of PCs in some parts of their business. However, instead of connecting dumb terminals to mainframes, PCs were linked to servers.

Probably the first general use high speed network that expanded beyond a single room or building ever constructed was built in July and August of 1989 by a small private liberal arts college called William Jennings Bryan College in Dayton, Tennessee. This college used Novell 286 software and ARCNet network cards to connect 4 dormitories, an administrative/academic building, an athletics building, and two other buildings elsewhere on campus together into one comprehensive network. The college allowed students who were interested to lease-to-own network-capable computers from the college. These students were then allowed to use these computers to connect to the network from their dorm rooms.

This network, called BryanNet, was configured as a token ring network. Token ring networks will be discussed later in this lesson. This network also had through put speeds of 2.5 mbps (megabits per second). This was considered very fast in 1989. The network used coaxial cable to connect between buildings and twisted pair wiring inside the various buildings.

The first major use the students put this network to was studying for art appreciation tests where they had to memorize various works of art and the artists who created them. The art appreciation teacher placed images of the pieces of art she wanted the students to memorize on the network so the students could study them from their dorms prior to the test. At test time, the teacher randomly chose some of the images for the students to identify.

ByranNet, and other early networks, used computers called servers as central storage areas where shared documents and other shared files were saved. Anybody who wanted access to a shared document or file got that document or file from the server, and when they were finished with it, they saved it back to the server complete with any changes they had made. Businesses had resolved the problem of how to make sure everyone was using the most recent copy of a document. Everybody simply used the same document that was stored somewhere on a server. Today, this is still a common use for networks, although additional capabilities have been added.

After this, things in the area of networking started progressing very quickly. The next thing businesses wanted was to be able to use the Internet just like universities and the military could. Later, individuals wanted the same access at home. Once people started getting access to the Internet at home, they wanted a more attractive way to view the information on the Internet. This was when the World Wide Web was invented.

The *World Wide Web (WWW)* is a service on the Internet that allows people to use special client software called a browser to view the content of different Internet sites in a more visually appealing manner. The initial development of the World Wide Web took place in the early 1990s. By the mid 1990s, the World Wide Web was established as a viable entity on the Internet.

One important point to understand is the difference between the Internet and the World Wide Web. Many people tend to think that the World Wide Web and the Internet are synonymous with each other. They are not. The World Wide Web and the Internet are two distinctly different things. The Internet is a hardware and software infrastructure composed of cables, routers, switches, servers, and other devices. All of these devices will be discussed in detail in later lessons. The World Wide Web, on the other hand is simply a service, or a software program, that runs on top of the infrastructure of the Internet. The World Wide Web uses the Internet infrastructure to support websites and to move data between websites and browsers. The World Wide Web is only one of many network services that use the Internet infrastructure to support it. A couple of other easily recognized services that use the Internet are e-mail and news groups. There are quite a few others as well that are not so well known.

Once the World Wide Web was developed, businesses started realizing what a great marketing tool this was and so more advanced ways of presenting data on various websites were developed. As websites became more complex, it began to take longer to download the content of websites so faster methods of accessing the World Wide Web were developed. These advances first made their way into businesses and finally into homes.

As the speed of network connections increased, so did the complexity of data that people wanted to download. Where people were once content with just text messages, they began to want color text messages. Next they wanted graphics added to their websites. Soon graphics were not enough and people began to want images and sound, then animated images and sound, and finally, movies. These different and more complex types of data forced networking technology to increase and become faster to meet the new demands. These changes worked their way from businesses into the homes of individuals, until we came to what we have today, ubiquitous access to pretty much any type of information you could want access to.

This book will help you understand how networking technology works. This book will also help you understand how the various networking technologies work together as a single unified whole. Hang on; it will be a fun ride.

Different Types of Networks

Data networks come in two major categories, with a third category sometimes being used to describe a network between the size of the first category and the second category. The two main categories are called *wide area networks* and *local area networks*. Based on the first letter or each word in their name, these networks are generally referred to as *WANs* and *LANs* respectively.

WAN AND MAN NETWORKS

A WAN is a very large network that can stretch across large geographical areas. The biggest WAN in existence is the Internet, however networks that connect several cities, states, nations, counties, and so on would also qualify as WANs. Many companies use WANs in offices or buildings in widely dispersed areas to keep all the facilities and employees of their company connected to each other. A WAN of this nature is sometimes called an *Enterprise network*.

Whereas a WAN can spread across very large geographic areas, LANs, as their name implies, are limited to a local area. LANs are usually limited to just one building, or at most, several buildings that are near one another. Sometimes LANs are limited to only certain rooms in a given building. The technologies used by LANs and WANs, while similar, are slightly different from each other. These similarities and differences will be discussed in more detail in later lessons.

TAKE NOTE*

The term MAN is falling out of usage and networks that exhibit the characteristics of MANs are often simply referred to as WANs or Enterprise Networks.

Networks that are larger than LANs, but are slightly too small to be considered WANs, are sometimes called *Metropolitan Area Networks (MANs)*. MANs are networks that are generally no more than about fifty kilometers across. MANs are used to link areas, from the size of a college campus up to the size of cities, together into a single data network that can be either privately owned by a company or publicly owned by a municipality. Some cities have set up MANs as public utilities so that local businesses and individuals may link computers and LANs together to share various network services provided by the city to individuals and companies that are linked to the MAN. MANs and WANs generally use the same technologies, although newer WAN technologies generally find their way into MANs before they spread out to the larger WANs. It is cheaper and easier to upgrade MANs than it is WANs, so MANs are upgraded more often.

CERTIFICATION READY
Can you explain the characteristics of a peer-to-peer network and a client/server network?
3.5

DIFFERENT TYPES OF LANS

LANs come in two major types. These types are peer-to-peer networks and client/server networks.

Peer-to-peer networks

In a *peer-to-peer network*, each computer in the network acts independently of all the other computers, but they can share data and resources such as printers with all the other computers in the network. Because each computer acts independently from the others, it is necessary to set up security and resource sharing on each computer separately. If you have five computers in a peer-to-peer network that are shared by five users, then you have to set up all five users on each computer. This makes it difficult to manage all the users because every time you need to make a change in a user's configuration or setup, you have to do it five different times. As you can see from this example, the more computers and/or users on a peer-to-peer network, the more difficult it is to manage that network.

Peer-to-peer networks are very easy to set up and work best when only a small number of computers and users are involved. Most network operating systems such as Windows XP, Windows Vista, Windows 7, MAC OS X, and Linux actually let you set up a peer-to-peer network simply by connecting several computers together with a hub or a switch. Once this is done, most of these network operating systems automatically find the other connected computers. This means that all the end user has to do is create additional users on each of the connected computers and decide what folders and/or printers and other resources they want to share on the network.

As stated previously, peer-to-peer networks work best with small numbers of computers. Microsoft operating systems do not allow more than 10 computers to be connected to the same resource in a peer-to-peer environment.

Peer-to-peer networks are actually quite common. If fact they may be more common than you realize. If a person has two or more computers connected to a switch or access point in his or her home in order to share Internet access, then that person is actually running peer-to-peer network. Home networks are the most common form of peer-to-peer networks.

Client/server networks

Client/server networks are a bit more complex and quite a bit more expensive than peer-to-peer networks. In a client/server network, one main computer called a server or domain controller handles network management. In this type of network, all the users and the resources they share are placed on one or more servers. Anytime a user wants to access the network or some resource on the network, that user's personal workstation has to first be authenticated or allowed on the network. Once the workstation has been authenticated, or allowed on the network, the workstation will receive an access token from the Domain Controller, which outlines what resources that workstation is allowed access to based on the user who logged on to it. After this, when the logged on user wants access to various resources on the network, the workstation compares the resource the user wants to the access token and only allows the user access to those resources on the network permitted to them based on the access token. Anytime a user asks for a resource they do not have permission to, they are declined access to that resource. All the information just discussed applies specifically to Windows-based networks. Networks based on other operating systems perform differently and grant or deny access to resources in ways that are specific to those operating systems.

Because a client/server network has a central sever that controls access to all the resources on the network, it is much easier to manage a client/server network than it is a peer-to-peer network. What this means in practical terms is that if you have 10 users on your network, instead of having to set up 10 users on 10 different computers like you would in a peer-to-peer network, you can set them up just one time on a central controlling server. After this, if you have to change a user's setup, all you need to do is go to the central controlling server and make the change. The change only has to be made in one place and you are done, unlike peer-to-peer networks where you have to do it in 10 different places.

Like everything else, there are some trade-offs for the convenience of using a client/server network. One of the biggest trade-offs is cost. In a client/server network, if you have 10 users that need to use 10 computers, you have to purchase 10 computers and connect them together with a hub or switch. This is fine; this is what you would have to do with a peer-to-peer network too. However, on top of the 10 workstations, you also have to purchase the server computer as well, which is generally a bit more powerful and therefore more expensive than a workstation. This means you would need 11 computers instead of just the 10 a peer-to-peer network would need. Besides this, you would have to buy a server operating system for the server. A standard workstation operating system from Microsoft cannot be used as a server operating system; a special, and more expensive, server operating system is required to set up a server using Microsoft software. This adds even more cost to the overall network.

A client/server network is often not a very cost-effective solution for just a small handful of computers on a network. For a small network, a peer-to-peer solution is all that is needed. However, if there are more than 10 computers that need to connect to and use the same network resources, then a client/server network is usually the best solution. In fact, when using Microsoft software, you must set up a client/server network if you have more than 10 computers because Microsoft hard codes its operating systems so that no more than 10 computers can be connected to the same resource simultaneously. With Microsoft operating systems, as soon as the 11th computer tries to connect to a resource on a workstation, the operating system denies access to that computer. Client/server networks are the most common type of LANs found in business today. Generally speaking, client/server networks are also the most cost-effective solution even for small businesses.

■ Basic Network Topologies

 THE BOTTOM LINE

In this section, you will learn what the term *network topology* means and how it is used in modern networks. The basic types of topologies available for a network are also discussed. Additionally, you will learn the difference between logical and physical topologies.

> **CERTIFICATION READY**
> Can you identify and explain common network topologies such as star, mesh, bus, ring, point-to-point, point-to-multipoint, and hybrid?
> 3.5

The term topology is used to refer to the shape of something. In this way, a topological map shows the shape of the land represented on the map. Computer networks also have shapes. The shape of a network is referred to as the network's topology. Networks can have both physical topologies and logical topologies. In the following sections, we discuss many of the basic shapes, or topologies, that networks can take.

Bus Topology

A *bus network topology* was one of the first networking topologies to be developed. Figure 1-1 illustrates what a basic network using the bus topology looks like.

Figure 1-1

Bus network topology

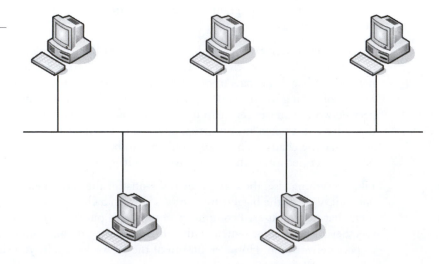

As you can see in Figure 1-1, in a bus network topology all the computers in the network are tied together by one main cable, called a backbone. This topology has the advantage of being easy to build and requiring only a minimal amount of cable. However, the bus topology does have drawbacks. The biggest drawback of this type of topology is that if the cable breaks at any point, the computers on the network lose the ability to communicate with each other. An additional drawback is that in the event of a cable break, it becomes very difficult to isolate the problem. The final main drawback is that only one signal can be sent down the main cable at a time. If more than one computer attempts to send a signal at the same time, the signals collide with each other and the data in both signals is lost. There are mechanisms put in place to deal with this last drawback and they are discussed in a later lesson.

Star Topology

The next topology is the *star network topology*. The star topology is the most commonly used networking topology today. Most networks that you are likely to come across use some variation on this topology. Figure 1-2 illustrates a basic star topology network.

Figure 1-2

Star network topology

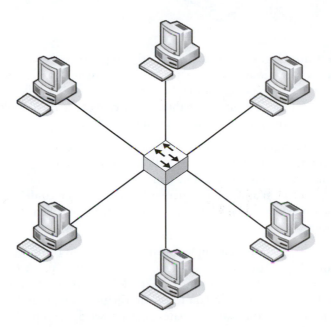

Looking at Figure 1-2, it is clear why this type of topology is called a star topology. In this topology, several workstations are connected together via one central device such as a hub or a switch. The symbol used for this central device in Figure 1-2 is the standard symbol for a switch. The main advantage of this type of topology is that if the cable to one of the attached computers goes bad, only that computer will be affected. Since only one computer on the network is affected, it becomes a rather easy matter to determine which computer has the problem. The one main drawback that this topology has is that if the central device that connects all the computers goes bad, the entire network will not work. However, this drawback is offset by the fact that if the entire network is down, then the problem is most likely at the central connecting device. This fact limits the places that you have to look to determine what the problem is. The only other slight drawback of this network topology is that it does require more cable than the bus topology and is therefore a bit more expensive.

Ring Topology

The *ring network topology*, like the bus topology, was one of the first networking topologies to be devised. Figure 1-3 illustrates this topology.

Figure 1-3

Ring network topology

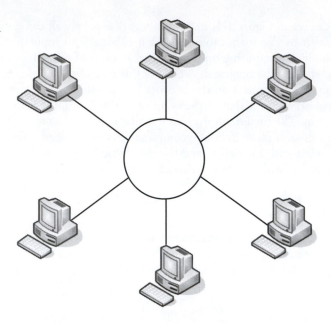

It is clear from Figure 1-3 that the term ring topology comes from the large ring that is used to connect the various computers together in a network configuration. The ring topology is similar to the bus topology in that both have a main cable, called a backbone, which is used to connect all the computers together. In the case of the ring topology that backbone cable is formed into a ring to connect all the computers together.

This ring configuration of the backbone has a couple of advantages over the bus topology. One advantage is that data can only flow in one direction, so data does not collide with data from another computer. The control mechanism for this is something called a token. The token used in a token ring network should not be confused with the access token discussed previously. These are two different types of tokens that are totally unrelated to each other.

In a token ring network a single token is passed from computer to computer. If a computer does not want to send data, it lets the token pass to the next computer. If a computer does want to transmit data, it takes control of the token and creates a data packet that is used to send data to the destination computer. Once the destination computer receives the data, it creates an acknowledgment packet, which it sends to the computer that originally sent the data. Once the computer that sent the data receives the acknowledgement packet, it releases the token to go on around the network looking for the next computer that wants to send data. This prevents the network from ever crashing because of too many computers trying to send data at the same time; however, if a number of computers do want to send data, the transmission of data can become very slow on this type of network.

The ring topology, because of its similarity to the bus topology, also shares one of the bus topology's major weaknesses. If the backbone is cut anywhere, it will bring down the whole network, which makes it difficult to locate where the break is. This drawback, coupled with the fact that the network becomes very slow when large amounts of data are being sent, has resulted in this topology, along with the bus topology, being largely replaced with the star topology.

Mesh Topology

The *mesh network topology* is most commonly used in a WAN environment. Figure 1-4 shows a diagram that illustrates what a mesh topology looks like.

Figure 1-4

Mesh network topology

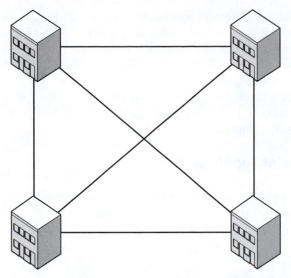

Because the mesh topology is primarily used as a WAN technology, buildings are used in the illustration rather than computers. As you can see in this figure, a mesh topology is quite a bit more complex than the previous topologies. In a full mesh topology, every computer or building is connected directly to every other computer or building in the network. This allows for a great deal of redundancy, but also gets to be very expensive.

One way to determine how many connections a mesh topology network requires is to use a simple formula. That formula is $n\,(n{-}1)\,/2$. In this formula, the n stands for the number of devices or buildings to be connected. To illustrate this, let us consider a four-device mesh network. Using this value, the formula would be filled in like this 4 (4–1) /2. The result of this equation is six. What this means is that a full mesh topology network with four computers in it would require six connections. By looking at Figure 1-4 and counting the total number of separate connections, you can see that the result of six connections is indeed correct.

As the number of computers grows, the number of connections required grows rather quickly as well. A full mesh network with five devices in it would require 10 separate connections, and a full mesh network with six devices would require 15 connections. As this illustrates, using a full mesh topology, despite its great redundancy, can get to be very expensive very fast.

It is because of the expense involved in a full mesh network that an alternative to the full mesh network was developed. This alternative is called a partial mesh network. An illustration of a partial mesh network can be seen in Figure 1-5.

Figure 1-5

Partial mesh network topology

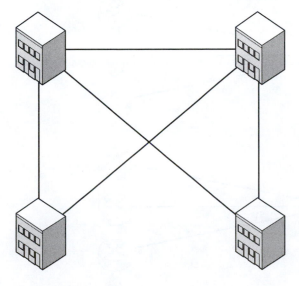

A *partial mesh network topology* has all the same advantages as a full mesh topology where redundancy is concerned; however, it also has the added benefit that it does not require as many connections. Since fewer connections are required, a partial mesh network costs less. For a partial mesh network to be truly redundant, each device on the network needs to be able to connect to at least two other devices. It is possible to have more than two connections per device, but a minimum of two connections per device are needed for the network to qualify as a mesh topology network. The largest partial mesh topology network in the world is the Internet.

Point-to-Point Topology

The *point-to-point network topology*, like the mesh topology, is primarily a WAN type topology. Figure 1-6 illustrates this point very well.

Figure 1-6

Point-to-point network topology

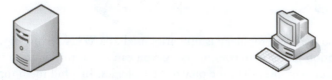

 X REF

More about remote access is discussed in Lesson 8.

Figure 1-6 clearly shows that in a point-to-point topology network, one, and only one, computer is directly connected to one other computer or device. This type of configuration is most commonly used when a computer outside the network needs to remotely connect to a computer or server inside a network. In this scenario, a point-to-point connection could be set up using some type of remote access technology to connect the computer outside the network to a computer on the inside.

Point-to-Multipoint Topology

The *point-to-multipoint network topology* is a variation on the point-to-point topology, but unlike the point-to-point topology, it is commonly used in both LANs and WANs. Aside from this last fact, the primary difference between point-to-point and point-to-multipoint topology is that in the point-to-multipoint topology, instead of having one device connect to just one other device, one device is connected to several other devices. Figure 1-7 illustrates this point.

Figure 1-7

Point-to-multipoint network topology

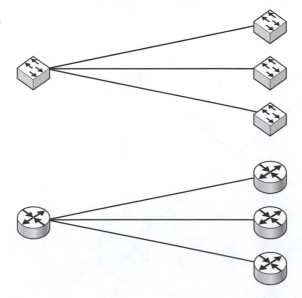

The point-to-multipoint network topology is very seldom used to connect one computer to multiple computers. It is much more likely that the point-to-multipoint topology will be used to connect one switch or router to multiple switches, routers, computers, or other network devices. Figure 1-7 shows a switch and a router connected to multiple switches or routers rather than a single computer connected to multiple computers.

The circle with two arrows pointing in and two arrows pointing out in Figure 1-7 is the standard symbol of a device called a router. This device is used to move data around in a WAN and to ensure that the most efficient route is used.

Routers and switches are discussed in greater detail in Lesson 6.

Hybrid Topology

The *hybrid network topology*, as its name implies, is a hybrid or combination of several network topologies. Most networks that you will come across will likely be some kind of hybrid network topology. Probably the most common is a star-bus hybrid topology. Figure 1-8 shows a hypothetical network that contains several network topologies combined into one hybrid network topology.

Figure 1-8

Hybrid network topologies

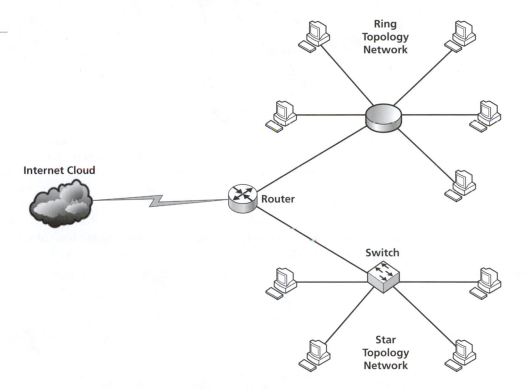

The two most prominent network topologies in Figure 1-8 are the ring topology at the top of the diagram and the star topology at the bottom. However, the network connection between the top ring, the middle router, and the bottom switch is an example of a bus topology. The connection between the router and the Internet cloud is an example of a point-to-point topology connection between the router and the *Internet Service Provider (ISP)* that provides access to the Internet for the entire network. The cloud symbol is a common networking symbol that is used to illustrate a network that you do not know the shape of.

There is one other way that a hybrid network can be formed. That way is by combining physical topologies with logical topologies. These two types of topologies are the topic of the next section of this lesson.

Physical vs. Logical Topologies

The best way to understand the difference between the physical topology of a network and the logical topology of a network is to think of it in this way. A network's *physical topology* refers to the shape of the wires. A network's *logical topology* refers to the shape of the path the data follows as it moves through the network. Figures 1-9 and 1-10 are two examples of networks that have one physical topology but a different logical topology.

Figure 1-9

Physical star topology using a logical bus topology

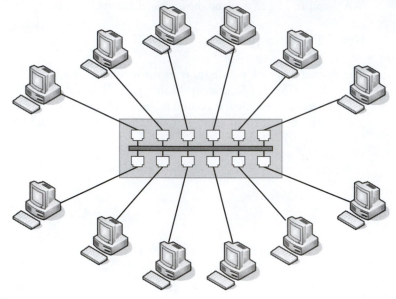

Figure 1-9 illustrates a network that is physically shaped like a star, but internally works like a bus. In this illustration, the large box with the ports on it represents a network device called a hub. This hub is used to connect all the computers together in a network. The thick line inside the hub illustrates how the hub works internally. Internally, this hub has the topology of a bus, but externally, the computers connected to the hub have the topology of a star—a star-bus network. Inside the hub, the data flows as if it were a bus network; that is the logical topology of the network. Externally the computers are hooked up to the hub in the shape of a physical star; that is the physical topology of the network.

Figure 1-10

Physical star topology using a logical ring topology

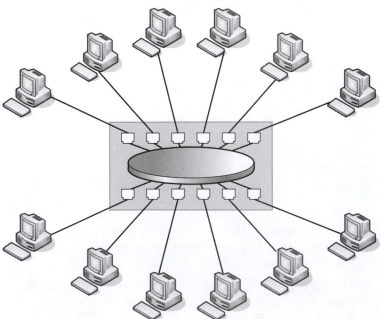

CERTIFICATION READY
Can you explain the difference between a physical topology and a logical topology?
3.5

Figure 1-10 is similar to Figure 1-9, with one main difference. Instead of the central hub having a bus topology on the inside, it has a ring topology on the inside. A device like this is sometimes called a Token Ring Hub or a Ring Hub. One of the official names of a device like this is a *MAU*, which stands for *Media Access Unit*. These type devices are only used in token ring networks. Figure 1-10 illustrates a star-ring network. The physical shape of the network is that of a star. However, the logical shape or topology is that of a ring. In this network, data flows from one computer to the other just like described in the earlier section on the ring; but when you look at this network on the outside, it looks like a star. Thus this network has a ring logical topology but a star physical topology. In short, it is a star-ring network.

■ Basic Network Configuration in Windows

THE BOTTOM LINE

In this section of Lesson 1, we present a basic introduction to configuring a Windows Vista machine to be used on a network.

Being able to configure a Windows Vista or Windows 7 computer is a very important skill to know and is used throughout this book during the labs. One thing to keep in mind when configuring Vista is that because of the high level of security Microsoft tries to include in Vista, there will be many extra steps that simply require you to click YES or OK or provide administrative passwords numerous times during the configuration process. To eliminate these warning dialog boxes, you will need to turn off the *User Account Control (UAC)* inside Windows Vista. This is less of an issue in Windows 7 and so there is no real reason to disable the UAC in Windows 7.

User Account Control is a feature of Windows Vista and Windows 7 that requires confirmation, and sometimes administrative passwords, in order to allow certain actions to be taken on a Windows Vista or Windows 7 computer, even when the person attempting the actions has administrative rights already. Many people turn this feature off in Windows Vista as they find it annoying. As mentioned earlier, Microsoft softened this quite a bit in Windows 7 and so it is not so much of an issue in that operating system.

Some people have questioned whether there is any utility to the UAC feature in Windows Vista and 7. Microsoft assures us that this feature is necessary for you to implement the highest level of security on your local computer. To a certain extent this is true because it makes things more difficult for malicious programs to make headway in compromising the Windows Vista and 7 operating systems. However, one thing that anyone who works with computers should keep in mind is that as soon as a technique to protect a computer comes out, there will always be someone else out there trying to bypass it.

If you are not sure of what you are doing and want to be warned anytime you are about to take an action that may have permanent consequences for your computer system, you may want to keep UAC turned on in Windows Vista. If you are sure of what you are doing and do not wish to see the pop-ups and warning every time you take actions that require administrative access, you may wish to turn UAC off. The choice is yours, and Vista can accommodate you in either circumstance.

To turn the UAC off, go into the control panel inside Vista. Once inside the control panel, double-click the Security icon to go to the Security Dialog box shown in Figure 1-11.

As you can see in Figure 1-11, the bottom menu option in the Security Dialog box is labeled "Other security settings." When this menu section is opened up, there are two settings that can be changed. One of those settings is the option to turn off User Access Control. Double-clicking on this option will allow you to turn off UAC and eliminate the pop-up screen messages and requests mentioned previously.

Figure 1-11

Windows Vista Security
Dialog box

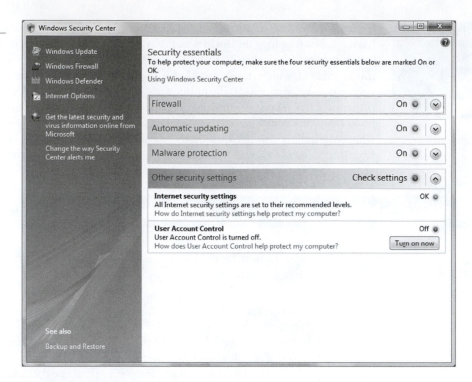

Now that the entire UAC issue is out of the way, it is time to discuss how to configure a Windows Vista or Windows 7 computer for network access. This topic is very detailed and will be covered often throughout this book. For now, we will simply address the basics of how to get into Vista's and 7's network configuration screens.

The key to configuring different network options is also found in the Windows Vista/7 control panel, specifically in the Network and Sharing Center applet. This is the place where all issues related to networking and sharing of files, folders, media, and so on are located. Figure 1-12 illustrates the dialog box that comes up when the Network and Sharing Center applet is double-clicked.

Figure 1-12

Windows Vista Network and
Sharing Center dialog box

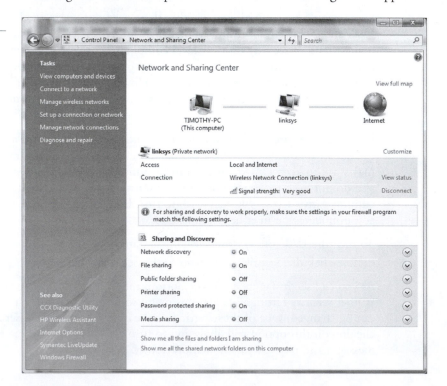

As you can see in Figure 1-12, there is a lot going on in this particular dialog box. In fact, there is actually a lot more going on in this dialog box than is apparent when you are first looking at it. Fortunately, one of the labs in this lesson deals with all the different items that can be found in this dialog box and how some of them can be used. However, the lab will use Windows 7 instead of Windows Vista because Windows 7 is more widely accepted in the corporate environment. The illustrations in the text here are from Windows Vista. I have chosen to use Windows Vista in the text and Windows 7 in the lab so that you can see both. Windows Vista and Windows 7 are quite similar in this area.

SKILL SUMMARY

IN THIS LESSON YOU LEARNED:

- A brief history of networking.
- The difference between the World Wide Web and the Internet.
- The difference between LANs, MANs, and WANs.
- What a peer-to-peer network is and some of its advantages and disadvantages.
- What a client/server network is and what its advantages and disadvantages are.
- Different types of network topologies and the advantages and disadvantages of each as well as how some of them are used.
- The difference between logical and physical topologies and some examples to help understand that difference.
- What the UAC is and how to disable it if you so desire.
- How to access the section of Vista that will allow you to configure different components of Vista's networking capabilities.

Knowledge Assessment

Fill in the Blank

Complete the following sentences by writing the correct word or words in the blanks provided.

1. The very first "computer networks" were jokingly referred to as _____.

2. The three main categories of networks are _____, _____, and _____.

3. A network that is limited to just one building or at most two or three buildings in close proximity is called a _____.

4. _____ networks are very common and are the type found in most homes that have networks.

5. A _____ network is a network that has one central server that controls access to it and is the type most commonly found in businesses.

6. Most modern LANs follow some form of the _____ topology.

7. When a network combines two or more types of network topologies in its structure, it is called a _____.

8. The physical shape of a network is referred to as the network's _____.

9. A network's _____ refers to the shape of the path that data takes as it flows through a network.

10. Microsoft's _____ is used to display warnings and ask for confirmation anytime a person wants to make some important change in Windows Vista that requires administrative access.

Multiple Choice

Circle the letter corresponding to the correct answer.

1. The infrastructure that the World Wide Web and other services reside on is called what?
   a. WAN
   b. Enterprise Network
   c. Internet
   d. E-mail

2. Services that use the Internet as their main support structure are which of the following?
   a. World Wide Web
   b. E-mail
   c. News groups
   d. All of the above

3. The organization that spearheaded the development of the Internet was which of the following?
   a. ARPA
   b. DARPA
   c. Novell
   d. Bubba's Computer Consulting, Ltd.

4. _____use technology similar to WANs but cover a smaller geographic area.
   a. LANs
   b. MANs
   c. Peer-to-peer networks
   d. Internet

5. Which of the following network topologies work best with 10 or fewer systems and users?
   a. Client/server networks
   b. LANs
   c. Enterprise Networks
   d. Peer-to-peer networks

6. Which of the following network topologies use a single main cable called a backbone? (Choose two.)
   a. Bus topology
   b. Star topology
   c. Mesh topology
   d. Ring topology

7. A ring topology network uses a _____ to control the flow of data on the network.
   a. MAU
   b. Token ring hub
   c. Token
   d. Data collisions

8. The most expensive network topology listed here is what?
   a. Sneaker net
   b. Star topology
   c. But topology
   d. Partial mesh

9. The shape of the path that data takes through a network is called its what?
   a. Local area network
   b. Logical topology
   c. Vulcan mindset
   d. Physical topology

10. In Windows Vista, where would you go to find the Network and Sharing Center dialog box?
    a. Control panel
    b. Security icon
    c. Other security settings
    d. Recycle bin

■ Case Scenario

Scenario 1-1: Building a Home Network

John wants to build a home network. He has three computers from which he would like to be able to access the Internet, but he only has one Internet connection coming into his house. Fortunately for John, his home is a relatively new home and has network jacks in every room with one central location where all the network jacks in his home come together at a central multiport jack. This location is also where John's Internet access comes into his home. What should John do to accomplish his goal?

Lab Exercises

■ Lab 1

Tour of a Working Client/Server LAN

The purpose of this lab is to familiarize the students with what a working local area network (LAN) looks like.

This lab is important to the student because the instructor can use the things seen during this tour in later lessons as a point of reference to help students understand different topics that will be discussed. If the student can visualize what the instructor is talking about, it will help their understanding and retention. This lab will provide a shared central point of reference for both the students and the instructor in later classroom discussions.

MATERIALS
- Notepad
- Pencil

DO THE LAB

In order to accomplish this lab, the instructor will need to arrange a tour with either a local business, or the IT department of the school at which the class is being taught. This tour needs to include the point where outside communications come into the business. The tour also needs to contain the location where the network is initially broken out into smaller sections. This section is usually called the main distribution frame. If the servers for the network are kept in a different location, this area needs to be seen too. If the site being toured is large enough to contain one or more intermediate distribution frames, one of these needs to be seen as well.

The tour needs to be led by someone who is knowledgeable about the network that is being toured. This person needs to identify all the equipment in the various locations viewed by the class and explain their function in the overall scheme of the network. The tour guide also should make a point of showing how the main distribution frame is connected to the intermediate distribution frame and how both of these areas are connected to the individual systems and rooms in the overall network. The tour guide should be prepared to answer any questions the students ask over the course of the tour.

The student should take notes during the tour. After the tour, the student should create a basic diagram of the high points of the network and how it all works together based on their notes and the information provided by the tour guide. Both the notes and the diagram should be turned in to the instructor as proof the student did the lab. The instructor should then return the notes and diagrams to the students so that they can be used as a reference point in later classes.

■ Lab 2

Configuring Network Related Components in Windows 7

The purpose of this lab is to familiarize the student with the tools used in Windows 7 to do basic network configuration. This is the lab that was referred to in the last section of this lesson.

This lab is important to the student because it familiarizes them with the mechanisms used in Windows 7 for configuring networks. This will help the student gain a better understanding of how Windows 7 works in regards to networking and will prepare them to configure Windows 7 in future labs.

MATERIALS

- A computer running Windows 7
- Connection to a functioning network
- Internet connectivity

Find and Open the Network and Sharing Center

1. Click on **Start** in the bottom left corner of the computer screen.
2. This will bring up the Start Menu.
3. Note the list of options down the right side of the menu. Write these down on a piece of paper.
4. Click on the option labeled **Control Panel**.
5. This brings up a Window similar to the one shown in Figure 1-13, click the down arrow located next to **View By:** at the top right side of the screen and choose the **Large Icons** option.

Figure 1-13

Windows 7 Control Panel

6. The icons in this Window are in alphabetic order. Each icon represents a program called an applet. Double-click the applet called **Network and Sharing Center**.
7. Double-clicking the Network and Sharing Center applet will bring up the Network and Sharing Center, which will look similar to the dialog box shown in Figure 1-14.

Figure 1-14

Windows 7 Network and
Sharing Applet

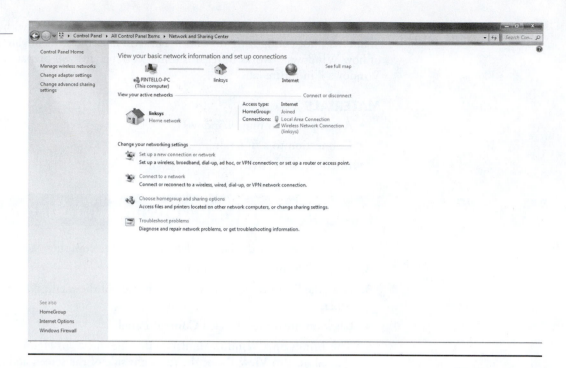

Familiarize Yourself with the Network and Sharing Center

1. The Network and Sharing Center has several different areas within it. At the top of the Network and Sharing Center are a few icons. The first icon should be labeled *This Computer* and should also contain the name of the local computer. Connected to this icon is another icon that shows some sort of network device or workgroup. Connected to this may be a third icon that represents the Internet or some other component of a larger network.

2. Click on the **computer icon**. Clicking this icon will show you what is located on the local computer, its drives, folders, and so on. This is the same information that can be obtained by double-clicking the Computer icon on the desktop. Close this dialog box.

3. Click the **second icon**. Clicking this icon will show you what is on the immediate network. When this icon is clicked, Windows 7 begins an inventory of the local network segment or workgroup your computer is on. Once this inventory is done, it will create a net dialog box that shows all the computers and other network devices in the immediate vicinity of your computer. Clicking on this icon will give you something similar to Figure 1-15. List the Name, Category, Workgroup, and Network Location for at least 3 devices on your network. Close this dialog box.

Figure 1-15

Windows 7 Network
dialog box

4. Click the **last icon** at the top of the Network and Sharing Center applet. If this icon is the Internet icon, it will take you to the default web browser for your computer. Write down the name of the application that came up. Close this application.

5. The lower section of the Network and Sharing Center has to do with setting up sharing different resources on your local computer. While there are several options down here, we will only look at a couple of them.

6. The first option on this lower list is labeled *Set up a new connection or network*. Click on this option. When you click on this option, it gives you a dialog box containing a list of connection wizards. Write down all the connection wizards available to you on a piece of paper. Close this dialog box.

7. Click on the second option labeled *Connect to a network*. This option brings up a list of all the networks that are currently available to you and gives you the option of connecting to one. This dialog box also tells you which network you are currently connected to. List on a piece of paper all the networks available to you and the one you are connected to. Close this dialog box.

8. To the left side of the Network and Sharing Center is a list of options than can be chosen. The options at the bottom of this section take you to different items related to networking that are not listed in the Network and Sharing Center. These items will vary depending on what software your local computer has and what the state of its networking capabilities are. The menu options at the top of this section are what we are currently interested in. Write down all the menu options listed on your computer from this upper area.

9. Locate the option labeled *Change Adapter Settings*. This brings up a very important dialog box that lists all the network connections available to you on your local computer. The dialog box should look similar to Figure 1-16 if your view options are set to *Detail*.

Figure 1-16

Windows 7 Network
Connections dialog box

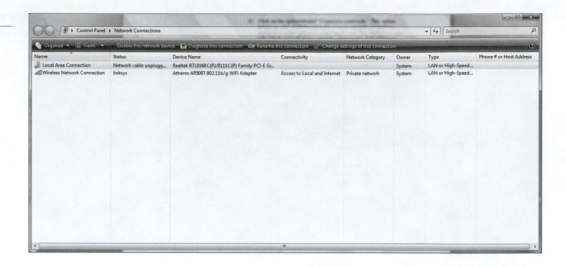

10. The *Network Connections* dialog box is of particular importance to us because it is one of the ways that we are able to get to the manual configuration menu for a specific network connection. Choose a network connection in this dialog box and double-click it. (Note: There may only be one connection in this dialog box.) Once you double-click the network connection of your choice you will get a dialog box similar to the one shown in Figure 1-17.

Figure 1-17

Windows 7 Local Area
Connection Status dialog box

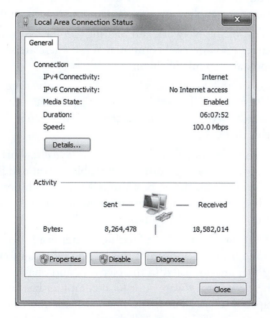

11. This dialog box shows the status of your connection and has several different buttons on it. The top button, the *Details* button, gives you detailed information about your NIC and connection. The buttons along the bottom are *Properties*, *Disable*, and *Diagnose*. The Disable button will disable the NIC. You can then re-enable it by clicking the button again, except that it will now be labeled *Enable*. The Diagnose button runs a basic diagnostic on the NIC to check it for any problems. The Properties button however is the one that we are interested in right now. This button will bring up the dialog box shown in Figure 1-18.

Figure 1-18

Windows 7 Local Area Connection Properties dialog box

12. This dialog box shows all the Clients, Services, and Protocols that are installed on this local area connection. The icon of a computer connected to a cable represents Clients, the icon of a computer sitting on top of a hand represents Services, and the icon of just a wire represents protocols. Protocols are basically different sets of rules that allow one computer to communicate to another or some other such thing. Protocols are covered in greater detail in Lesson 5. Write down on a piece of paper the Clients, Services, and Protocols running on your local computer.

13. Find the protocol labeled *Internet Protocol Version 4 (TCP/IPv4)*. Click on this protocol once so that it is highlighted. Now click on the dialog button labeled **Properties**. This will bring up a dialog box that looks like Figure 1-19.

14. This dialog box is where your computer's network addressing information is configured. Your local computer is probably set for "Obtain an IP Address Automatically." For now we will leave it there; however, in later labs it may become necessary to make changes in this area.

15. Click **Cancel** on the Internet Protocol Version 4 (TCP/IPv4) Properties dialog box.

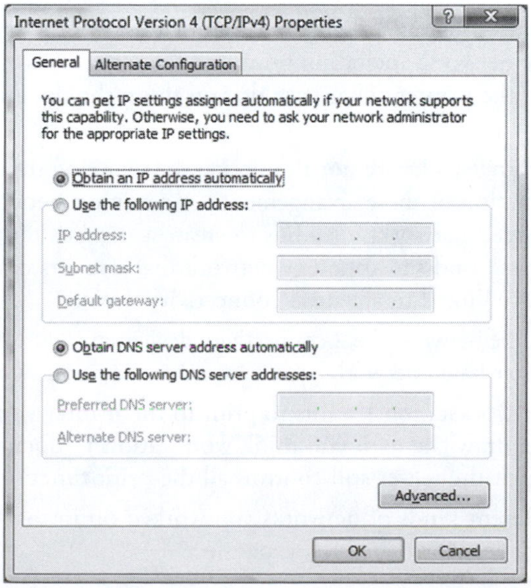

Figure 1-19

Windows Vista Internet Protocol Version 4 (TCP/IPv4) Properties dialog box

16. Click **Cancel** on the Local Area Connections Properties dialog box.

17. Close the Network Connections dialog box.

18. Close the Network and Sharing Center dialog box.

19. You are now finished with this lab. This lab has familiarized you with the Network and Sharing Center and some of the things that can be checked and configured in this location. In future labs, this applet will be used to help you configure your local computers to complete some of the other labs in this book.

■ Lab 3

Basic Diagramming of Star and Bus Topologies

During your career in networking, you will frequently need to interpret networks drawings, if not create them yourself. This lab will start you on doing some simple network diagrams.

Familiarizing Yourself with Star and Bus Topologies

1. Draw a basic bus topology with 4 computers attached to the backbone. Label the computers A, B, C, and D. (The book has an example of a bus topology in Lesson 1).

2. Imagine the user at computer A needs to open a file on computer D in a peer-to-peer fashion. What path do you think the data will follow from A to D and then from D to A? Add this path, as a dotted line, to your network diagram.

3. On the opposite side of your paper, using no more than half a page, draw a star-shaped topology with 4 computers attached to a central connectivity device. Label the workstations E, F, G, and H. (Note: At this point, none of these workstations are servers).

4. Imagine that the user at computer E wants to open a file that is on computer H's hard disk, in a peer-to-peer fashion. With a dotted line, draw the path you think data would take between these 2 computers.

5. Now add a printer and a server to your star topology network drawing. Make sure the printer is connected to the server and not directly to the network. With the addition of a server, you have changed the network from a peer-to-peer network to a client/server network. The printer has become a resource that all the workstation users can share.

6. Suppose the new server is configured to provide all necessary services to the entire star topology network, including print and file services. Now if computer G sends a document to the printer, what path do you think the document's data will take to the printer? Draw this path as a dotted line on your network.

7. Most modern networks are not simple star, bus, or ring topologies, instead, they are some combination of these arrangements. A common network design combines 2 or more star-shaped networks via a bus to create a star-bus topology. On the same sheet of paper, draw a second star topology network that consists of 3 workstations, labeled I, J, and K, that are linked to a central connectivity device.

8. Now draw a line between the 2 connectivity devices to indicate a bus-style connection between the star-based networks. You have now designed a hybrid star-bus topology network.

9. Suppose that workstation J wants to print to the printer you just added in step 5. Using a dotted line, draw the path you think workstation J's document will take to the printer. Remember that the server still controls all the print functions for that network.

10. Of the 3 different kinds of networks you worked on in this project, which one do you think would allow for the easiest expansion?

The OSI and TCP/IP Models

EXAM OBJECTIVE MATRIX

Technology Skill Covered	Exam Objective	Exam Objective Number
Introduction to the OSI Model	**Compare the layers of the OSI and TCP/IP models.** OSI model: • Layer 1—Physical • Layer 2—Data Link • Layer 3—Network • Layer 4—Transport • Layer 5—Session • Layer 6—Presentation • Layer 7—Application	1.1
	Classify how applications, devices, and protocols relate to the OSI model layers. • IP address • Frames • Packets • Cable	1.2
TCP/IP Model	**Compare the layers of the OSI and TCP/IP models.** TCP/IP model: • Network Interface Layer • Internet Layer • Transport Layer • Application Layer • (Also described as: Link Layer, Internet Layer, Transport Layer, Application Layer)	1.1
How the Layers Work Together		

KEY TERMS

Application layer	de-encapsulation	half-duplex
bits	duplex	header
compression	encapsulation	Internet layer
connectionless protocol	encryption	logical address
connection-oriented protocol	frame	Logical Link Control (LLC) sublayer
data	frame synchronization	Media Access Control (MAC) sublayer
Data Link layer	full-duplex	Network Interface layer

Network layer	Presentation layer	simplex
OSI Model	protocol	tailer
packet	protocol suite	TCP/IP Model
physical address	routing	translation
Physical layer	segment	Transport layer
port address	Session layer	

John works for XYZ Network Architects Consulting. One of his company's clients, ABC Software Wingdings has created a new application. They want John to determine how to program their new computer software to work on a network. John has to determine what needs to be done to make this happen.

■ Introduction to the OSI Model

↓ **THE BOTTOM LINE**

This section of Lesson 2 introduces the OSI Model and explains what it is. This section also examines each of the layers of the OSI Model and explains the functions that are carried out at each layer. This section also introduces the concept of encapsulation.

OSI stands for Open Systems Interconnection. This model was created by the International Standards Organization to describe the steps that data must go through in order to be transmitted across a data network. The OSI Model was never intended to *define* how data moves across networks; instead the OSI Model was intended to *describe* how data moved across networks. As such, the OSI Model is not a standard that all networking protocols must follow. In point of fact, the OSI Model was not even created until 1984, which is some years after TCP/IP, the most commonly used networking protocol, was first created.

CERTIFICATION READY
What are the 7 Layers of the OSI Model?
1.1

Since the OSI Model was not created to define how data flows through networks, why was it created? The *OSI Model* was created as a framework and reference model to explain how different networking technologies work together and interact. In this capacity, the OSI Model is an excellent place to start when you are trying to understand all the processes that are necessary for data to be moved around a data network.

What the OSI Model Looks Like

Figure 2-1 shows the various layers of the OSI Model and how they are organized in relation to each other. Each layer has specific functions it is responsible for and all the layers must work together in the correct order to move data around a network. The correct order of the layers from top to bottom is Application, Presentation, Session, Transport, Network, Data Link, and Physical.

Figure 2-1

The basic layers of the OSI Model

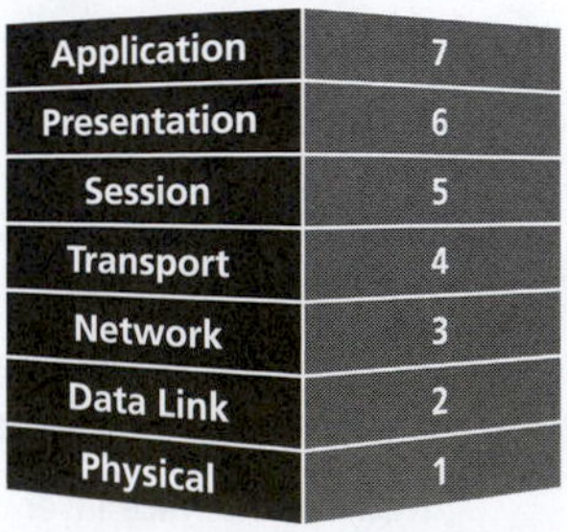

Application	7
Presentation	6
Session	5
Transport	4
Network	3
Data Link	2
Physical	1

There are many common mnemonics that people use to remember the correct order of the layers. To remember the order from top to bottom, the following mnemonic may help—**A**ll **P**eople **S**eem **T**o **N**eed **D**ata **P**rocessing. The first letter of each word in the mnemonic is the first letter of each layer of the OSI Model from top to bottom.

If you prefer to remember the OSI layers in the correct order from bottom to the top, a different mnemonic can be used—**P**lease **D**o **N**ot **T**hrow **S**ausage **P**izza **A**way.

Encapsulation

The next few sections of Lesson 2 discuss each of the layers of the OSI Model and the functions of each layer. However, before discussing the functions of the various layers of the OSI Model, the concept of encapsulation needs to be introduced.

In networking, *encapsulation* is the process of taking data from a previous layer of the OSI Model and carrying it forward into the next layer. The reverse of this process is called de-encapsulation. It is necessary to mention this process at this point because as data moves from one layer of the OSI Model to the next, different terms are used to describe it.

While data is in the top three layers of the OSI Model, the Application, Presentation, and Session layers, it is called *data*. When data enters the Transport layer, it then becomes known as a *segment*. As the segment is passed further down the OSI Model, to the Networking layer, the segment becomes known as a *packet*. Down in the Data Link layer, the packet is turned into a *frame*. Finally, when the frame reaches the bottom of the OSI Model and enters the Physical layer, it is converted into *bits*, which are then passed down the network media to the destination computer. When the bits reach their destination computer the reverse process takes place. The reverse process is called *de-encapsulation*. Bits become frames, frames then become packets, the packets become segments, and finally the segments are turned back into data as each passes through its respective layers.

Encapsulation will be discussed in more detail at the end of this lesson. Figure 2-2 shows what data is called at each point in the encapsulation process.

Figure 2-2

OSI Model layers and what data is called at each level of encapsulation

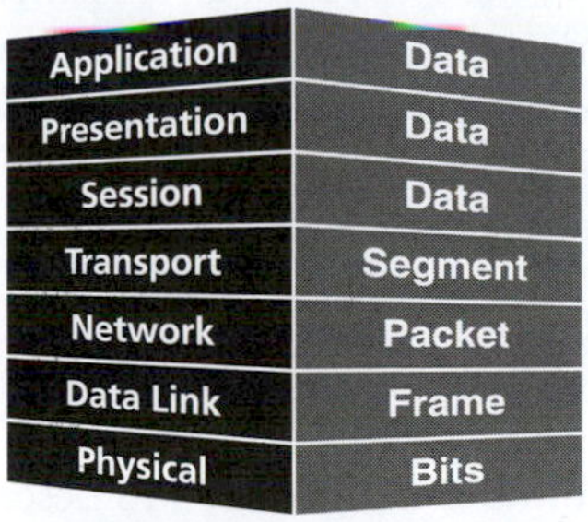

Application	Data
Presentation	Data
Session	Data
Transport	Segment
Network	Packet
Data Link	Frame
Physical	Bits

Physical Layer

Let's begin our discussion of the functions of the different layers of the OSI Model. The first layer we discuss is Layer 1, the *Physical layer*. The Physical layer, as may be expected from its name, deals with all aspects of physically moving data from one computer to the next. Specifically, cable standards are defined on this layer as well as the standards that define other means of data transmission such as wireless standards and fiber optic standards. The encapsulation unit on this layer is called bits because this layer is concerned with converting data from the upper layers into 1s and 0s that can be transmitted over various types of transmission media. Hubs are an example of the types of devices found on this layer of the OSI Model.

One of the areas defined on this layer of the OSI Model is the physical means that are used to transmit data across the network. Copper wiring, fiber optic cable, radio frequencies, anything that can be used to transmit data is defined on the Physical layer of the OSI Model. However, defining physical media specifications is not the only use for the Physical layer.

The Physical layer of the OSI Model is also used to define how data is encoded onto the media used to transmit the data. What this means is that the Physical layer defines how the data is converted to whatever medium is being used to transmit the data.

If copper wire is being used, the Physical layer defines how the data is converted to electrical impulses that are sent across the copper media. If fiber optic cables are being used, the Physical layer defines how the data being transmitted is converted to light pulses. Finally, if some sort of wireless media such as radio waves or microwaves are being used to transmit the data, the Physical layer is responsible for defining how the radio waves, microwaves, and so on are modulated to carry the data that is being transmitted.

Data Link Layer

The **Data Link layer** is the second layer of the OSI Model and the next layer to be discussed. The encapsulation on this layer is called a frame. Switches are an example of the types of devices found on this layer of the OSI Model.

While the Physical layer is concerned with media specifications and encoding, the Data Link layer is concerned with moving data from one computer to another. Another way of saying this is that the Data Link layer is responsible for moving frames from node-to-node or computer-to-computer. This is sometimes called *node-to-node communications*. The Data Link layer cannot move frames across routers; it can only move frames from one adjacent computer or device to another. This means that if a computer shares a network segment with another computer, then the computers in question can use the frame of the Data Link layer to move the data. To move the data to a different network segment, other means are needed and will be discussed later.

To move data around a network, a computer needs to know the address of the computer it is trying to communicate with. As such, the Data Link layer also contains an addressing mechanism for finding the computer or other device on the shared network segment it is trying to communicate with. This address is called a MAC address or a **physical address**. This address is called a physical address because it is hard coded into the network device. Each device to be communicated with on a network segment must have a unique physical address. This is an example of what a physical address looks like: 00-22-68-BF-F8-EA.

A couple of the better-known protocols that are defined on the Data Link layer are the Ethernet Protocol and the Point-to-Point Protocol (PPP). Simply defined, a **protocol** is a predefined and widely accepted set of rules that are used to describe exactly how a specific task is to work in a network environment.

Another thing to understand about the Data Link layer is that it is very unique because it has become necessary to divide it up into two sublayers in order to properly describe its full functionality. These two sublayers are called the **Logical Link Control (LLC) sublayer** and the **Media Access Control (MAC) sublayer**. Figure 2-3 shows how the Data Link layer is broken out into the Logical Link Control and the Media Access Control sublayers.

The IEEE 802.2 protocol defines these two sublayers in the Data Link layer. IEEE 802.2 is one of the protocols defined in the greater IEEE 802 protocol set, which was first proposed by a standards organization known as the Institute of Electrical and Electronic Engineers (IEEE). This standards organization has been around for approximately 125 years and has numerous standards to its credit. The IEEE 802 standards are one of the organization's biggest contributions to computer networking technologies.

X REF

The protocols mentioned here, along with many others, are discussed in more detail in Lesson 5 of this book.

Figure 2-3

OSI Model with the Data Link sublayers

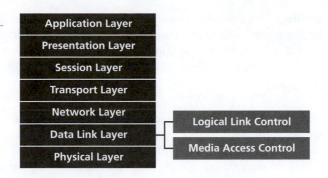

LLC SUBLAYER

In many ways, the LLC sublayer is the creation of the IEEE 802.2 standard, which was created to facilitate communications between the upper Network layer of the OSI Model and the lower Physical layer. In its original version, the Data Link layer ignored the networking issues of how addressing on the Data Link layer was to work and how to control data flow from the Physical layer up to the Network layer and vice versa was to be controlled. IEEE 802.2 addresses these issues.

In addition to the two previously mentioned critical areas, the LLC sublayer also addresses some optional areas—address notification and error correction.

MAC SUBLAYER

A greater discussion of these two Carrier Sensing technologies is found in Lesson 7 of this book.

The Media Access Control sublayer is in some ways what the original Data Link layer was until IEEE 802.2 brought its much-needed added functionality to the Data Link layer. One of the MAC sublayer's primary functions is to determine which computer has access to the network media at any given time. In other words, the MAC sublayer provides access control to the media just as its name implies. In the LAN environment, the primary way that the MAC sublayer does this is with something called Carrier Sensing Media Access/Collision Detection (CSMA/CD) in the wired world and Carrier Sensing Media Access/Collision Avoidance (CSMA/CA) in the wireless world.

Another function of the Media Access Control sublayer is to determine where one frame ends and the next one starts; this is called *frame synchronization*. Frame synchronization is the method used by a specific frame type or protocol to delineate, or define, to the computer the beginning and ending of any given frame.

There are four main forms of frame synchronization:

- **Time-based frame synchronization:** Places a specific amount of time between each frame in a stream of frames. After a set amount of time, the computer knows that the next frame has begun. The main drawback of this frame synchronization type is that extra time can creep into any given transmission due to external influences, which throws off the entire synchronization. Some external influences could be interference, attenuation of the signal, changes in media, or just plain distance.

- **Character counting:** Keeps track of how many characters are in a frame, as defined by one of the settings in a frame. Once the computer gets to the end of the count, it knows that the frame has come to an end and the next one has started. The main drawback to this method is that over time errors can creep into the frame, which results in characters being lost or added to the frame, throwing off the count and therefore the synchronization.

- **Byte stuffing:** Uses a predefined set of bytes to start off a frame and uses a different set of predefined bytes to end a frame. A byte is made of 8 bits, or eight 1s and 0s. When the computer sees the predefined series of bytes that indicate the end of a frame immediately followed by the other predefined set of bytes indicating the beginning of a frame, the computer knows that one frame has ended and another has started. Byte stuffing and bit stuffing are related to each other and are variations on the same idea.

- **Bit stuffing:** Uses several groups of eight 1s and 0s, a predefined series of bits, to indicate the beginning and ending of a frame. Aside from the substitution of a small number of bits for a series of bytes, the byte stuffing and bit stuffing methods work exactly the same way.

Network Layer

While the Data Link layer is responsible for moving the data from one computer or node to another, the **Network layer**, Layer 3, is responsible for moving the data in the form of packets from one end of the network to the other. This is sometimes called *end-to-end communications*. The Network layer does this via the use of something called **logical addresses**. While hard coded machine/physical addresses are used on the Data Link layer, logical addresses are logically assigned depending on the Networking layer protocol being used. In the case of the TCP/IP Protocol, the most commonly used networking protocol, the logical address is known as the IP address. This is what an IPv4 address looks like: 192.168.0.100. Routers are an example of the types of devices found on this layer of the OSI Model.

IP addresses will be discussed in greater detail in Lesson 4.

Logical addresses need to be assigned manually to every computer on a network. Also any computers that are directly connected to each other in the network or via routers and other connectivity devices need to have unique logical addresses as well. These addresses are used by the network as a kind of placeholder as data is moved across different computers in the network. While the physical address changes as a data frame is moved from one computer to another, the logical address does not change.

Logical addresses are used in one of the most important functions of the Network layer—routing. **Routing** is the ability of the various network devices and their related software to move data packets successfully from their source location to their destination locations no matter how far apart they are.

How physical and logical addresses work together will be described in more detail in Lesson 4 under the "How Physical and Logical Addresses Work Together" heading.

With logical addresses serving as placeholders, the Network layer devices and related software are able to use the logical address to determine the best route that a particular data packet can take to get to its destination. Every device along the path taken uses the logical address to keep the packet on track and to determine the next step the packet needs to take to get to its destination.

Transport Layer

The next layer up from the Networking layer is the **Transport layer** or Layer 4. The Transport layer is concerned with taking the data from higher levels of the OSI Model and breaking it down into smaller pieces called segments that can be sent along to lower-level layers for data transmission. Conversely, when data arrives into the computer, the Transport layer takes the data segments and reassembles them into data that the higher-level protocols and applications can use. Directly connected to this, the Transport layer is also concerned with sequencing the different segments so that they can be reassembled in the correct order when they arrive at their destination computer.

Aside from breaking the data into segments or reassembling segments back into data, the Transport layer is also concerned with the reliability of the transport of the data sent. One of the jobs of the Transport layer is to ensure that the data that has been sent has safely arrived at its destination. In order to do this, once a Transport layer protocol has sent its data segment or group of data segments, most of them will await a response from the destination computer that the data had arrived before sending out another data segment or group of data segments. The most common protocol of this type is the TCP protocol that is part of the TCP/IP protocol suite. If the sending computer does not receive the expected response, it will resend the data segment or segments it had just transmitted. Because of this function of the Transport layer, many of the protocols found on this layer are called connection-oriented protocols. However, it is important to note that not all Transport layer protocols verify that the destination computer actually received the data segments sent. In fact, one fairly common Transport layer protocol, UDP, actually does not check and because of this is called a connectionless protocol. Connection-oriented protocols and connectionless protocols will be discussed in more detail later in this lesson.

PORT ADDRESSING

Aside from the previously discussed functions of the Transport layer, this layer also makes sure that the data it has sent is able to get to the proper destination applications, services, or protocols once it reaches its destination, or vice versa. To do this, the Transport layer uses special addressing called port addressing. A *port address* is a unique address inside the computer that is associated with a specific protocol, service, or application. Some of these port addresses are predefined and cannot change, while others are assigned on the fly by the computer as the need arises.

Port addresses especially apply to the TCP and UDP protocols and are divided into three categories or ranges:

- **Well-known ports:** Have the range of 0 thru 1,023 and are pre-assigned by the Internet Corporation for Assigned Names and Numbers (ICANN) for the use of major networking protocols. These do not change no matter what computer or operating system you use.
- **Registered ports:** Have the address range of 1,024 thru 49,151 and have been registered with ICANN for specific uses usually for a specific company, vendor, application, or operating system for proprietary use.
- **Dynamic ports:** Have an address range of 49,152 thru 65,535 and are available for use by any application to communicate with any other application. Dynamic ports are also sometimes known as private ports.

CONNECTIONLESS VERSUS CONNECTION-ORIENTED PROTOCOLS

In discussing Network and Transport layer protocols, the concept of connectionless and connection-oriented protocols must be addressed. This is an important concept because the protocols on this layer and the Network layer fall into one of these two categories:

- A *connectionless protocol* is a network communications protocol that does not ask for verification that a data packet has successfully reached its destination. Basically if a connectionless protocol is being used, the data packet is thrown out on the network and it is just "assumed" that the packet successfully reached its destination. Video streaming and VoIP (Voice over IP) are examples of the types of applications that use connectionless protocols for communications.
- *Connection-oriented protocols* on the other hand ask for verification that a packet has successfully reached its destination before sending another packet out. Receiving a data file is a good example of a networking activity that uses connection-oriented protocols.

The vast majority of the Network layer protocols used in modern networks are connectionless. A good example of this is the IP protocol. However, when we look at the Transport layer, we find that one of the most widely used protocols on this layer, TCP, is actually a connection-oriented protocol. Another widely used protocol found on the Transport layer is UDP. UDP is a connectionless protocol used in various data-streaming network applications.

Session Layer

The *Session layer*, Layer 5, is responsible for managing the dialog between networked devices. The Session layer is able to establish, manage, and terminate connections between local and remote computers or applications. The Session layer provides duplex, half-duplex, or simplex communications between devices.

Duplex or *full-duplex* communication is true two-way communications between two devices. Either end of the connection can transmit or receive at the same time the other end is doing the same thing. *Half-duplex* communication is where a device can only send or receive while the device on the other end is doing the opposite. An example of this would be a CB or walkie-talkie where only one party can transmit at a time. Finally, *simplex* communication is pure one-way communications. Think of a radio or TV. A simplex device can either send or receive; it cannot do both.

Aside from all this, the Session layer also provides procedures for establishing checkpoints, adjournment, termination, and restart or recovery procedures. In the TCP/IP Model discussed later in this lesson, some of the jobs of the Session layer are taken up by the Transport layer and some are taken up by the Application layer.

Presentation Layer

The *Presentation layer* is concerned with how data is presented to the network. In order to properly present data to the network, the Presentation layer is primarily concerned with three tasks. These tasks are translation, compression, and encryption.

- *Translation* is the ability to take data transmitted by one type of computer and change it so that another type of computer can understand it. An example of this would be enabling a Macintosh or Apple computer to understand data sent by a PC or a Windows computer. However, with most computers now using the TCP/IP protocol to transmit data on most networks, this function is becoming less important.

- *Compression* is where data is made smaller in such a way that more data can be sent along the network in a given amount of time without making any changes to the hardware. This compression is usually done by taking redundant or repeated data out of a data stream. The opposite of compression is de-compression, which is the process of taking the compressed data stream and rebuilding it so that all the data that was originally present before compression is present again. De-compression is also a function of the Presentation layer. Most data that is sent across the Internet today is already compressed. This reduces the need for the data to be compressed again before it is transmitted; so, this function, like translation, is commonly ignored by networking protocols.

- *Encryption* is a process that allows data to be encoded in such a way that if an eavesdropper on the network is able to intercept the data being transmitted he or she still would not be able to understand it without knowing how to decode it. The reverse of encryption is decryption. If a computer is receiving encrypted data from another computer, then it is the Presentation layer's job to decrypt that data.

One of the best-known uses of network encryption is something called Secure Socket Layer (SSL). SSL is what is used to encrypt web pages. Anytime you see a web page that starts out with "https," that web page has been encrypted using SSL. Note that not all encryption has to take place on the Presentation layer. Many times lower-level protocols are used for encryption and decryption. An example of such a protocol is IPSec, which is really a Transport layer protocol used for encryption.

Application Layer

The *Application layer*, Layer 7, is the top layer of the OSI Model. The name of this layer sometimes confuses people. They tend to associate the term application with software programs such as Office, Outlook, Firefox, and so on. While this is a valid association, it is not what is meant by the term application when discussing the Application layer of the OSI Model. Instead, it is best to think of the Application layer as the layer of the OSI Model that contains all the services or protocols that are needed by the application software or operating system to communicate on the network.

A very good example to illustrate the point made previously is a web browser such as Firefox. Firefox is the application that an end user would use to browse the web; however, just having

Firefox running on your computer does not mean you can automatically view web pages. In order to view web pages, Firefox has to have an Application layer protocol called *HTTP (Hyper-Text Transport Protocol)* to view a web page. A similar example would be e-mail software such as Outlook. Outlook cannot automatically pick up and read or send e-mails. Instead, it has to have the Application layer protocol *POP3 (Post Office Protocol version 3)* in order to read e-mails and the Application layer protocol *SMTP (Simple Mail Transport Protocol)* to send e-mail. The Application layer of the OSI Model is where the various protocols and services that are used by computer applications to send and receive different types of data on a network reside.

How Data Moves Through the OSI Model

Now that we have discussed what each layer of the OSI Model does, we need to discuss how these layers are used in practice. Figure 2-4 illustrates this nicely.

Figure 2-4

Data from the OS moving down the OSI layers

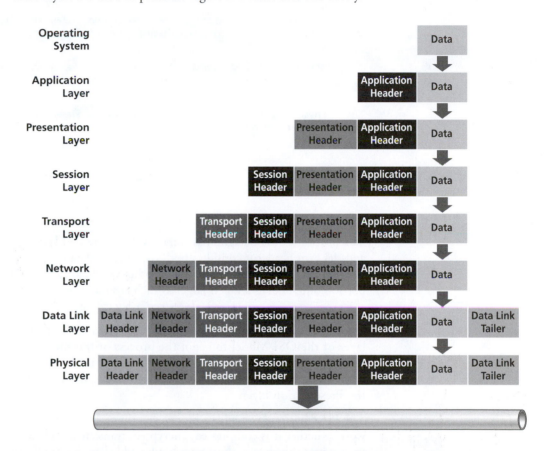

Figure 2-4 illustrates how each layer of the OSI Model adds its own ***header*** to the data that originated from the operating system. Each layer adds its own header in front of the header from the previous layer. This header contains information that describes what each layer of the OSI Model should do with the data. In addition to a header, the Data Link layer also adds a ***tailer***. This tailer contains additional information added by the Data Link layer that deals with error correction. Note: the only layer that does not add a header or tailer to the data is the Physical layer of the OSI Model. This is because the Physical layer of the OSI Model is only concerned with encoding the data to the media that is being used to pass the data down the network. This is illustrated by the wire that follows along the bottom of Figure 2-4 and the large arrow pointing to it.

Figure 2-5 shows how the data appears to the system as it moves through the OSI layers. You will notice that the shading of the headers changed to become the same shade as the

Figure 2-5

Data as it appears to the
system moving down the OSI
layers

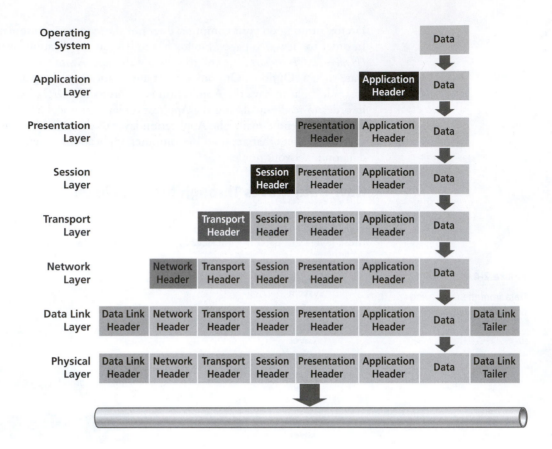

data portion of the datagram as is moves down the OSI layers. This is because as each layer adds its own header it considers both the original data and any headers added by any previous layers to be part of that layer's data. In other words, as far as each layer is concerned, the data portion of the datagram gets larger as each layer adds its own header information.

Figure 2-6 shows how data is sent and then received by another computer. On the sending end of the connection, the operating system (OS) sends the data to the Application layer of the OSI Model to begin the process of transmitting the data to the destination computer. The Application layer adds a header to the data indicating what protocol or service the data uses. The data with this new header information is then passed down to the Presentation layer.

The Presentation layer adds a header describing how the data is to be presented to the network, whether it is compressed, encrypted, translated, and so on. The Presentation layer then passes this data with its own header added to the Application layer's header down to the Session layer.

The Session layer then adds a header describing how the session the data belongs to is to be established, managed, terminated, and so on before passing it down to the Transport layer.

The Transport layer breaks the data up into segments and sequences them for passing on to the next computer for reassembly. The information the Transport layer puts in its own header describes how the data is segmented and sequenced. The Transport layer also adds source and destination port numbers to indicate what service, protocol, or application a particular data segment belongs to. You should note that the Transport layer copies the header information from the previous three layers to each of the segments before adding its own header information. Once this header information is added in front of all the previous headers, it is passed down to the Network layer.

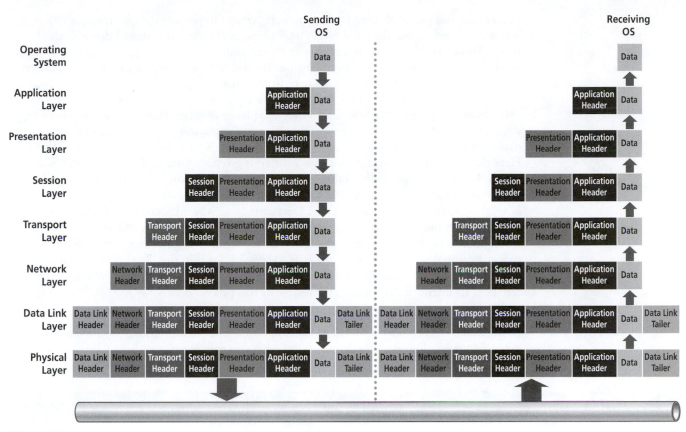

Sending
OS

Receiving
OS

Figure 2-6

Data as it moves through the OSI Layers as it is sent by one computer and received by another

The Network layer creates a header that adds source and destination logical addresses, along with a few other pieces of information, to each segment it receives from the Transport layer above. At this point, the segments become known as a packet. The source and destination logical address added by the Network layer ensures that each packet will be able to find the destination computer it is intended for. After doing all this, the Network layer passes the new packet down to the Data Link layer.

The Data Link layer takes the packet it received from the Network layer and adds the source physical addresses to the packet and the destination physical address of the next device down the line it needs to be sent to as determined by the destination logical address added by the Network layer. At this point, the packet becomes known as a frame. The Data Link layer places all this information into the Data Link header. In addition to this information being added into a new header, the Data Link layer also runs an error-checking algorithm on the data and puts that result in the Data Link tailer at the end of the frame. Once this is complete, the Data Link layer passes the whole ensemble of headers and data down to the Physical layer of the OSI Model.

The Physical layer encodes the data into whatever form is needed to place it onto the media being used to communicate with the destination computer. When the destination computer receives the signal on the Physical layer, the whole process described here begins in reverse until the data is finally passed on to the operating system, which then ensures that data is given to the software application it was intended for.

Another way to describe this is to follow an imaginary piece of data as moves down the various layers of the OSI Model and describe what happens at each layer. The data starts out originating with some program in the computer. That data is then sent to the networking sub-system of the operating system so that it can be sent to a different device on the network. The first stop of that data would be the Application layer. The Application layer contains the services and protocols used by the operating system to prepare data for transportation across a network. Once the Application layer prepares the data, it is passed down to the Presentation layer. Here the data type is identified and the data is compressed or encrypted if needed. After this, the data is passed down to the Session layer where a link is made between the two computers exchanging the data, and rules for sending the data are agreed on. Next the data is passed on to the Transport layerwhere the data is broken up into smaller manageable pieces called segments, which are given a sequence number. Here the data is also given a port address identifying the source and destination applications, protocols, or services the data is intended for. Once this is complete, the segment is passed down to the Network layer. Here the segment is converted into a packet that is given a source and destination IP address, which does not change, so that other devices on the network know how to pass the packet on to the next device along the path to its destination. After passing through the Network layer, the packet is handed down to the Data Link layer where it becomes a frame. The frame is given the source MAC address of the device it is currently on and the destination MAC address of the next directly connected device it needs to go to in order to move closer to its ultimate destination. Finally the frame is passed down to the Physical layer where it is converted to bits and sent down the media being used to transmit the data. When the data arrives at its intended destination, the reverse of this process occurs.

The entire process described in this section is called encapsulation, which is when the data comes down the protocol stack from the Application layer to the Physical layer. When the process is reversed on the other end, it is called de-encapsulation.

■ TCP/IP Model

THE BOTTOM LINE

This section of Lesson 2 describes an alternative networking model called the TCP/IP Model that is based on the TCP/IP protocol. This section describes each of the layers and what their functions are. Finally, this section describes how the TCP/IP Model correlates to the OSI Model.

TAKE NOTE*

The TCP/IP Model is an important model to know because most networks now use the TCP/IP protocol suite for transmitting data. As such, the TCP/IP Model, which is built around the TCP/IP protocol suite, is important to understand.

The OSI Model is not the only networking model out there. There is also a networking model called the *TCP/IP Model*. While the OSI Model was based on an idealized network environment and does not match any real protocol suites, the TCP/IP Model is built around the TCP/IP protocol suite. The TCP/IP protocol suite is called a *protocol suite* because it is made up of a large number of related protocols that all work together to accomplish the task of allowing computers in a network to communicate with each other. Each task that needs to be accomplished for any given session is carried out by different protocols in the suite. An example of this will be given later in this lesson.

As you can see in Figure 2-7, the TCP/IP Model only contains four layers as opposed to the seven layers of the OSI Model. While the names of the top two layers of the TCP/IP Model are the same as layer names in the OSI Model, the function of these two layers do not quite correspond to the layers of the same name in the other model. We discuss more about that as we look at each layer individually.

Figure 2-7

The TCP/IP Model

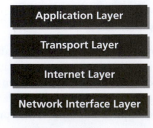

TAKE NOTE*

While some of the layers used in the TCP/IP Model and the OSI Model have the same name, their function is not identical. Layers with the same name in the two models have differences in functionalities.

Figure 2-8

TCP/IP Model and the OSI Model

CERTIFICATION READY
What are the layers of the TCP/IP Model?
1.1

Application Layer

The **Application layer** is the top layer of the TCP/IP Model. Even though it has the same name as the top layer of the OSI Model, it functions somewhat differently. The Application layer of the OSI Model simply deals with providing the protocols and/or services needed by the operating system and application software to communicate with the network. The Application layer of the TCP/IP Model does this and much more. In fact, the Application layer of the TCP/IP Model encompasses the same functions as the Application, Presentation, and Session layers of the OSI Model. This is illustrated in Figure 2-8, which compares the OSI and TCP/IP Models side by side.

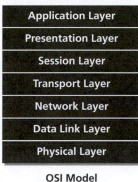

OSI Model   **TCP/IP Model**

As you can see in Figure 2-8, the Application layer of the TCP/IP Model occupies the same location as the Application, Presentation, and most of the Session layers of the OSI Model.

Transport Layer

If you look at the TCP/IP and OSI models in Figure 2-8, you will notice that the **Transport layer** in both models occupies the same location except that the Transport Layer of the TCP/IP Model occupies a small portion of the Session Layer of the OSI Model as well. This is because the Transport layer in both models functions essentially the same way. The only difference is that the TCP and other similar protocols take on some of the function of the Session layer as well. The TCP protocol in particular, along with everything else it does, is used to synchronize its source and destination computers to set up the session between the respective computers. In the OSI Model synchronizing the source and destination computer and setting up a session are part of what the Session Layer does. However in the TCP/IP Model, TCP and related protocols do this, even though they are technically Transport Layer protocols.

Internet Layer

CERTIFICATION READY
How do the layers of the TCP/IP Model match up to the layers of the OSI Model? Which layers are the same? Which layers are different?
1.1

As you can see from Figure 2-8, the **Internet layer** occupies more or less the same area on the TCP/IP Model as the Network layer on the OSI Model. That is because this layer performs pretty much the same job. However, you will also notice that the Internet layer extends slightly into the Data Link layer of the OSI Model as well. This is because the Internet layer also performs many of the functions of the Logical Link Control sublayer of the OSI Model's Data Link layer.

The primary protocol on the Internet layer of the TCP/IP Model is the Internet Protocol (IP). However, IP does not perform all the functions of the Internet layer by itself. IP has the help of several related protocols as well. Address Resolution Protocol (ARP) is one of the main ones, and it performs much of the LLC sublayer's job in the area of physical addressing.

Network Interface Layer

The last layer of the TCP/IP Model is the ***Network Interface layer***. This layer does much of the job of the MAC portion of the Data Link and Physical layers of the OSI Model. The TCP/IP Protocol does not say anything about what happens on this layer of the TCP/IP Model. Instead, TCP/IP protocol suite relies on the standards created by the various standards organizations concerning different media and how to encode bits onto them to do the work on this layer. Standards such as the standard for Ethernet, the 802.11 Wireless Standards, and various WAN media standards make up many of the protocols found on this layer of the TCP/IP Model.

Alternate Layer Names for the TCP/IP Model

While the layer names given earlier are considered the most common layer names for the TCP/IP Model, there are alternate names for the TCP/IP Model Layers. The reason for this is because the TCP/IP Model is not a formalized model defined in formal standards like the OSI Model was. This informality of the TCP/IP Model leads to alternative names for the model layers. The CompTIA Network+ objectives recognize two different naming schemes for the TCP/IP Model. The first is the one we have used in the previous parts of this section and the other is shown in Figure 2-9.

Figure 2-9

TCP/IP Model and the alternate layer names recognized by CompTIA Network + objectives

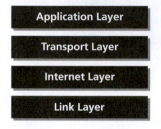

As can be seen in Figure 2-9, all the layers of the alternate TCP/IP Model naming convention are the same except for the last layer. The last layer of the TCP/IP model can alternatively be called the Link Layer. The alternate layers of the TCP/IP Model are Application Layer, Transport Layer, Internet Layer, and Link Layer. The actual functions of the Layers of the alternate TCP/IP Model are the same as the functions of the TCP/IP Model as described above.

■ How the Layers Work Together

THE BOTTOM LINE
This section describes how all the network layers work together to allow data to be moved across a network.

In order discuss how all the information in this lesson is pulled together, the TCP/IP Model will be used. The TCP/IP Model was chosen because there are real protocols with real jobs that can be used to illustrate how the layers of the TCP/IP Model work together. Figure 2-10 serves as a reference for discussing how everything works.

Figure 2-10 contains some of the more important protocols found in the TCP/IP protocol suite and their relative position in relation to the TCP/IP Model. Using this diagram, we discuss how everything works together. You should note that different protocols located on the Application layer of the TCP/IP Model connect to different Transport layer protocols. A big exception to this is that the DNS protocol on the Application layer connects to both TCP (Transport Control Protocol) and UDP (User Datagram Protocol) protocols on the Transport layer.

For this demonstration, we will use a scenario in which a web server needs to send a web page out across the network to a certain computer.

Figure 2-10

TCP/IP Model and its relation to protocols of the TCP/IP suite

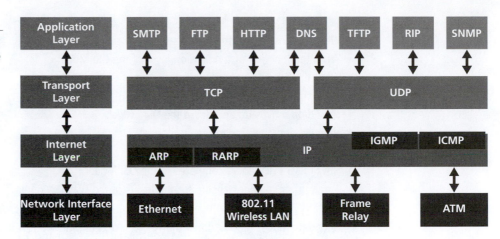

To start sending the web page, the first thing the web server needs to do is take the HTML (Hypertext Markup Language) code of the web page and encode it using the HTTP (Hypertext Transfer Protocol) to prepare the web page for transfer across the network. Once this is done, the encoded data is passed down to the TCP Protocol that sets up the session between the source and destination computers. After that, TCP breaks the data up into segments and gives each segment a sequence number so the segments can be put back together in the correct order once they reach their destination. Finally, just before sending the segments down to IP on the next layer, TCP gives each segment a source port number of 80 indicating that the data is using HTTP for transfer and the destination port number of the service, protocol, or program on the other end that will be receiving the segment.

Once the segment is passed down to IP (Internet Protocol) on the Internet layer, IP assigns the segments logical addresses for the source computer and the destination computer. This is to ensure that the data eventually is able to find a path to the destination computer. IP also uses the ARP (Address Resolution Protocol) to determine the physical address of the next device the packet has to go to. This job is usually part of the Data Link layer's job in the OSI Model, but is handled by the Internet layer in the TCP/IP Model. Assuming the destination computer is part of the Local Area Network (LAN), IP then passes the new packet to the Ethernet protocol found on the Network Interface Layer so that the packet can be encoded to be sent over the LAN.

Once the data reaches the destination computer, the reverse happens. Once the destination computer senses an Ethernet frame coming its way with its physical address, it accepts the data and passes it up to IP. IP verifies the logical address and passes it up to TCP. TCP puts the segments in the right order based on their sequence numbers and then sends them to the correct protocol, service, or program based on the destination port number. In this case, the destination port number would be whatever port number had been assigned to incoming HTTP datagrams. The HTTP protocol decodes the HTML code and passes it to a web browser so that the user of the destination computer can now view the web page on his or her screen.

X REF

More protocols will be discussed in Lesson 5 of this book. We will also go into much more detail about what each protocol does in that lesson.

SKILL SUMMARY

> **IN THIS LESSON YOU LEARNED:**
>
> - What the OSI Model is.
> - What the Physical layer of the OSI Model does.
> - What the Data Link layer of the OSI Model does.
> - What the two sublayers of the Data Link layer were and what they do.
> - What the function of the Network layer of the OSI Model is.

(Continued)

- What the function of the Transport layer of the OSI Model is.
- What the function of the Session layer of the OSI Model is.
- What the function of the Presentation layer of the OSI Model is.
- What the function of the Application layer of the OSI Model is.
- How data moves up and down the OSI Model.
- How headers function in the OSI Model.
- What the TCP/IP Model is.
- How the TCP/IP Model compares to the OSI Model.
- An alternate naming scheme for the layers of the TCP/IP Model.
- What some common protocols are at the various layers of the TCP/IP Model are.
- How data moves up and down the TCP/IP Model and how this relates to the protocols used.

■ Knowledge Assessment

Fill in the Blank

Complete the following sentences by writing the correct word or words in the blanks provided.

1. The primary function of the Physical layer is to _____.

2. The two sublayers of the Data Link layer are _____, and _____.

3. The primary job of the Network layer is to _____.

4. Two of the main jobs of the Transport layer are _____, and _____.

5. The three main functions of the Presentation layer of the OSI Model are _____, _____, and _____.

6. The process of moving data from one layer of the OSI Model to the next layer is called _____.

7. The Application layer of the TCP/IP Model corresponds to the _____ _____ layer(s) of the OSI Model.

8. A good mnemonic for remembering the layers of the OSI Model from top to bottom is A_____, P_____, S_____, T___, N_____, D_____, P_____.

9. The two most important protocols on the Transport layer of the TCP/IP Model are _____ and _____.

10. The most important protocol on the Internet layer of the TCP/IP Model is _____.

Multiple Choice

Circle the letter corresponding to the correct answer.

1. Which layer of the OSI Model contains all the services or protocols that are needed by application software or the operating system to communicate on the network?
   a. Presentation
   b. Session
   c. Data Link
   d. Application

2. Which layer of the OSI Model is responsible for segmenting data and sequencing it for the rest of the OSI Model?
   a. Transport
   b. Physical
   c. Network
   d. Presentation

3. Which layer of the OSI Model is concerned with reliably getting data from one computer to another?
   a. Presentation
   b. Session
   c. Transport
   d. Application

4. A _____ is a unique address inside the computer that is associated with a specific protocol, service, or application.
   a. Logical address
   b. Port address
   c. Physical address
   d. Socket

5. _____ are used for end-to-end communications on a network.
   a. Logical addresses
   b. Port addresses
   c. Physical addresses
   d. Sockets

6. _____ are used for node-to-node communications on a network.
   a. Logical addresses
   b. Port addresses
   c. Physical addresses
   d. Sockets

7. The encapsulation unit on the Presentation layer of the OSI Model is

   _____.

   a. Packet
   b. Segment
   c. Frame
   d. Data

8. The encapsulation unit on the Transport layer of the OSI Model is _____.
   a. Packet
   b. Segment
   c. Frame
   d. Data

9. The encapsulation unit on the Network layer of the OSI Model is _____.
   a. Packet
   b. Segment
   c. Frame
   d. Data

10. The encapsulation unit on the Data Link layer of the OSI Model is _____.
    a. Packet
    b. Segment
    c. Frame
    d. Data

Lab Exercises

■ Lab 1

How TCP/IP Protocols Work through the TCP/IP Model

The purpose of this lab is to familiarize the students with the TCP/IP Model and some of the protocols that are used in it.

This lab is important to the student because it takes the student through a thought experiment about how data would pass thorough the TCP/IP Model down from the computer and up through the destination computer. By doing this thought experiment the student will come to better understand how different protocols work together to accomplish a specific task.

MATERIALS

- Notepad
- Pencil
- Textbook

DO THE LAB

Follow Protocols Through the Layers of the TCP/IP Model

1. Read though the section of this lesson titled "How the Layers Work Together."
2. Carefully study Figure 2-11.

Figure 2-11

The TCP/IP Model and how it relates to some of the protocols that make up the TCP/IP Suite

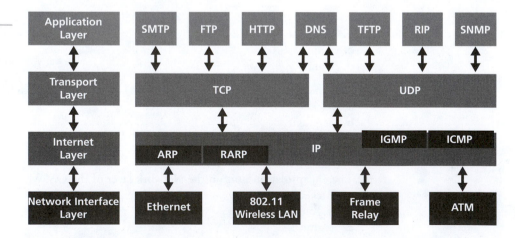

3. On a piece of paper, list the layers of the TCP/IP Model and then the protocols that the discussion you read says are used on each layer to move the data from one location on the network to another. The following is what your answer should look like:
   - Application Layer: HTTP
   - Transport Layer: TCP
   - Internet Layer: IP
   - Network Interface Layer: Ethernet

4. List the protocols as they correspond to the TCP/IP Model that you think would be used to send e-mail across the network. (Hint: You should start with the Application layer protocol SMTP.)

5. List the protocols as they correspond to the TCP/IP Model that you think would be used to send a file across the network using TFTP.

Lab 2

TAKE NOTE

This lab uses Windows 7. If you are using Windows Vista or Windows XP, you will need to make some slight variations to the lab.

Using the IPCONFIG Command

The purpose of this lab is to help students learn how to determine what their IP and physical addresses are when working on a computer.

This lab is important to the student because it familiarizes the student with the commands and procedures they will need to master in order to determine the logical and physical addresses of any computer they are using.

MATERIALS

- Notepad
- Pencil
- Computer running Windows 7 Professional

DO THE LAB

The IPCONFIG Command

1. Click the **Start** button at the bottom left of your Windows 7 Desktop Display in order to bring up the Windows 7 start menu (Figure 2-12).

Figure 2-12

Windows 7 Start Menu

2. Type **CMD** into the *Search Programs and Files* box at the bottom of the Start Menu and press **Enter**.

3. The Command Line Interface (CLI) Window will come up (as shown in Figure 2-13). The CLI is a window where you can enter commands into the computer in the form of text. This type of interface was how a person interacted with DOS. It is also how a person is able to currently interact with Linux if they choose not to use one of several graphical interfaces available for use with Linux.

Figure 2-13

Command Line Interface Window

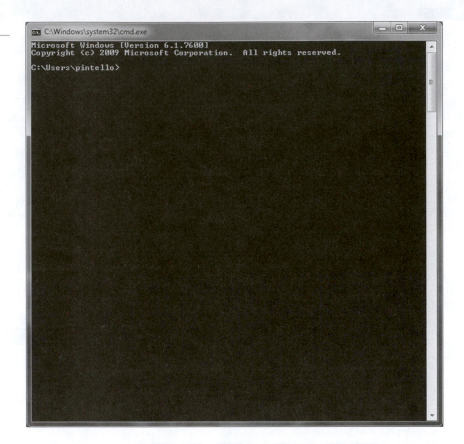

```
C:\Windows\system32\cmd.exe

Microsoft Windows [Version 6.1.7600]
Copyright (c) 2009 Microsoft Corporation.  All rights reserved.

C:\Users\pintello>
```

4. Once you have opened the Command Line Interface (CLI), type in the command **ipconfig**. When the ipconfig command is entered, the CLI changes to something similar to Figure 2-14. You should note that the information that appears when you enter "ipconfig" will differ from the information displayed here.

5. Write out on a piece of paper the name of the network adapter that appears in your CLI:
   • Write down the IPv6 address:
   • Write down the IPv4 address:
   • Write down the Subnet Mask:
   • Write down the Default Gateway:

6. Type the command **ipconfig ?** exactly as shown here. Be sure to include a space between the last letter of the command and the question mark. When you do this, the CLI reports back the correct syntax of the ipconfig command as well as a list of options that can be used with this command.

   • List 6 available options:

Figure 2-14

Command Line Interface
Window after entering the
"ipconfig" command

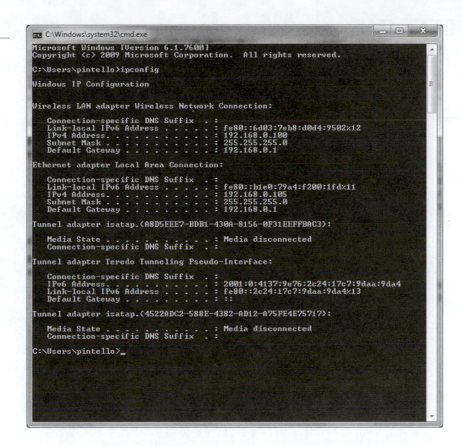

7. Next type **ipconfig /all** just as shown here, in the CLI. What additional information is presented that was not there when just "ipconfig" was entered?

   • List at least 6 additional pieces of information that you now have available to you for your network adapter card.

   • What is the physical address of your network adapter? List it here.

   • Why is it important to know what your physical address is? Write out your answer here.

8. Close the CLI by clicking the **X** in the box with the red background in the top right corner of the CLI window.

LESSON

Media

EXAM OBJECTIVE MATRIX

Technology Skill Covered	Exam Objective	Exam Objective Number

Copper Cabling and Its Properties	**Categorize standard media types and associated properties.**
	• Copper
	  • UTP
	  • STP
	  • CAT3
	  • CAT5
	  • CAT5e
	  • CAT6
	  • CAT6a
	  • Coaxial
	  • Crossover
	  • T1 Crossover
	  • Straight-through
	• Plenum vs. non-plenum
	• Distance limitations and speed limitations
	• Broadband over powerline
		3.1

	Categorize standard connector types based on network media.
	• Copper
	  • RJ-45
	  • RJ-11
	  • BNC
	  • F-connector
	  • DB-9 (RS-232)
		3.2

	Given a scenario, troubleshoot common physical connectivity problems. Cable problems: • EMI/Interference	3.6

Fiber-Optic Cabling	**Categorize standard media types and associated properties.**
	• Fiber
	  • Multimode
	  • Singlemode
		3.1

	Categorize standard connector types based on network media.
	 • Fiber
	  • ST
	  • SC
	  • LC
	  • MTRJ
		3.2

Installing Wiring Distributions	**Categorize standard connector types based on network media.**
	 • Copper
	  • Patch panel
	  • 110 block (T568A, T568B)
		3.2

	Identify components of wiring distribution. • IDF • MDF • Demarc • Demarc extension • Smart jack	3.8
Wireless Media	**Given a scenario, install and configure a wireless network.** • Wireless standards	2.2

	Compare and contrast different wireless standards.
	 • 802.11 a/b/g/n standards
	  • Distance
	  • Speed
	  • Latency
	  • Frequency
	  • Channels
	  • MIMO
	  • Channel bonding
		3.3

Tying it All Together		

KEY TERMS

100-pair cable	coaxial cable	half-duplex
110 block	cross-connect	hardware loopback
25-pair cable	crossover cable	intermediate distribution frame (IDF)
66 block	crosstalk	latched
attenuation	demarc	latency
bandwidth	demarc extension	light emitting diodes (LEDs)
baseband cable	Electromagnetic Interference (EMI)	local connector (LC)
BNC connector	F-connector	main distribution frame (MDF)
broadband cable	feeder cable	mechanical transfer registered jack (MT-RJ or MTRJ)
Broadband over Power Line (BPL)	full-duplex	

multimode fiber (MMF)	Radio Frequency Interference (RFI)	square connector (SC)
multiple-input/multiple-output (MIMO)	Recommended Standard 232 (RS-232)	straight-through cable
Network Interface Device (NID)	registered jack (RJ)	straight tip (ST) connector
noise	rollover cable	subscriber connector (SC)
patch cable	serial	T1 crossover cable
patch panel	shielded twisted pair (STP)	Thin Ethernet (Thinnet)
plenum	simplex	throughput
plenum-rated cable	single-mode fiber (SMF)	Universal Serial Bus (USB)
Public Switched Telephone Network (PSTN)	small form factor (SFF) connector	unshielded twisted pair (UTP)
	smart jack	

Bill works at a company called Computer Consultants, LLC. Bill's company has been contracted by Heralding Public Relations, Inc. to build a data network for their main office. Bill's job is to determine what the communications media needs for the new network will be. The information in this lesson will cover what Bill will need to know to accomplish his assigned task.

■ Copper Cabling and Its Properties

THE BOTTOM LINE

This section of Lesson 3 deals the different types of copper cables that have been used in the past and are used today for network communications. The topics we cover are unshielded twisted-pair cables and their connectors as well as different types of cables created from unshielded twisted-pair wires. Shielded twisted-pair and coaxial cables along with their relevant types and connectors are also discussed.

There are a number of types of media used in networking today. These types range from wireless communications methods using radio frequencies and microwave signals to fiber-optic cables and copper wires. This section of Lesson 3 deals with the different types of copper wiring currently used in data networks as well as some types of copper cables that were common in the past but not used so much today.

How Cable Is Denoted

When copper cable is being discussed, more often than not, it is being discussed in the context of LAN technologies because copper is not often used in WAN applications today. Fiber optic or some other form of wireless communications are generally used to make WAN connections today. When discussing LAN cabling, Ethernet is the most commonly used.

Ethernet cable types are described using a code that follows this format: *N<Signaling>–X*. The *N* refers to the signaling rate in megabits per second, *<Signaling>* stands for the signaling type—either baseband or broadband, and the *X* is a unique identifier for a specific Ethernet cabling scheme.

100Base-X is a common example of this code. The 100 in this example tells you that the transmission speed is 100Mb, or 100 megabits. The *X* value can mean several different things depending on the type of cable being used. If the cable is twisted pair, the X is replaced by a T. In this example, the cable would be denoted as 100Base-T. This is the standard for running 100-Megabit Ethernet over two pairs (four wires) of Category 5, 5e, or 6 UTP. In the same manner 1000Base-T would be how you would denote running 1 gigabit per second of cable across a twisted-pair cable. This is sometimes called Gigabit Ethernet and uses Category 6 or higher cable. You should note that some forms of fiber optic also use this scheme to describe them, but with different values in place of the X.

Unshielded Twisted Pair

CERTIFICATION READY
What is UTP cabling?
What is UTP used for?
3.1

Twisted-pair cables consist of multiple individually insulated wires that are twisted together in pairs. Sometimes a metallic foil-like shield is placed around them; when this is done it is called shielded twisted pair (STP). Twisted-pair cable without outer shielding is called *unshielded twisted pair (UTP).* Unshielded twisted-pair cable is used in all types of twisted-pair Ethernet networks.

Many people wonder why the cable is called "twisted" pair. The reason has to do with the fact that when electromagnetic signals are conducted on copper wires in close proximity, the signals begin to interfere with each other. This interference is called *crosstalk.* You can minimize crosstalk by twisting two wires together as a pair. Twisting the wires together can also minimize other types of interference as well. Twisted-pair cables are rated on the number of twist per meter and how many pairs are in the cable. Ratings in twisted-pair cables are called category. There are currently 10 categories of twisted-pair cables defined. More is discussed about this later in this Lesson.

There are several reasons why unshielded twisted-pair wire is preferred in modern Ethernet network configurations:

- It is cheaper than other types of cabling.
- It is easy to work with.
- It allows transmission rates that were impossible 10 years ago.

RJ CONNECTORS

CERTIFICATION READY
What are RJ connectors?
What types of RJ connectors are available?
What applications are the different RJ connectors used in?
3.2

Unshielded twisted-pair (UTP) wiring has unique specifications for its connectors. To fit a connector to UTP wiring, it is necessary to use a *registered jack (RJ)* connector. This connector is very familiar to most people because one version of this connector is used on most telephone lines to connect them to a wall jack.

There are three main types of RJ connectors:

- **RJ-11:** This connector is used to connect a phone to a phone jack. This connector is used with UTP cable similar to Category 1 cable and uses two pairs (four wires). RJ-11 connectors are not used for local area networks (LANs), however, aside from POTS (Plain Old Telephone Service). RJ-11 connectors are used for home Digital Subscriber Line (DSL) connections.

- **RJ-22:** This connector is used for handsets of older style telephones. In these phones, the extension wire that runs between the handset and the base of the phone generally used RJ-22 connectors. These connectors are not used in network communications and are not really of any concern for this book.

- **RJ-45:** This connector, which is used in Ethernet data networks, uses four pairs of wires (eight wires). Figure 3-1 shows a couple of RJ-45 connectors. RJ-45 is usually associated with Category 3 or higher UTP wires.

These connectors are attached to the cable with a device called a RJ connector crimper. This crimper is different from the crimper used with BNC connectors because the connectors are shaped differently and the crimper has to be built accordingly. Because of the different shapes of the connectors, the die that holds the connector is a different shape. Higher-quality crimping tools have interchangeable dies for both types of cables; however, it is often more cost effective to purchase separate crimping tools for each type of connector.

Figure 3-1

RJ-45 connectors

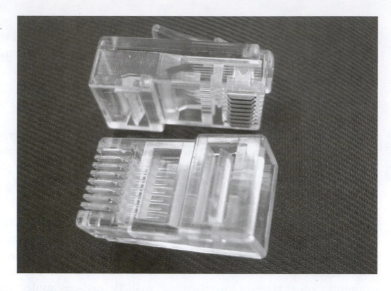

CERTIFICATION READY
What is category
cabling? Where is
category cabling used?
What variations exist in
category cabling?
3.1

CATEGORY CABLING

The number of twists and the direction the twists are turning in a given meter of wire can vary according to how much and what types of interference the twisted-pair wires are trying to minimize. To show this, twisted-pair wire is rated using "categories." The categories are known by the abbreviation CAT followed by a number. The most common grades of "category" twisted-pair wires currently used in LANs are CAT 5, CAT 5e, and CAT 6. These three category cables as well as several others are discussed next.

Category cabling also has standardized jacks that are used to connect it to wall jacks. Figure 3-2 shows a standard category cabling jack.

Figure 3-2

Standard category cabling jack

All the defined categories of twisted-pair cables include CAT 1, CAT 2, CAT 3, CAT 4, CAT 5, CAT 5e, CAT 6, CAT 6a, CAT 7, and CAT 7a. Here is a discussion of seven of the defined categories:

- **CAT 1:** Consists of two twisted wire pairs (four wires). It is the oldest type and is only voice grade, meaning that it is not rated for data communication. People refer to it as plain old telephone service (POTS). Before 1983, this was the standard cable used throughout the North American telephone system. POTS cable still exists in parts of the Public Switched Telephone Network (PSTN) and supports signals limited to the 1MHz frequency range.

- **CAT 2:** Consists of four twisted wire pairs (eight wires). CAT 2 handles up to 4 mbps, with a frequency limitation of 10 MHz, and is now obsolete.

- **CAT 3:** Consists of four twisted wire pairs (eight wires) with three twists per foot. CAT 3 can handle transmissions up to 16 MHz. It was popular in the mid-1980s for up to 10 mbps Ethernet. Today, however, it is limited to telecommunication equipment and is obsolete for data networks.

- **CAT 4:** Consists of four twisted wire pairs (eight wires) and is rated for 20 MHz. CAT 4 wire was never very popular and is now obsolete.

- **CAT 5:** Consists of four twisted wire pairs (eight wires) and is rated for 100 MHz. CAT 5 was very popular until the appearance of CAT 5e wire, which is now preferred because it is the same price as CAT 5 wire but with better capabilities. CAT 5 wires can carry 100 mbps worth of data in 100 meters.

- **CAT 5e:** Consists of four twisted wire pairs (eight wires) and is rated for 100 MHz. CAT 5e is enhanced because it is capable of handling the interference that comes from being able to transmit on all four pairs of wires at the same time instead of just the two pairs that CAT 5 and previous CAT cables used. This feature is needed for Gigabit Ethernet but is more commonly used to run Voice over IP (VoIP) and data on the same cable. In this situation, VoIP is run on two pairs, and data is run on the other two pairs. Categories below 5e really should not be used in today's network environments.

- **CAT 6:** Consists of four twisted wire pairs (eight wires) and is rated for 250 MHz. CAT 6 became a standard back in June 2002. In many applications, CAT 6 wiring is replacing older category standards and is the preferred standard for Gigabit Ethernet. These cables are also used as riser cable to connect floors together. When installing a network in a new building, CAT 6 wiring is the best option because it provides room to upgrade the network in the future as capabilities improve. Figure 3-3 shows a basic CAT 6 cable with four wire pairs twisted to reduce crosstalk.

Figure 3-3

Unshielded twisted-pair CAT 6 cable

TAKE NOTE*

If your goal is to have data rates faster than 100 mbps over UTP, ensure that all your components are rated to deliver this data rate and be careful when handling all components. If CAT 5e wire is pulled on hard during installation, it will stretch the number of twists inside the jacket, rendering the CAT 5e label on the outside of the cable invalid. Also, be certain to connect and test all four pairs of wire. Today's wiring usually only uses two pairs (four wires); the standard for Gigabit Ethernet over UTP requires that all four pairs (eight wires) be in good condition. In order to allow for upgrading to Gigabit Ethernet in the future it is important to keep this in mind.

Also be aware that a true CAT 5e cabling system uses rated components from end to end, patch cables from workstation to wall panel, cable from wall panel to patch panel, and patch cables from patch panel to switch. If any components are missing, or if the lengths do not match the CAT 5e specification, you will not have a CAT 5e cabling installation. You should also make an effort to certify that the entire installation is CAT 5e compliant. Certifying that your entire wiring installation is true CAT 5e can be expensive due to the special equipment needed to accomplish this.

TIA/EIA 568 STANDARDS

Inside a network cable, there are four pairs of wires twisted together to prevent crosstalk, EMI, and tapping. The same pins have to be used on the same colors throughout a network to receive and transmit. To ensure that all cables use the same color wires, two wiring standards have been agreed to by over 60 vendors including AT&T, 3Com, and Cisco. The two standards that have been agreed to are the TIA/EIA 568A and 568B. This means that some jacks will use one of these standards while others will use the other standard. This does cause some confusion, but looking at the jacks in any given network will help you know which one is in use. The difference in the two standards is the position of four wires on one side of the cable. There are eight wires in each UTP cable, however, pins 4, 5, 7, and 8 are not used in either standard and are simply there to help shield the wires that are used. The reason for the two different standards is something called a crossover cable.

Pins 1, 2, 3, and 6 are the pins used when creating data cables for Ethernet networks. If these pins are arranged so that green-white, green, orange-white, and orange wires go to pins 1, 2, 3, and 6, respectively, on both sides of the cable, then the TIA/EIA 568A standard is being used. If however, these pins are arranged so that orange-white, orange, white-green, and green wires go to pins 1, 2, 3, and 6, respectively on both sides of the cable, then the TIA/EIA 568B standard is being used. Wires arranged in either of these configurations create a regular patch cable. If TIA/EIA 568A is used on one end of a cable and TIA/EIA 568B is used on the other end, then a *crossover cable* is created. These two types of cables as well as two other types are discussed in more detail next.

TYPES OF COMMONLY USED CABLES

Ethernet cabling is an important topic to understand, especially if you are planning to work on any type of LAN network. There are different types of wiring standards available:

- Straight-through cable (568A)
- Crossover cable (568B)
- Rolled cable (rollover)
- Hardware loopback

In this section, we discuss each one of these types of cable. This section ends with some examples.

CERTIFICATION READY
What are the main types of patch cables? What applications is each type of patch cable used in?
3.1

Straight-through cable

The *straight-through cable* is used to connect a host to a switch or hub, or a router to a switch or hub. An easy way to recall this is to remember that straight-through cables are used to connect devices with dissimilar functions while crossover cables are used to connect devices with similar functions.

Four wires are used in a straight-through cable to connect Ethernet devices. Even though all 4 pairs, 8 wires, are used to create the cable, only 2 pairs or 4 wires, are used to carry data. The four wires used to carry data are 1, 2, 3, and 6. Wires 3 and 6 are split by the blue wires in order to cut down on interference within the cable. Figure 3-4 depicts the layout of the wires used to create a straight-through cable. Figure 3-4 uses the EIA/TIA 568B standard to make a straight-through cable. This means that orange-white wire goes to pin 1, the orange wire goes to pin 2, the green-white wire goes to pin 3, and the green wire goes to pin 6. This standard was chosen because it is the one that AT&T uses.

Notice that each pin is connected directly to the pin of the same number on the other side of the connection. If the pins are not connected directly to each other in this manner, the cable will not work. This cable configuration is only for a 10/100 Ethernet cable. This configuration will not work for 1000 mbps Ethernet, voice, Token Ring, ISDN, or anything else that is not 10/100 Ethernet.

Figure 3-4

Straight-through Ethernet cable pin out

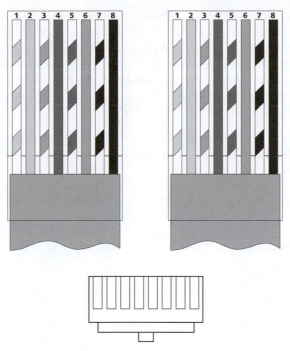

Crossover cable

The same four wires that are used in a straight-through cable are also used in a crossover cable, just with the wires arranged differently. Crossover cables can be used to connect these devices:

- Switch to switch
- Hub to hub
- Host to host
- Hub to switch
- Router direct to host

Figure 3-5, which demonstrates how each of the eight wires are arranged in a crossover Ethernet cable

Figure 3-5

Crossover Ethernet cable pin out

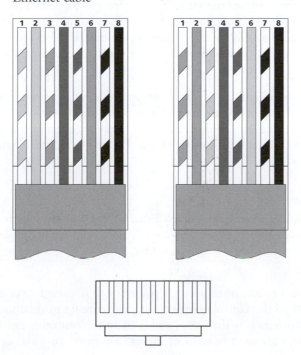

When looking at Figure 3-5 notice that instead of connecting pin 1 to 1, 2 to 2, and so on, the connections are pins 1 to 3, and 2 to 6 and so on, on each side of the cable. A crossover cable is typically used to connect two switches together, but it can also be used to test communications between two workstations directly, bypassing the switch. An easy way to remember when to use straight-through and crossover cables is to remember that straight-through cables are used to connect dissimilar function devices and crossover cables are used to connect similar function devices.

A crossover cable is used only in Ethernet UTP installations. It is important to remember however that it is possible to connect two workstation NICs or a workstation and a server NIC directly with it.

It is a good idea to always have a crossover cable in your tool bag along with a laptop computer. This can be useful when you need to ensure that a server's NIC is functioning correctly. In this situation, you can test this by simply connecting the laptop directly to the server's NIC using the crossover cable. It should be easy to log in to the server if both NICs are configured correctly.

T1 crossover cable

A **T1 crossover cable** is a specialized crossover cable used in T1 applications. T1 cabling is normally a type of wiring that is commonly used in WAN networks. However, in this case, a T1 crossover cable is a cable that is used in a local switch room to connect multiple devices that are used to setup T1 connections. In other words, if you had two devices that had T1 connections coming into them, but you needed to pass the signal from one of these devices to the other, you could use a T1 crossover cable. This is similar to how you could use a standard crossover cable to connect two LAN devices of similar function with RJ-45 ports to each other. Two computers or two switches are examples of LAN devices with similar functions.

Another example of a situation where a T1 crossover cable may be used is when two PBXs need to be connected together. PBXs are special switching systems that are used to control multiple phones in a conventional office phone system. In a conventional phone system, one phone line comes into a company and that phone line is then broken up into multiple phone lines within the premises so that more than one person working at a given location can have a phone. The device that used to break this single incoming line into multiple lines within the premises is called a PBX switch. It should be noted that this type of phone systems is quickly falling out of use in favor of phone systems that share the same cabling infrastructure as the data network.

As can be seen in Figure 3-6, a T1 crossover cable has the same pin out as a straight-through cable except that pins 1-2 are crossed with pins 4-5. It should be noted that an Ethernet crossover cable like the one described in a previous section of this Lesson cannot be used in place of a T1 crossover cable or vice-versa. Figure 3-6 illustrates what a T1 crossover cable pin out would look like.

Rollover cable

Rollover cables are not used to hook Ethernet connections together. However, they are used to connect a host to a router's console port. A router's console port is used by a WAN Engineer to program or configure a router. Switches have a similar port that is used for the same purpose.

To configure a router or a switch, a rollover cable is used to connect the PC's Serial (COM) Port to the console port on the device being programmed. HyperTerminal or a similar program is then used to log in to the router or switch and then configured. All eight wires are used in rollover cables to connect to serial devices, although not all

Figure 3-6

T1 crossover cable pin out

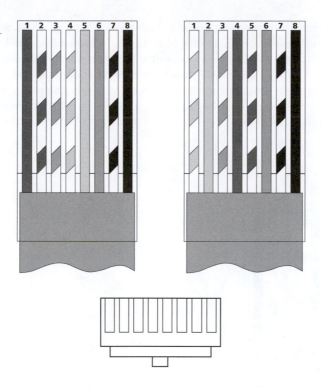

eight are used to send information (just as in Ethernet networking). Rollover cables are also sometimes called null modem cables. Figure 3-7 shows the eight wires used in a rolled cable.

Figure 3-7

Rollover Ethernet patch cable pin out

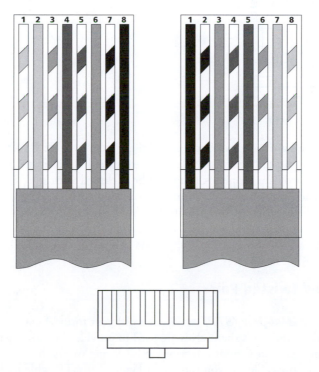

Hardware loopback

While a hardware loopback is not a wiring standard, it is still an important topic to discuss. A ***hardware loopback*** is a way to redirect data flow. Sometimes it is necessary to make a computer to think it has a live connection to a network when such a connection in reality does not exist. One reason to do this is to test a computer or because you need a "live" net-work connection to install a piece of software. In these cases, the loopback can be used to trick the PC into seeing its own output as input. A device that allows you to do this is some-thing called a loopback plug. A loopback plug works similarly to a crossover cable except that the transmit pins are connected directly to the receive pins, as shown in Figure 3-8. Such a device is often used by the NIC's software diagnostics software to test transmission and reception capabilities.

Figure 3-8

Hardware loopback and its connections

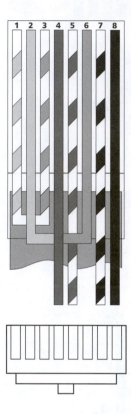

Usually, the hardware loopback is no bigger than a single RJ-45 connector with a few small wires on the back. If a NIC has hardware diagnostic software that can use the loop-back, the hardware loopback plug will be included with the NIC. To use it, simply plug the loopback into the RJ-45 connector on the back of the NIC, and start the diagnostic software. Select the option in your NIC's diagnostic software that requires the loopback, and start the diagnostic routine. These diagnostics will determine if the NIC can send and receive data.

Shielded Twisted Pair

Shielded twisted-pair (STP) cabling is a different form of copper twisted-pair wiring. In UTP wiring, the wires themselves are used to provide shielding against various forms of EMI by twisting them in various directions. STP wiring works the same way, but adds additional shielding to the cable. As you can see in Figure 3-9, STP cable looks just like UTP cable, except that STP cable adds extra shielding around the wires in the cable.

Shielded twisted-pair cables are actually not used very often these days. However, back when IBM Token Ring networks were more common than they are currently, many of them used STP cables. It is not very likely that you will see a network using STP today.

Figure 3-9

Shielded twisted-pair cable showing its shielding

CERTIFICATION READY

What are STP cables? How do they differ from UTP cables?

3.1

CERTIFICATION READY

What is coaxial cable? What applications was it used in during the past? Where are you most likely to find coaxial cable today? What are the two most commonly used types of coaxial cable?

3.1

TAKE NOTE *

It is no longer necessary to know much about most coax cable types used in data networks. The primary place that coaxial is used today is in cable TV and broadband Internet access from the cable TV providers. The cable used for cable TV is known as 75 ohm cable. RG-6 or cable TV coax is used in the broadband home Internet access market. Use of coaxial cables of any sort for Ethernet-based networks is pretty much a thing of the past.

Coaxial

Coaxial cable, referred to as *coax*, contains a center conductor made of copper that is surrounded by a plastic jacket. The plastic jacket then has a braided shield over it. A plastic such as PVC or Teflon covers this metal shield. The Teflon-type covering is frequently referred to as a plenum-rated coating. This coating is expensive; however, it is often mandated by local or municipal fire code when cable is hidden in walls and ceilings. Many municipalities require these coatings because if *plenum-rated cable* is used in a building that catches fire, it will not release toxic gases. Non-plenum-rated cables *do* release toxic gases when they are burned. Plenum rating applies to all types of cabling, including UTP and STP cables, and is an approved replacement for all other compositions of cable sheathing and insulation. There is more about plenum and non-plenum cabling later in this lesson.

Table 3-1 lists some specifications for the different types of coaxial cables. You should note, however, that we tend to use only RG-59 and RG-6 in modern day situations.

Table 3-1

Coaxial Cable Specifications

RG Rating	Popular Name	Ethernet Implementation	Type of Cable
RG-58 U	N/A	None	Solid copper
RG-58 A/U	Thinnet	10Base-2	Stranded copper
RG-8	Thicknet	10Base-5	Solid copper
RG-59	Cable television Low cost, short distance	N/A	Solid copper
RG-6	Cable television, cable modems Longer distances than RG-59; some power implementations	N/A	Solid copper
RG-62	ARCnet (obsolete)	N/A	Solid/stranded copper

continuation

Thin Ethernet or **Thinnet**, also referred to as 10Base-2, is a thin coaxial cable. It is basically the same as thick coaxial cable except it is only about one-quarter inch in diameter. Thin Ethernet coaxial cable is Radio Grade 58 or just RG-58. Figure 3-10 shows an example of Thin Ethernet cable.

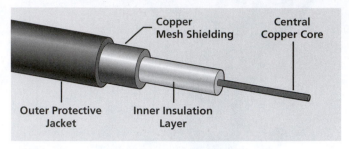

Figure 3-10

A diagram of a stripped-back Thinnet cable

The 10Base-2 designation indicates that Thinnet cables are able to carry 10 mbps data rates for up to 200 meters. In reality, Thinnet cables are only rated to carry data 185 meters, but the people who put the standard together decided to just leave it at 10Base-2 instead of 10Base-185. The "Base" part of the standard designation indicates that the cable is a **baseband cable** and can only carry one signal at a time. If the standard was able to carry multiple signals simultaneously then it would be a **broadband cable** and the term "broad" would be used in place of "base."

BNC CONNECTORS

When using Thinnet cable, something called a **BNC connector** must be used to attach stations to the network. Figure 3-11 shows a BNC connector. BNC connectors can be attached using a specialized crimper that looks somewhat similar to a pair of pliers. This crimper has a special die that allows it to crimp the connector. A simple squeeze of the crimper causes the BNC connector to be crimped to the cable. A screw-on BNC connector is also available; however the screw-on type BNC connectors tend to come off the cable more easily than the crimped-on type.

Figure 3-11

Male and female BNC connectors

F-CONNECTOR

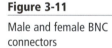

F-connectors are another type of coaxial cable connector. F-connectors are most commonly used in broadband and home video applications. If you have cable television and/or Internet in your home, the type of coaxial cables used to connect your TV to your cable input uses the F-connector. There is also a variation on the F-connector that is able to simply push over the treads of a device that requires an F-connector. Some of the older style VCRs came with this type of F-connector. Figure 3-12 shows a typical F-connector that you may use in your home to connect up cable television.

Figure 3-12

A male F-connector for a
coaxial cable

RG-59

This type of coaxial cable is used for low-power video and audio transmission. Typically this is the cable that is provided with DVD players and such to allow them to connect to a TV. This cable can also be used for data runs that are longer than the 100 meters, which are longer data runs than UTP is capable of. UTP is limited to 100-meter data runs. However, RG-59 is not often used in this capacity. This cable was also used in older cable TV installations. That role however has been taken up with RG-6 coaxial cable in recent years.

RG-6

The RG portion of the RG-6 and RG-59 stands for Radio Guide, which is an old and now obsolete military standard. However, even though RG cables are not often used in military applications anymore, RG-6 is still widely used in civilian applications. The largest civilian application of RG-6 cable is in the cable TV industry. RG-6 is used to run cable signals inside the house to the television as well as from the external drop point into the house. RG-6 coaxial cable is also used in fast broadband Internet connections from various cable companies. Figure 3-13 shows a photo of a stripped back RG-6 coaxial cable.

Figure 3-13

Stripped-back RG-6 coaxial
cable

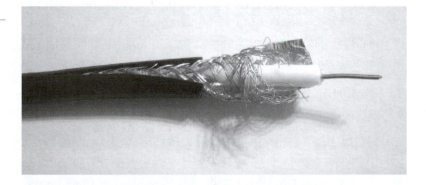

Broadband over Power Line

Broadband over Power Line (BPL) is a new technology that is emerging. While this technology may not help a great deal in areas where high-speed Internet is already available, rural areas and 3rd world areas could benefit a great deal from this technology. The idea behind BPL is that the standard power grid and power cables are used to not only carry electricity but also data. This technology uses the same cabling as the power in a house uses, so no new or different cabling is necessary. If BPL is available in an area, then data devices that can take advantage of BPL simply need to be plugged into an AC power wall outlet to get on a network. The IEEE 1901 standard describes BPL. It should be pointed out however that BPL is not actually available in the US and is mostly a technology that may see use in more 3rd world settings where there is not already an Internet access infrastructure in place.

CERTIFICATION READY
What is Broadband over
Power Lines (BPL)? What
is a situation where BPL
may be especially useful?
3.1

Serial

All the cable flavors discussed so far are considered serial cable types. In network communications, **_serial_** means that one bit after another is sent out onto the wire or fiber and interpreted by a network card or other type of interface on the other end. Each 1 or 0 is read separately and then combined with others to form data.

An alternative to sending data out on a cable in serial is to send out the data in parallel. In parallel communication, bits are sent in groups along multiple wires simultaneously and have to be read together to make sense of the message they represent. A good example of a parallel cable is an old-style printer cable, which is currently in the process of being replaced by the newer Universal Serial Bus (USB) cables. USB cables will be discussed later in this lesson.

RECOMMENDED STANDARD 232 (RS-232)

Recommended Standard 232 (RS-232) is the cable standard used for serial data cables connecting data-terminal and data-communications equipment. A familiar example of this would be using a computer's serial port to connect to an external modem. Today, serial connectors on many computers have been replaced with USB or FireWire. Most laptops do not even have RS-232 serial ports built into them anymore.

UNIVERSAL SERIAL BUS (USB)

Universal Serial Bus (USB) is now the default built-in serial bus for most motherboards. While most computer manufactures include 4 to 8 and occasionally more USB ports on their computers, USB can actually support up to 127 external devices. Along with the ability to theoretically support so many devices at once, USB is also a much more flexible peripheral bus than either serial or parallel. A much larger number of devices are designed to use the USB interface than ever existed for serial or parallel interfaces. USB can be used to connect printers, scanners, and a host of other input devices like keyboards, joysticks, and mice.

USB peripherals can be connected to a computer in two ways. One way is to directly connect a USB peripheral to a USB port on the PC. A second way is to connect them to a USB hub that is then connected to a USB port on the PC.

Hubs can be chained together to provide multiple USB connections. While the USB specifications allow for connecting up to 127 USB devices, it really is not practical to do so. The reason this is not practical is because all USB devices connecting to a computer share the same resources. The more USB devices sharing the same resources, the slower all the devices are going to perform. USB-enabled devices use a USB plug to connect to a computer. There are several varieties of USB connectors in various shapes and sizes, with USB ports to match. Depending on the types of devices you are using, you can have different types of USB ports on those devices. USB has gone through multiple versions since its introduction in 1996:

- **Version 1.0:** USB 1.0 was first introduced in 1996; however, it was not widely adopted because it had many problems that limited its utility. There were not many devices made that used it. USB 1.1 was introduced in 1998, and this version was very successful and widely adopted. USB 1.1 was so popular because it resolved most of the issues that existed in 1.0 making USB truly a usable external media connector. USB 1.0 and 1.1 had a low bandwidth throughput of 1.5 mbps (megabits per second); its higher bandwidth throughput was 12.0 mbps. It had a maximum cable length of 5 meters (16 ft) for full-speed devices and a 3-meter maximum length for low-speed devices.

- **Version 2.0:** USB 2.0 was released in 2000. It has a maximum data rate of 480 mbps and a maximum cable length of 5 meters. USB 2.0 is also known as high-speed USB. There have been many additions to the USB 2.0 standard since it was first release and it now has a large number of different connectors and ports that can be used to connect it to many different types of devices.

- **Version 3.0:** USB 3.0 is a new USB standard that was first released to manufacturers on November 17, 2008. However, no hardware has been manufactured for it yet, although it is expected that some will be created in 2010. Part of the reason for this slow adoption is that Intel has stated that they will not be supporting the new standard until 2011. Also, Windows 7's initial release did not come with support of the new standard either, although Microsoft says it is working on Windows 7 support. However, if USB 3.0 device drivers from USB 3.0 device vendors are installed USB 3.0 works fine in Windows 7.

When USB 3.0 devices are finally available, they will be a huge improvement over the older USB technologies. The USB standard calls for a superspeed data transfer support that will be up to 4.8 gbps (gigabits per second). In real terms, this means that USB 3.0 devices could potentially transfer data at 3.2 gbps. It is also estimated that USB 3.0 cables will be able to sustain this speed on cables up to 3 meters long.

Plenum versus Non-Plenum

The difference between plenum and non-plenum cable comes down to how each is constructed and where you can use it. Many large multistory buildings are designed to circulate air through the spaces between the ceiling of one story and the floor of the next; this space between floors is referred to as the *plenum*. The plenum is often the perfect spot to run all the cables that connect the numerous computers that are often located in these buildings. The insulating material of cable that can be run in the plenum must be composed of materials that do not release deadly gasses when burned. Any cable that meets this requirement is called plenum-rated cable. Any cable that does not meet this requirement is called non-plenum-rated cable. Additionally, for cable to be considered plenum-rated, the insulating material in the cable cannot burn so quickly that it acts as a type of wick. This requirement ensures that the cable does not help spread a fire quickly throughout a building. Because of these types of requirements, plenum-rated cabling is more expensive than non-plenum-rated cable.

CERTIFICATION READY
What is the difference between plenum and non-plenum cable?
3.1

The National Fire Protection Association (NFPA) demands that any cables run within a building's plenum be tested and guaranteed as safe. The cable used in this manner must be fire retardant and create little or no smoke and poisonous gas when burned. This means that non-plenum cable absolutely cannot be in the plenum. The NFPA does permit the use of non-plenum cable in other places where it is safe. Because of the cost difference between plenum and non-plenum cable, non-plenum cable is often used in this capacity where permitted.

Problems and Limitations Related to Copper

CERTIFICATION READY
What are some properties and limitations found in copper cabling?
3.1

There are a number of limitations that are inherent in using copper cabling for transferring data around a network. The most common limitations can be found in the distance that data can be sent, the speed the cable can transmit data, and Electromagnetic Interference (EMI). We will look at these limitations in reverse order.

ELECTROMAGNETIC INTERFERENCE

When electrons are pushed through two wires next to each other, it creates a magnetic field. The magnetic fields produced in this way result in noise. Anything that interferes with the transmission of information in a given environment is *noise*. An easy way to visualize this is to think of what it is like to sit in a very noisy room and talk to the person next to you. The various sound waves in the room, whether they are from machinery or people's voices, all work together to limit your ability to carry on a conversation with the person next to you.

The analogy of the crowded room works for electronic media also; however in electronic media, instead of noise being composed of sound, noise is composed of interfering electromagnetic fields. The more electromagnetic fields there are or the stronger those fields are the more noise, and therefore interference, the copper media has to overcome to get its signal through. This interference, which is termed *Electromagnetic Interference (EMI)*, can result in several problems.

One problem that results from this type of interference is that the copper cable can only be run a limited distance before the signal in the cable attenuates to the point where it is no longer readable. This problem, called *attenuation*, is the degradation of a signal due to the distance the signal has to travel. If the cable is run too close to sources of EMI such as electric motors, speakers, amplifiers, fluorescent light ballasts, and so on, then the distance a cable can successfully carry its signal becomes significantly less than the standard allows for.

Another problem that EMI can result in is something called *crosstalk*. Crosstalk is a form of EMI that results from two improperly shielded copper wires running too close together. In crosstalk, the signal being carried in one wire bleeds over to the other wire so that both signals are carried on the same wire, which results in both signals being degraded. A familiar example of this type of interference is when you tune into an AM radio station and end up hearing parts of broadcasts from two different stations simultaneously.

A third problem of EMI has to do with security and electromagnetism, rather than electromagnetic interference. As stated previously, when electrons move through copper cables they generate small amounts of electromagnetic radiation. Since the data flowing through the copper wires are in the form of 1s and 0s, a kind of pulsing of the resultant electromagnetic field takes place. With the right tools in hand, people can read the message in the wire without cutting it or even removing the insulation. This is one way people are able to create wiretaps like those used in law enforcement and espionage. In the past, high-security installations like the Pentagon actually encased communication wires in lead shielding to prevent them from being tapped.

The best way to solve the various problems caused by electricity flowing through copper wires is to not use copper wires at all. Fiber-optic cables, which are immune to the EMI problems previously mentioned, can be used in place of copper. However, because of the expense of fiber-optic cables, they may not be an option for every situation, and alternative solutions to EMI problems have been developed. The earliest solution was to wrap the data portion of a cable in a copper shield that helped protect the data wire from outside interference. This is the direction taken with coaxial cable and shielded twisted pair. In effect, the outer shield helps divert outside interference away from the data wire on the inside. A second, and cheaper, alternative is to wrap the wires in a cable around each other tightly so that the wires inside the cable partially shield themselves from outside interference. This is what unshielded twisted-pair cabling does. The amount of protection afforded by the tightness of the internal twist is what the various Category ratings are partially based on. It is important to note that neither one of these alternatives can protect the data wires from EMI completely, but they do offer some additional protection. The amount of protection offered depends on the choices made and the cost a person is willing to pay in order to accomplish his or her goals.

SPEED

Speed in a network is often used to refer to how fast data can be transmitted across a specific type of connection or media. The speed of a network connection is dependent on a number of different things. Here is a list of some of the more critical dependencies:

- *Bandwidth*: In wiring and other network media, the amount or number of signals that a wire can carry is measured as bandwidth. Another way of looking at this is to say that bandwidth is the theoretical maximum of how much data a specific cable or other media can carry. However, due to other issues such as latency, just because a media has a certain maximum bandwidth does not mean the media is able to carry that full bandwidth.

- *Latency*: The best way to illustrate latency is to think of a satellite link. To get data from a satellite connection, it is necessary for the source location to send the signal high up into space where the satellite then processes the signal and beams it back down to earth at a different location. Because signals to satellites can only travel at the speed of light, it takes time for the signal to go up to the satellite and come back down. If the satellite were in geosynchronous orbit, that would be around 35,000 miles straight up. If you are not sending the signal straight up but at an angle, the distance is even farther. That means that at a minimum the signal will have to travel at least 70,000 miles. Since light can only travel at approximately 186,000 miles a second, just the travel time will be close to one half a second. When you add to this the processing time at both ends of the connection and also at the satellite, the signal may take as much as a second to reach its intended destination. All media types have to deal with latency. This is also the reason an old-style 56 kbps modem could never truly send 56 kbps of data in real life.

- *Throughput*: Throughput is the amount of actual data that is being carried at any given time during a connection. Throughput takes into account both bandwidth and latency issues and gives us what the true functional speed of the network is. This is one reason it is better to use the term throughput when discussing how fast a network is rather than the terms speed or bandwidth. The two latter terms are only part of the picture, while throughput is the final sum.

DISTANCE LIMITATIONS

A deciding factor used in choosing what cable type to use is often the topology of a network and the distance between its components. Some network technologies can run much farther than others without communication errors, but all network communications technologies are prone to attenuation. As mentioned previously, attenuation can be caused by the distance signals have to travel, but it also could be due to the medium itself. Different types of noise on the cable also contribute to attenuation. Noise is described in more detail below. Some cable types suffer from attenuation more than others. For instance, any network using unshielded twisted-pair cable should have a maximum segment length of only 328 feet (100 meters). Other types of cable allow for longer lengths but cost more.

DUPLEXING

Communications come in three categories. The difference between these three categories is whether the communicating devices can broadcast and/or receive at the same time. The categories are simplex, half-duplex, and full-duplex:

- *Simplex*: A device can either broadcast or receive, it cannot do both. A good example of this is the radio in most cars. Your car radio is only capable of receiving a radio signal; it cannot transmit one. In other words, no matter how loud you yell at that talk show host you listen to during your morning commute, he or she cannot hear you.

- *Half-duplex*: A device can either send or receive communication, but it cannot do both at the same time. A pair of walkie-talkies is an example of this. When the button is pressed on the walkie-talkie, it turns the speaker off, and you cannot hear anything the other person is saying, however, you can talk to the person on the other end. Holding down the button on a walkie-talkie enables it to transmit. Letting off the button allows it to receive. It can only do one or the other at any given point in time; it cannot do both at the same time.

- *Full-duplex*: Both devices can send and receive communication at the same time. This means that the effective throughput is doubled and communication is much more efficient. Full-duplex is typical in most of today's switched networks.

X REF

Both full- and half-duplex communications are mentioned again in Lesson 7 where we discuss the various LAN technologies that are available, in particular, how Ethernet works.

■ Fiber-Optic Cabling

THE BOTTOM LINE

This section of Lesson 3 discusses fiber-optic cabling. The two different types of fiber optics and their advantages and disadvantages are discussed. Additionally several different types of fiber-optic connectors are mentioned as well as the pros and cons of each type of connector.

CERTIFICATION READY
What are the two main types of fiber-optic cables? How do they differ from each other?
3.1

Fiber-optic cable transmits digital signals using light impulses rather than electricity. Because of this, it is immune to electromagnetic Interference (EMI) and Radio Frequency Interference (RFI). This means that motors, fans, florescent lights, strong radio signals, and other types of interference that can interrupt transmissions through copper cables cannot interfere with signals through fiber-optic cables. This also means it is immune to technologies that are used to remotely intercept and read signals that travel through copper cables, making fiber-optic cables more secure.

Fiber cable works by allowing light impulses to be carried through either a glass or plastic core. Glass can carry the signal a greater distance, but plastic costs less. Whichever the type of core used, it works the same way. The fiber-optic cable is surrounded by a glass or plastic cladding with a different refraction index that reflects the light back into the core. Around this is a layer of flexible plastic buffer that can be wrapped in an armor coating usually composed of Kevlar. All of this is then sheathed in PVC or plenum.

The cable itself comes in either single-mode fiber (SMF) or multimode fiber (MMF); the difference between the two is in the number of light rays (the number of signals) each can carry. Multimode fiber is most often used for shorter-distance applications, and single-mode fiber is used for spanning longer distances.

Although fiber-optic cable may sound like the solution to many problems, it has pros and cons just like any other cable type. The pros to fiber-optic cable are as follows:

- Complete immunity to EMI and RFI
- Ability to transmit up to 40 kilometers, about 25 miles, in a single hop

The cons to fiber-optic cable are as follows:

- Difficult to install
- More expensive then twisted-pair
- Troubleshooting equipment is more expensive than twisted-pair test equipment
- More difficult to troubleshoot

Multimode Fiber

Multimode fiber (MMF) is a type of fiber-optic cable that uses light to communicate a signal; but with it, the light is dispersed on numerous paths as it travels through the core and is reflected back. A special material called *cladding* is used to line the core and focus the light back onto it. MMF provides high bandwidth at high speeds over medium distances (up to about 3,000 feet), but beyond that the signal begins to degrade. This is why MMF is most often used within a smaller area. If the buildings in a specific location are not too far apart, MMF is used to connect them. MMF is also used to make very long runs between different locations within one larger building.

MMF is available in a glass or plastic version that makes installation a lot easier and increases the installation's flexibility. MMF usually uses *light emitting diodes (LEDs)* for the light source of the data that is sent down the cable.

Single Mode Fiber

Single-mode fiber (SMF) is a very high-speed, long-distance fiber-optic cable that consists of a single strand—sometimes two strands—of fiberglass that carries the signals. Lasers are the primary light sources used with SMF. The light source is transmitted from end to end and pulsed to create communication. This is the type of fiber cable employed to span really long distances because it can transmit data 50 times farther than multimode fiber at a faster rate.

The transmission media of fiber-optic cable is made up of very small tubes designed to allow specific bands of light to pass down them. Because of this the installation of SMF can be very difficult and generally requires very specialized equipment and training. When installing fiber optics of any sort, the installer should be careful not to bend it too tightly. When working in switch rooms that contain fiber optics, the technicians should be careful how they handle the fiber-optic cables as well.

Fiber-Optic Connectors

There are many different types of connectors available for use with fiber-optic cables. However, the two most popular are the *straight tip (ST) connector* and *subscriber connector (SC)*, which is also sometimes called the *square connector*.

SUBSCRIBER CONNECTOR (SC)

The subscriber connector (SC) is one type of fiber-optic connector. As you can see in Figure 3-14, SCs are *latched*. This means that SCs use a mechanism to hold the connector securely attached and to prevent it from falling out.

Figure 3-14

Subscriber connector (SC)

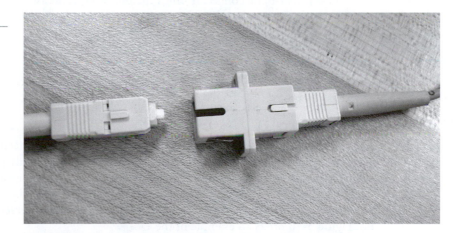

SCs work with both single-mode and multimode optical fibers and will last for around 1,000 matings. A mating is a way to refer to connecting a connector into its proper socket or jack. An SC is good for around 1,000 connections and disconnections before it wears out and needs to be replaced. SCs are being used more now but are still are not as common as ST connectors for LAN connections.

STRAIGHT TIP (ST) CONNECTOR

The ST fiber-optic connector (developed by AT&T) is one of the most widely used fiber-optic connectors; it uses a BNC style attachment mechanism similar to Thinnet, which makes connections and disconnections fairly frustration free. In fact, it is this feature that makes this connector so popular. Figure 3-15 shows an example of an ST connector. Notice the BNC style attachment mechanism.

Figure 3-15

Straight tip (ST) connector

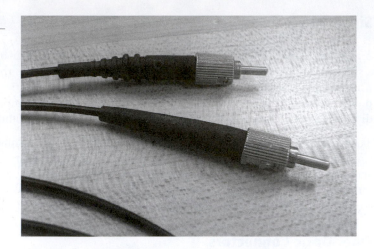

SMALL FORM FACTOR CONNECTOR

Another type of fiber-optic connector is the *small form factor (SFF) connector*. This type of connector allows more fiber-optic terminations in the same amount of space than its standard-sized counterparts. The two most common versions are the *mechanical transfer registered jack (MT-RJ or MTRJ)*, designed by AMP, and the *local connector (LC)*, designed by Lucent.

Mechanical Transfer Registered Jack (MT-RJ)

The MT-RJ fiber-optic connector was the first small form factor fiber-optic connector to be widely used and is only one-third the size of the SC and ST connectors it most often replaces. The MT-RJ fiber-optic connector offers the following benefits:

- Small size
- TX and RX strands in one connector
- Keyed for single polarity
- Pre-terminated ends that require no polishing or epoxy
- Easy to use

Local Connector (LC)

Local connectors (LCs) are a newer style of the SFF (small form factor) fiber-optic connector that is pulling ahead of the MT-RJ in popularity. It is especially popular for use with Fibre-Channel (FC) adapters and is a standard used for fast storage area networks and Gigabit Ethernet adapters. LCs have similar advantages to MT-RJ and other SFF-type connectors but are easier to terminate. LCs use a ceramic insert just as standard-sized fiber-optic connectors do. Figure 3-16 offers an example of the LC.

Figure 3-16

Local connector (LC)

CERTIFICATION READY
What are some commonly used fiber-optic connectors?
3.2

■ Installing Wiring Distributions

THE BOTTOM LINE

In this portion of Lesson 3, we discuss how to install wiring and distribute it across the network and topics such as horizontal and vertical cross-connects, patch panels, and Main Distribution Frames and Intermediate Distribution Frames and their related equipment. Additionally we examine how to verify that both your wire installation and wire termination are good.

CERTIFICATION READY
What are some of the main components of cable distribution in a network? What does each of those components do?
3.8

X REF

Lesson 6 in this book will go into much more detail about this topic.

There are many components involved in wiring a computer network. The components involved are not just the cables themselves but also connectors, devices the connectors go into, different types of cables based on purpose, and many other things. The following section of this lesson discusses some of those devices and types of cables.

Vertical and Horizontal Cross-Connects

A *cross-connect* is a location within a cabling system that facilitates the termination of cable elements, plus the reconnection of those elements with jumpers, termination blocks, and/or cables to a patch panel, and so on. In other words, the cross-connect is where all the wires come together. The cables used to make the connection from the switches to the computers have specific names and specifications that go with them.

Cables that run from communications closets to wall outlets are known as *horizontal connect cables*, because they are generally used on the same floor of a building. Sometimes a horizontal cable will run directly from a switch to a wall jack, but more often it will run from something called a patch panel (discussed next) to the wall outlet.

The cable that connects the patch panel with the switch is called a patch cable and is not considered part of the horizontal cable. The cable that connects the wall outlet to the actual computer is also called a patch cable. In other words, a *patch cable* is any cable that has a connector on both ends and is used to connect a network device to a network device, a wall jack to a network device, or a network device to a patch panel. Patch cables come in two main types and one secondary type. These types are straight-through, crossover, and rollover. These cables were discussed earlier in this lesson.

When using UTP cables for the horizontal connect cables, the cable should not exceed 100 meters, which includes the entire distance from the switch all the way to the computer at the other end. Any patch cables that are used to connect up the computers are included in the 100-meter length.

Here is a formula that is used to try and keep all this in perspective. The cross-connect cable that runs from the switch to the patch panel should not be any longer than 6 meters. The horizontal connect cable that goes from the patch panel to the wall jack should not be longer than 90 meters. Finally, the patch cable that connects the wall jack to the actual computer should not be longer than 3 meters. These values are not absolute, but they are a good point to start with and try to stay within. If you add up all the cable lengths, you end up with 99 meters. This is one meter within the Category specifications that define cable lengths for UTP cables, preventing you from exceeding the specification limit.

Backbone cables that connect equipment rooms, telecommunications rooms, and other physical termination points are referred to as *vertical connect cables*. This name came about because these cables often go from floor to floor in a building. All of these cables will eventually connect to each other and finish off the network cabling for the building. The exact pieces involved depend on the size of the installation, the needs of the organization, and the structure in which they are installed.

Patch Panels

CERTIFICATION READY
What is a patch panel and what is it used for?
3.2

A *patch panel* is usually a rack or wall-mounted structure that houses cable connections. A patch cable generally plugs into the front, while the back holds the punched-down connection of a longer, more permanent cable. The purpose of the patch panel is to give the administrator a flexible way to change the path of a signal quickly when needed. Figure 3-17 depicts a small patch panel. Figure 3-18 shows the reverse side of the patch panel shown in Figure 3-17.

Figure 3-17

Front view of a small patch panel

Figure 3-18

Back view of a small patch panel

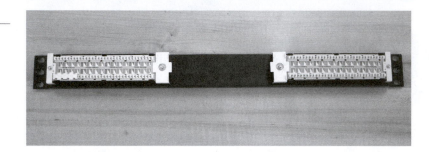

66 BLOCK

In the past, one of the most common types of patch panels was known as a *66 block*. Figure 3-19 shows a 66 block. Even though these are now considered legacy equipment, they are still listed as an objective on the exam. These devices are considered legacy equipment because they are large in comparison to newer wire-terminating devices and they have a relatively small (25-pair) capacity. The final reason these devices are considered legacy is because they are unsuited for any network communications speeds faster than 10 mbps. The most likely place to see one of these devices today is in some older telephone installations.

Figure 3-19

A 66 block

MAIN DISTRIBUTION FRAME (MDF)/INTERMEDIATE DISTRIBUTION FRAME (IDF)

The *main distribution frame (MDF)* is a wiring point that is generally used as a reference point for network and telephone lines. It is installed in the building as part of the prewiring process, generally when the building is first built, and the internal lines are connected to it. After that, all that is left is to connect the external (telephone and WAN/Internet company) lines to the other side to complete the circuit. Often, another wire frame called an *intermediate distribution frame (IDF)* is located in an equipment or telecommunications room. It is connected to the MDF by a backbone cable of some sort and is used to provide greater flexibility for the distribution of all the communications lines within the building. This is especially true when the building in question is too large to terminate all the cables in the building at one location. In a situation like this, one MDF and one or more IDFs are positioned within the building to allow for full coverage of the building without exceeding length limitations that are placed on different types of cables. Both the MDF and IDFs contain sturdy metal racks designed to hold the bulk of cables coming from all over the building.

25 pair

A *25-pair cable* consists of 25 individual pairs of wires all inside one common insulating jacket. This type of cable is not generally used for data cabling but is commonly used for telephone cabling. Cabling of this type is especially useful as backbone and cross-connect cables in a telephone setup because it reduces the cable clutter significantly. A 25-pair cable is often referred to as a *feeder cable* because it supplies a signal to many connected pairs. In Figure 3-17, a 25-pair wire is connected to the 66 block to provide connectivity to the IDF.

100 pair

100-pair cables can be used for very large telephone company installations. They combine 100 pairs of wires into one large, insulated cable. These large cables are also used in aerial installations and sometimes in buried and duct-type installations that run up and down a building. To keep the pairs unique, colors other than the traditional networking ones are used.

110 BLOCK

A newer type of wiring distribution point called a *110 block* has replaced most telephone wire installations and is also used for computer networking. On one side, wires are punched down; the other side has RJ-11 jacks (for phone connections) or RJ-45 jacks (for network connections). Figure 3-20 shows a small 110 block. 110 blocks come in sizes from 25 to more than 500 wire pairs, and some are capable of carrying 1 gpbs connections when used with Category 6 cables.

Figure 3-20

A 110 block

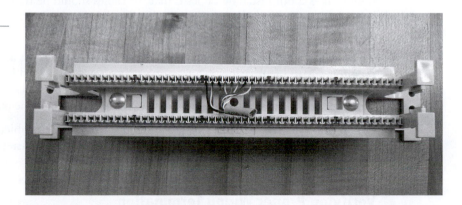

CSU/DSUs are explained in detail in Lesson 6.

DEMARC/DEMARC EXTENSION

The *demarc* (short for demarcation point) is the last point of responsibility of the service provider. It is often at the MDF in your building connection (if your building is large), but it is usually just an RJ-45 jack that your *channel service unit/data service unit* (CSU/DSU) connects into from your router to wide area network (WAN) connections.

CERTIFICATION READY
What does demarc stand for? Why is it important to know where the demarc is for a network?
3.8

When troubleshooting, network administrators often test for connectivity on both sides of the demarc to determine if the problem is internal or external. The length of copper or fiber that begins after the demarc but still does not reach all the way up to your office is referred to as a *demarc extension*. Demarc extensions are most often used when the external service enters your building somewhere other than the MDF. If this is the case, then the cable that runs from that point to the MDF would be considered a demarc extension.

SMART JACK

A *smart jack*, also called a *Network Interface Device (NID)* or network interface unit, is owned by the *Public Switched Telephone Network (PSTN)* and is a special network interface that is often used between the service provider's network and the internal network. You cannot physically test to an actual demarc because it is just an RJ-45 jack, but the service provider may install a NID that has power and can be looped for testing purposes.

The smart jack device may also provide for code and protocol conversion, making the signal from the service provider usable by the devices on the internal network like the CSU/DSU.

Verifying Correct Wiring Installation

After a wire installation has been completed on a site, it is very important to verify that all the installed wires are tested. This is important because there are many things that can go wrong in an installation. Many of these problems may not come to light unless a thorough testing is carried out. When doing a wire installation, it is not only important to check all the wires, it is also important to keep complete records of where and how the wires are connected in the network. It is not acceptable to test just a few cables and then assume that all of them are correct.

Following are some of the things that can go wrong in a cable installation. Sometimes copper cables can be placed a little too close to a magnetic source and can be affected by EMI. Occasionally cable jackets can be ripped off completely when pulling the cable through a tight space or around a corner. Cables can be cut wrong and extended beyond the maximum length for their type. Fiber-optic cables are very fragile and can be easily and expensively damaged if they are handled roughly or poorly installed. These are just a few of things that can go wrong and the best way to catch them is to test each cable separately. The best cable-installer companies assume that some of these things will go wrong, and therefore they will test, test, and test again. If you are handling your own installation, you should do the same things. The bottom line about installing cables is that the cables should be tested frequently during installation and again when the installation is done.

It is also general practice to install more cables than are absolutely necessary. The reason for this is that at some point a cable will go bad. When a cable goes bad, it is often not possible to simply rip it out and replace it with a new one. Given this fact, a good installer will install a handful of extra cables in any given room in a company's building so that if a cable does go bad in the future, there are already extra cables that can be used to take the place of the bad cable.

Finally it is very important to keep detailed records in case problems come up later. If such problems do come up, with detailed records it is much easier to track down and resolve the problem.

Verifying Proper Wiring Termination

Although many things can go wrong while pulling a cable, many more things can go wrong when terminating a cable, copper or otherwise. With a minimal amount of training and a little patience, almost anyone can pull a network cable without damaging it—at least, most of the time. Proper termination of copper cables to a punch-down block is much trickier and requires practice to get right. For this reason, it is best to always inspect the installation and verify that all wires are terminated properly in the right order as you go. If the wires get out of order or are punched down in the incorrect location, the whole network could fail to work. When this happens, sometimes it becomes necessary to actually start over the punch down process. It is much better to get it right the first time.

Fiber-optic termination requires specialized and expensive equipment and training. Unless the installers spend hours cutting, stripping, polishing, and terminating the fiber-optic cable and look for any mistakes or damage thoroughly, there is a good chance the installation will not be done correctly the first time. New connections should always be terminated using the appropriate tools.

■ Wireless Media

THE BOTTOM LINE

This section of Lesson 3 examines the 802.11 wireless standard and the four most commonly used amendments that have been made to this standard.

In recent years, wireless media has become more and more important. Now many LANs have a wireless component to them, even when they are primarily wire-based LANs. A few LANs even use wireless media for every connection.

IEEE 802.11

CERTIFICATION READY
What wireless standards are most commonly used today? What are the characteristics of each of the wireless standards that may be found in use today?
3.3

CERTIFICATION READY
How would wireless standards affect installing and configuring a wireless network?
2.2

The most prominent standard for wireless LANs is the IEEE 802.11 standards. The IEEE ratified the 802.11 initial or basic standard in 1997; however, subsequent standard updates and improvements have been released over the years. Of the 802.11 standards, four are the most common: 802.11a, 802.11b, 802.11g, and most recently, 802.11n. Each of these standards has maximum speeds, distances, and channels. Each of these four standards also has specific radio frequencies they are restricted to. These four standards will be examined next along with some characteristics of each standard. We will discuss some characteristics of each standard before we go on to discuss the specific standards and how the characteristics apply to them.

Distance

Distance is a measure of how far a data signal can be sent before the signal has to be renewed. Another term used to characterize this property is range. Different wireless standards have different distances or ranges they are able to transmit. These distances will be noted as each standard is discussed.

Speed

Speed is a measure of what a particular standard's throughput is. Throughput is best defined as how much data can be sent across the medium in a specific amount of time. This property is also often referred to as a specific technologies data transfer rate. Different wireless standards have different throughputs. It should be noted that the further a receiving device is from the origin of the data signal the lower the throughput, or the lower the amount of data, the device can receive will be in a given amount of time. The maximum data transfer rate of a particular standard will be noted for each standard that is discussed. You should always keep in mind that the further a receiving device is from the source or origin of the data signal is the smaller the actual data transfer rate, or speed will be.

Latency

Latency is the time it takes a signal to be passed from one device to another on a network. Latency does not just include the time it takes the signal to move from one device to another over the media. Latency also includes the processing time required on both the send end and the receive end of the connection. If a signal has to pass through multiple devices to get to its destination, then latency also includes the time each intervening device uses to process the signal.

A good way to help visualize latency is to think about news cast you have seen on TV where one reporter is in the middle of nowhere and the other reporter is in the news rooms. In those situations often times the reporter in the news room asks a question and then it takes a few moments for the reporter in the remote location to hear the question and answer it. The wait time between the reporter in the news room asking the question and the remote reporter answering it is the latency of the signal. The same situation happens with computer networks. The only difference is that the total latency time is usually too short to notice, unlike the latency taking place between the two reporters.

Frequency

In wireless networking frequency refers to the range of the electromagnetic spectrum that is used by a specific standard for wireless communications. For example the wireless standards that we will discuss below use either the 2.4 GHz (gigahertz) radio frequency range or the 5 GHz frequency range.

Channels

When discussing wireless networking, channels refer to specific sub-ranges of the assigned frequency of wireless networking standards. The channels are used to divide up the assigned frequencies of a specific standard so that multiple wireless LANs can be setup in the same location. Depending on the wireless standard used, you can have different numbers of channels available for different overlapping networks. Based on the standard being used, this places a maximum limit on how many different wireless networks can be in the same location.

One limitation to keep in mind when using channels is that two networks in the same location cannot have overlapping channels or they will interfere with each other. What this means is that when the frequency range that is assigned to a specific wireless standard is divided into channels, it is necessary to make sure that there is no overlap of the sub-frequency ranges that make up the channels.

Another limitation placed on channel creation is that each wireless standard specifies how large the frequency range has to be for each channel. This specification places an upward limit on how many channels may be created out of each frequency range. This channel number limit can range from 4 to 27 depending on what each specification stays. The number of channels each standard allows will be mentioned when the standards are discussed.

Channel bonding

Channel bonding is wireless communications technique where two or more channels are used together to increase the amount of data that can be sent across a network at the same time. Another way of putting it is that channel bonding is a way to increase a network's throughput by using more than one channel to transmit data between two devices.

Channel bonding is similar to a technique used in the old days of dial-up modems called shot gunning where two modems and two dial-up lines were used to double the throughput of a dial-up connection. The difference is that instead of using two modems and two dial-up lines to accomplish this, two or more wireless channels are used instead. This technique was introduced with the IEEE 802.11n amendment to the wireless standard and will be discussed in more detail later.

MIMO

Multiple-input/multiple-output (MIMO) is a wireless antenna technology developed to increase the range and throughput of a wireless network. This technology is used in the IEEE 802.11n standard to increase the reliability, range or distance, and throughput of wireless network signals. What MIMO does is it uses multiple antennas on sending and receiving devices to minimize the effects of a phenomenon called multipath. Multipath is a phenomenon that results when radio signals bouncing off of different objects causing the signal to split up and arrive at the destination at different times and/or multiple times. Using multiple antennas MIMO is able to mitigate some of these effects allowing the radio signal to travel further and not lose as much data as would happen with just a single antenna. This technique can also be tweaked to actually allow a station to transmit more data than normal by taking advantage of the multipath phenomenon to send out more data at one time. MIMO does this by deliberately using the split up signal paths to send more date than if just a single path were being used.

802.11a

The IEEE 802.11a amendment to the 802.11 standard was made in 1999. The theoretical maximum throughput for this standard is 54 mbps; however, realistically it is more like 22 mbps. The 802.11a standard has 8 non-overlapping channels, which means that the frequency ranges between specific channels are not shared. When a channel or frequency range is not shared or overlapping with another range, both ranges can be used to carry data without having to worry about interference between the different access points in a network. The more access points you have without having to reuse channels, the more flexibility you have in how you layout and design your wireless network. The maximum indoor distance for 802.11a is ~50 feet or 15 meters but the maximum outdoor distance is ~100 feet or 30 meters. The 802.11a standard uses the 5 GHz radio frequency range.

802.11b

Like the 802.11a wireless standard, the 802.11b amendment was also ratified in 1999 with the first products using the standard appearing in early 2000. The 801.11b standard allows for a theoretical throughput of up to 11 mbps, however, a throughput of 2.5 mbps is more realistic. The maximum indoor range or distance for 802.11b is ~150 feet or 45 meters. The maximum outdoor range is ~300 feet or 90 meters. 802.11b uses the 2.4 GHz radio frequency range. The 802.11b standard only has 3 non-overlapping channels. The non-overlapping channels are 1, 6, and 11.

802.11g

The 802.11g amendment to the 802.11 standard was actually widely adopted by consumers and manufacturers in early 2003 even though it was not officially ratified until June 2003. 802.11g uses the same frequency range and therefore the same channels as 802.11b. 802.11g also has the same distance capabilities as 802.11b. The main difference between 802.11b and 802.11g is the data throughput speeds. 802.11b has a maximum throughput of 11 mbps with a realistic throughput of between 2.5 and 5 mbps, 802.11g maximum and realistic throughputs in line with 802.11a. That means that the maximum throughput of 802.11g is 54 mbps with a realistic throughput of around 22 mbps.

The close relationship between 802.11b and 802.11g means that 802.11g is fully backwards compatible with 802.11b. What this means in practical terms is that if you have a computer equipped with an 802.11g network card it will be able to connect to any 802.11b or g network.

802.11n

802.11n is the most recent amendment to the 801.11 standards. The 802.11n standard was officially ratified in September 2009; however, industry had started migrating to it as early as 2007.

802.11n uses both the 5 GHz and 2.4 GHz frequency ranges. The maximum theoretical throughput for 802.11n is 300 mbps, although some people say it can go as high as 600 mbps. However, realistically most 802.11n installations run between 100 and 200 mbps. The maximum indoor distance for 802.11n is ~229 feet or 70 meters. The maximum outdoor distance is 820 feet or 250 meters.

The question of channels is a little bit more complicated when discussing 802.11n. If you are simply asking how many channels are possible with 802.11n, then the answer would be 3 non-overlapping channels in the 2.4 GHz range. An additional 24 non-overlapping channels are available in the 5 GHz range if each channel is 20 MHz wide, or 12 if each channel is 40 MHz wide.

As you can probably guess by the way the previous couple of sentences are worded, there is a catch when it comes to channels in the 802.11n standard. The catch is the addition of channel bonding. In channel bonding, two or more adjacent channels can be linked together to increase the overall throughput of the wireless network. This means that if one channel can carry 54 mbps of data by itself, when it is bonded with an adjacent channel of similar capability, the bonded channels can now carry 108 mbps of data. 802.11n allows two or more channels to be bonded. However, the more channels you bond together, the fewer overall channels you have to work with. Along with channel bonding, the 802.11n standard is also the only standard capable of using MIMO as discussed above.

As far as compatibility with previous 802.11 standards goes, 802.11n is backwards compatible to the 802.11a, 802.11b, and 802.11g amendments. The reason that 802.11n is so universally backwards compatible is because it uses the same frequency ranges of the previous 802.11 amendments; it has been deliberately designed to take advantage of that so that it would be compatible with all of them. Any new device that can connect to an 802.11n network can also connect to an 802.11a, 802.11b, or 802.11g network.

INSTALLING AND CONFIGURING WIRELESS MEDIA

There are several issues that are involved in configuring wireless media. Four important issues related to this are Access Point placement, antenna type, interference, and Service Set Identifier (SSID) configuration. A SSID is a 32 character identifier attached to the header of a packet being sent across a wireless network used to identify the wireless network being used. A SSID can also act as a kind of password that ensures the signal being sent across the wireless network actually belongs there. All four of these configuration issues will be covered in Lesson 7 in detail.

■ Tying It All Together

THE BOTTOM LINE

In the last section of this lesson, we examine why it is important for a person to know about the different types of media that are available for network communications.

The previous lesson discussed the theory behind how different devices and networks talk to each other using protocols and the various layers of the TCP/IP and OSI Models to explain the function of each layer. However, for a network to exist, some means of allowing the different devices to talk to each other needs to exist. Without that, all you have is a stand-alone computer. The means of tying, or connecting the different computers in the network together is called the media. In this lesson, we talked about the three most common types of media used to do this. Those media types were copper wires, fiber optic cables, and radio frequencies.

The Network Access layer in the TCP/IP Model and the Physical and MAC sublayer of the Data Link layer in the OSI Model both define how the 1s and 0s of electronic communications are encoded onto the media. However, without the correct media being connected in the correct manner to the rest of the network, all the encoding of 1s and 0s will accomplish nothing.

It is important to know what types of media connect to specific devices and in which order to ensure that communications take place. If you connect the wrong type of media to a device, or connect the media in the wrong place, then there is no network. For this reason, it is important for the people who support data networks to know what different types of media look like and how they are to be connected to different devices and ports. The purpose of this lesson was to ensure that the people supporting a network know this information.

The information covered in this lesson is also important for the effective troubleshooting of networks. Statistics show that the majority of problems that have to be resolved in network environments are at the physical level of the network. That means that most problems encountered in network environments have to do with broken media, incorrect media, incorrectly connected media, or media connected in the wrong way or at the wrong location. If a network support person knows the information found in this lesson, he or she will be able to more effectively identify these problems in real-world environments and know what to do to correct them.

SKILL SUMMARY

IN THIS LESSON YOU LEARNED:

- How cabling is denoted.
- The difference between different types of copper cabling.
- What unshielded twisted-pair (UTP) cabling is.
- The different types of connectors used in UTP cabling.
- What Category cabling is.
- Three types of commonly used patch cables.
- Some of the problems and limitations of copper cabling.
- What fiber-optic cabling is.
- The two modes used to transmit data across fiber-optic cables.
- Some of the different types of more commonly used connectors in fiber-optic cabling.
- What patch panels are and some of the technologies associated with them.
- The four most commonly used types of wireless media for LAN networks.
- Some of the limitations and capabilities of the four most common types of wireless media for LANs.

■ Knowledge Assessment

Fill in the Blank

Complete the following sentences by writing the correct word or words in the blanks provided.

1. The three main types of copper cabling used in LANs are _____, _____, and _____.

2. The two main types or RJ connectors are _____, which is used in telephone connections and _____, which is used in network connections.

3. In modern LANs, the two most commonly used types of Category cabling are _____ and _____.

4. The three types of patch cables that are used in networking are _____, _____, and _____.

5. _____ connectors are the types of connectors used in coaxial installations.

6. The two main serial standards in use today are _____ and _____.

7. The three types of duplexing are _____, _____, and _____.

8. _____ and _____ are the two methods used for sending data down a fiber-optic cable.

9. The three most commonly used wireless technologies in modern wireless LANs are
   _____, _____, and _____.

10. Four things that need to be taken into consider when configuring a wireless LAN are
    _____, _____, _____, and _____.

Multiple Choice

Circle the letter corresponding to the correct answer.

1. Which of the following is not a legitimate RJ-style connector?
   a. RJ-11
   b. RJ-52
   c. RJ-45
   d. RJ-22

2. The category of unshielded twisted-pair wires that is best used for gigabit Ethernet is
   which of the following?
   a. CAT 5
   b. CAT 3
   c. CAT 6
   d. CAT 5e

3. Which of the following types of patch cable is used to connect similar devices?
   a. Crossover cable
   b. Straight-through cable
   c. Rollover cable
   d. Horizontal cross-connect cable

4. Which of the following types of patch cable is used to connect dissimilar devices?
   a. Crossover cable
   b. Straight-through cable
   c. Rollover cable
   d. Horizontal cross-connect cable

5. USB _____ is capable of top theoretical throughput speeds of 480 mbps.
   a. RS-232
   b. Version 1.1
   c. Version 2.0
   d. Version 3.0

6. When a signal on a copper cable looses strength over time as it travels down the wire, it
   is called _____.
   a. Crosstalk
   b. Latency
   c. Duplexing
   d. Attenuation

7. When a signal on one wire interferes with a signal on an adjacent wire, it is called
   _____.
   a. Crosstalk
   b. Throughput
   c. Duplexing
   d. Frequency

8. In _____ fiber-optic cables, a laser serves as the light source.
   a. SC
   b. MMF
   c. SMF
   d. LC

9. In _____ fiber-optic cables, an LED generally serves as the light source.
   a. SC
   b. MMF
   c. SMF
   d. LC

10. The IEEE 802.11n wireless standard is backwards compatible with which of the following standards? (Choose all that apply.)
   a. IEEE 802.11a
   b. IEEE 802.11b
   c. IEEE 802.11g
   d. IEEE 802.11m

Case Scenarios

Scenario 3-1: Connecting Two Switches Together with a UTP Cable

You have been given several types of RJ-45 UTP cables. Based on the following diagram, which cable should you use?

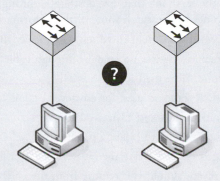

Scenario 3-2: Connecting a Small Network Together Using Several Different UTP Cables

You have been given several types of RJ-45 UTP cables and the following network configuration. How many of each type of cable will you need and where should you connect them?

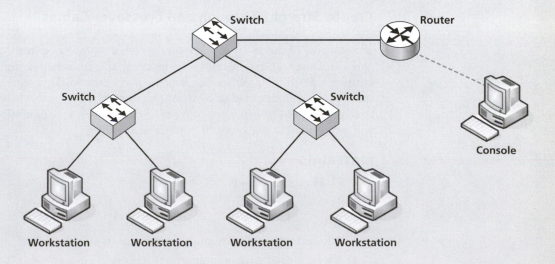

Lab Exercises

Lab 1

Patch Cables

MATERIALS
- Computer running Microsoft Office
- Internet connectivity
- Textbook

THE LAB

Get to Know Your Patch Cables

1. Read the section of the textbook that covers straight-through, crossover, and rollover cables. You may also need to research some of this information on the Internet.
2. Create a Microsoft Word document in which you answer the following:
   a. What are the differences between a straight-through cable and crossover cable?
   b. What is each type of cable used for?
   c. What is the TIA/EIA standard used for crossover cables?
   d. What do the acronyms TIA and EIA stand for?
   e. What three tools are needed to create a patch cable?
   f. What type of plug is used to create the crossover patch cables?
   g. How much of a sheath should you remove from the end?
   h. What is the difference between CAT 5 and CAT 5e?
3. Turn your answers in to your instructor.

Lab 2

Create Straight-Through and Crossover Cables

The purpose of this lab is to take you through the process of creating both a straight-through and a crossover cable. The reason we are doing this lab is familiarize you with the process of creating a patch cable. When you become part of the working world, you will be required at some point in their career to create one or more of these cables. It is not a question of *if* the student will need to make one or more of these cables, it is a question of *when* the student will be required to make one or more of these cables.

MATERIALS
- RJ-45 crimping tool
- RJ-45 connectors
- Two lengths of CAT 5 or higher UTP cable at least 4 feet long
- Wire stripper or telecommunications scissors
- Wire cutter or telecommunications scissors
- The pin-put diagrams for straight-through and crossover cables found in this lesson

THE LAB

Create a Straight-Through Cable

1. Strip about $1^1/_2$ inches of cladding off the end of the CAT 5 cable using either the wire stripping tool or the telecommunications scissors.

2. Untwist the wires in the CAT 5 cable so that you have them all spread out by color. Make sure that the solid colors are matched beside the white version of their color. See Figure 3-21.

Figure 3-21

Straight-through Ethernet cable pin out

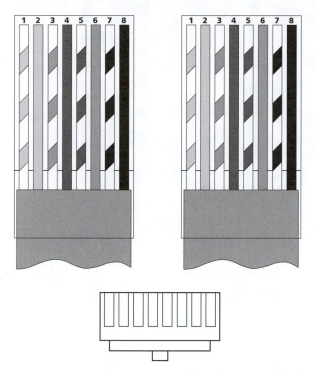

3. Arrange the small wires in the order indicated in the diagram for what a straight-through cable is to look like.

4. Without getting the small wires out of order, bring the small wires together until they are all side by side; also ensure that all the small wires are straight and not bent.

5. While holding the cable tightly in one hand without letting the small wires get out of order, use the wire cutter or telecommunications scissors to cut the ends of the small wires off in a straight line until only about an inch is left of the small wires sticking out of the sheathing.

6. Pick up a RJ-45 connector and make sure the tab is facing down, as shown in the diagram.

7. Carefully slip the RJ-45 connector on to the end of the CAT 5 cable. Make sure that each of the smaller wires goes into its own separate groove in the RJ-45 connector and that they remain in the correct order.

8. Push the CAT 5 cable into the RJ-45 connector until you can see the copper ends of the smaller wires directly up against the very end of the RJ-45 connector. If you look at the RJ-45 connector directly head on where you can see the ends of the smaller wires, they will look like little disks at the end of the connector. Also make sure that the outer sheathing of the CAT 5 cable is pushed all the way into the RJ-45 connector.

9. Using the RJ-45 crimping tool, crimp down the RJ-45 connector. Do not be afraid to use a lot of strength to do this because if you do not, the connections will not take and the cable will not work.

10. Repeat steps 1–9 on the other end of the cable.

11. You have now created a straight-through cable. Use a cable tester to verify that you have successfully completed the cable.

Create a Crossover Cable

1. Strip about $1^1/_2$ inches of cladding off the end of the CAT 5 cable using either the wire stripping tool or the telecommunications scissors.

2. Untwist the wires in the CAT 5 cable so that you have them all spread out by color. Make sure that the solid colors are matched beside the white version of their color. See Figure 3-22.

Figure 3-22

Crossover Ethernet cable pin out

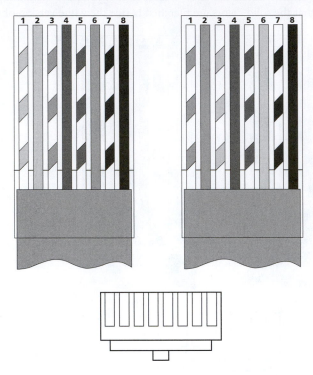

3. Arrange the small wires in the order indicated in the diagram for the left side of what the crossover cable is to look like.

4. Without getting the small wires out of order, bring the small wires together until they are all side by side; also ensure that all the small wires are straight and not bent.

5. While holding the cable tightly in one hand without letting the small wires get out of order, use the wire cutter or telecommunications scissors to cut the ends of the small wires off in a straight line until only about an inch is left of the small wires sticking out of the sheathing.

6. Pick up a RJ-45 connector and make sure the tab is facing down, as shown in the diagram.

7. Carefully slip the RJ-45 connector onto the end of the CAT 5 cable. Make sure that each of the smaller wires goes into its own separate groove in the RJ-45 connector and that they remain in the correct order.

8. Push the CAT 5 cable into the RJ-45 connector until you can see the copper ends of the smaller wires directly up against the very end of the RJ-45 connector. If you look at the RJ-45 connector directly head on where you can see the ends of the smaller wires, they will look like little disks at the end of the connector. Also make sure that the outer sheathing of the CAT 5 cable is pushed all the way into the RJ-45 connector.

9. Using the RJ-45 crimping tool, crimp down the RJ-45 connector. Do not be afraid to use a lot of strength to do this because if you do not, the connections will not take and the cable will not work.

10. Repeat steps 1–9 on the other end of the cable. Except in step 3, use the right side of the diagram for your reference for the correct order of the small wires.

11. You have now created a crossover cable. Use a cable tester to verify that you have successfully completed the cable.

Network Addressing

EXAM OBJECTIVE MATRIX

TECHNOLOGY SKILL COVERED	EXAM OBJECTIVE	EXAM OBJECTIVE NUMBER
Physical Addressing	**Classify how applications, devices, and protocols relate to the OSI model layers.** • MAC Address	1.2
	Explain the purpose and properties of IP addressing. • MAC address format	1.3
Logical Addressing	**Classify how applications, devices, and protocols relate to the OSI model layers.** • EUI-64	1.2
	Explain the purpose and properties of IP addressing. • Classes of addresses • A, B, C and D • Classless (CIDR) • IPv4 vs. IPv6 (formatting) • Subnetting	1.3
How Physical and Logical Addressing Work Together	**Explain the purpose and properties of IP addressing.** • MAC address format	1.3
	Explain the purpose and properties of routing and switching. • Broadcast domain vs. collision domain	1.4
Other Addressing Technologies	**Explain the purpose and properties of IP addressing.** • Classes of addresses • Public vs. Private • Multicast vs. unicast vs. broadcast • APIPA	1.3
	Given a scenario, install and configure routers and switches. • NAT • PAT	2.1
	Explain the purpose and properties of DHCP. • Static vs. dynamic IP addressing	2.3
	Given a scenario, install and configure a basic firewall. • NAT/PAT	5.5

KEY TERMS

60-bit Extended Unique Identifier (EUI-60)	MAC address
64-bit Extended Unique Identifier (EUI-64)	multicast
Automatic Private Internet Protocol Addressing (APIPA)	Network Address Translation (NAT)
binary	physical address
broadcast	Port Address Translation (PAT)
classful IP addressing	private IP address
classless inter-domain routing (CIDR)	private network
classless IP addressing	protocol suite
Dynamic Host Configuration Protocol (DHCP)	public IP address
dynamic IP addressing	public network
Extended Unique Identifier (EUI)	Source Network Address Translation (SNAT)
hexadecimal	static IP addressing
hop	subnetting
Internet Protocol (IP)	supernetting
IP version 4 (IPv4)	TCP/IP Protocol Suite
IP version 6 (IPv6)	unicast

John is the WAN Engineer for Dive Master Services Inc. His company has purchased another company called Diving Unlimited, Ltd. John has to figure out how to make the two networks work together. In order to do this he needs to come up with a uniform network addressing scheme that combines the two company's networks. How will he go about doing this?

■ Physical Addressing

THE BOTTOM LINE

This section of Lesson 4 discusses what physical addresses are and how they are used in computer networks. This section also briefly discusses what the hexadecimal numbering system is. This section also explains the usage differences between physical addresses versus MAC addresses. Finally, the practice of MAC Address Spoofing is discussed.

A *physical address* is the physical binary address that every network device is given when it is created by its manufacturer. In most cases, this address is binding on the device and cannot be changed. This address is also known as the device's *MAC address*. In any portion of a network where all the computers are connected to the same switch or hub, no two network devices can have the same MAC address. If two devices do have the same MAC address, then they will interfere with each other and cause problems on the network until one of the two network devices are replaced. This usually means replacing a network card in one of the interfering devices; however, it may require replacing the computer because many modern computers have the network cards built into their motherboards directly.

The physical address of a network device is 48 bits long. This means that the address is made up of forty-eight 1s and 0s. Because it is hard and confusing for a person to read forty-eight 1s and 0s together and be able to distinguish one address from another, physical address are generally expressed in something called *hexadecimal* format. This is a special base 16 numbering system that replaces every fourth 1 and 0 with the numerals 0–9 or the alphabetic letters A–F. The result of this is a string of 12 numbers and letters that are much easier for a human to read and distinguish between. To make things even easier, many times a dash (-) or a colon (:) is placed between every two hexadecimal numbers.

Using hexadecimal numbers, a physical address would look something like this—91-FC-5D-D9-A3-B0. In *binary* the same physical address would look like this—100100011111110001011101101100110100011110110000. Both numbers are the same except the first one is in hexadecimal and the second one is in binary. As you can see, the hexadecimal one is much easier to read.

The first half of those forty-eight 1s and 0s are made of up the manufacturer's portion of the physical address. Each network device manufacturer out there is assigned a 24-bit number that represents their company. Any network connectivity device that company manufactures is required to use those 24 bits as the first portion of the physical address. Companies can be assigned multiple 24-bit addresses for the manufacturing portion of the network devices they build. These first 24 bits are called the *Organizationally Unique Identifier*.

The last 24 bits of the physical address is called the host portion of the physical address. Each device made by the manufacturer needs to have a unique host portion of its physical address so that it does not interfere with the networks in which the devices will be placed. For each manufacturer portion of the physical address that a manufacturer has, they can produce 16,777,216 devices with unique host portions of their physical address.

After a manufacturer uses all 16 million plus host numbers, they will need to start reusing the host portion of the physical address. This is why, only on very rare occasions, a network will sometimes have two devices with the same physical address, especially if they get all their network devices from the same manufacturer. In the rare event that this happens, all the network support personnel have to do is replace one of the duplicate physical address devices with a network device that does not use the same physical address as some other device on the network. It is unlikely in the extreme that the device that replaces the duplicate physical device will have the same physical address as some other device on the network.

EUI-60 and EUI-64

There are a couple of variations on the conventional MAC address called *Extended Unique Identifiers (EUI)*. One of these variations is called *60-bit Extended Unique Identifier (EUI-60)*. This is simply a MAC address where the host extension is 36-bits long rather than 24-bits long. This allows for more host addresses for each manufacture's OUI before they are repeated. A second variation is called *64-bit Extended Unique Identifier (EUI-64)* where the host extension is 40-bits long, allowing for even more host addresses per OUI. EUI-64 is especially important because IPv6 can use this to create a unique interface identifier. This will be discussed in more detail later in this lesson when IPv6 is discussed.

MAC Addressing

As stated before, the MAC address and the physical address of a network device is the same thing. This is essentially correct. However, the term MAC address is generally used to refer to the function of the physical address, while the term physical address is used more often to refer to the actual thing.

The computer or network device uses the MAC address to move data frames from one computer or network device to an adjacent computer or network device. What this means is that each computer in a network knows the MAC addresses of all the other computers and network devices that it is directly connected to via a switch, hub, crossover cable, or other such device. If a computer needs to send data to one of the computers or network devices connected to it, it will use that computer or device's MAC address to indicate where the data frame is intended to go. All data in a computer network moves from one computer or network device to another computer or network device in this way. In fact, each time a computer or network device hands off the data frame to the next computer or network device down the line, it is called a *hop*. This concept is discussed in much more detail later in this lesson.

CERTIFICATION READY
What are the two main parts of a MAC address? How does a MAC address differ from a physical address, or are they the same thing?
1.3

CERTIFICATION READY
What is a MAC address and how does the computer use it?
1.2

TAKE NOTE *
You have probably noticed that I used the phrase "computer or network device" quite often in the previous paragraph. This is because it is not just computers that function in the manner described earlier. Routers, switches, bridges, brouter, gateways, and other devices all use the same technique to hand off data frames from one device to the next and move them around the network. The phrase "computers and network devices" is intended to be inclusive of this fact.

SPOOFING MAC ADDRESSES

As mentioned previously, MAC address, or physical address, are generally hard coded into modern network cards. Because of this, physical addresses cannot physically be changed in most devices. This does not mean that other computers or devices cannot be tricked into thinking the MAC address of one device is different from that device's actual physical address. A common practice among hackers is to trick other computers on a network into thinking that a certain computer's MAC address is one physical address when in reality it is a different physical address. This practice is called MAC address spoofing or MAC spoofing.

The fact that hackers regularly engage in the practice of MAC spoofing leads to the question of why they do this. Hackers attempt to spoof the MAC addresses of a network because they wish to trick the network into letting them have access to it when they do not rightfully have that access. Many networks, wireless ones in particular, use the physical addresses of the computers on the network as a security measure.

In the most basic form of this, the device that allows access to a specific network, such as a wireless access point, has a record of the MAC addresses of all the devices allowed on the network. If a computer or other device attempts to access the network without having a valid MAC address, the access point denies that computer access to the network.

To get around this security measure, hackers will attempt to trick the access point into thinking that the MAC address of their computer is one of the ones permitted. The hacker does this with software rather than hardware. Since the physical address of a computer is physically encoded into the network device, they use software to change this. What happens is the software that is designed to imitate a different MAC address, intercepts the MAC address of the local computer it is installed on before it is sent out on the network and substitutes that MAC address with a different one that is acceptable to the access point. In this way, the access point on the network does not see the actual address of the computer attempting to spoof the access point and instead sees the MAC address that the spoofing software wants it to see.

■ Logical Addressing

THE BOTTOM LINE

This section of Lesson 4 describes how logical addressing works. This section also discusses what subnetting is and how it is done with a Class C IP address. This section also compares IPv4 with IPv6. In the discussion of subnetting, binary to decimal conversion is explained. In the discussion comparing IPv4 with IPv6, binary to hexadecimal conversion is explained.

While physical addressing has to do with the physical address of a computer and is hard coded, logical addressing is something different. Logical addresses have to be assigned to a computer, and based on what protocol is being used; different protocols use different standards to do this.

Just like physical addresses, every computer on the network needs a unique logical address. This is actually more of a critical issue with logical addresses than it is with physical addresses because with physical addresses, only the computers or devices that are directly connected to each other via a switch or some other such device need unique addresses. With logical addresses, every computer or device in the entire network needs to have a unique address. This does not just apply to those devices connected to the local switch, but also those computers and devices connected to every other switch or router in the network as well. This makes for a very large number of unique IP addresses if you want every computer or network device in your network to talk to each other and get on the Internet.

CERTIFICATION READY
What is an IP address?
What is the difference
between an IPv4 and an
IPv6 address?
1.3

The function of logical addresses is different from the function of physical addresses as well. Physical addresses are used to move data frames from one computer or networking device to the next computer or network device. Logical addresses are used to make sure that the data packet can actually decide the best path to follow to get to the destination computer and not just move it to an adjacent computer or network device. It is important to note that both types of addresses are needed to effectively move data around on a network. How this is done is discussed later in this lesson.

The most commonly used protocol suite for networking is the *TCP/IP Protocol Suite*. A *protocol suite* is a group of protocols that are designed to work together to carry out all the functions needed for data to be communicated across a network. The protocol in the TCP/IP Protocol Suite that is responsible for finding the best path to a destination computer is the *Internet Protocol (IP)*, which comes in two main versions. The oldest and most widely used version is *IP version 4 (IPv4)*. The newest and least widely adopted IP is *IP version 6 (IPv6)*. Both protocol versions are discussed in this lesson.

Internet Protocol Version 4 (IPv4)

As the oldest version of IP currently in use, IPv4 is also the most limited. The logical address used in IPv4 is 32 bits long, and those 32 bits are broken up into 4 groups of 8 bits called octets. IPv4 addresses are generally expressed in 8-bit decimal format. This means that the IP address 11000000100000101110001100011011 could be expressed in 8-bit decimal format as 192.130.227.27.

Because IPv4 addresses are limited to just 32 bits, the largest number of computer and other networkable devices that can be assigned a unique IP address is 4,294,967,296. While over 4 billion addresses seems like a really big number, when you think about it globally, you realize it really is not that big a number after all.

To put this in perspective, every computer that gets on the Internet, every Internet-capable cell phone, every router or access point to the Internet, all have to have a unique IP address. When you add all those devices up, there are more devices that need to get on the Internet than there are IP addresses available to them, so what do we do? To overcome this problem, several different techniques have been worked out that basically act to stretch out the available pool of IP address. One of those methods, subnetting, will be discussed next. Other methods of stretching out the available pool of IP addresses are discussed later in this lesson.

SUBNETTING

In its most basic form, *subnetting* is taking a given IP address range and breaking it up into smaller pieces so that a given range of IP addresses can be used in more than one network. To do this, an IP address is broken up into two main parts. One part is called the network portion of the IP address and the other part is called the host portion of the address.

Subnetting can be illustrated by using the IP address that was mentioned earlier. That IP address was 192.130.227.27. The easiest way to break this IP address up into network and host portions is to choose one of the octets as the break point. In this case, we can decide that 192.130.227 will be the network portion of the IP address and 27 will be the host portion of the address. Alternatively, we can decide 192.130 will be the network portion of the IP address and 127.27 will be the host portion of the IP address. In the first example, the first three octets are used to decide what network a computer belongs to and the last octet is used to determine which host is being singled out in the network to receive data. In the second example, the first two octets are used to identify the network a computer belongs to and the last two octets are used to determine which computer on the network is intended.

The deciding factor about which portion of the entire IP address you want to use as the network ID versus which portion of the entire IP address you want to use as the host ID is really determined by how many hosts you need on your network. Each octet can have up to 254 possible numbers. If you want to use 178 computers as hosts, then it does not make sense to use both the third and fourth octets for the host portion of your network. That would mean wasting a lot of IP addresses that could have been used by other computers. Since you can

CERTIFICATION READY
What is subnetting?
Explain how subnetting is used.
1.3

have up to 254 hosts in a single octet and you only need to have room on your network for 178 hosts, you really only need to use the last octet of the IP address as your host portion of the network. This is especially true considering that if you use both the third and fourth octets, you are allowed well over 65,000 host numbers. That is way too many host IP addresses for just 178 computers.

ANDing

The next logical question related to subnetting is, "How does the computer know what portion of the network address is for the host and which part is for the network ID?" This is where something called the subnet mask comes in. The subnet mask is a series of 1s and 0s that the computer uses to determine which part of the IP address is the network ID versus which part is the host. The subnet mask is all 1s followed by all 0s. Ones are placed in the portion of a four octet IP address that is intended for the network, but 0s are placed in the portion of an IP address that is intended for host. The computer then compares the subnet mask IP address to the actual IP address of the computer to determine which part is which.

To illustrate this, we will use our example from earlier. The IP address we used previously was 192.130.227.27. Also we stated that 192.130.227 was the network portion of that address and the.27 part was the host portion of that address. Finally if you look back even earlier in this lesson, we said the binary value for this IP was 11000000100000101110001100011011. This is all well and good, but how do you tell the computer this? You tell the computer this by giving it the subnet mask 255.255.255.0.

The next logical question is, "How does this tell the computer anything?" The answer to that question comes from comparing the binary address of the computer to the binary equivalent of the subnet mask. The binary equivalent for the subnet mask 255.255.255.0 is 11111111111111111111111100000000. The computer uses a logical AND truth table to compare the full IP address of the computer to the subnet mask. The logical AND truth table resembles Table 4-1.

Table 4-1

Logical AND Truth Table

INPUT 1	INPUT 2	OUTPUT
0	0	0
0	1	0
1	0	0
1	1	1

Following the AND truth table rules shown in Figure 4-1, the computer compares the binary value of the IP address to the binary value of the subnet mask. The process of comparing the IP address with the subnet mask using the AND truth table is called ANDing. The result of ANDing looks something like Table 4-2.

Table 4-2

Result of ANDing 192.130.227.27 with the Subnet Mask 255.255.255.0

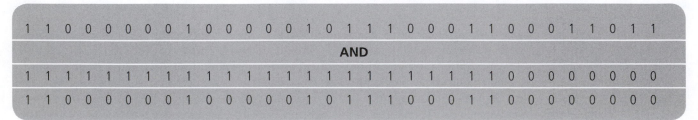

1	1	0	0	0	0	0	0	1	0	0	0	0	0	1	0	1	1	1	0	0	0	1	1	0	0	0	1	1	0	1	1
															AND																
1	1	1	1	1	1	1	1	1	1	1	1	1	1	1	1	1	1	1	1	1	1	1	1	0	0	0	0	0	0	0	0
1	1	0	0	0	0	0	0	1	0	0	0	0	0	1	0	1	1	1	0	0	0	1	1	0	0	0	0	0	0	0	0

The first row in Table 4-2 is the binary equivalent of the IP address 192.130.227.27. The second row of the table tells which truth table will be used—the AND truth table. The third row is the binary equivalent of the subnet mask 255.255.255.0. Finally, the fourth row contains the results of applying the values in the first row with the values in the third row using AND. When this is done, a very interesting pattern emerges. In the example we examined here, where the subnet mask binary is 1, the result of the ANDing process is the same as the binary equivalent of the IP address. However, where the binary portion of the subnet mask is 0, the result of the ANDing process is also 0. This pattern holds up, no matter what valid IP address you use or what valid subnet mask to which you compare it.

This is very important because the computer takes the result of the ANDing process to determine some very important information about the IP address. The computer uses the portion of the result that matches the original IP address to tell it which part of the overall IP address is to be used for the network ID. The remainder of the original IP address is used for the host portion of the IP address.

In the example here, the first twenty-four 1s and 0s of the result match up with the original IP address. That means that the first 24 bits of the original IP address refer to the network ID. The last 8 bits of the result are all 0s. This tells the computer that the last 8 bits of the original IP address are to be used for host IDs. In this way, every computer on the network knows which part of the different IP addresses they see are network IDs and which portion of the IP addresses they see are host IDs. By knowing this, the computers and other network devices can keep track of which hosts belong to which networks and route the data packets that pass though the network accordingly.

Classful IP addressing

Originally, when determining what part of an IP address was network ID and what part of the IP address was host, a class system was used. There were five classes created, Class A, B, C, D, and E. However, only the general population was only allowed to use the first three classes. This is called *classful IP addressing*. The classful method of determining what portion of an IP address is network ID and what portion of an IP address is used to denote hosts went out of general use around 1993. However, some routers and such that are still in use recognize class-based subnet masks and so this topic needs to be discussed.

When using classful IP addressing, the subnet mask for a Class A IP address is 255.0.0.0. The subnet mask for a Class B IP address is 255.255.0.0. Finally the subnet mask for a Class C IP address is 255.255.255.0.

Along with a predefined subnet mask, classful IP addressing also has predefined IP address ranges for each class of IP addresses, as well as a few ranges set aside for specific purposes. The range of IP addresses belonging in a specific class is determined by the first few bits of the entire 32-bit binary IP address. The range of the different classes of IP addresses as well as additional information about each IP class is shown in Table 4-3.

The first column in Table 4-3 lists the IP Class. The second column of Table 4-3 shows what the first portion of the 32-bit binary address is of a particular class that is used to define that class. Column three shows how many bits are set aside off the beginning of the binary IP address to define the subnet mask of that particular class. Notice that Class D and E do not have this defined. The fourth column gives both the dot decimal format of the subnet mask as well as the binary format of that particular class IP address. Notice that the number of 1s in the binary IP addresses of Classes A through C matches the value shown in column 3 if you were to count them. Again this is not defined for Class D and E addresses.

The fourth and fifth columns contain information about how many network IDs are available for use in each class and how many host IDs are available for each available network in each class of IP addresses. Class A addresses only allow for 128 unique network IDs but allow for 16,777,216 host IDs for each network. Class B IP ranges allow for 16,384 network IDs

IP Class	First Binary Bits Defining Class	Bits Used to Define Subnet Mask	Actual Subnet Mask in Decimal Format and then in Binary Format	Network IDs Available for Each Class	Host IDs Available for Each Class	Starting IP Address	Ending IP Address
Class A	0	8	255.0.0.0 11111111.00000000. 00000000.00000000	128	16,777,216	0.0.0.0	127.255.255.255
Class B	10	16	255.255.0.0 11111111.11111111. 00000000.00000000	16,384	65,536	128.0.0.0	191.255.255.255
Class C	110	24	255.255.255.0 11111111.11111111. 11111111.00000000	2,097,152	256	192.0.0.0	223.255.255.255
Class D	1110	Not defined	Not defined	Not defined	Not defined	224.0.0.0	239.255.255.255
Class E	1111	Not defined	Not defined	Not defined	Not defined	240.0.0.0	255.255.255.255

Table 4-3

IP Address Classes and Some of Their Defining Characteristics

and 65,536 host IDs for each network. Finally, Class C IP addresses allow for 2,097,152 networks, but only 256 host IDs per network. The last two columns of the table show what the beginning IP address is for each class and what the ending IP address is for each class.

IP ADDRESS RANGES RESERVED FOR SPECIAL PURPOSES. As briefly mentioned earlier, there are a few ranges in IPv4 that are set aside for specific purposes. For example all of Class D and E are reserved for special purposes. Class D, range 224.0.0.0 to 239.255.255.255, is reserved for something called IP multicasting. IP multicasting is where one device on a network sends out a message to all of a specific IP range or specific type of device. While this is not commonly used today, the Class D ranges of IP addresses have still been set aside for this purpose.

The Class E range of IP addresses, 240.0.0.0 to 255.255.255.255 has been set aside for "experimental" uses. Currently not much is being done with this class of IP address and it generally just sits there without being used. However, some companies and individuals have begun to use Class E IP addresses as if they are another range of IP addresses available for general use in private networks that do not connect to the Internet.

Aside from Class D and E IP address ranges that have been set aside for specific use, a few other smaller ranges have also been set aside for special uses in each of the three usable classes of IP addresses. Table 4-4 shows each of these ranges that have been set aside and what they have been set aside for.

Two IP address ranges of special interest that have been set aside are 169.254.0.0 to 169.254.255.255 and 127.0.0.0 to 127.255.255.255. The 169.254 range is of interest because this is the range Microsoft Windows uses when it has to automatically assign IP addresses to a computer. In other words, this is the range of IP addresses used by Microsoft Windows for automatic IP addressing.

Finally the loopback range is interesting. Loopback is used when you want to test your system. For example, when a loopback address is assigned to a network card, when the operating system sends a signal to that loopback address, it is treated as if the signal had left the system and come back in without actually going anywhere. If a computer can successfully do this, it indicates that everything above the Data Link layer of the OSI Model is working. If it fails to accomplish this task, it indicates that there is a software problem somewhere in the

Table 4-4

IP Ranges that have been set aside for various uses

Address Start Range	Address End Range	Range Use
0.0.0.0	0.255.255.255	Reserved
10.0.0.0	10.255.255.255	Class A private address block
127.0.0.0	127.255.255.255	Loopback address block
128.0.0.0	128.0.255.255	Reserved
169.254.0.0	169.254.255.255	Class B private address Block reserved for Private IP address allocation (i.e., Microsoft automatic private addressing)
172.16.0.0	172.31.255.255	Class B private address block
191.255.0.0	191.255.255.255	Reserved
192.0.0.0	192.0.0.255	Reserved
192.168.0.0	192.168.255.255	Class C private address bock
223.255.255.0	223.255.255.255	Reserved

system. To put things in a simpler form, if I can ping the loopback address, but cannot ping an IP address outside of my system, there is a good chance there is something wrong with my network card. If on the other hand, I cannot ping the loopback address, there is probably something wrong with my operating system.

One other thing that a loopback address can be used for is to simulate a port on a router or other network device that is not there. A loopback address can be used to define a nonexistent interface on a router, which can then be used to test the router's overall configuration. Since a loopback sends information back into the system as if a return signal is coming from that address, when a router sends a signal out a loopback port, the router's operating system reports it as if a success transmission has taken place even though no signal has actually gone anywhere.

IP ADDRESSES SET ASIDE FOR SPECIAL MEANINGS. Finally, there are two other IP addresses that are set aside for specific purposes. If an IP address has all 1s in the host portion of its address, all devices that contain the same network portion of that address should be sent the same signal. This is called a broadcast signal.

If all 0s are in the host portion of an IP address, it indicates that the whole network is being referred to. Another way of looking at this is to say that where there are all 0s in the host portion of an IP address, it means "this network" or "default network."

Classless IP addressing

As mentioned in the first paragraph of this section, classful addressing fell out of mainstream usage around 1993. What replaced it was something called *classless IP addressing*. In classless IP addressing, the class of an IP address is not even considered. Instead, the portion of an IP address that is host and the portion that is network is based solely on the subnet mask. So, the portion of the IP address 192.130.227.27 that is network versus the portion that is host can only be determined by knowing what the subnet mask is. If the subnet mask was 255.0.0.0, then the 192 portion of the IP address would be network and the rest would be host. If the subnet mask was 255.255.0.0, then the network portion would be 192.130 and the host portion would be 227.27. Finally if the subnet mask was 255.255.255.0, then 192.130.227 would be the network ID and 27 would be the host ID. As you can imagine from the previous example, in order for classless IP addressing to work, the subnet mask IP address must also be known. Without knowing the subnet mask, it is not possible for the computer to determine which portion of the IP address is to be network and which portion is to be host. For this reason, whenever a network address is assigned to a computer, it is also necessary to assign the appropriate subnet mask. Without doing both, the computer will be unable to communicate to the network.

Classless inter-domain routing (CIDR)

Classless inter-domain routing (CIDR) is a standard notation that came about as a form of shorthand that indicates what portion of a given IP address is to be used for network ID and what part is to be used for host ID. The CIDR notation takes a form similar to the following: 192.130.227.27/n. The IP address of a specific computer is placed first in the notation. This example uses 192.130.227.27, but really any IP address can go here. The /n part of the CIDR notation is the important part because it indicates how many of the total 32 bits of the IP address' binary form are to be used for the network IP portion. Put another way, the /n portion of the CIDR notation tells what the subnet mask is. To illustrate this let's look at the following example: 192.130.227.27/8 indicates that the subnet mask would be 255.0.0.0. If the CIDR notation was 192.130.227.27/16 the subnet mask would be 255.255.0.0. Finally, if the CIDR notation was 192.130.227.27/24, the subnet mask would be 255.255.255.0. However, the /n portion of the CIDR notation is not limited to just 8, 16, or 24. Really any number between 1 and 32 can be used, but realistically, only the numbers 2 through 30 would work to indicate the subnet mask. To be able to properly interpret CIDR notation beyond the basic 8, 16, or 24, you need to learn how to convert binary numbers to decimal numbers. It is also important to learn how to figure out subnet network ranges from larger network ranges. The next few sections of this lesson explain these concepts.

BINARY CONVERSION.   To learn how to do subnetting beyond the simple basics already discussed, the first thing that a student needs to learn how to do is to convert binary numbers to decimal numbers and decimal numbers to binary numbers. Since each octet in an IPv4 address only contains 8 bits each, we will only concern ourselves with converting binary numbers up to 8 bits long.

The first step to doing this is learning what number systems are. In the modern world, we use something called a base 10 number system. What this means is that each digit in a modern number is a factor of 10 larger than the digit directly to its right. Table 4-5 illustrates this point.

Table 4-5

The base 10 number system out to 8 digits

10^7	10^6	10^5	10^4	10^3	10^2	10^1	10^0
10,000,000	1,000,000	100,000	10,000	1,000	100	10	1

Using Table 4-5 we can solve basic base 10 numbers pretty easily. The number 14,609,182 can be placed into Table 4-5 as shown in Table 4-6.

Table 4-6

The number 14,609,182 placed into a base 10 number system table

10^7	10^6	10^5	10^4	10^3	10^2	10^1	10^0
10,000,000	1,000,000	100,000	10,000	1,000	100	10	1
1	4	6	0	9	1	8	2

Looked at this way, the number 14,609,182 can be expressed using the following formula:

$$((1 \times 10,000,000) + (4 \times 1,000,000) + (6 \times 100,000) + (0 \times 10,000) + (9 \times 1,000) + (1 \times 100) + (8 \times 10) + (2 \times 1))$$

The base 2 number system works in a similar way. Table 4-7 shows the base 2 number system out to 8 digits, called bits in computer terms.

Table 4-7

The base 2 number system out to 8 digits or bits

2^7	2^6	2^5	2^4	2^3	2^2	2^1	2^0
128	64	32	16	8	4	2	1

To convert a binary number up to 8 bits long, you place the binary value in the row below the decimal values for 2 to whatever power listed above it. To illustrate this explanation, we will look at the binary number 11100011, which is actually the third octet of the IP address we have been using in all our examples in this lesson. Table 4-8 has this binary value placed in Table 4-7 as described.

Table 4-8

Binary value 11100011 in base 2 number system out to 8 bits

2^7	2^6	2^5	2^4	2^3	2^2	2^1	2^0
128	64	32	16	8	4	2	1
1	1	1	0	0	0	1	1

Once we have filled in the table with the correct binary value, we simply add up all the decimal values that have a 1 under them. This gives us the simple equation 128 + 64 + 32 + 2 + 1. This equals 227, which is the value in the third octet of the IP address we have been using for our examples.

Converting a decimal value to a binary one is also pretty easy. Since we are only using 8 bits for our binary values, we will not use any numbers greater than 255 in our examples. The binary equivalent of 255 is 11111111 and so that is the largest 8-bit binary number we can use.

To illustrate converting decimal numbers into binary number we will use the value 130. We are using 130 because it is the value of the second octet of the IP address we have been using all along.

To convert 130 to binary you start with a table like Table 4-7. We will duplicate that here as Table 4-9 to simplify things.

Table 4-9

Base 2 number system out to 8 bits

2^7	2^6	2^5	2^4	2^3	2^2	2^1	2^0
128	64	32	16	8	4	2	1

Now, looking at the number 130, we see which number in the second row of the table is the largest number present that we can subtract from 130 without exceeding 130. In this case, 128 is the largest possible number we can subtract from 130. Therefore we place a 1 in the third row below 128 in the table. This is seen in Table 4-10.

Table 4-10

Base 2 number system out to 8 bits with a 1 in the 128 position

2^7	2^6	2^5	2^4	2^3	2^2	2^1	2^0
128	64	32	16	8	4	2	1
1							

After that, 130 minus 128 (130 − 128) gives us 2. The smallest number in Table 4-10 that can be successfully subtracted from 2 is 2, so we place a 1 in row 3 under the 2 as shown in Table 4-11.

Table 4-11

Base 2 number system out to 8 bits with a 1 in the 128 and 2 positions

2^7	2^6	2^5	2^4	2^3	2^2	2^1	2^0
128	64	32	16	8	4	2	1
1						1	

Since $2 - 2 = 0$ and there is no 0 place in the table, we are finished. All that is left is putting a 0 in all the positions that do not contain 1s and you have the binary equivalent of 130, which is seen in Table 4-12.

Table 4-12

Base 2 number system out to 8 bits with 1s in the 128 and 2 positions and 0s in all other positions

2^7	2^6	2^5	2^4	2^3	2^2	2^1	2^0
128	64	32	16	8	4	2	1
1	0	0	0	0	0	1	0

As you can see in Table 4-12, the binary equivalent of 130 is 10000010. You will be expected to convert binary values to decimal and decimal values to binary in some of the labs in this lesson using the techniques described here.

FIGURING OUT THE SUBNET MASK USING CIDR. In the CIDR notation such as 192.130.227.27/24, the /24 portion of the notation indicates how many 1s to use for the subnet mask. In examples like /8, /16, and /24 it is easy to figure out the subnet mask because each octet of the subnet mask has eight 1s in it and no 0s. Remember from earlier, that if you have 11111111 in binary, it equals 255 because that is the highest decimal number possible with 8 bits in a binary number. In other words, /8 is 255.0.0.0, /16 is 255.255.0.0, and /24 is 255.255.255.0. The problem comes in when the /n portion of the notation is something other than a multiple of 8.

What happens if the CIDR notation is 192.130.227.27/12? The easiest way to look at this is to realize that you can use the value 8 to determine the subnet mask in each octet. In the example 192.130.227.27/12, if we subtract 8 from this value, we end up with the value 4. That means that the first octet has eight 1s in it while the second octet uses the remaining four 1s. If an octet has eight 1s in it, it is going to be 255. So the first octet of the subnet mask is 255.

Now that the first octet has been determined, the remaining number, in this example is 4. With 4 now in the /n portion of the CIDR notation, that means the first four places in the second octet of the subnet mask starting with the leftmost place are all 1s. In binary it would look like 11110000. If this is plugged into Table 4-9, the value converts to 240. This means that the value 240 should be in the second octet of the subnet mask. Since 4 is smaller than 8, there are no 1s in the last two octets and so they will equal 0. The subnet mask that results from the CIDR notation 192.130.227.27/12 is therefore 255.240.0.0.

Let us look at another example to explain things in another way. This time we will use the CIDR notation 192.130.227.27/27. When 8 is divided into 27 the result is 3 with a remainder of 3. This means the first three octets of the subnet mask are all full of 1s, but the last octet only contains 1s in the first three left positions. In binary the subnet mask would look like 11111111.11111111.11111111.11100000. When converting each octet into decimal, the result is 255.255.255.224.

For one final example, let us use the CIDR notation 192.130.227.27/18. When 18 divided by 8 the result is 2 with a remainder of 2. This means the first two octets are full of 1s in binary, but the third octet only has 1s in the first two positions to the left. Since the last octet is not affected by dividing 18 by 8, it contains all 0s. In this way, we can determine that the subnet mask for 192.130.227.27/18 is therefore 255.255.192.0. Table 4-13 illustrates how 1s, added to the front of an octet based on the number remaining after being divided by 8, can be converted to decimal format.

Table 4-13

Bits remaining after dividing by 8 with the binary and decimal Values they represent

Bits Remaining After Dividing by 8	Binary Equivalent	Decimal Value
0	00000000	0
1	10000000	128
2	11000000	192
3	11100000	224
4	11110000	240
5	11111000	248
6	11111100	252
7	11111110	254
8	11111111	255

TAKE NOTE*

CIDR is the preferred method in the networking industry to express sub-network ranges. It is also important to understand how to read CIDR notation for the CompTIA Network+ Exam.

TAKE NOTE*

There are some other alternatives to how the theoretical company could resolve its IP addresses issue for its three networks that need access to the Internet. Some of those alternatives will be discussed later in this Lesson. For the purposes of explaining subnetting however, we will stick with the scenario as it is.

DETERMINING SUB-NETWORK RANGES USING CIDR. While CIDR notation can be used to determine subnet mask, it can also be used to determine sub-network ranges as well. A sub-network is where a specific network IP address is divided into smaller networks to make more efficient use of the available IP addresses.

For example, if a company has three networks they want to build, each network containing 25 computers, all needing to connect to the Internet, there are two approaches this theoretical company could take. One, they could lease rights to three Class C IP ranges from the ICANNA, the organization responsible for making sure duplicate IP addresses are not used on the Internet. This approach would work, but it would be rather expensive. Alternatively, this theoretical company could lease just one Class C IP range from ICANNA and divide it up into smaller networks that contain at least 25 IP addresses. This second option will cost three times less than the first option.

The key to subnetting a larger network is the subnet mask. In the case of the company in the example, a Class C IP range is all they need. A Class C IP range has a total of 256 IP addresses. The number 256 comes from the range of the last octet, which is 0 to 255. This includes the number 0 and gives a total of 256 IP addresses. The 0 IP address cannot be used because it is the network address. Also the 255 IP address cannot be used because it is the broadcast address. Only IP addresses 1 through 254 are actually usable.

For a real-world scenario, let us assume that the Class C IP address range that the company bought from ICANNA was 207.253.187.0/24 in CIDR notation. That means the actual IP address range that was available to the company would be 207.253.187.0 through 207.253.187.255. Given the network and broadcast addresses mentioned previously, the actual usable IP address range available to the company would be 207.253.187.1 through 207.253.187.254. That is a total of 254 possible IP addresses to use in a single network. However, the company needs three networks with a minimum of 25 IP addresses in each one. The solution for the company is to break up the network range 207.253.187.0 through 207.253.187.255 into smaller networks.

To understand how to do this, the first thing we need to do is take a look at Table 4-14. Understand what Table 4-14 is saying will help you greatly in understanding the subnetting process for Class C networks like in the earlier example. Subnetting larger Class A and Class B networks is discussed in more detail in a later lesson.

Table 4-14

Values in Subnetting Class C Subnets

Subnet Mask in Binary Format	Subnet Mask in Decimal Format	Subnet Network Increment Value	Networks Available	Usable Networks Available	Hosts Available per Network	Usable Hosts Available per Network
00000000	0	0	0	0	0	0
10000000	128	128	2	0	0	0
11000000	192	64	4	2	64	62
11100000	224	32	8	6	32	30
11110000	240	16	16	14	16	14
11111000	248	8	32	30	8	6
11111100	252	4	64	62	4	2
11111110	254	2	128	0	2	0
11111111	255	1	256	0	0	0

Table 4-14 contains all the information needed to successfully subnet a Class C network. The first three columns of the table are consistent for Class A, B, and C networks. The last four columns are specific to Class C networks.

Columns 1 and 2 contain the binary and decimal equivalents of what the last octet in a Class C network should contain. Even in Class A and B networks the octet that contained the last non-0 value would match up to these numbers.

To review what was previously discussed, if a Class C network with the following CIDR notation, 207.253.187.0/26 was given, then the subnet mask for that network would be 255.255.255.192. The last octet contains 192, because the value 26 is three greater than 24. Put another way 26 divided by 8 gives us 4 with a remainder of 2. This means that the fourth octet will use two 1s from the front of its binary value. This gives us the binary value of 11000000 in the fourth octet of the subnet mask. When we look at Table 4-14, the binary value 11000000 gives the decimal value of 192. This means that the subnet mask in decimal format of 207.253.187.0/26 is 255.255.255.192.

Now that we have determined the subnet mask, we need to determine what network ranges are available with the given subnet mask. To do this, we need to look at the third column. In that column, the increment that goes with the subnet mask value of 192 is 64. This means that the network range changes every 64th number in the fourth octet of the IP address. This works something like what is shown in Table 4-15.

Table 4-15

Value changes by increments of 64 in the last octet of 207.253.187.0/26

NETWORK NUMBER	NETWORK ID
Network 1	207.253.187.0
Network 2	207.253.187.64
Network 3	207.253.187.128
Network 4	207.253.187.192

As you can see in Table 4-15, by using the information from Table 4-14, it is possible to determine what values are used to create sub-networks under the network 207.253.187.0/26 using the subnet value determined by the /26 portion of this CIDR notation network.

Now for a little bit more information about sub-networking. Just like the first and last value in a normal network cannot be used, the first and last range in a group of sub-networks also cannot be used. That means that of the 4 potential sub-networks that 207.253.187.0/26 gives us, only the middle two are useable. The number of available networks versus the number of usable networks is illustrated in the fourth and fifth rows of Table 4-14.

As you remember from earlier in this lesson, the first IP address in an IP range is always the network ID and cannot be used for a host value. Keeping that in mind, the first usable network is the 207.253.187.64 network, and the second usable network is the 207.253.187.128 network. This means that the network ranges for each of the networks must begin with these IP addresses. Table 4-16 illustrates the absolute network ranges for all the networks created using the CIDR notation 207.253.187.0/26.

Table 4-16

Absolute network ranges using CIDR 207.253.187.0/26

NETWORK NUMBER	NETWORK ID	NETWORK RANGE
Network 1	207.253.187.0	207.253.187.0–207.253.187.63
Network 2	207.253.187.64	207.253.187.64–207.253.187.127
Network 3	207.253.187.128	207.253.187.128–207.253.187.191
Network 4	207.253.187.192	207.253.187.192–207.253.187.255

You need to remember that the first and last range in a group of related sub-networks cannot be used. Additionally you need to remember that the first and last IP addresses in any given range of networks also cannot be used. As such, the last table in this series, Table 4-17, shows what the usable network ranges are.

Table 4-17

Usable network ranges from all usable networks created using CIDR 207.153.187.0/26

NETWORK NUMBER	NETWORK ID	NETWORK RANGE	USABLE NETWORK RANGE
Network 1	207.253.187.0	207.253.187.0–207.253.187.63	Unusable
Network 2	207.253.187.64	207.253.187.64–207.253.187.127	207.253.187.65–207.253.187.126
Network 3	207.253.187.128	207.253.187.128–207.253.187.191	207.253.187.129–207.253.187.190
Network 4	207.253.187.192	207.253.187.192–207.253.187.255	Unusable

There are two more columns on Table 4-14. Those two columns are very important for resolving the problem that our fictitious company has to resolve. Those two columns have to do with how many hosts and usable hosts are available for each sub-network.

In the scenario we stared out this section of the lesson with, a fictitious company needed three networks that contained at least 25 hosts each. That same company also bought the Class C network range 207.253.187.0/24. Using the information contained in Table 4-14, it is easy to determine how to subnet the 207.253.187.0/24 network to accommodate the company's needs. Table 4-18 provides a good reference.

Table 4-18

Values in Subnetting Class C
Subnets

Subnet Mask in Binary Format	Subnet Mask in Decimal Format	Subnet Network Increment Value	Networks Available	Usable Networks Available	Hosts Available per Network	Usable Hosts Available per Network
00000000	0	0	0	0	0	0
10000000	128	128	2	0	0	0
11000000	192	64	4	2	64	62
11100000	224	32	8	6	32	30
11110000	240	16	16	14	16	14
11111000	248	8	32	30	8	6
11111100	252	4	64	62	4	2
11111110	254	2	128	0	2	0
11111111	255	1	256	0	0	0

Looking at the last row on Table 4-18, we see a list of the usable hosts that are allowed for each possible sub-network mask. Based on this table, both the 192 sub-network and the 224 sub-network, have the appropriate number of hosts available. Sub-network 192 has 62 usable hosts, and sub-network 224 has 30 usable hosts. However, our fictitious company also needs at least three networks. Column 5 in Table 4-18 tells us that 192 only has two usable networks, so it does not meet the company's needs. However, 224 has six available networks, which will work nicely for our company. This means that the subnet mask we need to use for our networks is 255.255.255.224. This can be written as 207.253.187.0/27 since column 1 shows us that three 1s are taken off the front of the last octet.

Using the third column of Table 4-18, we learn that each network in the 255.255.255.224 sub-network increases by a value of 32. This means, using a table similar to Table 4-19, we can map out the networks and IP address ranges we will need to use to accommodate the company's stated needs.

By subnetting the 207.253.187.0/24 network in the manner shown in Table 4-19, the company has 6 usable networks with each network containing 30 usable IP addresses. This meets the company's requirements of having three networks with at least 25 host IP addresses available for each network.

This entire section of Lesson 4 on subnetting is very important. There will be labs and scenarios related to the subnetting section at the end of this lesson.

Table 4-19

The 207.253.187.0/27 network

NETWORK NUMBER	NETWORK ID	NETWORK RANGE	USABLE NETWORK RANGE
Network 1	207.253.187.0	207.253.187.0–207.253.187.31	Unusable
Network 2	207.253.187.32	207.253.187.32–207.253.187.63	207.253.187.33–207.253.187.62
Network 3	207.253.187.64	207.253.187.64–207.253.187.95	207.253.187.65–207.253.187.94
Network 4	207.253.187.96	207.253.187.96–207.253.187.127	207.253.187.97–207.253.187.126
Network 5	207.253.187.128	207.253.187.128–207.253.187.159	207.253.187.129–207.253.187.158
Network 6	207.253.187.160	207.253.187.160–207.253.187.191	207.253.187.161–207.253.187.190
Network 7	207.253.187.192	207.253.187.192–207.253.187.223	207.253.187.193–207.253.187.222
Network 8	207.253.187.224	207.253.187.224–207.253.187.255	Unusable

TAKE NOTE*

IPv6 is a newer technology in the networking industry but is steadily growing in importance. The reason for the growing importance of IPv6 is because the available new IPv4 addresses ran out in January 2011.

Internet Protocol Version 6 (IPv6)

IPv6 is an updated version of the IPv4 protocol that we have just been discussing. As mentioned earlier, there are just over 4 billion IP addresses available with IPv4. Even with subnetting and some of the other techniques that will be discussed later in this lesson that number is not enough to meet our networking needs in the future. In response to this foreseen problem, IPv6 was developed and is now in the process of being deployed. That said; do not expect to see everything shifting to IPv6 overnight. It will take time to transition the old IPv4 infrastructure to the new IPv6 infrastructure. In fact, this transition has already been going on for several years. What you will see is an accelerated shift to IPv6 over the next few years as more and more of the infrastructure is transitioned.

There are a number of features of IPv6 that make it the Internet Protocol of choice. One of the biggest features is that IPv6 has a lot more IP addresses to dole out to different Internet capable devices. IPv4 was limited to only a little over 4 billion addresses because it only used a 32-bit addressing scheme; 2^{32} gives us 4,294,967,296. That means that 4,294,967,296 is the largest number of unique binary IP addresses that are possible with IPv4. When you add up the ever-growing number of devices that need access to the Internet, you quickly realize that 4,294,967,296 is really not a very large number. IPv6 on the other hand, uses 128 bits for its IP addresses. This is 2^{128}, which is equal to a number so large it has to be expressed in scientific notation. Essentially the number is 3.4×10^{38} or 34 followed by 37 zeros.

Another difference between IPv4 and IPv6 is that IPv6 addresses are expressed in hexadecimal numbers instead of decimal numbers. Hexadecimal numbers use the base 16 number system, just like physical addresses do. Hexadecimal numbers use 0–9 and then A–F to account for all 16 digits. One reason for this is because humans can separate 32 numbers and letters in our minds much easier than we can 128 1s and 0s. Furthermore, the 32 numbers and letters of the hexadecimal IPv6 address are broken up into two main parts. The first 16 hexadecimal digits are the network ID, and the last 16 hexadecimal digits are the host number or host ID. This eliminates the need for subnetting for the time being. The IPv6 address is further broken up for easy reading because each part of the address, the network ID and host ID, is broken into four sets of hexadecimal digits separated by a colon.

Another reason hexadecimal numbers are used in an IPv6 addresses is because it is very easy to convert between binary and hexadecimal numbers. Table 4-20 shows the binary equivalents of the hexadecimal characters.

Table 4-20

Binary to Hexadecimal conversion table

BINARY VALUE	HEXADECIMAL VALUE	BINARY VALUE	HEXADECIMAL VALUE
0000	0	1000	8
0001	1	1001	9
0010	2	1010	A
0011	3	1011	B
0100	4	1100	C
0101	5	1101	D
0110	6	1110	E
0111	7	1111	F

To convert a binary number to a hexadecimal number, you replace every four 1s and 0s with the equivalent hexadecimal value. To convert hexadecimal to binary, you replace every hexadecimal value with its binary equivalent.

To illustrate the conversion process, convert the following two examples. Place a space after every fourth binary digit to make it easier to read the binary numbers and see how they are converted.

The binary value 1100 1101 0011 0110 converts to the hexadecimal value CD36. By the same token, the hexadecimal number 40F9 converts to the binary number 0100 0000 1111 1001. As you can see in these two examples, converting between binary and hexadecimal numbering is very straightforward.

There are some other advantages and differences with regard to IPv6 versus IPv4, but the main ones are those described here.

One other issue related to IPv6 addressing is the fact that not all 16-bit groups in the IPv6 address need to be shown. If an IPv6 address has a group of 16 bits that is equal to all 0s then that 16-bit section can be skipped. This is shown with two colons next to each other. I will show you an example to illustrate this.

The first example is the hypothetical IPv6 address **13D4:FA97:0000:1258:AD8B:1009:34D6:1800**. This IPv6 IP address can be written as **13D4:FA97::1258:AD8B:1009:34D6:1800** using the method described above. Additionally, if there is more than one group of 16 bits next to each other that all have 0000 in them, then all of these groups can be skipped using the same technique. This can be illustrated using the IPv6 address **13D4:0000:0000:0000:0000:1009:34D6:1800**. This IPv6 address can be written as **13D4::1009:34D6:1800**. You can also use the double colon technique when multiple groups of 0000 are separated by hexadecimal groups other than 0000. In other words **13D4:0000:0000:0000: AD8B :0000:0000:1800** can be written as **13D4::AD8B::1800**.

EUI-64

Another capability of IPv6 is the ability of a host to automatically assign itself a unique 64-bit interface identifier. IPv6 is able to do this without requiring DHCP (discussed in Lesson 6) to provide it or having it manually assigned. The way IPv6 does this is by using the IEEE standard organization's EUI-64 format. This format is defined in the IEEE's Guidelines for EIU-64 Registration Authority and RFC 2373.

EUI-64 works in two steps. In the first step, the MAC address is divided between the Organizationally Unique Identifier (OUI) and the Host portion of the MAC address. Between these two portions of the MAC address the hexadecimal value FFFE is added. The value FFFE is used because it is the value specified in RFC 2373 and is reserved so that manufacturers cannot use it in their OUIs.

If only the first step is carried out then all that has been done is that a conventional 48-bit MAC address has been converted into a 64-bit MAC address called a EUI-64 address. While some 64-bit MAC addresses are used, most are of the traditional 48-bit type.

In the second step, as specified in the above documents, the 7th bit of the MAC address is inverted so that it is the opposite of what it was previously. This specific bit is called the universal/local flag. This bit is normally set to 0. To invert this bit, it has to be changed to 1. At this point the EUI-64 becomes a Modified EUI-64 address and can now be used by IPv6 as a unique interface identifier on a device connected to a network.

If IPv6 had a EUI-64 address to work with from the start, all it would have to do is step 2 in order to generate a Modified EUI-64 address. Once this is done, IPv6 can use the generated address as a unique interface identifier in the same manner as discussed above.

CERTIFICATION READY
What is EUI-64? How does it relate to IPv6?
1.2

■ How Physical and Logical Addressing Work Together

↓
THE BOTTOM LINE

This portion of Lesson 4 will discuss how logical addresses and physical addresses work together to make sure that data finds its way to the intended destination across a large network.

The purpose of this section of the lesson is to take all the information discussed previously and pull it together in a coherent way so that you can picture how the information discussed in this lesson is actually used in a simple model network. A series of diagrams is used in this section to show each step of addressing a network and how those different types of addresses are used to move data along in the network. A brief explanation is given after each diagram before moving on to the next. Each one of these diagrams will build on the one used before it. For the purposes of this discussion it is assumed that the represented network uses Ethernet for both its LAN and WAN portions. This is done to simplify the network and allow us to concentrate on how the overall network works rather than worrying about differences in technology. While it is still very rare to see networks that use Ethernet for their WAN communications the technology to do so exists and is gradually becoming more common.

Figure 4-1 offers a simple model of a basic internetwork.

Figure 4-1

Simplified form of an internetwork

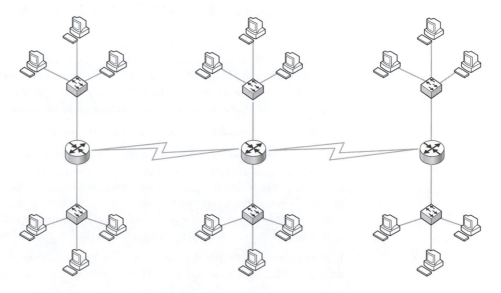

TAKE NOTE *

An explanation of how physical and logical addresses work together to move data around on a network is not part of the CompTIA Network + Exam. However, such an explanation is very important for understanding how networking actually works.

The symbols used in Figure 4-1 are all standard symbols used in networking diagrams to represent the various network components. To help you understand, here is an overview of what each symbol in the network diagram represents:

- **Circular symbols** with two arrows pointing outward and two arrows pointing inward represent standard routers.
- **Rectangular symbols** with two arrows pointing in one direction and two arrows pointing in the opposite direction represent standard switches.
- **Small computers** represent network workstations.
- **Lightning bolts** represent the WAN connection between each router.
- **Solid lines** between each computer and switch as well as each switch and router represent standard Ethernet connections.

Figure 4-2 is the same as the base diagram just introduced, except a new element has been added.

Figure 4-2

Internetwork with letters representing MAC addresses

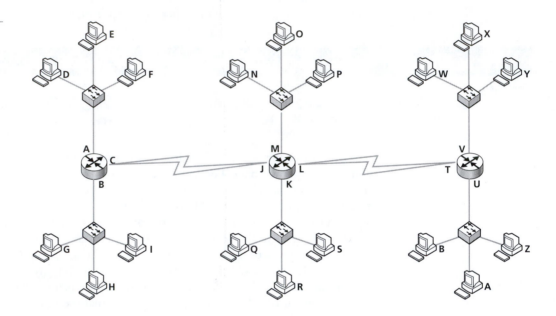

Figure 4-2 includes an added element of capital letters on each network interface. These capital letters represent the physical addresses, also called the MAC addresses, of each node on the internetwork. It is important to notice that along with each computer having a MAC address, each individual interface on the routers have also been assigned individual MAC addresses. You can think of each interface on a router as being a different network card, therefore it needs to have its own unique MAC address as well. You may also notice that the interfaces on the switches do not have a unique MAC address. For the purposes of this illustration, just assume that the each port on the switch takes on the MAC address of the computer that is attached to it.

Figure 4-3 shows the different segments or collision domains of the internetwork.

Any large network needs to be broken down into smaller components so that the number of computers attempting to communicate on any given network will not overwhelm the capacity of the network. Breaking a network down into smaller components or units also has certain security benefits. Each component that a network is broken down into is called a segment. Another word used to describe these individual segments are collision domains or broadcast domains. In Figure 4-3, routers are the devices used to break down this particular internetwork.

It is important to notice that all the network interfaces within a given segment must have unique MAC or physical addresses. If two or more network interfaces within a given segment

Figure 4-3

Internetwork segments

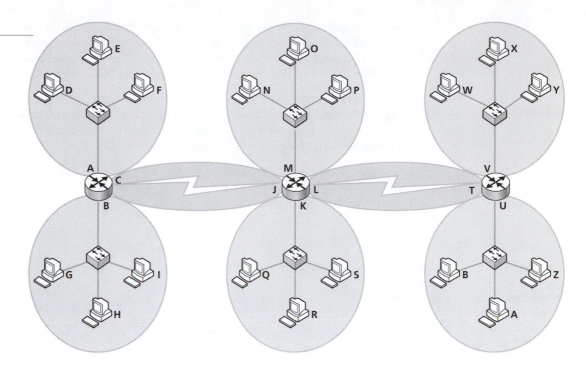

were to share a MAC address, communications would not work properly within that segment. Also, you should note that within the same internetwork it is possible to repeat MAC addresses so long as the repeated MAC addresses are not within the same segment.

Since routers were used to break this network down into segments, each segment must be given its own unique network or logical address as represented by IP addresses (see Figure 4-4). In wide area networks (WANs), this type of arrangement is common between different locations.

While it is expected that any given router interfaces and the workstations connected directly to them via a switch consist of a single network segment, each link between one router and the next

Figure 4-4

Internetwork segments with unique logical addresses

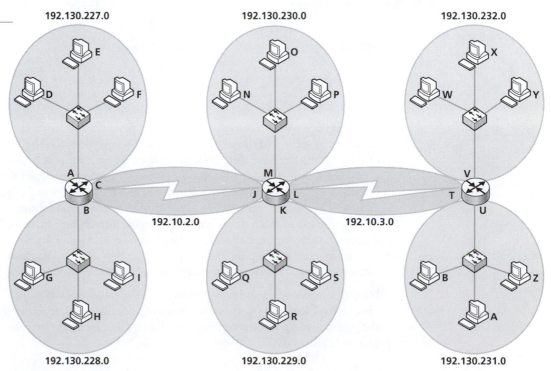

is also considered a network segment. The reason for this is based on how network devices communicate with each other and will be discussed in more detail later in this section. Since the connection between the interfaces of two directly connected routers is considered a segment, each of these mini-segments needs to have its own network address. This can be seen clearly in Figure 4-4.

While each segment must have a unique network address, each network interface within each segment must also have a unique network or logical address. The network address for each device with the segment must contain the network address of the entire segment as well as a unique identifier for each interface (see Figure 4-5).

In Figure 4-5, each network segment is given a logical address that ends in a 0 in the last section of the address. In this diagram, that is the logical address for that entire segment. The portion of the logical address that is not the number 0 in our diagram is called the network address.

Figure 4-5

Internetwork segments with unique logical addresses assigned to each device based on the network address of each segment

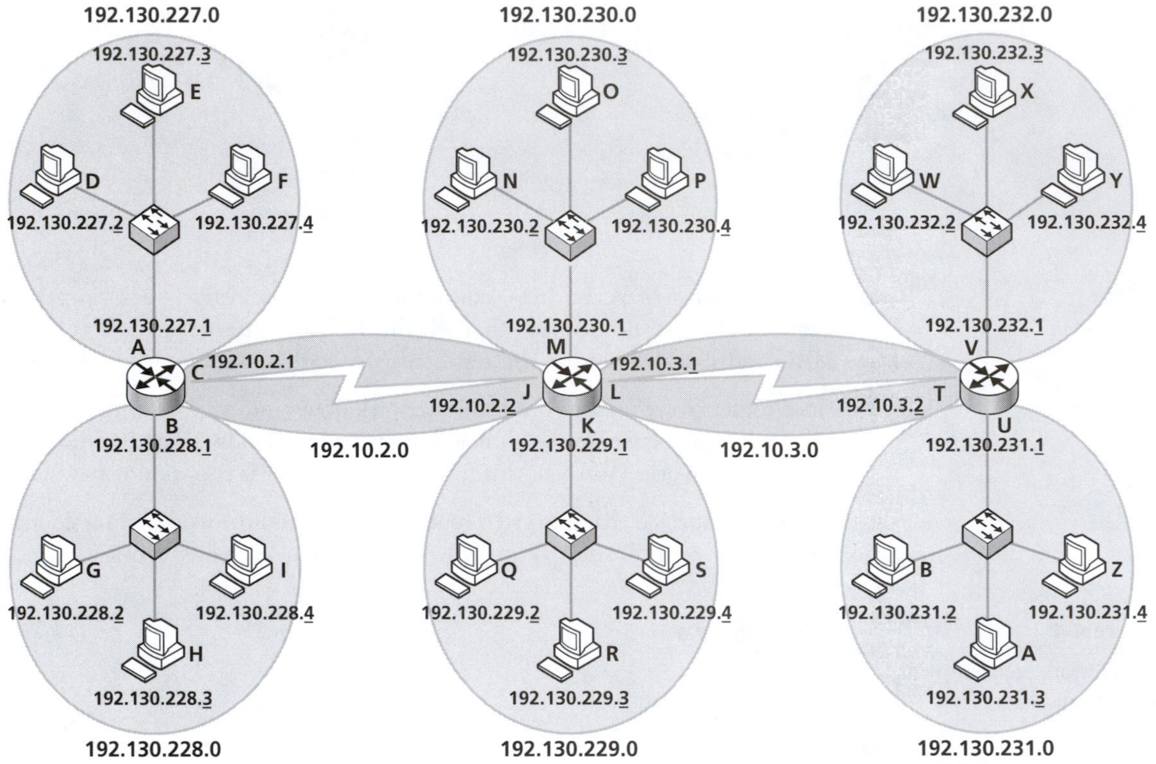

Each interface within a segment then uses the same network portion of the logical address; however, the last section of the address where the 0 was gets replaced by a different number. This part of the logical address is called the host number. By tradition, the router interface for a given segment receives the number 1 for its host number. For the purposes of this discussion, all the other interfaces in the segment receive a number between 2 and 254 in the host portion of their logical address. This number range is an effect of how IP network addressing works and is explained later in this lesson. Each device within the segment must have a unique host number in its logical address. If two or more devices have the same host number in a given segment, the logical address conflict message will appear. Please note, every device within a segment must also have the same network portion of their logical address. All of this is clearly illustrated by Figure 4-5.

Now that you understand how physical and logical addressing works in an internetwork system, we will look at how these two types of addresses work together to move data around in the internetwork. To illustrate this, a series of diagrams stemming from the previous series of diagrams are used.

Figure 4-6 shows a source computer with the logical address 192.130.227.2 and the physical address D which needs to send data to a destination computer with the logical address 192.130.231.4 and the physical address Z.

Figure 4-6

Source computer on one end of the internetwork and its intended destination on the other

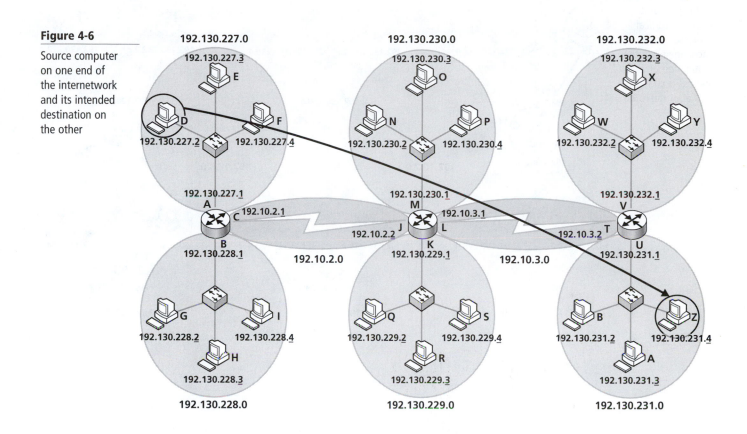

At this point it is important to note that frames can only be moved within a given segment by a computer. It is also important to note that a computer only contains a record of the physical addresses within its own segment. A computer is unable to know what the physical address of a computer located in a different segment is. In this scenario, the source computer needs to communicate to a computer in a totally different segment of the internetwork.

This presents a certain amount of difficulty if all we had to work with were physical addresses. However, we also have the logical address to help us. Put another way, the physical address is used to move a frame of data within a segment, and the logical address is used to determine the best route the frame can take to move across multiple segments. In order to move a data frame across an internetwork, it is necessary to reset the source and destination physical addresses at each step along the route, called a hop (Figure 4-7), while maintaining the same logical address so as to keep the frame on the proper course.

The source computer does not know the physical address of the destination computer; however, it does know the physical address of the router that is connected to the segment that it is part of. The computer also knows that if it does not know the physical address of the destination computer, it is to send the data frame to the router. In order to do this, the computer sets the destination physical address of the data frame to A, which is the router's physical address, while leaving the logical address set to the actual destination computer. This allows the computer to pass the data frame to the router and completes the first hop necessary to reach the data frame's ultimate destination. Moving the data frame from the source computer to the first router completes the first hop. The second hop is illustrated in Figure 4-8.

Figure 4-7

Source computer knows the physical address of the router that is part of its segment. Logical addresses are unchanged, but the destination physical address is changed to that of the route

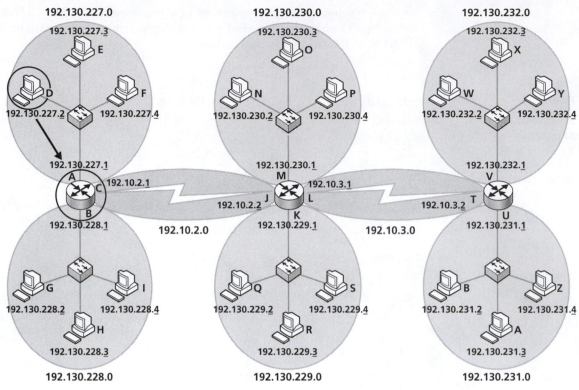

Figure 4-8

Logical addresses stay the same but the source physical address changes to A and destination physical addresses changes to J

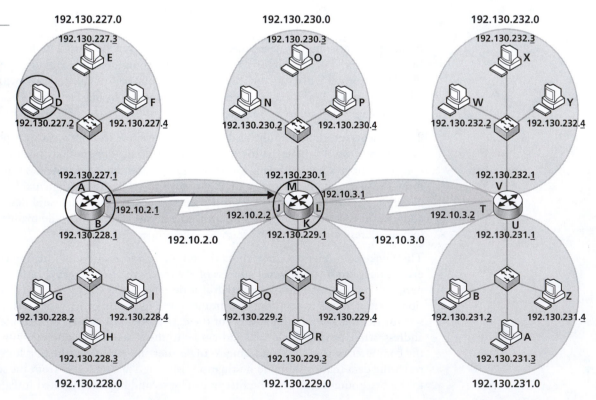

Once the router receives the data frame from the computer, it analyzes the logical address of the data frame to see if it should be passed on to a segment directly connected to the router. In this instance, the router is able to determine that the ultimate destination is not one of the segments directly connected to it, so it passes the data frame on to the next router down the network. In order to do this, the router leaves the logical addresses untouched, but changes the source physical address to its own address of A and changes the destination physical address to J, which is the physical address of the next router down the network. Now the data frame is able to travel to the next destination on its journey to its ultimate destination. Moving the data frame from the first router to the second router completes the second hop. The third hop is illustrated in Figure 4-9.

Figure 4-9

Logical addresses stay the same but the source physical address changes to J and destination physical addresses changes to T

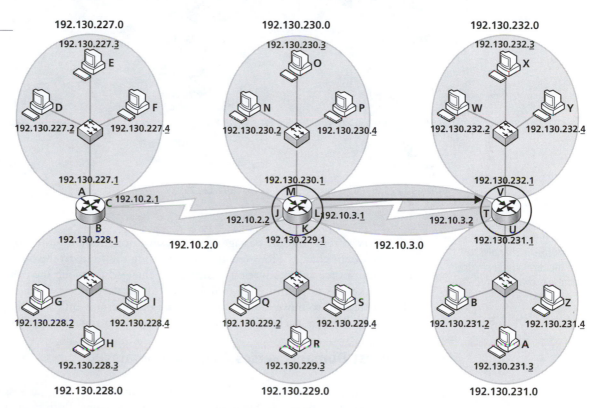

Once the next router receives the data frame from the previous router, it too analyzes the logical address of the data frame. Again the router determines that the destination of the data frame is not in a segment directly connected to it, so it again changes the source and destination physical addresses. The new source physical address is J and the new destination physical address is T. The logical addresses are not touched. Once more the data frame is passed on to the next router down the network. Moving the data frame from the second router to the third router completes the third hop. The final hop in this example is illustrated in Figure 4-10.

The third router also analyzes the logical addresses of the source and destination of the data frame and realizes that the destination logical address matches the logical address of a computer that is directly connected to one of the segments it controls. Once the router knows this, it changes the physical source to match its own physical address of T and changes the destination physical address to Z, which is the physical address of the computer the data frame is intended for. The data frame is then able to move from the router to the appropriate computer and in this way the data frame is able to reach its ultimate destination. This completes the fourth and final hop of the data frame.

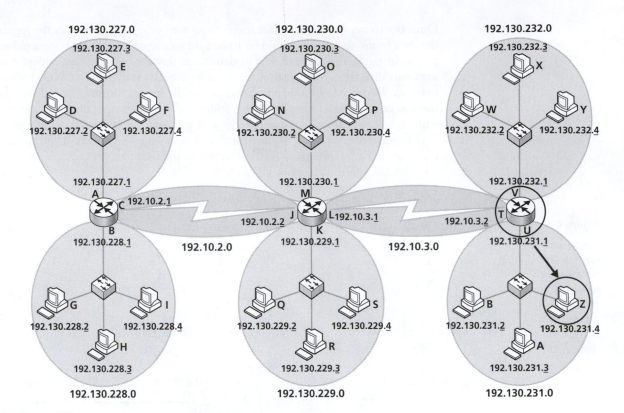

Figure 4-10

Logical addresses again stay the same, but the source physical address is changed to T and the destination physical address is changed to Z

In summary, throughout the passage of the packet through the internetwork, the logical addresses do not change. However, at each step along the route to the destination computer, the physical source and destination addresses are changed to match the computers or routers the packet has to pass through to reach its ultimate destination. In this way, physical addresses are used to move the data frame across the internetwork, while logical addresses are used to keep the data packet on course so that it is able to reach its appropriate destination.

Broadcast Domains verses Collision Domains

Two concepts that are related to addressing and how different types of addresses works together are the concepts of Broadcast Domains and Collision Domains. Both types of domains are similar but are also different.

When all the devices on a network or a segment are connected together in such a way that they are all able to receive the same broadcast signal from the one computer we have something called a Broadcast Domain. For a device to be considered part of a single broadcast domain, the signal received cannot pass through a switch, router, or similar device. This is called a broadcast domain because all the devices within the domain are able to broadcast a signal that can be received by all the other devices in the domain.

A collision domain is similar but slightly different. When two or more devices on the same segment or network are able to cause their signal to interfere with the signal from another device on the same segment or network we have what is called a Collision Domain. It is called a collision domain because when two signals interfere with each other in this way it is called a collision.

Following is a real world example that may help illustrate the differences between a broadcast domain and a collision domain. I you had a network device called a hub and connected as many computers to that hub as it will support, you can create both a collision domain and a broadcast domain. The resulting construct would be a collision domain because all the devices

CERTIFICATION READY
What is a broadcast domain? What is a collision domain? What is the difference between the two?
1.4

connected to the hub have the potential of their signals interfering with the signal of one or more other devices connected to the hub. The reason for this is based on the nature of how a hug works. At the same time, all the devices connected to the hub would also be a broadcast domain. The reason the resulting construct is a broadcast domain is because when one device on the hub sends out a broadcast; all the other devices on the hub will receive that broadcast.

Now let us take a similar situation but use a switch instead. A switch is especially designed so that any one device connected to the switch is only able to communicate directly to only one other device. As a result of this, a collision domain cannot form. The reason a collision domain cannot form is because the two devices communicating to each other know about the communication and so their signals do not interfere with each. If two or more signals cannot collide with each other, then a collision domain cannot form. However, if a device connected to the switch chooses to send out a signal using the broadcast address discussed previously, all the devices connected to the switch will receive the broadcast signal. In this way the switch does form a broadcast domain.

To summarize, when a network connectivity device called a hub is used to connect multiple devices together then both a collision and a broadcast domain are formed. However, if a network connectivity device called a switch is used in place of the hub, then a collision domain cannot form because of how a switch works, but a broadcast domain is formed.

■ Other Addressing Technologies

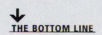 **THE BOTTOM LINE**

This section of Lesson 4 discusses different addressing technologies such as supernetting, NAT, DHCP, and the different methods computers on a network use to send packets to each other.

As previously mentioned, aside from subnetting, there are other technologies available to stretch out the limited number of IPv4 addresses that are available. Some of these technologies are discussed in this section.

Supernetting

The first technology to be discussed is ***supernetting***. Simply put, supernetting is the process of combining several IP ranges, usually Class C ranges, into one larger network. For example, in our opening scenario, if John had two IP address ranges, say 204.214.56.0 and 204.214.57.0, he could combine them, or supernet them, into one aggregate range of IP addresses. What John would have to do is use the CIDR notation of 204.214.56.0/23. The /23 portion of the CIDR notation, indicates that the first 23 bits of the IP address are the network ID while the last 9 bits are used for the host ID. This would result in a network range that supported one network with 512 hosts, minus the first and last host IDs, which are used for network ID and broadcast IDs, respectively.

Network Address Translation (NAT)

CERTIFICATION READY
What does NAT stand for? When is it used?
2.1

Network Address Translation, or *NAT*, and is another technology used to stretch out the limited number of IP addresses available with IPv4. This is a technology that many people use and do not even realize they are doing so. If you have more than one computer at home that can get on the Internet, but only one Internet connection coming into your house, you are using NAT technology.

NATing, the process of using NAT technology, works by taking an IP address coming in from an ISP or other location and using that one IP address to allow all Internet-enable devices to which it is connected to access the Internet. In this way, only one IP address is used to get on the Internet, and multiple devices can use that one IP address to do so.

One good example of this is the network located in the average user's home. One IP address comes into your house from the "modem" provided by your ISP. That "modem" is intended to connect directly to only one computer and only that computer is supposed to have Internet access. However, that is not what happens in most people's homes. Instead of connecting the "modem" to a single computer, most people connect the "modem" to a router/switch or some other type of access point. From that access point, they then connect all their computers and other network-enabled devices in the house. In order for all the different devices to access the Internet via just one IP address, the router/switch has to keep track of each device attempting to connect to the Internet and which device is asking for which connection. That is called NATing. Figure 4-11 illustrates how NATing works in a small home environment.

Figure 4-11

Diagram of a how a basic NAT setup may look in a home environment

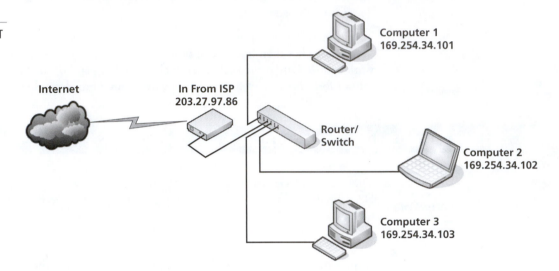

Figure 4-11 is a hypothetical setup for a home network. An ISP comes into the home via a "modem" and assigns the IP address 203.27.97.86 to allow access to the Internet via that modem. However, the family has more than one computer in the house from which they want to access the Internet. To accomplish this, instead of connecting the modem to just one computer and limiting their Internet access to just that computer, they connect the modem to a router/switch instead. The router/switch that the modem is connected to has the ability to take the one IP address from the ISP and match it to the IP addresses of all the computers in the home. This is called Network Address Translation, or NAT. When one of the computers connects to the Internet, the router/switch changes the source IP address of the requesting computer to the IP address given to it by the modem and then sends the request out onto the Internet. When the response comes back from the Internet, the router/switch remembers which port requested a response from that specific website and sends the response message out to the local computer that asked for it via the appropriate port on the router/switch.

The situation is also sometimes called *Network Masquerading* because with NAT in place, the effective result is to hide the entire network address space on the inside of the router/switch from the ISP allowing access to the network or the Internet as a whole. The "inside" of the router/switch refers to the side of the router/switch that connects to a local network. The "outside" of the router/switch is the side of the router/switch that connects to the ISP, the Internet, or any other network outside of the local network.

SOURCE NETWORK ADDRESS TRANSLATION (SNAT)

The previous description of how NAT works in a home environment is actually an example of a very specific type of NAT called *Source Network Address Translation* or *SNAT*. SNAT is an example of what happens when the router/switch in charge of the NAT process for a network changes the source IP address of the request going out of the local network. As changing the source address is the method used to trick the modem in the earlier example, SNAT is the NAT method used in that situation.

PORT ADDRESS TRANSLATION (PAT)

PAT or *Port Address Translation* is what NAT uses to keep track of which device asked for which piece of information. A table found in a device that is using PAT keeps track of public and private addresses so that data can be routed accordingly once it is received back at the network based on the stored port address.

Public versus private

Public versus private addresses refers to two types of IP addresses. *Public IP addresses* are IP addresses that can be used on the Internet. *Private IP addresses* on the other hand cannot be used on the Internet. There are two types of networks that refer to the type of IP addresses being used. If the network is intended to have direct access to the Internet, then it is called a *public network* and the IP addresses used on that network must be registered with a group called the Network Information Center. If a network is not intended to connect directly to the Internet, but uses an intermediary like NAT to allow access to the Internet, then the network is called a *private network*. The IP addresses used in a private network do not have to be registered with the Network Information Center.

In the case of private IP addresses, there are three ranges of addresses that have been set aside by the Network Information Center that can never be used on public networks. These are the address ranges that have been set aside for this purpose:

- 10.0.0.0 to 10.255.255.255
- 172.16.0.0 to 172.31.255.255
- 192.168.0.0 to 192.168.255.255

Many businesses will use one of these ranges for their own internal IP addressing schemes, and then use some form of NAT to link their internal private network to the Internet or some other public network.

Automatic Private Internet Protocol Addressing (APIPA) Service

Another IP address range that would be considered a private IP address range is a range that Microsoft has purchased. The range in question is 169.254.0.1 to 169.254.255.254. This range was purchased by Microsoft to be used in their *Automatic Private Internet Protocol Addressing (APIPA)* Service. This range is only used by Microsoft operating systems and acts as a failover in case there is a problem with trying to connect to an IP address range in some other way. Specifically APIPA is intended to take over if an automatic addressing protocol called DHCP does not work or is not implemented in a network. DHCP is discussed in the next section of this lesson.

The previous situation is most commonly seen in home network environments. In this case, if a home user has not set up DHCP or does not know how to set up DHCP, then Windows will take over the process of assigning IP addresses to the computers in the home network. The IP addresses assigned by Windows will come from the range specified earlier. This allows home computers to link together into a network without the end user having to know how to set things up.

Many router/switches that are designed for use in home environments will also automatically set up NAT based off the IP addresses assigned by Windows. This is why many home networks running Windows simply work without the end user knowing what is going on.

PULLING NAT ALL TOGETHER

Now that we have discussed what NAT, SNAT, PAT, public and private IP addressing, and APIPA are, we can now explain how it all works together. Figure 4-12 illustrates the whole process.

Figure 4-12

Diagram of a how a basic NAT setup may look in a home environment with SNAT and PAT

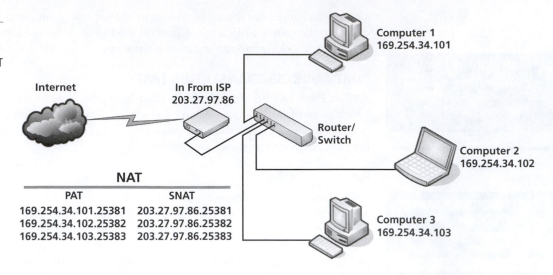

Figure 4-12 illustrates all five of the topics we just discussed. The IP address on the modem from the ISP is an example of a public IP address that is allowed to get on the Internet. The IP addresses on the home computers illustrate both private IP addresses and APIPA addressing. The IP addresses on the computers are private IP addresses because they are not allowed on the Internet. The same IP addresses are also part of the range that Microsoft uses for its Automatic Private IP Addressing Service. The computers received these IP addresses because the person who set up the home network simply let Microsoft assign IP addresses as it saw fit.

The final piece of Figure 4-12 is the NAT portion of the diagram. All the NAT functions take place on the router/switch. The first thing the router/switch does is take each of the private IP addresses it is connected to and assigns port addresses to them. This is seen below the PAT heading. The :25381, :25382, and :25383 that are added on the end of the IP address are the ports the router/switch assigned to each IP address. This process is called Port Address Translation or PAT.

Whenever one of the computers in the home network wants to connect to the Internet, the router/switch substitutes the IP address 203.97.27.86 for that computer's true IP address. However, the router/switch keeps the port address assigned by PAT the same. This is called Source Network Address Translation, or SNAT. Changing the source IP address allows the computer that wanted to get on the Internet to do so, while leaving the port address alone enables the router/switch to make sure that any response from the Internet gets to the correct computer on the home network.

PAT and SNAT working together in this manner is called Network Address Translation, or NAT. In order for NAT to work, a router/switch or other networking device needs to be able to do PAT and SNAT as both are components of NAT.

Assigning IP Addresses

Because IP addresses are logical addresses, they have to be assigned by the network administrators. There are several ways that network administrators can go about doing this.

STATIC ADDRESSING

The oldest way to assign IP addresses is called *static IP addressing*. In static IP addressing all IP addresses had to be assigned manually by the network administrator. This meant that the network administrator had to go to each computer individually and manually assign an IP address to it. This resulted in a lot of extra work and required very good record keeping on the network administrator's part to make sure that a particular IP address was not used more than once.

While static IP addressing required a lot of extra work, there are still some situations where it is preferred. The main situation where static IP addressing may be preferred is in the case of network security. In any systems that do not require that IP addresses be assigned manually, the IP addresses used on a network get broadcasted. This makes it possible for a hacker to listen in on a network and build a reliable map of the layout of the network over time. This makes it easier for the hacker to then come in later and compromise the network for his or her own purposes.

Static IP addressing is mainly used today in conjunction with dynamic IP addressing. In this situation, the majority of the network uses dynamic IP addressing, but specific routes or computers that you wish to remain hidden are assigned static IP addresses.

DYNAMIC ADDRESSING

Because of the large amount of administrative work required of the network administrator when static IP addressing is used exclusively in a network, computer scientists began looking for ways to automate the process of assigning IP addresses. After some experimentation, they settled on something called *Dynamic Host Configuration Protocol (DHCP)*, which is used for *dynamic IP addressing*.

Dynamic host configuration protocol (DHCP)

DHCP is a protocol that was developed to allow IP addresses to be assigned dynamically without requiring constant input from the network administrator. This new protocol greatly reduced the network administrators' workload and is the preferred method used in modern networks to assign IP addresses. Once DHCP is set up on a DHCP server, IP addresses are automatically assigned to client computers as they come onto the network or as their old IP addresses expire.

Figure 4-13 explains how DHCP is used in modern networks. One important thing to notice about this figure is that the clients as well as the DHCP server are all connected to the same switch. When computers and servers, as well as other network devices, share a common switch, that group of devices is called a segment. In Figure 4-13, the clients and the DHCP server are all on the same segment. This is important because for DHCP to work there must be a DHCP server on the same segment as the clients that wish to use the DHCP server to obtain IP addresses.

Figure 4-13

Network segment with a DHCP server and clients

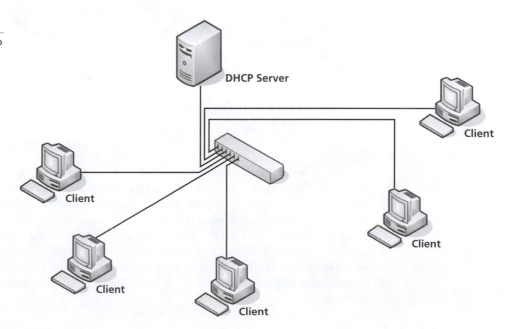

For the purposes of this illustration, we will assume that the DHCP server has been set up and configured correctly. Once this is done, any time a client comes onto the network the following DHCP steps take place:

- **DHCPDISCOVER:** This step originates with the client. First the client broadcasts a signal to the IP address 255.255.255.255. This IP address indicates that the packet is to go to every computer on the segment. The packet broadcasted by the client is a request for an IP address from any DHCP server that may be present. This step is called the DHCP Discovery.

- **DHCPOFFER:** This step originates with the server. Once the DHCP server receives the broadcasted request, it sends an offer to the client making the request. This offer contains the proposed IP address of the client matched to that client's MAC address. The offer from the DHCP server includes terms that specify how long the client is allowed to use the proposed IP address.

- **DHCPREQUEST:** This step originates with the client. Because there may be more than one DHCP server on a given segment, the client sends a second broadcast to the entire segment stating which DHCP offer it is accepting. Any DHCP servers that did not have their offer selected withdraw their offers when they receive this broadcast.

- **DHCPACKNOWLEDGMENT:** In this stage, the server whose offer was accepted by the client sends a packet directly to the requesting client defining the usage terms for the IP address and any additional configuration information the client may have requested or may need to automatically configure the new IP address.

Figure 4-14 illustrates the steps just explained. Additional information about DHCP will be discussed in Lesson 5.

Figure 4-14

Network segment with a DHCP server and clients

❶ DHCP client begins its boot up process.

❷ DHCP client issues a DHCPDISCOVER request.

❸ DHCP server processes the DHCPDISCOVER request and issues a DHCPOFFER message.

❹ DHCP client receives DHCPOFFER messages and issues a DHCPREQUEST message to the DHCP server it has accepted.

❺ DHCP server then issues a DHCPACK message to the client initializing the lease.

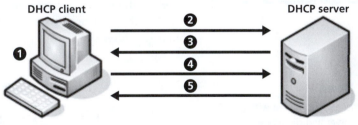

As DHCP is described here, a different DCHP server would be required for each network segment. If you have a network with a large number of segments, this may not be the optimal setup to have. In that situation, there are a couple of different solutions that are available. One such solution is to have a DHCP server attached to a port on a switch that is part of several VLANs. This solution is described in Lesson 6. A second alternative is to have DCHP Relay Agents running on your network. A *DHCP Relay Agent* is a protocol that relays DHCP messages between clients on one sub-network and a DHCP server located on a different sub-network if both sub-networks are part of a larger interconnected network.

Addressing Schemes

CERTIFICATION READY
What is unicast?
1.3

The Addressing Schemes discussed here, have to do more with how computers address or send signals to each other rather than how a person would go about giving them addresses. There are three main types of addressing that computers use to communicate with each other. Those three methods are unicast, broadcast, and multicast:

- *Unicast:* Refers to a computer sending a packet to only one computer at a time. The source computer sends a unicast packet only to the computer that the packet is intended for. Most network traffic uses this sort of communication for normal network activity.

- *Broadcast:* Communication from one computer to all available computers on the network. Where unicast sends communications from just one computer to one other computer, broadcast is used when a packet or message needs to be sent to all computers on a network or segment. We already saw one situation where a broadcast was used when we discussed DHCP. In DHCP, broadcast communications are used by the client for two purposes: to send a request out to the entire segment looking for a DHCP server and to send a message out to the entire network segment, which lets all computers know that it had chosen a specific DHCP server's offer. Another situation where a broadcast communication may be used is to alert all computers on the network about a problem on the network or to update the state of a router or other network device on the network.

CERTIFICATION READY
What is the difference between a multicast and a broadcast?
1.3

- *Multicast:* Multicast is kind of a compromise between unicast and broadcast. Multicast communications are used to send packets to multiple computers at one time, but not to all computers on the network. A multicast is used if several computers need the same information, but all computers do not. A good example of where a multicast may be used is to stream video to several computers on the network at one time.

SKILL SUMMARY

IN THIS LESSON YOU LEARNED:

- About physical addressing.
- About logical addressing.
- About IPv4 and its limitations.
- How to convert binary to decimal and decimal to binary.
- What subnetting is and how it works.
- How to determine subnets.
- About IPv6 and its advantages.
- How physical and logical addressing work together to move packets around a network.
- What NAT is and how it works.
- About public versus private addressing.
- How SNAT and PAT are necessary for NAT to work.
- About static IP addressing.
- About dynamic addressing.
- How DHCP works.
- What unicast, broadcast, and multicast are and when they are used.

Knowledge Assessment

Fill in the Blank

Complete the following sentences by writing the correct word or words in the blanks provided.

1. All network interface cards come with a built in address called a _____.

2. A _____ is an address that has to be assigned to a computer in some way once it is on a network.

3. The two main Internet layer protocols that are used in TCP/IP are _____ and _____.

4. _____ is the process used by a computer to determine which part of an IP address is to be used for the network IP and which part is to be used for the host ID.

5. The process of one computer communicating to just one other computer on a network is called _____.

6. When one computer sends data to multiple computers on a network but not all of them, it is called _____.

7. When one device on a network needs to communicate to every device on the network at the same time it is called a _____.

8. NAT stands for _____.

9. SNAT stands for _____.

10. PAT stands for _____.

Multiple Choice

Circle the letter corresponding to the correct answer.

1. The process of comparing the binary subnet mask with the binary IP address is called what?
   a. ANDing
   b. Classful IP addressing
   c. Logical addressing
   d. Supernetting

2. What is the first half of a physical address called?
   a. Port address
   b. MAC address
   c. Organizational Unique Identifier
   d. Subnet

3. What address range is used for APIPA?
   a. 10.0.0.0 to 10.255.255.255
   b. 169.254.0.1 to 169.254.255.254
   c. 172.16.0.0 to 172.31.255.255
   d. 192.168.0.0 to 192.168.255.255

4. The protocol most commonly used for automatically assigning IP addresses in large networks is which of the following?
   a. Dynamic IP addressing
   b. DHCP
   c. NAT
   d. APIPA

5. _____ is the name of the numbering system used to uniquely identify MAC addresses in a human readable format.
   a. Binary
   b. Octal
   c. Decimal
   d. Hexadecimal

6. An IP address that is not intended to be used on the Internet is called what?
   a. Private IP address
   b. Public IP address
   c. Static IP address
   d. Dynamic IP address

7. A group of network protocols that are designed to work together is called a _____.
   a. Protocol suite
   b. Automatic Private Internet Protocol Addressing
   c. Supernetting
   d. IP Protocol

8. _____ uses a dot decimal format to express its addressing in human readable format.
   a. IPv6
   b. TCP
   c. IPSec
   d. IPv4

9. A _____ is a network that can access the Internet directly.
   a. Private network
   b. CIDR
   c. Public network
   d. Multicast network

10. Classless IP addressing is IP addressing that is characterized by which of the following?
    a. A lack of manners
    b. By being very uncool
    c. The use of subnet masks to determine network IDs
    d. By using NAT to determine its host IDs

■ Case Scenarios

TAKE NOTE ★

It may be easier to complete the lab exercises before attempting to answer these two scenarios.

Scenario 4-1: Subnetting 201.144.32.0/24 for 2 Networks and 48 Hosts

You are the WAN engineer for Widgets International. Your company has just purchased the IP network range 201.144.32.0/24. Your company needs two networks with 48 hosts per network using this IP network range. How do you subnet this IP network? What is the subnet mask you should use? What network address would you use? How would you write this in CIDR notation? What are the usable networks and ranges that you can use to accomplish your company's directive?

Scenario 4-2: Subnetting 192.53.245.0/24 for 3 Networks and 30 Host

You are the WAN engineer for Diver Master Services, Inc. Your company has just purchased Divers Unlimited, Ltd. Between the two companies, you need three networks of at least 24, but no more than 30, computers each. When your company purchased Divers Unlimited, Ltd. your company also acquired the IP address range 193.53.245.0/24. As the WAN engineer, how can you break up this network range to create the networks your combined company needs? How would you denote this using CIDR? What subnet mask should you use? What network addresses should you use? What are the IP ranges of the three sub-networks you will need? What are the usable IP ranges of the three sub-networks you will need?

Lab Exercises

■ Lab 1

Converting Binary to Hexadecimal and Hexadecimal to Binary

The purpose of this lab is to familiarize the students with converting binary values to hexadecimal values and hexadecimal values to binary values.

This lab is important to the student because many values in network, programming, and computer troubleshooting are expressed in the hexadecimal number system. Some examples are physical addresses, IPv6 addresses, memory addresses, and I/O addresses. Throughout the students career he or she will need to recognize what hexadecimal numbering looks like and be able to translate it.

MATERIALS
- Notepad
- Pencil

DO THE LAB

Convert between Binary and Hexadecimal Values

1. Using Table 4-20 from the lesson, convert the following binary values to hexadecimal values. Write the hexadecimal value in the right column of this table.

1001 1101 1111 0010	
0010 0111 1000 0010	
0001 1010 0000 1101	
1111 0110 1001 0100	
0000 0111 1110 0110	
1001 0111 1100 0100	
0011 1100 0110 1111	
0100 1101 0010 1110	

2. Using Table 4-20 from the lesson, convert the following hexadecimal values to binary values. Write the binary value in the right column of this table.

A890	
72E5	
0010	
120F	
ABCD	
1234	
FEDC	
9D48	

■ Lab 2

Converting Binary to Decimal and Decimal to Binary

The purpose of this lab is to familiarize the students with converting binary values to decimal values and decimal values to binary values.

This lab is important to the student because many values in network, programming, and computer troubleshooting are expressed in the binary number system. Converting from decimal to binary and binary to decimal is also an important step in learning how to manually subnet a network.

MATERIALS
- Notepad
- Pencil

THE LAB

Convert between Binary and Decimal Values

1. Using Table 4-7 from the lesson, convert the following binary values to decimal values. Write the decimal value in the right column of this table.

10011100	
11111111	
11011100	
00111000	
00011000	
10000001	
11000110	
00000110	

2. Using Table 4-7 from the lesson, convert the following decimal values to binary values. Write the binary value in the right column of this table.

197	
23	
243	
255	
128	
160	
242	
192	

■ Lab 3

Determining the Subnet Mask of an IP Network Address in CIDR Notation

The purpose of this lab is to familiarize students with determining the subnet mask of an IP network address when the student has been given the IP network address in CIDR notation.

This lab is important to the student because it will help them begin to correctly interpret CIDR notation and help them on their way to being able to determine the subnet ranges of an IP network address when seeing it in CIDR notation.

MATERIALS
- Notepad
- Pencil

DO THE LAB

Determine the Subnet Mask

Using Table 4-12 from the lesson, the student needs to determine the subnet mask for the following IP Network Addresses presented in CIDR notation. Write the subnet mask in the right column of this table.

205.23.189.0/24	
157.234.0.0/16	
12.0.0.0/8	
209.34.81.0/27	
167.55.0.0/18	
15.0.0.0/12	
197.245.1.0/30	
201.23.143.0/26	

■ Lab 4

Determining the Subnet Mask and IP Ranges of a Class C IP Network Address in CIDR Notation

The purpose of this lab is to familiarize the students with determining the subnet mask and IP Address ranges of an IP Network Address when the student has been given the IP Network Address in CIDR notation.

This lab is important to the student because it will help them to begin to correctly interpret CIDR notation and help them on their way to being able to determine the subnet ranges of an IP Network Address when seeing it in CIDR notation. It will also begin to familiarize the student with the process of determine IP Address ranges in a subnet as defined by the CIDR IP Network Address. Once the student is able to successful interpret IP Address ranges for a Class C sub-network, they will have begun to understand the basics of interpreting the IP Address ranges of non Class C sub-network. This Lab will give the student a basic understanding to start with when the topic of interpreting non Class C sub-network ranges is discussed in a later lesson.

MATERIALS
- Notepad
- Pencil

DO THE LAB

Determine the IP Ranges and Subnet Mask from CIDR Notation

Using Table 4-14 from the lesson, determine and write down the subnet mask, all IP address ranges, the usable IP address ranges, and the usable IP addresses for the following IP network addresses presented in CIDR notation.

Using the information found in Table 4-14, create a table similar to Table 4-19 for each of these CIDR notation values:

193.56.132.0/26
206.112.213.0/28
199.123.45.0/27

Network Protocols

EXAM OBJECTIVE MATRIX

Technology Skill Covered	Exam Objective	Exam Objective Number
Protocol Suites	**Explain the purpose and properties of IP addressing.** • IPv4 vs. IPv6 (formatting)	1.3
	Identify common TCP and UDP default ports. • SMTP – 25 • HTTP – 80 • HTTPS – 443 • FTP – 20, 21 • TELNET – 23 • IMAP – 143 • RDP – 3389 • SSH – 22 • DNS – 53 • DHCP – 67, 68	1.5
	Explain the function of common networking protocols. • TCP • FTP • UDP • TCP/IP suite • DHCP • TFTP • DNS • HTTPS • HTTP • ARP • SIP (VoIP) • RTP (VoIP) • SSH • POP3 • NTP • IMAP4 • Telnet • SMTP • SNMP2/3 • ICMP • IGMP • TLS	1.6

	Given a scenario, use appropriate software tools to troubleshoot connectivity issues. • Ping • Tracert/traceroute	4.3
How Protocols Work Together		
Routing Protocols	**Explain the purpose and properties of routing and switching.** • EIGRP • OSPF • RIP • Link state vs. distance vector vs. hybrid • Static vs. dynamic • Routing metrics 　• Hop counts 　• MTU, bandwidth 　• Costs 　• Latency • Next hop • IGP vs. EGP • Routing tables • Convergence (steady state)	1.4
	Given a scenario, install and configure routers and switches. • Routing tables	2.1

KEY TERMS

checksum

convergence

Denial of Service (DoS) attack

distance vector routing protocol

dynamic routing

hybrid routing protocol

link state routing protocol

metrics

next hop

ping

port address

protocol

protocol stack

protocol suite

Request for Comment (RFC)

routed protocol

routing protocol

routing table

static routing

steady state

TCP port

TCP/IP Protocol Suite

TELNET

tracert

UDP port

John is the WAN Engineer for Dive Master Services Inc. His company has purchased another company called Diving Unlimited, Ltd. John has to figure out how to make the two networks work together. In order to do this he will need to come up with a uniform network addressing scheme that combines the two company's networks. How will he go about doing this?

■ Protocol Suites

THE BOTTOM LINE

This section of Lesson 5 will discuss what a protocol suite is with specific emphasis on the TCP/IP Protocol Suite because that is the protocol suite most in use today. Additionally, different protocols that are part of the TCP/IP Protocol Suite and where they belong in the overall scheme of the TCP/IP protocol suite will be discussed.

CERTIFICATION READY
What is a protocol? What is a protocol suite? What is the difference between a protocol suite and a protocol stack?
1.6

In computer networking, a ***protocol*** is a set of agreed on instructions designed to allow computers to communicate to each other across a network connection. There are many protocols used in networking. The reason there are so many protocols is because there are many different tasks that need to be done to allow computers to communicate with each other. A ***protocol suite*** is a group of networking protocols that are designed to work together to accomplish the separate little tasks needed to allow network communications.

Another word that needs to be defined that is related to the concept of a protocol suite is protocol stack. A ***protocol stack*** is all the protocols from a protocol suite that are currently being used to carry out specific functions of network communications within the computer. The protocol stack encompasses all the layers of the protocol model contained in the protocol suite being used. The protocol stack also allows for the moving of additional protocols in and out of the stack as additional functionality is needed for the communications tasks at hand.

TCP/IP Protocol Suite

The most widely used protocol suite in modern computer networking is the ***TCP/IP Protocol Suite***. This suite is built around the Transmission Control Protocol and the Internet Protocol. As you can guess by the name of the second major protocol in this suite, this protocol suite was originally used for Internet communications. However, over time, every major networking company has adopted the TCP/IP Protocol Suite as their networking protocol suite of choice. Even Apple and Novell, who both had their own protocol suites at one time, have given up their own protocol suites in favor of the TCP/IP Suite.

While TCP and IP are the two most important protocols in the TCP/IP Protocol Suite, they are not the only protocols in the TCP/IP Protocol Suite. There are literally scores of protocols that have been developed over the years to work with the TCP/IP Protocol Suite. These various protocols were designed to carry out specific tasks. A few of the more common or widely used protocols designed to be used with TCP/IP are discussed in this lesson.

NETWORK ACCESS LAYER PROTOCOLS

To understand the TCP/IP Protocol Suite we will first need to go back to Lesson 2 where we learned about the TCP/IP Model. In that model there were four layers. Each of those layers represented specific functions that are needed to carry out network communications. These layers listed in order from bottom to top are Network Access, Internet, Transport, and Application. Figure 5-1 shows the layers of the TCP/IP Model.

Figure 5-1

TCP/IP Model

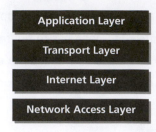

- Application Layer
- Transport Layer
- Internet Layer
- Network Access Layer

X REF

Other Network Access layer protocols will be discussed in Lessons 7 and 8.

On the Network Access layer of the TCP/IP Model, there are no unique protocols specific to TCP/IP. Instead, TCP/IP is designed to use the general Network Access layer protocols that are used by all networking protocols. Some examples of these are Ethernet, Frame Relay, Point-to-Point Protocol, IEEE 802.11 protocols, most of the other IEEE 802 standards, the UTP protocols, and many more. Some of these Network Access layer protocols were discussed in Lesson 3.

INTERNET LAYER PROTOCOLS

The Internet layer of the TCP/IP Model is the first layer to have TCP/IP ProtocolSuite specific protocols. The Internet Protocol (IP) is the most important TCP/IP protocol on this layer and is one of the two protocols used to name the TCP/IP Protocol Suite.

Internet Protocol version 4 (IPv4)

Internet Protocol or IP is used to move data packets from one location on a packet-switched network to another location based on the IP address of the packet being moved. A packet-switched network is one where each data packet is responsible for finding its own route from its source to its destination. In a packet-switched network, it is entirely possible that two packets can be sent from the same host to the same destination and take two totally different routes to get there.

CERTIFICATION READY

What is the IP protocol? What is its function and why is it important? What is the difference between IPv4 and IPv6?

1.3

One of the main functions of IP is to help packets on their way to finding the proper destination. This is why IP addressing is one of the main things defined by the IP protocol. IPv4, or standard IP addresses, are 32 bits long and no two hosts on the same network can share the same IP address. There are several methods to make sure this does not happen. Some of these methods were discussed in Lesson 4.

While IP is concerned with making sure packets are able to move from one location on the network to another, IP is not concerned with verifying that the packet actually got there. Verifying that data actually got to its intended location is the responsibility of higher-level protocols, which will be discussed later. A protocol that does not concern itself with whether data makes it to its destination is called a connectionless protocol. Connectionless protocols are also considered unreliable protocols because there is no mechanism in place to verify the data sent with them arrives at its destination successfully. As a result of this, IP is considered a best effort delivery protocol. IP makes its best effort to get the data to where it needs to be, but if it does not get there, IP is not concerned.

IP however is very concerned that the data it sent is sent to the right location. To ensure that a packet is sent to the correct location, IP has a mechanism in place to verify that the source and destination IP addresses in the IP packet are correct. To verify that the data in a packet is sent to the correct location, IP contains a header checksum. This means that when a network device receives a data packet from another network device, it runs an algorithm on the header of the IP packet and then compares the result of this algorithm with the result stored in the IP header. This process is called a ***checksum***. The area of the header that the checksum result is stored in is also called the checksum portion of the header. If the checksums match, the header of the IP packet is considered good and the packet is passed on to the next hop. If the checksum done on the header does not match up with the checksum stored in the header, then IP discards the packet and does not pass it on.

Because IP only verifies the header of a packet and not the data in the packet, several types of errors are possible when IP packets are sent. Some of these errors are:

- **Data corruption:** The date contained in the packet is corrupted. When this happens, although the data arrived at the correct destination, the data carried in the packet is useless because whatever data sent is not what has arrived.

- **Lost data packets:** Packets never reach their intended destination. This can be caused by any number of things. It can be something as simple as the header getting corrupted so that a networking device somewhere down the line discarded it or the connection between the destination and the source could have gone down, which meant the packet was not able to find an alternative route before it expired.

- **Duplicate arrivals:** More than one copy of the data packet arrived at the destination computer. This could happen because the source computer received a message that a packet was lost when it was not and so it sent a second packet. This can also happen if TCP, a higher-level protocol, expected a response from the destination computer and did not receive it and then ordered that a second packet be sent.

- **Out-of-order packet delivery:** Packets arrive in a different order than the one they were sent in. Most data sent across a network is too large to fit into the data portion of a single packet. As a result, most data sent across a network is broken up into multiple pieces and sent with different packets. However because different packets can take different routes to get to their destination, and take different amounts of time to arrive, there is a good likelihood that the packet could arrive in a different order from the one in which they were sent. When this happens, the receiving computer needs to know what the correct order should be. If it does not know this, then the data will be out of order and it will not be able to be effectively reassembled on the destination computer. When data is being sent that needs to be reassembled in a specific order, IP needs to use a higher-level protocol such as TCP to properly sequence data.

One of the important things to know about the IPv4 protocol is what the IP header portion of a packet looks like. Figure 5-2 shows this.

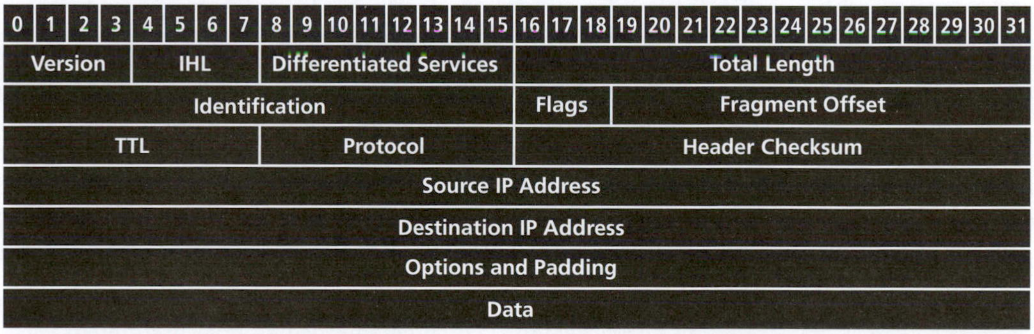

MORE INFORMATION
The following paragraphs will go into some detail about the headers of select protocols. This information is not needed for the CompTIA Network+ exam but is included for those students who may wish to become programmers. As programmers, they will need to write code for networking applications and in many cases this class may be the only class they have that covers networking. The additional information is included for these students.

Figure 5-2

Internet Protocol version 4 (IPv4) header

0	1	2	3	4	5	6	7	8	9	10	11	12	13	14	15	16	17	18	19	20	21	22	23	24	25	26	27	28	29	30	31
Version				IHL				Differentiated Services								Total Length															
Identification																Flags			Fragment Offset												
TTL								Protocol								Header Checksum															
Source IP Address																															
Destination IP Address																															
Options and Padding																															
Data																															

As you can see in Figure 5-2, there are many parts to an IP header. The first 4 bits of the header contain the IP *version* being used. This is important because IPv4 is handled a bit differently than IPv6 is by networking devices. The next 4 bits contain the *IHL*, which stands for the Internet Header Length and specifies how many 32-bit words are used to make up the IP header. The minimum value for an IP header to be valid is five. Because our example has six 32-bit words in it, it is a valid IP header. The next 8 bits are the *Differentiated Services* field, which is intended to show any differentiated services that are used by this IP packet. Differentiated services are a number of enhancements created for IP that are intended to help IP easily discriminate scalable services that are available on the Internet. Scalable services are services that can be built into net-work nodes and make it possible to quantify network performance based on peak performance, bandwidth, and so on, as well as more relative measures of performance. If you wish to know more about this, you can read up on it in RFC 2474. **RFC** stands for **Request For Comment** and all networking standards and protocols are defined by these various documents. Finally, the last 16 bits of the first 32-bit word in the sample IP header is *Total Length*. This section contains the total length of the entire packet in bits.

There are three sections in the next 32-bit word in the sample IP header. The first section is labeled *Identification* and it is used to differentiate the fragments of one IP packet from another. The value placed in this field must be unique for that specific source-destination pair of computers for the time that the packet is active in the Internet. What this means is that each source and destination pair of computers must have a unique number generated by the source computer in order to send packets. The next 3 bits of the send 32-bit word is labeled *Flags*. The first bit of the 3 is used to indicate if the packet is reserved. Generally this value should be 0. The second bit is used to indicate whether the data packet can be fragmented more if necessary. A 0 indicates that the packet, also called a datagram, can be fragmented whereas a 1 indicates that the datagram is not to be further fragmented. The last bit of the flag section is used to indicate if there are more fragments contained in the datagram or if this fragment is the last one. A 0 indicates that this is the last fragment, and a 1 indicates that there are more fragments to come. Finally, the last section is labeled *Fragment Offset*. This section is only used if there are multiple fragments in a datagram and they need to be reassembled.

The next 32-bit word contains the *TTL*, *Protocol*, and *Header Checksum* fields. The *TTL*, or time to live, field is 8 bits long and contains the number of times a specific packet can pass through other network devices before it is terminated. Each time a packet passes through a network device, the TTL is reduced by 1 until it reaches 0 at which point the packet is terminated. This is done to prevent a packet from bouncing around the Internet or other network indefinitely. If enough packets are bouncing around a network indefinitely, sooner or later all of a network's bandwidth will be used up and no more data will be able to pass through it. The *Protocol* field is used to tell a computer which protocol an IP packet needs to be handed off to at the next level up in the protocol stack. This is important because pretty much every protocol in the TCP/IP Protocol Suite passes though the IP protocol on the Internet layer. Finally the *Header Checksum* field contains the checksum value generated when the packet was first created. Each time a packet passes through a network device a checksum is done on the header of the IP packet, and the result is compared to the checksum value stored in this field to determine if the header has been corrupted or otherwise damaged.

The next 32-bit word in the IP header contains the 32-bit *source IP address* or the address of the computer sending the packet. The next 32-bit word in the IP header contains the 32-bit *destination IP address*. Finally, the last 32-bit word of the IP header contains some additional IP *options and padding* to be placed between the IP header and the data to keep the two parts of the datagram separated. The padding portion of the IP header varies depending on what additional options are used. After this, the *Data* of the datagram is found. This section varies in size based on the Network Access layer protocols such as Ethernet.

After discussing IPv4, it is necessary to look at a couple of additional protocols because they are tied closely to IPv4 and are needed by IPv4 in different ways so that IPv4 can carry out its intended task. Two particularly important protocols are Address Resolution Protocol (ARP) and Internet Control Message Protocol (ICMP).

Internet Protocol version 6 (IPv6)

IPv6 is the successor to IPv4 and is described in detail in RFC 2460 which was released in December of 1998. The biggest advantage of IPv6 over IPv4 is that it uses 128-bit address verses the 32-bit addresses used by IPv4. The term used to describe how large an address a particular protocol can create iscalled that protocol's address space. In the case of IPv6 the address space is 128-bits long whereas the address space of IPv4 is only 32-bits long. The advantage the larger address space gives IPv6 is that there is a much larger number of unique IP addresses that can be assigned when using IPv6 over using IPv4. In fact, this larger number of unique IP addresses was one of the main motivations behind creating the IPv6 standard in the first place.

Aside from the larger address space that IPv6 has, there are also other additional capabilities that are not found in IPv4. One of these additional capabilities is multicasting. Multicasting is the ability to send a signal to multiple specific destinations all at the same time without having to send the signal to all possible destinations. The ability to send a signal to all possible destinations at the same time is called broadcasting. While multicasting is an option with IPv4 that is widely used, it is part of the base specification for IPv6.

Stateless Address Configuration (SLAAC) is another advantage of IPv6. However for this to work, ICMPv6 also has to be implemented. ICMP will be covered later in this Lesson. When IPv6 is implemented in conjunction with ICMPv6, then network devices are able to configure their own addresses without using DHCP or some other automatic IP address assigning protocol. Like ICMP, DHCP will be discussed later in this Lesson and in even more detail in Lesson 6.

Another advantage of IPv6 is that some network security features are built into it directly rather than having to rely on additional protocols to implement network security. Specifically, instead of having to rely on the outside protocol IPSec to secure its data packets, IPv6 has a version of IPSec directly built into it. The topic of network security is covered in great detail in later Lessons.

IPv6 has also greatly reduced the overhead of the IP packet. It did this by taking out a lot of the flags and other options that were built into IPv4. While the IPv6 header is actually larger than the header of IPv4 do to how large the address space is, it actually takes less time for a router to process the IPv6 header. This results in faster processing of the routers on a network, which translates into an increase in network performance. There are actually a few other advantages of IPv6 over IPv4, but the ones mentioned are the more important ones.

As alluded to in the previous paragraph, the header for IPv6 looks quite a bit different than the header for IPv4. Figure 5-3 shows what the header of an IPv6 packet looks like.

Figure 5-3

Internet Protocol version 6 (IPv6) header

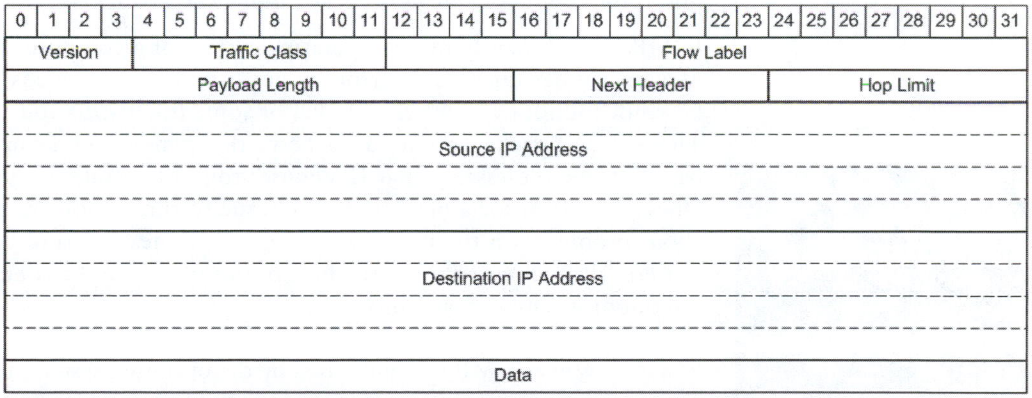

Like with IPv4, the first 4-bits of the header are reserved for the protocol version number. After this, everything is different. The next 8-bits are reserved for the Traffic Class field. This Traffic Class field is used to distinguish between different IPv6 class or priority packets. The next 20-bits are reserved for the Flow Label field. This field is used by IPv6 to sequence packets that have special handling request. RFC 3697 describes in how the Flow Label field is intended to work. The next 16-bits are reserved for specifying the Payload Length of the rest of the packet in number of octets. The Next Header field follows next and is 8-bits long. This field is used to identify the type of any header that may be following the IP header. This field uses the same values as IPv4 does. The Hop Limit field is used to state how many hops a packet has left before it is discarded by the router. Every time an IPv6 packet passes through a network device the value in the Hop Limit field is decreased by 1. Once this value reaches 0, the packet is discarded. Finally we have the Source and Destination Address fields. Each of these fields is 128-bits long and contains the source and destination IP addresses for the packet. After these two fields, the remainder of the packet is data.

Address Resolution Protocol (ARP)

CERTIFICATION READY
What does ARP stand for? What is the main function of the ARP protocol?
1.6

As we discussed in Lesson 4, in network addressing, when a packet is being passed along a network across routers, the MAC address is actually changed at each hop so that the data frame can move on to the next hop in its journey. What was not discussed in that lesson was *how* the MAC address is changed. The ARP protocol is responsible for this particular task. Part of ARP's job is to determine what the MAC address is for the next hop and then adjust the frame accordingly so that the frame can be moved to the next hop along the way.

To accomplish this, ARP in some ways actually needs to work on both Layer 2 (Data Link) and Layer 3 (Network) of the OSI Model. ARP works on Layer 3 in that it needs to be able to understand the IP address of the packet so that it can know where to look for the next MAC address. At the same time, it needs to be able to read and change MAC or physical addresses in the source and destination fields of the Layer 2 Frame in order to move the packet its next hop. Because of this dual role, ARP actually resides in the LLC (Logical Link Control) sublayer of the OSI Model. In a way, ARP acts as a translator between the pure software portion and the hardware portion of the OSI Model, much like the LLC sublayer does. If you would like to learn more about ARP, take a look at RFC 826. A simple Google or Bing search of the Internet will find this RFC for you.

Internet Control Message Protocol (ICMP)

CERTIFICATION READY
What does ICMP stand for? What is the main function of the ICMP protocol?
1.6

As discussed earlier concerning IPv4, it is a connectionless protocol and therefore simply sends off its data packets without checking to see if they successfully reached their destination. But, how then does IP know if a given route is good or not? The answer to that question is the Internet Control Message Protocol (ICMP).

ICMP is used mainly by the operating system of a computer to send messages about the network. When there is an error in the IP packet, a service is unreachable or down, a host not found, or a router is down, or some other situation, an ICMP message is sent. These ICMP packets are used for network diagnostic and routing purposes. It is partly based on these messages that IP chooses routes to send data packets down. ICMP messages are critical for a network to continue to run smoothly and to alert other devices about problems on the network. Using ICMP messages and routing tables found on routers, IP is able to choose the best routes to ensure that data packets are able to get to their appropriate destinations.

CERTIFICATION READY
What is ping? What is ping used for? What is tracert and what it is used for? What is the difference between ping and tracert?
4.3

PING.   While ICMP is mainly used by the operating system, there are a couple of exceptions to that. One of the exceptions where ICMP is used by something other than the operating system is the ping command. *Ping* is a network administration utility that is used to test connectivity to specific nodes on a network and to measure the round-trip time it takes for a packet to get to a specific destination and back.

Ping accomplishes all of this by sending an ICMP request for reply to a specific IP address and then waiting for a response. The response to this ping request is sometimes called a pong. Ping usually issues more than one request so that you can get a general feel for how the network is performing. Ping can be used to test connectivity, to test round-trip times to specific hosts, and to measure how many packets are lost in transit.

On a more negative note, hackers sometimes use ping to bring down a target network by ordering numerous computers to launch continuous ping requests at a target IP address. When this is done with a large enough number of computers, the target computer's network capacity can be overloaded and it can be brought down. This is called a ***Denial of Service attack*** or ***DoS attack*** for short. While ping is not the only way to cause a DoS attack, it was one of the earliest DoS attacks dreamed up by attackers. Today, most systems are hardened against ping-based DoS attacks.

Generally, when a network administrator uses ping to test a system, he or she runs several tests. The first test pings the loopback or the IP address 127.0.0.1. This test is used to verify that the actual network card hardware is working correctly. The next test to run is to ping the local computer's IP address. This verifies that the local NIC is configured correctly. The next test is to ping a different IP address on the same network segment. This verifies local connectivity. Test number four is to next ping the local gateway, which is usually the local router. This verifies that the local router is properly configured. After that, you can ping a host beyond the local router to verify that it is possible to connect beyond the local segment. If all these tests are successful but you still cannot connect to your desired target host, then the problem is beyond the first or second router. If you are in that situation, you will need to find out where the problem you are experiencing begins. To do this, a different utility called trace route is used. We discuss this ICMP utility next.

TRACE ROUTE.   Trace route is a utility used to report back each hop along a route to a specific IP destination. Some versions of trace route use ICMP and some use UDP or even TCP to carry out this function. In the case of ***tracert***, the Windows implementation of this utility, ICMP is used to determine each hop along the way to a specific destination, however, it does not use ICMP the same way that ping does. Trace route does not send just one packet to test each hop along a route, but instead sends several packets to test each hop. The specific number depends on which version is used and what parameters are chosen.

In tracert, the Windows implementation, the TTL (time-to-live) value is modified for each batch of packets used to test the hops to a specific destination. For the first group of packets, the TTL is set to 1. This elicits an ICMP message from the next hop reporting that the TTL of a packet has expired. For the second hop, the TTL is set to 2, thus eliciting the same ICMP message from that router. The group of packets intended for the third hop has their TTL set to 3, and so on until the destination IP address is reached. The computer sending the tracert packets uses the ICMP message to report TTL expirations at each hop and the IP address of that hop as well as relevant data such as how long it took the message to arrive at the machine sending out the trace route. All this data can then be used to diagnose a network and identify where a problem may be occurring. This is the first step in resolving problems. Unfortunately, hackers can also use this information to map out a network that they hope to break into. This is why many network administrators have chosen to filter out these types of packets and only use them internally to test their own networks.

Internet Group Management Protocol (IGMP)

Internet Group Management Protocol (IGMP) is used by IP hosts to manage their multicast groups' dynamic membership and by connecting routers to find those group members. IP multicasting is basically the ability of an IP host to send a datagram or data packet to all the IP hosts within a "host group." A host group consists of all the IP computers that are currently connected to a particular IP multicast host that are set to receive the same transmission from that host. These host groups can be set to contain 0 or more hosts.

Because multicast host groups use IP to transmit datagrams, there is no guarantee that the datagrams will reach the entire intended host group, or if they do that they will be in the correct order. In short, because IP is the protocol used to send the datagrams, all that can be expected by the receiving host is that IP will make its "best effort" to get the datagrams to where they need to go.

As indicated earlier, the membership of a host group is dynamic. This means that hosts can connect and disconnect from the host group at will. There are two types of host groups:

- **Permanent host group:** In this group, it is not the hosts that are a permanent part of the group, but rather the IP address that is permanent. What this means is that while hosts may join or disconnect at will, the IP address they connect to in order to be part of this group is permanent.

- **Transient host group:** This is a host group that is formed for a specific multicast and then disbanded after use. In this type of group, the multicast host creates the group and seeks out its members at the time the multicast group is in use, but after the multicast group is no longer needed, as indicated when the host membership reaches 0, the multicast group is disbanded and the resources are made available for another multicast group.

But where does IGMP come in to play in all this? The answer to that question is that it is IGMP's job to manage all this. IGMP is responsible for creating host groups and for adding hosts to and deleting hosts from those host groups. IGMP also is responsible for setting up a "deadman timer" procedure that forces members of a host group to periodically confirm their membership in the host group. Aside from managing and creating multicast groups, IGMP is also responsible for creating and maintaining the database structure that keeps tracks of all the IP hosts that are part of a specific multicast group. To sum up, IP hosts and their neighboring multicast agents use IGMP to create transient multicast groups, to add members to and delete members from those groups, and to require periodical group membership confirmation from member IP hosts.

If you wish to know more about IGMP, you can read RFC 988. This RFC is one of the shorter ones at only 20 pages long.

TRANSPORT LAYER PROTOCOLS

The two main TCP/IP protocols on the Transport layer of both the OSI and TCP/IP Models are Transmission Control Protocol (TCP) and User Datagram Protocol (UDP). TCP is a connection-oriented protocol, while UDP is TCP's connectionless counterpart.

Ports

Protocols on the Data Link layer have MAC or physical addresses that indicate the physical location of a device and are used to move data frames from one network device to another network device directly connected to it. Protocols on the Network layer have logical addresses that are used to determine the best route for a device to take to a specific distant location. Protocols on the Transport layer have port addresses. ***Port addresses***, also known as ***ports***, are used to determine which upper-layer protocols, services, and processes each data segment is intended for. Port addresses are used to make sure that the correct protocol, service, or process is able to get the data that is intended for it. The two main protocols on the Transport layer, UDP and TCP, both use port addresses or ports.

Port addresses, or ports, are in the number range from 0 to 65,535. These port address numbers come in three groups or classes:

- **Well known ports:** Port numbers in this group range from 0–1023. Well known ports can only be assigned by the Internet Assigned Numbers Authority (IANA). The ports in this range, according to IANA, can only be used by the system or root processes and by programs that are executed by privileged users. For the most part, port addresses in this range have been officially set aside by IANA for specific protocols, processes, and services. Port numbers that have been set aside by IANA can only be used by the protocol, process, or service that IANA has defined for each port address.

- **Registered ports:** The port range for this group is 1024–49151. If a company, organization, or individual wishes to use one of these ports, it should register it with IANA. When a program uses a registered port, that port is used consistently on all systems.

- **Dynamic or private ports:** These ports range from 49152–65535. These ports can be used by any program or user at any time and are assigned dynamically by the system as needed.

CERTIFICATION READY
What are ports? What function do they serve in networking? What layer of the OSI Model are ports found on?
1.5

TAKE NOTE*

These port addresses need to be learned to pass CompTIA's Network+ exam.

Table 5-1

Commonly used well-known port addresses

Table 5-1 lists some of the more commonly used well-known port addresses.

PORT ADDRESS	PROTOCOL USED	DESCRIPTION
20	TCP	File Transfer Protocol (FTP)—Data
21	TCP	FTP—Control (Used for commands)
22	TCP/UDP*	Secure Shell (SSH)—Used for secure logins, file transfers (Secure Copy [SCP] and Secure File Transfer Protocol [SFTP]), and port forwarding
23	TCP	Telnet protocol—Unencrypted text communications
25	TCP	Simple Mail Transport Protocol (SMTP)—Used for routing e-mail between e-mail servers
53	TCP/UDP	Domain Name System (DNS)
67	UDP	Boot Strap Protocol (BOOTP) Server and Dynamic Host Configuration Protocol (DHCP) Server
68	UDP	BOOTP Client and DHCP Client
69	UDP	Trivial File Transfer Protocol (TFTP)
80	TCP/UDP*	Hypertext Transfer Protocol (HTTP)
110	TCP	Post Office Protocol version 3 (POP3)—Used by local host to retrieve e-mails from remote e-mail servers using TCP/IP
123	UDP	Network Time Protocol (NTP)—Used for network time synchronization
143	TCP/UDP*	Internet Message Access Protocol (IMAP)—Used to retrieve, organize, and synchronize e-mail messages
161	UDP	Simple Network Management Protocol (SMNP)
162	TCP/UDP	Simple Network Management Protocol Trap (SMNPTRAP)
443	TCP	HTTPS (Hypertext Transfer Protocol over SSL/TLS [Secure Sockets Layer/Transport Layer Security])
3389	TCP	RDP (Remote Desktop Protocol)—Proprietary protocol from Microsoft developed to remotely take over a host's desktop across a network.

TAKE NOTE *

The port numbers listed here are only valid for the TCP/IP Protocol Suite. Different port numbers are used by other, no longer used, protocols. As such, these port numbers are sometimes referred to as TCP port numbers and may be referred to as TCP Ports on the Network+ exam.

The first column in Table 5-1 contains the commonly used port number. The second column contains the Transport layer protocol that most commonly uses that port number. Those ports that contain a TCP in this column are generally known as *TCP ports*, and those ports that contain a UDP in this column are generally known as *UDP ports*. You should note that some ports contain both TCP and UDP in this column because these ports are commonly used by both protocols. In point of fact, most ports can be used by TCP and UDP according to IANA, but only those that are commonly used by both have the TCP/UDP values in the second column. Finally the last column in Table 5-1 gives a brief description of which Application layer protocol each port number is used by. All the information in this table can be found at *http://www.iana.org/assignments/port-numbers*, which is the official IANA Database for Port Numbers.

There are a couple of additional notes that need to be made about this table. For purposes of the CompTIA Network+ Exam, those port numbers with an * beside the TCP/UDP should be understood as only being TCP port numbers. This is not absolutely true according to IANA, but it should be understood to be true for the Network+ Exam. One other note is that port numbers 68 and 162 are not listed by CompTIA as being on their Network+ Exam.

Transmission Control Protocol (TCP)

Transmission Control Protocol (TCP) is the most commonly used protocol on the Transport layer and is considered one of the core protocols of the TCP/IP Protocol Suite. While IP is mainly concerned with getting messages from one network device to the next in order to get the packet to its ultimate destination, TCP is concerned with the two end devices. The main function of TCP is to provide communication services between Application layer services, protocols, and processes and the IP. Another way of saying this is that while IP is concerned with getting data from one device to another device quickly, TCP is concerned with getting data from one network application such as an e-mail server or web server to another network application such as an e-mail client or web client. Some of the most popular Application layer services and that use TCP are e-mail, the World Wide Web, FTP, SSH, peer-to-peer file sharing, and some forms of media streaming.

In order for TCP to accomplish its function, there are several management tasks that it has to handle. Some of these tasks are flow control, managing network congestion, controlling segment size, controlling the rate at which data is allowed to move, and the number of segments permitted before an acknowledgment is required before additional data segments can be sent. Another task that TCP is responsible for is ensuring that data segments are reassembled into the correct sequence when they arrive at a specific destination.

TCP is optimized for the accurate delivery of data; it is not always able to deliver said data in a timely manner. Some of the reasons for this are that TCP has to wait for data that has to be resent or it has to wait for data that arrived out of sequence before reassembling it. Because of this, TCP should not be used for real-time applications such as Voice over IP (VoIP) or real-time video streaming. For these purposes UDP is provided.

Just like with IP, it is important to know what the TCP header looks like. Figure 5-4 shows the header portion of a TCP segment.

CERTIFICATION READY
What is the TCP protocol used for? How is the TCP protocol different than the IP protocol? Is TCP a connection-oriented protocol or a connectionless protocol?
1.6

Figure 5-4

Transmission Control Protocol (TCP) header

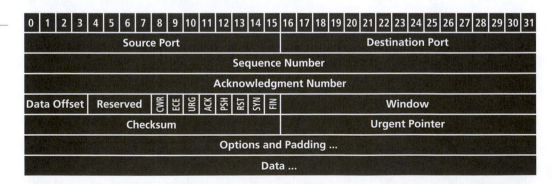

The first 16 bits of the TCP header contains the *Source Port* number. This is used to identify the sending port. The next 16 bits identify the *Destination Port* number. This is used to identify the receiving port on the destination computer. The *Sequence Number* takes up the next 32 bits of the heading. This field in the TCP header has two functions. If the SYN flag bit is set to 1 then it indicates that this is the first segment in a sequence of segments that are to come. If the SYN bit is clear, then this segment is one of several sent but it is not the first one. Each segment after the first segment contains the sequence number of the previous segment plus 1. In other words, if the first sequence number was 25, then the next one would be 25+1 or 26, the next would be 26+1 or 27, and so on until the last segment in a sequence is reached. The computer knows which segment is the last in a sequence because it will have the FIN bit set to 1.

The next 32 bits field is the *Acknowledgment Number*. When the ACK flag is set to 1, this field will show the sequence number that the receiving computer should expect next. This is one of the mechanisms in place with TCP to ensure that all segments safely arrive at their destination. If the segment in question is the first ACK segment sent to either end of a session, then each segment only contains the next sequence number but no data. This is used to set up a session between two computers running TCP.

The next 4 bits are called the *Data Offset* bits. These bits are used to specify how large a TCP header is to be in 32-bit words. The minimum number of 32-bit words needed to make a valid TCP header is 5 words or 20 bytes, while the maximum number is 15 32-bit words or 60 bytes.

The next 4 bits are *Reserved* for future use and currently should only contain all 0s. However, the next 8 bits are more interesting because they are the flag bits that were mentioned when discussing the Sequence Number and Acknowledgment Number fields. There are 8 of these flag bits, also called Control Bits, which are each one bit long. When a flag bit is set to 1, the flag is said to be set. Here are the 8 flag bits:

- **CWR:** When the CWR or Congestion Window Reduced flag is set, it indicates that that the sending host has received a TCP segment with its ECE flag set.
- **ECE:** ECE stands for ECN-Echo. This indicates two different things depending on if the SYN flag is set or not. If the SYN flag is set, then it indicates that TCP peer is ECN capable. If the SYN flag is clear, then it indicates that a packet with its Congestion Experienced flag set. ECN means Explicit Congestion Notification and was added to TCP and IP in RFC 3168. Not all TCP segments use ECN.
- **URG:** If this flag is set it indicates that the Urgent Point field, discussed later, is significant.
- **ACK:** If this flag is set it means that the Acknowledgment Field, discussed earlier, is important. All segments that are sent after the initial SYN packet from a client should have this flag set.
- **PSH:** This flag represents the push function. This flag is set when a system is asking that buffered data be pushed to the receiving application.
- **RST:** The RST flag means Reset. When this flag is set, the system is asking that the connection be reset.
- **SYN:** The SYN flag is very important. The SYN flag is set to indicate that the segment contains synchronizing sequence numbers. Only the first segment sent from each end of a connection should have this flag set. Also as previously noted, some flags change meaning based on what the SYN flag is set to. Some flags are only valid when SYN is set and others are only valid when SYN is clear.
- **FIN:** Finally we have the FIN flag. When this flag is set, it indicates that there is no more data coming from the sender.

The next field in the TCP header is the 16-bit *Window* field. This field is used to define the number of bytes TCP is willing to receive before it is required to wait for an acknowledgment. This windowing is part of TCP's flow control and is referred to as a sliding window. In an ideal situation, TCP send a set amount of data in bytes, as defined by the Window field, then waits for an acknowledgment before sending the next segments of data. If TCP does not receive the expected acknowledgment after a set amount of time, it will resend the data. If the buffer at the receiving end of the TCP connection is full, then the receiving TCP client sends a window size of 0. This tells the other end of the connection to stop sending data. Once the buffer is cleared, another TCP segment is sent with a new window size, and data transmission resumes. The window size of TCP can be as small as 2 bytes or as large as 65,535 bytes. This larger size is use in high-speed networks. RFC 1323, which is an extension of the TCP standard, actually creates a new option called Windows Scaling that allows for multiples of the 65,535-byte maximum. Once all the data has been sent, a termination of the session signal is sent and once the receiving end sends an acknowledgment, the transmission ends.

Following the Window field in the TCP header is the 16-bit *Checksum* field. This field is used to store a checksum value for the entire TCP segment. Unlike IP, the Checksum for TCP includes both the header and the data portions of the TCP segment.

Next in the header is the *Urgent Pointer* field. This field is 16 bits long and is only important if the URG flag is set. When the URG flag is set, this field contains the sequence number of the last segment of urgent data.

Finally we have the *Options and Padding* field. This field can be anywhere from 0 to 320 bits long, so long as it is divisible by 32. If the options are not divisible by 32, then the remaining space is used for padding so that the field is divisible by 32. There are a number of options that can be placed in this field, many of which are now obsolete. One of the options that can be placed here is the Windows Scaling option mentioned earlier that was introduced by RFC 1323. This RFC also defines some other options that can be placed in this field. After this, the TCP segment contains *Data*.

If you would like to learn more about the TCP standard you can look at RFC 793, RFC 1072, RFC 1146, as well as the previously mentioned RFC 1323, RFC 1644, RFC 2018, and RFC 2883. RFC 793 is the original RFC describing the current implementation of TCP, while the other RFCs are addendums or extensions of RFC 793.

User Datagram Protocol (UDP)

User Datagram Protocol (UDP) is connectionless counterpart of TCP. It does not guarantee reliable delivery and is primarily used to give other protocols such as IP access to datagram services like port number. Due to the limited functionality provided by UDP, the header is correspondingly much smaller and less complex. Figure 5-5 shows what a UDP header is to look like.

Figure 5-5

User Datagram Protocol (UDP) header

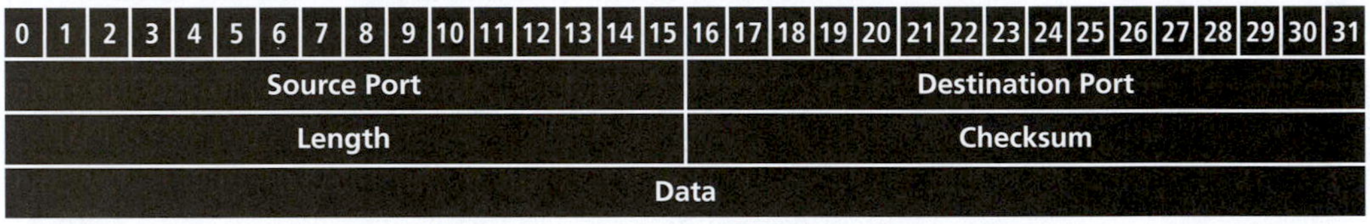

0 1 2 3 4 5 6 7 8 9 10 11 12 13 14 15	16 17 18 19 20 21 22 23 24 25 26 27 28 29 30 31
Source Port	Destination Port
Length	Checksum
Data	

CERTIFICATION READY

How is the UDP protocol different from the TCP protocol? Why is this difference important?

1.6

As you can see in Figure 5-5, the UDP header is much smaller and less complex than the TCP header. The first field is the *Source Port* field and contains the address port of the protocol, service, or process that is sending this data segment. This port should be used as the destination port when a service, process, or protocol on the other end needs to respond to this UDP segment. The next field is the *Destination Port* field, and it too is 16 bits long. Next we have the *Length* field. This field contains the length of the entire UDP segment. The minimum for this field is 8 bytes, and the theoretical maximum is 65,535 bytes; although, in reality the maximum length is determined by the IP packet that is using UDP. The minimum length is 8 bytes because that is the size of the UDP header. Finally we have the *Checksum* field. This field carries the Checksum value for the UDP header and the data contained within the datagram.

RFC 768 describes UDP. RFC 1122 also contains a small section about UDP and is a good overview of how Internet hosts are to communicate.

APPLICATION LAYER PROTOCOLS

Application layer protocols are protocols that are designed to carry out specific purposes or functions. There are many specific functions that these protocols carry out, such as file transfers, transferring web pages, transferring e-mails between servers, transferring e-mail from servers to clients, and many other jobs. None of the Application layer protocols can do their jobs alone; they always need lower-level protocols to carry out the transmission of their various services. In this section of Lesson 5, we discuss some of these Application layer protocols.

Dynamic Host Control Protocol (DHCP) and Domain Name Service (DNS) are two of the more important Application layer protocols we are going to talk about. You should note that in the event that DHCP does not work or goes down, the APIPA (Automatic Private Internet Protocol Addressing) protocol in later versions of Windows automatically goes into effect. This protocol was discussed in Lesson 4 if you need more details about it. The first Application layer protocol to be discussed is DHCP.

Bootstrap Protocol (BOOTP)

In order to discuss DHCP, it is first necessary to mention the Bootstrap Protocol (BOOTP). It is important to mention BOOTP not because it is widely used, but rather because it is what DHCP replaced. BOOTP was first introduced in RFC 951 and later updated in RFCs 1395, 1497, 1532, and 1542. All the updates to BOOTP were released in 1993.

BOOTP was intended to automate IP addressing across a network. BOOTP gets its name from the bootstrap process that takes place when a computer initially boots up. The very act of starting up a computer causes the initial BIOS program to begin running, which gets a computer ready to accept an operating system. This process is called the bootstrap process. BOOTP is used during this process. On the client side, while the computer is booting but has not yet initialized its operating system, BOOTP issues a request to a BOOTP server for an IP address. The server receives this request and sends the appropriate IP address to the computer booting up. After this, the computer is able to either request an OS from a Trivial File Transfer Protocol (TFTP) server or it loads the OS from its own resources. On the server side, BOOTP keeps a table of all the physical addresses found on a network and matches them to IP addresses. This database is used to assign IP addresses to the clients. Figure 5-6 illustrates the previously described BOOTP initialization process.

Figure 5-6

BOOTP Initialization Process

❶ BOOTP client begins its boot up process called bootstraping.

❷ BOOTP client issues a BOOTP request message.

❸ BOOTP server processes the BOOTP request.

❹ BOOTP server issues a BOOTP replay for the BOOTP client.

❺ If BOOTP client is a dump terminal, it sends out a TFTP request looking for an Operating System.

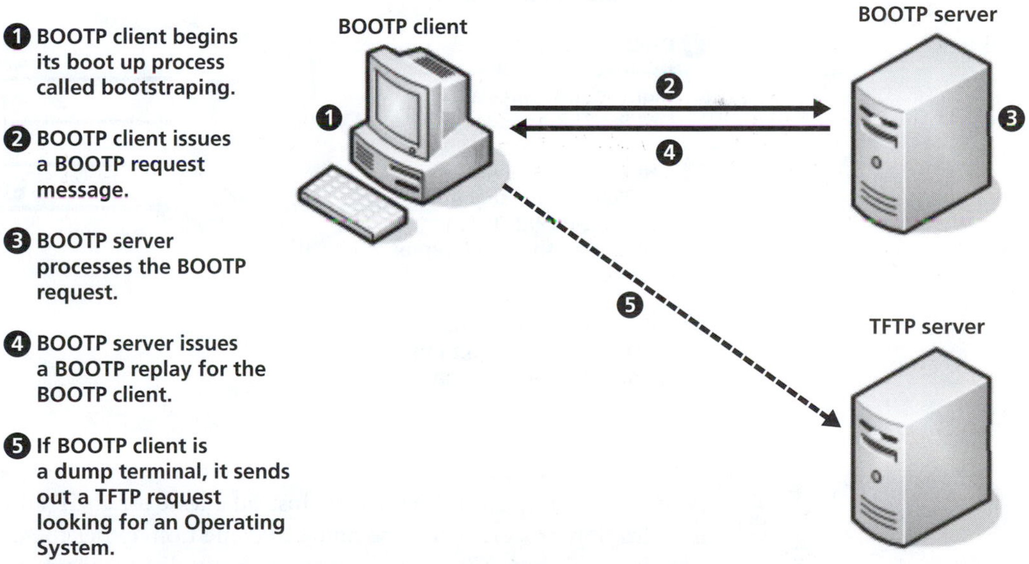

While BOOTP is not used very often these days, it may still be found in networks where the client devices do not contain any operating system or storage of their own. Such clients are often called dumb terminals. BOOTP uses UDP port 67 or the server and UDP port 69 for the client.

CERTIFICATION READY
What is DHCP? What type of situation would you use DHCP in?
1.6

Dynamic Host Control Protocol (DHCP)

This brings us to DHCP. DHCP was first introduced in RFC 1541 in 1993 and was intended as a replacement for the older and less wieldy BOOTP. DHCP has pretty effectively replaced BOOTP in most applications just like it was intended to.

While DHCP was initially built on top of BOOTP, it works a bit differently. Some of the differences are that DHCP does not require a table matching specific physical address to specific IP addresses. Instead DHCP holds a range of IP addresses to be assigned to clients and assigns them on an as-requested basis. Another difference is that DHCP can store complete IP configuration data for its clients. This means that aside from IP addresses for the clients, DHCP also stores information such as subnet mask, gateway, and DNS addresses.

In keeping with its roots in BOOTP, DHCP clients when they first boot up use the same message format BOOTP does to request an IP address, however the functionality is different. When a DHCP client comes up, it issues a DCHPDISCOVER message on its own network segment. The DHCP server then responds with a DHCPOFFER message, which contains an IP address and any other IP configuration data that may be located in the DHCPOFFER's options field. After a client receives one or more DCHPOFFER messages from various DHCP servers, it issues a DHCPREQUEST message to the DHCP server whose offer it has chosen. If more than one DHCP server is on a network, when the DHCPREQUEST is received from the client, those servers that the DHCPREQUEST was not intended for take that as a decline from the client. Once the DHCP server whose offer was accepted receives the DHCPREQUEST message, it binds that IP address to the physical address of the client so that the IP address will not be offered to another client. The DHCP server then sends a DHCPACK message to the client letting it know that it now has the proposed IP address and configuration. Figure 5-7 illustrates the DHCP initialization process just discussed.

Figure 5-7

DHCP Initialization Process

❶ DHCP client begins its boot up process.

❷ DHCP client issues a DHCPDISCOVER request.

❸ DHCP server processes the DHCPDISCOVER request and issues a DHCPOFFER message.

❹ DHCP client receives DHCPOFFER messages and issues a DHCPREQUEST message to the DHCP server it has accepted.

❺ DHCP server then issues a DHCPACK message to the client initializing the lease.

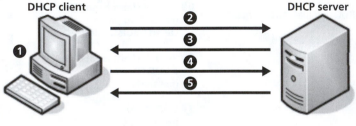

When a DHCP client receives an IP address from a DHCP server, the IP address is not permanently assigned to that client. Instead a lease for an IP address is negotiated during the initialization process. The lease time can come from either the client or the server, but a lease time is established. When the lease time on the client expires, it is required to go through the whole initialization process again to gain a new IP address.

After a lease is granted to a client, the client keeps two times in its memory—the renew time, which by default, is the point when the client has half its lease time remaining. The second time the client keeps in memory is the total time of the lease. When the renew time is reached the client attempts to renew the lease from the server by sending a RENEWING request to the server. If the server acknowledges the RENEWING request, then there is no problem and the client will continue to use that IP address and configuration under the renewed lease. If the server does not respond, the client waits half the remaining time and then tries again until it reaches 87.5% of its total lease time. At this point, the client attempts to issue a REBINDING request. If the server acknowledges the REBINDING request, then the lease is renewed and the client continues to use the assigned IP under the new lease. If the client does not receive an acknowledgment, then it again issues the REBINDING request after half the remaining time on the lease. If the client still does not receive an acknowledgment, it will continue to do this until there is only 60 seconds left on the lease. At this point, the client stops any networking processes that are running until it finally receives an acknowledgment from the server. During this time, the client will also attempt to go through the entire initialization process to receive a new DHCP lease. If the client either receives an acknowledgment for the REBINDING or RENEWAL of its former lease, or a new lease, it will reactivate its network processes. If the client receives a new lease, it must permanently relinquish its former lease in favor of the new one. DHCP uses UDP port 67 for the server and UDP port 68 for the client.

Domain Name System (DNS)

Domain Name System (DNS) is the next application layer protocol we discuss. This is a very important protocol and it makes it possible for us to use the World Wide Web the way we do. DNS is the protocol that converts all those URLs we can easily remember to IP addresses that the Internet can use.

CERTIFICATION READY
What is DNS? What is its main function on a network? Why is DNS needed to access the Internet?
1.6

There are a large number of RFCs that relate to DNS. However, RFC 830 was the RFC that first suggested that some sort of domain naming system was needed and proposed how that system could be implemented. RFC 920 was actually the first RFC to lay out the specific requirements for a Domain Naming System and even introduced the first 5 major domain names which are .gov, .mil, .com, .edu, and .org. This RFC also proposed the use of the standard English two-letter codes to be used for countries like.uk for United Kingdom or .us for United States, and so on. Many more RFCs have now been written that elaborate on and enhance DNS.

Several components are needed for DNS to work. Some of those components are name servers, authoritative name servers, cache servers, and resolvers:

- **Name severs:** Serve as the database of all the name domains on the Web. This database is distributed around the world and each domain sever has its own section of responsibility in this huge distributed database.

- **Authoritative name servers:** Are attached to domain servers and are responsible for answering any request they receive about the domain space they are part of. The authoritative name server can either be a master server, in which case it is the domain server, or it can be a slave server, which only holds a copy of the master server's database and uses that to answer request it receives about its name space.

- **Cache servers:** Maintain a database of requests that they have received for name resolution and provide the appropriate information if a new request is made for the same URL it had resolved previously. This database purges itself when a URL is not requested again after a certain amount of time, which is called the time to live or TTL of the initial request.

- **Resolvers:** Are the clients that make requests of the Domain Name System. These clients can be actual clients or even servers that are part of a larger network. They all have a small cache of their own, and if they are a server in their own right, they will have a larger cache.

Now that we have described the parts of DNS, we can discuss how DNS works. On the Internet, there are a whole series of domain servers. The most basic and most important domain server is the root server. Within its database, this server stores the IP address of every major domain server on the Internet. The major domain servers are those that are responsible for the .org domain, the .com domain, the .edu domain, the .net domain, the .gov domain, and so on. Each various domain server in turn contains in its database the IP address of every major server on its domain. For example, the .gov domain server's database may contain the IP address of the White House server, the Treasury Department server, the Justice Department server, the Pentagon server, and so on.

The following scenario illustrates how a DNS server is able to use the different servers listed earlier to resolve a URL to its IP address. In this scenario, you are attempting to access the URL www.support.widgets.com/widgets_specs.htm. When you open your web browser and enter this URL, the browser checks the local web cache to see if the IP address of the entered URL can be found. If it cannot be found, your computer sends a query to your ISP's DNS sever asking it for the IP address of the URL. The ISP's DNS server checks its cache in search of the IP address of the requested URL. If it does not find the IP address, it sends a query to the Root Domain Server asking it if it knows the IP address of the URL. The Root Domain Server replies back with the IP address of the .com domain server. The ISP's DNS server then sends a query to the .com domain server requesting the IP address of the URL. The .com domain server replies back with the IP address of the.widgets domain server. The ISP's DNS server then sends a query asking the .widgets domain server for the IP address of the URL. The .widgets domain server replies back with the IP address of the www.support.widgets.com web server. The ISP's DNS server then passes this IP address down to your client computer. Your computer then sends a query to the IP address of the www.support.widgets.com web server for the widgets_specs.htm document, which it then displays in the web browser on your client. Figure 5-8 is an illustration of the entire process. DNS uses UDP and TCP port 53.

Figure 5-8

DNS Name Resolution Process

❶ Client computer ask for the IP address of URL www.support.widgets.com/widget_specs.htm from the DNS server of the ISP.

❷ ISP DNS server queries the .root domain server for the IP address of the URL.

❸ The .root DNS server responds back with the IP address of the .com domain server.

❹ The ISP DNS server queries .com domain server for URL IP address.

❺ The .com domain server responds back with the IP address of the .widget domain server.

❻ The ISP DNS server queries .widget domain server for URL IP address.

❼ The .widgets domain server responds back with the IP address of the .support web server.

❽ ISP DNS server passes the IP address of the www.support.widgets.com web server to the client computer.

❾ The web browser on the client computer queries www.support.widgets.com web server for the widgets_specs.htm document.

❿ The www.support.widgets.com web server responds back with the requested document.

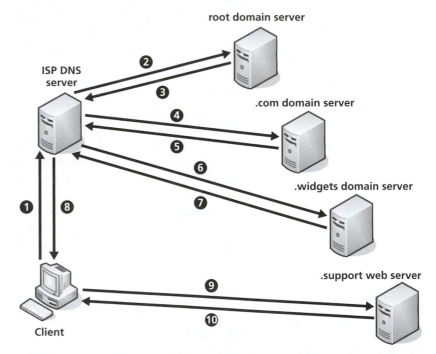

Hypertext Transport Protocol (HTTP)

The next Application layer protocol we discuss is Hypertext Transport Protocol (HTTP). As its name suggests, HTTP is used to transport Hypertext Markup Language (HTML) documents, otherwise known as web pages, over the Internet. However, this is not all that HTTP is used for. HTTP can also be used to retrieve graphics, images, and other types of media. The RFC that originally defined HTTP was RFC 1945 released in 1996. This RFC defined HTTP/1.0. However, HTTP had actually been used since 1990, and the format being used at that time was HTTP/.9. In 1999, RFC 2616 was released, which defined HTTP/1.1. This is the HTTP currently in use.

HTTP works in the following manner. When a browser or other client wishes to retrieve a specific file or web page from a known URL, it sets up a TCP session with the specific server and then sends an HTTP request to port 80. The HTTP request identifies the document or file it wants and sends a request to "get" that particular document or file. The server then responds back with an acknowledgment that contains a status line and the content requested, error message, or some other information. Once the response from the server is completed, the session is closed or additional information from the same server is requested.

The status line of the HTTP response is significant because there are several pieces of important information there. The two most important pieces of information are the content length and content type. The content length tells the client how much data to expect in bytes. The content type tells the client what form the data will take so that it can treat the data accordingly once it receives it. In the seven layer OSI Model, this last function would be the job of the Presentation layer, but since the Internet uses TCP/IP, defining the type of data to be sent needs to be done by HTTP because the upper three layers of the OSI Model are combined into the Application layer of the TCP/IP Model and Protocol Suite. HTTP uses TCP port 80.

Secure Sockets Layer (SSL)

Secure Sockets Layer (SSL) is a protocol that is used to secure Internet communications. SSL was initially introduced by Netscape and was used to secure Internet transactions in the Netscape browser. The first two version of SSL were not very effective, but the third version, which was introduced in 1996, resolved the problems of the first two versions. Over time, it has become a standard for securing Internet communications of all types no matter what browser is being used.

There are a couple of ways an end user can tell if SSL or a related security protocol called TLS, which is discussed later, is being used. One way is that the URL starts out with https instead of http. Another way to identify this is more web browser dependent. Some browsers such as Firefox change the color of the URL bar if the web site being accessed is secure. Other web browsers place a lock symbol next to the URL bar or down in the bottom right corner. Some browsers indicate a secure web site using two or more of the previously mentioned methods.

SSL works by inserting itself between the TCP protocol and any higher-level protocols such as HTTP that are being used to send data from one location to another. This is how SSL is able to secure a wide variety of higher-level protocols.

SSL is designed to carry out three basic tasks. Those tasks are as follows:

- Server authentication
- Client authentication
- Encrypt TCP sessions

The server authentication function of SSL allows a client to confirm the identity of a server to which it is preparing to send a transaction. This is important in verifying that the web server you are about to log on to in order to do your banking is indeed the bank the server claims to be, or to verify that the server you are about to send a credit card transaction to is the e-commerce server it claims to be. Many other examples can be used to illustrate the purpose of server authentication.

A server is authenticated with something called a certificate. A certificate is a security technique used to correctly identify and verify the identity of a specific computer over a network connection. In the case of SSL verifying the bank or credit card servers in our examples, both the client and the server would have a certain certificate key supplied by a trusted third-party certificate authority. When the client verifies that the server has the correct key, it is able to prove that the server in question really is the server it claims to be.

TAKE NOTE *

Some Internet sites use both forms of authentication simultaneously.

Client authentication is similar to server authentication except it works the other way around. Instead of the client verifying the identity of the server, the server is verifying the identity of the client. This type of authentication is important for a server sending confidential information to a specific client computer such as bank records or something else of a similar confidential nature. Client authentication uses certificates much like server authentication does except in the other direction.

The final function of SSL is to encrypt the TCP session. This means that all the data sent across the connection is encrypted at one end and decrypted at the other end. This way the data moving over the network cannot be understood by anyone who may be eavesdropping because that person would not know what key was used to encrypt the data. Another advantage of encrypting data before it is sent across the Internet is that it can give the person receiving the data strong confidence that the data was not tampered with or altered in transit. More about the topic of encryption is discussed in later lessons of this book. A very secure connection uses both client and server authentication and encrypts the data that is transmitted over the network connection. Because SSL is usually attached to some other Application layer protocol, it generally uses the TCP port that the protocol it is attached to uses. For example HTTPS or HTTP Secure uses SSL to secure the HTTP protocol and uses port 443 to do this which is the port assigned to HTTPS. HTTPS is also known as HTTP over SSL. SSL does not actually have a specific port address assigned to it.

Transport Layer Security (TLS)

The Transport Layer Security (TLS) protocol was first proposed in 1999 under RFC 2246 as an upgrade or enhancement of SSL. Since that time, TLS has undergone two major revisions—TLS v1.1 in 2006 under RFC 4346 and TLS v1.2 in 2008 under RFC 5246.

The main differences between SSL and TLS are not major, but there is enough difference that the two protocols are not interoperable. The main differences are in areas such as using different encryption algorithms and in the case of TLS enhanced authentication encryption and additional enhancements that allow it to have some additional extensions added to if for enhanced functionality with other protocols. Because TLS is usually attached to some other Application layer protocol, just like SSL, it generally uses the TCP port that the protocol it is attached to uses in the same way that SSL does. Like SSL, TLS does not have a specific port number attached to it.

Hypertext Transport Protocol Secure (HTTPS)

CERTIFICATION READY
What is the difference between HTTP and HTTPS? What does HTTPS do for network transmissions?
1.6

Hypertext Transport Protocol Secure (HTTPS) is a variation on HTTP. In fact, HTTPS combines HTTP and SSL/TLS. This means that SSL/TLS inserts itself between TCP and HTTP, which allows web pages to be authenticated and allows for the encryption of transmissions from web servers. HTTPS connections start URLs off with https:// rather than http://. Some browsers also denote HTTPS connections by changing the color of the background in an URL box or with a symbol of a lock somewhere on the web page. HTTPS uses TCP port 443.

File Transfer Protocol (FTP)

The next Application layer protocol to talk about is File Transfer Protocol (FTP). The most commonly used current version of FTP was first introduced in 1985 in RFC 959. However, the original form of FTP was introduced in 1971 using RFC 114.

FTP is used to send and manipulate files over a TCP/IP network. FTP can represent the data it sends in three modes:

• **ASCII mode:** Used for text files but is not a good mode for sending numeric data in binary, floating-point binary, or binary coded decimal formats.

• **Image mode (also called Binary mode):** Used for sending files byte by byte and is useful for all types of files.

• **EBCDIC mode:** Used by hosts to send plain text data. This mode uses the EBCDIC character set instead of the ASCII character set, but otherwise they are the same.

The first two modes are the most commonly used. Aside from representing data in three different modes, there are also three different transmission methods that FTP can use to send out data. Those transmission methods are:

- **Stream:** Data is sent in a continuous stream. This stream can have control information embedded in it or not. The main point is that the data comes off the FTP server in a continuous stream of data. Streaming transmission of data is the default setting for FTP.
- **Block:** Data is broken up into blocks that contain headers, which define how much data is in each block. This makes it possible to flag data as potentially corrupted. Additionally, block transmission allows the retransmission of data if that becomes necessary.
- **Compressed:** Data or error messages are compressed before sending.

Like HTTP, there is also a secure version of FTP. This is sometimes called Secure FTP, also noted as SFTP. It is indicated in URL bars as ftps://. Like HTTPS, FTPS uses SSL/TLS to secure its transmissions in much the same way. FTP uses TCP port 20 for data and TCP port 21 for control.

Voice over Internet Protocol (VoIP)

Voice over Internet Protocol (VoIP) is a general term that describes a group of technologies used to transmit voice data over packet-switched networks including but not limited to the Internet. VoIP has been implemented in several ways over the last decade or so.

The two main reasons that companies choose to use VoIP is because VoIP helps lower operational costs and is flexible. VoIP lowers operational costs by routing voice communications over the same network that data communications are run over. This eliminates the need for two parallel networks, one for telephone and the other for data communications. VoIP also helps reduce operational costs because, generally speaking, Internet services are billed differently and at a lower cost than telephone services are.

VoIP's flexibility may be its best feature. Multiple phone calls can be transmitted simultaneously over one broadband connection and messages can be encrypted easily because they use the same encryption technologies that regular TCP/IP network connections use. VoIP is also flexible because it is location independent. Traditional landline phones are tied to a specific location by their telephone service; however, VoIP simply needs a fast Internet connection to be used. Finally VoIP easily integrates with other Internet services such as video conferencing, message and file exchange, and many others.

SESSION INITIATION PROTOCOL (SIP). One protocol commonly used in setting up VoIP sessions is Session Initiation Protocol (SIP). This signaling protocol is used to set up multimedia communications sessions over the Internet. SIP can be used for voice and video communications. SIP can also be used to set up both unicast and multicast sessions. Unicast sessions entail communications between just two nodes, parties, or locations. Multicast sessions are used when one node, party, or location wishes to communicate to more than one other node, party, or location. Some of the actually applications that use SIP are online games, video conferencing, streaming video distribution, and instant messaging. SIP is an Application layer protocol that can use either TCP or UDP for is underlying Transport layer protocol. SIP generally uses TCP port 5060 or TCP port 5061 if combined with TLS.

REAL-TIME TRANSPORT PROTOCOL (RTP). Another protocol used to implement VoIP is Real-Time Transport Protocol (RTP). This protocol carries streaming media such as voice or video. RTP is commonly used in conjunction with other signal protocols such as SIP in order to carry out its voice or video streaming functions. Because RTP is used for voice streaming, it is one of the foundational technologies used in VoIP along with SIP and/or several other protocols. RTP is not pre-assigned to a specific port or range of ports. However, RTP commonly uses a UDP port number between 16,384 and 32,767.

Terminal Network (TELNET)

TELNET stands for *TEerminaL NETwork* and is used to provide bidirectional interactive command line access to either a remote or local host. TELNET was first introduced in 1969 in RFC 15. Later in 1983, TELNET was extended in RFC 854. TELNET client software can be found for pretty much every computer platform.

Because of how long ago TELNET was developed, security is its biggest failing. TELNET by default does not encrypt any data that is sends across a connection, including passwords. Furthermore, most TELNET implementations do not have the ability to authenticate onto a system. This means that TELNET does not have the ability to ensure that data across a connection is not being intercepted. Between the two security issues just mentioned, it is very easy to intercept data that is being sent across a TELNET connection with such software as Wireshark, which is introduced later. Additionally, when data is sent across a TELNET connection and is intercepted, it is in the clear, meaning no encryption has been used to make it more difficult to read. TELNET uses TCP port 23. On a side note, you will sometimes see TELNET spelled TELNET and at other times you will see it spelled Telnet or simply telnet. When it is spelled TELNET, it is referring to the TELNET command and protocol. However, sometimes when a person is talking about the action of remotely accessing a computer using the TELNET command they will use the term telnet or Telnet instead.

Secure Shell (SSH)

Because of the security limitations of TELNET, SSH (Secure Shell) was developed. SSH is used to remotely connect to other hosts just like TELNET is; however, unlike TELNET, SSH has some built-in security features. One security feature is the ability of SSH to use public key encryption to authenticate onto another network device. This allows SSH to send the necessary password to the destination computer encrypted instead of in the clear. SSH is also able to use an SSH extension called SFTP (SSH File Transport Protocol or Secure File Transfer Protocol) or SCP (Secure Copy) to encrypt and transport data across network connections. SFTP is an actual protocol that is used to encrypt data to transport across a remote connection, while SCP acts more like a command to accomplish the same thing. Both are based on SSH. SSH uses TCP port 22.

Remote Desktop Protocol (RDP)

Remote Desktop Protocol (RDP) is an Application layer proprietary protocol created by Microsoft to provide a user a graphical interface for application across a network to another computer. RDP is able to provide a graphical interface for most modern operating systems including Windows, MAC OS X, Android, Linux, and UNIX. RDP uses TCP port 3389.

E-mail Related Protocols

While the World Wide Web may be the most recognizable service running on the Internet, it is not only service running on the Internet. E-mail is another service that runs on the Internet, and it may actually be one of the larger services. There are several protocols that are related to e-mail. Those protocols are Simple Mail Transport Protocol (SMTP), Post Office Protocol version 3 (POP3), and Internet Message Access Protocol version 4 (IMAP4). Each of these protocols is discussed next.

SIMPLE MAIL TRANSPORT PROTOCOL (SMTP). Simple Mail Transport Protocol (SMTP) was first defined by RFC 821 in 1982 and last updated by RFC 5321 in 2008. As its name suggests, SMTP is a protocol that is used to transport e-mail from one server to another on IP networks. SMTP is intended for outgoing protocols and is used by mail servers and clients for this purpose. In the case of mail servers, SMTP is used to move e-mail from one server to another or from one location to the next as required. In the case of mail clients, SMTP is only used to move e-mail from the client to a mail server so that the e-mail can be relayed from there.

SMTP uses two other protocols (which has already been discussed) to accomplish its task of moving data from one e-mail server to another. The first protocol that SMTP uses is DNS.

SMTP uses DNS to determine the location of a specific e-mail server it needs to send e-mail to. SMTP then uses TCP to establish and control the session while it is sending the e-mail to its intended destination server. SMTP uses port 25 to accomplish this.

While SMTP works well to move e-mail from a client to an e-mail server or an e-mail server to another e-mail server, getting the e-mail from the final destination server to the appropriate client is another matter. The two protocols that are usually used to move e-mail from an e-mail server to the correct client are Post Office Protocol version 3 (POP3) or Internet Message Access Protocol version 4 (IMAP4).

POST OFFICE PROTOCOL (POP).   Post Office Protocol or POP is the oldest standard protocol used to retrieve e-mail from an e-mail server. POP was first introduced in RFC 918 in 1984. POP1 was soon superseded by POP2, which was introduced in RFC 937 in 1985. Finally in 1988, POP3 was introduced in RFC 1081 and then updated to the current specification by RFC 1939 in 1996. There have been a few extensions added since this time with the most recent being RFC 5034 in 2007, which added an authentication mechanism.

CERTIFICATION READY
What does POP stand for? What is the difference between POP3 and SMTP?
1.6

POP3 is used to connect to an e-mail server and retrieve any e-mails on that server before closing the connection. When POP3 retrieves e-mail it can either leave a copy on the server, or delete the e-mail from the server after downloading it to the client system. Additionally, POP3 supports encryption of the mail retrieval session using either SSL or TLS. POP3 uses port 110 to retrieve e-mail from an e-mail server.

INTERNET MAIL ACCESS PROTOCOL (IMAP).   IMAP was developed more recently than POP. IMAP was first developed by Mark Crispin in 1986 and was first put forward as a possible Internet standard in 1988 in RFC 1064 IMAP, which introduced it as Internet Mail Access Protocol version 2 (IMAP2). In 1994 in RFC 1730, which was the first introduction of IMAP4, IMAP was changed to mean Internet Message Access Protocol. IMAP4 was in need of some fairly serious revision, which took place in 1996 under RFC 2030. The current form of IMAP4 is found in RFC 3501, which came out in 2003. There have been several updates since then, but the basics of IMAP4 have remained the same. The current form of IMAP4 is more correctly known as IMAP4rev1. IMAP uses TCP port 143.

IMAP4 and POP3 generally do the same job and both are widely supported by various e-mail servers. However, there are some differences between them.

One difference is how POP3 and IMAP4 interact with their e-mail servers. POP3 only connects to the e-mail server long enough to download the appropriate e-mails. IMAP4 on the other hand generally stays up as long as the user interface is active. This means that IMAP4 can download content on demand, while POP3 requires a unique session be set every time content needs to be downloaded.

Another difference is in how many clients can be connected to a mailbox at the same time. POP3 only allows one client to be connected at any one time, while IMAP allows multiple clients to be simultaneously connected to a single mailbox.

Message state information is another way in which IMAP4 and POP3 differ. POP3 has no mechanism to indicate whether a particular e-mail has been read, replied to, or deleted. IMAP4 does have these flags built in. When you see an e-mail client that puts up little flags when an e-mail has been read or replied to, you know that IMAP4 is the mail retrieval protocol being used by your client.

Two other functions that IMAP4 has but that POP3 lacks are the ability to have multiple mailboxes for a single user on an IMAP4-enabled e-mail server. This means that a single user can make multiple mailboxes on the server and move content around between these mailboxes. From the end user's point of view, these mailboxes look like folders that are added in the e-mail client. The ability to request a server to search the e-mails of a specific user while they are still stored on the server is an additional ability that IMAP4 has that POP3 lacks. This means that end users do not have to download all their e-mail to their local computer before they can search them.

The two main weaknesses of IMAP4 are that it adds an additional level of complexity to using e-mail and it requires that TCP constantly keep up as session between the client and the server so that content can be downloaded as it comes in. These two main weaknesses are why IMAP4 has not replaced POP3. For the foreseeable future, both protocols will continue to be used for e-mail retrieval from e-mail servers.

Network Time Protocol (NTP)

Network Time Protocol (NTP) is the next protocol to discuss. NTP is a little known but very widely used Application layer protocol. NTP is the protocol used to synchronize clocks over packet-switched networks. Whenever computers on a network need to be synchronized, NTP is the protocol that is most likely used to do it. The NTP protocol has been in use for this purpose since at least 1985. RFC 1305, which was issued in 1992, standardized NTP to what we use today. NTP uses UDP and port 123 to carry out its synchronizations.

Simple Network Management Protocol (SNMP) 2/3

The last Application layer protocol to discuss is Simple Network Management Protocol (SNMP). SNMP primarily uses port 161 and UDP as its Transport layer protocol. As suggested by its name, SNMP is used to manage network systems.

RFCs for SNMP first appeared in 1988. Unlike the previous protocols discussed, instead of having one RFC that described SNMP, several RFCs were used to describe different aspects of SNMP. The first group of these RFCs was 1065, 1066, and 1067. While RFCs 1065 and 1066 described various aspects of network management, RFC 1067 titled "A Simple Network Management Protocol" discussed how the ideas in the first two RFCs could be implemented in network management protocol. It is from that title that we get SNMP. The proposed network management protocol came to be known as SNMPv1. The three RFCs listed above were updated two years later by RFCs 1155, 1156, and 1157.

In 1993 RFCs 1441–1452 were proposed. These RFCs revised the previous RFCs and became the basis for SNMPv2. RFCs 1901–1910 were added to RFCs 1441–1452 and created a community-based version of SNMPv2 called SNMPv2c and a user-based version of SNMPv2 called SNMPv2u. Some people consider the community-based version of SNMPv2 to be the de facto SNMPv2 standard. RFCs 1902–1908 describe the community-based version of SNMPv2. In 2002, RFCs 3411–3418 were released that described SNMPv3 and form the basis for the SNMP that we use today. All versions of SNMP use UDP port 161.

For a SNMP-managed network to work, three components are needed. These three components are managed devices, agents, and the network management system. Managed devices consist of any network devices or nodes that are running SNMP client software, which are able to share information with the network management system. Devices that can be managed devices are things like routers, switches, IP cameras and phones, printers, host computers, and pretty much any other device that can run on a network. Agents consist of client software that runs on the various managed devices. Finally the network management system is a device, usually a server, which runs the application that monitors and controls the various managed devices that are running on the network. There can be more than one server working in this capacity on a network.

Network management systems are very useful and can make a network administrator's job a lot easier when it comes to managing a network. However, with SNMP running on all devices on a network, there are some inherent security concerns. Some such concerns are that if a hacker gets a packet sniffer into a network, he will be able to map out the entire network. Another concern is that because SNMP exchanges a lot of information between its servers and clients, hackers using said packet sniffer running on the network could compromise sensitive information about different clients. SNMP running on a network is often named in network security threat lists produced by different security organizations. As a result of this, perhaps the best advice that a network administrator can follow in regard to SNMP is to only run it on the network when it is needed, otherwise keep it turned off.

■ How Protocols Work Together

THE BOTTOM LINE

In this portion of Lesson 5, we use a utility called Wireshark to analyze the traffic on a network and to visually see how the different protocols work together to carry out assigned network tasks.

Perhaps the best way to demonstrate how the same protocol suite or different protocols work together is to use a tool called Wireshark. Wireshark is a free and open-source protocol analyzer created by Gerald Combs, which was originally called Ethereal but was changed to Wireshark in 2006. It can easily be found on the Internet by doing a Google search for it. Pretty much every computer platform commonly in use has a version of Wireshark that works with it.

Protocol analyzers can capture packets as they go across a network and then open them to allow a network administrator to view their headers and content. One of the unique things about Wireshark is that it is programmed to actually understand the different protocols it is able to capture. This allows Wireshark to not only display the encapsulation and their fields, but to also tell you what they mean. Figure 5-9 is a screen shot of what Wireshark looks like with some captured protocols.

Figure 5-9

Wireshark with captured protocols

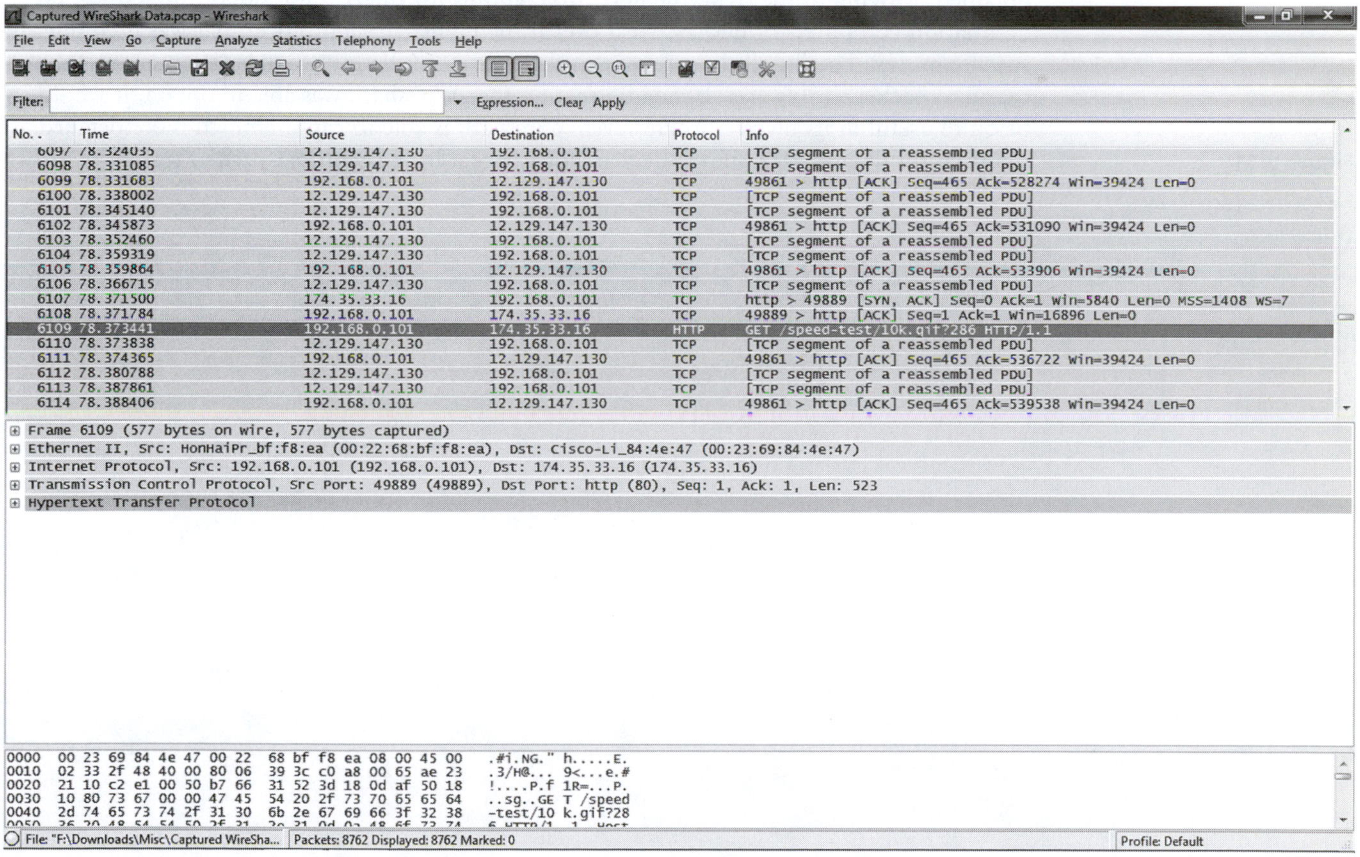

In this section of Lesson 5, Wireshark is used to explain how protocols work together. There is also be a lab at the end of this lesson where the student can become familiar with Wireshark.

As you can see in Figure 5-9, there are four major parts of the Wireshark screen. The top part of the screen is where the menu and shortcut icons are located to manipulate the Wireshark application. The window immediately below those icons shows the various packets and such that have been captured. Below the capture window is the detail window that gives the details of a protocol packet when it is highlighted. Finally the somewhat smaller window below the detail window contains the data payload of the packet being analyzed. If there is any text that was sent in the clear, it can be easily read in this window.

Figure 5-10 shows the first area of importance discussing how protocols work together.

Figure 5-10

Protocols captured by Wireshark

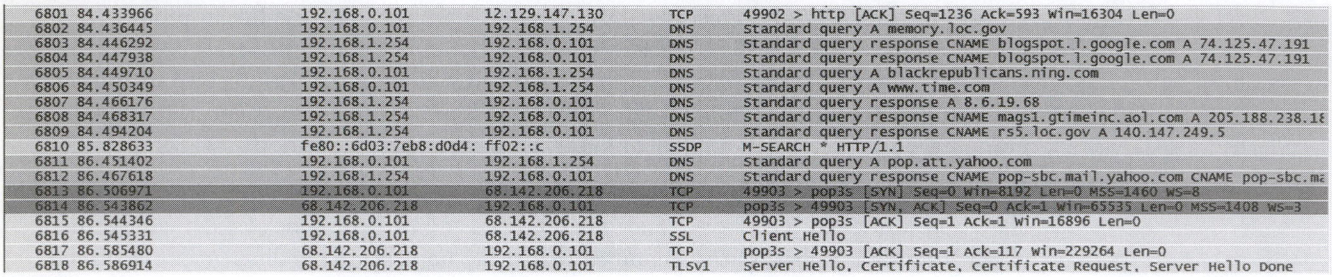

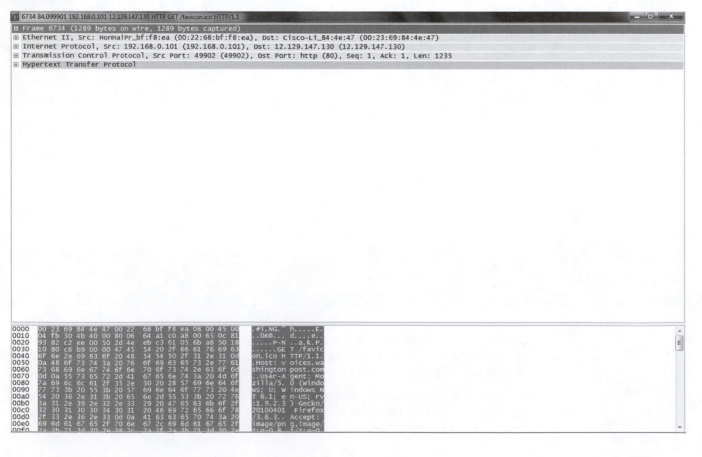

This window contains several pieces of important information. On the far left, it contains the frame number of the captured packet and the time after the start of the capture that it was obtained. Moving to the right, the next two columns list the IP addresses of the source and destination computers or devices. Next over is the highest-level protocol that was used in each specific packet. Finally, all the way over to the right is a little bit of information about the captured packet. If this was all the information that Wireshark was able to obtain, it would be quite useful in its own right. However, Wireshark is able to capture much more detailed information. Figure 5-11 shows the detail of a packet in the captured-packets screen.

Figure 5-11

Packet detail screen by Wireshark

This screen shot was obtained by double-clicking the packet whose detailed information was desired. When the packet is double-clicked, it opens a new window that shows details like those seen here.

At the top of Figure 5-11 is a list of protocols. In this case, the protocols listed from top to bottom are Frame, Ethernet II, Internet Protocol, Transmission Control Protocol, and Hypertext Transfer Protocol. These protocols are all the protocols that were encapsulated within the packet that was chosen by double-clicking it.

As you can see in Figure 5-12, each of the protocols in the detail list can in turn be expanded to show the header information. These headers contain valuable information for trouble-shooting or compromising a given network.

Figure 5-12

Packet detail screen by Wireshark with protocol headers expanded

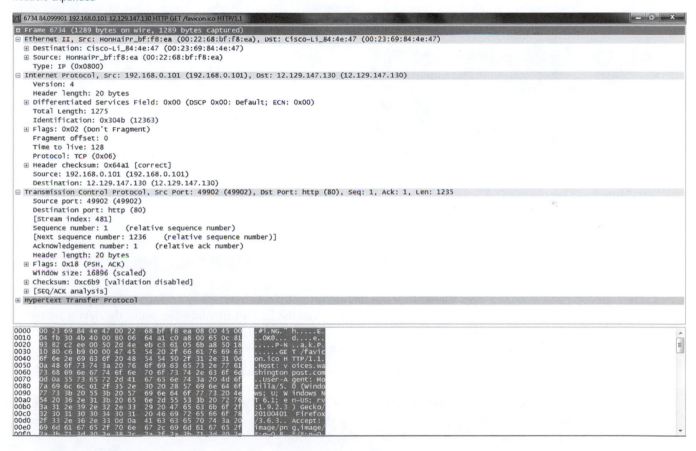

Figure 5-13 shows the fully expanded IPv4 header for the packet captured. If you compare the information in Figure 5-13 to the IPv4 header diagram previously shown in Figure 5-2, you can see that every field is accounted for and the information that is entered into each field is fully present. A similar comparison can be done with any protocol header that is available in the TCP/IP Protocol Suite when captured by Wireshark.

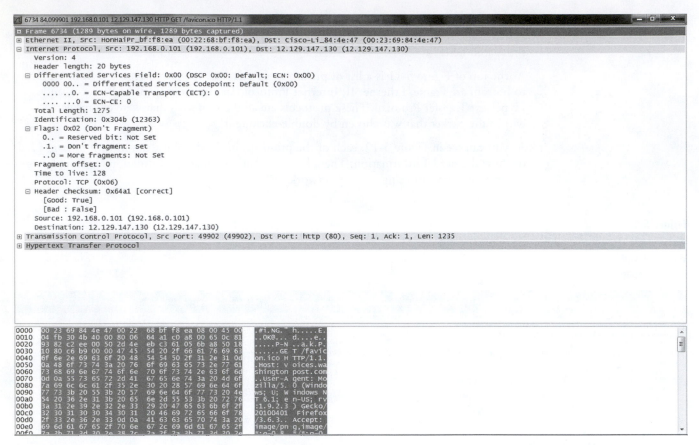

Figure 5-13

Packet detail screen
by Wireshark with Internet
protocol header fully expanded

The bottom windows in the Wireshark screen shot show the data content or payload of the packet. In Figure 5-14, the bottom window has been expanded to show as much of the payload as possible.

In this case, the payload is a request for a section of the *Washington Post* web page. We know this because the information is written in the English language section of the data window. We also know from the information found in the IP protocol that the source of the request is the local computer, while the destination is the *Washington Post* web server.

Now that Wireshark has been explained, we can use it to show how the different protocols work together to accomplish a given task. In the previous examples, we had an HTTP datagram that was used to carry part of a *Washington Post* story. However, HTTP could not pull down this web page on its own. If we look at Figure 5-11 again, we notice that there were five protocols involved in accomplishing this.

One protocol was the frame itself that was used to move the data onto the computer. The frame more or less described the length of the frame and what protocols were encapsulated within it. This is seen when the Frame protocol in the detail screen is opened. The frame mainly provides layer one information.

Next up was Ethernet II. When we open this protocol, we see the source and destination MAC addresses. Ethernet is the protocol used to move the previously described frame across the network.

Internet Protocol is listed next. When we open the Internet Protocol portion of the details window in Wireshark, we see that IPv4 was used. We also see the source and destination

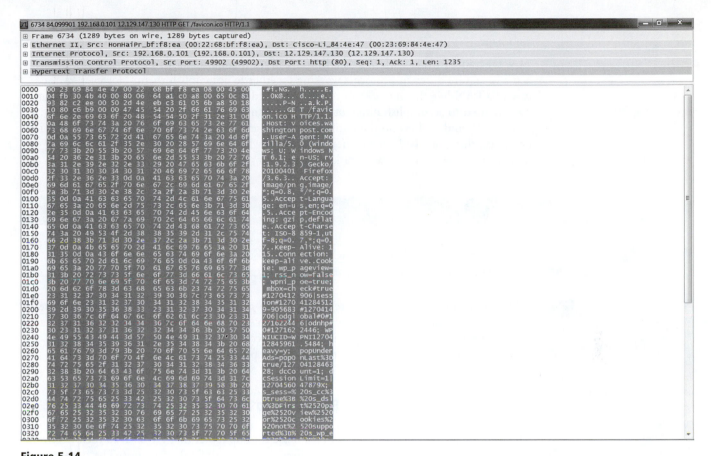

Figure 5-14

Packet detail screen by
Wireshark showing the data
window fully expanded

IP addresses. The protocol header also lists what flags and options were used and its header checksum. This Internet Protocol is used to find the best route from the local computer to the web server that contains the *Washington Post*'s article.

TCP is the next protocol listed. When TCP is opened, it tells us what the source and destination port numbers of the packet are. Additionally it tells us what the sequence number of the packet is as well as its acknowledgment number. Beyond this, we are also told what flags are set along with window size and the header checksum. TCP sets up the session that allows the *Washington Post* web server that contains the story to send it to the local computer running Wireshark.

The last protocol used was HTTP. This protocol sent the request for the html code that allows you to view the web page in a web browser. When we expand this protocol, we see lots of useful information, such as which version of HTTP is being used—version 1.1. We can also see that Firefox was the browser used to send the request for the web page and Windows NT 6.1, Windows 7, was the operating system used. We can also see that the specific host the web page expected to come from is voice.washingtonpost.com.

As you can see from this example, no single protocol in a given protocol suite can be used to accomplish everything that needs to be done. It takes multiple protocols working together to accomplish their assigned tasks. The physical limits of the frame are defines by the Frame protocol. Ethernet II protocol is used to move the datagram across the network based on MAC addresses. IP is used to navigate the datagram from its origination point to its destination point. TCP is used to establish the session that is needed to send the data back and forth, and HTTP is required to send the actual request for a specific web page.

As you explore further with Wireshark, you will see that all the tasks you do across a network actually require different protocols working together to accomplish them. However, in the case of a LAN like the one used in most homes and classrooms, even though different protocols are used to accomplish different tasks, pretty much all tasks will require at least a Frame, Ethernet II, and IP. Beyond these three protocols, at least when TCP/IP is the protocol suite of choice, things are wide open when it comes to what other protocols you may see being used on your network and what tasks they are being used for.

■ Routing Protocols

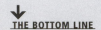 **THE BOTTOM LINE**

This section of Lesson 5 discusses what routing protocols are and the various concepts involving in routing protocols. We examine some specific routing protocols as well.

> **CERTIFICATION READY**
> What is the difference between a routed protocol and a routing protocol?
> 1.4

All the protocols discussed so far are called *routed protocols* or protocols that can be routed over a network via routers and other network devices. The protocols we discuss next are called *routing protocols*. This means that they are protocols that are used by routers to compile routing tables, which are then used to move those previously mentioned routed protocols around the network.

Purpose and Properties of Routing Protocols

> **CERTIFICATION READY**
> What is the difference between an interior gateway protocol and an exterior gateway protocol?
> 1.4

The purpose of routing protocols is to compose routing tables that are used to then determine the best routes to send data down as they head to their specific destinations. The properties of routing protocols are varied and are largely dependent on which routing protocol is being discussed. The first part of this section of Lesson 5 deals with different concepts that are connected to Routing Protocols. Afterward, we look as some specific routing protocols that are commonly used.

INTERIOR GATEWAY PROTOCOLS VERSUS EXTERIOR GATEWAY PROTOCOLS

Interior Gateway Protocols (IGPs) are those protocols that are used within an Autonomous System (AS) to discover the best routes, while Exterior Gateway Protocols (EGPs) are those protocols used to discover the best routes between various Autonomous Systems. Another way of looking at it is that IGPs are used only within specific networks, while EGPs are used to find the best routes between autonomous or separated networks that are still linked.

> **TAKE NOTE***
> There is an actual protocol called Exterior Gateway Protocol (EGP); however, this is an obsolete protocol that has been replaced by the BGP protocol. That obsolete EGP protocol is not the object of this discussion; the concept of exterior gateway protocols is the object of this discussion.

When the term Autonomous System, or AS, is being used, it refers to distinct networks that are still connected to each other by some exterior network link. The best way to think of an AS is to think of it as a network of routers that are internally connected without having to get on to the Internet to interact. If an AS is large enough, it is actually common practice to break it into several smaller ASs.

STATIC VERSUS DYNAMIC ROUTING

Static routing and dynamic routing are two different ways that routing tables can be built in a router. These routing tables are built and stored in different routers to be used by IP packets to find the best route to their intended destination.

The most basic way of building these routing tables is to manually create a routing table in a router. As new routes are needed on a network or old routes change, a person has to manually change or update the routing tables on the affected routers. This is called *static routing*. Unfortunately static routing is a time-consuming process and is prone to errors.

Because static routing is time consuming and error prone, routing protocols were created that are able to dynamically create their own routing tables and keep them updated. When a routing protocol is used to dynamically build and update routing tables in a router, it is called *dynamic routing*.

For most purposes dynamic routing is preferred. When using dynamic routing, each router broadcasts its routing table to those routers that are nearest to it. Over time as routers broadcast their routing tables to other routers and those routers add the new routes to their own routing tables, a map is built up in a router's memory of the entire network. In this way, routers are able to build routing tables in their memory, which are used by IP packets to determine the routes they should take to reach their destinations.

Even though dynamic routing is the most preferred method of building routing tables in a router, there are some special circumstances where it is better to use a static route. A static route is usually preferred when it is desirable to keep specific routes secret on a network for security purposes. If a static route is manually programmed into a router's routing table, the only time it is broadcast is when the static route has a change of state, which is where a route comes up or goes down for some reason. A static route is not broadcasted with the general routing tables that are broadcasted when dynamic routing protocols are used. Even if a hacker does manage to compromise a network, every time the routers update their routing tables by broadcasting them to other nearby routers, the static routes are not included and so the hacker cannot intercept them. In this way, using static routing for select routes protects them from hackers finding out about them simply by listening to the network traffic on a network.

ROUTING METRICS

The purpose of any routing protocol is to compile a table listing all the routes that are known to it so that the created table can be used by IP to find the best route to a specific location. The measurements used by a routing protocol to determine the best routes available to it are called *metrics*.

Metrics can be something as simple as hop counts, where a routing protocol determines that the best route to a specific destination is the route with the fewest number of hops. Alternatively, a routing protocol can take into account other things such as reliability, bandwidth, and delay to determine the best route to a specific destination. The more metrics a routing protocol can use to determine the best route to a specific destination, the better the routing protocol is considered to be. We will briefly go over some of the more common metrics used and exactly what they are.

Hop Count

Hop Count is the most basic metric used. Every time a packet passes through any type of network interface, it is registered as a hop. The hop count metric counts the number of hops between the source and destination and choose the route with the fewest number of hops. The biggest drawback to this metric when it is used by itself is that it does not take into account any other measurements. The following example illustrates this point. If it takes 3 hops over dial-up lines to get to a specific destination and 4 hops over high speed communications lines to get to the same detonation, a routing protocol using hop count as its only metric will always take the 3 hop dial-up route.

MTU (Maximum Transmission Unit)

A Maximum Transmission Unit or an MTU is a measurement of the maximum size permitted for a packet to be sent over a network. If a packet exceeds the MTU then the packet has to be broken up into smaller pieces that do not exceed the MTU. Breaking up a packet in to smaller units requires additional processing power on the part of the router attempting to transmit the packet. When MTU is used as a metric for determining the best route a particular packet can take, the router is checking what MTU size is allowed on a particular path. Generally a router will prefer a path that allows for packets up to the size of the packet it needs to transmit over a route that requires the packet to be broken up into smaller pieces. The reason for this is because if the packet has to be broken up into smaller units more processing power is required on both ends of the connections. More processing power is required on the sending end because the packet needs to be broken into smaller units to accommodate a route with a smaller MTU. On the receiving end, more processing power is required to put the fragmented packet back together.

Bandwidth

When a router uses bandwidth as a metric this means the router takes into account the network speeds of each possible route. Once the router has taken into account network speeds it chooses the best route based on which route can get the packet to its destination the fastest based on the network speeds available over the route. If bandwidth is being used as a metric then the scenario presented under the "Hop Count" heading will not happen. The reason the presented scenario will not happen is because the router will recognize that the high speed communication route is faster than the dial-up route regardless of hop count and choose the high speed communications route.

Cost

Cost is an arbitrary metric used by routers to determine the best route to a destination. The reason cost is arbitrary is because cost is set by the administrator of the network. The administrator assigns "cost" to each route based on which routes he or she prefers the routers choose. The administrator does this by setting routes he or she does not favor to a high cost while setting routes that he or she does favor to lower cost. The routers will then look at the relative cost of different routes and choose the one with the lowest overall cost. One big advantage of using cost as a metric is that the administrator can define which routes he or she prefers the routers take while still leaving up the less favorable routes. This is an advantage because in the event that something happens to bring down the favored route, the less favored routes will still be available to take up the slack.

Latency

Latency is simple the measure of how much time it takes a packet to travel from one location on a network to the other. When latency is used as a metric for choose the best path, the routers measure how long it takes a packet to make a round-trip to a specific location and back. Once the router knows what the round-trip times are for each route to a specific location, it will choose the route with the fasted round-trip time and send the packet down that route.

Latency differs from Bandwidth because with bandwidth as the metric the router is only concerned with how fast the communications links between two locations are. However, with latency, other factors that may slow down a round-trip such as delay, reliability, and load are taken into account.

UNDERSTANDING ROUTING TABLES AND HOW THEY APPLY TO PATH SELECTION

Routing tables are small databases that routers and other networked devices use to determine which route to take to get to a specific location on the network. A routing table can contain three types of routes in its database. The three types of routes are:

- **Gateway routes:** The route to another router or other similar type device.
- **Host routes:** The route to a specific host device such as a specific computer.
- **Default routes:** The route a packet is to take if the router does not know where the destination route is. This is sometimes called a gateway of last resort.

CERTIFICATION READY
What is the difference between bandwidth and latency when both are being used as a routing protocol metric?
1.4

TAKE NOTE*

Many people make the mistake of believing that only routers use routing tables. This is not correct. Most devices that connect to a network contain routing tables of one sort or another, including such devices as PCs and network-enabled printers.

There are several different information fields in routing table databases. The three most common are the network id of the destination network, the cost of the path the packet takes to get to the destination network, and the ***next hop***. The cost refers to the network cost, or metrics needed, in getting to the destination network. These metrics can be such things as the number of hops needed to get to a specific destination, the reliability of the bandwidth of the routes used to get there, or several other such values. Cost can also be a valued assigned by the network administrator. In that situation, a network administrator assigns a higher cost to less-preferred paths and a lower cost to more-preferred or favored paths. The next hop value is simply the IP or other protocol address of the next stop along the path to the desired destination.

Aside from the information discussed previously, some devices, especially routers, will contain additional information in their routing tables such as fields like quality of service, links to filtering criteria, and interfaces. The quality of service field contains information like whether a particular link is up or down. Links to filtering criteria are simply links to any access control list that may be applied to specific routes. Finally, interfaces refer to the specific interface of a router to which a routing table refers. This is a necessary field because most routers have multiple interfaces.

Distance Vector Routing Protocols

Routing protocols come in two types or a hybrid of those two types. The two types of protocols are distance vector routing protocols and link-state routing protocols. These two classes of protocols are based on how the protocol goes about determining its routing table.

The simplest type of routing protocol is a ***distance vector routing protocol***. In a distance vector routing protocol, each router periodically sends an update of its routing table to all the neighboring routers that are directly connected to it. In this way, periodically the entire network of routers gets updated. The time it takes for this update to take place is called ***convergence***. When the routers on a network remain in a converged state, it is said that they are operating in a ***steady state***. What this means is that all the routers in a network are updated and all they are doing is maintaining the status quo. This steady state is the state that you want a network to remain in as much as possible.

The main advantage of distance vector–based routing protocols is that they take less overhead to update each other and have less message traffic than the alternative link state routing protocol. The disadvantage of distance vector–based protocols is that they are susceptible to certain types of looping errors.

We can see an example of how a looping problem can come about by imaging a long line of routers. A Router_A on one end of a line of routers receives a message that a route has gone down. Router_A updates its own routing table to include this information and then passes it on the new routing table to the routers next to it. However, before the routing table update has had a chance to reach the other end of the line of routers, Router_A receives another message that the route is back up. Again Router_A updates its own routing table and tells the routers next to it about the change. By this time the original update has reached the end of the router line where it updates routing tables and sends out the update back down the line. In this way, these two routers are constantly updating their tables with a route being up and then down and passing that information on to their neighboring routers, thus perpetuating the problem.

To overcome this problem, counter measures such as route poisoning and split horizons have been developed. Route poisoning simply forces a route to stay down until an entire update cycle has been completed before it allows a new update to be passed down the line. In split

CERTIFICATION READY
What are routing tables? How are routing tables used by routers? What can happen if routing tables are not up to date?
2.1

CERTIFICATION READY
What is convergence? What are some commonly used metrics?
1.4

CERTIFICATION READY
What does it mean for a network to be in a steady state of operation?
1.4

horizon, updates are only allowed to go one way down the router line. Both of these solutions solve the looping problem just discussed.

As mentioned previously, distance vector routing protocols are protocols that use metrics such as hops, reliability, delay, and/or bandwidth to determine the best route to a specific destination. Second, distance vector routing protocols update their routing tables by broadcasting them to those routers directly connected to them. The Routing Information Protocol (RIP), the Internal Gateway Routing Protocol (IGRP), and the Border Gateway Protocol (BGP) are examples of distance vector routing protocols. We examine those protocols briefly next.

ROUTING INFORMATION PROTOCOL (RIP)

Routing Information Protocol (RIP) is one of the older routing protocols available. It was in use prior to 1988 and was formally described in RFC 1058 in that year. Because RIP is intended for use in local and wide area networks it is classified as an Internal Gateway Protocol (IGP). This means that it cannot be used to determine routes between WANs and other local networks. It can only be used to determine routes within single networks. The only metric used by RIP to determine best routes is hop count. However, RIP has a hop limit of 15. Any routes beyond this are out of reach of RIP, therefore, it can only be used on smaller networks.

A couple of other limitations that RIP has are the fact that it cannot be authenticated and cannot use a variable length subnet mask. This means that all the sub-networks within a specific class must be the same length. RIP is unable to use sub-networks that have been broken into smaller sub-networks after the original sub-network has been set.

Because of some of these deficiencies, RIP was updated to RIPv2 in 1993 in RFC 1388. RIPv2 as we use it today was finalized in RFC 2453 in 1998, with only one update added in 2007. While RIPv2 kept the 15-hop limit, it did add a few additional capabilities or improvements. Support for CIDR was added as well as a mechanism for allowing authentication.

Both RIP and RIPv2 are still in use today, though both were technically obsolete by IGRP. Ironically IGRP is not commonly in use today because it has been obsolete by other protocols in wide use such as EIGRP and OSPF.

INTERIOR GATEWAY ROUTING PROTOCOL (IGRP)

Interior Gateway Routing Protocol (IGRP) is a routing protocol that was invented by Cisco. It is considered a classful routing protocol because it only uses subnets based on the Class A, B, C standard for IP addresses. Because it was invented by Cisco, it is considered a proprietary protocol and was never a major routing protocol standard. The biggest contribution IGRP made to routing protocol standards is the fact that it used multiple metrics to determine the best route to specific destinations. The metrics accepted by IGRP are bandwidth, delay, maximum transmission unit (MTU), load, and reliability. IGRP is considered to be an obsolete routing protocol even by Cisco, but is mentioned here because of its relationship to EIGRP, which is discussed later.

BORDER GATEWAY PROTOCOL (BGP)

Border Gateway Protocol (BGP) is a very important protocol to know about in regards to how the Internet works. While very few network users ever actually use BGP themselves, the Internet Service Providers (ISPs) they connect to in order to get onto the Internet use BGP quite extensively. BGP, or more specifically BGP-4, is the routing protocol most ISPs use to create routing tables to help determine the best path between the Autonomous Systems (ASs) used by the different ISPs for their own networks. The routing tables created by BGP are what allow users to easily move around from one section of the Internet to another.

Unlike most vector-based routing protocols, the metrics used by BGP are a bit different because they are based on paths, network policies, and rule sets used by the various ISPs.

BGP was first introduced in RFC 1105 in 1989. Various revisions have been made to BGP up to RFC 1654, which proposed BGP-4. BGP-4 became the preferred version of BGP for border gateway routing in 1994. BGP was last updated by RFC 4271 in 2006 and is the basis for the version of BGP-4 used almost exclusively today by ISPs.

Link State Routing Protocols

Link state routing protocols are the other major type of routing protocols used by routers to construct their routing tables. In link state routing, instead of simply updating neighboring routers with its own routing table, each router constructs an entire map of all the routers connected together in a network and updates all the other routers in the network with its entire network map. Once the map is formed, the router calculates the quickest path to every node on the network and stores those paths in memory. This then is the routing table that link state routing protocols use. Aside from the main routing table, link state routing protocols also calculate an alternative route to the same nodes. In this way, if the main route is down, a link state routing protocol can immediately switch to the alternate route while it goes through the process of calculating a new routing table. Like with distance vector routing protocols, the time it takes all the routers on the network to update each other with the current routing tables is called convergence. Once the network is running in a converged state, it is said to be operating at a steady state, again like with distance vector routing protocols. Again, the goal is for the network to operate in a steady state as often as possible.

The main advantage of link state routing protocols is that they have a map of the entire network stored in memory and are able to calculate the most efficient route to any given node based on that map. Link state routing protocols also only send updates when there are changes in the state of the network instead of every so many seconds like distance vector routing protocols do. The main disadvantage is that link state maps take more resources on the router and network than vector-based routing tables would because of all the data that needs to be updated to the other routers. It also means that more processing power is given over to compiling maps, updating maps, and determining routing tables. A couple of examples of link state routing protocols are Open Shortest Path First (OSPF) and Intermediate System to Intermediate System (IS-IS).

OPEN SHORTEST PATH FIRST (OSPF)

Open Shortest Path First (OSPF) is a link state routing protocol designed to be used in IP networks. OSPF works with both IPv4 and IPv6. OSPF is also classified as an interior gateway protocol because it can only be used in the confines of an AS. Metrics used by OSPF include round-trip time (RTT), which is a measure of the distance to a specific router, network throughput of a link, or a link's reliability and availability.

In order to overcome the high traffic disadvantage of link state routing protocols, OSPF nominates a designated router (DR) and backup designated router (BDR) in a particular segment of an OSPF network. The DR and its backup limit the updating messages that are sent between the routers. Instead of each router updating all the routers near it every time the network state changes, the update is forwarded only to the DR and BDR if present. The DR and BDR keep a complete and updated map of the network in their memory. When the DR receives news of a change of state on the network from a router in its segment, it then multi-cast that update to each of the routers in the segment it oversees. In this way the update message traffic on that segment of the overall network is reduced. If something happens to the DR, then the BDR becomes the DR and a new BDR is designated. This provides redundancy and prevents an interruption of the network being updated. OSPFv2 was first introduced by

RFC 1247 in 1991 and has since been updated many times as technologies have changed and since IPv6 was introduced.

INTERMEDIATE SYSTEM TO INTERMEDIATE SYSTEM (IS-IS)

Intermediate System to Intermediate System (IS-IS) is an interior gateway protocol used to determine routing tables within an AS using link state routing. IS-IS is pronounced i-sys when being discussed.

IS-IS functions similarly to OSPF and was developed at about the same time. The primary difference between the two protocols is that OSPF is defined specifically for IP while IS-IS is not. There is also some difference in how the two protocols define the areas of the network for which they are creating routing tables. OSPF uses router interfaces to define AS areas, while IS-IS uses routers to define these areas.

Although IS-IS is not commonly used in enterprise network environments, it is used by some ISPs. IS-IS is not considered an Internet standard, but it is defined in the Open Systems Interconnects (OSI) reference design documents.

CERTIFICATION READY
What are the two main types of routing protocols? What are a couple of examples of each type of routing protocol?
1.4

Hybrid Routing Protocols

Both distance vector and link state routing protocols have advantages and disadvantages. In an attempt to develop routing protocols that included the advantages of each while minimizing their disadvantages, *hybrid routing protocols* were developed. A hybrid routing protocol uses the distance vector metrics-based method of determining best routes, while using the link state method of updating the other routers in the network. This minimizes the calculations needed to determine the best routes and keeps the link state protocol's ability to only have to update fellow routers when a change is detected on the network. This has the advantage of limiting the processing the each router has to do to find routes while also limiting the number of updating packets that have to be sent by routers to make sure that all routing tables are up to date. One of the more commonly used hybrid routing protocols is one from Cisco called Enhanced Interior Gateway Routing Protocol (EIGPR).

ENHANCED INTERIOR GATEWAY ROUTING PROTOCOL (EIGRP)

Enhanced Interior Gateway Routing Protocol (EIGRP) is a Cisco proprietary protocol that is based on Cisco's IGRP protocol. EIGRP has advanced distance vector-based capabilities. It also uses some techniques of link state routing protocols and is for this reason considered a hybrid protocol; although, there are those who would debate whether EIGRP is a true hybrid.

There are several distance vector routing protocol capabilities that EIGRP has. One such capability is using distance vector metrics to determine the best route to a specific destination. The metrics used by EIGRP are the same ones used by IGRP. Those metrics are bandwidth, load, delay, reliability, and MTU (maximum transmission units). Another feature of distance vector routing protocols shared by EIGRP is that it updates its directly connected neighbors instead of all the routers on the AS or a specific DR (designated router) like OSPF does.

EIGRP differs from other distance vector routing protocols in several ways. When EIGRP updates its neighbor routers, it does not send the entire routing table, instead it only sends those portions of it that have changed since the last update. EIGRP also does not send updates at specific intervals. Instead EIGRP only sends updates when a new route is added directly adjacent to the router on which it resides, or when a change of state has taken place on a router connected to or within the router on which EIGRP resides.

To determine the best route to a packet's destination, EIGRP uses three tables to store the data used:

- **Neighbor table:** Contains information about the routers that are directly connected to the current router.
- **Topology table:** Works as an aggregation of the routing tables of all the routers directly connected to the current router. In effect, this is a topology of only the immediate network a few routers out.
- **Routing table:** Contains the routes to the various destinations reachable by the router. This is used to send a packet on its way to the next stop on its route. The routing table is built from the topology table.

SKILL SUMMARY

IN THIS LESSON YOU LEARNED:

- About protocols suites.
- About the TCP/IP Protocol Suite.
- The different layers of the TCP/IP Protocol Suite.
- Some of the protocols used by the Internet layer of TCP/IP.
- Some of the protocols used by the Network layer of TCP/IP.
- Some of the protocols used by the Transport layer of TCP/IP.
- Some of the protocols used by the Application layer of TCP/IP.
- What port addresses are and what port addresses certain TCP/IP protocols use.
- How protocols from different layers work together to move data around a network.
- What routing protocols are and how they differ from other protocols.
- About distance vector routing protocols.
- About link state routing protocols.
- The difference between Internal Gateway Protocols and External Gateway Protocols.
- Some distance vector-based protocols.
- Some link state protocols.
- What static routing versus dynamic routing is.
- How routing tables are used to in regard to path selection.

Knowledge Assessment

Fill in the Blank

Complete the following sentences by writing the correct word or words in the blanks provided.

1. A group of protocols that are designed to work together is called a
   _____.

2. The most important protocol suite for networking is _____.

3. _____ is the TCP/IP protocol that is used to determine the best path a packet can take to reach its destination.

4. A connectionless protocol that is used to establish a TFTP session between two computers is _____.

5. DNS uses port _____.

6. An Application layer protocol that is used to reliably transfer files between one computer and another is _____.

7. _____ routing is where a route is manually written into a router's configuration.

8. A group of routers that are internally connected to each other is called an _____ _____.

9. A generic term for a routing protocol that is used to create routing tables within an AS is called an _____.

10. A generic term for a routing protocol that is used to create routing tables between different ASs is called an _____.

Multiple Choice

Circle the letter corresponding to the correct answer.

1. Which of the following best describes what the ICMP protocol is used for?
    a. Sending Internet Protocol control messages to other computers.
    b. Sending messages to a specific group of computers.
    c. Altering the physical addresses of packets so that they can be sent to their next destination.
    d. Managing networks.

2. What two ports does FTP use? (Choose two.)
    a. 80
    b. 20
    c. 21
    d. 143

3. What port does DNS use?
    a. 123
    b. 23
    c. 69
    d. 53

4. What port does HTTP use?
    a. 23
    b. 80
    c. 25
    d. 22

5. What port does Telnet use?
    a. 25
    b. 23
    c. 53
    d. 69

6. What port does SMTP use?
    a. 21
    b. 22
    c. 25
    d. 161

7. What protocol is used in conjunction with HTTP to make it secure?
   a. SSL/TSL
   b. SSH
   c. POP3
   d. SIP

8. What two protocols are components of VoIP? (Choose two.)
   a. SIP
   b. TCP
   c. IMAP3
   d. RTP

9. What protocol is used to help match IP addresses with URLs?
   a. TFTP
   b. CIDR
   c. DNS
   d. SNMP

10. What is the currently most commonly used link state routing protocol?
   a. IGP
   b. EGP
   c. IS-IS
   d. OSPF

Lab Exercises

■ Lab 1

Acquiring and Installing Wireshark

The purpose of this lab is to help students obtain the software program Wireshark and teach them how to install it.

MATERIALS

- Computer with access to the Internet
- Paper
- Pen or pencil

DO THE LAB

Install Wireshark

TAKE NOTE *

If you are unable to find this URL do a Google search for Wireshark Download. You will find a downloadable setup file for Wireshark somewhere on the Internet.

1. Go to the URL www.wireshark.org.
2. Click on the **Download Wireshark** button.
3. The purpose of the next four steps is to find the most recent version of Wireshark available and download it in preparation for installation:
   a. Find the box near the top of the web page titled *Stable Release* with a series of numbers in parenthesis after it.
   b. Look at the available releases listed.
   c. Choose the release that best fits the computer and operating system you are using.
   d. Download the release to a location on your hard drive.
4. The purpose of the next five steps is to install the version of Wireshark you downloaded in the previous steps:
   a. Go to the location where you chose to save your downloaded file.
   b. Double-click the installation file and let Wireshark install itself.
   c. When Wireshark's installation process asks if you want to install WinCap 4.1, or a later version, click **Yes**.
   d. Click on the **check box** to have Wireshark run after installation.
   e. Do not close Wireshark because it will be used in the next lab.

■ Lab 2

Capturing Network Traffic with Wireshark

The purpose of this lab is to walk the student though the process of capturing network traffic using Wireshark.

MATERIALS

- A computer with Wireshark installed

DO THE LAB

Use Wireshark

1. Make sure that Wireshark is running on your computer. If it is not, start it either from the Desktop or the Start Menu of Windows.

2. Wireshark's opening screen should look like Figure 5-15.

Figure 5-15

Opening Screen of Wireshark

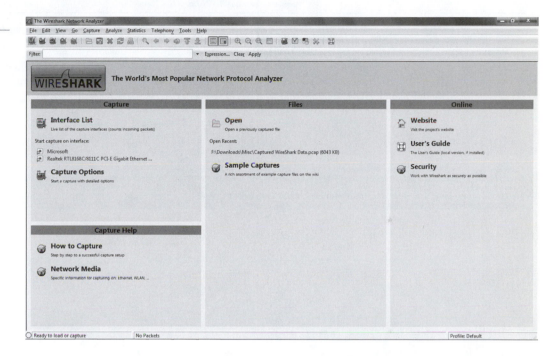

3. Click on the **Interface List** icon under the *Capture* section of the screen. Results should look similar to Figure 5-16.

Figure 5-16

Wireshark with Interface List icon selected

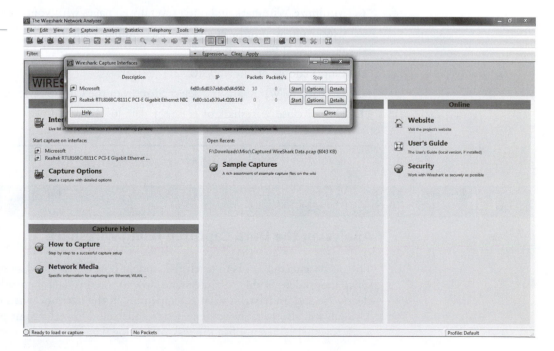

4. Click the **Start** button next to the network interface that is currently being used.

5. When you do this a screen similar to the one pictured in Figure 5-17 should appear.

Figure 5-17

Wireshark screen soon after a Capture has been started

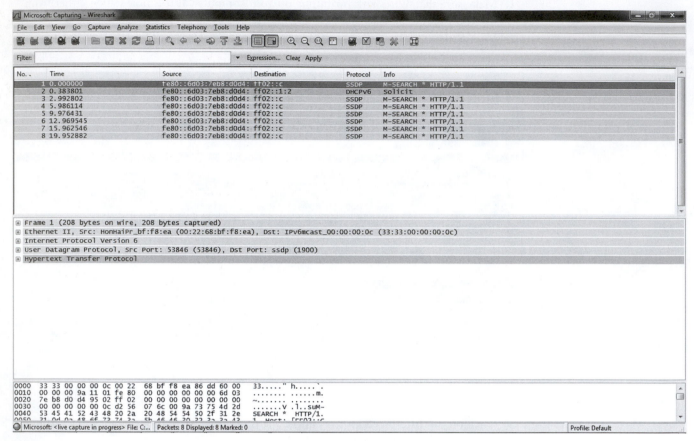

6. Minimize Wireshark and open several web pages with your browser.

7. Close your web browser and open a command screen.

8. Ping several known IP addresses.

9. Ping a couple of known URLs.

10. Go back to Wireshark and select **Stop** from the Capture Menu option in the top menu.

11. Do not close Wireshark or erase the data just obtained because it will be needed for the next lab.

■ Lab 3

Analyzing the Data Captured Using Wireshark

The purpose of this lab is to teach the student how to use the data obtained by Wireshark. Once the student is able to understand how to use this data, he or she will be able to more clearly see and understand what is happening on the network when data is moving across it. This lab will also help the student better understand how different protocols on the network work together to accomplish the task of moving data around the network.

MATERIALS
- Computer running Wireshark
- Paper
- Pen or pencil

DO THE LAB

Read and Interpret the Data Provided by Wireshark

1. What IP address keeps appearing in either the source or destination column? Write it down.

2. Why do you think this IP keeps appearing in one of these two places? Write down your answer.

3. List 6 or 7 protocols appearing in the column labeled *Protocol* in the Wireshark capture data. Write the protocols down.

4. Click on one of the protocol entries in the top screen and then list the lines that appear in the middle window. Write down you answer.

5. Repeat step 4 for two other entries in the top window that contain different entries in the protocol. Write down the information.

6. What do you notice about the information you have written down?

7. What two or three lines appear in each of the lists you copied earlier? Why do these lines appear consistently? Write down what you think the answer is.

8. Click the + sign next to the Frame line. What type of information appears? Write this down. Close the – sign.

9. Click the + sign for the rest of the lines in the middle windows. What are the heading lines and what data appears under each heading? Write this down.

10. What is all this information showing you? How do you think it could be used? Write down your answers.

11. What does this information tell you about how protocols work together on a network?

_____

Networking Devices

EXAM OBJECTIVE MATRIX

TECHNOLOGY SKILL COVERED	EXAM OBJECTIVE	EXAM OBJECTIVE NUMBER
Network Interface Cards	**Classify how applications, devices, and protocols relate to the OSI model layers.** • NIC	1.2
Modems		

Media Converters	**Categorize standard media types and associated properties.**
	• Media converters:
	  • Singlemode fiber to Ethernet
	  • Multimode fiber to Ethernet
	  • Fiber to Coaxial
	  • Singlemode to multimode fiber
		3.1

Repeaters and Hubs	**Classify how applications, devices, and protocols relate to the OSI model layers.** • Hub	1.2
Bridges and Switches	**Classify how applications, devices, and protocols relate to the OSI model layers.** • Switch • Multilayer switch • Bridge	1.2
	Explain the purpose and properties of routing and switching. • Spanning Tree Protocol • VLAN (802.1q) • Port mirroring	1.4
	Given a scenario, install and configure routers and switches. • VLAN (trunking) • Managed vs. unmanaged • PoE • Diagnostics • VTP configuration • Port mirroring	2.1

Channel Service Unit/ Data Service Unit (CSU/DSU)	**Identify components of wiring distribution.** • CSU/DSU	3.8
Routers and Firewalls	**Classify how applications, devices, and protocols relate to the OSI model layers.** • Router	1.2

	Given a scenario, install and configure a basic firewall.
	• Types:
	  • Software and hardware firewalls
	• Firewall rules:
	  • Block/allow
	  • Implicit deny
	  • ACL
		5.5

Servers	**Summarize DNS concepts and its components.** • DNS servers • DNS records (A, MX, AAAA, CNAME, PTR) • Dynamic DNS	1.7
	Explain the purpose and properties of DHCP. • Static vs. dynamic IP addressing • Reservations • Scopes • Leases • Options (DNS servers, suffixes)	2.3
	Explain the purpose and features of various network appliances. • Proxy server	4.1
Additional Specialized Network Devices	**Classify how applications, devices, and protocols relate to the OSI model layers.** • Encryption devices	1.2
	Explain the purpose and features of various network appliances. • Load balancer	4.1

	Categorize different types of network security appliances and methods.
	• IDS and IPS:
	  • Behavior based
	  • Signature based
		5.6

Wireless Devices	**Given a scenario, install and configure a wireless network.** • Compatibility (802.11 a/b/g/n)	2.2

	Compare and contrast different wireless standards.
	• 802.11 a/b/g/n standards
	  • Distance
	  • Speed
		3.3

Virtual Networking	**Identify virtual network components.**	1.9
	• Virtual switches • Virtual desktops • Virtual servers • Virtual PBX • Onsite vs. offsite • Network as a Service (NaaS)	

KEY TERMS

Access Control List (ACL)	gateway proxy server	port mirroring
active hub	hardware firewall	port-based authentication
asymmetric loading	hub	Power over Ethernet (PoE)
bandwidth shaper	implicit deny	priority activation
bandwidth shaping	intelligent hub	repeater
behavior-based detection	Intrusion Detection System (IDS)	reservation
block/allow	Intrusion Protection System (IPS)	reverse proxy server
bridge	lease	router
buffering	load balancer	scope
caching	media	signature-based detection
collision domain	media converter	Spanning Tree Protocol (STP)
Channel Service Unit/Data Service Unit (CSU/DSU)	modem	stateful protocol analysis
DHCP options	Network Interface Card (NIC)	switch
Dynamic DNS	Network Interface Controller (NIC)	traffic shaping
Encryption Devices	offloading	trunking
firewall	packet shaping	virtual LAN (VLAN)
Fully Qualified Domain Name (FQDN)	passive hub	wireless access point (WAP)
	port authentication	

Roberta is a WAN engineer with Solar Systems Inc., which has a network with over 400 computers. She has been directed by management to find a way to break the network into smaller units of no more than 50 computers that can only talk to other selected smaller units. How can she accomplish this task?

■ Network Interface Cards

THE BOTTOM LINE

In this section of Lesson 6, we discuss Network Interface Cards and their use in networking. We also discuss some of the features of Network Interface Cards.

CERTIFICATION READY
What is a NIC? What function does it perform in a network environment?
1.2

The *Network Interface Card (NIC)* is one of the most basic components in a computer network. Without the NIC, a computer is unable to access the network or share data with other computers on the network. NICs can be expansion cards or even directly built into a computer's motherboard. In most newer computers, the latter option is usually true. Because NICs more often than not are built directly into a computer's motherboard, the term Network

Figure 6-1

PCI Network Interface Card

Interface Card is considered by some to no longer be the best term for this device. People who think that Network Interface Card is no longer appropriate for this device generally refer to it as a ***Network Interface Controller***. Either way, the abbreviation NIC works just fine. Figure 6-1 shows a basic PCI NIC Card.

Most NIC devices also have several Light Emitting Diode (LED) indicators on them. These indicators help diagnose different network problems. Although different NICs may have different indicators, two LED indicators found on all NICs are the link light and the activity light. The link light is used to determine whether the NIC is linking, or connecting, to the network. If the NIC is correctly linking to the network the link light will be on. The activity light is the other LED indicator found on all NICs. This indicator is used to determine if there is any network activity reaching the NIC. Both indicators can tell you important information about your network. For example, if the link light is on but the activity light in not blinking, then the NIC is able to see the network, but it is not detecting any activity on it. This could be an indication that the port the NIC is connected to is not able to see the rest of the network. With this knowledge as a starting point, you are better situated to determine what problem the network may be experiencing.

Figure 6-2 shows a basic NIC card with indicator lights. The one labeled LNK is the link light, and the one labeled ACT is the activity light. The last indicator on this particular NIC is labeled 100 TX. This light lights up to indicate that the network is running at a full 100 Mbps and is running in full-duplex mode.

Figure 6-2

PCI Network Interface Card with indicator lights

Means of Communication and Media Used for Communication

Before discussing NICs in any further detail, there are two terms that you need to understand about network communications. Those two terms are the *means* of communications versus the media used for that communication. For the purposes of this discussion, the means of communications refers to whatever is used to communicate data across a network such as electrical impulses, light pulses, or radio wave/microwave modulations. The **media** used for communications is whatever carries those communications across a network. Copper wires carry electrical impulses, fiber optics carry light pulses, radio waves carry radio wave modulations, and microwaves carry microwave modulations. The NIC takes data coming down the protocol stack in a computer and encodes it into the appropriate means of communication needed to send data across the media being used for network communications. There are many different standards and technologies used to do this. Some are familiar to us, like wire-based NICs, and wireless NICs, while others like fiber-optic NICs are not commonly seen by the average end user. However, all NICs have one thing in common, they take the data coming off a computer and convert it to the appropriate means of communication used by a particular technology to send that data down the media that is intended to carry it.

To do its job, a NIC has to work on both the Data Link layer and the Physical layer of the OSI Model. The NIC acts as a translator between the software in the upper layers of the OSI Model and the physical components of the media. When data is moving through the upper five layers of the OSI Model, it is completely logical; it has no physical component to it. However, when data is moving down a physical media, it needs to interact with the world of physics. In the case of copper wires, data needs to be presented as electrical impulses that are conducted by copper wires. In the case of fiber optics, data needs to be presented as packets of photons, or light, that fiber optics is designed to conduct. The job of a NIC is to get from the 1s and 0s of data to the electrical impulses or light pulses of the physical media, and to be able to go back the other way when it is *receiving* electrical impulses or photon packets. To do this, the NIC has to straddle the two worlds. Because the NIC exists on the Data Link layer it is able to understand the 1s and 0s coming from the upper layers of the OSI Model. Because the NIC exists on the Physical layer it is able to interact directly with the means of communication and media used to transfer the physical phenomena carrying data across a network.

Because NICs work directly with the physical layer of a network, it is very important that the correct NIC is used on a network. Only a NIC that is designed to work with a specific type of media and its associated means of communication can be used in a computer that connects to the same kind of media. It is not possible to use a fiber-optic NIC to connect to an unshielded twisted-pair network. It is also not possible to use a UTP NIC to connect to a coaxial network. The NIC used in a particular network has to match the type of media being used by that portion of a network specifically. Not only is the *media* important, but the *means* of communication is also important. If a network segment is transmitting data across a network segment at 100 mbps, a network card that is only designed to read data at 10 mbps cannot be used.

In the same way that media and means need to be taken into account when deciding on a NIC, the technology standard being used also has to be taken into account. If the Ethernet LAN technology standard is being used on a network segment, a NIC designed for the Token Ring LAN technology standard cannot be used. Only a NIC designed to read the Ethernet LAN technology standard can be used.

If you want a NIC to work on a network segment, several different things have to be taken into account when purchasing that NIC. The NIC needs to be designed to use exactly the same media that your network uses. The NIC needs to be designed to read and write the data in exactly the same means and at the same rate as your network. Finally, the NIC needs to be

---

TAKE NOTE *

You should know what media is and how it impacts the decisions you make regarding other equipment used on the network. You should be able to differentiate between the media used to carry the signal and the physical phenomena used to propagate the signal within the media.

designed to match the same technology standard your network uses. In summary, for a NIC to be usable on a specific network segment it must be designed to use the same:

- Media
- Means of communication and data rate
- Communication technology standard

Addressing

If you would like to review the topic of physical and logical addressing and how they work together, you can reread the section of Lesson 4 titled "How Physical and Logical Addressing Work Together."

In order for an NIC to convert data into electrical impulses and such and get it to or from its proper destination, it needs to know where data is coming from or where a particular piece of data is intended to go. The NIC uses physical addresses to do this. Each NIC comes from the manufacturer with a unique physical address or serial number programmed into its ROM chip. This serial number is also known as the NIC's physical address or MAC address, and it is used to move a frame from one network device to another within a particular network segment as discussed in Lesson 4.

The physical address assigned to a NIC by its manufacturer is 48 bits long. Because of the way this address is divided up into two 24-bit parts, each manufacturer has only 16 million or so unique addresses they can use before the manufacturer has to begin reusing physical addresses. While normally this does not have any impact on the performance of a network, occasionally it may because no two NICs on any given segment of a network can have the same physical address. If there are two NICs with the same physical addresses within the same network segment, it can make the whole network behave in an unstable manner. This instability can manifest itself as intermittent problems on the network and lost frames. When these kinds of symptoms manifest themselves on a network, it is a good idea to check MAC addresses on the network to find the duplicate addresses. If duplicate MAC addresses are found, simply replace one of the NICs that is carrying the duplicate MAC address, or if the NIC is built into a computer, move it to a different segment of your network.

■ Modems

THE BOTTOM LINE

In this portion of Lesson 6, we discuss Modems. Some of the features found in modems are also discussed as well as their present obsolescence.

Modem stands for Modulator/Demodulator. A modem is a networking device that is used to modulate an analog signal in such a way that it can encode digital information or to demodulate the encoded signal so that it can be decoded back into something a computer can read. Any device that is used to encode digital information onto analog communications links, regardless of throughput, can rightfully be called a modem. However, many devices today are called modems that use digital encoding on digital media to transmit digital information. In the most correct sense of the word, these types of devices are not really modems.

In the past, the most commonly used and most recognizable modem was the one that was used, and in some cases is still used, to modulate the analog signal of a regular telephone line to encode digital information into it and then to demodulate return signals to view digital content from outer sources. These types of modems started out achieving only very slow data rates, but they gradually increased in speed. By the late 1990s, the modems used in home computers were able to attain speeds approaching 56.6 kilobits per second (kbps). Using data compression these devices enhanced their speed and were able to encode and transmit data across standard phone lines. Speeds approaching the 56.6 kbps rate however were on the upper end of the theoretical limits of such devices. Because of this limitation, other technologies were pursued.

Modems such as the ones used in home computers in the 1990s and later came in two types—external and internal. An external modem connected to a computer via the computer's COM port and later via a computer's USB port. An internal modem was placed into a computer using an expansion slot. One type of internal modem—a soft modem or Win modem—used the operating system, drivers, and hardware of the motherboard to accomplish its task. This resulted in a drain on the hardware of the computer and the computer's performance. This also meant that a soft modem could only be used with the operating system for which it was designed. Soft modems were usually designed for the various Windows operating systems, which is why these devices were often called Win modems. These devices were not compatible with alternative operating systems such as Linux.

The other type of internal modem—hardware modem—did not rely on the operating system and the hardware built into the motherboard to carry out its task, instead it relied on its own hardware and the software built into the modem itself to fulfill its task. The hardware modem was the better type because it was not limited to one operating system. However, hardware modems were more expensive.

XREF

These technologies are discussed in Lesson 8. There is also more discussion about dial-up connectivity in Lesson 8.

After the 1990s, newer technologies began to be developed that allowed access speeds far in excess of the speeds allowed by dial-up modems. It was the advent of these technologies and their pricing in ranges that were accessible to most American households that caused the use of dial-up modems to decline. Today most people access the Internet from their homes via cable broadband connections, various DSL-type technologies, or other usually wireless technologies.

■ Media Converters

↓ **THE BOTTOM LINE**

The two main types of media converters are discussed in this section of Lesson 6. One type is a wire-to-wire media converter, and the other type converts not just the wires but also the signal. Finally, we examine the role that some switches play in media conversion.

Media converters are devices used to convert one type of media to another type. Such devices are used to convert coaxial to twisted pair or fiber to copper. These types of devices are important for allowing two different types of technologies in the same network. Figure 6-3 shows a 9-pin serial connector converted to a RJ-45 connector. This type of media converted is essentially a wire-to-wire conversion.

Figure 6-3

A 9-pin serial connection converted to a RJ-45 connection

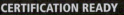
CERTIFICATION READY
What are media converters? In what circumstance would you use one?
3.1

Some types of media converted are also transceivers. A transceiver is used as a media converter when the data coming in on one side of the media converted needs to be retransmitted in a different format before sending it out the other end of the converter because the signals are not completely compatible. Figure 6-4 shows such a device.

The device shown in Figure 6-4 is intended to convert a serial interface signal into a 10BaseT Ethernet signal or vice versa. As you can see in the figure, one end contains the 15-pin male serial interface and the other end contains the RJ-45 Ethernet interface. Because the two types of signals are not fully compatible, the transceiver-converter has to take the signal coming in from one side and retransmit it as either an Ethernet or serial signal on the other side depending on which side of the device the signal originated from.

One of the more common situations where media converters are needed is when fiber optics are used to connected to switches together in a LAN but copper cables such as twisted pair is used to connect to the individual computers. In this situation, the media converted is usually built directly into the switch in question. That switch takes the fiber-optic cable coming in from another switch and converts it to electrical impulses that are then used to communicate to the computers or patch panel connected to the switch. This situation is illustrated in Figure 6-5.

Figure 6-5

Switches with fiber-optic cable
coming in and UTP copper
cables going out

In Figure 6-5 the thin cables coming into the two switches are multi-mode fiber-optic cables and the thicker cables going out are UTP CAT 5e Ethernet cables. Some special purpose media converters that are commonly used are discussed in the next few sections.

Fiber to Ethernet

There are many types of media converters used in the networking industry. Singlemode or multimode Fiber to Ethernet is one such converter. This type of media converter is used to convert different types of fiber optic cables to Ethernet. Some things you need to consider when doing this is how fast the Ethernet is you are trying to convert to and what type of fiber technology you are converting from. If you are running Ethernet using singlemode or multimode fiber then in reality all you may be doing is converting from the appropriate type of fiber to UTP or something similar. In this situation, you are still running Ethernet but you are changing cable types. This requires a media converter that does not need to do anything but convert the signal. However, you do need to make sure that the media converter you use is for either singlemode or multimode fiber depending on which type you are converting from.

On the other hand, you may be using the fiber optic cable to carry Ethernet, but you may need to convert from 10 gigabit or 1 gigabit Ethernet to 100 megabit Ethernet using UTP. In this case, you need to not only convert cable types but also data speeds. This requires a more capable media converter than the original scenario.

One other situation to keep in mind is that you may not be using the fiber to carry Ethernet signals. Instead, you may be using the fiber to carry T1, T3, or some other type of signal. In this case, not only do you need to convert the signal from fiber to copper, you also need to convert signal types or technologies. In this situation, the media converter you use needs to be able to not only convert the appropriate type of fiber to Ethernet, but also be able to convert the signal type as well. This particular scenario is particularly common when a signal is coming into the network from outside the network. For example, you may have your ISP coming into your corporate network using a T3 signal, but you are using 100 megabit Ethernet inside the corporate network. In this case, the T3 signal needs to be converted to an Ethernet signal that is actually a bit faster and the media type needs to be converted as well. When you are in this situation, you need to make sure that you have the appropriate conversion devices available so that you can get the ISP signal into your network. A bit more about this will be discussed later in this Lesson when we talk about CSU/DSUs.

Fiber to Coaxial

In the above section, we discussed converting fiber to some form of UTP Ethernet. However, UTP is not the only type of copper media that can be converted. It is also possible to convert between fiber and coaxial cables. This is most commonly done by cable television companies. These companies will sometimes run fiber optic cables into a certain neighborhood and then convert to coaxial when they get there. The reason they do this is because fiber can carry much greater bandwidth a much longer distance than coaxial cable can. However, once you are in the home, it is actually easier to use coaxial cable. One of the reasons it is easier to use coaxial in the home is because most home devices have connections for various copper media, including coaxial, but do not have connections for fiber media. Most of the same considerations that apply to converting fiber to Ethernet also apply to converting fiber to coaxial. The main difference is that a different copper media is being used.

Singlemode Fiber to Multimode Fiber

So far we have discussed converting fiber to copper, but we have not discussed converting fiber to fiber. The reason a person may want to do this is because part of a network may use singlemode fiber while another part may use multimode fiber. Perhaps singlemode fiber comes into a site from outside, but the main backbone of the site may be multimode fiber. In this scenario it becomes necessary to convert from singlemode to multimode at the site. Singlemode and multimode fiber use different techniques to encode data, so a media convert needs to be able to go from one encoding technique to another. A singlemode to multimode fiber converter may also need to be able to accommodate different data rates for the two types of fiber as well, as in some situations, the singlemode fiber may actually transmit data faster than the multimode. You need to know exactly how you network works in order to know what type of converter you are going to need when doing any type of media conversion in a network.

■ Repeaters and Hubs

↓ **THE BOTTOM LINE**

This section of Lesson 6 discusses repeaters and the three types of hubs that are available. Those three types of hubs are passive, active, and intelligent hubs. The concept of collision domains is also discussed in this section.

Repeaters and hubs are closely related devices. In fact, you could say that hubs are multiport repeaters. A *repeater* is a device that repeats a signal it receives in order to rebroadcast it, thus extending the range of a particular cable run. A repeater is always active and requires a power source. The main thing about a repeater is that it has one cable coming in and one going out.

Use a rule of thumb—the 5-4-3 rule—to determine how and where to connect these devices to a network. This rule only applies to networks that are connected together with repeaters and hubs. The 5-4-3 rule works like this. A network connected together with repeaters and hubs can only have 5 segments on it. The 5 segments can only be connected with 4 connecting devices linking them together. Finally, only 3 of those segments can contain computers. The 5-4-3 rule can be summed up like this, 5 segments, 4 connecting devices, and 3 segments with computers connected.

A similar device to a repeater is a *hub*. One thing to keep in mind is that hubs work as if they were the bus of a larger network. When a computer that is connected to one port of a hub needs to connect to a computer that is connected to a different port on a hub, it has to broadcast the signal to all the devices connected to that hub. This is how a hub acts as a bus.

Aside from working like a bus network, hubs come in three varieties: passive, active, and intelligent. A *passive hub* is really nothing more than a cable splitter. If you have seen old cable TV connections where one coaxial cable is connected to a cable splitter and two or more cables come out, you have seen what is essentially a passive hub. These types of devices are not very commonly used in data networks.

An *active hub* works very much like the previously described repeater. It needs to have power connected to it, because it repeats a signal from one computer connected to it to the other computers connected to it. This allows for connecting the various computers together at distances longer than the maximum distance of a single cable run. You do however need to be careful not to exceed the 5-4-3 rule.

Active hubs also act as a bus. When a hub repeats the signal from one computer, it repeats it to all the other computers or similar devices connected to that hub. This also applies when several hubs are connected together. If any device sends a signal to any other device connected to the various hubs, the signal is repeated to every device connected to every hub on the network. In effect, when using hubs, all devices connected to the network via one or more hubs are part of the same collision domain. Figure 6-6 shows an example of an active hub.

Figure 6-6

An active hub

A collision domain refers to the part of a network where one computer sends a signal to another computer and all the other computers see the signal. No matter how many computers you have on a segment of your network, when one computer sends a signal, all the other computers are able to see it. While this is a security risk, it is also a functionality issue. Because only one computer on a segment can send a signal at one time, the more computers on a segment, the more communications traffic there is. The more traffic there is, the more likely it is that two signals will hit each other. This is called a collision, which means the signal has to be resent and all the computers on the segment have to wait. A network segment where computer signals may collide with each other is called a **collision domain**. If there are too many computers on a single collision domain, a network can reach a point where there are so many collisions, that no computers are able to actually communicate with each other. Therefore, the goal of a hub-based network is to have as few computers as possible on a single collision domain. The devices we discuss in the next section can be used to reduce the size of these collision domains.

The last device we discuss in this section is called an **intelligent hub**. Intelligent hubs work like active hubs but have additional features and capabilities. One of the main features found in many intelligent hubs is diagnostics capabilities. Intelligent hubs with diagnostics capabilities are able to not only tell if there is a problem on the network but also, in many situations, they can determine where the problem is and the nature of the problem to some extent. Intelligent hubs also have data management capabilities. Intelligent hubs with data management capabilities are able to adjust their throughput to match that of slower devices so that both slower and faster devices can use the same data connections. Some intelligent hubs even have the ability to control which data line a specific packet uses. This can help streamline data throughput. Switches have a similar capability.

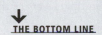

CERTIFICATION READY
What is a hub?
What role do hubs
play in a networking
environment?
1.2

Bridges and Switches

↓ **THE BOTTOM LINE**

This section of Lesson 6 discusses bridges and switches. The basic function of a bridge is described and the various types of switches that are available are also mentioned. Additionally several of the more commonly used features of switches such as VLANs, trunking, port mirroring, and port authentication are discussed. Finally the Spanning Tree Protocol is mentioned and Power over Ethernet is briefly discussed.

Repeaters and hubs are Layer 1 devices on the OSI Model. Bridges and switches are Layer 2 devices. In the case of some of the more advanced switches, they can be higher layer devices. This section of Lesson 6 discusses bridges and switches.

Bridges

CERTIFICATION READY
What is a bridge? How
does it function? What
role does a bridge play in
a network environment?
1.2

Bridges are devices intended to break up networks into smaller sections. These devices are able to do this by being more intelligent than your average hub. Since bridges work on Layer 2 of the OSI Model, they are able to read and make sense of MAC addresses. Based on these MAC or physical addresses, bridges can determine if a frame is allowed to pass through to the other side of the bridge. Using this capability bridges are able to break up network traffic into smaller collision domains.

A bridge will read each frame that comes its way. In doing this, a bridge is able to form a table of all the devices on either side of it. Using this table, the bridge determines if a frame needs to pass through it to the other side to reach its destination, or if it needs to stop the frame because its destination is on the side of the bridge the frame is already on. In doing this, a bridge is able to break a network into smaller sections called collision domains. By limiting where a frame is allowed to go based on its MAC address, a bridge is able to limit the number of frames on a given segment of a network thereby reducing the number of collisions on each segment. This is called breaking up the network into smaller collision domains. Figure 6-7 explains how this works.

In Figure 6-7 we see a basic bridge. Notice that the bridge has one side labeled Segment 1 and the other side labeled Segment 2. Each segment has a number of computers on it. The bridge contains a database/table that lists each segment attached to it and the computers located in each segment. The bridge uses this table to determine which frames to allow across the bridge to the segment on the other side and which frames not to allow to cross over the bridge to the segment on the other side. In the Figure 6-7 example, if Computer 1 tried sending a frame to Computer 4, that frame would be stopped at the bridge because the frame had already reached its destination. However, if Computer 1 tried sending a frame to Computer 7, the frame would be allowed to pass through

Figure 6-7

How a basic bridge would work

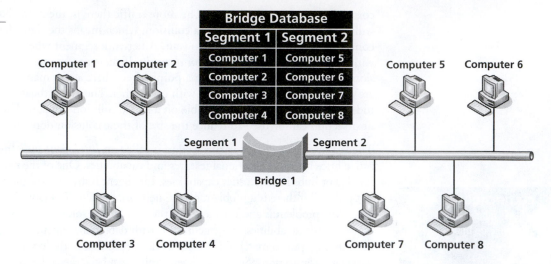

the bridge because Computer 7 is on the other side of the bridge. This is how the bridge controls traffic on the network—only allowing frames that need to go from one segment to the other to pass through while stopping those frames that do not need to go from one segment to the other.

Switches

CERTIFICATION READY
What is a switch? What role do switches play in a network environment?
1.2

Switches like bridges work primarily on Layer 2 of the OSI Model however, some types of switches can work on higher layers. If a switch is able to work on multiple layers at the same time, it is referred to as a multilayer switch.

Switches are used to connect multiple computers together on a local area network (LAN). A company called Kalpana introduced the concept of a multiport network switch in 1989, and they introduced the first Ethernet switch in 1990. In 1994, Cisco Systems acquired Kalpana.

BASIC SWITCH

The simplest and most common type of switch found in the networking world is the *basic switch*. This type of switch is essentially a multiport bridge. It is used to connect multiple networking devices, usually computers, together to form LANs. A basic switch can be called a multiport bridge because like a bridge, it is able to separate a network into multiple collision domains. The big difference is that in a switch each port is essentially its own collision domain. Any two devices that are connected together via a switch form their own collision domain. In essence, in a 48-port switch, if the computer connected to port 23 sent a frame to the computer connected to port 41, then an individual collision domain between port 23 and 41 would be formed. When this happens, any other communications on the switch would be unaffected by the connection between ports 41 and 23, and ports 41 and 23 would be unaffected by any other connections. In the case of a 48-port switch, 24 such unique collision domains can be established at one time. These collision domains can also shift and change as they need to in order to establish and disconnect links between ports as needed for communications on the network through the switch. Figure 6-8 shows a 24-port switch.

Figure 6-8

A 24-port switch

Another important function of switches is to convert media from one type to another. This means that switches can be used to take fiber-optic data input and break it out to twisted-pair ports. This is actually a pretty common use for switches because they are often placed in intermediate distribution frames (IDFs) to break out a signal to the different network devices in their section of a network, and they are connected to the main distribution frame (MDF) or other sections of a larger network via multimode fiber-optic cable or something of that sort. Figure 6-9 shows a switch being used to convert fiber to UTP in an MDF.

Figure 6-9

Switch in an IDF used to convert fiber optic to copper UTP

CERTIFICATION READY
What are the different types of switches? How do they differ from each other in their functioning and role in a network environment?
1.2

In a home environment, the ability of switches to convert one media type is expressed in a different way. Fast Internet connectivity is brought into the home via some type of copper. However, most people do not have copper connections running all over their homes and do not want to have this because it is usually not very neat unless the home was originally built with the copper connections built into the walls. To get around this, many people use some type of wireless network connectivity to connect to their Internet service where it comes into the house. The Internet comes into the house via some sort of "modem" from the ISP provider. It is then usually connected via twisted pair to some type of wireless access point, which has copper coming into it and may even have several other twisted-pair ports. It will also allow a computer to connect to itself via some wireless technology. This wireless access point is a switch that is also able to convert signals coming into it via copper, into radio signals that then go out to the various computers in the house and vice versa.

Interface Configuration

Many switches do not have a default setup. Instead you have to manually configure them in order to use them in your network. Configuring a switch is basically programming the switch to behave in the manner you wish it to using the operating system of the switch.

Many of the most recent switches, especially those intended for average consumers, actually come with a graphical interface to allow programming of them. In this situation, it is really a manner of pointing and clicking icons and inputting the required specification when the dialog box comes up. However, to have a very fine control over how a switch operates, it is often necessary to use command line interface (CLI) commands in order to correctly program a switch. Much of the Cisco CCNA certification is built around learning to use the CLI of Cisco routers and switches.

Much of the configuration done on switches revolves around configuring VLANs and Trunking. Both these topics will be discussed later in this Lesson. The most basic way to understand

VLANs is to simply look at it as determining which port or ports on a switch need to connect to a specific network and then group the ports accordingly. Trunking is simply determining which VLANs need to talk to each other and then configuring them to do so.

DIAGNOSTICS

In the case of switches, diagnostics during configuration refers to verifying that a switch is configured correctly by testing it out. However, diagnostics can also refer to determining what went wrong with a switch when it stops working like it was configured to. In both cases, there are a number of tools built into the switches to test them for both configuration issues and hardware issues. Diagnostics in a broader sense is knowing how to use these tools provided by the switch in order to determine what is wrong when something does not work as expected. This is another topic that is covered quite extensively in the Cisco CCNA certification material.

MULTILAYER SWITCH

Multilayer switches are switches that work on more than one layer of the OSI Model. The biggest advantage this gives a switch is the ability to move data from one type of network to another type of network. For example, multilayer switches can be used to move data from a Token Ring network to an Ethernet network. Multilayer switches can also route data frames between different VLANs. This will be discussed in more detail later in this lesson when we discuss VLANs.

CONTENT SWITCH

Load balancing is another activity that is performed by multilayer switches. Switches that are specifically used for this purpose are called *content switches*, or content service switches. These switches take the load from two or more servers and automatically share it across a network. This sharing is usually done based on TCP port numbers. The most common services that are load balanced by content switches are HTTP, HTTPS, and VPN; however, any protocol or service that has a TCP port number can benefit from the load sharing that content switches are capable of.

In addition to load balancing, there are some other services that can be performed by content switches. One such service is the ability to perform NAT at the speed of the network. Another task performed by content switches is SSL encryption/decryption and the centralized management of digital certificates. While there are other functions that can be handled by content switches, those listed here are among the most common.

MANAGED SWITCHES VERSES UNMANAGED SWITCHES

Switches come in two main categories. Those two main categories are managed switches and unmanaged switches.

An unmanaged switch is the type of switch most home users may have. An unmanaged switch comes with a default preconfigured setup and can only operate within the bounds of that preconfigured setup. When setting up a switch for home purposes where simplicity of configuration is important, an undamaged switch is the preferred type of switch to have.

If you need your switch to perform complex filtering or need it to segregate different ports into VLANs then a managed switch is the preferred technology to use. A managed switch gives you the ability to configure the switch to perform in exactly the way you desire it to and does not rely on a default configuration. This is the type of switch that was described earlier when interface configuration was discussed. Most large companies use managed switches while most home users and small companies with only a single office or site tend to use unmanaged switches. Depending on what you need to do, either a managed or an unmanaged switch can be your best choice. If you have limited computers, limited time, limited personnel, and only need a switch to connect your handful of computers together and to the Internet, then an unmanaged switch is the best choice for you. Alternatively, if you have a complex network, need extensive filtering, and have multiple subnetworks in your company, they managed switches are your best choice.

Virtual LAN (VLAN)

Virtual LAN (VLAN) in its most basic form refers to the ability to break up a much larger network into smaller networks using Layer 2 of the OSI Model. A VLAN refers to a group of hosts that share a common set of communications requirements that are grouped together via Layer 2 of the OSI Model regardless of whether they are attached to the same device. Aside from being able to break up a network into smaller segments, VLANs can also be used to make a network more secure. This use of VLANs will be discussed in more detail in a later lesson. Figure 6-10 shows the most basic way that VLANs can be formed.

Figure 6-10

VLAN formation

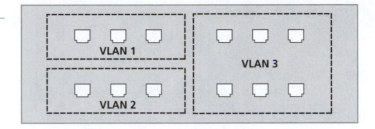

Figure 6-10 illustrates the most basic method used to define VLANs. The most basic way to form VLANs is to physically assign different ports or groups of ports on a switch to different VLANs in the configuration of the switch. Figure 6-11 illustrates how different switches can be used to spread a VLAN across multiple switches.

Figure 6-11

One VLAN stretched across more than one switch by configuring multiple connected switches on the same network with the same VLAN number

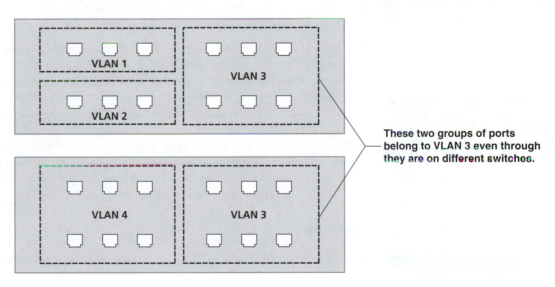

As you can see in Figure 6-11, it is not necessary to limit a VLAN to just one switch. When configuring switches, it is possible to spread a VLAN across more than one switch as long as all the switches that share the VLAN are interconnected. This is set up when the switches are configured. You may want to spread a VLAN across more than one switch if you need more ports than you have on just one switch, or you could have more complex reasons doing this.

You may have both data connections and VoIP connections in the same network and want to create two different VLANs: VLAN 1 for VoIP and VLAN 2 for data communications. You would use the two different VLANs to keep the two different types of communications separate. If a particular connection is intended for VoIP, then you would connect it to a port assigned to VLAN 1. If a particular connection is intended for data communications, you would connect it into VLAN 2. By spreading the two VLANs across multiple switches, as your company grew, you would just add a new switch and divide it into two VLANs with one being used for VoIP and the other for data communications. Figure 6-12 illustrates this scenario.

Figure 6-12

VoIP VLAN and a data VLAN stretched across two switches

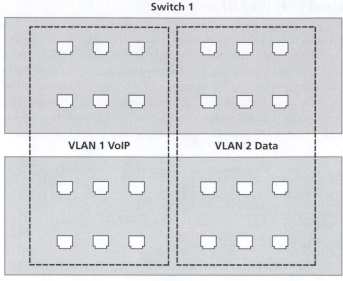

Another reason for breaking up a network into multiple VLANs may be to give a certain amount of bandwidth to one VLAN and a different amount of bandwidth to another VLAN. A way to illustrate this point is to continue using the example of one VLAN for VoIP and another for data. Aside from simply keeping the different types of communications separate, you can also use the different VLANs to assign different amounts of bandwidth to the two different types of communications.

In a real-world example of this, in a network that was initially set up, both VoIP and data were used to share the Internet bandwidth available to the organization. However, when 9/11 happened, the data side of the network took up so much bandwidth from people trying to find out what was happening that the site was not able to receive voice calls over the VoIP communications systems. As a result of this experience, the organization broke its network up into one VLAN for VoIP and other VLANs for data. They then assigned a set amount of bandwidth exclusively to the VoIP VLAN in order to ensure that the VoIP communications system would always have enough. The remaining bandwidth was shared by the various data VLANs. This prevented a repeat of the circumstances that knocked out the organization's ability to receive VoIP communications when the rest of the network was using too much bandwidth.

Trunking

Related to switches, *trunking* is basically VLAN multiplexing. Data from multiple VLANs are carried across a single cable or other network link. To accomplish this, special "trunking" protocols are needed. One such protocol is IEEE 802.1Q. This is an open protocol that works by adding a special tag in the header of an Ethernet frame that identifies the frame as belonging to a particular VLAN.

Cisco also has a proprietary protocol that it uses for trunking. That protocol is called the Inter-Switch Link protocol. The Cisco Inter-Switch Link protocol works differently from IEEE 802.1Q. Instead of adding a flag to the Ethernet frame heading, the Inter-Switch Link protocol wraps the whole Ethernet frame in a special wrapper or encapsulation that does pretty much the same thing as IEEE 802.1Q. IEEE 802.1Q is the most common way to carry out trunking.

Cisco has another proprietary protocol related to managing VLANs across multiple switches. That protocol is called VTP or VLAN Trunking Protocol. This protocol is used by Cisco Catalyst switches to advertise all the VLANs available in a group of related switches. This group of related switches is called a VLAN Domain. VTP can only be used by the Catalyst Switches that share same VLAN Domain. The purpose of advertising the VLANs available in a given VLAN Domain is to reduce the need to manually configure the shared VLANs on multiple switches as well the configuration of the trunk used between those multiple VLANs.

CERTIFICATION READY
What is a VLAN? How is a VLAN configured?
1.4

CERTIFICATION READY
What types of network situations are VLANs used in?
1.4

CERTIFICATION READY
What is trunking? How is trunking related to switches? What is trunking used for?
2.1

CERTIFICATION READY
What is VTP? What are some basic guidelines that should be followed when configuring VTP?
2.1

Cisco lists some basic guidelines when configuring VTP on a Cisco Catalyst switch. These basic guidelines are as follows.

- All switches being configured with VTP have to have the same VTP domain name
- All the switches sharing a VTP domain have to use the same version of VTP
- If the switches in a VTP domain are using a password, they all have to have the same password
- All VTP server switches should use the same revision number

All the information above can be found as Cisco's website. Specifically the information listed above–in much more detail–can be found at the URL "http://www.cisco.com/en/US/tech/tk389/tk689/technologies_configuration_example09186a0080890607.shtml."

Port Mirroring

Port mirroring is simply the act of sending a copy of the frames from one or more ports on a switch to another port on the same switch. This port mirroring can be done on a per port basis or even on a VLAN basis. Port mirroring allows you to monitor what is going on in the switch. Intrusion Detection Systems, or IDSs, are one example of this type of monitoring that will be looked at later in this lesson. Setting up a monitor port allows you to take all the frames or data packets that pass through a switch and send a copy of them to a specific port. The frames or packets that are sent to this monitor port are in turn connected to a device that allows the network administrator or another computer to analyze what is going through the switch. This type of monitoring can be done for security purposes or simply to identify problems before they become widespread.

Port Authentication

Port authentication or *port-based authentication* is the ability limit access to a specific port to just certain MAC addresses. This provides security to the entire network because it limits access to the network via a particular port to pre-authorized MAC addresses. This provides security for the entire network because the rest of the network, if port-based authentication is configured network wide, will only allow devices access to certain areas of the network if a port using port authentication gives them authorization.

This could work out in a real-life example if you want to limit access to a specific server to only devices with specific MAC addresses. If the server in question is connected to a port with port authentication set up, then that port would only allow access to pre-approved MAC addresses, which enables you to limit access to any sensitive data residing on the server in question.

Spanning Tree Protocol (STP)

Spanning Tree Protocol (STP) is the protocol used by switches when multiple switches are used in the same network. STP is a Layer 2 protocol and is primarily used to prevent loops from developing in switch-based LANs. The Spanning Tree Protocol gets its name from a mathematical algorithm called "spanning tree." What the spanning tree algorithm does is takes a group of points and connect them all together without allowing any loops to form. Figure 6-13 illustrates this concept.

In Figure 6-13, a grid of points or dots are connected together by lines. Each dot in the grid is connected to all the other dots in the grid, but none of the connections form loops. This is what Spanning Tree Protocol does for switch-based networks. STP makes sure that all switches and their ports on the network are able to connect to all the other switches and their ports on the network without forming any loops in the communications patch. If a loop were to form in a switch-based network, then switches that are part of the loop would be cut off from the rest of the switches on the network. STP ensures that this does not happen.

Power over Ethernet (PoE)

PoE stands for *Power over Ethernet*. Simply put, PoE is the protocol used to safely transfer power over Ethernet cabling. For PoE to work, either a specialized switch that is designed to

Figure 6-13

A Spanning Tree

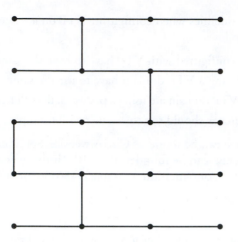

send power over Ethernet cabling needs to be used, or a secondary device designed to inject power into an Ethernet network needs to be used.

PoE was first ratified in 2003 and uses RJ-45 connectors to carry power along with data. There are several types of devices that typically use PoE, but the most common use for PoE is with VoIP installations where power is needed for the phone to work properly.

The IEEE 802.3af and 802.3at standards are used to define PoE. The 802.3af standard was ratified in 2003 and allows up to 15.4 W of power to be transmitted over the PoE connection. However 802.3af only assures 12.95 W at the other end because some power is lost over the transmission length. The 802.3at standard was ratified in 2009 and allows for up to 25.5 W of power to be transmitted, though some vendors claim to get as much as 51 W of power transmitted while still complying with the standard.

■ Channel Service Unit/Data Service Unit (CSU/DSU)

 THE BOTTOM LINE This section of Lesson 6 discusses what a CSU/DSU is and how it is used.

CERTIFICATION READY
What does CSU/DSU
stand for? What role
does a CSU/DSU play in a
network environment?
3.8

A ***Channel Service Unit/Data Service Unit (CSU/DSU)*** is used to convert a digital signal from one frame format to another. Most commonly it is used to convert Frame Relay or T-1 signals to Ethernet signals.

A CSU/DSU can come in a couple of different form factors. The oldest form factor has two different devices each about the size of an external modem or a brick that are connected to each other via a linking serial cable of some sort. Later, the functionality of a CSU/DSU was combined into a single device about the size of an external modem. More recently, CSU/DSUs have been reduced to the size of a single expansion slot that is placed into some sort of data terminal equipment (DTE) such as a router or a switch.

The CSU side of a CSU/DSU receives and transmits signals from some type of WAN connection such as a T-1 or Frame Relay connection. The DSU side converts the LAN signal to or from the CSU side and manages the connection and is capable of time-division multiplexing when necessary. The DSU side of a CSU/DSU also handles signal regeneration and timing errors.

■ Routers and Firewalls

 THE BOTTOM LINE The difference between routers and firewalls are discussed in this section of Lesson 6. Also, ways that firewalls are used in real-world networks are also explained.

Two other devices that are used in networks are very closely related. Those two devices are routers and firewalls.

Routers

Routers are networking devices that are used to move packets around a larger network. To do this they have to be very intelligent and read data packets to know where they are intended to go and where they have come from. This information allows the router to send the data packet on to its next stop as it journeys to its intended destination. Routers use different protocols, discussed in the previous lesson, to help accomplish this task. Routers work primarily on Layer 3 and Layer 4 of the OSI Model. Figure 6-14 shows a stack of 5 unconfigured routers in a rack.

Figure 6-14

Stack of five routers

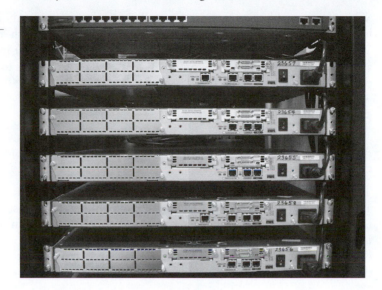

INTERFACE CONFIGURATION

Like switches, routers need to have their interfaces configured as well. Some new routers contain GUI interfaces like many of the newer switches, but such interfaces are rarer in routers. The primary method used to configure, or program, a router is to use a CLI. There are a lot more CLI commands related to router configuration than there are to switch configuration. This is because router configuration is a more complex task than switch configuration. One of the reasons router configuration is more complex than switch configuration is because there are more variables in router configuration. The Cisco CCNA certification spends a lot of time dealing with all the options available when configuring a router.

PORT SPEEDS.   One of the important variables that you need to be taken into account when configuring a router is ***port speed***. Port speed refers to how fast a specific port on the router is able to send and receive data. When manually configuring a router it is very important to remember to set the correct port speed depending on what type of port is being configured.

There are two basic types of ports on a router. Those two basic ports are serial ports and Ethernet ports. In the case of serial ports it is very important to set the proper clock speed on the serial port you are configuring otherwise the serial port will not work and you may not be able to connect to the network you are attempting to connect to. Another issue related to clock speed on a serial port is which end of the communications channel you are on. Only one end of a serial communications channel needs a clock rate. If a clock rate is put on the wrong end of the communications channel or on both ends of the communications channel, a serial connection will not work.

Ethernet ports also need to have the correct port speed. When configuring a router it is important that a Fast Ethernet port be designated as such. Standard Ethernet ports and Gigabit Ethernet ports also have to be correctly designated. If an Ethernet port is designated as the wrong type of Ethernet port, the configuration will not work as intended.

ROUTING TABLES

Routing tables are what routers use to determine the best route to send a packet down in order to help it reach its destination. Routing tables are exactly what their name implies them to be, tables. In the case of routing tables the table contains the router name, the IP address of the network each interface it is configured to connect to, and the interface identifier for each interface. To send a packet to the correct destination, the router looks at its routing table, determines which interface connects to the next hop on the way to the packet's destination and then directs the packet to the correct interface.

While routing tables can be setup manually in a router, most WAN administrators choose to let routers build their own routing tables. This makes things much less complicated for the WAN administrator and also makes it less likely errors will be put into the routing tables of a router. There are a number of protocols that are used by routers to accomplish this. These protocols were discussed back in Lesson 5.

Firewalls

A *firewall* is a networking device or networking software used to prevent unauthorized packets from getting into your network.

To better understand the roll of a firewall, you should think of the firewalls that are built into apartment complexes and other larger buildings with many rooms. The role of those firewalls is to stop or slow down a fire that starts in one apartment or room from spreading to another. Is short, a firewall is a physical barrier used to stop or slow down a fire from spreading. In computers, a network firewall does the same thing. However, instead of stopping or slowing down a fire, it is designed to stop or slow down a hacker attack.

FIREWALL RULES

In order for firewalls to work, they need to have rules set up in them so that they can tell what packets to block and what packets to allow. The rules for a firewall are found in a special list on the router or other device acting as a firewall. This list is called *Access Control List (ACL)*.

ACCESS CONTROL LIST (ACL)

ACLs can be set to block everything from specific IP addresses and ranges all the way up to specific ports and protocols. If one or more ACLs are in place in a router, when a router opens a packet to see what its destination is, it also runs a test on the packet to see if any ACL running on the router causes the packet to be rejected. If the packet has an IP address or contains a protocol or port that an ACL says is not to be allowed into the network, the router will discard the packet and not allow it entry into the network. This process is called the *block/allow* method of controlling entry into the network or device being protects. In some firewalls, if a specific port or IP address is not explicitly allowed in the ACL then it is automatically denied passage through the firewall. This method of controlling access to the network or device being protected by the firewall is called *implicit deny*.

Hardware Firewalls

Aside from routers acting as firewalls, there are also special-purpose devices that are classed as firewalls. These special-purpose devices are called hardware firewalls. *Hardware firewalls* are effectively routers with a large number of ACLs built into them that are designed to recognize numerous different activities that can be interpreted as attacks on the network and counter them. Many of these special-purpose firewalls also have intrusion detection software running on them. Intrusion Detection Systems (IDSs) will be discussed later in this lesson.

Hardware firewalls are placed in different locations in a network to help protect it. A couple of examples of common uses for firewalls are shown in the next couple of figures. Figure 6-15 illustrates the basic usage of a hardware firewall in a network.

Figure 6-15

Firewall in a basic network

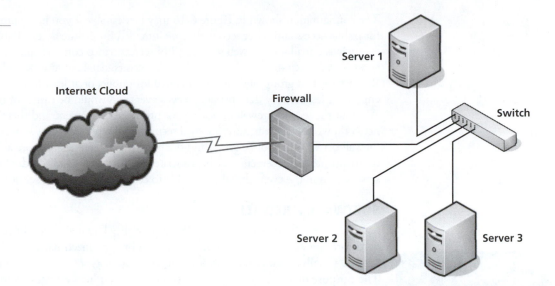

In this example, a firewall is placed between the Internet and the switch that connects the rest of a private network as the first line of defense between the private network and the Internet. The firewall is positioned to intercept unwanted packets before they are able to enter the private network. Also, with the firewall in this position, it can be used to prevent packets that are not intended for the Internet from getting out. Figure 6-16 shows a more complex but also very common use for firewalls.

Figure 6-16

Two firewalls used to create a DMZ

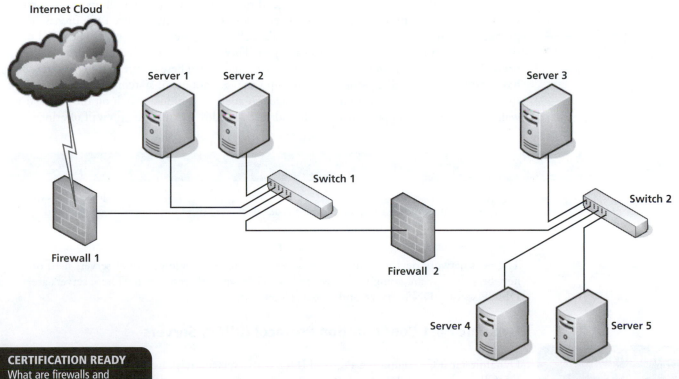

CERTIFICATION READY
What are firewalls and routers? How are firewalls and routers related? What roles do firewalls and routers play in a network environment?
5.5

In Figure 6-16, two firewalls are positioned to create a Demilitarized Zone (DMZ), which creates a special neutral zone where servers and other devices that are intended to access the Internet can reside without exposing the rest of the network if those specific servers and devices are compromised by hackers. With two firewalls in place, the servers between the two firewalls have less protection than those behind both firewalls.

The configuration shown in Figure 6-16 may be desirable if you have some servers that are intended for public access and other servers that are intended for private access. Public access servers are servers such as e-mail servers, web servers, VPN servers, video conferencing servers, and so on. Private access servers include domain controllers, file servers, database servers, and other such servers. Because the first group of servers is intended for public, or at least Internet access, it would inherently have less security than private access servers and would be easier for hackers to compromise. Without the second firewall in place, your private access servers, and therefore the rest of your network, would have the same lessened security as the public access servers. By placing the second firewall between the public access and the private access servers, you are able to increase the security of the private access servers and the associated network making it harder for hackers to attack those servers even in the event that they are able to compromise the first set of servers.

SOFTWARE FIREWALL

Software firewalls are similar to hardware firewalls. The main difference between the two is that hardware firewalls generally reside on a router or specialized hardware device while a software firewall usually resides on a computer or some other type of host. That said the job is the same. The purpose of a software firewall is to prevent unauthorized packets from getting into the device that is being protected. The difference is that you can purchase or download a software firewall and install it on your computer like any other program, assuming it does not already come with one. A hardware firewall on the other hand comes as a complete device that is placed on your network between an outside network such as the Internet and the inside network.

Windows Vista and Windows 7 come with pretty decent software firewalls built into them. However, if you are using Windows XP you may want to get a third party software firewall. One good third party firewall that can be legally downloaded for free is ZoneAlarm Free edition. As long as you are only using this firewall on a personal computer or are a student, you can legal use this software firewall. If you intend to use this software firewall on a computer you use for business purposes or want some enhanced features you will need to purchase the profession version of this firewall. Symantec also sells a software firewall that is effective but they require you to purchase a renewal each year. There are also a number of other software firewalls available for download that are both legal and free. These different software firewalls have varying levels of effectiveness and take up varying amounts of system resources, but all of them are better than having no firewall protection at all. If you do a search on the word "firewall" under www.filehippo.com you will find several additional software firewall offerings.

CERTIFICATION READY
What is the difference between a software firewall and a hardware firewall?
5.5

■ Servers

THE BOTTOM LINE
This section of Lesson 6 mentions several types of servers used in modern networks and the roles they play in the overall functioning of networks.

The next network devices to discuss are servers. There are a wide variety of servers used on networks, but we are going to discuss three specific types of servers here. Those servers are DHCP servers, DNS servers, and proxy servers.

Dynamic Host Configuration Protocol (DHCP) Servers

CERTIFICATION READY
What is DHCP? What are some of the issues involved with DHCP servers and configuring them?
2.3

Dynamic Host Configuration Protocol (DHCP) servers are responsible for controlling DHCP on the network. To review what was covered in a previous lesson, the purpose of a DHCP server is to automatically assign IP addresses to devices on a network so that the task does not need to be done automatically. Figure 6-17 reminds us how DHCP works.

DHCP Servers are the servers responsible for automatically assigning IP address on the network and do this by responding to the DHCPDISCOVER request from clients and sending

Figure 6-17

DHCP Initialization Process

❶ **DHCP client begins its boot up process.**

❷ **DHCP client issues a DHCPDISCOVER request.**

❸ **DHCP server processes the DHCPDISCOVER request and issues a DHCPOFFER message.**

❹ **DHCP client receives DHCPOFFER messages and issues a DHCPREQUEST message to the DHCP server it has accepted.**

❺ **DHCP server then issues a DHCPACK message to the client initializing the lease.**

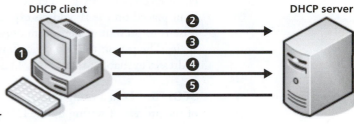

back a DHCPOFFER. When the client responds to the offer with a DHCPREQUEST the DHCP Server also is responsible for sending out the DHCPACK. A DHCP server is first configured with a range of IP addresses that are valid on a specific VLAN. The DHCP server issues and keeps track of all IP addresses on the VLAN it is attached to and makes sure that no duplicate IP addresses are issued.

One DHCP server can be used for several different VLANs as long as the port it is connected to on the switch is a part of each of the VLANs for which the DHCP server is responsible. The DHCP server must be configured to recognize the different VLANs it is attached to and be given different IP address ranges for each one. This situation is illustrated in Figure 6-18.

Beyond what has already been discussed, there are also some other issues related to DHCP servers and DHCP server configuration. Those issues will be discussed next.

Figure 6-18

One DHCP Server can service multiple VLANs at the same time

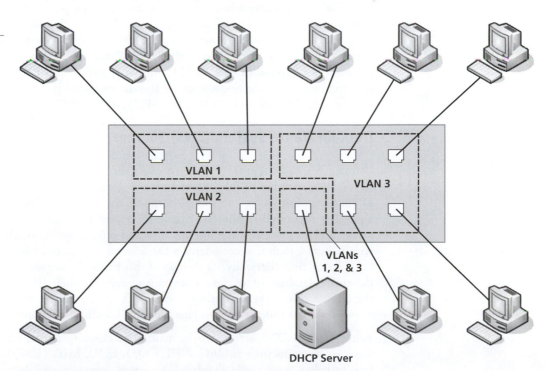

The DHCP server is able to serve VLANs 1, 2, & 3 because the port in the switch the DHCP server is attached to is assigned to all three VLANs in the switch's configuration.

LEASES. As already mentioned, once a client fines the network, one of the first things it does is request an IP address from the DHCP server. Once the process described above has been completed the DHCP client has an IP address it can use to access the network. However, the IP address that the client has available to it is not indefinite. The IP address the client receives is only good either until the client is rebooted or logged off, or until the time limit placed on the IP address expires. This time limit is called a *lease*. The purpose for the lease is to prevent a client from obtaining an IP address from the server that cannot be used again. The reason this is a concern is because a DHCP server only has a finite amount of IP addresses available to it for use. This finite amount of IP addresses will be discussed next.

SCOPES. When using DHCP it is necessary to setup the protocol in the DHCP Server. Part of the process of setting up the DHCP protocol is telling the server the range of IP addresses it has available to it to assign to DHCP clients. This range of available IP address to give out is called the DHCP Server's *scope*. The scope must always be predefined, and once the server hands out all the IP addresses in its scope, it is not able to assign additional IP addresses until previously assigned IP addresses are released by a client back to the server. The way a client can release an IP address is by being logged off, rebooted, or by having its lease expire.

RESERVATIONS. While normally it is not desirable to have an IP address assigned to a computer on the network indefinitely, there are some special circumstances where a permanent IP address is not only desirable, but preferred. One such situation may be that of a server or printer that must always use the same IP address for operational purposes. When this situation arises, a DHCP server can be configured to set aside an IP address permanently for that specific client. When this is done, it is called creating a reservation. A *reservation* is when a DHCP server is configured to only assign a specific IP address within its scope to a specific client. When an IP address is reserved I this manner, that IP address cannot be used by any other client or be handed out by the server except to the specific client the IP address in question has been reserved for.

OPTIONS. There are a large number of configuration parameters and control information that can be carried in DHCP Message packet. The specific field where these configuration parameters and control information can be found is the "options" field portion of the DHCP Message packet and are therefore called *DHCP options*. A complete description of these options can be found in RFC 2132 from March 1997. Additional options have been added over the years since the original release and can be found in subsequent RFCs. Some of those subsequent RFCs are RFC 2610, 3046, 4039, 4578, 4833, and 5192 amount others.

Domain Name System (DNS) Servers

Domain Name System (DNS) servers make the Domain Name System work. To be a DNS server, the server has to fulfill several criteria. First, the server has to be registered to join the DNS. Second, it has to run special-purpose DNS software. Third, the server has to be given a publicly registered IP address. Finally, the server must contain a database of other network names and addresses for the Internet host and other computers. If a server meets all these requirements, then it is considered a DNS server. Figure 6-19 reminds us how DNS works. DNS has a clear hierarchy. At the top of this hierarchy are the root servers, which contain the entire database of all the top domain servers and their IP addresses. There are 13 of these DNS root servers worldwide. Ten DNS root servers reside in the United States, the others reside as follows, one in Japan, one in London, UK, and one in Stockholm, Sweden.

Below the root DNS servers are the main DNS domain servers, which control different top-level domains such as ORG, NET, COM, EDU, MIL, GOV, US, UK, AU, and so on. Finally, below these reside all other DNS severs. Some control domains like Microsoft, Cisco, Google, and so on. Even lower-level DNS servers may reside on local networks and provide access to the large DNS for those networks such as the ISP DNS server shown in Figure 6-19.

1 Client computer ask for the IP address of URL www.support.widgets.com/widget_specs.htm from the DNS server of the ISP.

2 ISP DNS server queries the .root domain server for the IP address of the URL

3 The .root DNS server responds back with the IP address of the .com domain server.

4 The ISP DNS server queries .com domain server for URL IP address.

5 The .com domain server responds back with the IP address of the .widget domain server.

6 The ISP DNS server queries .widget domain server for URL IP address

7 The .widgets domain server responds back with the IP address of the .support web server.

8 ISP DNS server passes the IP address of the www.support.widgets.com web server to the client computer.

9 The web browser on the client computer queries www.support.widgets.com web server for the widgets_specs.htm document.

10 The www.support.widgets.com web server responds back with the requested document.

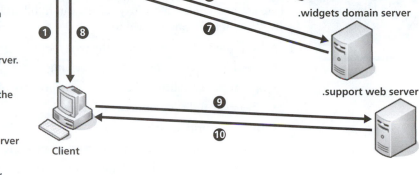

Figure 6-19

DNS name resolution process

CERTIFICATION READY
What are some common record types used by DNS?
1.7

DNS RECORDS. When describing DNS we mentioned that DNS needs to contain a database of network names and addresses in order for it to work. We also mentioned that the database in a DNS server contains network names and addresses from other computers and Internet host. This database is made up of a number of different record types depending on what type of network the DNS server is functioning in. While there are many record types possible in a DNS server, for the purposes of the CompTIA Network+ exam, five are important. Those five record types are A, MX, AAAA, CNAME, and PTR.

The A record type is used to store a 32-bit IPv4 IP address. While this is most commonly used to map IP addresses to hostnames, it can also be used to store a subnet mask. The A record type is described in RFC 1035.

The AAAA record type is similar to the A record type except it stores 128-bit IPv6 IP addresses instead of 32-bit IPv4 addresses. The AAAA record type is described in RFC 3596.

The MX record type maps domain names to a list of software agents that are responsible for transferring electronic messages from one computer to another. These software agents are called message transfer agents which are abbreviated MTA. The MX record type is described in the same RFC as the A record type is described.

The CNAME record type is used to records one alias name for another alias name. When the CNAME record type is used recorded alias is used in an attempt to access the appropriate location. NSLOOKUP uses this record type. The CNAME record type is also described in the same RFC as the A and MX record types.

The final record type to discuss for the CompTIA Network+ exam is the PTR record type. This record type is similar to the CNAME record type except that it only records the alias and reports it back, it does not attempt to use the recorded alias to access the network location. Reverse lookups will use this record type. Like the previous record type, this one is also described in RFC 1035.

DYNAMIC DNS. *Dynamic DNS*, which is sometimes referred to as DDNS, is a standard that has been added to the normal DNS standard. What Dynamic DNS does is allow a host with a changing IP address to use a permanent *Fully Qualified Domain Name (FQDN)*. A FQDN is basically a permanent URL or computer name within a defined network domain. The way Dynamic DNS allows a host with a changing IP address use a permanent FQDN is by automatically sending an update message to the DNS server every time the IP address changes. The RFC that fully describes Dynamic DNS is RFC 2136.

Proxy Servers

CERTIFICATION READY
What is a proxy server? What are some of the roles proxy servers are used for?
4.1

Proxy servers act as intermediaries between a client and other servers. Figure 6-20 is a diagram of how a generic proxy server would be used.

There are many roles that proxy servers can fulfill and they can be used for many different jobs. Proxy servers can be used to:

- Keep the computers behind the proxy server anonymous
- Speed up access to resources via caching
- Set up access policies to different network services and/or content
- Create an audit log of network usage
- Bypass security or services
- Scan inbound or outbound content for malware or other security risks
- Circumvent or get around any regional restriction you wish to avoid

Figure 6-20

Role of a Proxy Server

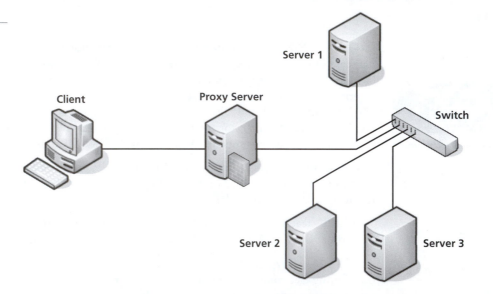

The two main ways that proxy servers are used are as gateway servers and as reverse proxy servers. A *gateway proxy server* passes requests and replies in an unmodified form. *Reverse proxy servers* are used to protect a private network from hosts on the Internet. In this way, it acts in the reverse of a standard proxy server. Reverse proxy servers act as front ends between a private network and the Internet. Reverse proxy servers can be used for load balancing, authentication, decryption, or caching. Some additional roles that proxy servers can take on:

- **Caching proxy server:** Used to cache the result of requests made by clients in order to pass the information directly to additional clients requesting the same information. This saves the caching proxy from having to look up the same content over and over. A good caching proxy server stores content locally that is commonly requested so as to minimize the data flow and conserve the bandwidth usage across a large enterprise network.
- **Web proxy servers:** Act as a caching proxy server for web content.

- **Content-filtering web proxy server:** Allows network administrators to control what type of web content is allowed into a network. These types of web proxy servers are often used to enforce rules about acceptable Internet use in corporate environments as well as schools and other places.

- **Anonymizing proxy server:** Helps a user remain anonymous on the Internet by acting as an intermediary between a user and the larger Internet. When a user uses an anonymizing proxy server, all requests that the user makes for Internet resources first go through the anonymizing proxy and then on to the greater Internet. In this way, when a request is tracked back to a system, the system it is tracked back to is the anonymizing proxy instead of the actual user that made the request for information.

- **Hostile proxy servers:** Used to intercept data and pass it on to its destination without the end user knowing so that the data can be used for nefarious purposes. Some spyware and phishing sites are designed to do this.

- **Intercepting proxy servers:** Used to intercept data and pass it on to its destination and to prevent users from avoiding acceptable use policies in place in a corporate network. Intercepting proxy servers help reduce the administrative burden on a network or limit data flow by intercepting common resource requests and diverting those requests to caching proxy servers. The difference between intercepting proxy servers and hostile proxy servers really is all in intent.

■ Additional Specialized Network Devices

THE BOTTOM LINE

In this section of Lesson 6, we introduce a few additional network devices such as multifunction network devices, intrusion detection/intrusion protection devices, load balancers, and bandwidth shapers. We also discuss the role these devices play in how a network functions.

In addition to multilayer switches, content switches, CSU/DSUs, and various types of servers, there are a few other network devices that serve specialized purposes. We will discuss a few of these devices next.

Multifunction Network Devices

As the name would imply, a multifunction network device is a network device that is designed to perform multiple functions at the same time. A wireless router switch or a network switch that contains a CSU/DSU port can be considered such a device. However, in the corporate world, possibly the most widely used multifunction network device is by a Cisco Catalyst Device. Figure 6-21 shows a Cisco Catalyst 8500 device.

In Figure 6-21, the Cisco Catalyst 8500 contains nine expansion cards, which is the full number this particular Catalyst can support. The first expansion card is a supervisor/router card. The second is also functioning as a router and even has the ability to take smaller expansion cards. The third card is a fiber-optic switch. Finally, the last six expansion cards are all Fast Ethernet switches containing 48 ports each.

Cisco Catalyst devices are true multifunction network devices because they are designed to perform pretty much any networking function possible so long as the correct cards are installed and configured correctly in the expansion slots. While the Cisco Catalyst 8500 is a large device with many large slots on it, all modern Cisco Catalyst devices can act as multifunction devices in one form or the other.

The reason that all Cisco Catalyst devices can act as multifunction network devices is that they are all designed with the ability to take different expansion cards of various sizes and

Figure 6-21

Cisco Catalyst 8500 with a full set of expansion cards

types. Even the routers seen in Figure 6-14 are Cisco Catalyst devices. Although the devices in Figure 6-14 are smaller than the Catalyst 8500, they still have the ability to add expansion cards of two different sizes and various functions.

Intrusion Detection Systems (IDS) and Intrusion Protection Systems (IPS)

Intrusion Detection Systems (IDS) and Intrusion Prevention Systems (IPS) are related technologies. An *Intrusion Detection System (IDS)* usually sits on the inside of a network and monitors the activity of the network. When something suspicious is noted, the IDS will notify the network administrator so that he or she can take steps to stop the suspect activity. Because an IDS only monitors activity, it is considered passive. Alternatively, an *Intrusion Protection Systems (IPS)* is active. An IPS works much like an IDS and in fact uses much of the same technology an IDS does, however when an IPS detects a suspicious activity, instead of just alerting the network administrator, it actually takes steps to stop the questionable activity by shutting down a connection or service that is acting suspiciously or logging out a user that has the suspicious activity coming from it. IPSs can also block IP addresses, applications, ports, and protocols as a response to what it considers suspicious activity. An IPS is often put on the perimeter of a network, whereas as IDS is often placed inside the network.

While the response to an intrusion is different for an IDS versus an IPS, the way the two devices detect an intrusion is the same. There are three techniques used by IDSs and IPSs to detect intrusions:

CERTIFICATION READY
What are IDSs and IDPs? What are they used for? How do they accomplish their function?
5.6

- *Behavior-based detection:* The IDS/IPS creates a baseline for a network's normal activity or behavior and then uses that baseline to look for any activity or behavior on the network that differs from what it considers to be normal activity. When such a divergence from the baseline is detected the IDS/IPS takes the action it is programmed to do against the threat. The main weakness of behavior-based detection is that it tends to produce a high number of false-positive detections. This means that it has a tendency to report activity as malicious that is not.

- *Signature-based detection:* The IDS/IPS has a database of known attacks available to it and uses signature-based detection to compare incoming activity to its signature database. When incoming activity matches a signature, the IDS/IPS responds as it was programmed to when malicious activity is detected. Signature-based detection tends to have a high number of false-negative detections where it misses or fails to detect a high number of attacks. This is generally because attacks that do not have a signature in its database are missed.

- *Stateful protocol analysis:* The IDS/IPS analyzes each packet that comes through the system and checks it for any settings or flags in its header that do not belong there. This type of analysis is also able to look at the data portion of a packet and identify any malicious code that may be present and act as it is programmed to when a malicious intrusion is detected. The main drawback of stateful protocol analysis is that if an attack or intrusion is not based on manipulating a datagram, the system will miss it.

The best IDS/IPS will use more than one of these detection methods to detect intrusion.

Encryption Devices

Encryption devices are hardware or software components that are used to encrypt information. For information or data to be encrypted means that the data is encoded in such a way that only the person or device possessing the correct key is able to read it. Some encryption devices are used to encrypt data locally while other encryption devices are used to encrypt data as it flows across a network. Devices that encrypt data as it moves across the network are called network encryption devices.

According to the NSA encryption devices come in 4 types. Type 1 encryption products or devices are endorsed by the NSA for securing classified and sensitive US government information. Type 2 encryption products or devices are endorsed by the NSA to be used in telecommunications and automated information systems. Type 3 encryption products or devices are endorsed by the NSA for use with unclassified documents or information. Finally Type 4 encryption devices or products have been registered with the NIST (National Institute of Standards and Technology) but are not endorsed by the NSA and cannot be used to secure classified documents and information. Generally devices and products that use lower levels of encryption such as 40-bit encryption are classified as Type 4 encryption devices.

> **CERTIFICATION READY**
> What are encryption devices and what are the four types recognized by the NSA?
> 1.2

Load Balancer

A *load balancer* is a network device used to balance the traffic on a network. The purpose of load balancing is to spread the traffic on a network across more than one device, segment, or connection in order to allow more traffic across the balanced network and to not overload one section of the network. Load balancing can be accomplished in a number of different ways. Some of the methods used for load balancing include asymmetric loading, priority activation, offloading, buffering, and caching.

Asymmetric loading involves varying the throughput to various devices or sections of a network based on the speed and capacity of the devices or segment receiving the data. This ensures that different parts of a network that work at different speeds or have different capacities do not get overwhelmed by data traffic or are not underutilized because an administrator is having to slow down, or throttle, throughput across the whole network so as not to overwhelm one part of the network.

Priority activation is sending data packets to a specific device or segment of a network based on their priority. This ensures that data from more important sources are sent to their destination first and are not slowed down or lost because of limited network capacity.

Offloading is where packets containing specific protocols such as SSL or TCP are sent to one server while other packets are sent to another. Packets that require more processing, such as SSL packets, are sent to a dedicated server so that servers that handle general data are not bogged down with handling packets that contain processing intensive packets, which prevents general traffic from being properly or promptly handled.

> **CERTIFICATION READY**
> What is a load balancing?
> 4.1

Buffering and caching are similar technologies, but they serve different functions. When data is intended for a slower computer or device, it is placed in a special memory location set aside to serve as a buffer. The data is then released from the buffer at a slow rate so as to not overwhelm the destination device with too much data. This is called *buffering*. The purpose of buffering is to allow a faster network device to process a request from a slower network device quickly and store it in the buffer. The data stored in the buffer is then released back at a rate the slower device can handle. While the data is being released from the buffer, the faster device can dedicate its processing capacity to the next request without having to slow down its function for the slower network device.

Caching also uses a set aside memory location, but for a different reason. In caching, a specific memory location is set aside on a network device where frequently requested information is stored so that the network device does not have to go and retrieve the frequently requested information every time it is asked for. The network device with the cache simply has to redirect the request to the cache and move on to the next request.

Bandwidth Shaper

Before we can discuss bandwidth shapers, we first need to understand what bandwidth shaping is. In short, ***bandwidth shaping*** is managing and/or controlling network usage in order to optimize how a network uses its available bandwidth. Controlling the usage of bandwidth on a network is one way of doing this. Bandwidth shaping is also known as ***traffic shaping*** or packet shaping. In the case of ***packet shaping***, it is the specific practice of limiting packet types, sources, or content as the means to do bandwidth shaping.

One of the more prominent examples of bandwidth shaping to appear in the news recently is the ongoing efforts of several ISPs to prevent people from using bit torrents and other related technologies. ISPs wish to prevent these technologies from being used because when they are in use only a handful of users end up using the majority of the available network capacity to download large amounts of data such as movies and music. Aside from the fact that much of this content is illegal, it also results in only a minimal amount of bandwidth being available for the majority of an ISP's users because of the small handful of users engaged in using the bit torrents and related technologies.

Now that we know what bandwidth shaping is, we need to discuss bandwidth shapers. A ***bandwidth shaper*** can be either in the form of a hardware device or software that is used to shape the bandwidth of a network in the manner described earlier. If the bandwidth shaper is a hardware device, it is usually in the form of a proxy server or network appliance.

■ Wireless Devices

 THE BOTTOM LINE   This section of Lesson 6 discusses wireless devices and how they are used in conjunction with wired devices in a network environment.

The final category of networking devices to be discussed is wireless network devices. Wireless network devices are simply the counterparts of the previously discussed network devices, except that they use radio waves as their communications medium instead of wires or cables.

Wireless NICs

Wireless NICs are used the same way that conventional NICs are used and do the same jobs. Wireless NICs come built-in in most portable computing devices such as notebook computers, netbook computers, tablets, and so on. Occasionally, you will even find a desktop computer that has a built-in wireless NIC. Aside from being built into a device, wireless NICs can also be add-on devices.

One way a wireless NIC can be added to a desktop computer is to add it as an expansion card. Figure 6-22 shows a PCI wireless NIC for a standard desktop computer.

Figure 6-22

802.11g wireless NIC

CERTIFICATION READY
How does compatibility affect installing and configuring a wireless network?
2.2

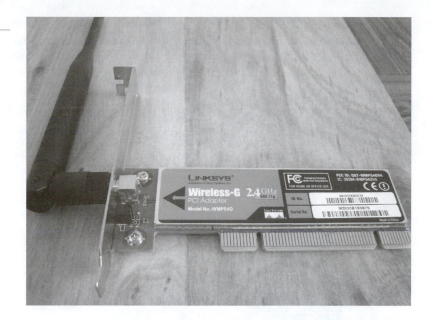

When you look at Figure 6-22, you will notice that it says Wireless-G. This means that it is a wireless NIC that complies with the IEEE 802.11g standard. There are three standards that are commonly used in wireless networks these days. Those standards are the IEEE 802.11b, IEEE 802.11g, and IEEE 802.11n. The slowest and oldest of these standards is the 802.11b standard. This standard allows for up to 11 Mbps throughput and has a range of approximately 100 feet at its highest throughput. IEEE 802.11g came out later and is backwards compatible to 802.11b. The theoretical maximum throughput of 802.11g is 54 Mbps with a range of approximately 100 feet at its highest throughput. The device in Figure 6-22 follows the 801.11g standard. Last, we have the IEEE 802.11n standard. This is the newest standard out and it has a theoretical maximum throughput of 600 Mbps, though so far only devices with a theoretical maximum throughput of 150 Mbps have been produced. The approximate maximum range of an 802.11n device is 200 feet at maximum throughput. A device that complies with 802.11n is backwards compatible with the earlier 802.11b and 802.11g standards.

While wireless NICs can take the form of expansion cards; more and more, wireless NICs are taking the form of USB devices. Figure 6-23 shows a wireless g-n device that is in the form of a USB device.

Figure 6-23

802.11g-n wireless NIC in the form of a USB device

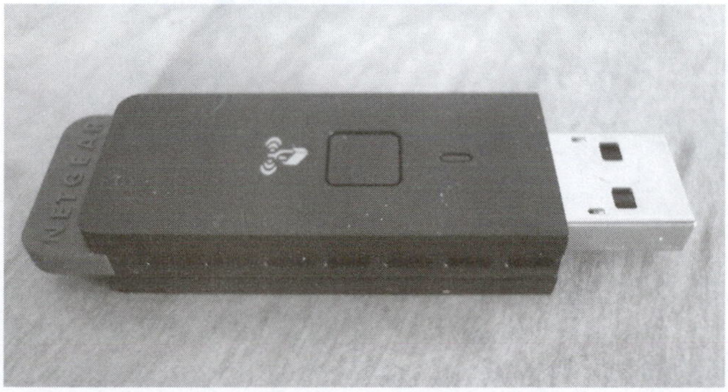

CERTIFICATION READY
What are the most commonly used wireless standards? What are some of the differences between the standards in regard to throughput speed and signal range or distance?
3.3

Figure 6-23 shows a Netgear USB 802.11g & n NIC, which means it can be used to connect to either an 802.11g or 802.11n network. It is also likely that the device would be able to connect to an 802.11b network.

Wireless USB NIC devices can be used in any computing device that has a USB port on it. Oftentimes wireless USB devices will also come with a stand that the USB device can be plugged into and then connected to a USB port. Figure 6-24 shows the device from Figure 6-23 in such a stand. These stands are usually intended to be used when a desktop computer is using the USB device.

Figure 6-24

802.11g-n wireless NIC in the form of a USB device in its stand

Wireless Access Points

The second major category of wireless networking devices we discuss is wireless access points. A *wireless access point (WAP)* is a wireless device that combines the roles of a switch and a router in smaller wireless networks. Figure 6-25 is an image of a newer model Cisco/Linksys home WAP.

Figure 6-25

Cisco wireless access point (WAP)

X REF

More is discussed about how wireless access points operate in Lesson 7.

Generally speaking, wireless access points are connected to larger networks and allow access to them via wireless media. In this way, WAPs act as switches to allow wireless devices access to a specific network.

In a home network, a WAP is often connected directly to a modem for an Internet connection coming in to the home from the outside. Figure 6-26 shows the wired connections that can be found on a home WAP for this purpose.

The wired network connections seen in Figure 6-26 are there to allow a WAP to connect various wireless devices to the network. In the case of Figure 6-26, the port with the Internet label is where a "modem" for a home Internet connection would be connected. The WAP would then

Figure 6-26

Cisco WAP with wired connections

act as a router and NAT the network IP addresses of the various wireless devices in the home network to the ISP's IP address. This allows the rest of the wireless devices in the home network to link to the home Internet connection. In a home environment, home gaming consoles such as Nintendo would be included in the devices allowed access to the Internet via the WAP.

Aside from allowing wireless devices access to the Internet and the home network, a WAP such as the one shown in Figure 6-26 can also be used to connect a small number of wired devices to the network. The four Ethernet ports are used for this purpose. When NATing the network, any devices connected to these would also be included.

■ Virtual Networking

↓
THE BOTTOM LINE

Finally we will discuss virtual network, what it is, and some of the technologies that are able to take advantage of virtual networking.

CERTIFICATION READY
What is a virtual network? How can a virtual network be useful?
1.9

Virtual networking is a new area of networking technology that combines hardware and software resources into a single entity for administrative purposes. Virtual networks come in two overall varieties, external and internal. In an external virtual network, the resources and hardware from multiple networks are combined into a single software environment for administrative purposes. An internal virtual network on the other hand is where a single device has been configured in such a way as to give network like functionality to every software container on the device. This is often done to consolidate the functionality of multiple servers into a single hardware and software platform.

The parent company of VMWare has produced a good online document found at http://www.vmware.com/files/pdf/virtual_networking_concepts.pdf which describes many of the concepts related to virtual networking.

The reason you may want to create virtual networks would be to save money. It cost less to purchase one or two very powerful servers and virtually construct a network in them than to purchase dozens of individual smaller servers and the supporting hardware. Once the very powerful servers are purchase and up and running, the network administrator then only has to create the various servers, switches, and other components needed to run the network inside the memory of the large servers. As long as the large servers are running, the virtual network functions just like a normal network similar to what is currently found in the real world minus the extra hardware and support cost.

Virtual Switches

A virtual switch is similar to a physical switch in that both server the same function. The function that both types of switches serve is to look up MAC destinations and sources, forward frames according to their MAC addresses, and even create VLANs inside the virtual network. One way that virtual switches differ from physical switches is that the Spanning-Tree Protocol is not needed to protect from loops as the process of vitalizing any switches in a virtual network does not allow for loops to take place.

Perhaps the biggest difference between physical switches and virtual switches is that a virtual switch does not exist in the physical world. Instead a virtual switch is a software construct inside a virtual network, which is also a software construct. The purpose of a virtual switch is to allow virtual devices such as workstations and servers to communicate with each other through the software environment.

Virtual Desktops

When talking about virtual networking, a virtual desktop is simply a virtual operating system setup in a virtual environment to allow end users to run software programs. It may be better to think of virtual desktops as virtual workstations since the term virtual desktop has been used in the past to refer to multiple desktop environments with the GUI of a windows type operating system. In one of the labs in this Lesson, we will be setting up a virtual workstation environment on a local computer.

Multiple virtual workstations can be created on a local computer and then linked together to create a simulated networking environment. In this situation the local computer's processing power, host operating system, and system resources are used to create the virtual networking environment.

CERTIFICATION READY
What are some of the components that may be found in a virtual network?
1.9

Virtual workstations can also be stored on a virtual server somewhere and run inside a physical device physically connected to the server containing the virtual workstations. In this situation all processing is done by the server but the environment on the local device looks and acts like the actual operating system being virtualized. This allows the end user to run operating systems and software that is not native to the physical platform being used.

An extreme case of running a virtualized operating on a different platform would be to appear to run Windows 7 on an iPad 2.0. The iPad cannot of course run Windows 7; however, a special client virtualization software called VSphere from VMWare can run on the iPad. The way this scenario would work is that a VMWare ESX virtual server somewhere would contain Windows 7 virtual workstations. The iPad would contain the VMWare client software called VSphere. The iPad would then connect to the virtual server via a physical network connection and run the Windows 7 virtual workstation inside the VSphere client. This would give the appearance of running Windows 7 and related software on the iPad when in reality, the Windows 7 virtual machine and related software is really running on a VMWare ESX server somewhere. The described scenario is actually currently possible using the software and hardware mentioned.

Virtual Servers

Virtual servers can be one of two things. They can be server programs that are designed to create and support virtual networks. An example of this type of virtual server would be the ESX Server from VMWare.

Another type of virtual server would be a server that is setup in a virtual environment to support some function that a real server would do in a physical network environment. Any function carried out by a physical server in a physical network can be carried out by a virtual server in a virtual network environment. Virtual servers can even be used as domain controllers in virtual network environment.

Virtual PBX

As the name suggest, a virtual PBX is a PBX switch that has been virtualized on a network. A virtual PBX switch works just like a physical PBX switch in that it is used to switch voice calls to the appropriate destination. The difference is that instead of purchasing specialized equipment to do this, a virtual PBX can be setup on a server to do the same job. Using a virtual PBX is usually much cheaper than using dedicated equipment to do the same thing.

On-site verses Off-site

The terms On-site and Off-site in this situation simply refer to where the hardware containing your virtual network is located. If the hardware containing your virtual network is located on the site it is being used at, it is called on-site. If the hardware being used to contain your virtual network is located somewhere other than the site where it is being used, it is called off-site.

There are a couple of advantages to having an on-site virtual network. One advantage to an on-site virtual network is that if anything were to go wrong with the hardware housing it you will have easy access to it and may more easily fix the problem. Another advantage is that the network speeds of a LAN are generally greater than the speeds of a WAN and so you can access the virtual network more quickly. The biggest disadvantage is that if you have more than one site, it becomes more difficult to keep all the sites updated to each other and synchronized. Other disadvantages may include higher equipment cost and greater backup costs.

There are also a couple of advantages to using off-site virtual networks. One such advantage is that if you have many smaller sites, rather than having to setup a network in each site, all you have to do is create a single virtual network in one site and allow the other sites to access it over a WAN connection. This cuts down significantly on hardware cost for each site. Another advantage is that with the entire virtual network centralized to one location, keeping multiple sites synchronized is not a problem as they are all effectively using the same network. A disadvantage is that WAN connections tend to be slower than LAN connection and so accessing the virtual network may take more time. Another disadvantage is a single point of failure. If all sites use the same off-site virtual network, if something were to happen to the hardware running it, all sites would no longer be able to function until the problem is resolved.

Network as a Service (NaaS)

Network as a Service is a new idea in networking that has only recently become possible with the ability to virtualize networks. Rather than selling access to a specific physical network such as the AT&T Network or the Verizon Network, NaaS proposes that vendors should sell network access period. With NaaS, who the hardware of the network belongs to does not matter; rather what matters is the network service consumers are purchasing.

> **CERTIFICATION READY**
> What is Network as a Service (NaaS)?
> 1.9

The idea of Naas has initially been strongly resisted by various vendors because they want to have control over who can access their hardware and what those accessing it can do with it. This is a reasonable concern given how much money these various vendors have invested in their network infrastructures. However, recently some of this resistance has weakened. One indication of this resistance weakening has come from Cisco. Cisco proposed an Openstack:NaaS model that provides open source APIs and protocols needed to make NaaS work back in April of 2011. We will have to wait and see where this all will go. As a side note, NaaS is sometimes referred to as Cloud Computing.

SKILL SUMMARY

IN THIS LESSON YOU LEARNED:

- About various network connectivity devices such as NICs, modems, and wireless NICs.
- What a media converter is and how it is used in modern networks.
- What repeaters and hubs are and the role they play in networking.
- What bridges and switches are and how they are related.
- About some of the various types of switches that are available for use in modern networks.
- What VLANs are and how they are configured and how they are used in networking.

- About some advanced switch-related topics such as port mirroring, port authentication, trunking, and PoE.
- What a spanning tree is and how it is used by a switch.
- What CSU/DSUs are and the role they play in networking.
- Some basic information about routers and how they are used in a network.
- What firewalls are and some of their basic function in networking.
- About several different types of servers that are commonly used in modern networks.
- About some additional network devices that are used in various types of networks such as multifunction devices, IDS/IPS, load balancers, and bandwidth shapers.
- About common wireless network devices that are in use today and how they are used in conjunction with wired network devices.

Knowledge Assessment

Fill in the Blank

Complete the following sentences by writing the correct word or words in the blanks provided.

1. NIC can stand for either _____ or _____.

2. Modem stands for _____.

3. A device called a _____ is used to convert one type of cable or wired technology to another.

4. One way to describe a hub is to describe it as a multiport _____.

5. Bridges use _____ to determine which frames to allow through and which frames to not allow through.

6. _____ are used to break up a larger LAN into smaller LANs based on which port a device is connected to on a switch.

7. The algorithm used by a group of switches to ensure that no loops are set up between the switches is called _____.

8. The technology that is used to send power over a LAN connection is called _____.

9. _____ are used to control access to a network based on packet headers.

10. When two firewalls are set up in a network, the area between them is called a _____, and is used to isolate certain publicly accessed devices such as web and e-mail servers from private network devices such as domain controllers and file servers.

Multiple Choice

Circle the letter corresponding to the correct answer.

1. Which term best describes a device that is built into a computer's motherboard that allows that computer to access a network?
   a. Network Interface Card
   b. Network Interface Controller
   c. Bridge
   d. Bandwidth Shaper

2. What device is used to convert analog signals to digital signals and digital signals to analog signals?
   a. Media converter
   b. Repeater
   c. Modem
   d. CSU/DSU

3. What is the technique called where all communications within a switch are repeated to one particular port?
   a. Port authentication
   b. Trunking
   c. Bandwidth shaping
   d. Port mirroring

4. The ability of a switch to send data from multiple VLANS through the same data link is called what?
   a. Trunking
   b. Load balancing
   c. Port mirroring
   d. PoE

5. A device that is used to change a digital signal from one frame format to another frame format such as Frame Relay to Ethernet or Ethernet to Frame Relay is called what?
   a. Modem
   b. Media converter
   c. CSU/DSU
   d. IDS/IPS

6. What does CSU/DSU stand for?
   a. Carrier Sensing Unit/Data Sensing Unit
   b. Channel Service Unit/Data Service Unit
   c. Carrier Service Unit/Data Service Unit
   d. Channel Sensing Unit/Data Service Unit

7. What type of server is used to convert URLs to IP addresses?
   a. DNS server
   b. DHCP server
   c. Proxy server
   d. Domain controller server

8. What networking device is used to detect network intrusion?
   a. Firewall
   b. Switch
   c. IDS
   d. IPS

9. What functions can a proxy server perform? (Choose all that apply.)
   a. Keep the computers behind the proxy server anonymous
   b. Set up access policies to different network services and/or content
   c. Bypass security or services
   d. Scan inbound or outbound content for malware or other security risks

10. What network device is used to distribute the load of a network evenly between multiple devices?
    a. Bandwidth shaper
    b. Proxy server
    c. DNS
    d. Load balancer

Lab Exercises

Connecting Two Computers Using Crossover Cables

The purpose of this lab is to show the student how to connect two computers together using a crossover cable. In order to do this the student will learn how to share files using Windows XP and connect computers using NICs and a crossover cable. After completing this lab the student will have a basic understanding of how to connect computers together into a peer-to-peer network.

MATERIALS
- Two computers running Windows XP Professional
- The crossover cable created in the Lesson 3 Lab
- Paper
- Pen or pencil

DO THE LAB
Write down three things you need to be able to do/have based on the above.

Connect the Computers Together

1. Make sure both computers are turned off.
2. Connect one end of the crossover cable to the network card in computer 1; it does not matter which end.
3. Connect the other end of the crossover cable to the network card in computer 2.

Configure the Two Computers

1. Turn both computers on. It does not matter which one you turn on first.
2. Sign in to Windows on both computers, as you normally do.
3. Wait until both computers have fully loaded Windows and all startup programs are shown in the System Tray.
4. With the left mouse button, click **Start** in the bottom left corner of the screen.
5. With the right mouse button, click **My Computer**, which should be located on the right pane of the *Start Menu*.
6. With the left mouse button, click **Properties** at the bottom of the *pop-up menu*.
7. With the left mouse button, click on the **Computer Name** tab.
8. Observe the *Workgroup name* listed on computer 1 and write it down exactly as shown on the screen.
9. On computer 2, with the left mouse button, click on the **Change...** button.
10. Type the **Workgroup name listed on computer 1** in the *Workgroup* textbox in computer 2 exactly as it was shown in computer 1.

11. With the left mouse button, click **OK**.

12. A message box appears that says something like *Welcome to the "Workgroup Name You Typed" workgroup*.

13. With the left mouse button, click **OK**.

14. Another message box will appear saying, **You must restart this computer for the changes to take effect**.

    With the left mouse button, click **OK** when you see this message.

15. The *System Properties* dialog box reappears with the *Computer Name* tab selected.

    With the left mouse button, click **OK** when this dialog box appears.

16. A message box will appear saying something like *You must restart your computer before the new settings will take effect. Do you want to restart your computer now?*

    With the left mouse button, click **Yes** when this message box appears.

17. Computer 2 restarts and both computers are now in the same workgroup.

18. Before proceeding to the next step, follow steps 7–11 to verify that both computers are showing the EXACT same workgroup name.

19. With the left mouse button, click **OK** on both computers, to close their *System Properties* dialog boxes.

Enable Sharing

1. With the left mouse button, click **Start**.

2. With the left mouse button, click **My Computer**.

3. With the right mouse button, click on the **Windows (C:)** or **Local Disk(C:)** hard disk drive or whichever other hard disk drive you may want to be able to exchange files with.

4. With the left mouse button, click **Sharing and Security...**.

5. With the left mouse button, click on the link **If you understand the risk but still want to share the root of the drive, click here**.

6. With the left mouse button, click on the link **If you understand the security risks but want to share files without running the wizard, click here**.

7. Select **Just enable file sharing**, by clicking on the circle with the left mouse button. When a circle is selected, a green dot will appear in that circle, indicating it has been selected.

8. With the left mouse button, click **OK**.

9. With the left mouse button, click on **the check box** next to *Share this folder on the network*. Once the box is selected a green check mark will appear in the box indicating it has been selected. The hard disk drive name will appear in the *Share name* text box as the default name "Share name." If you do not want to use the default name, you can rename it.

10. With the left mouse button, click on **the check box** next to *Allow network users to change my files*. Again, a green checkmark will appear in the box indicating it has been selected. When you do this step, it will allow you full access to the drive and its files.

11. With the left mouse button, click **OK**.

12. The *Setting folder permissions...* dialog box will briefly appear. Once it does, the *My Computer* window will reappear with a hand holding the hard disk drive, indicating that it is now shared.

13. With the left mouse button, double-click on **Windows (C:)** or **Local Disk(C:)** hard disk drive. If you changed drives before sharing them, then double-click on whichever hard disk drive the files and folders are located on that you want to gain access to.

14. With the left mouse button, double-click **Documents and Settings**.

15. With the right mouse button, click on **the folder** or **User Name** where the files and folders are located that you want to gain access to.

16. With the left mouse button, click on the **Sharing and Security...** link.

17. With the left mouse button, click on **the check box** *Make this folder private* to remove the check mark from the box. If there is no check mark in the box already, skip down to step 18.

18. With the left mouse button, click on **the check box** next to the *Share this folder on the network* link to place a check in the box. The user's folder name will appear in the *Share name* text box as the default *Share name*. Again you can rename it to a different share name if you so desire.

19. With the left mouse button, click on **the checkbox** next to *Allow network users to change my files* to place a check in the box.

20. With the left mouse button, click **OK**.

21. The *Setting folder permissions...* dialog box will briefly appear.

22. A hand holding the folder appears, indicating the folder is now shared.

23. With the left mouse button, click the **Close** button to close the *C:\Documents and Settings* window.

24. Repeat steps 18–23 to share other folders on the other computers.

> **TAKE NOTE** *
>
> It could take up to 15 minutes for the computers to start showing up. It is a known issue with the Windows XP Computer Browser function. It is quicker to just restart all computers, if one of them is not showing up.

Verify the Share in Network Places

1. With the left mouse button, click **Start**.

2. With the left mouse button, click **Control Panel**.

3. With the left mouse button, click **Network Connections** or **Network and Internet Connections**, then **Network Connections**.

4. With the left mouse button, click on **My Network Places**, below *Other Places*, on the left side of the screen.

5. With the left mouse button, click on **View workgroup computers**, below *Network Tasks*, on the left side of the screen.

6. With the left mouse button, double-click on **one of the computers** to view the shared folders/files on it.

7. You will see your computers. It is best practice to have all computers in the same workgroup, so they will show up on the other computers.

8. If you do not see your computers, then you may have a "firewall" of sorts running on your computer. You will need to either configure your firewall to allow file sharing between computers or temporarily shut the firewall down.

9. You can now exchange data between the two computers.

■ Lab 2

Connecting Multiple Computers Together Using a Switch or Hub

The purpose of this lab is to connect more than one computer together using a switch or a hub. Using switches is preferable for this lab because switches are what a student is most likely to see in the corporate world. After completing this lab, the student will be familiar with what is involved in connecting multiple computers together via a switch or hub.

MATERIALS

- More than one computer with NICs in them and running Windows XP
- The straight-through cable created in Lesson 3 lab
- A switch or hub
- Paper
- Pen or pencil

DO THE LAB

Build a Network Using a Switch or Hub

1. Make sure all the computers are off.
2. Connect each computer to the switch or hub by using a straight-through cable to connect each computer's NIC to a port on the switch or hub.
3. Go through the steps laid out under the heading *Verify the Share in Network Places* in Lab 1 to verify that all the computers connected to the switch or hub can see each other and share data. If a computer cannot be seen on the network, go through the necessary components of Lab 1 for each computer that is not seen on the network so that it can be seen.

Lab 3

Connecting Multiple Switches or Hubs Together in a Single Network

The purpose of this lab is to teach the student how to link multiple switches or hubs together in a single network. After completing this lab the student will be familiar with the concepts behind linking multiple switches or hubs together in a single network. As in Lab 2, switches are preferable to hubs for this lab because the student in more likely to see switches in the corporate world than they are to see hubs.

MATERIALS

- Two or more networks from Lab 2
- Straight-through cables to connect the various switches or hubs together
- Paper
- Pencil

DO THE LAB

Connect Multiple Networks Together Using Switches or Hubs

1. Link two or more switches with their computers still connected together using a straight-through cable.
2. Check whether the computers connected to the different switches are all part of the same workgroup using the appropriate steps from Lab 1. If they are not, change the workgroup names in the computers so that they all use the same workgroup name. Do this by following the appropriate steps in the first section of Lab 1.

3. Go through the steps laid out under the heading *Verify the Share in Network Places* in Lab 1 to verify that all the computers connected to the switch or hub can see each other and share data. If a computer cannot be seen on the network, go through the necessary components of Lab 1 for each computer that is not seen on the network so that it can be seen.

■ Lab 4

Creating a Virtual Workstation using VMPlayer

In this lab the student will download, or have their professor download ahead of time, the installation file for VMPlayer and an ISO for a Linux distribution, sometimes called a Linux distro. For the purposes of this lab I have chosen to use MintOS 11, which is a Windows like variation of the Linux distro called Ubuntu.

In the first part of this lab the student will install VMPlayer and look at some of its capabilities. In the second part of this lab the student will use VMPlayer to create and install a virtual machine of the Linux distro they downloaded. Once they have created and installed the virtual machine, they will then use it and explore the Linux operating system.

This lab will introduce the student to concepts of virtual computing, software related to virtual computing, how to install a Linux operating system, and how to use the Linux operating system with a graphical interface.

MATERIALS

- The file VMware-player-3.1.4-385536.exe or a newer version
- The ISO linuxmint-11-gnome-cd-nocodecs-32bit.iso or the ISO of a Linux distro of your professor's choice
- A computer running Windows XP or later
- Paper
- Pencil

TAKE NOTE *

VMPlayer is a fully functional educational and personal use version of VMWare's VMWorkstation software and does not have a usage time limit on it. The only difference between VMPlayer and VMWorkstation is that VMWorkstation had some additional functionality that VMPlayer does not.

DO THE LAB

Obtaining the Needed Files

1. The two files listed above can be downloaded both legally and free from the Internet.
2. To download the VMware-player file go to www.filehippo.com and search for VMPlayer.
   a. Once you have found the file listed above, or a later version of it, download it to the local computer.
   b. Alternatively your professor can download the file ahead of time and store it in a network location.
   c. Write down the location where this file is saved on the local computer.

3. To download the Linux ISO listed above you will need to go to the website http://www.linuxmint.com/edition.php?id=83. The version being downloaded from this location is the 32-bit CD no Codex version.

   a. Once you have found the ISO file listed above, download it to the local computer.

   b. Alternatively your professor can download the file ahead of time and store it in a network location.

   c. Write down the location where this file is saved on the local computer.

Install VMPlayer

1. Navigate to the VMPlayer installation file downloaded previously.

2. Double click the MVPlayer installation file. Figure 6-27 shows what the installation dialog box should look like.

Figure 6-27

VMPlayer initial installation dialog box

3. Press the <Next> button and take the default options until you reach a dialog box similar to Figure 6-28. Once you see this dialog box, click on <Continue>.

Figure 6-28

VMPlayer's "Ready to Perform Requested Operations" dialog box

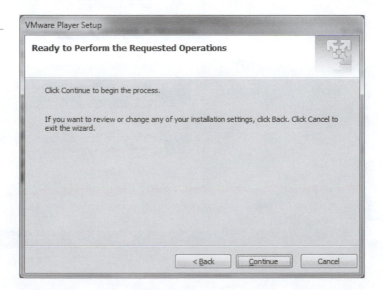

4. Once the VMPlayer installation program has completed its installation, the dialog box in Figure 6-29 will be displayed. When you see this dialog box, close all open programs and click on the <Restart> control button in the "Setup Wizard Complete" dialog box.

5. Once the system has restarted, locate the VMPlayer icon on the Desktop and double-click it. This will load the VMPlayer program. When loaded, VMPlayer will look similar to Figure 6-30.

6. VMPlayer is now installed and running in Windows.
7. Look around in VMPlayer and view some of the Help options available in VMPlayer.
8. Close VMPlayer.

Creating Your First Virtual Machine

1. Once you have installed and restarted your computer, you need to Double Click on the icon for VMPlayer and bring up the same dialog box as shown in Figure 6-30.

2. In the left hand pane of VMPlayer you will notice for icons. Double Click the icon labeled "Create a New Virtual Machine".

3. Once you have completed step 2 a dialog box similar to the one in Figure 6-31 will come up.

Figure 6-31

VMPlayer New Virtual Machine Wizard

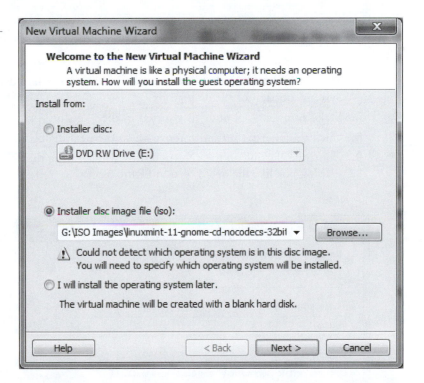

4. Click on the radial button labeled "Installer disc image file (iso):"

5. Click on the <Browse> button located to the left of the above radial button and browse to the location where your ISO image has been stored. This will point the new virtual machine to where it needs to go in order to install the guest operating system. Once you have clicked on the ISO you want to use, click on the <Next> button. After clicking on the <Next> button you will get a dialog box that looks like Figure 6-32.

Figure 6-32

VMPlayer New Virtual
Machine Wizard "Select Guest
Operating System" dialog box

Figure 6-32

VMPlayer New Virtual
Machine Wizard "Select Guest
Operating System" dialog box

6. Make sure that the radial button labeled "Linux" is selected in the "Guest Operating System" portion of the dialog box.

7. Make sure that "Ubuntu" is selected in the "Version" part of the dialog box.

8. Click the <Next> button to move on to the next dialog box.

9. Continue clicking on the <Next> button while leaving the default settings until you reach a dialog box like the one shown in Figure 6-33.

Figure 6-33

VMPlayer New Virtual Machine
Wizard "Name the Virtual
Machine" dialog box

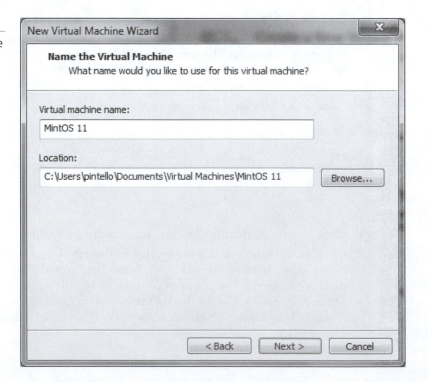

10. In the "Virtual Machine Name" portion of the dialog box, type a name that will tell you what this virtual machine is. As you can see from Figure 6-33, I named my virtual machine "MintOS 11" you can use whatever name reminds you exactly what the virtual machine is.

11. Take the default setting in the "Location" portion of the dialog box.

12. Click <Next> and continue taking default settings until you reach a dialog box similar to Figure 6-34.

Figure 6-34

VMPlayer New Virtual Machine Wizard "Ready to Create Virtual Machine" dialog box

13. Click the <Finish> button in this dialog box. If a dialog box comes up talking about removable devices simply click the <OK> button for that dialog box. Once you have done this, a dialog box similar to the one found in Figure 6-35 will come up.

Figure 6-35

VMPlayer New Virtual Machine Wizard "VMWareTools" dialog box

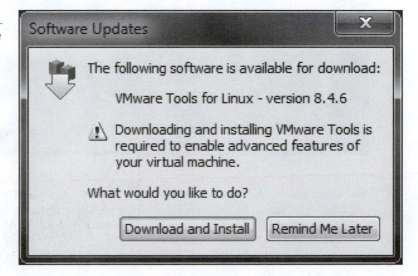

14. It is very important that you click the <Remind Me Later> button in this dialog box because you cannot install VMTools in a Linux Guest Operating System like you can a Windows Quest Operating System. The next part of this Lab will walk us through the process of installing VMTools in a Linux Guest Operating System. Once you click the <Remind Me Later> button a screen similar to Figure 3-36 will come up.

Figure 6-36

VMPlayer MintOS virtual
machine with message box

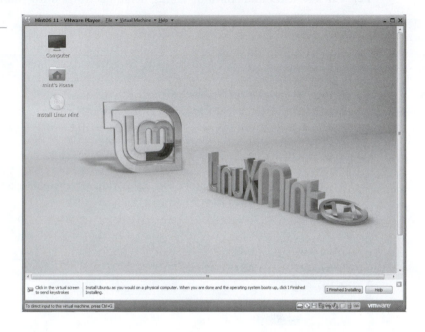

15. On the bottom part of the screen there is a message box. Click on the "I Finished Installing" button to make that message box go away. When you do, you will have a screen like Figure 6-37 where that bottom message box has disappeared.

Figure 6-37

VMPlayer MintOS virtual
machine without message box

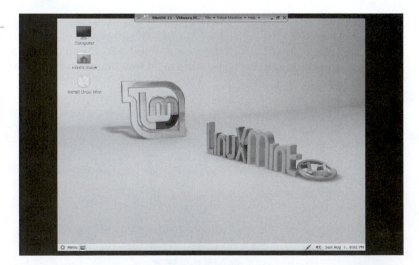

16. Once you have a screen similar to Figure 3-37 up, fine the icon on the MintOS desktop that says "Install Linux Mint". This icon will allow you to install MintOS as a full blown virtual machine that will act just like a computer where the MintOS operating system is installed directly into the computer.

17. Double Click the "Install Linux MintOS" icon. When you do this a screen similar to Figure 6-38 will come up.

Figure 6-38

VMPlayer MintOS virtual machine "Allocated Space" install dialog box

18. Make sure that the radial button labeled "Erase disk and install Linux Mint" is highlighted like in Figure 6-38 and then click on the <Forward> button.

19. Continue clicking on the <Forward> button and taking the default options until you come to a screen like the one shown in Figure 3-39.

Figure 6-39

VMPlayer MintOS virtual machine "Erase and install Linux Mint" install dialog box

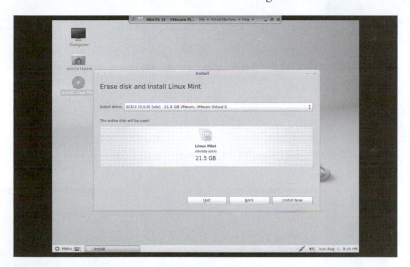

20. Once you have a screen like the one shown in Figure 6-39 up, click on the <Install Now> button. Once the <Install Now> button has been clicked a screen similar to the one in Figure 6-40 will come up.

Figure 6-40

VMPlayer MintOS virtual machine "Who are you" install dialog box not populated

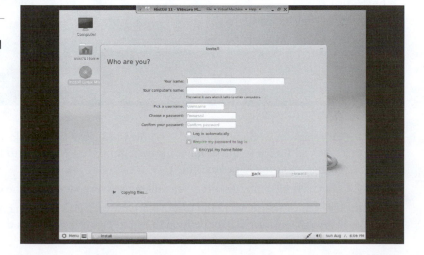

21. In the dialog box like the one that appears in Figure 6-40 type your first name in the text field labeled "Your Name". When you do this the field labeled "Your Computer's Name" will automatically be populated.

22. In the field labeled "Pick a Username" you can enter the username you would prefer to use.

23. Finally choose a password and type it in the "Choose a password" field and retype it in the "Confirm your password" field. When you get done your dialog box should look something like the dialog box shown in Figure 6-41.

Figure 6-41

VMPlayer MintOS virtual machine "Who are you" install dialog box populated

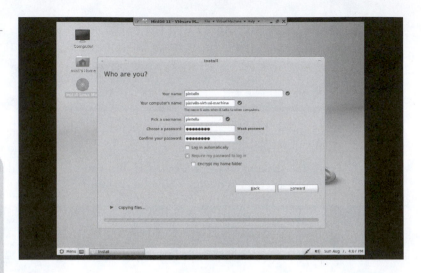

TAKE NOTE *

It is very important to note that Linux is case sensitive. This means that if you choose to use a capital letter in your username you will have to make sure you use the capital letter whenever you log into Linux as well.

24. When the "Who are you" dialog box is completely filled out click on the <Forward> button.

25. Keep clicking the <Forward> button and accepting the default settings until you reach a dialog box that looks like the one in Figure 6-42.

Figure 6-42

VMPlayer MintOS virtual machine "Installation Complete" dialog box

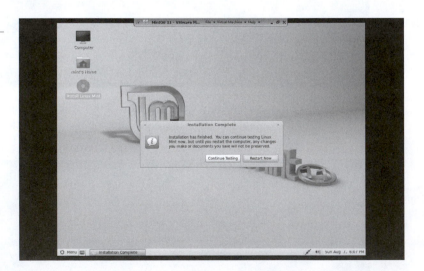

26. Once you have the dialog box up shown in Figure 6-42 click the <Restart Now> button. This will force the quest operating system inside VMPlayer to restart and make all the changes you made permanent.

27. Once MintOS has restarted you will get a screen similar to the one shown in Figure 6-43.

28. Click on your username and enter your password. This will bring up the MintOS desktop. This will look just like the desktop shown in Figure 6-37 minus the "Install Linux Mint" icon.

Figure 6-43

VMPlayer MintOS virtual machine logon screen

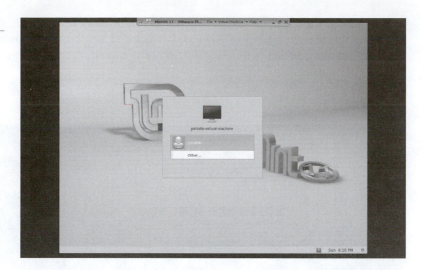

29. Congratulations, you have successfully installed Linux MintOS into VMPlayer. The Linux installation process you followed here is exactly the same installation process you would have followed to install this Operating System directly onto a computer.
30. Leave MintOS open and active for the next section of this Lab.

Installing VM-Tools inside Linux

VMTools is not absolutely necessary for using a virtual machine inside VMPlayer. However, VMTools do make it easier for the Guest operating system running inside VMPlayer to interact with the Host operating system that VMPlayer is running on more smoothly.

When installing a Windows based Guest operating system, VMTools can be installed at the time the Guest operating system is installed. However, when running a Linux or Unix based Guest operating system VMTools needs to be installed separately. This section of Lab 4 will take you through the process of installing VMTools on the MintOS Guest operating system using the Graphical Software Management Tool that comes with MintOS.

1. Make sure that the Linux MintOS Quest operating system is running and that your are on the MintOS desktop that you ended on in the last section.
2. Click on the "Menu" button in the bottom left hand side of the MintOS desktop and a Start Menu similar to the one shown in Figure 6-44 will come up.

Figure 6-44

MintOS start menu

3. On the left hand side of the MintOS start menu under the heading "System" is a program button labeled "Software Manager". Click on the "Software Manager" menu option. When you do a program dialog box similar to the one shown in Figure 6-45 will come up.

Figure 6-45

MintOS Software Manager program dialog box

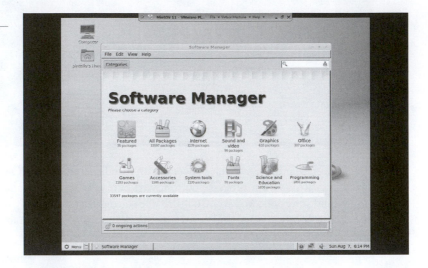

4. As can be seen from the screen shot in Figure 6-45, there are over 33,000 packages available for download. All the programs are free. Some time you may want to look at the different programs available in the different categories to see what is available. For our purposes we will use the search tool in the upper right hand corner of the package manager to look for VMTools. To do this, place the word "vmware" in the search tool like shown in Figure 6-46.

Figure 6-46

MintOS Software Manager program dialog box with "vmware" in the search tool

5. Once you have searched for "vmware" you will notice that 7 packages came up. The package we are interested in is the one labeled "open-vm-toolbox". Double click on the package named "open-vm-toolbox". When you do the screen shown in Figure 6-47 will come up.

Figure 6-47

MintOS Software Manager
install screen for "
open-vm-toolbox"

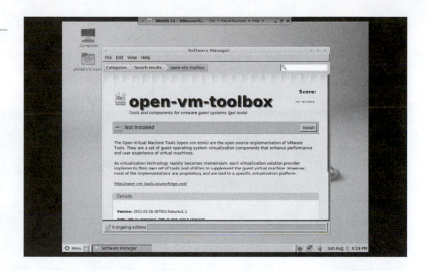

6. When the screen shown in Figure 6-47 comes up click on the button labeled "install". Once this package is done installing, all components needed for VMTools. Click the X in the upper right hand corner to close the Software Management Tools.

7. Once VMTools is installed, look around MintOS and get a feel for it. You may also want to go back into the Software Management Tool and see if there are other programs you would like to install.

8. List some things you like about MintOS.

9. List some things you did not like about MintOS.

10. How do you think MintOS compares to Windows?

11. Once you are finish looking around in MintOS, go back to the start "Menu" button and Quit MintOS. The Quit button will be the Menu option at the very bottom of the Start Menu on the left hand side. When you click on the Quit option, the Shutdown Computer dialog box will come up as shown in Figure 6-48.

Figure 6-48

MintOS Shutdown Computer screen

12. To complete shutting down MintOS, click the "Shutdown" option. Once you do that you will be taken back to the VMPlayer main screen. This will look like Figure 6-49.

Figure 6-49

VMPlayer opening screen with MintOS shown in the left hand pane

13. If you wish to go back into the MintOS virtual machine, simply open up VMPlayer and Double-Click the MintOS option in the left hand pane. This will begin the process of loading the MintOS virtual machine so that you can begin using it again.

LAN Technologies

EXAM OBJECTIVE MATRIX

TECHNOLOGY SKILL COVERED	EXAM OBJECTIVE	EXAM OBJECTIVE NUMBER

LAN Technologies	**Compare and contrast different LAN technologies.**
	• Types:
	  • Ethernet
	  • 10BaseT
	  • 100BaseT
	  • 1000BaseT
	  • 100BaseTX
	  • 100BaseFX
	  • 1000BaseX
	  • 10GBaseSR
	  • 10GBaseLR
	  • 10GBaseER
	  • 10GBaseSW
	  • 10GBaseLW
	  • 10GBaseEW
	  • 10GBaseT
	• Properties:
	  • CSMA/CD
	  • CSMA/CA
		3.7

Other LAN Concepts	**Compare and contrast different LAN technologies.**
	• Properties:
	  • Broadcast
	  • Collision
	  • Bonding
	  • Speed
	  • Distance
		3.7

Wireless LAN Technologies	**Given a scenario, install and configure a wireless network.** • WAP placement • Antenna types • Interference • Frequencies • Channels • SSID (enable/disable)	2.2

	Given a scenario, implement appropriate wireless security measures.	5.1
	• Encryption protocols:	
	• WEP	
	• WPA	
	• WPA2	
	• WPA Enterprise	
	• MAC address filtering	
	• Device placement	
	• Signal strength	
SOHO Network Technologies	**Given a set of requirements, plan and implement a basic SOHO network.**	2.6
	• List of requirements	
	• Cable length	
	• Device types/requirements	
	• Environment limitations	
	• Equipment limitations	
	• Compatibility requirements	

KEY TERMS

ad hoc wireless network

baseband

bit

bonding

broadband

broadcast

broadcast networking

Carrier Sense Multiple Access with Collision Avoidance (CSMA/CA)

Carrier Sense Multiple Access with Collision Detection (CSMA/CD)

channel

channel bonding

collision

collision domain

contention-based access method

distance

encryption

Ethernet

Ethernet_802.2

Ethernet_802.3

Ethernet bonding

Ethernet DIX

Ethernet II

Ethernet SNAP

gigabits per second (gbps)

infrastructure wireless network

kilobits per second (kbps)

link aggregation

MAC address filtering

megabits per second (mbps)

Multilink trunking (MLT)

Network Fault Tolerance (NFT)

Novell Ethernet

port bonding

Redundant Array of Independent Nodes (RAIN)

Service Set Identifier (SSID)

Small Office Home Office (SOHO)

speed

Synchronous Optical Network (SONET)

terabits per second (tbps)

George is a network engineer at a local hospital. He has been tasked by his boss to come up with a way for all the records of a patient who is in the hospital to be accessed from anywhere in the hospital. The solution George comes up with must also ensure that all changes to a patient's records be updated as soon as any changes are made to their record. What technology can George use to accomplish this task?

■ LAN Technologies

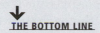

THE BOTTOM LINE

This section of Lesson 7 discusses some of the current LAN technologies that are available as well as some older technologies that are not in general use anymore. A particular emphasis in this section is placed on Ethernet technologies and CSMA/CD, which is used by Ethernet to access a network.

As has been previously discussed previously in this book, networking technologies come in two types, wide area network (WAN) and local area network (LAN) technologies. While there is beginning to be a convergence in these two technology areas, it is still in the very early stages. For the time being, the two technologies are still very distinct and different from each other. Because of this, these technologies are discussed as separate topics in this book. This lesson concentrates on those technologies that are used in LAN networks. Lesson 8 deals with WAN technologies.

Ethernet Frames

Ethernet is one of the oldest and the most widely used LAN technologies in use today. A group headed by Xerox Corporation first developed Ethernet between 1973 and 1975. Because of how old it is, initially there was not a set standard for Ethernet. The four types of Ethernet available are the result of different frame types that have been used for it over the years. The most widely used Ethernet frame type is called *Ethernet II* or *Ethernet DIX*. The DIX stands for (DEC, Intel, and Xerox), which are the three companies that worked together to develop this Ethernet frame type. Ethernet II or DIX is the most commonly used Ethernet frame today, mainly because it can be used directly by the Internet Protocol (IP).

Back when Xerox and company first developed Ethernet, Novell wanted to standardize it and approached the IEEE to do so. However, when the IEEE went to create an Ethernet standard, they did not take into consideration the implementation already used by Xerox and company or how the Ethernet standard was to work in the overall OSI Model. Put simply, they forgot, did not consider, or simply overlooked the fact that a Layer 2 Data Link protocol needed a Layer 2 Data Link identifier to work. However, in their defense, Novell claims that at the time of the development of the IEEE 802.3 standard, such an identifier was not needed. The end result is that this standard became Ethernet standard IEEE 802.3 (raw), which is sometimes referred to Ethernet_802.3. As a result of the way that Ethernet 802.3 was constructed, it can only run with Novell's IPX packets, and because of that, some people have called it *Novell Ethernet*.

Because *Ethernet_802.3* does not have an identifier number to enable it to work with the Data Link sublayer of the OSI Model, IEEE had to modify their standard. This modification became known as the Ethernet IEEE 802.2 Logical Link Control (LLC) standard, which is sometimes referred to as *Ethernet_802.2*. Basically, what this standard does is add the capability to the Ethernet_802.3 frame header that enables it to have an identifier so that it works with the Data Link sublayer of the OSI Model. This allows this Ethernet frame type to work with more than just the IPX protocol.

One of the main limitations of Ethernet_802.2_LLC is that its header can only support 128 protocols. While this is a large number, in point of fact there are more than protocols than that in the TCP/IP Protocol Suite. In order for a network to use Ethernet_802.2_LLC it had to be limited to 128 protocols on a single network. This did not sit well with the Internet community, so Ethernet_802.2_LLC was modified to allow a larger number of protocols to run on the network. This became known as ***Ethernet SNAP*** or Ethernet Subnetwork Access Protocol.

Ethernet Communications Methods

We have just finished discussing the different frame types available for Ethernet. The next topic of discussion is how Ethernet transfers data on a network. There are generally two main ways that Ethernet does this. One method is called Carrier Sense Multiple Access with Collision Detection (CSMA/CD), and the other is called Carrier Sense Multiple Access with Collision Avoidance (CSMA/CA). Both methods are considered contention-based access methods. In a ***contention-based access method***, the different nodes on the network segment compete to see which node is able to send out its packet first. Both methods are very much first-come, first-serve methods of access. The first node to get its packet on the network is the one to send its packet first. The next two sections of Lesson 7 will discuss these two methods.

CARRIER SENSE MULTIPLE ACCESS WITH COLLISION DETECTION (CSMA/CD)

Carrier Sense Multiple Access with Collision Detection (CSMA/CD) is the primary method that Ethernet uses to access wired LANs. Ethernet uses a different method to access wireless LANs.

When Ethernet was first created it was intended for bus-based networks. As a result, it needed to have a way to access a bus-based network without having packets constantly colliding into each other. To accomplish this, CSMA/CD was developed. The way that CSMA/CD works is as follows.

Figure 7-1 illustrates the process that is used when Ethernet sends data across a LAN using CSMA/CD. When a computer or node on a network needs to send a packet to another computer or node on the network, the first thing it does is listen to the network to make sure that another node is not in the process of sending a packet. If a different node is in the process of sending a packet, it waits for a time and listens again. If no other node is sending on the network, the node that needs to send a packet sends it. This part of the process is the Carrier Sense Multiple Access part of sending a packet on an Ethernet network using CSMA/CD.

Figure 7-1

Bus-based network using CSMA/CD to send a packet

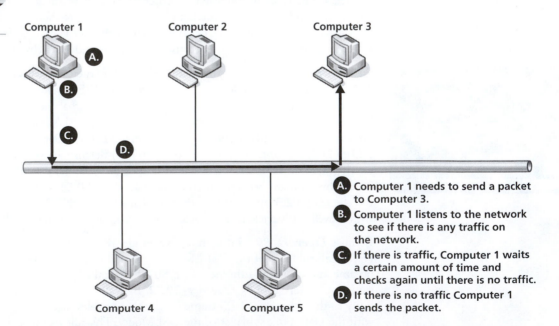

A. Computer 1 needs to send a packet to Computer 3.

B. Computer 1 listens to the network to see if there is any traffic on the network.

C. If there is traffic, Computer 1 waits a certain amount of time and checks again until there is no traffic.

D. If there is no traffic Computer 1 sends the packet.

There is one main weakness with CSMA/CD as a means of accessing a network. That weakness is that more than one computer can send data across the network at one time. This happens when two different computers need to send data at the same time. Both computers will listen to the network and neither computer will hear any activity on said network. This leads both computers to conclude that it is clear for them to send data. The result is that both computers end up sending data packets simultaneously; however, because only one data packet can be on the network cable at one time, a collision occurs. The collision results in a power spike on the network as well as the data in the two different packets being destroyed. Figure 7-2 shows what this collision looks like. In Figure 7-2 Computers 1 and 5 send data packets at the same time resulting in the collision that is symbolized by the starburst where the two data paths meet.

Figure 7-2

Bus-based network using CSMA/CD to send a packet when a collision occurs

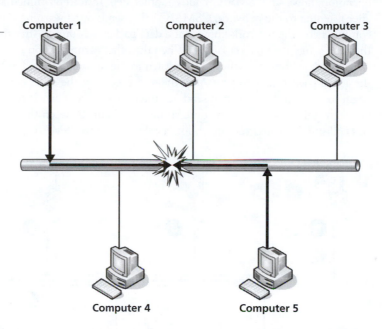

Fortunately, CSMA/CD has a mechanism in place for collisions. When the power spike that results from the two packets colliding occurs, all the computers on the affected network segment are able to "hear" it. When the computers on the network segment hear a collision on the network, they all immediately activate something called a hold down timer. A hold down timer is a clock that activates in each NIC on the network and starts counting down from a randomly set point of time. While the clock on a particular NIC is counting down, it is unable to send any packets. As each computer on the network segment finishes its random countdown it is able to begin listening to the network again in order to find an open point where it can begin to send its data packet.

Figure 7-3 shows a network segment immediately after a collision has occurred. Each computer on the segment has its hold down timer set for a random amount of time from which it will begin to count down before it can send its data.

Figure 7-3

Bus-based network using CSMA/CD immediately after a collision

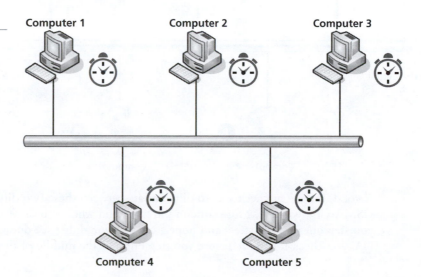

CARRIER SENSE MULTIPLE ACCESS WITH COLLISION AVOIDANCE (CSMA/CA)

Like CSMA/CD, *Carrier Sense Multiple Access with Collision Avoidance (CSMA/CA)* is a method used by Ethernet to access a local area network. Where CSMA/CD is most commonly used for *wired* networks, CSMA/CA is most commonly used for *wireless* networks.

Figure 7-4 illustrates how CSMA/CA works. CSMA/CA and CSMA/CD are very similar in operation; however, CSMA/CA adds another step. Instead of immediately sending its data packet after listening to the network, CSMA/CA first sends out a warning message letting all the other computers on the network know that a data packet is coming. After this warning is sent out, then the actual data packet is sent. When the other computers on the network segment hear the warning, they know that they cannot listen to the network to send out their own data until after the actual packet has come by. After the packet goes by, the other computers on the segment can begin to listen and compete to send out their own packet next. If two computers attempt to send out their warnings at the same time, a collision occurs between the two warning messages and this collision is treated very much like a collision in the CSMA/CD access method.

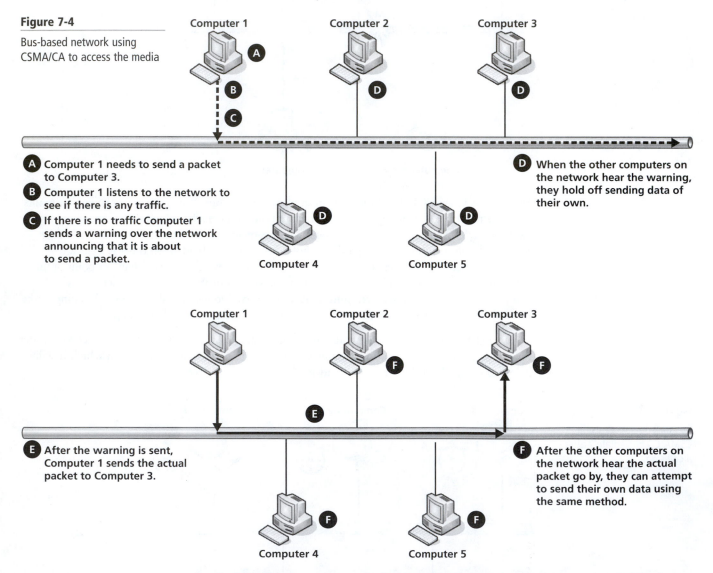

Figure 7-4

Bus-based network using CSMA/CA to access the media

A Computer 1 needs to send a packet to Computer 3.

B Computer 1 listens to the network to see if there is any traffic.

C If there is no traffic Computer 1 sends a warning over the network announcing that it is about to send a packet.

D When the other computers on the network hear the warning, they hold off sending data of their own.

E After the warning is sent, Computer 1 sends the actual packet to Computer 3.

F After the other computers on the network hear the actual packet go by, they can attempt to send their own data using the same method.

A good, tongue in cheek way to differentiate between these two different methods: In CSMA/CD, you check for traffic in the street and when you don't see any oncoming cars, you step out into the street and hope a car that you didn't see doesn't hit you. In CSMA/CA, you check for traffic before you step out into the middle of the street, and if you don't see any oncoming cars, you put your little bother out in the road with a sign telling any cars you didn't see to stop before you step out and hope he doesn't get hit.

Baseband Ethernet Technologies

Ethernet is a baseband technology. What **baseband** means is that a cable can only carry one signal one way at one time. In the case of most modern Ethernet cables, this means that there is one line for sending signals and another line for receiving signals. This is why collisions can take place on Ethernet setups. Since only one signal can travel down a wire at one time, if two signals attempt to use the same wire at the same time, a collision takes place. This explains why CSMA/CD or CSMA/CA is needed when Ethernet attempts to access media.

CERTIFICATION READY
Explain the naming convention used to differentiate types of LAN technologies that communicate data over a network?
3.7

In modern LAN configurations switches go a long way to alleviating collision issues. Switches do this by treating every network connection on the LAN as a microsegment that only has two computers connected to it, each with separate send and receive wires.

Over the years, LAN communications technologies have changed a great deal. To indicate these different changes a special naming convention has been worked out. A way to visualize and understand this naming convention is to think of it as *X*Base-*Y* naming convention. The *X* portion of the naming convention indicates the transfer rates possible for that particular media type. Usually this is some multiple of megabits per second (mbps). Thus a 10 would indicate a transfer rate of 10 mbps, and so on. If there is a capital G after the number, then that is the number of gigabits per second (gbps). In this way, 10G would indicate a 10 gbps transfer rate. The Base part of the naming convention indicates that it is a baseband media type.

CERTIFICATION READY
What are the different types of Ethernet technologies used to transfer data across various LANs? What are some older types of technologies used to transfer data across a LAN? What are the current types of technologies used to transfer data across a LAN? What are some technologies that may be used in the future to transfer data across a LAN?
3.7

If Broad is used in this location instead of Base, then that would indicate that the media type is broadband instead of baseband. A **broadband** media type is one that can carry multiple data signals on the same wire using some type of multiplexing. Finally, the *Y* indicates the type of media being used. Different letters indicate different types of media. For example a T usually indicates that the media used is unshielded twisted pair (UTP). A TX indicates that the media is full-duplex UTP. The best way to remember what the *Y* portion of the *X*Base-*Y* convention means is to simply memorize the *Y* portion because there is not set standard for how the *Y* portion is to be expressed.

Most of the various *X*Base-*Y* standards to be discussed here were set forth in the IEEE 802.3 standard or amended to that standard at a later date. Because of this, we include information about which IEEE 802.3 standard is used to specify each *X*Base-*Y* standard.

10BASE-5

10Base-5 was the first version of Ethernet that was widely used. Because it used thick coaxial cables to carry data, it was called Thick Ethernet. Both the original Ethernet II standard put forward in 1982 and the original IEEE 802.3 standard put forward in 1983 defined this type of Ethernet. The only difference between the two is how they defined certain fields in the header portion of the frame. 10Base-5 was a baseband technology that used thick coaxial cables for transmission. It had a 10 mbps throughput and a range of up to 500 meters.

> **TAKE NOTE***
>
> 10Base-5 and 10Base-2 Ethernet standards as well as some of the other Ethernet standards discussed here are rather old and are no longer likely to be found in real-world installations. Because the older Ethernet cabling standards can theoretically still show up on CompTIA Network1 exam, they are discussed here.

10BASE-2

10Base-2 was developed a couple of years later and was defined as the IEEE 802.3a standard. The main difference between 10Base-5 and 10Base-2 was that 10Base-2 used a thinner coaxial cable and only had a range of up to 185 meters. 10Base-2 came to be known as Thin Ethernet as opposed to 10Base-5, which was known as Thick Ethernet.

10BASE-T

The first twisted-pair version of the *X*Base-*Y* standard we will discuss is the 10Base-T standard. While this was not the first *X*Base-*Y* standard developed, it was the first developed for twisted pair. In 1990, IEEE 802.3i formalized the 10Base-T standard, which used CAT 3 UTP and could carry 10 mbps of throughput for a distance of 100 meters. 10Base-T was a baseband technology. This standard became known as Twisted Pair Ethernet.

100BASE-T

After Ethernet was introduced, 10 mbps remained the fastest Ethernet available until IEEE 802.3u was introduced in 1995. This standard permitted Ethernet to start functioning at speeds of 100 mbps and became known as Fast Ethernet as opposed to standard Ethernet of 10 mbps. Both copper and fiber versions of Fast Ethernet were introduced at the same time. 100Base-T4 and 100Base-TX were the copper standards introduced for Fast Ethernet at this time. A couple years later in 1998 IEEE 802.3y was introduced as 100Base-T2 for lower quality twisted-pair cables. Collectively, all these 100 megabit copper Ethernet technologies are referred to as 100Base-T or sometimes 100BaseT.

Any Ethernet standard that runs at 100 megabits per second is also called Fast Ethernet. The Fast Ethernet designation refers to both copper and fiber based versions of Ethernet that runs at 100 megabits per second.

100BASE-TX

Of the three copper standards, 100Base-TX became the most widely implemented because it actually allows 100 mbps in both directions simultaneously by using one pair for sending data and a different pair for receiving data. The patch cables created back in Lesson 3 were based on the 100Base-TX standard. 100Base-TX is a baseband technology and has a throughput of 100 mbps over a distance of 100 meters on UTP copper wire. 100Base-TX uses a minimum of Cat 5 UTP cable to do this.

100BASE-FX

100Base-FX is the version of Fast Ethernet that is intended to be used over fiber-optic cable. 100Base-FX was introduced at the same time as 100Base-TX and was part of the same IEEE 802.3y standard. 100Base-FX can be used in either half-duplex mode or in full-duplex mode. If 100Base-FX is used in half-duplex mode, then only one wire is needed, but collisions will occur. If 100Base-FX is used in full-duplex mode then two fiber wires are needed—one for transmitting and the other for receiving.

100Base-FX can also be used with both multimode fiber and single-mode fiber. 100Base-FX delivers a throughput of 100 mbps in all usage modes. With multimode fiber at half-duplex, 100Base-FX has a range of 400 meters. If you shift from half-duplex to full-duplex, 100Base-FX's range increases to 2,000 meters or 2 kilometers. When 100Base-FX is used with single-mode fiber instead of multimode fiber, it needs to be used at full-duplex, but its range increases to 10,000 meters, or 10 kilometers.

1000BASE-X

In 1998, 1000Base-X was released under the IEEE 802.3z standard. This was the first 1,000 megabit or 1gigabit Ethernet standard to be released and is also known as Gigabit Ethernet. 1000Base-X was intended for use with fiber-optic cables and as such came with several variations. The main variations defined in the IEEE 802.3z standard were 1000Base-SX and 1000Base-LX. All variations of the 1000Base-X standard had a throughput of 1,000 mbps or 1 gigabit; however, the ranges and type of fiber-optic cable used varied. 1000Base-SX was designed to be used over shorter distances using multimode fiber and had a range of 200 meters. 1000Base-LX was designed for longer length runs and could be used with either multimode or single-mode fiber. When 1000Base-LX was used with multimode fiber, it could achieve a range of up to 550 meters. When 1000Base-LX was used with single-mode fiber its range was extended out to as much as 5 kilometers.

1000BASE-T

1000Base-T is the copper version of Gigabit Ethernet and was standardized one year later in 1999. Copper-based Gigabit Ethernet used the IEEE 802.3ab standard. 802.3ab was designed to use Cat 5, 5e, or 6. This allowed businesses to use Gigabit Ethernet on their current installations. While 1000Base-T can reach 100 meters on Cat 5 cable, it is recommended that you use at least CAT 5e for twisted-pair Gigabit Ethernet implementations.

10 GIGABIT ETHERNET

There are a couple of differences between 10 Gigabit Ethernet and earlier versions of Ethernet. One of the biggest is that 10 Gigabit Ethernet only supports full-duplex communications. The other really big difference between 10 Gigabit Ethernet and earlier Ethernets is that it does not support CSMA/CD. This requires you to purchase specialized NICs and other networking equipment in order to run 10 Gigabit Ethernet. Generally speaking it cannot use existing infrastructure and therefore needs to have purpose-based infrastructure installed before it can be used effectively.

10 Gigabit Ethernet was first proposed under the IEEE 802.3ae standard in 2002. This standard put forward a number of fiber-optics-based 10 Gigabit Ethernet solutions. The Ethernet standards proposed under 802.3ae were 10GBase-SR, 10GBase-LR, 10GBase-ER, 10GBase-SW, 10GBase-LW, and 10GBase-EW. The 10G in front of the Base portion of the naming convention indicates 10 gigabits. What this means is that each of these standards are able to carry a throughput of 10 gbps (gigabits per second). Here are some details about each of the types of 10 Gigabit Ethernet:

- **10GBase-SR:** Intended for use with multimode fiber. 10GBase-SR can be used over a cable that is up to 300 meters long. The SR portion of the name stands for short range.
- **10GBase-LR:** Intended for single-mode fiber. 10GBase-LR can carry 10 gbps of data for 10 kilometers. The LR stands for long range.
- **10GBase-ER:** Intended for single-mode fiber. 10GBase-ER can carry 10gbps for up to 40 kilometers. The ER stands for extended range
- **10GBase-SW:** Uses the same specifications as 10GBase-SR, except that the SW stands for short wave. The main difference between 10GBase-SR and 10GBase-SW is that 10GBase-SW is designed to connect to *Synchronous Optical Network (SONET)* equipment and is usually a WAN technology. SONET is a standardized multiplexing protocol that is used to transmit multiple different data streams over a fiber-optic cable.
- **10GBase-LW:** Uses the same specifications as 10Base-LR. However, the difference between LR and LW is that 10GBase-LW is intended to connect to SONET equipment just like the 10GBase-SW standard.
- **10GBase-EW:** Shares the same specification ions with 10GBase-ER. The difference is that EW is intended to connect to SONET equipment where the ER standard is not.

One side note about the 10GBase-E technologies is that they actually have the potential to become an alternative to different WAN technologies. The advantage to using some form of Ethernet for both LAN and WAN technologies is that conversion is not needed between the LAN and the WAN. This results in a reduction in the amount of equipment used to connect LAN and WAN technology networks. We will have to wait and see if the industry agrees with this assessment.

- **10GBase-T:** Can use either shielded or unshielded twisted-pair wiring. This particular standard was formalized in the IEEE 802.3an standard in 2006.

In order for 10GBase-T to be used in a LAN environment, specialized NICs as well as switches need to be purchased. Unlike 1000Base-T, 10GBase-T cannot use an existing LAN infrastructure. This means that not only do the NICs and other networking equipment need to be replaced in order to run 10GBase-T in a network, the entire cabling infrastructure

TAKE NOTE*

It is good to note that while 10GBase-T cannot use the wiring infra-structure of older versions of Ethernet, older versions of Ethernet can use 10GBase-T's wiring infrastructure.

also has to be replaced. This has resulted in a slow adoption of this technology. In order for 10GBase-T to be used effectively with a range of up to 100 meters in a LAN environment, CAT 6A wiring needs to be in place. Standard CAT 6 can work in some situations, but it is not able to achieve the full 100-meter range that CAT 6A can achieve.

40/100 GIGABIT ETHERNET

40 Gigabit and 100 Gigabit Ethernet are the latest Ethernet standards available. Both are defined under the IEEE 802.3ba standard that was released in June 2010. 40/100 Gigabit Ethernet is full-duplex just like 10 Gigabit Ethernet and is intended to be used with multi-mode fiber, single-mode fiber, and copper cabling. 100 Gigabit Ethernet is also intended to have a range of up to 40 km using single-mode fiber. 40/100 Gigabit Ethernet also does not support CSMA/CD just like the previously discussed 10 Gigabit Ethernet. Finally 40/100 Gigabit Ethernet is intended as a bridge technology between current Ethernet standards and an eventual Terabit Ethernet standard that has not been developed yet.

■ Other LAN Concepts

THE BOTTOM LINE

In this portion of Lesson 7, the basic LAN concepts of broadcasting, collision, bonding, speed, and distance are discussed. This section of Lesson 7 also explains how distance needs to be taken into account when designing a new network. Additionally, a few concepts related to networking and particularly to LANs are discussed.

Broadcast

CERTIFICATION READY

What are broadcasts? How are they used in networking? How does this relate to Ethernet?

3.7

In its simplest terms, a ***broadcast*** is where a computer sends data across a network by sending the data frame containing the data to all computers directly connected to it on a local network. In ***broadcast networking***, broadcasts, as described here, are used to send data across a local network. Ethernet is a broadcast-based network technology.

In the case of Ethernet, when a computer on a local network wishes to send data to another computer on the local network, it creates a data frame. This data frame contains the data that a computer needs to send across the network as well as its own physical address and the physical address of the computer for which the data frame is intended. The sending computer then releases the prepared data frame to all the computers on the local network. The computers on the local network listen to every data frame that comes by and read their physical destination addresses. If the physical destination is the same as that of the computer looking at it, the computer retrieves the data frame and processes it. If the destination physical address does not match that of the computer looking at it, the data frame is ignored and not opened.

COLLISION

CERTIFICATION READY

What is a collision? When do collisions occur?

3.7

A ***collision*** is where two different data frames from two different computers interfere with each other because they were released onto the network at the same time. The previously discussed broadcast-based networking technologies create the circumstances that allow collisions to take place. Because a data frame is sent to all the computers on a local network segment, if any two computers on that segment send data at the same time, a collision is inevitable.

Collisions are inevitable because every data frame sent out by one computer is going to every other computer on the network. Sooner or later the two data frames that were released at the same time will collide. CSMA/CD and CSMA/CA were developed so that a network would be able to do two things: (1) limit the number of collisions that take place on a network and (2) so the network and the computers on it would know how to recover when a collision did take place.

Switches were developed to eliminate collisions almost completely by basically prescreening each frame that is released on the network. By prescreening each frame, a switch can set up a dedicated circuit between the source computer and the destination computer. A switch is able to do this because its primary job is to manage all its ports. When a frame is released from a computer onto the network, the first device that sees the data frame is a switch, which is designed to be able to read the MAC or physical destination address of a data frame. Once the switch knows what the destination physical address of a specific frame is, it links the port with the physical address of the source computer directly to the port with the physical address of the destination computer. This results in a direct connection between the two computers that no other computer connected to the switch is able to take over. With a dedicated link between two different computers set up, the possibility of a collision with a data frame from another computer is eliminated. The only way a collision could take place is if both of the directly connected computers sent a data frame to each other simultaneously. The possibility just mentioned is mitigated if a full-duplex connection is used with separate wires being dedicated to send and receive respectively. UTP in full-duplex mode uses different pairs of wires for send and receive. As a result, in modern networks where switches are used instead of hubs, collisions are very rare.

Collision domain

Collision domains, as the name implies, are related to collisions. In a network, a ***collision domain*** is all the computers physically connected to each other via a shared medium that could potentially have data frames collide. Another way of saying this is a collision domain is a group of computers on a network that are connected directly together without any intervening network equipment such as bridges that would act to separate them from each other, thereby blocking a collision between data frames of two of the connected computers.

Figure 7-5 illustrates two different types of collision domain. The first collision domain is formed because all the computers connected to the network share the same main cable. The second collision domain is formed because all the computers are connected to a single hub. One hub works much like a bus topology, so all computers connected together via one or more hubs form a single collision domain. If a switch was used in place of the hub, no collision domains would be formed because the switch acts to mitigate collisions. Without collisions, a collision domain is not created.

Figure 7-5

Two different types of collision domains

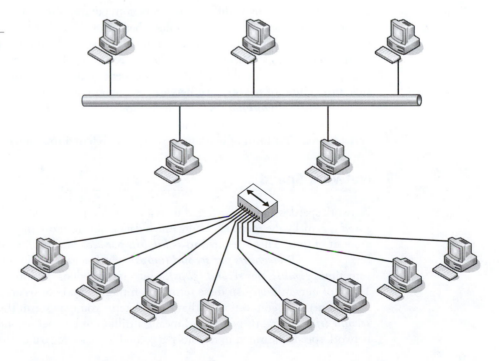

TAKE NOTE *

The process just described in the main text is referred to as RAID 0. A RAID 0 does not have any redundancy capability. This means that if even one of the disks that are part of the RAID 0 goes bad, then all the data on all the disks is lost. To compensate for this, RAID 0 is used in conjunction with other RAID methods that do provide redundancy. Alternatively something called RAID 5 is used, which is similar to RAID 0 except it provides redundancy at the cost of not being as fast as RAID 0.

Bonding

Bonding seems like an odd networking term, but it is a valid technique used in networking to increase network throughput. In simple terms, *bonding* is using two or more NICs, channels, or connections to push data through instead of just one. This works somewhat like disk striping in a RAID setup. While a RAID is more a topic of discussion in a Windows Server or an A+ class, we discuss it briefly here as a means to understand how bonding works.

RAID stands for Redundant Array of Independent Disks or Redundant Array of Inexpensive Disks depending on who you ask. A RAID takes multiple disks and spreads data storage across all the disks as a way to have redundant storage, a faster way to read and write data, or both. The second reason is the one we are concerned about here. In order to store data faster, such as in a database environment, that data is divided into equal parts depending on how many disks there are available in the RAID. If there are three disks, then the data is divided up into three equal parts; if there are five disks, then five equal parts; and so on. Once the data is divided into equal parts, it is then sent simultaneously to each of the disk drives that make up the RAID. Dividing the data as described results in being able to write data to the disks three times, five times, or however many times you have disks. This is faster than if you were only storing the data onto one disk.

This is all interesting, but what does it have to do with bonding? In bonding, just like in a RAID as described here, the data is broken into equal parts depending on how many NICs, connections, channels, and so on. However, instead of saving the data onto a group of hard disks, the data is sent out onto a network using different NICs, connections, or channels. More data is able to be sent out at the same time based on the number and throughput of the channels, NICs, or connections being bonded.

In fact, one term describing this process, even comes from the idea of a RAID. However, instead of calling it a RAID, it is called a RAIN. *RAIN* stands for *Redundant Array of Independent Nodes*. Additional terms used to describe this process are Ethernet bonding, channel bonding, link aggregation, network bonding, NIC teaming, and several others. Depending on what is being bonded, the name tends to change. If channels are being bonded, then the term *channel bonding* is used. If Ethernet connections are being bonded then it is called *Ethernet bonding*. If links are being bonded it is called *link aggregation*.

Bonding is used in many different network configurations for several different purposes. One purpose is to increase throughput as described before. Another purpose is to provide redundancy for a network connection. When bonding is done for the purpose of network redundancy, it is often referred to as *Network Fault Tolerance (NFT)*. To get very high speeds in an 802.11n network channel, multiple wireless radio frequencies are bonded together to increase the possible throughput of the 802.11n network configuration. There is even a variation on trunking called *multilink trunking (MLT)*, which allows you to bind two or more ports together on certain switches to allow for fault tolerance or greater throughput between switches or a switch and a router. This form of bonding is sometimes referred to as *port bonding*.

Network Speed

Network speed is variously referred to as a network's speed, bandwidth, or throughput. Network *speed* is actually the measure of how much data is able to move through the network in a given amount of time. This is referred to as *kilobits per second (kbps)*, which means thousands of bits per second; *megabits per second (mbps)*, which means millions of bits per second; and sometimes *gigabits per second (gbps)*, which means billions of bits per second. A *bit* is a single 1 or 0 of network data, so these terms mean that many 1s or 0s are being or can be sent across a network connection at that time. A term you may see in the future is *terabits per second (tbps)*. Terabits per second means a trillion of bits per second. Being able to achieve network speeds measured in terabits per second is an active goal of the networking industry.

CERTIFICATION READY
What is speed in a
networking sense? How
is speed measured?
3.7

There are two different aspects to speed. One is the network's actual speed or a specific connection's *actual* speed at any given time. This can be measured by going to sites such as www.speedtest.net and other similar sites. The other aspect of speed is the *potential* speed of a network or network connection at any given time.

When buying network services and technologies, what you are purchasing is the potential speed of the technology, not its actual speed. When we say that something is 1 Gigabit Ethernet, we are not saying that you will always get a speed of 1 gbps; we are saying you can potentially get a speed of 1 gbps from your network. In the same way, when you purchase an Internet service for your home or business, you are purchasing the service based on the potential speed of the service, not its actual speed. A good service will usually give you more speed than what you actually purchased, whereas a poor service may give you less actual speed than you purchased.

The actual network speed you get depends on a number of factors. One factor is how many people are currently using the network. If large numbers of people are currently connected to the network you are on, whether that network is an ISP's network or your work's network, then your network speed will be down. If only a few people are connected to the network you are on at a given time, then that network's speed will be up. Aside from how many people are using a network, how far you are from the nearest switch or router may also affect your speed. Also how close or far you are from the central office of your ISP can affect your network speed. If you are closer to your ISP's central office, you will most likely get better network speed than someone who is further away.

Distance

CERTIFICATION READY
What is distance in
networking? Why is it
important?
3.7

In networking, the most basic definition of ***distance*** is how far data has to travel to get from one point on a network to another. This however is only a basic and general definition of distance in reference to networking. Depending on the context in which the term distance is used, it can actually refer to several different things. First, it can refer to how far data has to travel to get from one point to another as already mentioned.

When talking about media, distance refers to how far a data signal can travel before it needs to be rebuilt. In this situation, when we say CAT 5 cable can carry a 100 mbps signal for a distance of 100 meters, what we mean is that CAT 5 cable can carry 100 mbps of data 100 meters before the data needs to be regenerated by some device such as a switch. Different types of media have different distances they can carry data before the data signal deteriorates to the point that it cannot be understood. When you are building a network and choosing the media you wish to use for it, how far the media can carry data reliably is an important consideration to take into account.

Also, the actual distance a type of media can carry data and the subjective distance data can be carried are two different things. To explain this we will go back to the example of CAT 5 cabling used earlier. CAT 5 cabling can indeed carry 100 mbps of data 100 meters reliably. However, this does not mean that we can run a cable from a switch to a computer that is 100 meters away and expect the CAT 5 cable to carry the data. This is mainly because there is almost never a straight run from one destination in a building to another. The cable has to be run along specific paths that are actually longer than the direct straight distance between two network devices. This subjective distance needs to be taken into account when determining how far away you can put a network device without having to use another network device to regenerate the signal.

Because the subjective distance between a switch and the end computer can be so different from the actual distance, it is recommended to assume all computers and other end devices can be no more than 50 meters from the switch or similar device it is connected to. By limiting the distance between a switch and its end devices to 50 meters, the different twists and turns the cable has to make to get to the appropriate end device is taken into account. Figure 7-6 shows how this is taken into account.

Figure 7-6 shows a fictitious building's floor plan. Based on the scale in the lower left hand side of the diagram, the building is roughly 90 meters long and 50 meters wide. In order to

Figure 7-6

The distance a cable is able to carry data can affect placement of IDFs and the MDF

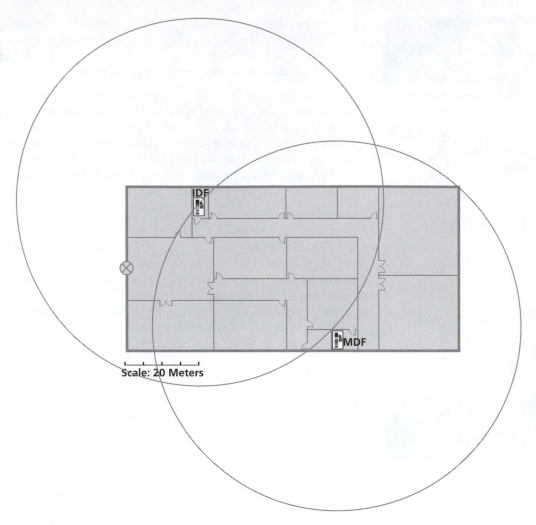

determine the placement of the IDF in the building, a circle with a radius of 50 meters based on the provided scale was drawn. The reason a circle of 50 meters instead of 100 meters is used is because 50 meters is half of the total range of a 100Base-TX or 1000Base-T network cable. The full 100 meters is not used because by the time you have run a cable with all the twists, turns, and changes of directions needed to get it to its destination, the cable will be considerably longer than a straight line of 100 meters to the destination. Using half the maximum length is a way to safely ensure that you do not end up running a cable so long that it is not able to carry a signal all the way to the intended destination.

The center of the 50-meter circle is placed on the MDF. The location of the MDF is generally where the outside communications lines come into a building, so there is not much choice about its placement. As you can see from Figure 7-6, the 50-meter radius of the circle did not cover the entire building. Because of this, an IDF has to be provided to achieve full coverage for the building. Once an appropriate location for an IDF has been found on the building's floor plan, a new 50-meter radius circle is drawn and centered on the proposed location of the IDF. As you can see in the figure, the second 50-meter radius circle provided coverage for the remainder of the building. Using this diagram, computers are connected to either the IDF or the MDF, based on where they are located in relation to the coverage shown by the 50-meter radius circles. One upside of the placement of the IDF in this proposed network site is that it is just within the CAT 5 range of the MDF. As a result, fiber does not have to be used to connect the MDF to the IDF, although that can be done if the network designer wishes it.

Wireless LAN Technologies

THE BOTTOM LINE

Wireless LAN technologies are discussed in this section of Lesson 7. Specifically we examine installing wireless NICs and access points. While discussing wireless access points (WAPs), we talk about configuration and some of the options available when configuring them. We will also discuss Service Set Identifiers (SSIDs), channels, and beacons. We also spend some time discussing the proper placement of access points and things to consider when making placement decisions.

Now let's look at some wireless technologies that are used to set up wireless LANs. Specifically, let's look at issues related to actually installing and configuring a wireless LAN. For the purposes of this section of Lesson 7, we will be using a Linksys WRT54GS2 Wireless-G router and the Windows 7 operating system. A different WAP or different operating system may result in slightly different results.

Install Client

Installing the client involves installing the wireless NIC in your computer. With most modern laptop and smaller computers, a wireless NIC is already built in and so no installation is needed. In the rare situation where you have a portable computer that does not contain an already built-in wireless NIC, you have two choices about the NIC technology you wish to use.

One option is that you can install a wireless NIC using your laptop's PCMCIA slot, also known as PC card slot. In some very old portable computers, this is the only option available. When installing a PCMCIA wireless NIC, the first step is to read the manual to make sure you understand all the steps involved. Generally speaking, you need to install the drivers for your PCMCIA card first. After that, generally you are required to restart the computer. Once restart is complete, you can insert the PCMCIA card into the appropriate slot. This causes the computer to activate the card and start searching for available wireless networks.

The second option for allowing a portable computer to connect to a network without a built-in wireless NIC is to use a USB port–based wireless NIC. This is actually the most common solution used today. Like with the PCMCIA card, the first thing you need to do is read the manual in order to ensure that you understand all the steps involved in installing your wireless NIC. Once you have done this, again, it is likely that you need to first install the drivers for your USB port–based wireless NIC. After installing the drivers, you may or may not have to restart your portable computer. Most likely you will need to do a restart. Once the restart has completed, all you have to do is plug the wireless USB port–based NIC into an appropriate USB slot. The portable computer will then activate the USB wireless NIC and begin searching for available wireless networks. Occasionally, additional steps may be needed to set up a USB-based wireless NIC. If additional steps are necessary, you will need to follow them as laid out in the manual you were supposed to have read prior to installing the wireless USB NIC.

With a desktop computer, the USB option is one way to make your computer access a wireless network. However, with desktop computers, you have one other possibility that you do not have with portable computers. That possibility is to install a wireless NIC in the appropriate expansion slot. In most modern desktop computers, the appropriate expansion slot to use is a PCI expansion slot. As always, the first step is to read the manual that came with the PCI or other wireless NIC. Depending on the wireless NIC being used, it may or may not be necessary to install your wireless NIC drivers first. You will know which is necessary for your particular installation because you would have already read the manual.

After you have determined whether you need to install the drivers first and have done so if it is required, you need to do the following to install your PCI wireless NIC. First, open your computer and locate an empty PCI slot. Remove the external cover for that slot location.

Connect the PCI card correctly into the PCI slot. After this, you can secure the PCI card into its slot by using a securing screw and then close the cover. Alternatively, you can choose to leave the card unsecured and the case open while testing the card before you secure the card and close the case. Either way, you need to restart your computer after placing the PCI card in the appropriate slot. Your computer will boot up and hopefully find the wireless NIC. It will either ask for the drivers or begin running a set up program of some sort. It is best to use the wireless setup and installation wizard that comes with Windows when using that operating system because third-party setup and installation software sometimes does not work correctly under Windows. This is especially true in the case of Windows XP.

Access Point Placement

CERTIFICATION READY
How do you determine the best place to install a wireless access point (WAP)?
2.2

Wireless access point (WAP) placement is an important issue when setting up a wireless network because you want to get the greatest possible coverage at the greatest possible speed for your site or home using your WAP. One thing to keep in mind with WAPs, the further your computer is from the access point, the slower the data throughput for your computer will be. With this fact in mind, when using a single access point, you should locate it as centrally as possible in relationship to where your computers are located. This gives the best possible throughput for all the computers connected to the wireless network via the WAP. If you place the access point in such a way that it is closer to one group of computers than to another group of computers, then some users will have very high throughput speeds while others will have very slow throughput and possibly even intermittent data loss.

Figure 7-7 shows the result of a poorly placed WAP. The Wireless Access Point (WAP) is the cone-shaped device on the right end of the building labeled WAP. In Figure 7-7 the circle centered on the WAP shows the effective range of this particular WAP. As you can see, those computers closest to the door are barely within range of the WAP and some may in fact only receive data from the WAP intermittently. Also, each row out from the WAP center will likely have lower throughput than those closer to the WAP. One other thing to keep in mind when using wireless networks—there is a very good chance that a WAP may extend to outside of the building it is located in, unless precautions are taken to make sure this does not happen.

Figure 7-7

A poorly-placed WAP

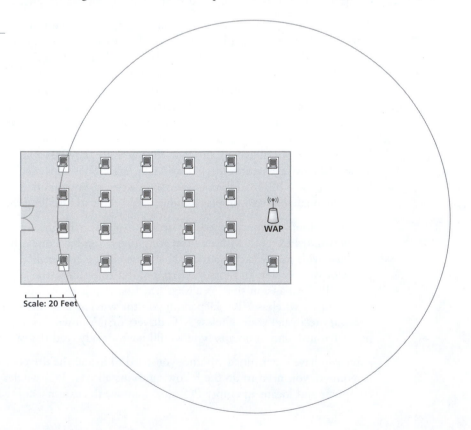

Scale: 20 Feet

Figure 7-8 shows a much better way to place the WAP in the same situation as shown in Figure 7-7. Instead of placing the WAP on one end of the building, it is located on a table in the center of the room, thus allowing the maximum available access to all computers in the room. This arrangement also ensures that all computers in the room are well within the WAP's range.

Figure 7-8

A well-placed WAP

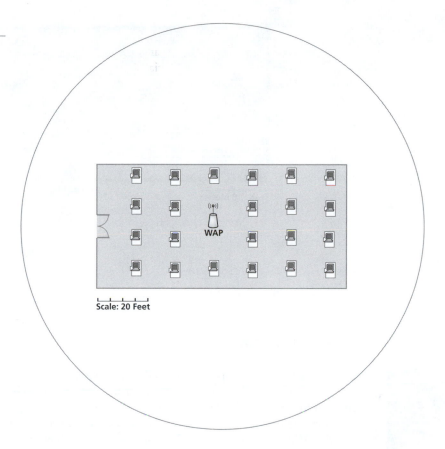

Scale: 20 Feet

When using multiple access points, placement becomes even more important. This is because there are only so many channels for which a WAP can be programmed, and two WAPs with different networks on the same channel cannot have their ranges overlap. In the case of 802.11n this is less of a problem because a relatively large number of nonoverlapping channels are available. As the network administrator, you just need to make sure that no WAPs that are on different networks are next to each other using the same channel. With 802.11g things are a bit more problematic. In the 802.11g, realistically there are only three nonoverlapping channels, so you must place WAPs in a way that does not allow any duplicate channels to overlap. This is illustrated in Figure 7-9.

In Figure 7-9 we are going back to the floor plan that was used earlier. However, this time we are concerned with placing WAPs for a large wireless network. WAPs are placed in the MDF and IDF because they are where network equipment would be located anyway; however, just placing WAPs in these locations does not give full coverage of the site. Like in previous examples, we are using circles with their centers placed on different WAPs. Because this is a 802.11g network, we are making the radii of the circles 30 meters instead of 50, because that is approximately the range that 802.11g has when used indoors. With our first two WAPs placed, we can see that we need three more WAPs to effectively cover the entire site. Based on the circles, placing WAPs in the NE, SE, and SW corners of the building will accomplish full coverage.

Now we need to set their channels so that WAPs whose ranges overlap will not interfere with each other. To do this, we need to set the WAPs in the NE and SW corners of the building to Channel A. Additionally, we need to set the WAPs the IDF and the SE corner of the building to Channel B. Finally, we need to set the WAP in the MDF to Channel C. Now we can see from our diagram that no overlapping WAPs have the same channel, so they will not interfere with each other.

Figure 7-9

Well placed WAPs in a large
network so as to ensure that
no WAP Channels overlap

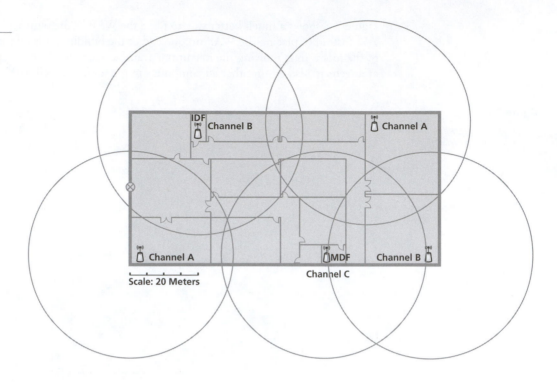

Install Access Point

CERTIFICATION READY
When installing a
wireless access point,
what configuration issues
have to be considered?
What are some
configuration options
that you will have to
decide about while doing
the configuration of the
WAP?
2.2

Once the WAPs have been placed, they need to be installed. The best way to do this is make
sure they are linked to the main server of their network via a switch and a wired network connection. While it is possible to do this wirelessly, you will have greater bandwidth if direct-wired
connections are used. Once all WAPs have been connected directly to a computer, you need
to run the WAP setup software on that computer. This will enable the computer to find the
different WAPs and allow you to configure them.

If you are only using one WAP in a home network environment, it is probably best to simply
allow the setup software to set up the WAP however it sees fit. If you wish to have a secure
network, there are several things you will want to make sure of during the setup process.

One thing you will want to do is make sure that the *Service Set Identifier (SSID)* is changed
from its default. The SSID acts as the network name for a particular WAP. If you are using
multiple WAPs in the same network, then they all need to have the same SSID. In Linksys
WAPs, the SSID can be up to 32 characters. A safety precaution you may want to take when
setting up a WAP is to have it configured so that it does not broadcast its SSID. If an SSID is
broadcasted, then a hacker can intercept it and use it for nefarious purposes.

Another thing you will want to do to ensure that your wireless network is as secure as it can
be is to change the default password on it. For Linksys WAPs, the default password is admin.

MAC ADDRESS FILTERING

Enabling *MAC address filtering* may be another thing you will want to do if you want
to make your wireless network as secure as possible. MAC filtering means that only preprogrammed MAC addresses will be allowed access to a specific WAP. This is a very useful
security measure because it means that only those computers and other devices whose MAC
addresses have been entered into the MAC address filtering configuration will be able to use
the WAP. There is however one drawback to enabling this. You will have to find out what
the MAC addresses of all the devices you want on your network are and then manually

enter them into the configuration screen. If you make a mistake while entering a particular device's MAC address, then until the mistake is found and corrected, the device in question will not have access to the wireless network. Some of the devices you may want on your home network may include gaming terminals such as a Wii or PS2. These devices also have to have their MAC addresses manually entered into the MAC address filtering screen. Any devices not entered into the MAC filtering configuration will not have access to the network. Any time a new device that needs access to your wireless network is brought in; it will also need to be manually added to the MAC filtering configuration before it can be used on the wireless network.

To get into the MAC address filtering screen on your WAP after its initial installation, you will need to do several things. First, access your WAP directly by using your web browser and entering the Default Gateway IP Address into it.

To get your Default Gateway IP Address in Windows, go into your command line interface. To do this go down to your *Start* button and type **cmd** in the *Search programs and files* box just above the *Start* symbol and press **Enter** on the keyboard. Figure 7-10 shows what your screen should look like once you have completed these instructions.

CERTIFICATION READY
What is MAC Filtering?
What role does it play in Wireless Networking?
5.1

Figure 7-10

Windows 7 command line interface

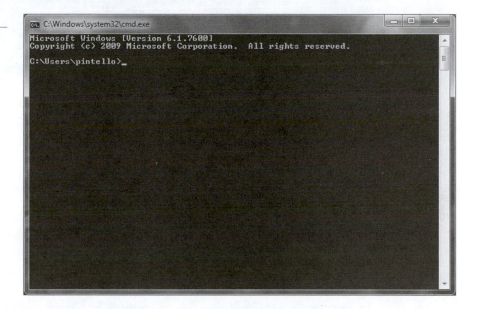

Once you have the command line interface open, you need to enter the command **ipconfig** at the prompt inside the black box, which is the command line interface. Figure 7-11 shows what the result of entering **ipconfig** should look like. I have expanded the command line interface window slightly to show the entire result at one time.

Looking at the command line interface window in Figure 7-11, you will see *IPv4* followed by an IP address, *Subnet Mask* followed by a subnet mask IP address, and *Default Gateway* followed by a third IP address. It is the Default Gateway that you are interested in. In this figure, the Default Gateway is 192.168.0.1. You need to write down your own Default Gateway.

Now that you have your Default Gateway address, you need to open a web browser. I will be using Firefox to do this, but you can use your preferred web browser.

Once you have opened your web browser, you need to type the entire Default Gateway in your URL line with no additional information. Figure 7-12 shows an image similar to what you will see on your system.

Figure 7-11

Windows 7 command line interface after ipconfig command has been entered

Figure 7-12

Windows 7 after the Default Gateway has been entered into a web browser

If you have already created a username and password for you WAP, then go ahead and enter that. Otherwise, just enter **admin** without the quotes in the *Password* field and leave the *Username* field blank. After you do this, click **OK**. This will take you into the WAP's configuration screen (see Figure 7-13).

Once you have gotten this far, you can navigate around in the configuration screen very easily. To enter the MAC addresses that you want to be filtered, go to the *Wireless* menu option. Under that menu option, you will see a menu option that says *Wireless MAC Filter*. From there you will need to enable *Wireless MAC Filter*. Once that is enabled, a button will come up that says *Edit MAC Filter List*. Clicking on that button brings up a window where you can enter the MAC addresses you want to filter. We will be doing more with WAP configuration in the Lab portion of this Lesson.

CONFIGURE APPROPRIATE ENCRYPTION

Encryption is where a device such as a computer or a WAP takes the data that it is sending out and runs an algorithm on it so that it cannot be read without first having the key to read it. This capability increases the security of a network by making it more difficult for an outsider to read what is passing across a network. This is especially important for a wireless network because pretty much anybody with a laptop computer and a wireless NIC can eavesdrop on them. By first encrypting the data that is sent over the wireless network, it becomes harder for someone to listen in casually.

The encryption settings for a WAP are found in the same general place as MAC Filtering. It is located under the *Wireless* menu options and then under the *Wireless Security* sub-menu

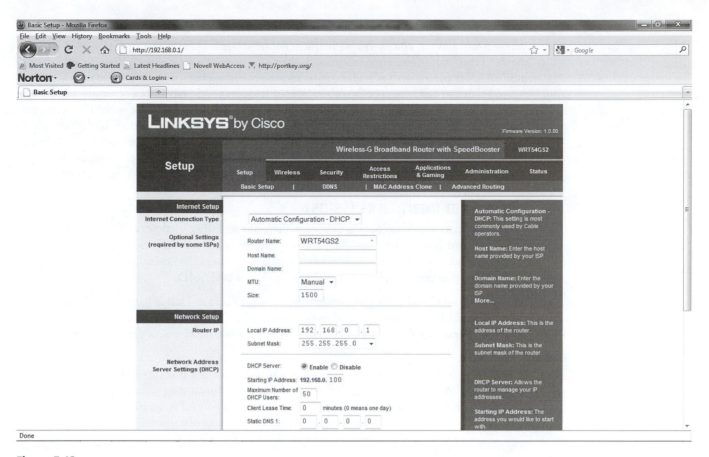

Figure 7-13

Initial configuration screen for a Linksys WAP

option. The available encryption schemes are WPA Enterprise and Personal, WPA2 Enterprise and Personal, RADIUS, and WEP. Of these options, WPA2 Enterprise is the strongest and WEP is the weakest. We will discuss WEP and the various versions of WPA in the next two sections of this lesson.

WEP

WEP stands for wired equivalent privacy. WEP was ratified in 1999 along with original IEEE 802.11 standard. WEP included both encryption and authentication capabilities. WEP was originally intended to have security capabilities similar to that of a more traditional wired network, however was not able to fulfill that promise. WEP2 was intended to be a stop gap measure that addressed some of the weaknesses of WEP, but this too did not live up to the expectation and was dropped.

WPA

WPA which stands for Wi-Fi Protected Access is a wireless protocol and certification program created by the Wi-Fi Alliance. The purpose of WPA is to help secure wireless computer networks as an intermediate security standard until the IEEE 802.11i wireless security standards could be ratified. WPA implements many of the security features that have been included in the 802.11i standard.

WPA2 came out in 2004 and is effectively the implementation of choice for the IEEE 802.11i wireless security standard. WPA2 provides much stronger encryption and authentication capabilities over the older WEP standard. Starting in 2006, any devices that carried the Wi-Fi logo have to meet the WPA2 standard for wireless security.

CERTIFICATION READY
What is the difference between WPA and WPA2?
5.1

CERTIFICATION READY
What are some encryption protocols used in Wireless Networking? How do these encryption methods differ from each other?
5.1

CHANNELS AND FREQUENCIES

When using a WAP, *channels* and frequencies are related. IEEE 802.11g for example uses the 2.4 GHz radio-frequency range for communications. This frequency range is broken up into 22 MHz pieces with a 5 MHz separation between each. This results in channels being created that are basically specific sub-ranges of frequency that have been set aside within the larger 2.4 GHz range. This gives 802.11g up to 14 channels it can work with. However, for these channels to all be used on the same network, there can be no overlap. Unfortunately, with 22 MHz channel ranges, and only 5 MHz between the start of one channel and the start of the next, there is a lot of overlap. While there may be 14 channels available for 802.11g, only three of those channels can effectively be used without overlap occurring.

SERVICE SET IDENTIFIERS (SSIDS)

We have already discussed SSIDs, however, there are actually two types of SSIDs. One type is an Extended Service Set Identifier (ESSID) and the other is a Basic Service Set Identifier (BSSID). Both types are used to identify a wireless network. However, how that wireless network is set up depends on whether it gets a BSSID or an ESSID.

BSSIDs are used to identify independent wireless networks, which is basically a stand-alone wireless network that does not need to be connected to another network in order for it to function. These independent wireless networks can either be ad hoc wireless networks or have a central access point controlling them.

An *ad hoc wireless network* is formed when a wireless network is composed of only independent wireless computers where each device participates in forwarding wireless packets. An ad hoc wireless network has no central WAP to monitor and control it. In effect, an ad hoc wireless network is the wireless network version of a peer-to-peer network.

Alternatively, a wireless network can be something called an *infrastructure wireless network* where WAPs are used to control access to the wireless network and are often connected to a larger wired network. Security is better on infrastructure wireless networks than it is on ad hoc wireless networks.

ESSIDs are used when two or more independent wireless networks are tied together. The WAPs used to tie the independent wireless networks together are each given their own ESSID. This ESSID is then used to help control the flow of data frames between the various devices on the different networks.

An SSID is generally set when a wireless network is first configured. Some WAPs allow you to change the SSID manually at a later date and others do not. Generally speaking when an SSID is changed on a WAP, the whole network needs to be reset. That means the WAP needs to be shut down along with all the other network devices using it. The WAP is then brought back up and the various wireless network devices using the WAP can then reconnect. Sometimes it is necessary to change the settings on the devices connected to the WAP as well as the WAP itself when a wireless access point is reset.

ANTENNA TYPES

There are two broad categories or types into which antennas fall. These antenna types are directional and omni-directional. What you intend to do with the wireless link you are setting up determines which type of antenna you need to use.

Omni-directional antenna

An omni-directional antenna broadcasts a signal in all directions. This type of antenna is often seen on handheld communications devices and in wireless access points. The advantage of this type of antenna is that you do not have to be facing the antenna or have your antenna pointing at it in order to receive a signal from it. The flexibility this gives you for communications is why it is often use in wireless networking.

Even though there are definite advantages to using an omni-directional antenna, there are also several disadvantages to using this type of antenna. One disadvantage is that an omni-directional antenna wastes a lot of power sending the signal in all directions. This wasted power directly results in the second notable disadvantage of omni-directional antenna. The second disadvantage is that omni-directional antennas have limited range. With the power being used to send the signal in a spherical pattern around the antenna, the power is not available to send that signal a long distance. The final disadvantage to an omni-directional antenna is that the signal being broadcast by the antenna is easy to intercept. The device being used to intercept the signal can be anywhere in the range of spherical pattern of the signal being broadcast.

Directional antenna

Directional antennas address some of the problems of omni-directional antennas, but they also lose some of the flexibility that omni-directional antennas have. A directional antenna is designed to send a signal in only one general direction. This means that all the power being fed into the antenna can be used to focus the signal in only one direction instead of being wasted sending the signal in all directions.

The advantage of sending the signal in only one direction is that the extra power can be used to increase the range of the signal. Alternatively power requirements can be reduced if you only want a minimal range for your antenna. It also becomes harder to intercept a wireless signal because the device being used to intercept signal must be directly in the path of the signal. This increases the chances that the device attempting to intercept the signal will be noticed.

The biggest disadvantage of directional antennas is that they can only be used to send a signal in only one direction and so do not lend themselves well to being a central access point for a wireless network.

CERTIFICATION READY
What are some issues related to configuring a wireless network?
2.2

INTERFERENCE

In wireless networking interference is any electromagnetic signal that interferes with passing data over a wireless network. This interference can have a number of sources. One common source is a device in the vicinity of the wireless network that sends out electromagnetic signals that overwhelm the devices on the wireless network so that they signals are not able to push through each other. Electric motors and microwave ovens have been known to create electromagnetic noise strong enough to do this.

Another way that wireless signals can be interfered with is if there is something in the environment that acts to redirect wireless signals. A good example of this type of interference is a building that uses steel studs in its walls rather than wooden ones. When this happens, the steel studs can act to re-direct the path of wireless signals so that they are not able to reach their destinations. A well known manifestation of this type of interference is trying to use a cell phone is a building with lots of steel studs in the walls. In a situation like that it can be very hard to send or receive cell phone calls unless you are next to a window that is not shielded against wireless radio signals.

SIGNAL STRENGTH

Signal strength has to do with how strong a wireless signal is when you are trying to send or receive information across a wireless network. One factor in signal strength is how close you are to a wireless access point. If you are close to the access point then you will have strong signal strength. The further away from the access point you position yourself, the weaker the signal strength will become.

Another thing that can affect signal strength is interference. Interference of either type discussed above will reduce signal strength. It is possible to have such strong interference in a given environment that all signal strength is lost no matter how close to the access point you are. In fact, one of the ways military communications jammers work is to flood a specific area with so much electromagnetic interference that all signal strength is lost and wireless communications cannot be used.

BEACON FRAMES

A wireless beacon frame is a frame that is periodically broadcasted by a WAPoint in order to announce the presence of the wireless network. The beacon frame contains several pieces of information. First it contains a MAC header identifying its MAC address. Next it contains a body with relevant information about the wireless network. The information contained in the body of the beacon frame contains a timestamp, the interval the beacon frame is broadcast on, and finally a basic summary of the capabilities of the broadcasting device or network. Some WAPs allow you to change the interval on which a beacon frame is sent; however, they do not allow you to change the actual contents of the frame. The Linksys router we have been working with has a default internal beacon of 100 milliseconds.

Verify Installation

Finally, once you have set up a wireless network, you need to verify that it is working properly. First, you should verify that you have changed the default SSID and password and know what the correct ones are. Then you should verify that all the devices on the network know what the SSID of the network is. Next, if you are using MAC filtering, verify that all the devices that need access to the network are actually entered into the MAC filter list and that they are entered correctly. Finally, test the wireless network to make sure that data is flowing across it. Once you have done all these things, you should have a wireless network that runs reliably for quite some time.

■ SOHO Network Technologies

 THE BOTTOM LINE

In this section of Lesson 7 we will discuss *Small Office Home Office (SOHO)* and some of the technologies related to it.

A SOHO is a special category of small LANs used for home offices or small business offices. This type of network has only a small number of devices in it and is usually well integrated with any other network devices in the home or office where it is setup.

List of Requirements

CERTIFICATION READY
What is a SOHO? How does it differ from a corporate style network?
2.6

CERTIFICATION READY
What are some issues you need to consider when planning to create a SOHO network?
2.6

When setting up a SOHO network there are a couple of things to consider. One thing to consider is if you wish to use a wireless network or a wired network in your SOHO. The wired network has the advantage of being more secure. However the wireless option is generally more flexible and does not require running wires all over the home or office being setup. Many recently built homes and small office spaces already have data communications wiring in them and so in those situations a wired SOHO becomes for reasonable.

Once you have determined what type of media you want to use for your SOHO network, you need to determine if you want your SOHO network to be peer-to-peer based on client-server based. A peer-to-peer network is easier to setup and does not require any specialized equipment, but is also inherently less secure. The client-server option is more secure but requires the additional equipment and cost. Client-server networks also require a different level of expertise to run. Also, if there are more than 10 devices attempting to use the SOHO network, a peer-to-peer network cannot really be used because of the 10 host restriction placed on non-server Windows operating systems.

Finally you need to decide where you want your SOHO network. If you are setting up a small office somewhere then this is less of a problem as you will probably want to network the entire small office. However, if you are setting up a home office, you need to determine if the SOHO network is going to be limited to your home office, or if you want to be able to access it from anywhere in the house. If you choose to go with the second options, you will need to check with either the company you are working for or a legal consultant as having a

SOHO network for business may not allow you to use it all over the house. A personal use SOHO network is not affected by this consideration.

Cable Length

If you choose to use a wired solution for your SOHO network then the same cable length restrictions used in corporate networks apply to SOHO network. The main exception to this may be if you choose to use a network over power lines option from your power company. If you choose to go this route you will need to see what kinds of cable length restrictions apply to the technology your power company is using for their power line based networks.

Device Types and Requirements

The types networking devices used in a SOHO networks are the same types of devices used in corporate style networks. However, you will want to look into smaller versions of the standard network devices used in larger corporate style networks. Many companies actually provide a SOHO line of their networking devices for just this situation.

The reason you will want to look into SOHO lines of devices from various companies is because they will generally be cheaper than the more conventional network equivalents. The reason SOHO versions will cost less than conventional versions of the devices is because they are designed with only a limited number of ports and such. Another advantage of SOHO specific versions of networking devices is that because of the more limited use they are intended for, they will also be easier to configure. Many SOHO specific devices actually have nice graphical interfaces and wizards for configuration or even have a default configuration built into them that will work in most SOHO network situations. The main drawback to SOHO specific network devices is that they will generally not have the full range of security features and/or capability you may find on similar devices intended for a large network.

Environment Limitations

The very nature of a SOHO network places some limitations on its environment. The biggest limitation is number of devices. Another limitation is the devices that are used in a SOHO network are often multiuse devices.

The technology used to connect to a larger network such as the Internet is also a limitation placed on a SOHO network. Often times SOHO networks are limited to the same options that a home user has when connecting to the Internet. Someone creating a SOHO network will usually not have available to them the same WAN options that are large corporate network has available. This is partly because of cost and partly because of location.

While WAN technologies will be discussed in the next Lesson, the example of a T-3 will work here to illustrate this point. T-3 lines are a WAN technology that many business networks use to connect to larger external networks. However, a typical T-3 line will cost hundreds if not thousands of dollars a month to lease and is only available to specific areas in a city based on where the businesses are. It is very unlikely that a person creating a home office based SOHO network will be able to get a T-3 line ran out to their home in a large residential area. Even if they could, it would end up costing a great deal of money for them to do so. Instead the person putting together the home office based SOHO network will have to settle for DSL or some other option available in the residential area they live in.

Equipment Limitations

While there are limits to the network environment that exist in a SOHO, there are also limitations to the equipment that is used in a SOHO. As mentioned previously, many of the devices used in a SOHO are multifunction devices. One example of a multifunction device is a printer that is also a fax machine and a copier. While this works well in a SOHO environment where only one or may be two people are using that device, in a large corporate network, this device would be too expensive to maintain. The reason this device would be too expensive to maintain in a corporate environment is because it is only designed to be used a limited amount. As a result of this the consumable items used by the device such as toner or ink is provided in smaller quantities. In a corporate environment it is actually more cost effective to use dedicated equipment that has large reservoirs of these consumables.

SOHO devices also tend to be slower and less heavy duty than dedicated equipment intended for a corporate environment. The reason for this is to make the devices more affordable and cost effective for the SOHO user. It is possible to get a multifunction device that is appropriate for a corporate environment, but that device will either need to be leased at hundreds of dollars a month or bought right out at thousands or tens of thousands of dollars. Neither possibility is really practical for a SOHO owner as almost all SOHOs are small business run from home or similar situations. Because of the nature of a SOHO business, most times the owners of the SOHO can only afford to spend a few hundred dollars on any given piece of office equipment. The owners also often cannot afford to spend several hundred dollars every time they need to replace a consumable. Because of this the manufactures of SOHO devices keep the reservoirs of consumables small compared to the reservoirs of corporate type devices so as to keep down the total cost of maintaining the office device.

Another reason manufactures of SOHO devices keep the reservoirs for the consumables small is to make sure that the consumable does not dry out, harden, or otherwise go bad before the SOHO owner can use it. This is an important consideration because SOHO equipment is not as heavily used as corporate equipment. While a corporate office may go through the large toner cartridge of a corporate style printer in just a couple of weeks, a similar size toner cartridge in a SOHO printer may actually go bad before the owner of the SOHO can finish using it. This ends up forcing the SOHO owner to buy a new toner cartridge before he or she has completely used the original. The smaller cartridges used in SOHO style equipment prevents this type of thing from happening.

A good source for SOHO style equipment is stores similar in nature to Office Depot, Staples, and Office Maxx. Much of the equipment sold in these types of establishments is intended for the SOHO environment. These types of stores are also good places to purchase the consumable items used by SOHO devices.

Compatibility Requirements

The last thing to consider when building a SOHO network is compatibility requirements. Most SOHO networks are not put together all at one time and then left alone. Instead, SOHO networks are usually built up a little at a time as it become apparent that additional technology is needed for the business to continue to function and grow. Because of this, the person using a SOHO network needs to be aware of what technologies are already being used in the SOHO network and only buy additional devices that are compatible with the existing technology in the SOHO network.

Following is a couple of examples of compatibility based issues that may come up in a SOHO network. One example is the person who is using all Microsoft software and wants to upgrade their computer system. When it comes time to upgrade their computer system, they need to be sure that they buy another Microsoft based computer rather than buying a MAC computer, even though they may like the MAC better. They need to do this in order to make sure that the software they are currently using will continue to be useful on the new systems.

Another example of a SOHO network compatibility issue could be wireless devices. If the person with the SOHO network has an old 802.11a network, they need to make sure that any new devices they purchase are compatible with the old 802.11a wireless network standard. Alternatively, they may decide that it is more cost effective to switch to 802.11n for their wireless network. They would do this knowing that the 801.11n standard is backwards compatible with the 802.11a standard. This will allow them to continue using all their old 802.11a wireless devices while purchasing new ones compatible with the 802.11n standard.

SKILL SUMMARY

IN THIS LESSON YOU LEARNED:

- About the most commonly used LAN technology of Ethernet.
- What CSMA/CD is and how it works.
- What CSMA/CA is and how it differs from CSMA/CD.
- About various cable-based Ethernet technologies.
- How broadcast is used to transfer data around a network.
- What collisions are.
- About collision domains and how they are broken up.
- What bonding is and how it applies to networking.
- What network speed is.
- How distance applies in networking and how it can affect the design of a network.
- What wireless NICs are and how to install them in different situations.
- What access points are and how to configure them.
- About the proper placement of access points.
- What SSIDs are.
- Some of the configuration options that apply when setting up a wireless LAN.

Knowledge Assessment

Fill in the Blank

Complete the following sentences by writing the correct word or words in the blanks provided.

1. _____ is one of the oldest and most widely used LAN technologies in use today.

2. The four types of Ethernet frames are _____, _____, _____, and _____.

3. Ethernet _____ and _____ are the same Ethernet frame type but with different names.

4. In Ethernet DIX the DIX stands for _____.

5. CSMA/CD stands for _____.

6. CSMA/CA stands for _____.

7. _____ is primarily used in wireless networks today.

8. The first widely used Ethernet cabling technology was_____.

9. A _____ takes place when two devices on an Ethernet network attempt to send data frames at the same time on the same wire.

10. All the computers on an Ethernet network that could potentially have a data frame collision are called the network's _____.

Multiple Choice

Circle the letter corresponding to the correct answer.

1. In 10Base-T the T stands for what?
   a. Terminated
   b. Twisted pair
   c. Trunked
   d. Bob

2. In 100Base-TX the 100 indicates what?
   a. The cable has a 100-meter range
   b. You can have up to 100 connections on the same network
   c. The cable has a throughput of 100 mbps
   d. 100 people can access the network at the same time

3. On an Ethernet-based network, computers communicate to other computers via
   _____.
   a. Broadcasts
   b. Collisions
   c. Bonding
   d. Collision domains

4. IEEE 802.11g has a total of _____ channels.
   a. 3
   b. 22
   c. 5
   d. 14

5. The following are options you may find in a Wireless Access Point's configuration screen. (Choose all that apply.)
   a. Encryption
   b. Beacon interval
   c. Collision domain interval
   d. MAC filtering

6. The LAN concept that deals with combining multiple channels on a network to increase throughput is called _____.
   a. Bonding
   b. Speed
   c. Bandwidth
   d. Distance

7. The name or number that identifies a wireless network to other wireless network devices is called a _____.
   a. SID
   b. WNID
   c. SSID
   d. NID

8. When deciding where to place a WAP, what needs to be taken into consideration? (Choose all that apply.)
   a. Range or distance of the WAP
   b. WAP encryption
   c. MAC filtering
   d. WAP channels to make sure they do not overlap

9. Which of the following are good security practices to carry out when setting up a Wireless Access Point (WAP)? (Choose all that apply.)
   a. Change the default SSID
   b. Change the default password
   c. Set up signal encryption
   d. Turn on and configure MAC filtering

10. A word that is often used synonymously with speed when discussing this LAN concept is_____. (Choose all that apply.)
    a. Distance
    b. Collisions
    c. Throughput
    d. Bandwidth

Lab Exercises

■ Lab 1

Accessing a Wireless Access Point

The purpose of this lab is to show the student how to access a wireless access point (WAP). After completing this lab, the student will know how to access and enter information into the configuration screen of a WAP similar to the one found in many homes.

MATERIALS

- A computer running Windows Vista or Windows 7
- A web browser
- A wireless access point set to factory defaults
- Paper
- Pen or pencil

PART 1:

Determine the Gateway

1. Go to the *Start* button on your computer and enter the command **cmd** in the *search* bar at the bottom of the menu and then press the **Enter** key. Figure 7-14 shows the *Start Menu* with the *Search Bar* at the bottom.

Figure 7-14

Windows 7 Start Menu showing the Search Bar

2. After hitting the **Enter** key, you will be taken to a command line interface window. Figure 7-15 shows the command line interface window.

Figure 7-15

Command line interface window

3. In the command line interface window type the command **ipconfig** and press the **Enter** key. Figure 7-16 shows a screenshot after the *ipconfig* command has been entered.

Figure 7-16

Command line interface window after the ipconfig command has been entered

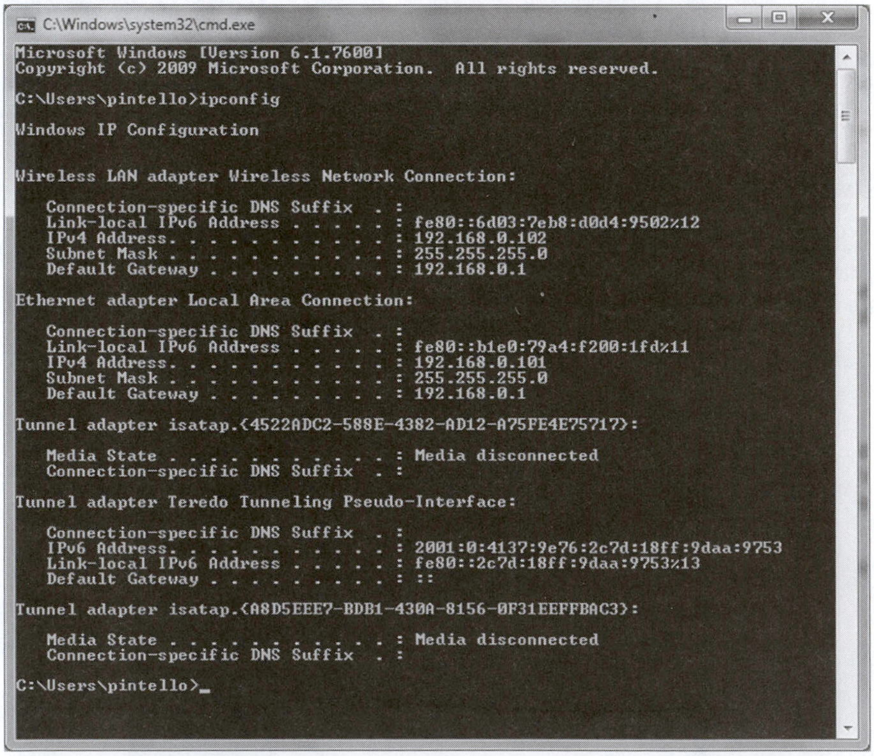

4. Notice that the *ipconfig* command results in a list of the NICs found in the computer and address information for those NICs. Look at the top NIC, if there are more than 1 listed and write down the IP address that comes after *Default Gateway* in the space here. Your Default Gateway will likely be different than the one shown in Figure 7-16.

5. Close the command line interface window after writing down the Default Gateway.

PART 2:

Open a WAP's Configuration Screen

1. Begin by opening the web browser found on your computer.

2. In the URL line, enter the IP address of the Default Gateway that you wrote down earlier. See Figure 7-17 for an example.

Figure 7-17

Web browser with the Gateway IP entered the URL line

3. Hit the **Enter** key on your keyboard. A screen similar to the screenshot in Figure 7-18 should come up. The screen will vary slightly depending on the manufacturer and model of the WAP used.

Figure 7-18

The WAP access dialog box open

4. If you are using a Linksys WAP set to factory defaults, then it does not have a username set and will only need a password. The password you will need to enter is **admin**; leave the *User Name* line blank. Once you have entered the password, click **OK** in the dialog box. The result should be a configuration screen similar to the one shown in Figure 7-19.

(Note that different WAP manufacturers and even different models of WAPs from the same manufacturer may have quite different configuration screens.)

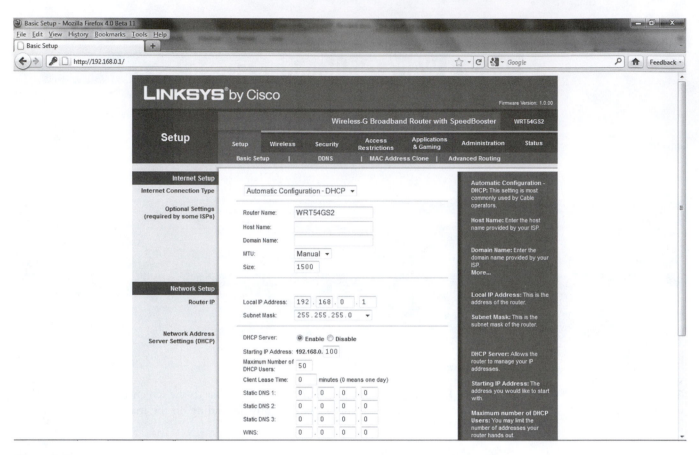

Figure 7-19

Configuration screen for a
Linksys WRT54GS2 WAP

5. Keep this screen open for the next lab.

■ Lab 2

Becoming Familiar with a WAP Configuration Screen

The purpose of this lab is to familiarize the student with some of the options available when configuring a WAP. After this lab, the student will understand what some of the available options are when configuring a WAP and what those options mean.

MATERIALS

- A computer running Windows Vista or Windows 7
- A web browser
- A WAP set to factory defaults
- Paper
- Pen or pencil

THE LAB

Become Familiar with Common Options Available in WAPs

1. Look at the opening WAP configuration screen. If they are shown, write down the following information on a separate piece of paper.

   Router Name:

   Local IP Address:

   Is DHCP enabled (yes or no):

2. List each of the main menu options as well as the submenu options available for the WAP you have entered. For the WAP in Figure 7-19, the main menu options are: Setup, Wireless, Security, Access Restrictions, Applications & Gaming, Administration, and Status.

   The sub-menu options for Setup are Basic Setup, DDNS, MAC Address Clone, and Advanced Routing.

   Write down all the main menu and sub-menu options for the WAP you have entered on a separate piece of paper.

3. Does the WAP you have entered give descriptions for what each of its settings do and what they are? The WAP shown in Figure 7-19 does; the information on the right side of the screen is a description of each setting and what it does.

   Choose three settings on your WAP, write down the three settings and their description on a separate piece of paper.

4. Open the various menus and sub-menus available on your WAP and read the descriptions of each of the options that are available.

   Choose three that catch your attention and write down the setting name and its description on a separate piece of paper.

WAN Technologies

EXAM OBJECTIVE MATRIX

Technology Skill Covered	Exam Objective	Exam Objective Number

Types of Circuit Switching	**Categorize WAN technology types and properties.**
	• Properties:
	  • Circuit switch
	  • Packet switch
		3.4

Transmission Media	**Categorize WAN technology types and properties.**
	• Types:
	  • DWDM
	  • Satellite
	  • Cellular
	  • WiMAX
	  • LTE
	  • HSPA+
	  • Fiber
	  • PON
	• Properties:
	  • Speed
	  • Transmission media
	  • Distance
		3.4

Various WAN Technologies	**Categorize WAN technology types and properties.**
	• Types:
	  • T1/E1
	  • T3/E3
	  • DS3
	  • OCx
	  • SONET
	  • SDH
	  • ISDN
	  • Cable
	  • DSL
	  • Dialup
	  • Frame relay
	  • ATMs
	• Properties:
	  • Speed
	  • Transmission media
	  • Distance
		3.4

	Describe different network topologies. • MPLS	3.5
Remote Access	Explain the methods of network access security. • Tunneling and encryption: • VPN	5.2

KEY TERMS

asymmetric digital subscriber line (ADSL)

asynchronous time division multiplexing

Asynchronous Transfer Mode (ATM)

broadband

cell

circuit switching

customer premise equipment (CPE)

demarc

demarcation point

Dense Wavelength Division Multiplexing (DWDM)

dial-up

digital subscriber line (DSL)

E-1

E-3

fractional T-1

Frame Relay

geostationary orbit (GSO)

geosynchronous orbit (GEO)

high-bit-rate digital subscriber line (HDSL)

Integrated Services Digital Network (ISDN)

Integrated Services Digital Network-Basic Rate Interface (ISDN-BRI)

Integrated Services Digital Network-Primary Rate Interface (ISDN-PRI)

last mile

leased line

local loop

Low Earth orbit (LEO)

Medium Earth orbit (MEO)

message switching

Molniya orbit

Multiprotocol Label Switching (MPLS)

network termination

OC-x

packet switching

Passive Optical Network (PON)

plain old telephone service (POTS)

Private Branch Exchange (PBX)

private network

public network

Public Switched Telephone Network (PSTN)

remote access

Remote Access Services (RAS)

remote access VPN

satellite communications

server-side compression

site-to-site VPN

symmetric digital subscriber line (SDSL)

Synchronous Digital Hierarchy (SDH)

Synchronous Optical Network (SONET)

T-1

T-3

T-Lines

terminal equipment

time division multiplexing

V.44

very-high-bit-rate digital subscriber line (VDSL)

virtual circuit switching

virtual private network (VPN)

Worldwide Interoperability for Microwave Access (WiMAX)

X.25

Will Smith is a WAN engineer. The company he works for has just bought a larger company that was going out of business, which brings several different locations from around the country together into one corporation. He has been tasked by the company to come up with a comprehensive plan for the company's WAN communications for all the new locations that have been acquired. He will need to set up main lines of communications as well as backup lines of communications. Additionally, Will needs to do this in a cost-effective and efficient manner. Where should Will start? What options does Will have that will allow him to carry out his company's directive?

■ Types of Circuit Switching

THE BOTTOM LINE

In this section of Lesson 8, we discuss various technologies used to send data across networks. Specifically we discuss circuit switching, packet switching, message switching, and virtual circuit switching.

Circuit switching by its most basic definition is a type of communications that establishes a dedicated communications channel for the duration of a given transmission. There are several options by which this is done. One option is called circuit switching after the operation that is being carried out. Another is virtual circuit switching. Finally, the last means of carrying out this type of communications is with packet switching. Each of these three methods functions differently, but all of them are used to establish communication channels for transmission of data.

Circuit Switching

Actual circuit switching is the oldest means by which communications channels were established. Probably the oldest and most well known example of a basic circuit switched network is the telephone service. The earliest examples of this network have been around since the late 1800s. When a phone call is made, different physical network segments are linked together to create a single unbroken telephone circuit for each phone call. The best way to visualize this is to think about an old movie you may have seen where a phone operator had to physically connect different lines together for a phone call to go through. Today this is done with specialized automatic phone switches, but the idea is still the same. Figure 8-1 illustrates what circuit switching looks like. The heavier line is the pre-established connection that the communications will flow down.

> **TAKE NOTE** *
>
> It should be noted that circuit switching is not limited to just voice communications. Any situation where a dedicated line is needed to be continuously up is a good candidate for circuit switching. Many dedicated lines between two fixed locations are circuit switched.

Figure 8-1

In circuit switching, a connection is established from one end of the communications link to the other before data is sent

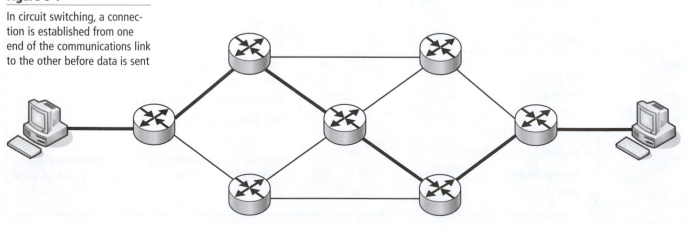

Packet Switching

Packet switching is a network communications technology that only opens up connections long enough for a small data packet to move from one network segment to another. In a data packet, data regardless of type, content, or structure is broken up into small blocks of data called packets. Each packet is then given enough information to find its own path to its intended destination.

One of the main differences between packet switched networks and circuit switched networks is that dedicated communications circuits are not required to send data to its intended destination. The advantage of this is that if a circuit is broken for whatever reason, the follow-on packets simply find a different path to their intended destination. This makes it very difficult for a single point of failure to bring down a larger network. In fact, this very reason is why the military developed packet switching in the first place. They were concerned that an enemy strike on a single location could bring down all data communications.

Figure 8-2 illustrates how packet switching works. The data to be communicated is broken up into discreet packets and then those packets are sent out on the network. Each packet is responsible for finding is own route to its destination and so different packets end up taking different routes. Once the packets reach their destination, they are most likely going to be out of sequence. Because of this, they will need to be put back into their original sequence before the data can be processed.

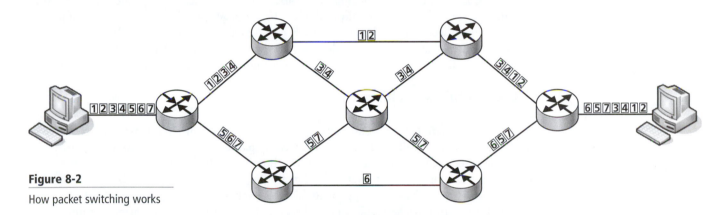

Figure 8-2

How packet switching works

The military's goal of creating a network that could not be taken down by the destruction of a single critical node has been empirically proven successful. The attack on the World Trade Center on September 11, 2001 was an attempt by a foreign terrorist to destroy up to one-quarter of America's entire communications capacity and an even larger percentage of America's financial data communications.

If the attack had worked, riots, food shortage, fuel shortages, and economic chaos and collapse would have likely resulted. In short, the attack on the communications center known as the World Trade Center in New York was an attempt to utterly destroy the economic capacity of the United States for a decade or more. Worse, if the first attempt on the World Trade Centers in 1993 had been successful, the goal of those terrorists would have most likely been realized.

What saved the United States in 2001 was the advent of packet switching technology on a large scale. When the central communications node known as the World Trade Center was destroyed, the data packets that would have traveled through them found alternative routes. The result was that while network communications slowed slightly until additional capacity was added elsewhere to make up for the capacity lost with the World Trade Center, America did not lose its ability to communicate or send financial transactions. Stores use these electronic financial transactions to pay for food, fuel, and goods. In short, from the point of view of the true goal of the attack on the World Trade Center, it was an utter failure. However, that attack did result in changes to the American way of life that we feel even today.

For all its advantages, there are disadvantages to using packet switching technology as well. The biggest disadvantage is that it incurs delays in communications that are not felt with circuit switching. There are several reasons for these delays. One reason is that each packet has to stop numerous times it its journey to wait in queues while it is processed and sent on to the next hop on its journey to its ultimate destination. Another cause of delay is the fact all the data packets that are part of a specific data communication have to arrive and then be rearranged into their proper sequence before they can be processed. Virtual circuit switching is an attempt to overcome these problems with packet switching; that concept is discussed in more detail later.

Message Switching

Message switching is another network communications technology and is related to packet switching. In fact, message switching was the precursor to packet switching and led to the development of packet switching. *Message switching* is a data communications technology that routes whole messages to their destination one hop at a time. Leonard Kleinrock first developed this technology in 1961. Over time, the message switching idea evolved into what we call packet switching today. With message switching, the entire message is sent out one message at a time. In packet switching the message is broken up into smaller packets and then sent out.

Message switching today is more likely to be known as store-and-forward. The biggest technology currently using this method of switching is e-mail. In an e-mail server, messages are stored and then sent out as a group to the next stop down the line. Even though e-mail servers use a form of message switching to send e-mails, the server is likely to use circuit switching or virtual circuit switching to send out the messages. The biggest advantage of store-and-forward is that messages can be stored during high-traffic times and then sent out later when network traffic has slowed down.

Virtual Circuit Switching

Virtual circuit switching is an attempt to keep the efficiency of circuit switched technology while taking advantage of the flexibility allowed by packet switched technology. In virtual circuit switched technology, a communications link is established between two points in a larger network such as the Internet. Additionally the data to communicate is broken into discreet packets just like what happens in packet switching. Once a link is established and the data broken into packets, the data packets are then sent to the destination computer using the pre-established communications path. Figure 8-3 illustrates how this works.

Figure 8-3

How virtual circuit switched communications work

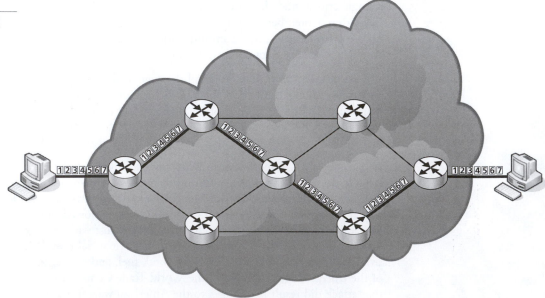

In Figure 8-3 the large cloud indicates a large unknown network such as the Internet. The heavier line linking the computer on one end to the computer on the other end represents the pre-established link through the network between the two computers. Once the communications link is established, the packets are allowed to flow through it to the destination. This makes the communications faster than packet switching because all the packets are following the same route to their destination and are kept in order. Another advantage is that since the packets are following a pre-established communications link, they do not need to wait in queue to be processed at every router so they can be sent on their way. The full route is already predetermined and all the packets have to do is follow it. Once the data one computer needs to communicate to the other computer is sent and received by the computer on the other end, the link is torn down. If the computer needs to establish a new link to the destination computer, a new dedicated link is established that may or may not follow the same route as the previous link. VPN is an example of a technology that makes extensive use of virtual circuit switching through the Internet.

■ Transmission Media

THE BOTTOM LINE

This portion of Lesson 8 discusses different types of media that are available for WAN network communications. Specifically we will discuss copper cables, fiber-optic cables, microwave signals, satellites, and radio frequency media in the form of cellular networks.

WAN networks, just like LAN networks, use different types of media to transmit data across them. While some of the media used for WAN data transmissions is similar to those used for LAN data transmissions, some are unique to the WAN environment. However, even in the WAN media that is similar to the transmission media found in LANs, the implementation is different. Copper wires, fiber-optic cables, and radio frequency (RF) signals are used in both LANs and WANs, though their implementation is different. Other types of media such as microwaves and satellite communications are different and are generally not found in LAN implementations.

Copper Cables

Copper cables are the oldest network transmission media used. Copper cables use pulses of electricity down a copper wire to transmit network communications. However, in WAN environments copper has pretty much been replaced by other media. About the only place in a WAN environment that copper media is still used is when the network is in the last segment leading up to the LAN. Examples of this would be the digital subscriber line (DSL) coming into homes and small businesses, or the broadband used by cable companies for the same purpose. Phone lines also still use copper in the last part of the network connections. However up to distribution boxes on the street and often coming directly into businesses, fiber-optic cables are now the preferred media for WAN networks.

Fiber-Optic Cables

As stated in Lesson 3, fiber-optic cables are the dominant transmission media used in WAN environments. Fiber-optic cables in their most basic form are very small hollow glass tubes with a reflective coating that allow them to reflect pulses of light down the tube as a means of transmitting network communications. Fiber-optic cables come in two different modes:

- **Single-mode fiber** is thinner than multimode fiber and carries very compact light pulses. Single-mode fiber is generally baseband and can carry signals much farther than multimode fiber is able to.

- **Multimode fiber** is a bit thicker than single-mode fiber and carries less compact pulses of light. Multimode fiber cables are able to carry broadband signals and is usually used for shorter range applications because the less compact nature of the light pulses it transmits cannot carry as far as the more compact light pulses used by single-mode fiber.

PON

- PON stands for *Passive Optical Network*. PON is a point-to-multipoint fiber optics network. This means that a signal from once source goes out to multiple end points. It works similar to broad band in that an Internet Service Provider will have one fiber optic cable going out from its main office but then splits the signal up with a passive splitter to send the signal to several destinations.

- When going downstream from the central office, the signal is broadcast to all destinations the fiber optic cable goes to. Oftenencryption is used to ensure the privacy of the different destinations the fiber optic cable connects to. Upstream, a form of *time division multiplexing* is used to ensure that all the locations connected to the fiber optic cable have equal access to the media. Time division multiplexing is where a signal is broken up into different time segments and each location on the fiber optic cable is assigned its own time segment.

DWDM

- *DWDM* stands for *Dense Wavelength Division Multiplexing*. DWDM is a type of multiplexing that uses wavelength to place more data on a cable rather than time segments. DWDM assigns different signals to different wavelengths of light. Because DWDM uses fiber optic cables it is able to transmit multiple wavelengths of light at the same time thus increasing the bandwidth of the fiber optics cable. ATM, SONET, and SDHare all WAN technologies that are able to use DWDM. We will be discussing each of the WAN technologies just listed later in this Lesson. For now you just need to understand that these technologies are able to use DWDM to send data across fiber optic cables.

Microwaves

Microwaves are a form of wireless communications seen in WAN environments. Microwaves use the electromagnetic spectrum between the frequencies of 300 MHz and 300 GHz. This range effectively covers all RF wireless technologies available. This includes Wi-Fi, Bluetooth, and Cellular technologies. Up until the advent of fiber-optic cables for communications; microwaves were the preferred method for sending phone signals long distances. As you can see from this list, microwaves are still quite commonly used in both LAN and WAN environments.

However, when WAN engineers discuss microwave communications used in WANs, they usually have a specific technology in mind—a point-to-point wireless technology. The way this is most often implemented is with two directional microwave transceivers facing each other. These transceivers are then used to send signals back and forth between the two locations.

The main drawback of this technology is in the point-to-point configuration just discussed, the transceivers need to be line of sight. This means that the transceivers need to be placed in high locations because if the transceivers are below the curve of the Earth from each other, the signals cannot be received. This line of sight is the biggest range limitation for this technology. As long as the transceivers are within line of sight of each other, distance is not really a limitation.

WiMAX

WiMAX stands for *Worldwide Interoperability for Microwave Access*. WiMAX is a wireless communications standard that uses microwaves as the communications media of choice. The

IEEE 802.16 standard introduced WiMAX. This microwave based communications system is used in some cellular phones but is mostly used as an alternative to DSL or Cable internet access in metropolitan areas. Alternatively WiMAX is used as a wireless medium for VoIP, IPTV, and other data communications services.

The most current version of WiMAX is 802.16m. This standard allows for a data rate of up to 40 megabits per second on mobile platforms and up to a 1 gigabit per second data rates on fixed platforms. WiMAX has a maximum fixed platform range of 30 miles and a maximum mobile platform range of 3 to 5 miles. The LTE, Long Term Evolution, standard is being developed in parallel to WiMAX as an alternative technology that basically does the same thing as WiMAX. We will discuss LTE later in this Lesson.

Satellite Communications

Satellite communications are a variation on microwave communications as both the ground stations and the satellites themselves use microwave signals to communicate with each other. With satellite communications, instead of two microwave towers communicating to each other, a ground station communicates to one or more satellites in orbit. The satellites then either relay the communications to a different ground station out of the line of sight of the original ground station, or another satellite in orbit within its line of sight. Since the satellites are using microwave signals to communicate with each other, they too are limited by line of sight just like microwave towers; however, with satellites being so far up in space, they have a much longer line of sight to each other. Another limitation with satellite communications is latency caused by the time it takes a signal to travel all the way up to the satellite and then all the way back down. The higher up a satellite is the longer it takes a signal to reach it. Latency can also be caused by the amount of time it takes to process the signal both on the ground and in the satellite.

CERTIFICATION READY
What are satellite communications? What advantage does satellite communication have over other types of communication?
3.4

Depending on how high up a satellite orbits, it can have a lesser or greater line of sight. The drawback to this is that the higher the satellite's orbit, the stronger the microwave signal has to be to get to it from a ground station and the greater the latency caused by distance. The trade-off just described works something like the following example. The higher a satellite's orbit, the fewer satellites are needed to be able to see every point on the earth but the more power it takes to signal them and the longer the signal takes to travel. The ideal position for seeing the largest area is something called *geosynchronous orbit (GEO)*, which is also known as *geostationary orbit (GSO)*. Satellites in this orbit maintain their position over a set geographic position at all times. Additionally, only three satellites are able to see most positions on the Earth. For a satellite to be in geosynchronous orbit, it must be 35,786 kilometers up and orbit along the Earth's equator. Because of the position geosynchronous satellites must maintain, they are not able to be reached by ground stations in higher latitudes. This includes areas like Canada or Russia. In other words, a satellite in geosynchronous orbit is not able to communicate with sites in the more northern parts of Russia, Canada, and Alaska.

To resolve this problem, an orbit called the Molniya orbit was developed. The Molniya orbit was named after a group of Soviet era satellites that used this orbit. The *Molniya orbit* is an orbit designed to cover locations in far northern regions. Russia makes great use of this orbit dynamic. With three satellites in Molniya orbits, 24-hour coverage of far northern regions can be achieved. Molniya orbits vary between 200 and 1,000 kilometers from the Earth's surface. It is the higher side of this orbit that is used for communications in higher latitudes. The diagram in Figure 8-4 illustrates what a Molniya orbit generally looks like.

While a combination of the Molniya orbit and geostationary orbits can give worldwide coverage for WAN communications, because of how high geosynchronous orbit is, a great deal of power is still needed to send microwave signals those distances, not to mention the latency issues. Because of this power requirement, two other general orbit ranges have been developed. These ranges are *Low Earth orbit (LEO)* and *Medium Earth orbit (MEO)*.

Figure 8-4

Molniya orbit

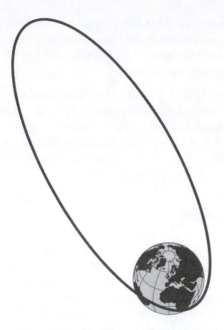

Low Earth orbit is commonly used for handheld satellite communications. LEO is generally considered to be any orbit between 160 kilometers up and 2,000 kilometers up. Because of how low this orbit is, it is easier to create a handheld device that can send a signal this distance. There are several companies using satellites in this orbit for communications in remote areas. Two of these companies are Global Star and Iridium. Iridium has a constellation of 66 satellites being used for communications in LEO. Another advantage of LEO orbits is that they are below the Van Allen Radiation belts. Most human spaceflight has taken place in LEO. The primary exceptions to this are the various Apollo trips to the Moon.

The other commonly used Earth orbit is something called Medium Earth orbit (MEO), which has a very wide range of orbits. These orbits are all between 2,000 kilometers and about 34,780 kilometers up. The primary use for this particular orbit is the various GPS networks that have been put into space.

Figure 8-5 is a graphic of most of the orbits discussed here. Table 8-1 is the legend for Figure 8-5.

Figure 8-5

Primary orbits in use for satellite communications networks

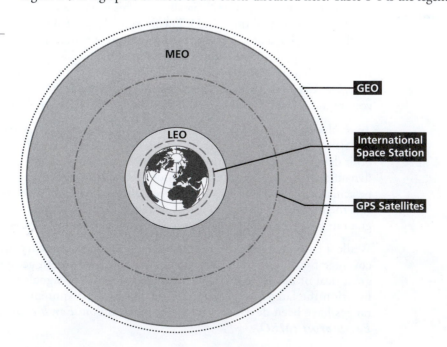

Table 8-1

Legend for Figure 8-5

Graphic Description	Legend	Distance above Surface of the Earth (in kms)
Earth	globe in center	0
Low Earth orbit (LEO)	light gray tinted area	160–2,000
Medium Earth orbit (MEO)	dark gray tinted area	2,000–34,780
International Space Station (ISS)	dashed line	350
Global Positioning System (GPS)	dash-dot-dot-dash line	20,230
Geostationary orbit (GEO)	Black dotted line	35,786

Radio Frequency (RF)

Finally, we can discuss radio frequencies that are used in WAN communications. This, like the satellites just discussed, is actually a subset of microwave communications. Any network communications technology that uses radio frequencies for communications is really a subset of microwave communications. In the case of WANs, cellular networks are the most common form of radio frequency WAN media.

The term cellular comes from the way a cellular network functions. Each transceiver tower in a cellular network is able to broadcast up to a set range based on the technology used; generally, each one of the cellular transceiver towers can broadcast in a radius between 1 and 30 kilometers wide. Each of these broadcast circles is called a cell, thus any network that uses this technology is called a cellular network.

While early cell networks used antenna that broadcasted in an omni-directional manner, modern cell networks do not because directional antenna can get a longer range for the same amount of power. Today, when a cell tower is being set up, it is usually equipped with three directional antennas pointed 120 degrees away from each other, allowing full coverage in a circle around the tower while pushing the range of the tower out farther. Because of this configuration, cells are generally represented as hexagons with a cell tower at each corner. Each of the antennas on the tower also uses a different channel so that none of the channels on a tower overlap. This configuration also allows the tower to service three different signals. As long as no two adjacent towers use the same channels, there will be no cross-channel overlap in a cellular network.

Figure 8-6 shows a hexagonal cellular network design. Notice that all the channels are at least three towers away from any other tower with the same channel. This is done so that the cellular channels do not overlap one another. Well-known cellular networks such as 2G, 3G, and 4G use this method to create WAN communications networks.

CELLULAR

CERTIFICATION READY
What are some widely used Cellular standards?
3.4

A cellular network is a radio frequency based communications network spread over a large land area. A cellular network is made up of individual transceiver points that slightly overlap the range of other transceiver points adjacent to it. Each of these transceiver points is called a cell and is where we get the term cellular network from. The most well-known cellular network is the mobile phone or cell phone network.

There are a wide variety of technologies that are used to make up the cells used in cellular networks. Table 8-2 is a list of all the various cellular technologies that have been used or proposed. It is not required that you know this table for the CompTIA Network+ exam but it is useful for seeing how the different cellular technologies relate to each other and which cellular technology families, or organizational development groups, they belong to. We will discuss a few of the more current cellular technologies after Table 8-2.

Figure 8-6

Cellular network and channels

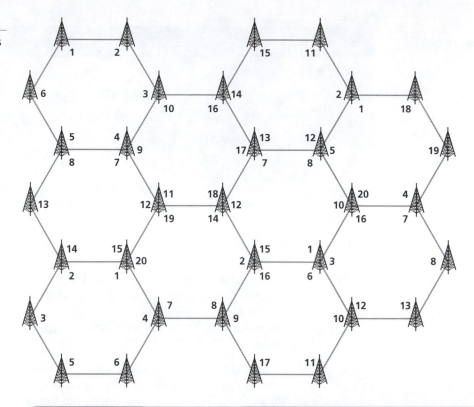

Table 8-2

Cellular technologies and how they are related to each other

TECHNOLOGY NAME	TECHNOLOGY FAMILY	TECHNOLOGY STANDARDS WITHIN FAMILY
0G (Radio Telephone)	None	MTS, MTA, MTB, IMTS, MTD, AMTS, OLT, Autoradiopuhelin
1G	AMPS	AMPS (TIA/EIA/IS-3, ANSI/TIA/EIA-553), N-AMPS (TIA/EIA/IS-91), TACS, ETACS
	Other	NMT, Hicap, Mobitex, DataTAC
2G	GSM/3GPP	GSM, CSD
	3GPP2	cmdaOne (TIA.EIA/IS-95 and ANSI-J-STD 008)
	AMPS	D-AMPS (IS-54 and IS-136)
	Other	CDPD, iDEN, PDC, PHS
2G Transitional (2.5G, 2.75G)	GSM/3GPP	HSCSD, GPRS, EDGE/EGPRS (UWC-136)
	3GPP2	CDMA2000 1X (TIA/EIA/IS-2000), 1X Advanced
	Other	WiDEN
3G (IMT-2000)	3GPP	UMTS (UTRAN), WCDMA-FDD, WCDMA-TDD, UTRA-TDD LCR (TD-SCDMA)
	3GPP2	CDMA2000 1xEV-DO Release 0 (TIA/IS-856)
3G Transitional (3.5G, 3.75G, 3.9G)	3GPP	HSPA, HSPA+, LTE (E-UTRA)
	3GPP2	CDMA2000 1xEV-DO Revision A (TIA/EIA/IS-856-A), EV-DO Revision B (TIA/EIA/IS-856-B), DO Advanced
	IEEE	Mobile WiMAX (IEEE 802.16e), Flash-OFDM, IEEE 802.20
4G (IMT-Advanced)	3GPP	LTE Advanced (E-UTRA)
	IEEE	WiMAX-Advanced (IEEE 802.16m)
5G		Research concept not under formal development

LTE

LTE stands for Long Term Evolution and is a result of the 3rd Generation Partnership Project also known as 3GPP. It is intended to be a replacement for the 3G cellular communications protocol. LTE is often marketed as 4G in the United States, however it does not comply fully with the IMT Advanced 4G standards which are the "true" 4G standard.

LTE Advanced

LTE Advanced is an updated version of the LTE standard. This standard has been approved by the ITU and has also been approved by 3GPP as a significant improvement on the older LTE standard. The IMT Advanced 4G standard organization has also given its approval to the LTE Advanced standard. The LTE Advanced fully implements all parts of the 4G standard and so is "true" 4G unlike its predecessor LTE.

HSPA

HSPA stands for High Speed Packet Access and is one of the most widely deployed mobile broadband implementations worldwide. HSPA combines the HSDPA (High Speed Downlink Packet Access) protocol with the HSUPD (High Speed Uplink Packet Access) protocol to give both downlink and uplink capabilities to HSPA. The result of this technology is the ability to both send and receive data at much higher data rates than other technologies allow. The term downlink is used to refer to the speed at which a technologies can receive data while the term uplink refers to the speed a technology can use to send data.

HSPA+

HSPA+ or Evolved High Speed Packet Access is a newer version of HSPA and gives even greater downlink and uplink speeds. A number of companies have announced plans to deploy the newer Evolved HSPA in their broadband wireless cellular networks.

■ Various WAN Technologies

THE BOTTOM LINE

In this section of the lesson, we discuss the various WAN technologies that are used to move data across WANs including dial-up, ISDN, DSL technologies, broadband technologies, Frame Relay, and ATM.

Over the years various specific WAN technologies have been developed to communicate data over large networks. This section of Lesson 8 will discuss some of these specific technologies. Some of these technologies are obsolete, while some are just old technologies that are still in use today. It will also discuss some of the new technologies that are now available.

Dial-Up

Dial-up is one of the oldest WAN network communication technologies available and is still used in some areas of both the United States and abroad. *Dial-up* works by using a device called a modem to connect a computer to a *plain old telephone service (POTS)*. POTS is just what it sounds like, it is the standard telephone service that pretty much every household in America has access to.

One of the biggest advantages to dial-up network communications, which really comes down to dial-up Internet access, is that it does not require any additional infrastructure beyond a standard telephone connection and a modem card. Modem cards are an inexpensive and readily available technology. Another advantage of dial-up Internet service is its cost. In many places dial-up is actually available for free. Where it is not free, it can be obtained for a very minimal charge of between $5 and $10 a month. Finally, dial-up access is generally available anywhere in the United States and around the world, even when other types of Internet access are unavailable.

The single biggest drawback of dial-up Internet access is speed. Dial-up Internet is limited to about 50 kbps transfer rates. While speed is the biggest limiting factor for using dial-up to access the Internet, some interesting modern technologies are making attempts at minimizing that problem.

One modern technology attempting to work around the speed limitations for dial-up is a compression standard called *V.44*. V.44 can compress text transmitted across a dial-up Internet connection by a factor of 6. This means that if a dial-up connection normally runs at a speed of 50 kbps, using V.44 compression, the effective speed of transmission becomes around 300 kbps for text files. Unfortunately, V.44 does not work as well on other types of files such as ZIP files, JPEG images, MP3 audio files, MPEG video files, and other already compressed file types.

In addition to using the V.44 compression standards, many dial-up service providers are beginning to use *server-side compression* on a proxy server before sending out data across a dial-up connection. The compression achieved with server-side compression is even more impressive that the compression that can achieved using V.44. Using server-side compression techniques, text files can actually be compressed to as little as 5 percent of their original size, and compressed graphics and other such files can be compressed potentially to as little as 15 percent to 20 percent of their original size. The drawback to compressing already compressed files is that the quality of the original data suffers. However, service providers that do compress already compressed data allow for the option of downloading the data without being additionally compressed. This however effectively eliminates the reason for compressing the data a second time in the first place.

While these compression rates are not always achieved with server-side compression, large compression rates are still achievable. This results in sending more data in a compressed form across dial-up connections in the same amount of time. This can potentially create effective transmission rates anywhere from 250 kbps to as much as 1,000 kbps for dial-up connections under the right circumstances. This does not mean that the actual transmission rate is anywhere near these speeds; it just means that the apparent transmission rate is at these speeds. The actually transmission rate will still be around 50 kbps.

PUBLIC SWITCHED TELEPHONE NETWORK (PSTN)

Public Switched Telephone Network (PSTN) refers to the entire worldwide telephone network. PSTN uses circuit switching to establish connections between different phones. Any copper cables, fiber-optic cables, microwave signals, satellite communications, or cellular networks that are used to allow any phone anywhere in the world to connect to any other phone in the world is part of the PSTN. The term POTS, or plain old telephone service, is sometimes used interchangeably with PSTN, but in reality it specifically refers to that part of the PSTN used for more conventional voice grade services.

The PSTN has multiple parts. The first part of the PSTN is the customer's home or business. Where the PSTN service provider comes into a local home or business is called the *demarc* point, which is short for *demarcation point*. The responsibility of the PSTN or other network providers ends here. What goes on inside the customer's home or business is the customer's responsibility. What happens from the demarc point outward is the service provider's responsibility.

From the demarc point to the remote switching facility is the next portion of the PSTN. The remote switching facility is basically the green or silver box located somewhere in your neighborhood, or underground in the nearest PSTN provider's manhole in some cases. This is sometimes also called the *last mile*; although the last mile can be either much shorter or much longer than one mile, depending on where you live. In rural areas, the last mile tends to be very long and it is often a technological challenge to get data from the remote switching facility to the demarc in a customer's home in such areas. This is much less of a challenge in towns and cities because of how much closer homes and businesses are together.

From the remote switching facility to a location called the central office is the next part of the PSTN. The central office is generally a building somewhere within a few miles of your home or business in towns and cities, although it may be a few tens of miles in more rural areas. The central office is where all the remote switching facility boxes terminate. The whole thing from a customer's demarc to the central office is called the *local loop*. The size of your local loop is very important because the size of your local loop and your proximity to the central office can affect the performance of your telecommunications equipment. The closer you are located to the central office, the better your dial-up and to some extent your digital subscriber line (DSL) speeds will be. Figure 8-7 illustrates both what the local loop is as well as what the last mile refers to.

Figure 8-7

The last mile and the local loop

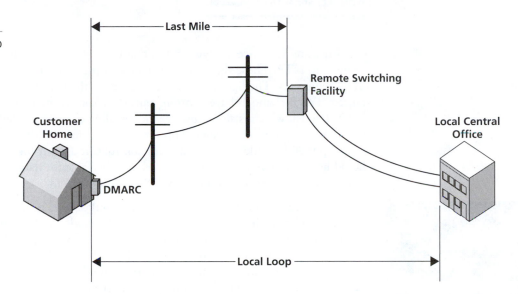

After your local office, you have a regional office. The regional office is where the local offices terminate and allow communications to take place outside of the local loops connected to the central office.

Finally, the regional offices are linked together by national and then international offices. National offices allow communications to take place between regional offices. The national office allows one region in a larger country such as the United States to communicate to other regions within the United States. Smaller nations may not have a need for regional offices due to their size. In these situations, the local offices connect directly to the national office. International offices allow communications to take place between national offices. It is the international office that allows communications to move out of one country and into another country. For communications to work around the world, multiple international offices are required to link the various national offices together. These international offices are interconnected to each other.

TAKE NOTE*

Satellite communications and the Internet have the ability to bypass national and international offices.

Integrated Services Digital Network (ISDN)

ISDN stands for *Integrated Services Digital Network* and is a set of standards that have been designed to carry voice, video, data, and other services in a digital format over the PSTN. Because ISDN is intended to be used over the PSTN, it uses circuit switching technology to establish, maintain, and release connections. Even though ISDN is a circuit switched technology, it does allow access to packet switched networks as well. Aside from higher speeds, the biggest advantage of ISDN over dial-up is that it is able to integrate voice and data over the same lines. ISDN allows 64 kbps to be transmitted over a single channel. ISDN also has the ability to bind multiple channels together for higher data rates. Figure 8-8 illustrates how a basic ISDN network and device may be set up.

TAKE NOTE*

ISDN is an older technology, but it is still listed in the CompTIA Network+ objectives and so may appear on the Network+ exam. Because of this, ISDN still needs to be covered.

Figure 8-8

Basic configuration of an ISDN networked device

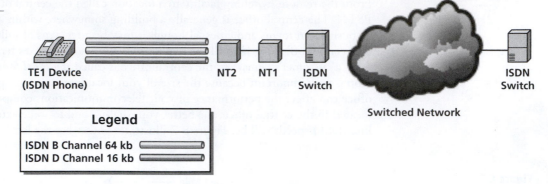

The first thing to notice in Figure 8-8 is that there are three conduits where the ISDN phone connects to NT2. Those three conduits represent the three different channels that a basic ISDN setup uses. The light gray conduits represent the two B channels that are used for data transfer. The B channels have a throughput of 64 kbps each. The dark gray conduit represents the D channel, which is also known as the signaling channel or control channel. The D channel has a throughput of 16 kbps. This means that a basic ISDN circuit has 128 kbps of data throughput and an additional 16 kbps of control throughput for a total of 144 kbps. It should however be noted that only 128 kbps is available for data. It is for this reason that some people say that basic ISDN has 128 kbps throughput.

As you can also see in Figure 8-8, there are several devices needed to make ISDN work. The first device in the figure is labeled TE1. TE stands for *terminal equipment*. Simply put this is the phone, computer, or other device that is connected to the ISDN network. After this device, there are two devices labeled NT2 and NT1. The NT stands for *network termination*. Network termination devices are used to convert the 4-wire subscriber line to the conventional 2-wire setup coming into most homes via the local loop. The NT type 1 or NT1 device is considered *customer premise equipment (CPE)* in the United States and it is generally the responsibility of the customer to provide this equipment, often by leasing it from the ISDN provider. In other parts of the world, the NT1 device is considered part of the network and is provided by the carrier.

NT type 2 or NT2 device is a more complicated device and is usually part of the *Private Branch Exchange (PBX)*. A PBX is a telephone exchange, or telephone switch, that serves a private business or office rather than one owned by a phone company. NT2 devices are intelligent and work on both Layers 2 and 3 of the OSI Model. The functionality of both the NT1 and NT2 devices can also be combined into one device, which is sometimes referred to as NT1/2. The network termination devices are then connected to the ISDN switch, which is how the ISDN network is able to connect to the larger switched network. This is represented by the cloud in Figure 8-8. Finally, the other end of the ISDN connection is another ISDN switch. The ISDN network on the destination end is configured more or less like the ISDN network on the source end.

INTEGRATED SERVICES DIGITAL NETWORK-BASIC RATE INTERFACE (ISDN-BRI)

Integrated Services Digital Network-Basic Rate Interface (ISDN-BRI) is an entry-level version of ISDN and is the most commonly used version. ISDN BRI is able to achieve both upstream and downstream data rates by bonding to 64 kbps channels together. These data channels are called B channels and are known as bearer channels. In addition to the two 64 kbps channels, ISDN BRI has one 16 kbps signaling a channel called a delta channel or a D channel. This channel carries the Q.931 protocol, which is a set of protocols related to establishing and breaking circuit switched connections as well as some more advanced calling features. In simple terms Q.931 is used by ISDN on the D channel to signal the other end of the connection. This is why the D channel is sometimes referred to as the signaling channel. When you add up all three channels that are used by ISDN-BRI, you get a total data rate of 144 kbps, though only 128 kbps of that data rate can be used to carry data.

INTEGRATED SERVICES DIGITAL NETWORK-PRIMARY RATE INTERFACE (ISDN-PRI)

The PRI portion of *ISDN-PRI* stands for *Primary Rate Interface*. This version of ISDN is very similar to ISDN-BRI except that instead of just two B channels bonded together, it has more. Additionally, the D channel for ISDN-PRI has a throughput of 64 kbps instead of 16 kbps.

In the United States, ISDN-PRI is commonly carried over a T-1 line of 1.544 mbps. This gives ISDN-PRI in the United States 23 B channels of 64 kbps and one D channel of 64 kbps for a total of 1.544 mbps. In other parts of the world, ISDN-PRI is carried on E-1 lines, which contain 30 B channels of 64 kbps and one D channel of 64 kbps. This means that an E-1 line is able to carry a total throughput of 2.048 mbps.

Digital Subscriber Line (DSL) Technologies

There are several variations on *digital subscriber line (DSL)* technology, but all of them have some common attributes. The main attribute in the various DSLs is that they are able to use the PSTN. DSL is able to do this because it uses a higher frequency than voice communications do to carry data. This means that line filters can be used to filter out the DSL signal for voice communications so they are not interfered with by the DSL data signal.

Because DSL uses higher frequencies for data communications, there are a couple of things that have to be set up in the phone system for DSL to work. Some older phone systems are not able to handle DSL.

To be able to support DSL, a phone system has to be able to cleanly carry the higher frequency signal of DSL data. Some older phone systems are not able to support these frequencies, and DSL cannot be used in these situations. However, most modern phone systems can support DSL.

Phone systems that support DSL also need a special terminal adapter on the customer end. This device is sometimes called a DSL modem. However it does not really do the job of a modem. What the adapter does is convert the digital signal of the computer to a signal of a suitable voltage level supported by the phone system. This means that the so-called DSL modem is connected directly to the computer usually via Ethernet while the other end of the terminal adapter is connected directly to the phone line where DSL comes in or goes out depending on the direction of communication.

While the DSL modem described here carries out the basic functions necessary for a phone system to use DSL, many modern DLS providers supply devices with additional functionality. Some terminal adapter can act as routers and switches in addition to providing the signal conversion of the standard DSL terminal adapter. In the case of a DSL terminal adapter that also works as a switch, some level of programming and security configuration is also available.

ASYMMETRIC DIGITAL SUBSCRIBER LINE (ADSL)

The *asymmetric digital subscriber line (ADSL)* is one of the most common forms of DSL found today. ADSL is called asymmetric because it provides a different data throughput for upstream communications than it does for downstream communications. Upstream communications refer to communications that go from the consumer or end user up to the ISP or server. Downstream communications refers to communications down to the consumer or end user. Depending on the ADSL standard being used, downstream transmission rates can range from 1.5 mbps all the way up to 12.0 mbps. For upstream transmissions, the rates range from .5 mbps to 1.8 mbps.

CERTIFICATION READY
What does DSL stand for? What is DSL? What are some variations on DSL that are used? What do the initials of those variations stand for?
3.4

In addition to various regular ADSL standards, there are also some ADSL2 and ADSL2+ standards. ADSL2 standards have downstream data rates from 1.5 mbps to 12.0 mbps and downstream data rates from .5 mbps to 3.5 mbps. The lower 1.5 mbps for downstream communications is for a version of ADSL2 that does not require a splitter for phone communications. The ADSL2+ group of standards has downstream communications rates of 24.0 mbps and upstream communications rates from 1.0 mbps to 3.5 mbps.

SYMMETRIC DIGITAL SUBSCRIBER LINE (SDSL)

A *symmetric digital subscriber line (SDSL)* has both a wide usage sense and a very specific usage sense. In the wider usage sense, SDSL refers to a group of DSL technologies that offer the same data rates for both downstream and upstream communications, which is the opposite of ADSL.

In a narrower more specific sense, SDSL refers to a specific DSL technology that supports only a single data line and does not support analog communications at all. Like in the wider usage of the term SDSL, this line offers the same data rate in both directions.

In this more narrow usage of SDSL, a single pair of copper wires is used to carry data over a SDSL connection. The data rate for this type of DSL is the same as that of a T-1 or E-1 line; SDSL used in this manner has a data rate either 1.544 mbps or 2.048 mbps depending on if the circuit is based off of U.S. standards or European standards. This type of SDSL has a range of 10,000 feet or roughly 3,000 meters and is targeted at small businesses that would like a dedicated T-1/E-1 line, but cannot afford the high cost of such a line. SDSL is usually price pointed between the cost of ADSL and T-1/E-1 lines.

CERTIFICATION READY
What are some of the differences between the various types of DSL?
3.4

HIGH-BIT-RATE DIGITAL SUBSCRIBER LINE (HDSL)

High-bit-rate digital subscriber line (HDSL) was developed to use twisted-pair copper and can carry both voice and data. HDSL uses T-1 lines and is often used to interconnect local carriers. When HDSL is being used to interconnect local carriers, repeaters are generally placed every 1.2 miles or so to accommodate this.

VERY-HIGH-BIT-RATE DIGITAL SUBSCRIBER LINE (VDSL)

Very-high-bit-rate digital subscriber line (VDSL or sometimes VHDSL) can provide very high data transfer rates. In fact, VDSL can offer up to 52 mbps downstream rates and up to 16 mbps upstream. The VDSL standard was first approved in 2001, and an updated and improved standard known as VDSL2 was approved in 2006. In the United States, AT&T, Verizon, and Qwest offer VDSL in some areas.

Broadband and Cable Modems

Broadband is a technology used by cable companies to provide data communications capabilities for their customers. In a more technical sense, broadband refers to any technology that sends more than one signal over the same communications media.

In the more technical sense just mentioned, cable television is the ultimate example of broadband. In cable television, a large number of channels are carried over the same media. In this case that media is coaxial copper cables. Cable companies use frequency multiplexing to do this. When the cable reaches the house, it is filtered twice. The first time it is filtered is at the pole. A filter is placed on the cable at the pole that filters out any major frequency ranges used for channels that the end user at that location is not paying for. The cable signal is then filtered at the television. In this case, a tuner is used to filter out all the frequencies, or channels except for the one the customer wants to view. The filter at the television is called a tuner, which is basically a variable frequency filter.

CERTIFICATION READY
What is a cable modem? What relationship does a cable modem have with broadband Internet access?
3.4

In modern network communications, cable companies add some additional frequencies or channels to accommodate Internet data communications as well. However, computers generally are not designed to receive these types of signals or do this type of filtering. As a result, a device called a *cable modem* is needed. In its most basic sense, a cable modem is a network bridge that follows the IEEE 802.1D standard to convert Ethernet frames into frames that can be read by the coaxial networks of the cable companies. The modem part of the name cable modem comes from the fact that this device needs to *modulate* the signal from the computer to use over the coaxial network of a cable company and *demodulate* the data coming from a cable company so that it can be read by the Ethernet port on a computer. However, the modulating and demodulating is not used to convert digital signals to analog signals and back again as a traditional modem does, mainly because most modern cable companies use digital signals from end to end.

X.25

X.25 is a technology that was developed in the 1970s as a means to use packet switched communications in a WAN environment. This technology is not as widely used today because it has been replaced by newer alternatives. X.25 was originally designed as an analog technology. It also does error checking on the packets it passes through.

Originally, X.25 had devices called packet-switching exchange (PSE) nodes that were used to connect different systems to the X.25 network as well as connecting the various PSEs in the X.25 network. These PSE nodes were connected in turn to data carrier equipment (DCE) that was then used to connect to different types of data terminal equipment (DTE) devices. Some of the DTE devices that connected to X.25 networks via the DCEs were computers, mainframes, communications switches, and local packet assembly/disassembly (PAD) facilities. PADs were used to connect dumb terminals to the X.25 network. Figure 8-9 illustrates the theoretical X.25 network just mentioned.

TAKE NOTE*

X.25 is another one of those technologies like ISDN that are no longer widely used but may appear on a Network+ exam.

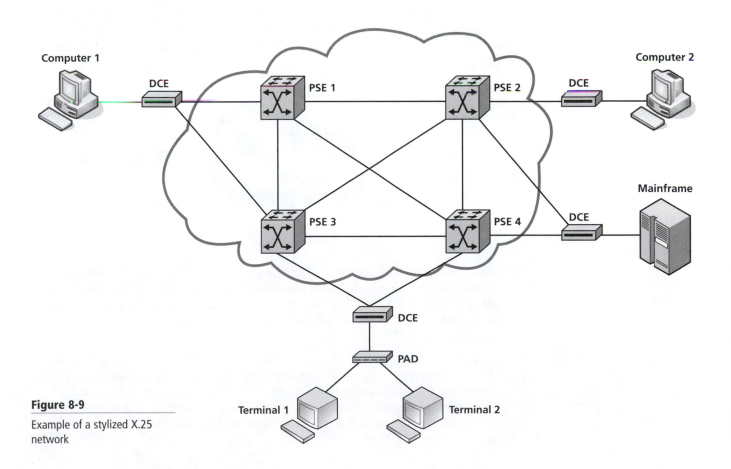

Figure 8-9

Example of a stylized X.25 network

Figure 8-9 shows what an X.25 network configuration could look like. Inside the network cloud there are four PSE nodes. These notes are then connected to various DCEs. Notice that a DCE can be connected to just one PSE or more than one PSE. The reason for connecting to more than one is to create redundancy in the network. Finally, the DCEs are connected to different types of equipment that serve as DTEs. In the upper left and right corners, the DTE is a computer or a workstation. In the lower right, the DTE is a mainframe computer. Finally, in the lower left corner, a PAD is serving as the DTE. The PAD is in turn connected to two dumb terminals, which can actually serve as interfaces to the mainframe that is located elsewhere on the X.25 network.

Frame Relay

Frame Relay is a WAN service that is designed to connect two points that require only intermittent communications. Put another way, Frame Relay is intended to connect different LANs or the endpoints of two WANs that do not require continuous connectivity to each other. This looks like a permanent virtual circuit to the end user, but it does not provide a continuous connection. Instead, the service provider determines the best route to a specific destination for each frame. Frame Relay gives the impression of a dedicated line like a T1 to the end user without the associated cost. What the end user is doing is effectively paying for a set amount of communications bandwidth between two different points, but not paying for a dedicated line to achieve that bandwidth.

This is a win-win situation for both the provider and the end user. The end user has a dedicated amount of bandwidth between two points of interest to him without paying for the cost of a dedicated connection that he does not need. And, the provider does not have to commit a full line to a specific end user and so can share that line's capacity between multiple end users so long as the end users have the full bandwidth they paid for when they need it. The end user is able to save money while the provider is able to make additional money. If at some point the end user finds that he or she does need a dedicated line, then they still have the capability to pay additional money each month and get one. Figure 8-10 illustrates how Frame Relay works.

Figure 8-10

How Frame Relay works

In Figure 8-10, a Frame Relay line running at 1.544 mbps, which is T1 speed, connects two WAN locations. While there is a dedicated connection bandwidth, the path the Frame Relay connection takes though the cloud is unknown. In this way, a service provider is able to guarantee a set bandwidth to a client company without having to set up a dedicated line between the client company's two WAN sites.

Frame Relay is able to offer full T1 service to end users as well as something called fractional T1 services without charging the full cost for such connection. A *fractional T1* is where a T1 connection is divided into 24 channels of 64 kbps each. Each fractional T1 channel is then leased to end users at less than full T1 cost. Frame Relay also works well with ISDN connections because they are made up of 64 kbps channels, just like fractional T1 channels.

Frame Relay is one of the new technologies that are replacing X.25 because Frame Relay is faster. X.25 was intended for older error-prone lines; this is why it has error-correction capabilities built into it. Alternatively, Frame Relay is intended for newer, less error-prone communications lines. For this reason, Frame Relay does not have error correction built into it and is designed to allow error correction to be handled by the end points. As a result, Frame Relay can push frames of variable sizes out over the Frame Relay connection without worrying about error correction. The end result of this is that Frame Relay is able to move data at a faster rate than X.25 due to less overhead.

T-Lines

CERTIFICATION READY
What is a T1? What are some variations available with T1 technologies? What is the European equivalent to T1 lines?
3.4

CERTIFICATION READY
What is another common designation for a T-Line?
3.4

T-Lines, also called T-carriers and sometimes T-CXR, refer to a group of technologies that used various means of digital multiplexing used in telecommunications. This technology was originally developed by Bell Labs and is used primarily in North America, Japan, and South Korea. Similar technology used elsewhere in the world is called E-carriers or E-Lines, where the E stands for European.

T-Lines are distinctive from other telecommunications technologies because they are made up of a number of smaller channels, which are created using multiplexing technology. By using multiplexing to create the smaller channels, one media cable can carry multiple channels. In the case of T-Lines, these smaller channels, or sub-channels, are 64 kbps in bandwidth.

T-Lines come in several different levels: Fractional T-Lines, *T1*, T1C, T2, *T3*, T4, and T5. The most commonly used levels however are T1, T3, and T5. Table 8-3 lists the various T-Line levels and their throughputs. Occasionally you will also find T-lines referred to as DS lines. This is seen in the table below. DS stands for Digital Signal.

Table 8-3

T-Line levels and specifications

T-LINE LEVEL	COMMON NAME	T-LINE THROUGHPUT	NUMBER OF 64KBPS CHANNELS
Level 0	Fractional T-Line or DS0	64 kbps x number of channels (but less than 24)	Number of channels purchased
Level 1	T1 or DS1	1.544 mbps	24
Intermediate Level	T1C or DS1C	3.152 mbps	48
Level 2	DS2	6.312 mbps	96
Level 3	T3 or DS3	44.736 mbps	672
Level 4	DS4	274.176 mbps	4,032
Level 5	T5 or DS5	400.352 mbps	5,760

Table 8-3 is fairly self-explanatory; however, the fractional T-Line may need an additional explanation. The reason the throughput of the fractional T-Line is listed as "64 kbps x number of channels (but less than 24)" is because a fractional T-Line is made up of a T-Line that does not use all 24 channels. In a fractional T-Line, customers lease a set number of channels from their provider and that number of leased channels times 64 kbps becomes the throughput of whatever the customer leased.

As mentioned earlier, T-carrier technology is used in North America, Japan, and South Korea, but the rest of the world generally uses a similar technology called E-carrier technology. Functionally, it is the same as T-carrier technology, but it has different specifications. Table 8-4 is the E-Line counterpart to Table 8-3.

Table 8-4

E-Line levels and specifications

E-LINE LEVEL	COMMON NAME	T-LINE THROUGHPUT	NUMBER OF 64KBPS CHANNELS
Level 0		64 kbps	1
Level 1	*E1*	2.048 mbps	32
Level 2	E2	8.448 mbps	128
Level 3	*E3*	34.386 mbps	512
Level 4	E4	139.264 mbps	2,048
Level 5	E5	565.148 mbps	8,192

As you can see when comparing Table 8-4 to Table 8-3, the specifications are quite different. Aside from different specifications, the European carriers also have a consistent, less confusing naming convention.

Asynchronous Transfer Mode (ATM)

ATM stands for Asynchronous Transfer Mode. The name comes from the fact that ATM uses asynchronous time division multiplexing to break communications into small frame-like segments called *cells*. *Asynchronous time division multiplexing* is a multiplexing technique that uses time slots to break a communications signal into different channels. It differs from conventional time division multiplexing, which breaks a signal into a set number of channels at all times without regard to whether the channels are actually being used in any given time slot. Asynchronous time division multiplexing only breaks the signals into the number of time slots needed to create the number of channels needed for current communications flow in any given time frame rather than a set number of channels such as T1s use. This allows ATM communications to more efficiently use the bandwidth available to it for communications purposes.

CERTIFICATION READY
What does ATM stand for? What is ATM? How does ATM differ from Frame Relay or T-Lines?
3.4

The ATM cells mentioned earlier are a fixed size. So, unlike frames, which they resemble, they are not able to have variable sizes. The set size of ATM cells is 5 bytes for a header and an additional 48 bytes for data. Therefore, the total size of an ATM cell is 58 bytes. The ATM uses such small cell sizes to speed up transmission across a network connection. The small set cell size makes is easier for hardware to switch ATM channels and cells because it does not have to take into account differing packet or frame sizes. This results in less delay and therefore higher throughput.

There are two types of ATM cells. One type is the NNI ATM cell, which means Network-Network Interface ATM cell (NNI). NNI ATM cells are specifically designed to manage network-to-network communications. The other type of ATM cell—the UNI ATM cell or User-Network Interface ATM cell (UNI)—is intended for use on a user-owned network as opposed to connecting two networks owned by different users. The UNI ATM cell is the most commonly used cell type. Figure 8-11 is a diagram of a UNI ATM cell. Notice how much it differs from some of the other protocol diagrams seen earlier in this book.

ATM is a connection-oriented protocol that works on the Data Link layer of the OSI Model. ATM's cell model uses properties from both circuit switched networks and small packet switched networks, making it a good choice for real-time transport for media such as voice and video. ATM is a core protocols used over both SONET backbones, which will be discussed next, and ISDN backbones, which were discussed previously.

Figure 8-11

UNI ATM cell

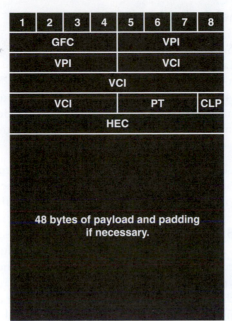

Legend
GFC – Generic Flow Control (4 bits)
VPI – Virtual Path Identifier (8 bits)
VCI – Virtual Channel Identifier (16 bits)
PT   – Payload Type (3 bits)
CLP – Cell Loss Priority (1 bit)
HEC – Header Error Control (8 bit CRC)

Synchronous Optical Networking (SONET) and Synchronous Digital Hierarchy (SDH)

Synchronous Optical Networking (SONET) and the related technology *Synchronous Digital Hierarchy (SDH)* are multiplexing protocols used to transfer multiple digital bit streams, also called channels, over fiber-optic cables using either lasers or LED (light emitting diodes). Both multiplexing protocols can also be used to send multiple digital bit streams over copper wires at data rates slower than those possible with fiber optic. SONET and SDH are essentially the same technology. The only real difference is that SONET is used in the United States and Canada, while the rest of the world uses SDH. Although SONET and SDH were originally intended for use with T-carriers, they are now used with such protocols as ATM, TCP/IP, and even Ethernet.

OC-X

SONET has several different level carriers to choose from. These levels are called SONET optical carrier levels and are abbreviated *OC-x* where *x* is the actual multiple of the base level called OC-1. The basic OC-1 level data rate is 51.84 Mbps. Each optical carrier level in turn has its own unique frame format. Table 8-4 lists different optical carrier levels, the associated frame format, and the data rate available with the associated OC-x level.

Table 8-4

SONET OC levels and associated frame formats and data rates

SONET Optical Carrier Level (OC-x)	SONET Frame Format	Associated SONET Data Rate (in Mbps)
OC-1	STS-1	51.84
OC-3	STS-3	155.52
OC-12	STS-12	622.08
OC-24	STS-24	1,244.16
OC-48	STS-48	2,488.32
OC-192	STS-192	9,953.28
OC-768	STS-768	39,813.12
OC-3072	STS-3072	159,252.48

Multiprotocol Label Switching (MPLS)

CERTIFICATION READY
What does MPLS stand for? How does MPLS work? What are some protocols that can work with MPLS?
3.5

Multiprotocol Label Switching (MPLS) is a relatively new standard approved by the Internet Engineering Task Force (ITEF), which is a standard organization for Internet technologies. MPLS's signaling protocols were laid out in RFC 3468, while its framework was laid out in RFC 3469. Both these RFCs came out in February 2003. The multiprotocol part of the name means that MPLS can interact with a wide variety of protocols used in network environments. Some of these accessible protocols are ATM, SONET, Ethernet, and even IP.

The purpose of MPLS is to speed up the movement of data across a larger network. MPLS does this by adding a label to a group of packets that need to be passed on to a specific destination. The number of hops needed to get to the specific destination is listed on the label added by MPLS. This speeds up transmission because it bypasses the need for the router to determine the next hop for each packet as it arrives. MPLS is especially efficient for end-to-end connections where all the hops leading up to a specific destination are known. A router designed and configured to use MPLS simply needs to check the MPLS label for the next hop and then send the packet on its way to its intended destination. No independent processing is needed, which speeds up transmission by eliminating a certain amount of processing overhead. A router that can use MPLS is sometimes called a *label edge router* or LER. MPLS works with a number of access technologies including T-1s, ATM, Frame Relay, and DSL.

◼ Remote Access

THE BOTTOM LINE
An explanation of remote access is discussed in this section of Lesson 8. The remote access technologies RAS and VPN are also introduced. More detailed information about how to secure RAS and VPN are found in a later lesson.

X REF

More detailed information about RAS and VPN can be found in Lesson 10, especially how these technologies can be made more secure.

Remote access technologies allow end users to access a network and the information located on it as if they were directly connected to that network even when they aren't. This capability is widely used by employees who need access to their company's network and/or proprietary information, but due to the nature of their job are not able to work on a company site. Two common examples of the types of employees that fall into this category are field engineers and sales representatives. There are of course other positions depending on the company that may also fall into this category, but these are two of the more common.

Two technologies commonly used in pursuit of remote access are RAS and VPN. Both of these technologies are introduced in this section of Lesson 8.

Remote Access Services (RAS)

Remote Access Services or *RAS* refers to a group of technologies used to facilitate remote access to a computer network. Generally speaking, most RAS technologies are software based. Many operating systems such as Windows have some type of RAS built into the core of the operating system. However, third-party software can also be used for this. One of the bigger providers of RAS is Citrix.

For RAS to work, generally both a server and client component are necessary. Many companies that provide remote access to their networks have one or more servers dedicated to managing that remote access. Usually, along with a RAS server, you also have to set up a RAS client on the client end. If Windows is used on both the client and server side, then the RAS client and servers provided by Microsoft are used. Occasionally, alternatives like Citrix are used if access is needed to a large database residing on a mainframe. Citrix also provides third-party alternatives for the native Microsoft software when additional functionality that is not part of Windows is needed, or when the company for some other reason does not wish to use the functionality in Windows.

A third-party version of RAS may also be desired if Linux or another non-Windows operating system is being used for a company's network. Though again, other operating systems may support other RASs natively. In the case of Linux, there are some versions that have RASs built in and some that do not.

Virtual Private Network (VPN)

A *virtual private network (VPN)* and is a technology commonly used by corporations to allow their users to gain remote access to their corporate servers. VPN is commonly used for this purpose because it is able to use the Internet to establish these connections. This means that field workers can effective gain access to the corporate network anywhere they can get access to the Internet. Put another way, VPN is a private method to connect remote sites and users together using a public network.

A *private network* is one that is owned by a specific entity such as a company for its own personal use. These networks are sometimes called enterprise network. A *public network* is a network that is available for general public access. The biggest example of a public network is the Internet.

There are two major categories or types of VPN networks. Perhaps the most widely known type of VPN is a *remote-access VPN*. The purpose of a remote-access VPN is to connect remote users to a corporate network via a public network of some sort, usually the Internet.

The second major type of VPN is what is called a *site-to-site VPN*. This type of VPN is used to connect different company-owned sites to each other without going the route of using dedicated leased lines such as T1s or ISDN circuits between sites. A *leased line* is a network communications line such as T1s or ISDN that is leased from a telecommunications company and is then dedicated to the sole use of the person or company leasing it.

Both types of VPN networks work more or less the same. The main difference is the source of the media being used to connect them, whether that media is private or public.

For VPN to work properly there has to be both a client and a server. The server end of the VPN generally resides at the company site where the private network being remotely accessed is located. The client end of the VPN can be located anywhere on the node to the public network that is being used to access the private network. One interesting feature of a VPN is that depending on how it is configured either the client or server end can initiate a VPN connection. Figure 8-12 illustrates a remote access VPN.

In Figure 8-12, a public network is shown with a specified path created for the VPN session. Depending on how the VPN is configured, either the client or the server can initialize the session. Once the session is initialized, then the client can use the VPN session to gain access to the file server on the destination private network via the VPN server. Because the VPN server has authorized the VPN client, it is then able to access the private network server as if it were directly connected inside the network. The established data path is what the client and server use to send data back and forth for the duration of the session.

Figure 8-12

Virtual private network (VPN)
used for remote access

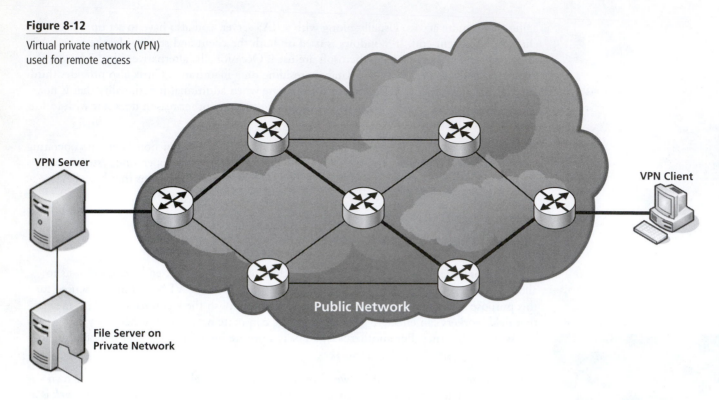

You may have noticed that Figure 8-12 looks remarkably like the Virtual Circuit Switched
Network discussed earlier in this lesson. This is because VPNs use virtual circuit switching to
create their remote access connection. Using various protocols such as PPP and PPTP or
L2TP and IPSec, VPNs establish and secure a virtual circuit through a public network. Once
the virtual circuit is established, it becomes the VPN circuit for the duration of the VPN session being used. As soon as the VPN client or server terminates the session, the virtual circuit
is released back to the public network. If a new VPN session is then established, a new virtual
circuit will be created which will most likely follow a different path than the last one.

SKILL SUMMARY

IN THIS LESSON YOU LEARNED:

- About the different types of circuit switching.
- The difference between circuit switching and virtual circuit switching.
- How packet switching works and how it affects network operations in a practical situation.
- What message switching is.
- The different types of transmission media are used in WANs.
- How broadcasts are used to transfer data around a network.
- How microwaves are used in WAN communications.
- How satellites are used in WAN communications.
- How wireless WANs based on Radio Frequencies work.
- How cells are used in wireless WANs.
- What dial-up is and how it works.
- How DSL works.
- How broadband and cable modems are used.
- The different types of DSL.

- What X.25 is.
- What Frame Relay is.
- How T-Carriers work.
- What ATM is and how it works.
- What SONET and SHD networks are and how they work.
- About the new MPLS networking technology.
- What Remote Access Services are and how they are used.
- What VPN is and what the two main types of VPNs are.
- How VPNs work.

■ Knowledge Assessment

Fill in the Blank

Complete the following sentences by writing the correct word or words in the blanks provided.

1. The oldest technology used to switch circuits is called _____.

2. _____ is a variation on circuit switching that establishes a circuit only for the duration of a specific network session.

3. The type of switching the Internet uses is _____.

4. E-mail is a good example of _____.

5. _____ is one of the oldest technologies that is still sometimes used for creating WAN connections.

6. The type of ISDN that uses two data channels and one control channel is _____.

7. _____ is a catchall name for the type of DSL that has different upload and download speeds.

8. _____ is a type of wired high-speed WAN connection that uses small set-sized frames called cells.

9. Those services used by an operating system to allow computers in remote locations to connect to them is called _____.

10. A common type of remote access that uses a public network such as the Internet to provide access to a private network is called _____.

Multiple Choice

Circle the letter corresponding to the correct answer.

1. The maximum speed dial-up can achieve is _____.
   a. 1.5 mbps
   b. less than 56.6 kbps
   c. 128 kbps
   d. 64 kbps

2. Each B channel in an ISDN circuit is _____.
   a. 64 kbps
   b. 16 kbps
   c. 1.544 mbps
   d. 144 kbps

3. A satellite orbit that allows for satellite communications in the far north is called what kind of orbit?
   a. Geostationary
   b. Lagrange
   c. Geosynchronous
   d. Molniyar

4. Which of the following are commonly used T-Lines in North America. (Choose all that apply.)
   a. T1
   b. E1
   c. E2
   d. T3

5. OC-x lines are multiples of what network speed?
   a. 64 kbps
   b. 1.544 mbps
   c. 51.84 mbps
   d. 128 kbps

6. SONET can be used with which of the following protocols? (Choose all that apply.)
   a. Ethernet
   b. TCP/IP
   c. Token Ring
   d. ATM

7. Satellites commonly use _____ to transmit data.
   a. Light
   b. Shortwave radio waves
   c. Cables
   d. Microwaves

8. POTS stands for _____?
   a. Plain Old Telephone Service
   b. Public Switched Telephone Network
   c. Publicly Owned Telephone System
   d. Publicly Owned Telecommunications System

9. VPN most commonly uses a _____ to access a _____. (Choose two.)
   a. Dial-up
   b. Public network
   c. Private network
   d. ISDN

10. Which operating systems have some form of RAS built into them? (Choose all that apply.)
    a. Windows 7
    b. Windows Server
    c. Most Linux Distros
    d. DOS

Lab Exercises

Researching Local WAN Providers

The purpose of this lab is to have the student research local ISPs in order to determine what WAN technologies are available in their area. After completing this lab, the student will know what local ISPs provide WAN services and what WAN services are available. They will also know the general cost of such WAN services.

(Note: This project can be done individually or in groups. If done in groups, this is a great project to teach students how to do group presentations and projects. Working on a project as a group is something the student will often have to do in the working world.)

MATERIALS

- A computer with access to the Internet
- Paper
- Pen or pencil

THE LAB

Find Out Which Local ISPs Provide WAN Services in Your Area

1. Get on the Internet and search for local ISPs that are found in your area. Some examples may be AT&T, Verizon, Cox Cable, Bright House, Century Link, and others.
2. Once you have determined what ISPs are found locally, go to their company web sites and determine which ones provide WAN services.
3. After determining which ISPs provide WAN services, find out how to contact them and ask them what specific services they provide and what their rates are. You may have to call them or e-mail them, or the information may be found directly on their web sites.
4. If you have to call or e-mail the ISPs to find out about their WAN services, let them know that you are a student doing a research project for school. Upon hearing that you are a student doing a school project, most ISPs will be more than willing to help you.

Report What You Discovered about Local ISPs

1. Once you have gathered all the information you can from the various ISPs in your area, you will need to put it all together in a report and/or a presentation.
   a. The types of technologies available from the ISPs.
   b. A cost comparison of the various WAN technologies offered by the different ISPs.
   c. The advantages and disadvantages of each of the WAN options.
   d. Any additional benefits offered by the ISP for choosing specific WAN options.
   e. What you or your group's recommendation is of the best option to choose and why.

2. The information gathered can be presented in the form of a report, proposal, or PowerPoint presentation. The final form of the report should cover all details outlined here as well as any additional criteria the instructor decides is relevant. If the PowerPoint format is chosen, it is recommended that the students all be required to present their presentations so they can have some practice giving PowerPoint presentations to a group of people. Being able to effectively present a report using PowerPoint is a very important skill that is often called upon in the working world.

■ Lab 2

Setting Up a VPN Using Windows 7

The purpose of this lab is to familiarize the student with what they will need to do to set up a VPN in a Windows 7 environment from the client's side. After completing this lab, the student will be able to set up a client VPN connection using Windows 7.

MATERIALS

- A computer running Windows 7
- Paper
- Pen or pencil

THE LAB

Set Up VPN

1. Go to the *Start Menu* and type **Setup VPN** in the *Search Bar*. Figure 8-13 illustrates the result of doing this.

Figure 8-13

Entering **Setup VPN** in the Start Menu Search Bar

2. Click on the option that says *Set up a virtual private network (VPN) connection*. There is a good chance that this is the only option available to you.

After clicking on this option, your screen will look similar to Figure 8-14.

Figure 8-14

VPN Connection Creation Wizard

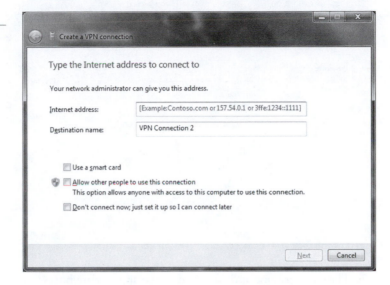

3. Write down all the options you see available in the VPN Connection Creation Wizard on a separate piece of paper.

4. Place the IP address or the server name your instructor tells you to on the line labeled *Internet Address*. If your instructor does not have an IP address or server name for you, any random IP address will do for the purposes of this lab. However, if a random IP address is used, you will not be able to establish a VPN connection.

5. Make sure that a check is placed in the box next to the *Don't connect now; just set it up so that I can connect later* label.

The reason for doing this is so that the Wizard can be completed in the event that you do not have a VPN server to connect to. When you are done, your screen should look similar to Figure 8-15.

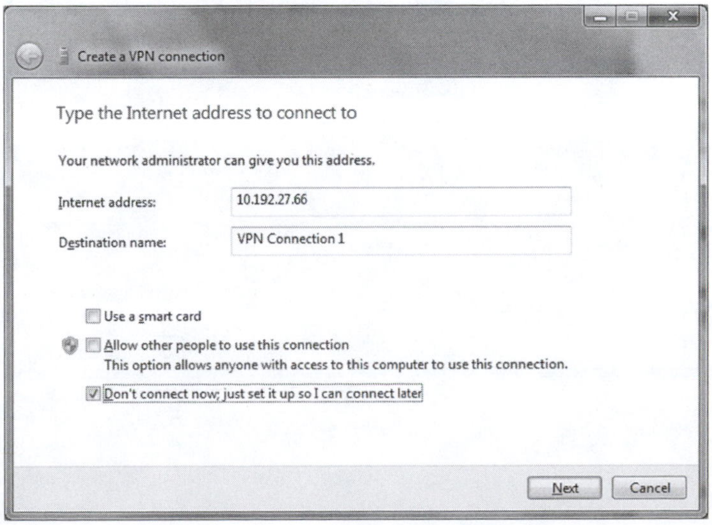

Figure 8-15

VPN Connection Creation Wizard after it has been filled out according to the instructions presented in this lab

6. Click the **Next** button. A window similar to the one shown in Figure 8-16 should come up.

Figure 8-16

VPN Connection Creation Wizard after the **Next** button has been clicked

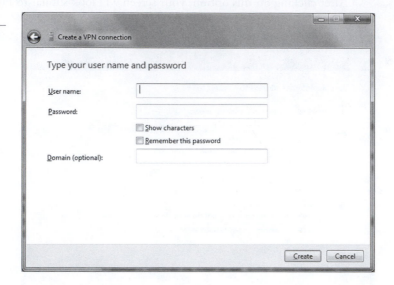

7. Place a username and password in the appropriate boxes.

If you are setting up a real VPN connection, make sure that both the username and the password you enter are valid. Also make sure that you enter the valid Domain if needed. Your instructor can help you determine the information needed if you are setting up a real VPN connection.

If you are not setting up a real VPN connection, then place any username and password you wish in the appropriate boxes. A Domain is not needed.

When you are done, your screen should look similar to Figure 8-17.

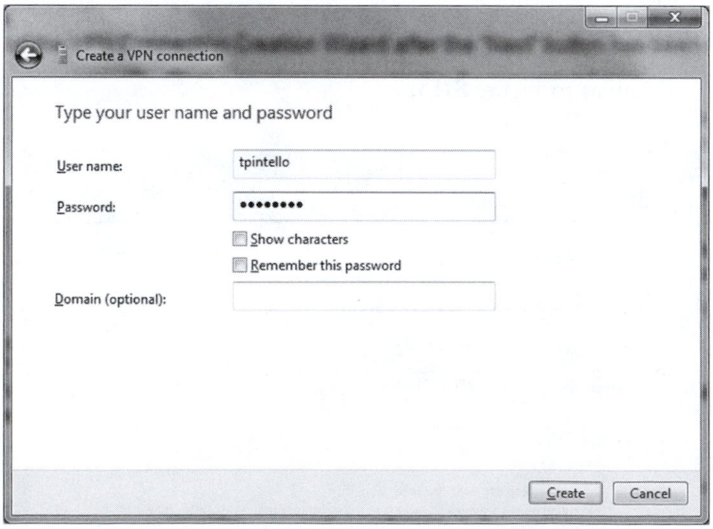

Figure 8-17

VPN Connection Creation Wizard after all the relevant user information has been entered

8. Click on the button labeled **Create** at the bottom of the window. A screen similar to the screenshot found in Figure 8-18 will come up.

Figure 8-18

VPN Connection Creation Wizard after clicking the **Create** button

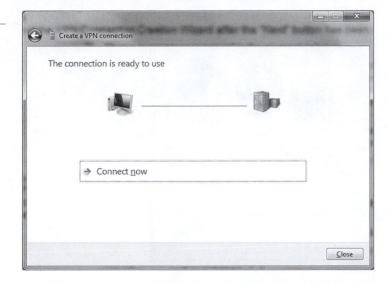

9. You are not able to connect to your newly created VPN by clicking on the *Connect* now bar. Click on the **Close** button to close the VPN connection window.

10. If you wish to use the VPN connection in the future, simply click on the **Network Icon** found in the *System* portion of the taskbar found at the bottom of the Windows Desktop. You will see a pop-up window telling you all the network connections that are available to you. Figure 8-19 shows what the Network Connections pop-up window looks like.

Figure 8-19

Network Connections Pop-Up Window

11. Left-click on the connection you just created and a *Connect* button will appear in the Network Connections pop-up window. Left-click on the **Connect** button. Figure 8-20 shows you what will come up.

Figure 8-20

VPN Connection Window

12. If you created a real VPN connection, then put in the appropriate Username, Password, and Domain and then click the **Connect** button. This will connect you to the VPN you just set up. If you did not create a real VPN connection, then simply click the **Cancel** button.

Basic Network Security

EXAM OBJECTIVE MATRIX

Technology Skill Covered	Exam Objective	Exam Objective Number
Network Security Considerations		

Basic Network Security Threats	**Explain common threats, vulnerabilities, and mitigation techniques.**
	• Wireless:
	  • War driving
	  • War chalking
	  • WEP cracking
	  • WPA cracking
	  • Evil twin
	  • Rogue access point
	• Attacks:
	  • DoS
	  • DDoS
	  • Man-in-the-middle
	  • Social engineering
	  • Virus
	  • Worms
	  • Buffer overflow
	  • Packet sniffing
	  • FTP bounce
	  • Smurf
		5.4

Countering Basic Security Threats	**Given a scenario, use the appropriate network monitoring resource to analyze traffic.** • SNMP • SNMPv2 • SNMPv3	4.4
	Explain methods of user authentication. • PKI • Kerberos • AAA (RADIUS, TACACS+) • Network access control (802.1x, posture assessment) • CHAP • MS-CHAP	5.3

	• EAP • Two-factor authentication • Multifactor authentication • Single sign-on	

After an Attack Has Occurred	**Explain common threats, vulnerabilities, and mitigation techniques.**
	• Mitigation techniques:
	  • Training and awareness
	  • Patch management
	  • Incident response
		5.4

Network Tools that Can Be Used for Good or Bad		

KEY TERMS

802.11x

AAA (authentication, authorization, accounting)

attackers

authentication

botnet

certificate

certificate authority

Challenge-Handshake Authentication Protocol (CHAP)

Denial of Service (DoS)

digital certificate

dumpster diving

Extensible Authentication Protocol (EAP)

File Transfer Protocol (FTP)

fraggle attack

holder

Hypertext Transfer Protocol (HTTP)

Hypertext Transfer Protocol Secure (HTTPS)

identity theft

intrusion detection software (IDS)

intrusion prevention software (IPS)

Kerberos

local access

macro

macro virus

malicious software

man-in-the-middle attack

Microsoft Challenge-Handshake Authentication Protocol (MS-CHAP)

Network Access Control (NAC)

packet analyzer

packet sniffer

phishing

physical security

port scanner

private key certificate

private key encryption

Public Key Infrastructure (PKI)

remote access

Remote Authentication Dial-In User Service (RADIUS)

Remote Shell (RSH)

rogue access point

Secure Copy Protocol (SCP)

Secure File Transfer Protocol or SSH File Transfer Protocol (SFTP)

Secure Shell (SSH)

Simple Network Management Protocol version 3 (SNMPv3)

smurf attack

social engineering

spyware

TELNET

Terminal Access Controller Access-Control System Plus (TACACS+)

Trojan horse

virus

worm

Allen Fox is the IT manager of a large call center. There have been a number of problems in his call center related to basic security threats such as spyware and viruses. Allen determines that one way he can minimize these problems is to educate the people who work in the call center about basic security problems. What things should Allen include in his education plan for the call center employees?

■ Network Security Considerations

THE BOTTOM LINE

Networking leaves computers susceptible to security threats. This lesson covers security threats, how to combat threats, and what to do after a security violation has taken place. If a computer is attached to a network in any way, it is vulnerable to outside attack. Therefore, if you have a network of any sort in your home or work, you need to take into consideration what network security threats are there and how to deal with them.

The first step to minimize network security threats in a corporate or business environment is to have a comprehensive network security policy for your business. Your policy should address the following security considerations:

- What security threats does your organization have to combat?
- What can you do to combat a security threat?
- What should you do after a security violation has taken place?

This lesson deals with each of these considerations in detail.

■ Basic Network Security Threats

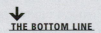
THE BOTTOM LINE

This portion of Lesson 9 outlines the various threats that are typically seen on a computer connected to or on a network. This section discusses various types of malicious software. Additionally, the differences between viruses, worms, and trojans are discussed. Finally, this section of Lesson 9 outlines a couple of common attacks and vulnerabilities found on networks.

CERTIFICATION READY
What are some common security threats to a network? What are some ways to mitigate those threats?
5.4

First, you need to answer the following questions: "What security threats does my company have to combat?" and "Are there security threats that are common to the entire network?" Next, you need to look at the unique threats that exist for your company or for specific portions of your company. It is important to realize that different companies in different lines of business have different priorities and needs when it comes to network security. This fact leads different companies to take different measures in addressing threats that they consider specific to their situation. The most important thing is that a company is looking at security threats and trying to address them. As long as a company is at least aware of the specific threats out there to their own line of business, and are taking steps to address them, they are on the right track. As the saying goes, "knowing is half the battle."

Too often, companies—especially smaller ones—do not even think about these things. A company that is not thinking about security issues is already at great risk and vulnerable to attack from outside groups or individuals. However, this issue is not limited to companies or businesses; it is also a problem in our homes as well. In fact, many small-time hackers (sometimes called script kiddies) actually actively target home computers. As the very first sentence of this lesson said, any computer connected to any type of network is vulnerable to being attacked. The Internet is the biggest and least controlled network out there. This means that any computer connected to the Internet is by definition at risk and you should take steps to protect it.

Social Engineering

CERTIFICATION READY
What is social engineering? Why is social engineering considered a network security threat? What is the best way to mitigate social engineering?
5.4

With all this talk about network security vulnerabilities, people tend to think of hackers in dark rooms with lots of computers trying to break into the computers and networks of unsuspecting individuals and companies or of secret agencies in one country trying to break into another country's computer systems. While all this does go on and people like this are most definitely a threat, they are not the biggest or most dangerous threat to a network. In fact, the most dangerous threat to a network does not even need to include a computer!

How can that be? How can something be a threat to a computer network without even needing a computer? The answer is something called social engineering. *Social engineering* has been around for as long as one group or person wished to hide something from another group or individual. The goal of social engineering is to trick or manipulate a person into revealing important information. Once the important information has been revealed, it can in turn be used for other nefarious purposes.

Some of the most effective means of social engineering do not even require the use of a computer, and these means can be wide and varied. A social engineer may convince you he or she is your friend in order to get you to reveal important information. They can engineer different social situations where you feel you can give them the information they wish to know. They can get to know information about you and use that to deduce the information they wish to know. The means a social engineer can use to manipulate a person are endless. The 2002 movie *Catch Me if You Can* illustrates this point very well. What makes this movie so good is that it is about a real person, and the exploits, while presented in a humorous light, are based on real things this person did.

A famous hacker named Kevin Mitnick once commented that it was much easier to trick a person into revealing a password to a system than it was to actually crack into the same system. You can find out more about Kevin Mitnick's comments in the books on hacking that he has co-authored.

This in a nutshell is what social engineering is all about. Social engineers manipulate people in order to gain access to a network rather than spending the time and effort needed to break into the network in a more "traditional" manner. The so-called traditional method of breaking into a network takes lots of know-how and time, and hackers run a higher risk of getting caught. Manipulating people on the other hand carries a lower risk and is often less time consuming. The best way to avoid social engineering is to make your employees aware of the danger and train them to report people they believe are trying to manipulate information out of them.

PHISHING

In the simplest terms *phishing* is using various means to trick people into revealing passwords, account numbers, social security numbers, and various other sensitive pieces of information. This is done under the disguise of asking users to providing the information to legitimate organizations. Many times e-mail and instant messaging are used in this attempt.

There are several pretty common scenarios that all qualify as phishing. One common scenario is getting an e-mail from Nigeria or some other place explaining how if you send them a certain amount of money you can make a lot more. This scenario went around a few years back. The goal of this phishing attempt was to get you to send bank information or money to the people perpetrating the phishing scam.

Another common phishing scam is an e-mail that purports to be from a reputable bank, maybe even the bank at which the user banks. In this version of a phishing scam, a reason is given as to why the person receiving the e-mail needs to update their banking information. The e-mail usually contains a hyperlink to a web page that looks like the legitimate website of the bank the e-mail is supposed to come from. The website then asks for information like account numbers, passwords, and/or pin numbers. The perpetrator of the attack then uses the provided information to raid the victim's real bank accounts.

One way to tell a fake website from a real one is to look at the URL. If the website you are sent to is bogus, it will not contain the domain name of the bank the website purports to represent.

Another thing to keep in mind is that banks and other legitimate institutions are not going to ask for sensitive personal data to be input into a public website. If the bank or other financial institution really does need your personal information, they will ask you to come into a local branch to confirm the information.

Websites have developed a few ways to counter these kinds of threats. One of the most common is to have an identifying picture that the end user has to verify before they are able to access their personal information or money. Another way is to have identifying questions that have to be answered before access in granted. Other methods have also been developed.

STEALING PASSWORDS

Stealing passwords can be done in a number of different ways. The reason hackers attempt to steal passwords is because it is easier to steal a password to break into a computer system, than it is to use brute force to break into the same computer system. Phishing as discussed earlier is one way to steal passwords, but there are many more ways as well.

Part of what makes it easy for others to steal passwords is the nature of the passwords that many people use. They use obvious phrases like the names of their children or friends, their birth dates, their favorite color, the name of their pets, and others. People do this because it is easier to remember these kinds of passwords. The problem is that if a password thief spends just a few minutes talking to the user and asking questions about family, pets, friends, and so on, they will gather enough information to be able to guess the user's password.

This brings us to another way that passwords can be stolen. If passwords are written down somewhere, then they can be found and used by someone else. In point of fact, if you were to go into any place of business where computers and passwords are widely used by the employees, you would be surprised at the number of passwords you would be able to find, simply by looking around the premises. If you were on the custodial staff and worked after hours, you would especially be able to find a large number of passwords because people often write down their passwords and then hide them so that no one can find them. Passwords are "hidden" under the desk calendar, under the telephone, under the mouse pad, in the desk drawer under the paperclip tray, under the computer keyboard, in a desk drawer stuck to the bottom side of the desk on a sticky note, hidden in a "note" written on the desk calendar, under a book, under a knickknack on the shelf, or any number of similar locations. Looking in these and other similar places could yield a large number of company passwords. The best way to avoid passwords being exposed in this way is to train your employees to not write down passwords by teaching them how to create passwords that they can easily remember but that are hard to crack. What follows is one such method.

In order to make a password harder to guess, but still easy to remember, there are a couple of different tricks that you can use. One really good trick to make a password easy to remember but hard to guess is to use a phrase and modify it in a way that's personal to the person creating the password. A good example is the phrase "Coke is the one for me" from an old commercial. To make it harder to guess, you could modify it to be CokeIsTheOneForMe. This causes the password to include upper- and lowercase letters. It could be further modified to CokeIsThe14Me. This adds numbers. Finally you could substitute special characters for specific letters. An example of this is (okeI$The14Me. This replaces the letter C with the "(" symbol and the "s" with the "$" symbol. Taken together, this creates a very complicated password that is also easy to remember. If this password is placed in the password strength checker at www.passwordmeter.com, it receives a strength rating of 100%. This same technique can be used on any phrase that is significant to a person with similar results. It is also almost impossible to guess unless you tell someone about the technique you have used to create your password.

IDENTITY THEFT

Identity theft is one type of social engineering that has been in the news in recent years. *Identity theft* is the act of presenting yourself as someone you are not in order to steal in one way or another from the person you are presenting yourself to be. One of the more common ways of doing this is to steal a pin and/or bank account number and present yourself as being the legitimate owner of the bank account and then withdrawing money that does not belong to you. Other ways of stealing an identity involve using phishing techniques to steal more elaborate personal information and use it to do anything from stealing money directly from people's accounts to establishing credit accounts in the other person's name without them knowing about it.

One way to protect yourself from identity theft is to keep a close eye on any financial activities that take place in your name. You can do this yourself by getting regular credit reports from the various credit reporting agencies such as Equifax and others. All of these credit reporting agencies provide services that allow you to access your credit reports online. Sometimes obtaining these reports costs money and sometimes they can be obtained free on a limited basis. There are only three credit reporting agencies in the United States, and you should get regular reports from each of them if you want to protect your identity.

Alternatively, you can pay a third-party organization to constantly monitor your financial activities for you and report to you when something happens outside of your normal activities. You should also make sure that the third party you hire gives you regular activity reports either on a monthly or quarterly basis. You should also make a point of actually reading the reports they give you in case they missed something.

There are several third-party organizations that specialize in protecting your identify. Most of them advertise on television and radio and through other media. You should research multiple identity guarding organizations before making a choice about which one to use. You should also know that many credit card companies provide similar services and you should look at them as well before making a final decision about who will help protect your identity. If you choose the services of a third-party organization in this endeavor, you should regularly evaluate whether they are continuing to serve your needs or if you need to find a new service. These organizations work for you, not the other way around, and they should treat you accordingly.

DUMPSTER DIVING

Dumpster diving is another form of social engineering, but is not limited to just obtaining information about people. Put simply, *dumpster diving* is the act of going through someone's garbage looking for personal information that can be used to steal their identity in one way or another. One very popular target of dumpster divers is preapproved credit card applications. A dumpster diver can use that application and pretend to be the person the application is for, thereby opening a credit card account in that person's name. Even though the person whose name appears on the card doesn't know about the credit card, they are still responsible for paying the bills run up by the other person. The best way to avoid this kind of situation is to use a paper shredder to shred any documents that can be used in this manner before throwing them out.

As mentioned before, while dumpster diving can be used to steal a person's identity, there are other things that dumpster diving can be used for. Really any personal or private information that can be found in a person or company's garbage is fair game for dumpster divers. A good case in point is what supposedly happened some years to a software company. One of that company's developers had a hard copy of the source code for one of the company's programs. When the developers were done with the hard copy, they accidentally threw it out with the trash. A dumpster diver found the source code and published some of it on the Internet. Assuming the story is true and not a hoax, it is a case where dumpster diving was used for something other than identity theft.

Malicious Software

Malicious software is a broad category that includes any software that is used against a company or person. The intent behind the malicious software can vary widely. It can be intended simply as a harmless prank all the way up to a deliberate attempt to cause extreme harm to a person's or company's computer systems. Malicious software can also be intended to capture information from someone that they would not normally release. This stolen data can be used for anything from stealing an identity to carrying out targeted marketing.

SPYWARE

As its name implies, *spyware* is a category of malicious software that is intended to spy on a computer system's user and obtain information that the user would not normally allow to be know. The purpose of spyware is to obtain personal or private information without the user being aware that the information is being taken.

There are quite a few different ways that people use to place spyware on unsuspecting victims' computers. Some obvious methods are to add the spyware into an attachment on e-mail so that when a person opens the attachment, the spyware is installed. This used to be a common way to place spyware on a computer, but it is not very effective today because most e-mail providers take measures to prevent that from happening.

A more subtle way to slip spyware onto a computer is to have it install when some other piece of "legitimate" software is installed. This is by far the most common way to place spyware on someone's computer. One of the first programs to do this is a program called Comet Cursor. This program from the 1990s gave the person who installed it the ability to have multiple cursors and to change them. Unfortunately, it also placed software onto the computer that reported back to the creator of Comet Cursor what a person's Internet surfing practices were. This information was then sold to marketers who used it to target those specific people for goods and services via e-mail.

Another early program trick used to plant software from the late 1990s is something called Webshots. This program allowed people to take electronic pictures and use them as rotating backgrounds and screensavers. It was extremely popular in its day and is still around today. However, what the people who loaded this program on their computer did not know was that it also loaded a program called Gator that stole any personal information they typed into their computers and passed it back to the creators of Gator. The catch with Gator was that there was no way to remove it from the computer short of a registry edit. This meant removing it was beyond the ability of most end users even if they did an Uninstall through the Add/Remove apps in the Control Panel of their computers.

Aside from using spyware to steal information for marketing and other purposes that most end users would not want on their computers, there is also a more sinister use for spyware—to steal people's credit card numbers for use in identity theft. Additionally, hackers can use spyware to gather all the information they need to gain control of your computer for their own purposes.

One extreme case of this happened in the 1990s when a ring of criminals gained access to the IP addresses and names of shared folders on people's computers. These criminals then used those shared folders to store illicit pictures on the computers of the unsuspecting victims. Before law enforcement finally figured out what had happened, a number of good and upstanding people were charged with possession of various types of illicit pictures and had their names dragged all through the national press, even though they had not actually done anything wrong. Many of these people were pillars of the community they lived in, and their reputations were utterly destroyed. Even though the charges were later retracted, the damage to these people's reputations had already been done. Many of them lost their jobs and positions in the community, and some of them even to this day have not fully recovered from it. Because of these events, laws were changed about when possession charges of various illicit types of images can be made public.

VIRUSES

CERTIFICATION READY
What is a virus? How does a virus differ from a worm or a Trojan?
5.4

Computer virus is a kind of catchall term that many people use to describe a wide variety of malicious types of programs. However, the term virus technically refers to a very specific type of malware. Specifically, a *virus* is a type of malicious software that modifies the code of existing programs in an attempt to cause harm, reproduce itself, and/or to escape detection.

To illustrate how a virus works, we discuss a specific type of virus—a macro virus—that was common in the mid to late 1990s. A *macro virus* is a virus that attaches itself to the documents produced by common software applications. Using the macro language of the software application in question, a macro virus is able to alter documents created within that application. A *macro language* is built into a software application that was intended to automate specific tasks within that application. A macro language is very specific to a particular application; there is no single universal macro language used by all applications. Automations and alterations of a document via a macro language are attached to the document and are generally called *macros*. Depending on how versatile the macro language of the software application is, macros can be used to do everything from automatically filling in common information and altering the appearance of the document to changing how the entire application behaves and even to wiping whole files and even hard drives.

Microsoft Office was a favorite target of macro viruses; it was targeted so often because it was widely used in the business world and had a very powerful macro language. It was even possible to wipe whole hard drives using the Microsoft Office macro language. There were macro viruses in Microsoft Word that changed normal polite words to vulgar and rude words, caused letters to drop randomly off a document, and even replaced whole paragraphs of a document with rude messages.

These macro viruses spread by attaching themselves to any Word documents they found on any drive they were currently residing on. When a worker took a document on a floppy disk home to work on it on their infected home computer, any document they had on their home computer would see the uninfected document on the floppy disk and infect it. Then the worker returned to work the next day and copied the infected file to their local work computer. The macro virus was now attached to the file they brought from home and would seek out any uninfected viruses on the new local computer and infect them. When any file was then shared from that computer to other computers in the company, those computers would also become infected.

Later macro viruses can actually take code from different documents infected with different macro viruses and randomly combine the infected code to change the effect the macro virus has on a document. Sometimes the combined code negates itself; sometimes it makes the virus weaker and less of a threat; sometimes in makes the virus much worse. There simply is no way to tell what will happen until the virus shows up.

In an attempt to counter macro viruses, as well as other types of viruses, different solutions were developed. One such solution, and the one that ultimately turned out to be the best, was the invention of anti-virus software. This software was designed to go looking for viruses and destroy them before they could cause damage. The role of this software has since expanded to combat other types of malicious software threats, including spyware.

Microsoft also took steps to limit damage by macro viruses by not allowing Office to run macro code in an application without first warning the user that macros are present in a specific document. Once the end user is warned that macros are present in a specific document, they are given the option of either continuing to run the document or turning off the macro. Microsoft still does this today, but not many documents actually use macros any more. You will however, occasionally see the message pop-up.

WORMS

Worms are often called viruses, but in point of fact they are a totally different type of malware. A *worm* is a malicious program that is placed on a computer and then activated. When a worm is activated, it executes a program that is designed to cause some kind of harm to the computer or user using the computer. The way worms get on computers varies. Most commonly worms are snuck onto a computer as attachments to e-mails or as addendums to web pages. When a worm gets on a computer, it attempts to replicate itself and carry out whatever function it was programmed to do. These malicious functions can be as benign as copying personal information from the computer to the worm's originator or as malevolent as formatting an entire hard drive.

The key to identifying a worm as opposed to some other type of malicious hardware is in how it presents itself. A virus adds additional code to an already existing program to cause problems. A worm does not try to add code to another program or to masquerade as a legitimate program. A worm is a full program by itself. There are a number of ways that worms can get on a computer. E-mail attachments at one point were one of the most common ways to

CERTIFICATION READY
What is a worm? How does a worm differ from a virus or a Trojan?
5.4

achieve this. The very act of opening an e-mail with a worm attached was enough to load the program. Many of the "free" programs you are able to download onto your computer and use actually contain worms. This is a very common way that spyware gets on people's computers. When you download and install a free program that does some useful or cool thing that people want, an additional program is added to your computer. This additional program is a worm that is designed to do something that you may not want it to do such as collect information about your web surfing habits and forward them to the company that created the "free and useful" program you just installed. Some of these worms even ask permission to be placed on a computer. This is done by having a check box automatically turned on that adds some kind of browser add-on or other program that is actually the worm/spyware that was the main reason the free and useful program was created in the first place. If you do find a free program that you really want to use on your computer, make sure that there are no hidden programs or agendas attached to it before installing. You should be warned that even some "open source" programs will have worms as spyware attached to them; although, with true open source programs you always have the option of turning off the add-on before you install.

TROJANS

Trojans, also known as *Trojan horses*, are malicious programs that are very similar to worms. However, instead of just attempting to enter a computer via some secondary avenue like worms do, Trojans actively masquerade as legitimate programs that belong on your computer. Your computer runs the malicious program without being aware that it should not. The creator of a Trojan will take a legitimate program such as a "winsock.dll" program, or other programs, and replace it with a different program of the same name and place it in the same location. Then, when a Trojan is snuck onto a computer, the computer will see it as a legitimate program and not interfere with it. This allows the Trojan to do whatever it was designed to do without interference from the system and gives the originator of the Trojan several advantages. One it allows the program to sneak onto the target system without the system realizing it does not belong there. More troubling, once the Trojan gets on the target system, it can start running without the system reacting to it because the system thinks it is a legitimate program doing what it is supposed to do. Many "botnet" programs work like this.

A *botnet* is a group of computers that have been compromised by a single hacker or a group of hackers. Once these computers have been compromised, the hacker can use the computer to do things that the owner would not want it to do. The worst thing about a botnet is that botnets allow multiple computers to work on different pieces of the same problem, which allows much more difficult problems to be solved than what a single computer could do by itself.

A legitimate example of how botnets can solve very complicated problems more quickly and efficiently than a single computer is a project from the 1990s called SETI@Home. This project got people to knowingly and voluntarily put a program on their computers that was designed to take data from radio telescopes and analyze it looking for signals that may have deliberately been sent by extraterrestrial civilizations. Because of the huge amount of data recorded by radio telescopes around the world, it was impossible for even a supercomputer to analyze the available data looking for that one small signal that may have been sent by ET. In fact there was so much recorded data that it would have taken even a supercomputer many decades to analyze all the stored data, not counting any new data that was captured. As a solution to this, the SETI people came up with the idea of getting millions of computers to analyze small amounts of recorded data looking for ET instead of having just one large computer analyzing all the recorded data looking for ET. By chopping up this huge problem into many very small pieces and allowing millions of computers to analyze it, the impossible task before SETI became doable in just a couple of years. The program given out by SETI@Home to analyze the data only took a small portion of any computer's processing time to work, so it did not interfere with the user's normal computer usage. Incidentally, they never did find a signal from ET.

Hackers use the same idea, but for malicious purposes instead of benign purposes. Hackers sneak a program onto a computer in the form of a Trojan so the computer will run it as if it were a legitimate program. However, the end user is not told about the program, nor is their permission asked to place the program on their computer. Once a hacker, or group of hackers, feel they have enough computers with their malicious Trojan installed on them, they then send an order out to the compromised computers to carry out some task the hackers assign them. These tasks can be a wide range of things. One use for botnets in the past, and still in the present, has been to launch Denial of Service (DoS) attacks against specific computers with the goal of making those computers unable to do what they are supposed to. More about DoS attacks will be discussed later in this lesson.

Botnets have also been put to use cracking passwords captured from a network. In fact, not too long ago, a rather large financial institution had a large number of accounts and their passwords compromised by a hacker using the method just described. After the hacker captured a large number of accounts and their passwords from the large financial institution, they used a botnet to crack the passwords on the compromised accounts.

Table 9-1 contains a summary of each of the malicious software types just discussed. It contains the name of the malicious software type and a brief description of each type. This table is useful for keeping the four malicious types of software discussed straight and for learning the differences between them.

Table 9-1

Summary of Different Types of Malicious Software

Malicious Software Type	Characteristics
Spyware	Software that is slipped onto a computer for the purpose of gaining private information about the target computer or how the computer is used. Spyware can be slipped onto computers via web browsers, by tricking people into installing it along with software they intended to install, through e-mail, or by other means.
Viruses	Malicious code that attaches itself to legitimate programs and/or data files that are then altered so that they do something malicious in addition to or instead of their normal activities. The malicious code usually contains instructions on how the virus can replicate itself.
Worms	Complete stand-alone programs that are smuggled onto a computer via some legitimate-seeming method. These programs are designed to carry out specific instructions that are detrimental to the computer or its user in some way. Many spyware programs are actually worms in nature. Worms are also used to take control of computers without their users being aware of this. E-mail and Instant Messaging programs are favored methods used by hackers to smuggle worms onto targeted computers. Worms often carry code within them that allows them to smuggle copies of themselves onto other computers.
Trojans	Trojans are similar in their behavior to worms. However, where worms are full-blown programs that try to secret themselves onto computers, Trojans use existing legitimate programs and replace them with false programs using the same name and file location on the computer. This causes operating systems and other programs to execute the Trojans instead of the legitimate program they think they are executing. When this is done, the Trojan then carries out its true malicious intent instead of the legitimate actions the program it is replacing would carry out. Trojans are a favorite method used by hackers to get illegitimate access to computers and networks.

Threats from Attackers

There is a common thread found throughout our discussion of malicious software so far: *attackers* or hackers are attempting to get something from or do something to end users that the end users do not want them to get or do. The following discussion is about what some of those threats are and what the hackers are trying to accomplish by carrying them out.

SOCIAL ENGINEERING

We have already discussed social engineering. However, it needs to be repeated that social engineering is perhaps the single biggest threat from an attacker that a network can face. The only way to effectively guard against a social engineering attack is to make sure that all the people that have access to a network understand what social engineering is and be trained to recognize it when they see it. You can also make sure that all the users of a network are trained to take steps that make it harder for attackers to social engineer the network. Some of these steps could be using passwords that are not based on a personal piece of information and not writing down passwords under any circumstances. You should also train your network users to report cases of social engineering that they may see going on around them or when they suspect that someone is trying to social engineer them.

DENIAL OF SERVICE (DOS) AND DISTRIBUTED DENIAL OF SERVICE (DDOS) THREATS

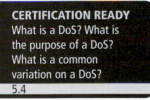

CERTIFICATION READY
What is a DoS? What is the purpose of a DoS? What is a common variation on a DoS?
5.4

Denial of Service (DoS) attacks do exactly what they sound like they do, they attempt to deny computer services in some way or another. This may sound like a small thing, but in reality, it is quite large. In fact, some of the most financially damaging attacks against computer networks to date have been of this type. An example of this happened back when Amazon.com, eBay, Yahoo, and other companies were still fairly new. A group of hackers decided to launch a massive DoS attack against these companies and others and managed to bring their web presences down all at once for anywhere from hours to a few days. The estimated financial damage caused by these attacks in the form of lost revenues was in the many millions of dollars. This happened back in February 2000. Interestingly enough the attack was accomplished by using a number of an early kind of botnet called zombie networks, which were built using Trojans, specifically a variation of a Trojan called *SubSeven*.

The type of DoS attack just described is called a *Distributed Denial of Service (DDoS)* attack. A DDoS is a DoS that is launched from many points at the same time using large numbers of compromised computers. These DDoS attacks can be launched from multiple locations against just one target, or against multiple targets all at once. Figure 9-1 contains a diagram showing how computers are subverted into becoming zombie networks or botnets. In the figure, an attacker has used the Internet to infect numerous home computers with some type of worm or Trojan allowing the attacker to control all the infected computers in some way.

Figure 9-1

Forming a zombie network or botnet

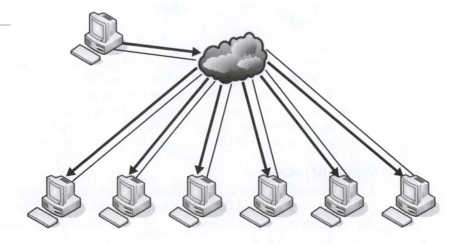

There are many ways a DoS attack can be carried out. Some DoS attacks target resources on a system such as overflowing a device's buffer memory so legitimate packets cannot be processed, consuming a server's communications bandwidth so it cannot communicate to the outside world, or even overloading a device's processing power by making more requests than the processor can handle. The bottom line is that the objective of a DoS attack is to take away the ability of the target to carry out its normal function, thus denying the use of that device to those who legitimately need it. Another way to cause a DoS attack is to exploit a flaw in a device's hardware or software, including the operating system, so that the device is not able to work properly. A sufficiently severe attack against the right kind of target can even cause a device to be physically unusable. This can be done by physically damaging some part of the device such as its hard drive by causing it to be trashed to the point of physical damage. A system or device can also be taken out by forcing a re-install of its software. This could cause so much damage to the operating system or other software that only a fresh install of the software will restore the system. In Figure 9-2, the hacker first (1) uses the Internet to compromise a large number of personal computers. The hacker then (2) takes control of the computers that have been compromised. And finally, (3) the hacker orders the compromised computers to flood a target server with large numbers of requests in order to overload and disable the system.

Figure 9-2

Distributed Denial of Service (DDoS) attack using a zombie network or botnet

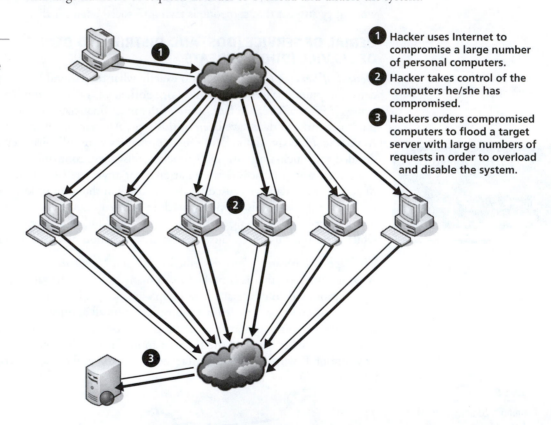

1 Hacker uses Internet to compromise a large number of personal computers.

2 Hacker takes control of the computers he/she has compromised.

3 Hackers orders compromised computers to flood a target server with large numbers of requests in order to overload and disable the system.

There are many devices other than computers that can also be brought down by a DoS attack. All it takes is a proper understanding of how a specific type of device works and how you can cause some part of that device to no longer function properly. Routers, switches, web servers, DNS servers, credit card payment gateways, and even domain root servers have all been targeted by DoS attacks over the years. Each type of device needs a different sort of attack to be successful, but people who would cause malicious harm are always inventive in their methods.

SMURF ATTACKS

A *Smurf attack* is a DoS attack in which the target server or network is flooded with Internet Control Message Protocol (ICMP) replies. This overloads the inbound lines on a network and can result in bringing it down. This attack is carried out by infiltrating computers that are able to broadcast IP protocols directly to a specific target. The attacker then convinces the hijacked computers to send ICMP replies to the target computer as if they had received an ICMP request for reply from the target computer. If enough computers can be convinced to do this, the target computer can be brought down by overloading its inbound connections. This attack is named after the Smurf Trojan that is used to set up the attack on people's computers. A similar DoS attack is something called a *Fraggle attack*. This attack works just like the Smurf attack except that UDP echo replies are used instead of ICMP replies.

When Smurf attacks first came out, they did a fair amount of damage. However, today Smurf attacks are not commonly launched because they are easy to counter and most modern networks are set up so that broadcasted ICMP requests or request for replies are now blocked.

BUFFER OVERFLOW

To understand what a buffer overflow is, you must first understand what a buffer is. A buffer is a section of memory that has been set aside by the writer of a program so that the program can use that memory section for actions related to that program. A buffer overflow, sometimes called a buffer overrun, occurs when the memory assigned to a specific function by the program has too much data put into it thus causing the data in the buffer to overflow and start taking up space in adjacent memory locations. When this happens, the data that is overflowing the buffer can interfere with programs and processes that have been assigned the adjacent memory locations. A buffer overflow attack is an exploit that intentionally forces the buffer to overflow its memory range, or bounds, and deliberately causes interference with other programs in memory.

Buffer overflow attacks vary depending on what operating system is being attacked, what memory address range the buffer is assigned to. The type of buffer overflow attack being carried out can also depend on the programs that are currently running in memory. These and many other variables can affect what type of buffer overflow attack is being used and what the goal of that attack is.

Depending on the type of attack being used, there are quite a few different results that attackers are trying for. One basic result that attackers use buffer overflow attacks to achieve is to cause a particular network or devices on a network to be unusable. This type of buffer overflow attack is one way of effectively causing a DoS attack. Servers, routers, switches, and other network devices can be the target of this type of buffer overflow attack. Another goal of a buffer overflow attack could be to force data out of a protected memory location into an adjacent memory location where the attacker can capture the data. Some buffer overflow attacks are even designed to change the behavior of a program or process so that it does something to favor the attacker. As can be seen from this small sample, buffer overflows can be effective tools for attackers to compromise a network.

MAN-IN-THE-MIDDLE ATTACKS

A man-in-the-middle attack is exactly what its name implies. In a *man-in-the-middle attack* a person positions him- or herself between two other people and eavesdrops on them. The man-in-the-middle also needs to be able to pass messages from each of the people he is between in such a way that they do not know that they are being eavesdropped on or their data is being retransmitted to their intended recipient. Man-in-the-middle attacks are referred to by a number of different names. The commonly recognized abbreviation for this kind of attack is *MITM attack*. A MITM attack can also be referred to as bucket-brigade attack, fire-brigade attack, monkey-in-the-middle attack, *session hijacking*, *TCP hijacking*, TCP session hijacking, and other names. These attacks are commonly used to intercept HTTP and HTTPS communications, e-mail communications, encryption key exchanges, and many other things.

A common way to explain the man-in-the-middle attack is to use the examples of Alice, Bob, and Mallory. Alice and Bob are regular computer users who are using their e-mail to communicate with each other. Mallory is a malicious computer user who wants to cause problems for

Bob and Alice. With this in mind, Mallory places a Trojan on Bob's computer or uses some other method that acts to relay any packets that originates on Bob's computer to Mallory instead of its intended recipient. Mallory is then able to read any data sent out from Bob's computer and then do several different things to that data before sending it on. One, she can send the data on to the intended recipient as it is. Two, she can choose not to send the data on at all. Third, she can send altered or even entirely different and/or false data and make it look like it came from Bob. With this ability, Mallory can do any number of things to make Bob's life especially difficult, such as sabotage Bob's relationships, sabotage his work, or even steal Bob's personal information and use it for her own purposes. Figure 9-3 illustrates how this can be done with Bob being the primary victim of Mallory.

Figure 9-3

Mallory perpetrating a man-in-the-middle attack against Bob

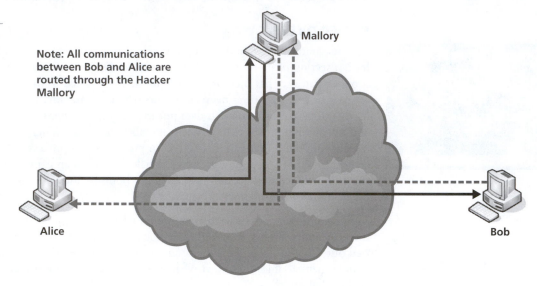

In Figure 9-3, the hacker Mallory has managed to insert herself between Bob and Alice's communications routes. From this point, Mallory is able to manipulate the communications between Bob and Alice in all the ways described earlier and more.

PACKET SNIFFING

Packet sniffing is the practice of capturing packets as they go by on the network and then open them to see what is in them. Doing this attackers can over time map out a network so that they know what addresses, both physical and logical, are found on a network. They may do this in order to spoof an address later. Additionally packet sniffing can be used to determine what protocols are running on a network. If a protocol is running on the network with known weaknesses, attackers can use that protocol to compromise the rest of the network. Depending on what protocols are running on a network, packet sniffing can even be used to view the content of the captured packets thus obtaining information about the user or computer the packet came from. In fact, when you did the WireShark lab a few Lessons back, you were running a packet sniffer and capturing network packets. The information captured and then analyzed in this way could have in turn been used to find vulnerabilities in the network that could be exploited.

FTP BOUNCE

The FTP bounce attack is an exploit against the FTP protocol in which the attacker uses the PORT command to indirectly gain access to ports that are opened on the computer they are attempting to attack. FTP bounce can be sued by attackers in an attempt to scan the open ports on a specific computer. The reason an attacker may want to scan for ports is because if they are able to find an open port that is unused, they can then use then reassign that port to some other purpose that suits the attacker. An indirect approach such as the FTP bounce attack is used so as to hopefully minimize the chances of the scan being detected.

One widely used network management tool that can utilize the FTP bounce attack to scan for ports is the program nmap. A graphical version of the nmap program will be used in a lab associated with Lesson 11. It should be noted that modern FTP servers are generally configured to refuse the PORT command from any system but the original host by default. This makes the FTP bounce less effective than in the past.

Wireless Threats

Wireless threats are attacks that are targeted specifically at wireless networks. There are a wide variety of wireless specific threats, but we will only discuss some of the more common ones.

WAR DRIVING

War driving is perhaps one of the most basic wireless threats out there and is often used in conjunction with other wireless threats by attackers. Specifically war driving is the practice of driving around in a car in an area or neighborhood looking for open wireless networks that can be used by the person doing the war driving for their own purposes. An open wireless network is one that does not have any security built into it. Once an open wireless network is found, the attacker will then use that wireless network for accessing the Internet or whatever else they wish to do. If an attacker does not find an open wireless network, then he or she will use other wireless attacks to break open access to the wireless network they are attempting to hack into.

Warchalking

Warchalking (war chalking) is a variation on war driving. The main difference between Warchalking and war driving is that once a wireless network is found, symbols are placed on an outdoor surface indicating the availability of the wireless access point and the type of wireless access point that is available. Figure 9-4 illustrates the most common Warchalking symbols used.

CERTIFICATION READY
How are war driving and
Warchalking related?
5.4

Figure 9-4

Commonly used Warchalking symbols

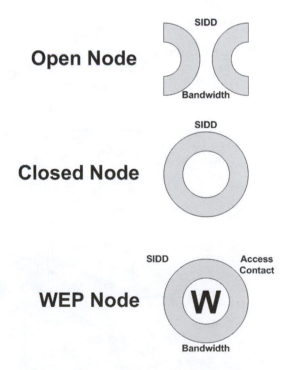

WEP CRACKING

Cracking refers to the ability to break or decode an encryption scheme used for passwords, wireless network access, or any other encrypted object. Thus WEP Cracking refers to the ability to break the encryption on a wireless network that uses WEP to encrypt its communications. WEP is actually among the easiest encryption schemes to crack. There are a number of tools that can be downloaded that make cracking a WEP wireless network very easy.

Perhaps the most comprehensive source of various network management tools that can also be used for nefarious purposes is the Backtrack distribution of Linux. This distribution of Linux contains several tools in it that can be used to test as well as cracking WEP protected wireless networks.

WPA CRACKING

WPA cracking is the same as WEP cracking except the encryption protocol targeted in WPA instead of WEP. One thing to keep in mind about WPA is that WPA has both encryption and authentication functions. Some of the same tools that can be used to test and crack WEP can also be used to test and crack WPA. Again the Backtrack distribution of Linux is a good source for finding and using these tools.

A good source of information about both WEP and WPA and how they are cracked is the PDF found at the URL shown below: http://www.hsc.fr/ressources/articles/hakin9_wifi/hakin9_wifi_EN.pdf.

ROGUE ACCESS POINTS

CERTIFICATION READY
What is a rogue access point? What are some ways that a rogue access point may come to be set up?
5.4

A rogue access point is a component often used in many man-in-the-middle attacks launched against wireless networks. Simply put, a ***rogue access point*** is an unauthorized access point that has been added to a wireless network. Not all rogue access points are created with malicious intent. Sometimes rogue access points can be added simply because a well-meaning employee wants to access the company's network wirelessly. In this situation, an employee may simply go out and buy a wireless access point from Wal-Mart or wherever and attach it to their network jack without telling IT. While this creates a rather major security breach in a company's network, the employee's action was not malicious.

However, many rogue access points *are* placed with malicious intent. When a rogue access point is placed with malicious intent, it is usually used to compromise a company's network as a first step to causing harm to the company. Once a rogue access point is put in place, it can be used to gain unauthorized access to the company's network or as the means by which a man-in-the-middle attack is carried out against a company or individuals within that company. Figure 9-5 illustrates a rogue access point.

Figure 9-5

Rogue access point

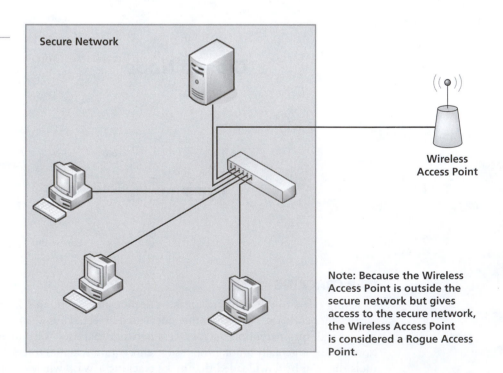

Secure Network

Wireless Access Point

Note: Because the Wireless Access Point is outside the secure network but gives access to the secure network, the Wireless Access Point is considered a Rogue Access Point.

Earlier it was said that not all rogue access points are created with malicious intent. This is true; however, once the rogue access point is in place, there really is nothing stopping somebody else from using it for his or her own purposes, malicious or otherwise. A favorite pastime for some hackers is looking for rogue access points and trying to compromise them for later use. This is why network personnel should always be on the lookout for rogue access points in their company.

There are several ways that IT personnel can determine if an access point is legitimate. One thing IT personnel can do is to check it to see if it is on the company's list of managed access points. If it is not, then it is a rogue access point by definition, no matter who placed it. Even if the access point was placed with the authorization of the IT department, if it is not on a managed list, it can easily be compromised by a user with malicious intent without that malicious user being noticed.

A second way that IT personnel can use to determine if an access point is rogue is to determine if the access point is connected to the company's secure network. Because of the security risk and limitations inherent in wireless access points, companies do not connect them to the secure networks within the company. Often, separate wireless network are set up in the company with gateways established and monitored between the wireless network and the more secure wired network. Companies do this for the express purpose of making it difficult for someone accessing the wireless network to gain access to the wired network within a company. Therefore, if a wireless access point is found that is directly connected to the wired network, thereby bypassing the steps taken to isolate it from the main network, it is a rogue access point and a security threat.

Evil Twin

<table>
<tr><td>CERTIFICATION READY
What is an evil twin?
How is evil twin related
to rogue access point?
5.4</td></tr>
</table>

An evil twin is a special case of a rogue access point. In the case of an evil twin, a rogue access point is setup, but it is not intended to be used as a backdoor into a network, instead it is intended to trick users into using it as a means to access the Internet and thus allowing the hackers in control of the evil twin to gain information about those people using the rogue access point.

An example of what an evil twin may look like would be setting up a rogue access point in a public use area. The access point looks like a legitimate wireless access point and so unsuspecting users will use it to access the Internet and simply use it for their general Internet usage. The hackers that set up the evil twin hope to capture passwords, account number, PINs, etc. from the people who are using the evil twin access point unawares.

A more sophisticated version of the evil twin access point would be where the rouge access point is slipped into a legitimate public wireless access area. In this situation the evil twin is slipped into the legitimate public wireless access area and takes over processing users from the legitimate wireless access point that was there. In this way the evil twin masquerades as the legitimate wireless access point at the site.

■ Countering Basic Security Threats

THE BOTTOM LINE

This section of Lesson 9 will discuss various ways to secure a network against basic security threats. First, we talk about device security. Next, we discuss topics such as secure and unsecure protocols as well as passwords, encryption, and certificates. Finally, we discuss authentication and the various protocols used to authenticate clients on a network. The last topic of discussion is Network Access Control.

Now that several security threats have been discussed, it is time to discuss some ways those threats can be countered. Specifically security on the device level will be discussed as well as additional topics such as passwords, encryption, and authentication.

Device Security

Device security has to do with what can be done to secure a network by securing the devices that use that network. Measures used to secure network devices range from physically securing them to securing who has access to them and their resources on the network. The protocols that are used on the network can also contribute or take away from a network device's security. Another way to secure a device is by judicially using passwords, encryption, security certificates, and authentication.

PHYSICAL SECURITY

Physical security is the first area of device security we examine. Many people overlook the importance of physical security, but in reality, it is one of the most important areas of network security. The truth of the matter is that if a hacker can get physical access to a computer, there really is not much that can be done to protect the data stored on that computer. This simple fact makes physical security a topic of utmost importance.

There are a number of things that can be done to physically secure a computer. One thing to do is to make sure that all computers containing important data are located in a locked location. This is especially true of servers. Beyond making sure that your servers are in a locked location, you should also very strictly limit access to the locked location of your servers. No one who does not have an actual need to access the servers should be permitted where the servers are located.

Another safety precaution that you can take to physically secure your servers is to place them in a location that can be seen by a large number of people. This at first sounds contradictory to the statement just made about access to the servers, but it really is not. You should lock your servers up in a room securely, but you should also have large windows in the room facing out so that everyone else in your company can see what is going on in the server room. This includes making sure that lights are always on in the room so that it is easier to see into. If a large number of people can see into a server room at all times, someone with malicious intent is less likely to physically access that room for fear someone will see them doing it and report things.

RESTRICTING LOCAL AND REMOTE ACCESS

Restricting access simply has to do with limiting who is able to gain entry into a network or a computer. *Local access* refers to the ability to gain entry into a computer via the LAN. *Remote access* refers to the ability to gain entry into a computer via a WAN connection.

The most basic way to secure access to a network, either remotely or locally is to use usernames and password. Depending on if a person is trying to access a computer remotely or locally, different protocols are used. There are also different considerations from an administrative and security point of view depending on if a person is logging on to a network locally or remotely.

Local access is the easiest to secure because the local network administrator has control of all equipment on the network. This makes it much easier to secure things. Additionally there is a basic level of trust between the users and the local network. This level of trust comes from the fact that it is generally assumed that if a person is logging on to a network locally, he or she already has some level of permission to be there. This does not preclude a hacker breaking into the local network and masquerading as a legitimate user on the network; but generally speaking, if people already have usernames on the local network, they are assumed to belong there because people who are logging on to a network locally are already inside the facility that houses that network.

Remote access is a more difficult type of access to restrict because when gaining remote access to a network, unsecured networks such as the Internet are used. An administrator does not have any real control over who uses the Internet or what is on it beyond the people and machines that are accessing it from within the local network. This means that an administrator cannot assume that people who are remotely accessing the network belong there, or are even who they say they are. Because of this, a number of additional steps need to be taken to

CERTIFICATION READY
What is local access?
What is remote access?
5.3

make sure that someone who does not belong on the network is not able to access it through remote means. Some of these methods are discussed in later sections of this lesson.

SECURE ACCESS METHODS VERSUS UNSECURE ACCESS METHODS

Secure access methods are those methods of network access that have some built-in means to limit who may access the network or what they may use to access the network. *Unsecure access methods* do not have a built-in means to limit access to a network. Alternatively, unsecure access methods can be easily bypassed. Many times, in cases where the access method is unsecure, no security is better than poor security. With poor security, the illusion of security is there but the reality is not. This may result in users being complacent and behaving in ways they would not if they knew their network was not secure.

Methods used to secure a network come in three types or flavors:

- **What you know:** Access methods that require usernames and passwords, security phrases, personal questions to verify your identity, pin numbers, and even pictures that you recognize. Most methods used to secure network access fall into this category.

  What you have: Access methods in which you possess something that shows you have legitimate access to a network. My house key would be a good example of this. The fact that you have a key to the front door of a house shows that you have some level of permission to use that house. In the computer world, a similar concept is used. However instead of traditional keys, items like swipe cards, smart cards, and key generating USB sticks are used. If you possess a secured swipe card or some such, it shows that you have some level of permission or right to access the network that the swipe card belongs to. A good everyday example of this would be your ATM card. The fact that you have the ATM card indicates that you have permission to access the bank account to which that ATM card is connected. An ATM card is also an example of using multiple types of secure access to a network. Just having the ATM card (what you have) does not give you automatic access to the attached bank account; you also have to know the correct pin number (what you know).

- **What you are:** Access methods that use something that is inherently unique to each user. Security methods of this type are what biometrics is built around. *Biometrics* refers to using unique characteristics of a person's body as the basis for securing a network or some other item. Unique characteristics that can be used in this manner include a person's fingerprints (*fingerprint scanner*), the pattern of the blood vessels found in a person's eye (*retina scanner*), the pattern of colors and shapes found in a person's iris (*iris scanner*), the shape of a person's fingers or hand (*finger and hand pattern recognition*), and even the shape of person's face (*face recognition*). There are other unique characteristics being used as a basis of biometric security as well. Scientists are even looking at using a person's DNA as a means to biometric security.

Secure protocols

Protocols are predefined standardized sets of rules that are used to communicate on a network. *Secure protocols* are predefined standardized sets of rules that are used to secure communications on a network.

For a protocol, or anything else for that matter, to be considered secure, it needs to provide three things—confidentiality, integrity, and authentication. *Confidentiality* refers to a protocol's ability to secure a communication so that a hacker cannot read it as it goes by on the network. *Integrity* refers to a protocol's ability to ensure that the data that arrives at a destination is the same data that left the source. In other words, integrity refers to a protocol's ability to ensure that data has not been modified in any way. Finally, *authentication* refers to a protocol's ability to ensure that the data came from a valid source or where it claims to have come from. If a protocol does not provide these three features, it is considered an insecure protocol. Alternatively, if a protocol does provide these three features, it is considered a secure protocol.

There is no single secure protocol that takes care of all security issues on a network, partly because people are constantly coming up with new ways to communicate across a network. Every time someone comes up with a new network technology, protocols to communicate across that network technology as well as ways to secure those communications have to be developed. Another reason no single security protocol exists is because every time a method of securing network communications is developed, hackers eventually discover a way to circumvent it. As a result, network technology developers are constantly looking for new methods of securing their network communications. Finally, there is no single ultimate security protocol because different network communications require different security methods. In the sections of Lesson 9 that follow, we discuss some secure network protocols and then we examine some unsecure network protocols.

SECURE SHELL (SSH). *Secure Shell (SSH)* was first proposed in 1995 as an alternative to TELNET. This older version became known as SSH-1. In 2006 an updated version of SSH was proposed. This version of SSH became known as SSH-2.

TELNET, the protocol SSH was intended to be an alternative for, was used to communicate between two different computers in command line terminal mode. The problem with TELNET was that it was not secure. In fact, TELNET sent passwords across the network in *plaintext*, which means that there was no encryption used to conceal the password. If a packet that contained the password was captured by a hacker, then all he/she had to do to read the password was to look at the content of the data portion of the packet using a tool like Wireshark.

The main advantage of SSH over TELNET is that SSH actually authenticates the user attempting to gain access to a system using encrypted passwords. SSH can also be used in conjunction with other protocols such as TCP, SFTP, and SCP to help open sessions for those protocols and to also secure them. SSH is assigned port 22 and is often used to secure remote connections on Linux systems. SSH, aside from securing sessions with secure authentication, can also be used to issue commands across a network and to transfer files. This gives it slightly more functionality than TELNET.

HYPERTEXT TRANSFER PROTOCOL SECURE (HTTPS). *HTTPS* stands for HTTP Secure or *Hypertext Transfer Protocol Secure*. HTTPS is also sometimes referred to as HTTP over SSL because HTTPS is not a protocol by itself, instead HTTPS is HTTP combined with the SSL/TLS protocol to secure a connection on the Internet, or some other unsecure network, and to make sure that the hypertext data being transferred over that connection is also secured. Because HTTPS encrypts web pages that are sent across the HTTPS session, it helps protect against eavesdropping and man-in-the-middle attacks. Generally HTTPS is assigned port 443 and HTTP is assigned port 80 on a network.

Although HTTPS helps secure communications across an unsecure network, it does have limitations. The biggest limitation of HTTPS is how it is implemented in a browser. If HTTPS is implemented in a browser but the browser only uses weak encryption keys, then the security provided by HTTPS can be severely compromised. How well HTTPS is implemented on the server side of things can also place a limit on HTTPS' effectiveness. You should also note that even though a communication may be secure as it travels across a network, if the destination or source computer has been compromised, then so has the HTTPS communication.

One final note of warning about HTTPS' effectiveness: the root encryption key used in both SSL and TLS protocols has been broken. While this does not allow a hacker to decrypt a packet as it goes by on the Internet, it is a different story if the packet is captured for later analysis. If a person manages to capture an HTTPS communication, he or she will eventually be able to decrypt it even without the key used to encrypt the data in the first place. This can be done because the root key used for SSL and TLS has as of right now been broken. The industry is currently working on alternatives to SSL and TLS but those aren't expected for some time.

SIMPLE NETWORK MANAGEMENT PROTOCOL VERSION 3 (SNMPV3). *SNMPv3* stands for *Simple Network Management Protocol version 3*. SNMP is a set of protocols that were developed in the early 1980s and used to manage and monitor complex network systems. SNMP has three parts:

- **Managed devices:** can be computers, switches, routers, access servers, IP phones, IP cameras, printers, and just about anything else that can be connected to a network.

CERTIFICATION READY
What is SNMPv3? How does SNMPv3 differ from SNMPv1/2?
4.4

- **Agent:** A software component that ran on the managed device. The agent is used to gather information about the managed device it resides on and to forward that information to the network management.

- **Network management system:** The final component used to do the managing, stores information about the managed device that has been gathered by the agent. The network management system stores this information in a specialized database called a *Management Information Base (MIB)*. Other software can then use the MIB to report back the condition of the various devices on the network.

As you can see from this description, SMNP is a set of protocols that you would want to be able to secure. However when SNMP was first developed, no security was built into it. The first attempt to build security into SNMP was called SNMPv2. This version of SNMP was first developed in 1993; however, it was not widely adopted primarily because many network administrators thought SNMPv2 really did not do much to secure their networks.

As a result of the poor reception of SNMPv2, developers went back to the drawing board so to speak and developed SNMPv3 in 2002. Rather than try to fix SNMPv2, developers decided to start from scratch with SNMPv1 and add security. This ended up working out quite well and SNMPv3 was born. Using the three features of a secure protocol mentioned earlier, SNMPv3 meets them in the following way. The encryption of its packets by SNMPv3 is also used to prove its packets' integrity. If the data of the packets are modified in any way, then they would not be able to be decrypted when they arrive at their destination on the network management system. Finally for authentication SNMPv3 uses the HMAC-MD5-96 authentication protocol. This and other components of the security found in SNMPv3 are found in RFC 3414. If you are interested in doing more research on SNMPv3, then RFC 3411 through RFC 3418 deal with this protocol extensively.

SECURE FILE TRANSFER PROTOCOL (SFTP). As you may have guessed, *SFTP* stands for *Secure File Transfer Protocol* or *SSH File Transfer Protocol*. SFTP was developed by the Internet Engineering Task Force (IETF) as a way to provide file access, file transfer, and file management over secure network communication sessions. The main limitation of SFTP is that it makes several assumptions whenever it is being used. One, SFTP assumes that it is already being run over a secure channel. Two, SFTP assumes that the server has already authenticated the client that is running SFTP. Finally, SFTP assumes that the client's identity is available to it. As of 2006, the most resent version of SFTP is version 6.

SECURE COPY PROTOCOL (SCP). *SCP* stands for *Secure Copy Protocol* and is another protocol that is based on SSH. Like SFTP, SCP is used to transfer files securely over a network. For the most part, SFTP has superseded SCP for this function because SFTP is a more comprehensive protocol with a greater breadth of capabilities than SCP.

Unsecure protocols

Unsecure protocols do most of the functions described in the previous protocols but without the security provided by them. You may ask why use unsecure protocols when there are secure equivalents of all of them. The simple answer to this question is that secure protocols require more computer overhead. In order to use a secure protocol, more memory, processing power, and data bandwidth is required. When security is an important consideration, it is a reasonable expectation to have to pay the price for that greater security. However, if security is not an issue, why pay the penalty when you do not have to. An example would be a web page. If a web page only contains general information that is not of a sensitive nature, why should additional resources be used to secure the transfer of that web page across the Internet? The answer is of course that the extra resources should not be used to secure the transfer of that web page. Without using extra resources, the page can be transferred faster and the web page can be accessed more often in the same amount of time. These are all good reasons not to spend the extra resources if you do not have to.

TELNET. The first unsecure protocol to be discussed is TELNET. *TELNET* has been around for a long time and is a terminal emulation tool that is used to enter commands into another computer or other device remotely across a network. TELNET sends usernames and passwords across the connection in plaintext and really has no security to speak of built into it. In a situation where you are connected directly to a device using a console cable or some other means of direct connection, TELNET's lack of security is not an issue. After all, if a person has direct access to your hardware equipment, it is generally assumed that they belong there. If they do not belong there, then you have much worse things to be worried about. However, if you are trying to access a device and manage it across a network of any sort, especially a public one, you really do not want to be using TELNET because of its lack of security. In these situations, SSH is a better choice.

HYPERTEXT TRANSFER PROTOCOL (HTTP). *HTTP* stands for *Hypertext Transfer Protocol* and is used to transfer web pages across a network, most commonly the Internet. Because HTTP does not have any security features built into it, it has a very low overhead cost and is a fast and efficient way to transfer web pages across a network. If the information being sent via a web page is sensitive, then some additional protocols need to be used in conjunction with HTTP. When additional protocols are used in conjunction with HTTP to secure the data being transferred using HTTP, then HTTPS is being used.

FILE TRANSFER PROTOCOL (FTP). *FTP* stands for *File Transfer Protocol* and is used to transfer files across the Internet much like HTTP is used to transfer web pages and SMTP is used to transfer e-mail. The main drawback of FTP is that it is an unsecure protocol. In 1999 RFC 2577 listed some of the vulnerabilities found in FTP. Some of the vulnerabilities listed were bounce attacks, spoof attacks, brute force attacks, packet capturing, username protection, and port stealing.

In *bounce attacks*, a hacker can use the PORT command found in FTP to indirectly access other ports on the computer where FTP is being used. *Spoof attacks* are where one person or machine successfully masquerades as another person or machine by falsifying data that allows the attacker access to the system. In a *brute force attack*, an attacker tries every possible combination to resolve an encrypted piece of data, such as a password, until the attacker finally hits on the combination that matches the actual piece of data. The longer the piece of data being attacked via brute force and the more complex that data is, the longer it takes to hit the correct combination. This is why longer passwords are favored over shorter ones. *Packet capture*, which is also known as *sniffing*, is the ability of a hacker to capture a packet and read the information contained in that packet. This is actually what Wireshark does. *Username protection* refers to the ability of a system or protocol to protect the usernames being used by that system or protocol from attackers. In the case of FTP, username protection is a vulnerability because it does not have a mechanism in place to protect usernames. Finally, *port stealing* is the ability of an attacker to take over a port that is being used for one purpose and assign it to another purpose that is detrimental to the system. Hackers will use this ability to create a port for their malicious software so as to provide illegitimate access to a system.

FTP is vulnerable to all these attacks because it was not designed to encrypt its traffic. All transmissions coming from FTP are in *clear text*. In other words, all passwords, usernames, data, and commands are sent in plaintext across the network. The result of this is that anyone who is able to use packet capture software on the network will be able to see everything sent across the network using FTP. The worst part is that anyone can also send data across the network using FTP without having to worry about their packets not working. This means that a hacker can essentially highjack any devices running FTP on the network and use them for their own purposes within the limitations of what FTP is capable of doing. Unfortunately protocols such as TELNET, SMTP, POP, and IMAP suffer from this same problem.

REMOTE SHELL (RSH). *RSH* stands for *Remote Shell* and is a small computer program that can be used to issue command line commands remotely across a network. This is similar to what TELNET and SSH can do. However, unlike SSH, RSH does not have security built into it and so is vulnerable to attackers if it is used on a network. Because of this, it is very unlikely you will see this program running on any modern computers. About the only place you may see RSH is in UNIX- or Linux-based systems where it may be used to remotely access other devices that are directly connected to the device using RSH.

FIBRE CHANNEL PROTOCOL (FCP). *FCP* or *Fibre Channel Protocol* is the interface protocol used to transfer SCSI (Small Component System Interface) commands and data over Fibre Channels. These *fibre channels* are the channels used in fibre channel networks to connect workstations, mainframes, supercomputers, storage devices, and displays together at very high speeds. *Fibre Channel Networks* are proposed as alternatives to current networking technology. To date, these types of networks have only been deployed in limited numbers and situations. This protocol does not have security features built into it.

SIMPLE NETWORK MANAGEMENT PROTOCOL VERSIONS 1 AND 2 (SNMPV1/2). SNMP refers to Simple Network Management Protocols versions 1 and 2. These two protocols are earlier versions of SNMPv3, which was discussed earlier, but versions 1 and 2 did not have the built-in security features that SNMPv3 has. Both protocols have been superseded by SNMPv3.

Passwords

Passwords are another way to secure a system against unauthorized access. Passwords are used to verify that the person attempting to access a system is the person they claim to be. There are only a few rules that need to be followed when using passwords. First, a password should be complex enough that it cannot be easily guessed. Earlier in this lesson, we discussed methods that accomplish this. The second rule is that passwords should be renewed and changed periodically. Forcing a password change periodically protects against the possibility that a hacker may have compromised a previous password. Constant renewal reduces this threat because it makes older passwords that may have been compromised invalid. The third rule to follow in regards to passwords is not to use the same password for everything. If you use the same password for everything, and someone compromises one password, then everything you secure with that password is also compromised. If you use different passwords for different items, when one of your passwords is compromised, then only the items protected by that password are compromised. All your other items protected by different passwords remain secure.

Encryption

CERTIFICATION READY
What does PKI stand for?
What is PKI used for?
How does PKI work?
5.3

Encryption is the process by which a mathematical algorithm is run on a set of data to make it unreadable to someone who does not know the mathematical algorithm used to encode it. Encryption can be done on data before it is sent out on a network or on data that is stored on a media of some sort. Either way, the process is intended to make the data that has been encrypted readable only to someone who knows how the data was encrypted in the first place. The reverse of encryption is decryption. The data that has been encrypted is called cipher text.

There are two major forms of encryption—private key encryption and public key encryption. In *private key encryption*, a person has to have a copy of the original encryption key in order to decrypt a cipher text. This is the kind of encryption that was used in World War II where countries had codebooks that were used to create encrypted messages and to decrypt encoded messages. In this environment, it became a high-priority espionage goal to steal the enemy's codebook without them knowing it. Figure 9-6 illustrates how private key encryption works. Step 1 in the figure takes an e-mail message and encrypts it on the sending computer using a stored private key. In step 2, the e-mail in an encrypted form is sent across the network to the destination computer. In the final step, the e-mail is decrypted on the destination computer using a copy of the same key with which it was encrypted.

Figure 9-6

Private Key Encryption

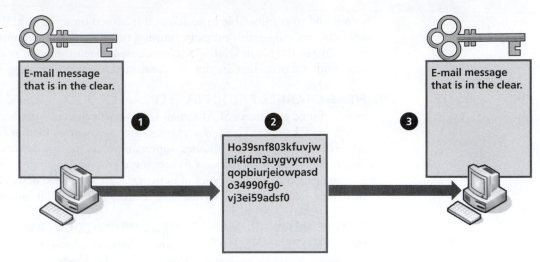

① E-mail message is encrypted on the sending computer using a stored private key.

② E-mail in encrypted form is sent across the network to the destination computer.

③ E-mail is decrypted on the destination computer by using a copy of the same key it was encrypted with.

Public key encryption is only somewhat similar to private key encryption. Figure 9-7 illustrates public key encryption. With **public key encryption**, you still start with a secret private key. However, instead of using the private key to encrypt a message, you use the private key to generate a public key (step 1) that is then used to encrypt a message (step 2). Once the public key is generated and used to encrypt a message, the public key is sent to the destination computer (step 3) either before the encrypted message was sent or along with the encrypted message (step 4). This public key is then used on the destination computer to decrypt the message that was sent to it (step 5).

Figure 9-7

Public Key Encryption

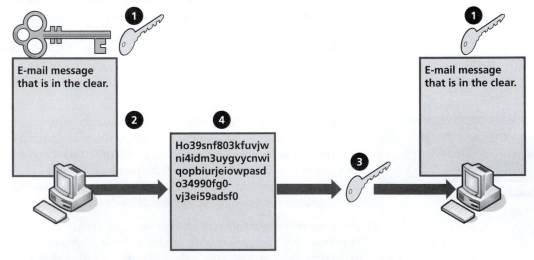

① A private key stored on the sender computer is used to generate a public key.

② E-mail message is encrypted on the sending computer using the newly generated public key.

③ The public key is sent on ahead to the destination computer.

④ The encrypted e-mail message is sent to the destination computer.

⑤ The e-mail is decrypted on the destination computer using the public key.

The public key generated by the private key can be used in one of several ways. First, it can be used as a single-use encryption key. This means that the key is used only to decrypt the one message that it was used to encrypt. After this, the public key is no longer valid. The next two ways that a public key can be used are related. The public key can be used for a set number of messages before it is made invalid, or revoked. Alternatively, it can be set to be valid for a certain period of time before it is revoked. In this situation, the public key is set to be valid for a month from the time it was created. At the end of that month, the public key is revoked and a new one is generated for additional use. In both cases, a copy of the generated public key is kept on the computer that generated it until the public key is no longer valid.

Now that we understand what encryption is, we need to ask the question, how is encryption used to secure a network. In point of fact, encryption can be used in two of the three areas previously mentioned to ensure that a network is secure. Those two areas are confidentiality and integrity. Encryption aids in the confidentiality of a piece of data by ensuring that it cannot be casually read by someone snooping on the network. Encryption does this by turning the data into cipher text, which cannot be easily read unless the one reading it also possesses the correct encryption key.

Public key encryption in particular is also useful for ensuring the integrity of data being sent across the network because data sent by public key encryption can only be decrypted by the corresponding public key. If data is altered after it has been encrypted with a specific public key, then when that data arrives at its destination, the public key possessed by the destination computer will not be able to decrypt it. If the data cannot be decrypted by the public key, that means the data was somehow altered after it was first encrypted but before it arrived at the destination computer.

Certificates

Certificates are basically certifications that a public key is valid. They are often called *public key certificates* or *digital certificates*. Generally, a certificate is a digital document that is added to a public key to certify the origins of the public key and its validity. Digital certificates identify the person who is the owner of the public key (generally referred to as the *holder*). It also contains the actual public key of the holder. Finally, the certificate contains information that identifies the issuer of the public key and digital certificate in question. The computer (usually a server) that issued the certificate is referred to as a *certificate authority*. The data security infrastructure that uses certificates is called the PKI, which stands for Public Key Infrastructure.

TEMPORAL KEY INTEGRITY PROTOCOL (TKIP)

TKIP stands for Temporal Key Integrity Protocol. TKIP is an encryption standard designed to be used with IEEE 802.11 wireless standards. What TKIP does is wrap additional layers of encryption around existing wireless encryption standards such as WEP. This allows TKIP to work with older wireless LAN security standards. While TKIP does increase the security of a wireless frame, wireless networks are still inherently unsecure. You should note that the encryption that TKIP was based on has recently been broken. For this reason, the same warning given for SSL/TLS applies here. If you are only trying to minimize the chances that someone will be able to eavesdrop on your packets as they go by then TKIP is fine. However, if you are trying to secure a network so that captured packets cannot be read at the hacker's leisure, then TKIP really is not an option for you. Of course, if your data is that sensitive, then you probably should not be placing it on a wireless network in the first place.

Authentication

CERTIFICATION READY
What is authentication?
Why is it important?
5.3

Before permitting access to the computer or network being queried, a user or computer is verified to be who or what they claim to be using a process called *authentication*. There are many different protocols that are used for authentication. However, they all have one thing in common, they are designed to verify the identity of the person or computer seeking access to whatever is being queried.

The most common authentication method uses a username and password. In this type of authentication, if you know the password associated with a specific username, then it is assumed that you are the person attempting to access the system. The main weakness of this authentication method is that passwords can be stolen. Because of this, some alternative methods of authentication have been developed. Some require knowledge of more than just a password, while others require that the user possess a specific item or have a certain characteristic. Alternatively, some authentication protocols use certificates as part of the authentication process.

We will discuss a couple of authentication methods below. After the discussion of different authentication methods, we will next look at several different authentication protocols.

Multi-factor authentication

The first step in understanding what multi-factor authentication required that us understand what authentication factors are. There are generally three recognized categories of authentication factors. These categories are something the user knows, something the user has, and something the user is. Examples of something a user knows could be a username, password, the answer to a security question, the ability to recognize a security picture, or a PIN number. Something a user has could be a security fob, a smart card, a bank card, an ATM, a key, or any number of other items a user has in their possession. Finally, something a user is would involve unique characteristics of a person. Some examples of this would be finger prints, iris pattern, DNA pattern, the pattern of blood vessels in the retina of the user's eye, a voice print of the user, the geometry of a user's hand or face, or a number of other unique features a user possesses.

CERTIFICATION READY
What are authentication factors? List and describe a few authentication factors.
5.3

Multi-factor authentication is a form of authentication that requires the user to present more than one proof of who they are before they are allowed access to whatever it is they are attempting to access. If you do have seen the animated movie *The Incredibles*, you have seen a humorous example of multi-factor authentication. In that movie, to gain access to her lab where she created the superhero's suits Edna had to use multi-factor authentication. In the movie, Edna had to have a security card, a password, a hand print, a retina scan, and a voice print recognition. The card was something Edna had, the password was something Edna knew, and the hand print, retina scan, and voice print match were all something Edna was.

Many websites that give access to financial information or bill paying will have a username, password, security question, and/or security picture. The person attempting to access this site needs to know all these pieces of information before they are allowed to access a back account, credit card account, or other items of financial importance. In this illustration multiple pieces of information are needed to gain access to the website being accesses. However, despite having to know all these pieces of information, this is not an example of multi-factor authentication. This is in fact an example of single-factor authentication. The reason this is single-factor authentication is because all the things used to identify the user are things the user knows. They do not require the user to possess anything or to be anything. Because only one factor is used, what the user knows, it is not considered multi-factor authentication.

CERTIFICATION READY
What is required for an authentication method to be considered multi-factor authentication?
5.3

On the other hand, access to an ATM machine does require multi-factor authentication. In the case of the ATM machine, the user needs to possess the correct ATM card and they need to know the correct PIN number. In this case, two factors are being used and so this can be considered a multi-factor authentication system. The two factors being used are something the user has, the ATM card, and something the user knows, the PIN number.

TWO-FACTOR AUTHENTICATION. Two-factor authentication is a special case of multi-factor authentication. In two-factor authentication the user attempting to gain access to whatever they are attempting to gain access to needs two factors that prove they are who they claim to be. The ATM example above is in reality a two-factor authentication system.

Disney and many other amusement parks also use two-factor authentication. In the case of Disney, they require each person attempting to gain access to the park on some kind of pass to possess both the appropriate pass card and to have the matching finger print or hand geometry. This prevents more than one person from using one pass card on different days to gain access to the Disney amusement park. Even if the pass card can be given to a different person, the hand geometry or finger print of the original pass purchaser cannot be passed by a different person. In this case the two factors being used for authentication are something the user has, the pass card, and something the use is, the finger print or hand geometry.

Single sign-on

CERTIFICATION READY
What is single sign-on?
What is the advantage to single sign-on? What is the disadvantage to single sign-on?
5.3

Single sign-on is the practice of using a single password, username, or authentication device such as a smartcard to sign-on to multiple systems. The advantage of a single sign-on system is that the end user does not have to remember multiple passwords and usernames or possess multiple authentication devices. The disadvantage of the single sign-on system is that if the user forgets their password and/or username they will not be able to access the system. Even worse, if a single smartcard is being used, should that smartcard fall into the wrong person's hands, it can be used to access multiple systems or locations.

PUBLIC KEY INFRASTRUCTURE (PKI)

PKI stands for *Public Key Infrastructure*, which is a set of people, policies, software, and equipment needed to handle digital certificates for various applications. Some of the main components in this infrastructure are as follows. The end user is the person that wishes to make use of the PKI to carry out some online activity. The registration authority (RA) is used to verify that a specific public key belongs to a specific end user. The certificate authority (CA) is used to issue a digital certificate to the end user. The CA also sends information about the digital certificate on to a validation authority (VA), which verifies the certificate when an e-commerce site or other online service seeks to have the certificate verified. Finally, we have the e-commerce sites and other online services that use the PKI to verify digital certificates for various reasons. All these components are needed for PKI to function properly.

In a general sense, PKI is intended to bind public keys to digital certificates so that the digital certificates in turn can be used for online authentication in many different capacities. PKI-generated digital certificates can be used for activities as diverse as verifying the sender of a sensitive e-mail to verifying that a person has the right to make an online purchase.

E-commerce is one area in which PKI is heavily used. Figure 9-8 illustrates how PKI can be used to carry out an online commerce transaction. In Figure 9-8, the following steps are carried out. First, an end user must have a private key from which he/she can create a public key to bind to a digital certificate in the PKI. The end user then sends the generated public key to a registration authority (RA) to have his identify verified (step 1). In step 2, the RA then sends the verified public key to a certificate authority (CA). The CA, based on the information provided by the RA, issues a digital certificate to the end user that binds his public key to his online certificate (step 3). The CA also sends information about the generated certificate to the validation authority (VA) so that when the VA receives the digital certificate it will know that it is a valid one (step 4). The end user then uses his digital certificate to order some merchandise from an e-commerce site (step 5). The e-commerce site takes the certificate the end user gave it and verifies it with the VA (step 6). Once the VA verifies the digital certificate as valid, the e-commerce site then removes the set amount of money from the end user's account and credits the end user with the merchandise they just purchased (step 7). Once the end user is credited with the order merchandise, the e-commerce site then sends the merchandise to the end user via the appropriate means.

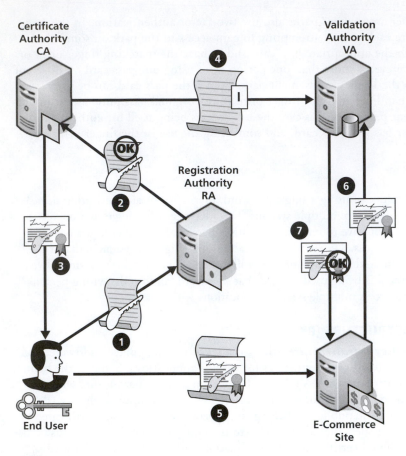

Figure 9-8

How PKI works

1. End user applies to the RA for a certificate using a public key generated with his private key.

2. The RA confirms the identity to the End User and sends this confirmation to a CA.

3. CA issues a certificate to the End User.

4. CA sends information about the certificate to a VA.

5. End User uses his certificate to order merchandise from a E-Commerce Site.

6. The E-Commerce Site verifies the End User with the VA.

7. VA confirms the certificate and identity of the End user to the E-Commerce Site and the End User is permitted to purchase his merchamdise.

While Figure 9-8 shows how PKI and digital certificates can be used in e-commerce, there are many other applications in which digital certificates and the PKI can be used.

KERBEROS

Kerberos is an authentication protocol that is commonly used to authenticate clients over an unsecured network, most commonly LANs. Kerberos is the authentication protocol most commonly used by Windows-based client/server networks. A Kerberos system is composed of an *authentication service (AS)*, a *ticket granting service (TGS)*, and a *network services (NS)*. In the case of a Windows domain network, the AS and the TGS are usually located on the same computer, which is also a domain controller. Network Services can be found on any server connected to the domain that provides a service. These services can be anything from file services to e-mail services, or anything in between. Figure 9-9 illustrates in a broad general way how Kerberos works in a Microsoft domain environment.

As you can see in Figure 9-9, the whole authentication process begins when a client wants access to network services. When this happens the client issues an authentication request to the Kerberos AS (step1), which in a Windows environment exists on the domain controller. The AS responds by sending the client a *ticket granting ticket (TGT)* that the AS requires the client to correctly decrypt (step 2) and respond back with. Once the client correctly decrypts the TGT, it sends it back to the ticket granting service (TGS) (step 3), which is part of the AS, as proof that it deserves a *service ticket (ST)*. After verifying that the TGT has been decrypted properly, the TGS then issues an ST to the client (step 4). Once the ST is issued to the client, the client is able to use the ST to gain access to any network services to which it is permitted (step 5).

Figure 9-9

How Kerberos works in a
Windows environment

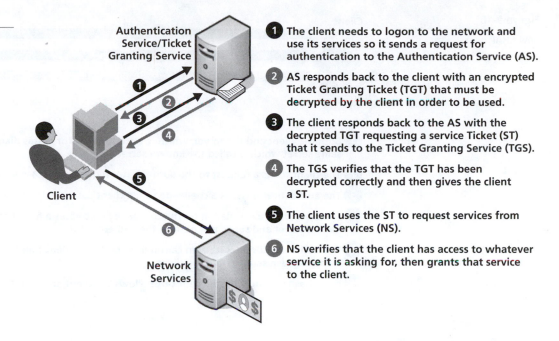

This ST is good for a set amount of time (usually around 8 hours) during which the client can use the ST to access any network services it needs. However, the ST also contains an *Access Control List (ACL)* delineating all the network services the client has access to and what permissions it has related to those services. Any time a client wants access to a network service, the ST is checked to verify that the client has access to the service being requested and what permissions it has in that service. Once a client's access permission is verified using the ST, the client is then allowed access to that network service (step 6). If the client's ST does not confirm that a client has access to a specific service, either additional authentication is requested or access is denied to the network service the client is requesting.

CHALLENGE-HANDSHAKE AUTHENTICATION PROTOCOL (CHAP)

CHAP stands for *Challenge-Handshake Authentication Protocol*. CHAP is an authentication method used by *PPP (Point-to-Point Protocol)* to verify the identity of a client after a connection has been successfully established. PPP is a protocol that establishes a dedicated connection between two different points that last for the duration of the session being used. The interesting thing about CHAP is that it sends the challenge and response in clear text, but still maintains a certain level of security by having both the client and the server know what the secret (i.e., password or secret phrase) is and using that secret to establish each other's identity without actually sending the secret across the connection. It does this with a three-way-handshake. Figure 9-10 shows this process.

Figure 9-10 shows all the steps necessary to allow authentication on the server or authenticator. Step 1 is that both computers know the same secret password or phase. This is called the Known Secret. The client that wishes access to the server must issue a request for access to the server (step 2). This is called the Request. The server responds back with a challenge phase or password that the client has to encrypt into a hash using the Known Secret (step 3). This is called the Challenge. Once the client has created the hash, it sends it back to the server in a response (step 4). This is called the Response. The server does the same calculation on the challenge the client did using the Known Secret to create its own hash (step 5). If the two hashes match up, then the server allows the client access to the network (step 6). The Request-Challenge-Response sequence is what is called the *three-way-handshake* mentioned

Figure 9-10

How CHAP works

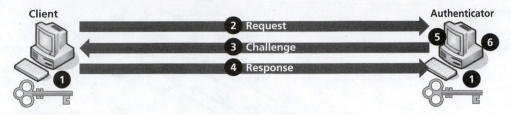

1. Both the client and the server, which is the authenticator in this diagram, know the same secret which is called the known secret.

2. The client sends a request to the authenicator requesting access to the network.

3. The authenticator issues a challenge to the client based on the known secret.

4. The client does a calculation on the challenge and creates a hash based on the known secret and sends this hash to the authenticator.

5. The authenticator does its own calculations on the challenge and compares it to the response hash sent to it by the client.

6. If the hashes match, the authenticator allows the client access to the network.

earlier. After this, the server periodically sends a new challenge to the client and tests the client's response in order to verify that the correct client is still accessing the network.

The main type of attack CHAP defends against is a *replay attack*. A replay attack is where a hacker captures the response from the client and replays it to the server in an attempt to fool the server into thinking it is the true client.

CHAP was first discussed in RFC 1334 in 1992. In 1996, CHAP was updated by RFC 1994. CHAP was again updated by RFC 2484 in 1999.

MICROSOFT CHALLENGE-HANDSHAKE AUTHENTICATION PROTOCOL (MS-CHAP)

CERTIFICATION READY
What is CHAP? What is MS-CHAP? How do CHAP and MS-CHAP differ?
5.3

MS-CHAP stands for *Microsoft Challenge-Handshake Authentication Protocol*. It is very closely related to standard CHAP but is designed to work closely with Microsoft operating systems. This allows MS-CHAP to work with the authentication protocols and capabilities built into the various Windows operating systems. There are only three main differences between MS-CHAP and CHAP beyond MS-CHAP being designed with Windows. Those differences are as follows. MS-CHAP:

- Does not require the authenticator to store a clear text or reversible encryption secret.
- Includes mechanisms for allowing retries and changing passwords.
- Has a set of reasons for failure codes that it can return to the client if the client has failed to authenticate on the authenticator.

RFC 2433 describes MS-CHAP version 1, and RFC 2759 describes MS-CHAP version 2.

EXTENSIBLE AUTHENTICATION PROTOCOL (EAP)

CERTIFICATION READY
What does EAP stand for? What is EAP used for?
5.3

EAP stands for *Extensible Authentication Protocol*, which is an authentication protocol that is primarily used in wireless communications, although it can also be used with PPP connections. EAP defines a wide variety of methods to authenticate packets on a network. There are currently something like 40 different methods related to EAP defined in various RFCs.

EAP was first defined in RFC 2284 in 1998 and was originally defined as an authentication protocol for PPP. In 2004, RFC 3784 was proposed which updated EAP to include other lower layer protocols besides PPP. This proposal allowed EAP to be used with wireless access technologies. RFC 5247 proposed in 2008 included various key management capabilities for

EAP. Because of all these changes, EAP is able to support the wide variety of authentication methods previously mentioned. EAP has become an important authentication protocol for wireless communications. Both WAP and WAP2 use EAP authentication methods.

802.11X

802.11x is a standard that is used to secure *wireless LANs (WLANs)* that follow the various 802.11 standards. 802.11x allows a user on a WLAN to be authenticated by a central authentication authority. For any messages that need to be exchanged during the authentication process 802.11x uses EAP.

To understand how 802.11x works, we need to define a couple of terms. First is the term *supplicant,* a supplicant is any wireless device wishing to gain access to a WLAN. The access point through which a wireless device is seeking access to the WLAN is called an *authenticator*. The server that the authenticator has to get permission from to allow the supplicant onto the network is called the authentication server. Finally a state called the *unauthorized state* is a special state the supplicant is placed in while the authenticator queries the authentication server about allowing the supplicant access to the network. In the unauthorized state, only EAP message can be passed to and from the supplicant. Once the supplicant has been allowed on the network by the authentication server, its state is changed to authorized. In this state, the supplicant is allowed full access to the network. Figure 9-11 illustrates how 802.11x works using these terms.

Figure 9-11

How 802.11x works

1 Client, also known as the supplicant, wishes to access the WLAN that the access point, also as the authenticator, controls.

2 Authenticator places the supplicant into unauthorized mode so that only EAP message can be sent to and from supplicant and requests the supplicant's identity and credentials.

3 Supplicant responds back with its identity and credentials.

4 Authenticator forwards the supplicants identity and credentials to the authentication server.

5 Authentication server verifies the supplicants identity and credentials and sends a message to the authenticator allowing it to permit the supplicant full access to the WLAN.

6 The authenticator changes the state of the supplicant to authorized so it has full access to the WLAN.

As you can see in Figure 9-11, a supplicant or client wishes to gain access to a WLAN that the access point, or authenticator, controls and sends a request for access to the authenticator (step 1). The access point, which also serves as the authenticator, intercepts the access request and sends the supplicant a message that places it into unauthorized mode (step 2). While in unauthorized mode, the supplicant can only send and receive EAP messages. The authenticator uses these EAP messages to request the supplicant's identity and credentials, which the supplicant sends to the authenticator (step 3). The authenticator then passes the supplicant's identity and credentials on to the authentication server (step 4). The authentication server verifies the supplicant's identity using the credentials provided and then sends a message to the authenticator (step 5) either allowing or denying the supplicant full access to the WLAN. If the supplicant is allowed full access to the WLAN, the authenticator passes on a message to the supplicant switching it to authorized mode, which allows the supplicant full access to the WLAN (step 6). If the supplicant is denied full access to the WLAN, then the authenticator blocks the supplicant from having access to the WLAN.

AUTHENTICATION, AUTHORIZATION, AND ACCOUNTING (AAA)

CERTIFICATION READY
What does AAA stand for? What does AAA refer to?
5.3

AAA is a network security term that refers to authentication, authorization, and accounting. *Authentication* refers to any process by which an entity's identity is verified. *Authorization* refers to any process that is used to verify that an entity has permission to perform some activity or has access to some resource. Finally *accounting* refers to ability to track various events on a network.

Any protocol that has all the abilities just listed is referred to as an AAA protocol. Some protocols that are considered AAA protocols are RADIUS, Diameter, TACACS, and TACACS+. We discuss RADIUS and TACACS+ next in this lesson.

Remote Authentication Dial-In User Service (RADIUS)

CERTIFICATION READY
What is RADIUS? What is it used for?
5.3

Remote Authentication Dial-In User Service (RADIUS) provides a method of centralized authentication, authorization, and accounting between a computer and a managed network. Despite its name, RADIUS is not limited to dial-in services with a modem. That is merely the original method used to access a network. In point of fact, many modern ISPs use RADIUS to manage access to the Internet. Companies also use RADIUS to manage access to their internal networks. RADIUS is a very flexible protocol and can be used with modems, access points, DSL, web servers, network ports, VPNs, and other access technologies. RADIUS was first introduced in 1991 and is still being updated and adjusted today. The most recent RFC related to RADIUS was issued in August 2010.

RADIUS provides authentication, authorization, and accounting to the network it is used to access. On the authentication side, RADIUS allows or grants access to the network to specific users and/or devices. On the authorization side of things, once a user or device is on a network, RADIUS restricts the user or device only to the specific network services they have been granted permission to use. Finally, on the accounting side of things, RADIUS keeps a record of which users and devices accessed or attempted to access specific network services.

Terminal Access Controller Access-Control System Plus (TACACS+)

CERTIFICATION READY
What is TACACS+? What is TACACS+ used for? What is the difference between TACACS+ and RADIUS?
5.3

TACACS+ stands for *Terminal Access Controller Access-Control System Plus*. TACACS+ is a similar protocol to RADIUS. However where RADIUS is an open protocol TACACS+ is a Cisco proprietary protocol. Also TACACS+ is used more for routers, network access servers, and other similar devices while RADIUS is more often used for client access. However, TACACS+, like RADIUS does provide mechanisms for authentication, authorization, and accounting. TACACS+ was first introduced in a draft RFC in 1996 by Cisco. The final draft RFC came out in 1997.

TACACS+ is similar but unrelated to an earlier protocol called TACACS. TACACS was an open protocol that was first developed for UNIX systems. However, later protocols like RADIUS made TACACS all but obsolete. Cisco responded to RADIUS with TACACS+. This protocol did many of the things that TACACS did but had better security and was more efficient. TACACS+ was also proprietary to Cisco unlike TACACS.

There are some significant differences between TACACS+ and RADIUS beyond the fact that RADIUS is an open protocol and TACACS+ is a proprietary protocol. Some of those differences are as follows. One of those differences is that RADIUS uses UDP for its transport layer protocol while TACACS+ uses TCP. Because of this fact, some administrators see TACACS+ as more reliable than RADIUS. Second, TACACS+ uses more types of authentication request and response codes than RADIUS does. Next, TACACS+ supports more protocols than RADIUS does. RADIUS is pretty much limited to TCP/IP while TACACS+ is able to use TCP/IP, IPX/SPX, and Apple Talk protocols. Finally, while TACACS+ encrypts the entire body of the packet, RADIUS only encrypts the password in the access request packet and leaves the rest unencrypted. On a final note, Cisco is committed to supporting both protocols.

NETWORK ACCESS CONTROL

Network Access Control (NAC) is not a specific protocol or application so much as an overall approach to computer security. The purpose of NAC is to limit what a host, client, or device can do on a proprietary network. NAC includes authentication, but it also includes additional security assets that that can be used on a network to enhance the security of that network. These additional assets may include things such as intrusion detection/prevention software, antivirus software, anti-spyware components, and other similar security measures. The way these different security measures are employed is directly related to the network security policies of the entity using the NAC system. NAC is ideal for network environments where administrators can tightly control the network. However, many administrators feel that the more diverse the devices and capabilities in a network, the less effective NAC becomes.

Posture assessment

Simply put a posture assessment is an evaluation of how good a company or network's security is. Companies should evaluate their network security on a regular basis and update that security as needed. As new patches or security technology that is relevant to a company come out, they need to be added to the company's network. If a company waits to implement security improvements they run the risk of becoming vulnerable to new threats as they come out or are discovered. The Lesson later in this book on Network Management will discuss some of the policies and actions a company can carry out to ensure that their security posture remains up to date.

■ After an Attack Has Occurred

THE BOTTOM LINE

An explanation of what needs to be done after an attack has happened is the topic of discussion in this section of Lesson 9.

There is one rule that it is very important to learn when it comes to network security. The goal of network security is not to make your network invulnerable to attack. It is impossible to make your network so secure that it is invulnerable. Instead, the goal of network security is to make your network harder to get into than the other guy's so that the hackers will bother him and not you. The corollary to this rule is that if a hacker knows you have a piece of data and he or she wants it bad enough, they will figure out a way to get it. That said, the obvious best defense for a network is not to let people know what you have on it unless they have a need to know. All of this leads to another inescapable fact; sooner or later your network will be attacked. What should you do after the attack has occurred?

The answer to this question starts before the attack even occurs. Your company should have policies in place ahead of time that outline what should happen after an attack has been discovered. It does not matter if the attack is successful or not, what you do remains the same. After a policy is set for what you should do after an attack occurs, you should also assemble a team of people whose job is to evaluate every attack that occurs.

Mitigation Techniques

Mitigation techniques are things that can be done to limit the impact that security threats and/or breaches can have on a network. A few of these mitigation techniques will be discussed in this Lesson. However, a later Lesson on Network Management will go into more detail on some of these topics.

TRAINING AND AWARENESS

Perhaps the best mitigation technique that a company has available to it is its network users. If a company's users are trained to recognize and react properly toward threats to the corporate network posed by such things as virus and spyware, then these types of things will have less impact on the functioning of the network. Additionally, if users are taught the importance of things like passwords and how to make complex but easily remembered passwords then the network will inherently become more secure because the user passwords will be more effective and they will not feel the need to write them down. Finally, if users are taught about social engineering and how to spot it, they will recognize when someone is attempting to social engineer them and react appropriately. All these things can make a network much more secure and all of them involve training users in what these threats are, how to recognize them, and how to respond to them. When this is done it has the effect of making a network's users more aware of what is going on around them and this in turn makes it harder for attackers to cause problems on the network.

PATCH MANAGEMENT

CERTIFICATION READY
What is patch management important and why is it important?
5.4

Patch management has to do with making sure that all devices and software on the network has the latest patches installed on them. This is important because patches are released for the purpose of fixing security problems or holes that were discovered after the hardware or software product initially came out. By keeping all software and hardware devices on the network properly patched, it makes your network less vulnerable to attack.

Incident Response

CERTIFICATION READY
Why is it important to respond to an incident correctly?
5.4

Whether the attack was successful or not, the first thing the team should do is assess the attack. They can do this using various networking tools available to network administrators and hackers alike. Some of these tools are discussed later in this lesson.

There are a variety of things the after-attack team should look at. How did the attacker gain access to the network? They should evaluate how effective the network was at keeping them out. Were the attackers stopped before they got whatever they were after? If the attacker did get stopped, were they stopped at the perimeter of the network, or did they get some distance into the network before they were stopped? If the attacker got a certain distance into the network before being stopped, what can be done to stop similar attacks closer to the outer edge of the network?

The after-attack team should also try to determine what data the attacker was after or what action they were attempting to accomplish. If they are able to determine what the attacker was after, then additional steps can be taken to protect that particular bit of data or that particular service because if a hacker tried once for a piece of data or to access a service and failed, they may make follow-up attempts to accomplish what they had failed to do the first time.

If the attack was successful, then the after-attack team has to answer many of the same questions. If the attacker got into the network, then the team has to determine how they got into the network. Once they know this, they can then take actions to close that pathway of vulnerability in the future.

The team also has to try to determine what the hackers did or stole from the network. This is important because what the hackers took or what they did to the network could have long-term consequences for the company. If they stole sensitive data, then steps need to be taken to minimize the impact of that data getting out. If the attackers compromised some network service or application, then steps need to be taken to counter their actions and make it so that in the future hackers will not be able to do that to your network again.

The most discouraging part of all this is that very often, even if you know you were attacked, you cannot determine what the hacker did or attempted to do, nor can you determine what they took or attempted to take. When that is the situation, the only thing the members of the after-attack team can do is determine to the best of their ability how the hackers got in, and instate countermeasures to prevent the same thing from happening again in the future. Even more discouraging is that many attacks go undiscovered or are discovered so long after the event that there is really no way to tell what the attacker did or how they did it.

■ Network Tools that Can Be Used for Good or Bad

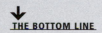

THE BOTTOM LINE

This section of Lesson 9 describes various tools used by administrators to manage their networks and by hackers to break into the same networks the administrators are trying to protect.

There are many tools available for network administrators to use that allows them to better protect their networks and to take actions when someone is invading their networks. However, many of these tools have dual uses. Network administrators may use them to protect their networks or hackers may use them to compromise their networks. We discuss some of these network tools in this section of Lesson 9. A few of the tools are useful primarily against attacks while a few are of use primarily by attackers. The rest are dual use.

Intrusion Detection Software (IDS)

Intrusion detection software (IDS) is software that is able to detect an intruder that has broken into a network or a computer. This software is often called a software firewall. Some popular examples of this type of software are ZoneAlarm, Windows Firewall, and Norton Internet Security. While this type of software is often called a firewall, it is not what would traditionally be considered a firewall. Traditionally, a firewall is a networking device specifically designed to prevent intruders from entering a network. Firewalls are designed to prevent attackers from getting into a network. IDS, because it resides on top of an operating system, only works after the attacker has gotten in and is able to be detected. It is this last distinction that prevents IDS from qualifying as a traditional firewall.

IDS detects intruders using many of the same techniques that antivirus software uses to detect malware. One tech technique used by IDSs to detect intruders is definitions. In antivirus software, definitions are a database of what different viruses look like. Antivirus software uses these definitions determine using comparison if a virus may be present in a scanned file. In IDSs, definitions are a database of what different types of intrusions look like. The IDS uses these definitions to compare observed network activity to the database to determine if it looks like an intrusion. The main problem with definitions is that they only cover known attacks. If a hacker comes up with a new type of attack, then that type of attack may not yet have a definition available and so an IDS relying solely on definitions would not be able to identify the attack.

Another way that IDS detects intruders is to compare baseline activity of the computer or network to current activity. If there is a very large difference in what is considered normal activity on a network or computer and what is currently happening, then this is an indication that an attack may be under way.

No matter what detection method IDS uses to detect an attack, the software's response is the same. When IDS uncovers some activity that looks like an attack, it warns the network administrator of the suspect activity. It is then up to the network administrator to investigate the activity and determine if an attack is indeed going on. If an attack is taking place, the administrator then has to decide what needs to be done to stop it.

Intrusion Prevention Software (IPS)

Intrusion prevention software (IPS) is an extension of IDS. Most of the IDSs mentioned earlier actually have IPS components built into them. Where IDS is only able to detect intruders and report it, IPS is able to take action against the intruder. This action can cover a wide range of activities including closing ports, blocking specific protocols, and blocking suspiciously behaving IP addresses. In point of fact, most modern IDSs could more accurately be called IDS/IPS because when most modern IDSs detect suspicious activity, not only do they report it, they also take preprogrammed steps to stop the intrusion.

Packet Sniffers

Packet sniffers, which are also called *packet analyzers* are programs designed to capture networkt packets and break them apart to analyze them. When a packet sniffer breaks the packets apart, you are able to see the various protocols that make up the packet as well as read the data that is encapsulated in the packet. This reveals information that is valuable to both network administrators in protecting their networks and hackers in invading networks. Some of the information found using packet sniffers includes source and destination logical addresses, source and destination MAC addresses, the protocols used to transport the data, the kind of data being transported, the actual data itself if it has not been encrypted, and much more. This is all information that can be used to detect intruders and take action to stop them. It is also information that an intruder can use to compromise any network they are targeting.

Packet sniffing software is very useful software and something you have already been exposed to. The Wireshark program used earlier in this book is in fact a packet sniffing program that you have used and are somewhat familiar with. While Wireshark is a packet analyzer you have been exposed to, there are quite a few other ones out there. Some examples of other packet sniffing software are dSniff, The Dude, Cain and Able, and even the Network Monitor that comes with most Windows operating systems. These tools are very common and very useful for those with both good and bad intentions.

Port Scanners

Port scanners are software programs that are designed to search a host or a network server for port addresses that are open but not being used. Network administrators use these tools to look for open ports on their network servers and computers that need to be closed so that they cannot be exploited by hackers. Hackers use port scanners to look for open ports on networks and computers so that they can be exploited. This tool, just like the protocol analyzer, is one that can be used by both the good guys and the bad guys.

Key Loggers

Key loggers are software programs or hardware devices that can be loaded onto a computer or plugged into a computer to record the keystrokes that are typed into the keyboard. In the case of a hardware key logger, a device is placed between the keyboard and the keyboard interface on the computer.

Key loggers are a tool that can be useful for finding out what an end user is doing on their computer in order to troubleshoot what they are doing wrong in a program. Hackers can also use key loggers to capture passwords without having to crack them. Some key loggers, especially those of the software variety, can also capture screen shots of what a person is doing on their computer making them even more useful for both hackers and network administrators alike.

Hackers use key loggers in the following way. A hacker slips a key logger onto a victim's computer and sets it to activate every time the victim starts up their computer. The key logger then makes a log of every keystroke the user types on their computer during the day. The hacker later retrieves the log created by the key logger. The hacker can do this by either retrieving the actual log or retrieving the device if it is hardware based. Once the log has been retrieved, the hacker sifts through the data collected to determine any usernames and password the victim used during the day. This tool also allows the hacker to circumvent other security measures such as any security questions. Anything requiring a typed response can be captured by a key logger.

On a more positive side, parents can also use key loggers to monitor what their kids are doing on the computers when the parent is not present to see. This is done much like the hacker would, except the parent has easy physical access to the computer, which a hacker may not have, and the parent is using the key logger for totally different reasons. Key loggers are tools that can be used by both the good guys and the bad guys, but are more likely to be used by the bad guys.

Password Capturing/Cracking Software

Password capturing software is exactly what its name implies; it is software that is used to capture passwords. The way password capturing software differs from key loggers is that it sits passively on a computer or network looking for usernames to go by and then it captures them in their encrypted form. A good example of software of this type is a program called PasswordDump. The password capturing software is slipped onto a vulnerable computer and quietly makes copies of all usernames and passwords that go by it on the network. The hacker is then able to retrieve the data captured by the software and use another program called a password cracker on it.

A password cracker is a software program that is designed to take a captured password hash and decrypt it so that the plaintext of the password can be seen. The hacker is then able to use this plaintext password to break into a target computer or network.

There are two main methods used by password crackers to break, or crack, passwords. The first is a simple *dictionary attack*. In a dictionary attack, a large database of possible passwords and their encrypted hash is used to compare the captured hash in the hopes of finding a match that will reveal the plaintext password. These databases of passwords are called *wordlists*. There are some very good wordlists available on the Internet for those interested in experimenting with them. Because computers are very good at making huge numbers of comparisons very quickly, a dictionary attack can break a password rapidly assuming the password was located in the dictionary to start with. A large percentage of all passwords can be broken very quickly using this method.

If a dictionary attack fails, then the password cracking software has to resort to another method to break the password. In a *brute force attack* the password cracker keeps substituting letters, numbers, and special characters and encrypting them with the same encryption method used by the computer that originally created the password until it finds a hash that is a perfect match for the hash captured. The more characters and the more types of characters in a password, the longer it will take a computer to break a password using the brute force method. This is why you should try to make your password at least eight characters long and use uppercase, lowercase, and numbers in them. For additional security, special characters such as most of those found above the number keys on a keyboard can be used as well.

SKILL SUMMARY

IN THIS LESSON YOU LEARNED:

- What network security considerations you should have.
- What social engineering is and how it is the most successful method to circumvent security measures.
- What phishing is and how to avoid it.
- How passwords are stolen.
- A method for creating very secure passwords that are easy to remember.
- What identity theft is and ways to avoid it.
- About different types of malware.
- What the difference is between viruses, worms, and Trojans.
- Several different types of attacks used by hackers to cause harm on networks.
- What a Denial of Service attack is.
- What a man-in-the-middle attack is.
- What rogue access points are and different ways locate them.
- You learned different methods of countering some of the attacks covered in this lesson.
- How physical security is just as important as other types of security on a network.
- That one of the most successful ways to counter hackers is to train your end users.
- The difference between secure and unsecure protocols.
- Some examples of secure and unsecure protocols.
- How encryption works.
- What certificates are and how they are used in networking.
- What authentication is.
- What RADIUS and TACACS+ are and how they are different.
- What CHAP, MS-CHAP, and EAP are and how they differ from each other.
- What Network Access Control is.
- Some commonly used networking tools that can be used for good and bad purposes.

Knowledge Assessment

Fill in the Blank

Complete the following sentences by writing the correct word or words in the blanks provided.

1. The single most common method used to penetrate network defenses and steal information that a company has is _____.

2. _____ is a method used to steal passwords and account information that commonly involves e-mails and bogus web sites.

3. A form of malware that is used to steal personal information and web surfing habits is called _____.

4. A _____ is a form of malware that changes already existing files in an attempt to cause harm to a computer.

5. A _____ is a form of malware that conceals itself as a legitimate program it has replaced.

6. A form of malware that attempts to sneak itself onto a computer without being noticed and then executing itself without trying to replace a legitimate program is called a _____.

7. When a hacker tries to overload a system by flooding it with irrelevant network traffic, the hacker has launched a _____ attack.

8. A _____ is a wireless access point that does not belong on a network.

9. A piece of software that is designed to look for and detect network intrusions is called _____.

10. _____ is an open authentication protocol that uses a three-way-handshake to authenticate a client to a server.

Multiple Choice

Circle the letter corresponding to the correct answer.

1. A secure protocol used to transport HTML pages across the Internet is _____.
   a. HTTP
   b. FTP
   c. HTTPS
   d. SSL

2. _____ is a secure protocol used to manage devices on a network.
   a. SCP
   b. SNMPv3
   c. SNMPv1/2
   d. SSH

3. Which of the following does AAA stand for?
   a. Authentication, Authorization, Accounting
   b. Access, Authentication, Accounting
   c. Accounting, Access Control, Authorization
   d. Access Control, Accounting Control, Authorization Control

4. Which of the following are considered unsecure protocols? (Choose all that apply.)
   a. HTTP
   b. Telnet
   c. RSH
   d. SFTP

5. _____is a form of encryption that requires each party to have the same key.
   a. Public key encryption
   b. RSH encryption
   c. Codebook encryption ring
   d. Private key encryption

6. A software program that is able to detect when a hacker intrudes into a network and is able to take steps to stop the attack is called what?
   a. Intrusion detection software
   b. Intrusion prevention software
   c. Phishing software
   d. PKI software

7. The authentication protocol most commonly used by Windows domain controllers to control access to their domains in a LAN environment is called what?
   a. RADIUS
   b. TACACS+
   c. EAP
   d. Kerberos

8. _____is a proprietary authentication protocol that uses a three-way-handshake to allow access to a network.
   a. MS-CHAP
   b. CHAP
   c. TKIP
   d. PKI

9. _____ is a form of encryption generally used with wireless LANs.
   a. EAP
   b. AAA
   c. TKIP
   d. PKI

10. Which of the following are important functions of both RADIUS and TACACS+? (Choose all that apply.)
    a. Authentication
    b. Access Control
    c. Authorization
    d. Accounting

Lab Exercises

Installing Malware Detection and Protection Software

The purpose of this lab is to teach the student what malware detection and protection software is and how it can benefit them. This will be done by having the student install a commonly used malware detection software program that is free and then have them use it.

MATERIALS

- A computer running Windows XP, Windows Vista, or Windows 7
- Access to the Internet
- A web browser
- Paper
- Pen or pencil

THE LAB

Download the Software Malwarebytes

1. Place www.filehippo.com in the URL bar of your web browser.

   (Note: www.filehippo.com was chosen as the URL to download this software program because it has been around a very long time and keeps copies of all versions of any program it makes available for download.)

2. Look around this site. What kind of site is it?

3. Write down some programs that you find interesting.

4. Go to the search bar found on the File Hippo site and type **malwarebytes**.

5. What comes up?

6. What version of Malwarebytes is shown?

7. What kind of software does the description say Malwarebytes is?

8. Click on the **Download** link.

9. Where does this take you?

10. What do you notice over on the right side of the new web page?

11. Click on the **Download Latest Version** link in the top right corner.

12. When the dialog box to save or run the file mbam-setup-x.xx.exe comes up, either save the setup file to a specific location on your computer or run it from this dialog box.

    (Note: If you chose to save the file in a specific location on your computer, write down the path used to save it on a separate piece of paper.)

Install Malwarebytes Anti-Malware Software

1. If you chose the run option from the dialog box mentioned earlier, then skip the next step. Malwarebytes either has been installed on your computer or is in the process of being installed.

2. If you chose to save the file nbam-setup-x.xx.exe, then navigate in your computer to the location where you chose to save the file and double-click it. This will begin the process of installing Malwarebytes to your computer.

3. As Malwarebytes begins to install on your computer, it will ask you some installation questions. Just take the default options.

4. When Malwarebytes is finished installing, start it up if it does not start itself automatically.

Use Malwarebytes

1. What different tabs are available in Malwarebytes. Write them down.

2. What are the differences between the various types of scans? Which scans can you perform with the free version of this software? Write them down.

3. Click on the **Protection** tab. What additional features do you get if you purchase Malwarebytes? Write them down. Write down the purchase feature you think most valuable.

4. Click on each of the other tabs. What features are revealed when you open the other tabs?

5. Write down the tab number under which the tool called *File Assassin* is found. What does File Assassin do? What does this mean?

6. Go back to the *Scanner* tab. Click on **Perform Quick Scan** to do a quick scan of your computer. Was any malware found on your computer? If so, list some examples of what was found. Have Malwarebytes remove any malware it found.

7. If you have time and your teacher allows it, run a full scan. What is the difference between a quick scan and a full scan? Did the full scan find any malware the quick scan missed? If so, what?

8. Do you think this is a useful program to know about? Why or why not?

■ Lab 2

Installing Intrusion Detection and Protection Software

The purpose of this lab is to teach the student what intrusion detection and protection software is and how it can benefit them. This will be done by having the student install a commonly used intrusion detection software program that is free and then have them use it.

MATERIALS
- A computer running Windows XP, Windows Vista, or Windows 7
- Access to the Internet
- A web browser
- Paper
- Pen or pencil

THE LAB

Download the Software ZoneAlarm

1. Place www.filehippo.com in the URL bar of your web browser.

2. Go to the search bar found on the File Hippo site and type **ZoneAlarm**.

3. What version of ZoneAlarm is shown? How big is the download?

4. Click on the name **ZoneAlarm**. What additional information comes up?

5. What tabs appear? Write down the type of information found under each tab?

6. What is found under the description information on the **Description** tab?

7. Click on the **Download Latest Version** link in the top right corner.

8. When the dialog box to save or run the file zaSetup_xx_xxx_xxx_en.exe comes up, either save the setup file to a specific location on your computer or run it from this dialog box. (Note: If you chose to save the file in a specific location on your computer, remember where you saved it.)

Install the ZoneAlarm Intrusion Detection Software

1. If you chose the run option from the dialog box mentioned previously, then skip the next step. ZoneAlarm either has been installed on your computer or is in the process of being installed.

2. If ZoneAlarm setup ran automatically, then you will need to close all open programs before it can fully install.

3. If you chose to save the file zaSetup_xx_xxx_xxx_en.exe, first shut down all running programs and then navigate in your computer to the location you chose to save the file and double-click it. This will begin the process of installing ZoneAlarm to your computer.

4. As ZoneAlarm begins to install on your computer it will ask you some installation questions. Just take the default options.

5. When ZoneAlarm is finished installing, you will need to restart your computer. Do this, and then start ZoneAlarm up if it does not start itself automatically.

Use ZoneAlarm

1. When ZoneAlarm starts up, what boxes appear on the interface? Write them down. Why are some boxes one color and the others a different color?

2. What functionality comes with the free version of ZoneAlarm. Write it down.

3. When you click the **Firewall** icon, what comes up? Write down some of the options you see there.

4. What happens when you click the **Anti-Virus/Anti-Spyware** icon? Write down the result. Why do you think this happened?

5. What do you see over on the left side of the dialog box? Write down the main options there. Which one is currently active?

6. Click on the **Firewall icon** on the left side of the interface. Write down the two main options under the Firewall icon.

7. What is showing in the main portion of the Dialog box while *Main* is active?

8. What shows when you click the **Zones** link under the Firewall icon on the left side of the dialog box? Copy on a piece of paper the table you see in the main portion of the dialog box. What do you think the table means?

9. What buttons are found in the bottom part of the main dialog box? Write them down. Click on **Edit**, what do you see? Close *Edit* without making any changes.

10. Look at the ? in a circle in the bottom portion of the left side of the dialog box. Click on the question mark. What comes up? Close it.

11. Click on the **Programs Control** icon in the left side of the dialog box. What does this show?

12. What happens if you click on the **Programs** link under the *Program Control* icon? Write down some of the programs you see listed.

13. Do you see any programs that are checked as un-trusted? Why do you think they are un-trusted?

14. Do you think this is a useful program to know about? Why or why not.

15. Close ZoneAlarm by clicking on the X in the upper right corner of the window the dialog box is in.

16. If your instructor tells you to, uninstall ZoneAlarm because it will interfere with any other IDS that may be running on your computer.

Network Access Security

EXAM OBJECTIVE MATRIX

Technology Skill Covered	Exam Objective	Exam Objective Number
Firewalls	**Given a scenario, install and configure routers and switches.** • Interface configurations • MAC filtering • Traffic filtering	2.1
	Explain the purpose and features of various network appliances. • Proxy server • Content filter	4.1

	Explain the methods of network access security.
	• ACL
	  • MAC filtering
	  • IP filtering
	  • Port filtering
		5.2

	Given a scenario, install and configure a basic firewall.
	• Types:
	  • Software and hardware firewalls
	• Port security
	• Stateful inspection vs. packet filtering
	• Firewall rules:
	  • ACL
	• DMZ
		5.5

	Categorize different types of network security appliances and methods.
	• IDS and IPS:
	  • Network-based
	  • Host-based
	• Methods:
	  • Honey pots
	  • Honey nets
		5.6

Tunneling and Encryption	**Explain the purpose and features of various network appliances.** • Load balancer • Proxy server • Content filter • VPN concentrator	4.1

	Explain the methods of network access security. • Tunneling and encryption 　• SSL VPN 　• VPN 　• L2TP 　• PPTP 　• IPSec 　• ISAKMP 　• TLS 　• TLS1.2 　• Site-to-site and client-to-site • Remote access: 　• RAS 　• RDP 　• PPPoE 　• PPP 　• ICA 　• SSH	5.2	
Wireless Authentication and Encryption	**Given a scenario, implement appropriate wireless security measures.** • Encryption protocols: 　• WEP 　• WPA 　• WPA2 　• WPA Enterprise	5.1	
Best Practices	**Explain common threats, vulnerabilities, and mitigation techniques.** • Mitigation techniques: 　• Training and awareness 　• Patch management 　• Policies and procedures	5.4	

KEY TERMS

Access Control List (ACL)

access policies

algorithm

application layer firewalls

Authentication Header (AH)

best practices

cipher

content filtering

definition

Demilitarized Zone (DMZ)

Directory Services

dual firewall configuration

e-Directory

Encapsulating Security
　Payload (ESP)

encryption

filtering

firewall

Graphical User Interface (GUI)

host-based firewalls

Host-Based Intrusion Detection
　System (HIDS)

Host-Based Intrusion Prevention
　System (HIPS)

Host-to-host communications

Internet Key Exchange (IKE)

Internet Protocol Security (IPSec)

Layer 2 Forwarding (L2F)

Layer 2 Tunneling Protocol
　(L2TP)

Lightweight Directory Access Protocol (LDAP)

Link Control Protocol (LCP)

MAC address filtering

network-based firewalls

Network Control Protocol (NCP)

Network Intrusion Detection System (NIDS)

Network Intrusion Prevention System (NIPS)

network layer firewall

network security policy

network-to-host communications

network-to-network communications

packet filters

password policies

plaintext

Point-to-Point Protocol (PPP)

Point-to-Point Protocol over Ethernet (PPPoE)

Point-to-Point Tunneling Protocol (PPTP)

policy

port security

procedure

proxy server

Remote Access Services (RAS)

Remote Authentication Dial-In User Service (RADIUS)

Remote Desktop Connection

Remote Desktop Protocol (RDP)

Remote Desktop Service

scanning services

Secure Sockets Layer (SSL)

Secure Sockets Layer VPN (SSL VPN)

signature

signature identification

single firewall configuration

stateful firewall

stateful inspection

stateful packet inspection

stateless packet inspection

System Intrusion Detection Software (SIDS)

System Intrusion Prevention Software (SIPS)

Terminal Services

Terminal Services Client

transport mode

tunnel mode

Temporal Key Integrity Protocol (TKIP)

tunneling

virtual dial-up

Virtual Network Computing (VNC)

Virtual Private Network (VPN)

VPN concentrator

Web VPN

Wi-Fi Protected Access (WPA)

Wired Equivalent Privacy (WEP)

X11

zone-based firewall

Ray Bath is a network administrator. Management has tasked him to develop policies for the company to follow regarding network access and security. What types of things does Ray need to consider while he is creating these policies?

■ Firewalls

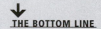 **THE BOTTOM LINE**

In the first section of Lesson 10, we discuss firewalls—how they are used, where to locate them, and what technologies they use to carry out their jobs.

CERTIFICATION READY
What is a firewall? What is the difference between host-based and network-based firewalls?
5.5

Firewalls are used in apartment complexes or other large buildings with numerous rooms. In such buildings, the firewall is a specially built wall that is designed to prevent fire from entering an apartment or to limit its ability to spread from one room to another within the larger building. In networking, something similar is used. However, in networking the objective of the firewall is not to limit how fire can spread but to prevent security threats from spreading. The purpose of a network *firewall* is to prevent a hacker or other security threats from entering the network, or baring that, to limit their ability to spread through the network. In this lesson, we spend a lot of time discussing these firewalls. These firewalls come in two very broad categories—network-based firewalls and host-based firewalls. We are going to discuss the network-based firewall category first.

Network-based Firewalls

Network-based firewalls reside on the network. They are usually hardware in nature but are augmented with additional software. In fact many firewalls are built into or on top of routers. This type of firewall would be considered a true firewall because its job is to prevent a threat from actually entering the network it is protecting. Other firewalls that may be built further into the network are designed to prevent any threats that may have entered the network from spreading further into the network.

There are two common firewall configurations that are used in the industry. The simplest and most basic configuration uses only one firewall to protect the network. The type of firewall is sometimes referred to as a ***single firewall configuration***. Figure 10.1 illustrates a single firewall configuration.

As you can see in Figure 10-1, a single firewall configuration uses one firewall. In this configuration, a single firewall is placed between the external network, usually the Internet, and the internal network. This configuration also allows for the servers to be segregated from the main internal network as well. In this configuration, a threat has to break through the firewall before it can either attack the servers or the internal network.

Figure 10-1

Single firewall configuration

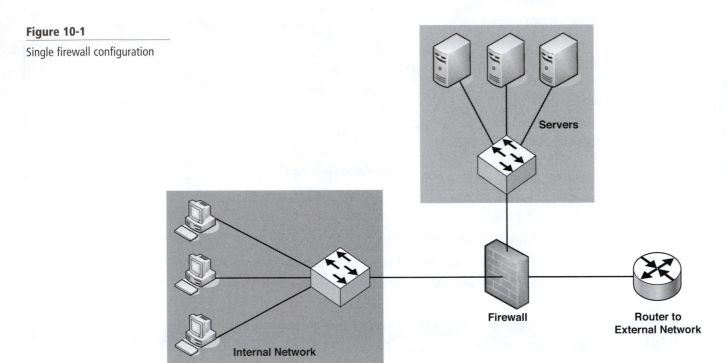

The ***dual firewall configuration***, also known as the DMZ configuration, is also very commonly used. In fact, the dual firewall configuration is actually the preferred configuration because it places an extra layer of defense between your internal network and the external network. Figure 10-2 illustrates a dual firewall configuration.

In the dual firewall configuration as seen in Figure 10-2, two firewalls are used instead of one. One firewall blocks off access to the external network while the other firewall blocks off access to the internal network. The area in between the two firewalls is called the ***DMZ*** or ***Demilitarized Zone***. This means the area acts as a buffer between the internal and external networks.

Often, certain types of servers such as e-mail servers, DNS servers, web servers, FTP servers, and others are placed in this area. These types of servers are placed here because they are servers that generally need access to both the internal and external networks. Placing these servers in the DMZ area gives them access to the external network without comprising the internal network. Hackers commonly target these types of servers because they need access to the external network. By placing servers that are common hacker targets in the DMZ, even if they become compromised, they will not expose the internal network.

Figure 10-2

Dual firewall configuration

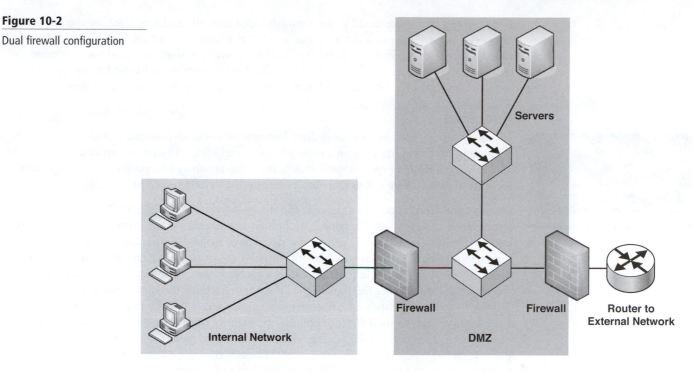

Servers that do not need access to the external network like file servers, database servers, domain controllers, and similar type servers are not placed into the DMZ. These types of servers should only be accessible to those within the network. If they were placed in the DMZ, they would be more accessible to hackers and other security threats found on the external network. These types of servers should be placed in the internal network. Placing them there gives them an added layer of defense from hackers. This is especially important because these are also the servers that most likely contain information of interest to hackers. Figure 10-3 shows how these servers would be placed if a DMZ were present.

Figure 10-3

Server placement with a DMZ

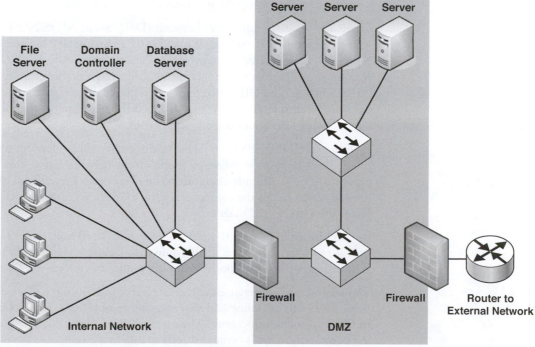

Before going into more detail about network based firewalls and how they are used to protect networks, we will look at a different but somewhat related technology. This technology is called a proxy server. Proxy servers are related to firewalls in that they reside on the network and are used to manage traffic on the network. Proxy servers are even used to increase network security in some situations. However, they are different because they are not firewalls.

Proxy server

Proxy servers are used as an intermediary between networks and servers. A proxy server can be a purpose built device, installed on a network device including in some circumstances a router, or an application running on a server somewhere on the network. The purpose of having a proxy server is to intercept signals to specific servers or other devices before passing them on.

Once a proxy server receives a signal it can do several different things with it. One thing the proxy server can do with the signal is evaluate it and decide to pass it on or not to pass it on based on criteria stored in the proxy server. The proxy can also intercept the signal and attempt to service the request based on information the proxy server has stored in its memory from previous similar request. This is called a cache. If the proxy server is unable to service the request it then passes the signal on to the original device the signal was intended for. This is done to reduce demands on the device the request was originally made to. Another thing a proxy server can be used for is to conceal the identity of the person making a request from the network. This concealment can be done for privacy reasons or for more nefarious purposes such as by passing security or parental consent controls. Proxy servers can even be used to alter request coming into a network or going out of a network. This may be done to circumvent restrictions placed on the network or some of the content located on the network.

NETWORK INTRUSION DETECTION SYSTEM/NETWORK INTRUSION PREVENTION SYSTEM (NIDS/NIPS)

NIDS stands for *Network Intrusion Detection System* and *NIPS* stands for *Network Intrusion Prevention System*. Both of these products work just like the IDS and IPS discussed in Lesson 9. Also, like with the IDS and IPS counterparts discussed in Lesson 9, pretty much all NIDS currently on the market also contain NIPS functionality. In the cases of both IDS/IPS and NIDS/NIPS, the software is designed to look for evidence of intruder activity, report it, and act to stop the intrusion that has been detected.

There are two main differences between IDS/IPS and NIDS/NIPS. The first difference is where you locate the software. While IDS/IPS are generally located on local computers, NIDS/NIPS are located on network appliances. Specifically NIDS/NIPS is a program that runs on specialized hardware that is intended to be a platform from which to run the NIDS/NIPS software. The NIDS/NIPS are often placed on specialized routers or a computer that has been custom built to serve as a NIDS/NIPS platform. In the case of a custom computer, the operating system of choice is often Linux.

Once your NIDS/NIPS is on its host platform, the host platform needs to be positioned on the network somewhere where all traffic on the network has to pass through the NIDS/NIPS platform. This location is often on the line between a firewall and the switch that links the firewall to the rest of the computer. Figure 10-4 shows possible locations of NIDS/NIPS platforms using the DMZ diagram.

As you can see in Figure 10-4, the possible NIDS/NIPS placement locations are where data flow is restricted down to a single connection before spreading out to multiple connections. Like in Figure 10-4, it is possible to have multiple NIDS/NIPS on a network.

The second main difference between IDS/IPS and NIDS/NIPS is that NIDS/NIPS software is used for both incoming and outgoing communications, while IDS/IPS is mostly restricted to incoming communications. The reason NIDS/NIPS is used for both incoming and outgoing communications is because threats to a network can come from both internal and external sources and a NIDS/NIPS needs to be positioned to detect both types of threats. Another

Figure 10-4

Possible NIDS placement
locations

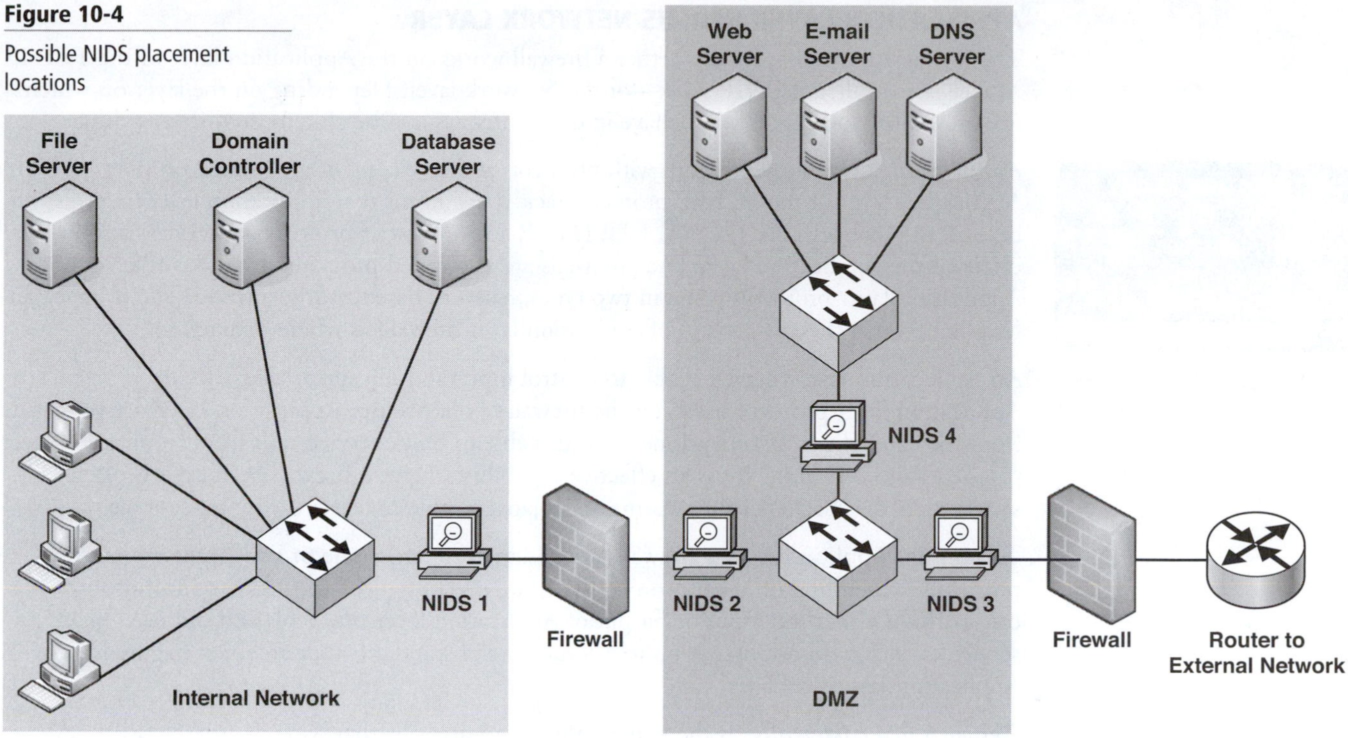

reason to have NIDS/NIPS handling both incoming and outgoing communications is to give the network administrator the ability to use data collected by the NIDS/NIPS to determine what is happening during an ongoing attack against your network. If your NIDS/NIPS analyzes both incoming and outgoing communications, it becomes easier to get an accurate picture of what the attack is doing, which makes it easier to counter.

Host-based Firewalls

Host-based firewalls are basically software packages that run on a computer platform. These firewalls have the ability to evaluate packets that arrived in the host and determine whether they are malicious. Host-based firewalls can evaluate and filter packets just like a more conventional network-based firewalls such as the ones previously discussed. The main difference between a host-based firewall and a network-based firewall is that a network-based firewall is designed to stop threats from entering the network whereas a host-based firewall is designed to stop threats once they have reached the host they are protecting. In this sense, a host-based firewall is not a true firewall because it only works after the threat has gotten to the host.

Firewalls that are host based are sometimes called *Host-Based Intrusion Detection System* or *HIDS*. Occasionally it may also be referred to as *SIDS*, which stands for *System Intrusion Detection Software*. However, most commonly, this software is simply referred to as a computer's firewall. Either way, most HIDSs also contain the ability to prevent intrusions or to take action against the intrusion once it is detected. In this way, a HIDS works just like a NIDS.

When a HIDS has the ability to prevent an intrusion or take action against a detected intrusion, it becomes a *Host-Based Intrusion Prevention System* or *HIPS*, which is sometimes referred to as a *SIPS* or *System Intrusion Prevention Software*. In this way, most HIDSs are also HIPSs; so when you refer to a HIDS, it is assumed that the software in question also has the ability to prevent intrusions, not just detect them.

Common Features of a Firewall

Whether a firewall is network based or host based there are some common features they all share. In this section of Lesson 10, we discuss those common features.

APPLICATION LAYER VERSUS NETWORK LAYER

The first feature to discuss is whether a firewall works on the Application layer of the TCP/IP Model—also called TCP/IP stack—or the Network layer. Depending on the layer on which the firewall is working, it will behave in different ways and be able to do different things.

Application layer firewalls work with protocols and services that are located on the Application layer of the TCP/IP protocol stack. This means that application layer firewalls can be used to block TELNET, DNS, FTP, HTTP, and any other protocols or services also located on the Application layer. Such firewalls are also called proxy servers. Like other firewalls, Application layer protocols come in two types, network based and host based. The primary difference between these two types of application layer firewalls is where they reside.

An Application layer firewall is able to control input and output or access to, from, or by any Application layer protocol based on the firewall's policy setup. Application layer firewalls aside from the capabilities just mentioned, are also able to block service calls from Application layer protocols and services. This is an effective capability to give a firewall because it is often via service calls that hackers using worms or Trojans are able to affect computer systems.

To sum up, Application layer firewalls are designed to target one or two Application layer protocols, depending on what protocols they are preconfigured to filter. Application firewalls can work on either the input or output of Application layer protocols and can even block service calls that do not match up to a certain set of standards that are preconfigured in the Application layer firewall.

Network layer firewalls, as the name implies, are firewalls that work on the Network layer of the TCP/IP protocol stack. This means that they primarily target packet communications. Because Network layer firewalls tend to target packet traffic on a network, they are often referred to as *packet filters*. The packets filtered by a Network layer firewall can be filtered by a wide variety of criteria. Some of these criteria are source and destination IP address, port addresses, what higher-level protocols the packet contains, and many other criteria. The criteria used are limited by what the network administrator configures into the firewall.

Another advantage of Network layer firewalls is their speed. Because the packets filtered by a Network layer firewall usually only have to read the header of a packet, they tend to be able to test their packet criteria very quickly. This allows the Network layer firewall to move data quickly through its checks.

There are two general types of Network layer firewalls in use. Those two types are called stateful and stateless firewalls. We examine these two types of Network layer firewalls next.

Stateful versus stateless

The easiest way to approach the differences between stateful and stateless firewalls is to explain the more complex of the two—stateful firewalls. A *stateful firewall* is a firewall that filters packets based on their state. This process is called a *stateful packet inspection* or *stateful inspection*. For a stateful packet inspection to happen, there are a couple of things that have to be in place. One, the firewall doing the stateful inspections needs to be able to keep track of all the network connections currently flowing through the router. This includes both TCP and UDP sessions. Next, the router needs to know what state every connection is in at any given moment. A connection's state includes such things as IP address, port number, sequence number, and packet type (i.e., an acknowledgment packet, synchronization packet, keep alive packet, and so on). Once the firewall is able to keep track of each session and the state each connection is currently in, it then has the ability to inspect each packet to make sure that the packet belongs to the session it claims to belong to and that the packet contains the expected state of the next packet that is supposed to be a part of that session. Keeping track of all this information causes the network to run slower because of the overhead involved. Additionally, because of the extra processing power and memory needed for stateful firewalls, they tend to cost more money.

CERTIFICATION READY
What is stateful inspection and what is stateless inspection? What is the difference between the two?
5.5

Using a stateful firewall makes it very difficult for a hacker to hijack a session because not only is the firewall monitoring the protocols and IP that belongs to each session, it is also keeping track of what type of packet is supposed to arrive next for each session. If a sequence number is wrong, or a synchronization packet is arriving out of place or when an acknowledgment packet is expected, the firewall knows to block that packet. Also if a synchronization packet arrives when a data packet is expected, again the router knows to block that packet.

A firewall that is able to recognize synchronization (SYN) packets and what is supposed to come after them makes it much more difficult for Denial of Service (DoS) attacks to be used against a computer because many modern DoS attacks are of the SYN attack variety. This type of DoS attack is where the hacker attempts to flood a target computer or server with a continuous flow of SYN requests. The hacker does this with the hopes of overflowing, or using up, the memory of the target router or switch so that the target network is no longer able to access its network. With a firewall in place that can perform stateful inspections, the firewall is able to recognize what is happening and deny the malicious SYN requests access to the network it is protecting, thereby preventing the SYN attack from being successful.

Stateless packet inspection is another way for firewalls to monitor traffic coming into a network. Stateful packet filtering requires the firewall to know the state of each connection in order to properly filter packets. Stateless packet filtering firewalls, on the other hand, treat each packet as if it were a separate entity. This means that each packet is evaluated on an individual basis without regard to which session they are part of or what the state of that session is. The result is that data is able to move very quickly around the network as compared to stateful packet inspection because of the lower overhead needs. However, the downside is that networks that use stateless firewalls are more vulnerable to hackers hijacking them. As with everything, it is a trade-off. If security is your most important goal, then stateful firewalls are your best option. If speed is your primary goal, then stateless firewalls are your best option. Stateless firewalls, because of the lower overhead requirements, and therefore lower processing and memory requirements, generally cost less than stateful firewalls.

SCANNING SERVICES

CERTIFICATION READY
What are scanning services and what do they scan?
4.1

Scanning services are simply the ability of a firewall to scan packets and protocols for specific threats. For example, a firewall with scanning services can scan http traffic for spyware or viruses. Similarly, a firewall with scanning services set to scan SMTP could scan e-mail for things like spam. In short, scanning services are firewall services set to scan different types of traffic for threats related to the type of traffic for which they are scanning.

CONTENT FILTERS

CERTIFICATION READY
What is content filtering?
4.1

Content filtering is similar to scanning services but it goes quite a bit further. In the case of scanning services, specific threats are looked for in the packets being scanned. Content filtering is a bit less specific. In content filtering, the firewall or other device doing the filtering looks at the actual content of the data coming into the device and evaluates it against a predefined set of guidelines about what is allowed through. While scanning services may block spam simply because of its source IP, content filtering blocks spam because of its content, regardless of where it came from.

Another example of content filters are programs like Net Nanny, Cyber Patrol, and others that do not allow specific websites through a web browser based on predefined content restrictions. In these cases, if it has been predefined that websites containing specific words be blocked, then any website with one of the banned words will not be allowed to download to the web browser. Many businesses do exactly this kind of blocking of websites with specific content restriction criteria to prevent harassment lawsuits or because certain content violates their Internet policies. Parental controls, which are now built directly into Windows 7, are also a form of content filters.

There are a wide variety of content filters. The main thing that makes a filter a content filter, rather than a filter of some other type, is the fact that content filters actually look at the data coming into a network or computer and filter based on the content of that data. Other types of filters use other criteria such as specific addresses, protocols, ports, and so on, but not the content of the data. In other words, if you have an antivirus program that looks for viruses by actually testing the data of incoming traffic, then that antivirus program is a content filter. However, if you have an antivirus program that simply compares virus patterns and definitions against the patterns seen in incoming traffic, then your antivirus program is not a content filter. Good antivirus software will do both.

SIGNATURE IDENTIFICATION

Signature identification is the process used by many firewalls, IDSs, and antivirus programs that use something called signatures or definitions to identify threats. Many threats, whether viruses or network attacks, have unique patterns that uniquely identify them. These patterns are called *signatures* or *definitions*. In the case of viruses, each virus creates a unique pattern or code in the infected file that allows antivirus software to identify it. In the case of IDSs or firewalls, each type of attack follows a unique pattern that identifies it from other types of attacks. By collecting these patterns and placing them in a database called a definition or signature base, threats can be compared to current activity on a network or computer to see if the activity matches threat profiles, or signatures, in the database. If the current activity matches, then the antivirus software or the IDS knows that a threat to the system is currently active. Once the threat has been identified, the software can notify the administrator and act in a preprogrammed way to counter the threat.

The biggest flaw with this type of threat assessment system is that it can only work against threats that are known by the antivirus or IDS software in use. If the signature database of the software does not contain a threat's signature, then the software is not aware the threat even exists. The best defense against this happening is keeping your antivirus or IDS signature database up to date. Keeping the database up-to-date is why many software programs of this type automatically update their signature database without requiring input from the system administrator.

Even with up-to-date signatures, if a threat was not previously known, your system or network is vulnerable to it. Because of this vulnerability to unknown threats, it is a good idea to not just rely on signature identification as your only way to identify and respond to threats. Good IDS and antivirus software uses more than one of the methods discussed, as well as some methods not discussed, to identify threats. If your software does not use multiple threat identification methods, you should probably consider getting a software that does.

ZONES

Zone-based firewalls create firewalls on a router based on groups of interfaces instead of individual interfaces as the previously discussed firewall methods did. When using zone-based firewall configurations, there are three rules that always apply and are the basis for allowing or disallowing communications to pass through the firewall. These rules are as follows:

- Interfaces that share the same zone can *always* talk to each other.
- Interfaces in one zone *cannot* talk to interfaces in another zone unless there are explicit rules written into the firewall configuration that allows different zones to talk to each other.
- Interfaces that *are not* part of a zone *cannot* talk to any interfaces that *are* part of a zone.

Figure 10-5 helps explain these rules and helps you visualize how zone-based firewalls work.

In Figure 10-5, we see a router with six interfaces labeled E0 through E5. Interface E0 is assigned to Zone 1; interfaces E1 and E2 are assigned to Zone 2; interface E3 is not assigned to a zone; finally, interfaces E4 and E5 are assigned to Zone 3. Keep the basic rules listed earlier in mind when you examine the rules as they are applied in Figure 10-5:

- **Rule 1:** Interface E1 and E2 or interfaces E4 and E5 can *always* talk to each other.
- **Rule 2:** Interfaces E1 and E2, E4 and E5, and/or E0 can only talk to each other if they are explicitly allowed to in the router's configuration.
- **Rule 3:** Interface E3 *cannot* talk to any of the other interfaces.

Figure 10-5

Zone-based firewall

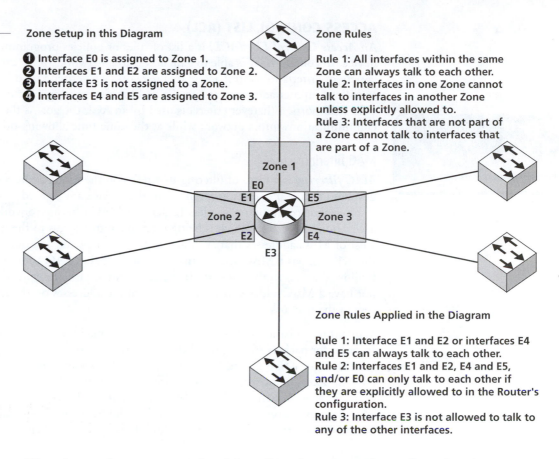

Zone Setup in this Diagram

❶ Interface E0 is assigned to Zone 1.
❷ Interfaces E1 and E2 are assigned to Zone 2.
❸ Interface E3 is not assigned to a Zone.
❹ Interfaces E4 and E5 are assigned to Zone 3.

Zone Rules

Rule 1: All interfaces within the same Zone can always talk to each other.
Rule 2: Interfaces in one Zone cannot talk to interfaces in another Zone unless explicitly allowed to.
Rule 3: Interfaces that are not part of a Zone cannot talk to interfaces that are part of a Zone.

Zone 1
E0
E1   E5
Zone 2   Zone 3
E2   E4
E3

Zone Rules Applied in the Diagram

Rule 1: Interface E1 and E2 or interfaces E4 and E5 can always talk to each other.
Rule 2: Interfaces E1 and E2, E4 and E5, and/or E0 can only talk to each other if they are explicitly allowed to in the Router's configuration.
Rule 3: Interface E3 is not allowed to talk to any of the other interfaces.

The primary advantage to zone-based firewall configuration is that it allows the administrator to apply rules to groups of interfaces on a router all at once rather than to each individual interface. This simplifies the job of the network administrator when it comes to creating firewall policies for their network. To explain this, look at the following example.

If you have a router with multiple interfaces and three of those interfaces all connect to your internal network, you could simply create a zone for those three interfaces and create rules for that zone rather than having to make separate rules for each one of the three interfaces. Using zones also allows you to block one or more interfaces in the router from the other interfaces without having to make a set of rules that explicitly do this. This can be accomplished simply by not putting the interface you want blocked in a zone. Alternatively, you could create a special zone for the interface you wish to block and not make any rules allowing it to connect to the other zones on your router. Either way, you have blocked the interface without having to tell all the other interfaces what you have done.

The end result is that complex firewall configurations can be somewhat simplified by the use of zones. Zones also give the network administrator an added level of control when it comes to permitting or not permitting interfaces on the same router to communicate with each other.

Filtering

Filtering is one of the methods used by firewalls to protect a network from malicious attacks. Filtering comes in many varieties. We have already looked at some types of filtering such as stateful and stateless filtering. However, there are some other methods used in filtering that we will look at now. Any time a characteristic of a packet such as its IP address or port address is used to allow or block IP packet traffic on a network it is called packet filtering or sometimes traffic filtering. Generally the terms packet filtering and traffic filtering are used interchangeably when discussing filtering based on characteristics of IP packets. Several of these types of filtering methods will be discussed below.

CERTIFICATION READY
What is filtering? What types of filtering are there? How do those types of filtering work?
5.2

CERTIFICATION READY
What is another term for packet filtering?
2.1

ACCESS CONTROL LIST (ACL)

An *Access Control List (ACL)* is a list of rules or policies programmed into a router, or other device, to control what is able to gain access to a network. ACLs can be used with a wide variety of criteria to control access to a network. The criteria used by ACLs can range from a specific computer addresses, to specific address ranges, to specific protocols and even to specific TCP ports. Whatever criteria is used by an ACL the goal is the same, to prevent specific communications into a network while at the same time allowing others to pass freely.

CERTIFICATION READY
What is an ACL? What does ACL stand for? What are ACLs used for?
5.2

MAC filtering

MAC filtering is a form of filtering that relies on the MAC address or physical address of a device to decide if communications from that device are allowed into the network. This type of filtering is common on wireless LANs. For MAC filtering to work on a wireless LAN, the access point or router, which is being used to control access to the network, needs to contain a list of MAC addresses that are allowed into the network. If a device attempting to access the network has a MAC address that matches one the MAC addresses on the list, the device is allowed access to the network. If the device attempting to gain access to the network does not have a MAC address that matches one of the addresses on the list, it is not allowed access to the network.

While this is a basic form of protection found on many wireless LANs, it is not foolproof. In order for hackers to get around this protection, all they have to do is listen to the network long enough to find a valid MAC address and then spoof their devices so that the device tells the access point that its MAC address is one of the MAC addresses recognized as valid. Software is used to intercept the MAC address of the device used by the hacker before the MAC address leaves the wireless NIC and a valid MAC address is substituted in its place. Software to do this can commonly be found on the web, especially at hacker sights.

IP filtering

IP filtering is similar to MAC filtering, except that it uses IP addresses instead of MAC addresses. Also, while MAC filtering is commonly used on wireless LANs, IP filtering is more commonly used on wired networks. Functionally, however, they do the same job. One advantage of IP filtering over MAC filtering is that IP filtering allows you to block or allow whole ranges of IP addresses. With MAC filtering, you have to program specific MAC addresses into your router if you want them blocked or allowed.

IP filtering is commonly used in routers to control access to networks and/or specific devices on networks. In fact, a Cisco router called a Standard Access Control List is an ACL that relies solely on IP filtering to permit or deny access. If you want to do more advanced filtering beyond simple IP filtering on Cisco routers, you need to create something called an Extended Access Control List. Extended ACLs, while they allow filtering via IP address, also allows a more advanced filtering technique called packet filtering, which we look at next.

Port filtering

Port filtering is the practice of filtering out specific protocols from a data signal based on the TCP or UDP port address of the protocols to be filtered. For example, if a network administrator wished to filter out web traffic from a data signal they would block port address 80, which is the TCP port address of the HTTP protocol. In the same way, if a network administrator wished to block out e-mail from a data signal they would block TCP port 25.

CERTIFICATION READY
What is port filtering? How does it work?
5.2

Another way port filtering can be used is to block all protocols except for a specific protocol. In this way, only specific protocols will be allowed into a network device. Using the previous examples, if a network administrator wanted only web traffic to come through a specific network node, they could block all ports except for port 80. In the same way, if a network administrator wanted only e-mail traffic to come through a specific node they could block all port numbers except for port 25.

Port filtering is also not limited to just one port or all ports except one either. It is entirely possible to combine different rules in a router or a firewall, which allows certain specific network protocols through while at the same time blocking certain specific other protocols as well. All of this is done with the ACLs discussed previously in this Lesson.

Port security

In networking, one way an attacker may attempt to get around the safeguards placed by firewalls is to attach a regular switch with no security features on it, called a dumb switch, into a network and connect it to a single port on a switch that has access to the resources the attackers are trying to gain access to. While this requires the attacker to have physical access to the network, it also allows the attackers to share the switch port with the legitimate user, thus gaining access to the desired resources without tipping off the regular user.

Port security is a capability of Cisco switches that is designed to counter the above described technique. If a switch has port security capabilities, the network administrator responsible for programming the switches can program ports on a switch to only allow specific MAC addresses through and to block all other MAC addresses. When this is done, even if an attacker does manage to slip a dumb switch between the attacking computer and the port on the network switch with access to the resources the attacker is trying to gain access to, the attacker will still be unable to access those resources. The reason the attacker will not be able to access the desired resources is because the port on the switch the attacker is attached to will not recognize the attacker's MAC address and so block all attempts to gain access to the protected resources.

Honey Pots

Honey pots are not directly related to routers and firewalls but they are network security tools. The purpose of a honey pot is to provide a target for hackers so that they will attack the honey pot rather than the network it is intended to protect. The purpose of this is twofold. One it can be used to distract a hacker. Two, it can be used to analyze an attack to see what the hackers did before they are able to use the same trick against a production network.

In the first instance, distracting the hacker, honey pots are setup as a deliberate target for a hacker. It is hoped that a hacker will attack the honey pot thinking he or she is attacking the real network. If this fails, then the honey pot acts as a kind of early warning system for the network. While the hacker is distracted attacking the honey pot, warnings are tripped to alert the network administrators that the network is under attack. It is hoped that while the attacker is attempting to get through the honey pot, additional defenses for the real network can be brought on line by installing more equipment or software during the time the hacker is busy with the honey pot before he realizes he is attacking a decoy.

In the second instance mentioned in the first paragraph, the honey pot becomes a research laboratory. A honey pot is deliberately setup with information in it that is deliberately enticing. The information may be real or fabricated. It is hoped that a hacker will take the bait and attempt to attack the honey pot. While the attacker is doing this, the person that setup the honey pot watches what the hacker is doing and then takes steps to block those same actions in a real network or computer. There are honey pots online that have been setup by network security companies for the sole purpose of being targets for hackers. These honey pots will often have an advertised object of value in them and hackers are then encouraged to try to penetrate the honey pot. The network security research company then monitors the honey pot it setup to see what hackers do to attempt to penetrate it. The company can then use what they learned from the honey pot to protect real networks from the same attack techniques.

If there are two or more honey pots on a network, it is called a honey net. The goal of a honey net is to simulate a full-blown highly interactive network.

■ Tunneling and Encryption

 THE BOTTOM LINE This section of Lesson 10 will deal with the concept of network tunneling. We will also discuss topics related to tunneling as well as technologies that use tunneling.

Tunneling and encryption are two methods used to protect communications over public networks. The primary public network in view here is the Internet. Before we can discuss tunneling, we need to discuss something called Point-to-Point Protocol (PPP) because of how dependent different tunneling protocols are on PPP.

Before going into more details about tunneling and encryptions, it would be a good idea to review a few concepts that are related to tunneling and encryption in different ways. The first related topic s site-to-site and client-to-site tunnels. Next, we will look at a couple of protocols that are related to securing tunnels. Those protocols are SSL and the related TLS protocols. Finally, we will look at the ISAKMP protocol that is related to setting up security associations and encryption. The reason we want to look at these initial topics is because while they are not directly connected to creating tunnels, they are important when it come to securing tunnels once they are created.

SITE-TO-SITE AND CLIENT-TO-SITE. When talking about the different connection topologies known as site-to-site and client-to-site, it is important to know the main difference between the two is the identity of the objects being connected. If two different remote networks are being connected via a point-to-point connection then it is called a site-to-site connection. However, if a single computer is being connected to a remote network, then we are discussing a client-to-site connection.

SSL. As discussed in Lesson 5, SSL stands for Secure Socket Layer and is a protocol used to manage the security of a message over an Internet connection. SSL was initially developed by a company called Netscape for securing communications over the Internet between browsers. Over time SSL became the de facto standard for securing communications over the Internet until it was superseded by a more recent security standard.

SSL is used to secure a connection between a client and a server. Once the connection is secured with SSL, any amount of data can be safely passed over the connection. SSL is also used in conjunction with other protocols to help secure them as well. SFTP and HTTPS both use SSL for their security component. The security standard that superseded SSL is TLS.

TLS. TLS stands for Transport Layer Security. The TLS standard was built based on the SSL standard and has become the successor to SSL. TLS has two different layers or components. These two layers are the TLS Record Protocol and the TLS Handshake Protocol. The TLS Record Protocol is used to provide security for the connection it establishes and allows that connection to be encrypted using DES or similar encryption protocol. TLS Handshake Protocol is used by the client and server to authenticate each other and to negotiate the encryption algorithm used by the TLS Records Protocol. It should be noted that TLS does not require encryption be active for it to be used.

Since TLS was first introduced in January 1999 in RFC 2246, it has undergone several updates. The most recent update it to TLS 1.2 was introduced in August of 2008 via RFC 5246.

On a side note, SSL and TLS are not interoperable. However, a message sent by TLS can be handled by SSL. The reverse is not true. It should also be noted that this interoperability was revoked in March of 2011 with RFC 6176 where TLS was disallowed to use components of SSL 2.0 to negotiate a connection.

ISAKMP. ISAKMP stands for Internet Security Association and Key Management Protocol. ISAKMP is a protocol originally specified in 1998 under RFC 2408 and used to establish Security Associations and cryptographic keys in an Internet environment. To understand what all that means we need to look at what a Security Association is and what cryptographic keys are. A Security Association occurs when two separate networks have established a communications channel and have agreed on the security attributes that the two networks will use to secure the communications between them. When all this is done, it is said that the two networks have established a Security Association. Part of ISAKMP's job is to help establish that Security Association and is what the first 3 letters of the name refer to.

A cryptographic key is a piece of variable information that is used by an encryption algorithm to either encrypt or decrypt data that is being secured on a computer or in transmission across a network connection. There are a number of different algorithms used by computers to encode or decode data as just described. The cryptographic key is the piece of data used as a baseline for that encryption. A cryptographic key can be a secret password or passphrase, a specific series of numbers, or a specific string of 1s and 0s. Whatever it is, it needs to be remembered and managed in order for either encryption or decryption takes place. If the wrong cryptographic key is used on an encrypted packet or document, the document or packet cannot be decoded.

Part of cryptographic key management is to make sure that the right cryptographic key is used on the right piece of encrypted data or data needing encryption in order to successfully decode or encode the data. The last part of ISAKMP, the KMP part, refers to the responsibility of this protocol to ensure that accurate key management takes place. This means that part of ISAKMP's job is to make sure that the right key gets to the right piece of data so that it either is encrypted or decrypted successfully.

All taken together, ISAKMP has the following responsibilities. One, it is used to help to networks form a reliable Security Association between them over the Internet. Two, ISAKMP is used to make sure that the data exchanged between the networks in the Security Association use the correct cryptographic keys on the correct data set to either encrypt or decrypt the data being exchanged between the networks in the Security Association.

POINT-TO-POINT PROTOCOL (PPP). Now that we have looked at a couple of side issues related to tunneling we can look directly at the mechanics of how tunneling works. The first protocol we need to look at in regards to tunneling is the Point-to-Point protocol or PPP. *Point-to-Point Protocol (PPP)* was first proposed in 1989 with RFC 1134. PPP became a full-blown standard three years later with RFC 1548. PPP has since gone through several updates and revisions. The most current form of PPP is described in RFC 5072, released in September 2007, which allows for PPP over IPv6 and RFC 5172, released March 2008, which discusses PPP and compression over IPv6.

CERTIFICATION READY
What is PPP? What is PPP used for?
5.2

PPP is made up of three main components. The first component is that it contains a method to encapsulate multi-protocol datagrams. This means PPP has the ability to work with multiple Network layer protocols and wrap them up in such a way that they can be transported over a wide variety of OSI Physical and Data Link layer technologies. The second component PPP contains is a *Link Control Protocol (LCP)*. This means that PPP contains a protocol that allows it to establish, configure, and test any OSI Data Link layer connections it uses to transport other protocols. Finally, PPP has a family of *Network Control Protocol (NCP)* protocols to allow it to establish and configure different OSI Network layer protocols.

PPP works in the following way. First PPP sends some LCP packets to establish, configure, and test a data link connection. Once the connection has been established, PPP sends some NCP packets to choose and configure one or more Network layer protocols. Once the Network layer protocols have been chosen and configured, datagrams from the configured Network layer protocols can then be sent over the PPP link or connection. This PPP then remains open until it is explicitly closed down by a LCP or NCP packet. This allows the transmission of multiple Network layer packets across a pre-established point-to-point link across a public network, which helps ensure that the packets arrive at their destination in sequence and without having to find their own routes to the destination. The makes for a quicker and more efficient connection that can be better secured because the point-to-point path as been determined and can be secured accordingly using related protocols for tunneling, which are discussed next.

TUNNELING. *Tunneling* is the process of establishing a connection through a public network that looks like a point-to-point connection to the devices on either end of it; although in reality, it is not. For tunneling to work, three different protocols are needed:

- **Carrier protocol:** The protocol used by the network over which the protocol is carried. In many situations, the carrier protocol is a Point-to-Point Protocol (PPP). PPP is used to establish a direct connection between the two ends of the communication link.

- **Encapsulating protocol:** The protocol used to create a tunnel around the connection created by the carrier protocol. There are several protocols that are commonly used for this purpose. Some of these protocols are GRE, PPTP, L2F, L2TP, and IPSec. These protocols are effectively wrapped around the original data in order to carry it over the connection established by PPP. More about the protocols just listed is discussed later in this lesson.

- **Passenger protocol:** The protocol that the data originally used when it was traveling over its own network before being wrapped up by the encapsulating protocol and carrier over the PPP link. The most common protocol that acts as a passenger protocol is the IP protocol.

To sum up this section and explain it, we use the following illustration. Suppose you ordered a book from Amazon.com. The UPS or FedEx delivery truck acts like the carrier protocol. The box the book is packed in acts like the encapsulating protocol. Finally, the book itself acts like the passenger protocol. Figure 10-6 offers a visual that explains this further.

CERTIFICATION READY
What is tunneling? How does tunneling work? Where is tunneling used? What protocols use tunneling?
5.2

Figure 10-6

How network tunneling works

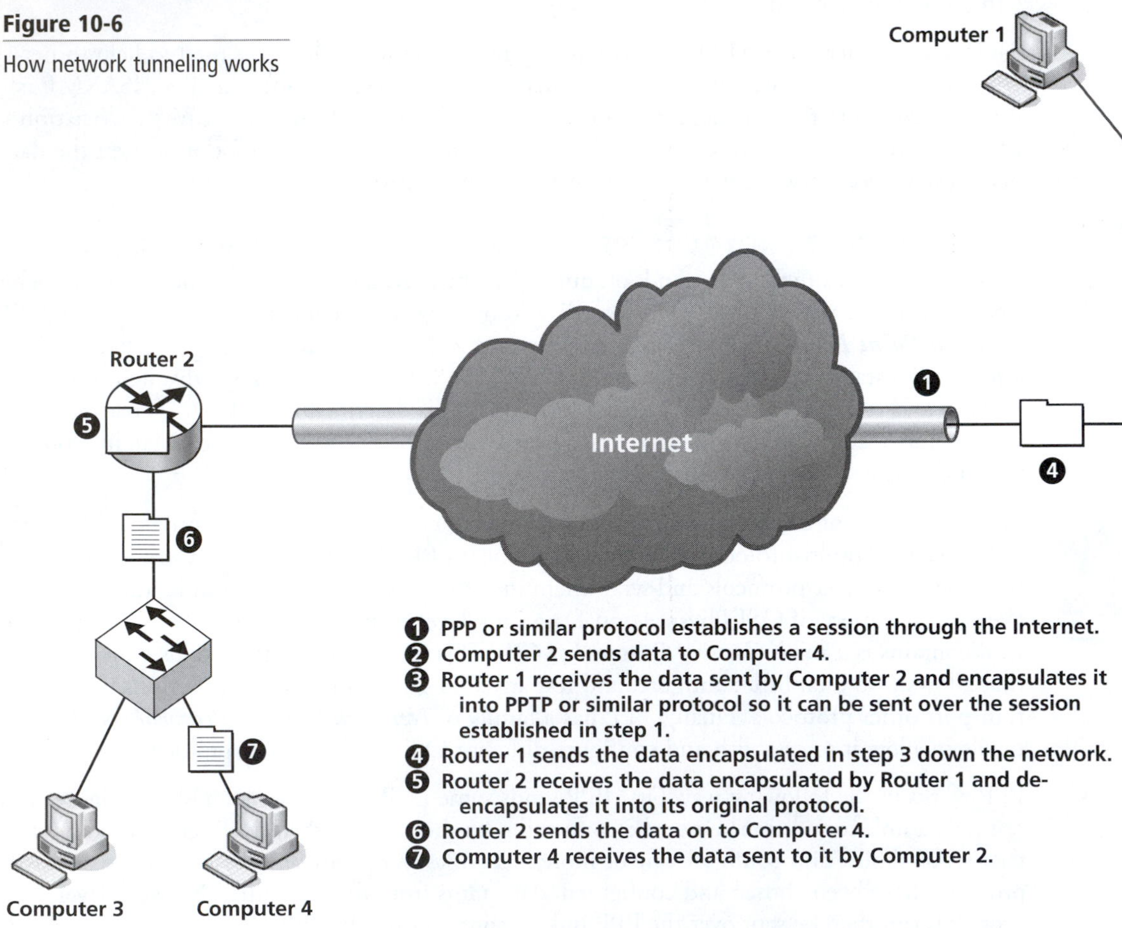

1. PPP or similar protocol establishes a session through the Internet.
2. Computer 2 sends data to Computer 4.
3. Router 1 receives the data sent by Computer 2 and encapsulates it into PPTP or similar protocol so it can be sent over the session established in step 1.
4. Router 1 sends the data encapsulated in step 3 down the network.
5. Router 2 receives the data encapsulated by Router 1 and de-encapsulates it into its original protocol.
6. Router 2 sends the data on to Computer 4.
7. Computer 4 receives the data sent to it by Computer 2.

As you can see in Figure 10-6, the tunneling process works something like this. Before Computer 2 can send data to Computer 4 via the public network, PPP or a similar protocol needs to establish a session over the Internet (step 1). Once PPP or similar protocol establishes a session over the Internet, Computer 2 is able to send its data (step 2). When Router 1 receives Computer 2's data, it encapsulates the data using PPTP or similar tunneling protocol before it sends it over the session established by PPP (step 3). Once Router 1 has encapsulated the data in its tunneling protocol, it sends it down the network toward Computer 4 (step 4). When the data finally reaches its destination network, Router 2 de-encapsulates the data back into its original network protocol (step 5) and sends it on to Computer 4 (step 6). Computer 4 receives the data sent to it by Computer 2 (step 7).

ENCRYPTION. *Encryption* is the process by which an algorithm is used to encode either the header or the entire packet of a network communication so that it cannot be read simply by opening it and looking at the content. If a communication packet is not encrypted, it is called *plaintext*. An *algorithm* is a mathematical formula that is applied to a communications packet or packet header so that the clear text or plaintext of the message is obscured. Another name, that you may see more commonly used, for algorithm is *cipher*.

The goal of encrypting communications is to ensure that only the person who has special knowledge of the key used to encrypt the data is able to read it. To decode or decrypt a packet, two pieces of information are needed. One, the destination computer has to know which algorithm was used to encode the data. Two, the destination computer needs to know the key used by the algorithm to encode the data. Without both pieces of information, a packet cannot easily be decrypted. The more complex the algorithm and the more difficult it is to guess the key, the more difficult it is to break the encryption.

There are quite a few encryption algorithms out there. Some of the most commonly used ones are Advanced Encryption Standard (AES), Blowfish, and Data Encryption Standard (DES). Scientists are constantly on the lookout for more complex algorithm standards to use, because the better the algorithm, the more difficult it is for hackers to break an encryption using brute force. There is a lot more to say about encryption. If you take a course that prepares you for CompTIA's Security+ certification, you will learn much more about them.

Layer 2 Tunneling Protocol (L2TP)

CERTIFICATION READY
What is L2TP? What is L2TP used for? How does L2TP differ from PPTP?
5.2

The *Layer 2 Tunneling Protocol (L2TP)* is a fairly recent protocol that was first introduced in RFC 2661 in 1999. L2TP was designed as an extension of PPP and allows PPP to establish a Layer 2 connection that allows the endpoints to reside on two different devices as long as they are connected by a packet switched network. In other words, L2TP is designed to create a tunnel across a public packet switched network (i.e., the Internet) that PPP is then able to use. L2TP allows ISPs and others to operate VPNs over their networks.

When L2TP was developed, it included some features that are found in some other tunneling protocols. The two protocols it borrowed most heavily from were PPTP and L2F. PPTP is a tunneling protocol developed by Microsoft, and L2F is a tunneling protocol developed by Cisco. Both are discussed in more detail next.

Point-to-Point Tunneling Protocol (PPTP)

CERTIFICATION READY
What is PPTP? What is PPTP used for?
5.2

Microsoft developed the *Point-to-Point Tunneling Protocol (PPTP)*, and RFC 2637 was produced for it in July 1999. Although Microsoft developed PPTP, they did it with the help of a consortium that consisted of 3COM, Ascent Communications, and others. Like L2TP, PPTP was specifically developed for VPN and tied into the existing PPP to do this.

While PPTP ties into PPP to establish connections, it uses an enhanced version of the Generic Routing Encapsulation (GRE) mechanism to provide flow and congestion encapsulation service for PPP. The "enhanced" version of GRE used with PPTP uses a nonstandard packet format and includes some fields in its header that other GRE packets do not. Additionally, PPTP does not describe any encryption or authentication mechanisms. However, when PPTP is bundled in Microsoft Windows operating systems, mechanisms for both encryption and authentication are included via other Microsoft components.

Layer 2 Forwarding (L2F)

Layer 2 Forwarding (L2F) is a protocol developed by Cisco and introduced in RFC 2341 in May 1998. L2F was specifically designed so that PPP could be tunneled over the Internet and used in VPNs. L2F does not provide encryption or confidentiality for itself. Instead, L2F relies on the protocols it is tunneling to provide these things.

Interestingly enough, Cisco used the term "virtual dial-up" to refer to VPN in the RFC where L2F was introduced. By the time PPTP and L2TP were introduced about a year later, *virtual dial-up* had come to be known as VPN and was referred to as such in the related RFCs.

Internet Protocol Security (IPSec)

Internet Protocol Security or *IPSec* is a suite of protocols designed to provide security options to IP. It is important to remember that IPSec is a suite of protocols rather than just one specific protocol. The security options offered by IPSec work on the Internet layer of the TCP/IP Model rather than the Application layer on which other security protocols operate. IPSec, using different protocols available in its suite, can offer both authentication and encryption to IP packets. IPSec is widely used in securing VPN connections. Another advantage of IPSec is that applications do not need to be specifically designed to use IPSec like they do for other security protocols such as TLS/SSL.

IPSec was first introduced in 1998 using RFC 2401, but it builds on RFC 1825 that was introduced in 1995. Even though RFC 2401 built on RFC 1825, it also made RFC 1825 obsolete. RFC 2401 was itself was made obsolete in 2005 by RFC 4301, which elaborates on and enhances IPSec. At the time RFC 2401 was introduced, several other RFCs were also introduced that addressed different aspects of IPSec and the protocols associated with it. The RFCs introduced at this time were RFCs 2402 through 2412. At the time RFC 4301 was released, RFCs 4302 through 4312 were also released, which made the corresponding 24xx RFCs obsolete as well.

A couple of the protocols related to IPSec that were introduced when IPSec was introduced are IKE, AH, and ESP:

- *Internet Key Exchange (IKE):* Used to handle the negotiations of protocols and algorithms. Additionally, IKE is used to generate the encryption and authentication keys used by IPSec.
- *Authentication Header (AH):* Used to authenticate data packets, but it cannot encrypt them. By using AH for authentication, IPSec is able to provide integrity to the datagram it is authenticating. The authentication provided by AH also helps protect a packet from replay attacks.
- *Encapsulating Security Payload (ESP):* Used to authenticate and encrypt data. However, one drawback of ESP is that while it is able to encrypt the data, or payload, of a packet it cannot encrypt the header, something AH can do. ESP supports combined authentication and encryption for packets as well as authentication-only and encryption-only for packets. However, it is generally not recommended to use only one or the other; instead, you should use both.

IPSec works in two modes. Those two modes are *transport mode* and *tunnel mode*. In transport mode, only the payload or the data in a packet is encrypted. However, in tunnel mode, the entire packet is encrypted and then surrounded by a new IP packet containing a new IP header. VPN uses tunnel mode and can be used for network-to-network communications, network-to-host communications, and host-to-host communications. *Network-to-network communications* occur when a router on one network communicates to a router on a different network. *Network-to-host communications* occur when a router on one network communicates to a host, or workstation, on another network. An example of this type of communication is remote access. Finally, *host-to-host communications* occur when one host, such as a workstation, communicates to another host. An example of this type of communication is a private chat. Figure 10-7 illustrates these different types of communications.

Generic Routing Encapsulation (GRE)

Generic Routing Encapsulation or GRE was first introduced in 1994 in the informational RFCs 1701 and 1702 from Cisco. However in March 2000, GRE was proposed in RFC 2784 as a full standard. That standard was updated in September 2000 in RFC 2890.

Figure 10-7

Different types of network communications

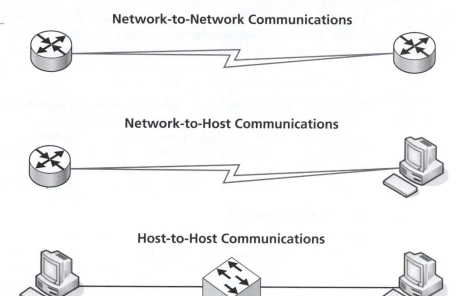

Network-to-Network Communications

Network-to-Host Communications

Host-to-Host Communications

GRE is a generic method that can be used to encapsulate any arbitrary Network layer protocol over any other arbitrary Network layer protocol. This means that GRE can use pretty much any Network layer protocol and encapsulate it so that it can be transported by pretty much any other Network layer protocol. The most common protocol to do this with is IP. However, IP is not by any means the only Network layer protocol that can use GRE in this way. Aside from proposing GRE as a full standard, RFC 2784 also describes how to specifically use IP with GRE. When IP is used with GRE it is sometimes referred to IP type 47.

Virtual Private Network (VPN)

CERTIFICATION READY
What is VPN? What is VPN used for? What protocols are involved in using VPN?
4.1

As you remember from Lesson 8, *VPN* stands for *Virtual Private Network*. As you undoubtedly also remember, VPN is a method used to establish a connection from a client computer outside of a local network to an Enterprise LAN using the Internet or other public network. VPN establishes this connection over the Internet using tunneling, which we just discussed in this lesson.

For VPN to work, there are several steps that have to be followed. First, a VPN client has to be present on the end user's computer in order to connect to a VPN server on the corporate side of the connection. Next, the point-to-point connection used by VPN has to be established. This link is usually established by PPP. Next, the data packets have to be wrapped up in a tunneling protocol in order to use the link established by PPP. Two protocols that are often used for this are GRE and PPTP. Additional protocols used for this purpose are L2TP and IPSec. Once a standard protocol such as IP has been encapsulated into a form that can transverse the tunneling link, the data packet is sent on to the other end of the connection. Once the data packet reaches the other end of the tunnel, the tunneling packet is de-encapsulated or unwrapped so that the original IP packet can be seen. Once the original IP packet can be seen or is restored, it is passed on to the destination computer on the private network it was intended for. Figure 10-6 describes how VPN works as well as the more generic tunneling process it was originally drawn to illustrate and can be used to understand this process. In a way, VPN is just a specific form of network tunneling.

SECURE SOCKETS LAYER (SSL) VIRTUAL PRIVATE NETWORK (VPN)

CERTIFICATION READY
What is SSL VPN? How does it differ from standard VPN?
5.2

SSL VPN is a specific implementation of VPN that allows secure VPN sessions to be set up from within a browser. Any browser that supports *Secure Sockets Layer (SSL)* can be used for SSL VPN, which is also sometimes known as *WebVPN*.

The advantage of SSL VPN to a company is that it allows any employee in a remote location to have access to the corporate private network. In order to make SSL VPN work, an employee in a remote location only needs a web browser that supports SSL and an Internet connection. This means that specialized VPN client software does not need to be present for an SSL VPN connection to be established.

Because SSL VPN uses the SSL protocol, the connection established between the client and the server can also be secured. SSL or its successor TLS helps secure SSL VPN by encrypting the communications traffic between the client and the VPN server. Because SSL secures the traffic between the VPN client and server, it means that the actual tunnel or link that SSL VPN is using for the VPN session is encrypted, not each individual packets being sent across the link. It is possible to encrypt both the tunnel and the packets, but that requires the use of additional protocols.

VPN CONCENTRATOR

VPN concentrator are purpose built devices created by Cisco that are designed to concentrate multiple VPN connections into a single device. There are several advantages to using a VPN concentrator to provide remote VPN access to a network. One advantage is that they provide high availability for VPN access into a network. By using a VPN concentrator, you can establish a large number of VPN connections to your network. Aside from high availability, VPN concentrators also provide high performance. High performance is achieved because VPN concentrators are designed specifically for VPN. You do not need a general-purpose device such as a server serving this function. This allows you to commit more resources to establishing VPN connections within the machine rather than having those resources support services that are not really necessary for the task at hand. Finally, VPN concentrators are scalable. This scalability is brought about because Cisco has designed their VPN concentrators to allow for expansion and the addition of more VPN connections as they are needed. By allowing additional components to be added to a VPN concentrator, its capacity and capabilities are extended.

Remote Access

As discussed in Lesson 8, remote access technologies allow end users to access a network and the information located on it as if they were directly connected to that network even when they aren't. In this lesson, we discuss some of the specific protocols and other technologies used for this purpose. We also discuss some of the security issues related to them.

Remote Access Services (RAS)

Remote Access Services (RAS) refer to all the technology, hardware, and software used to make remote access to a network possible. One of the security issues related to RAS is verifying that the user attempting to gain access remotely to the network is actually permitted to do so. Another security-related issue with RAS is making sure that users are only able to access those resources that they have permission to access once they have access to the network remotely. A final security consideration is making sure that the communications between the local network and the remote user are not being eavesdropped on by hackers.

The first issue in verifying that the user attempting to gain access to the network remotely is who they claim to be is accomplished via authentication. There are quite a few different authentication methods available to do this. Several of these authentication methods were discussed in Lesson 9. One of the most important things to remember about authentication methods is that none of them are perfect. For every authentication method, there are plenty of hackers trying to circumvent it. Sooner or later, someone will figure out how to do it. This is why you should never rely on a single method of security and should instead apply multiple layers of security to every network. This is also why you should never become complacent and assume your network is secure simply because you do not know of anybody who has penetrated it. The other side of this coin is that just because you do not know of a security breach in your network, does not mean that one has not happened or is not already there.

CERTIFICATION READY
What is a VPN concentrator? What is the purpose of a VPN concentrator?
4.1

CERTIFICATION READY
What is remote access? What are some protocols that are related to remote access?
5.2

CERTIFICATION READY
What is RAS? How is RAS related to remote access?
5.2

The second issue mentioned earlier was making sure that a user in the network only has access to those resources you want them to have access to. This issue can be resolved through the use of access control lists (ACLs). We discussed ACLs and other methods of controlling what a user has access to on a network earlier in this lesson.

One method of controlling access to a network not discussed so far is something called directory services. **Directory Services** is a networking service that controls access to the resources on a network via a user access list. Directory services contain several different lists. One is a list of all users on a network. Another is a list of all the resources available on the network. Finally, a directory service also has a list of what resources on the network each user has permission to access. When a user attempts to access a resource, the network server compares the username of the user attempting access with the permitted access list of each resource. Access to the resource is either permitted or denied based on what that list says.

In Windows 2000 and later, directory services are called Active Directory. In the SUSE Linux environment from Novell you may see something called e-Directory. **e-Directory** is the directory services environment created by Novell for Linux. Finally a more generic directory service used in all environments is something called **Lightweight Directory Access Protocol (LDAP)**, which is the basis for the various different directory services just mentioned. Active Directory and e-Directory are originally based on LDAP, although both have significantly modified the environment initially created for LDAP.

Finally, we need to address the problem of eavesdroppers. This security issue related to RAS is generally handled in two ways: encrypting the communication between the remote client and the server that is located on the local network or by creating a tunnel as discussed earlier in this lesson between the client and the server on the local network. Finally, many times the two different solutions are combined. A tunnel is created between the client and the server, and the communications being sent through the tunnel are also encrypted. With some tunneling technologies there is also the possibility of creating a tunnel between the two endpoints, encrypting the data packets as they travel through the tunnel, and also encrypting the tunnel itself. This last way of protecting the communications between two endpoints is the most comprehensive, but it also requires the most network overhead.

How important it is to you to prevent your communications from being captured by a malicious hacker determines how much network overhead and how many resources you are willing to commit to preventing the problem. In other words, if all you are doing is streaming public video over a public network, it really does not make much sense to spend a lot of resources and overhead in securing that communications link. However, if you are sending information about a top secret company project across a public network, it becomes very important to secure the communications link; so, you may be more inclined to spend as many resources and as much network overhead as necessary to secure the communications link. It all depends on what is most important to you in your particular situation.

Point-to-Point Protocol over Ethernet (PPPoe)

CERTIFICATION READY
What is PPPoE? How does PPPoE differ from PPP?
5.2

Both PPP and PPPoE are remote access technologies. However, since we discussed PPP earlier in this lesson, we will concentrate on PPPoE here. The first thing to be sure of is that the user does not confuse PPPoE with PoE. PoE is Power over Ethernet and is not discussed in this lesson. **PPPoE** is **Point-to-Point Protocol over Ethernet**. PPPoE is most commonly used in connection with the various DSL technologies in general use today.

In the most basic terms, PPPoE is a method, developed in 1999, that allows PPP to be used in an Ethernet environment. For PPP to work over Ethernet, a stage, or possibly a pre-stage, had to be developed so that Ethernet could be used as the main Data Link frame technology for the PPP connection. The new stage that was developed for this was called the discovery stage. In the discovery stage, PPP seeks to discover what the MAC address of the client and server computers are on the network so that a PPPoE session identification

Figure 10-8

Point-to-Point Protocol over
Ethernet Discovery Stage

① PPPoE host determines to establish
a PPPoE session and enters into the
PPPoE Discovery Stage.

② Host sends out a PPPoE Active
Discover Initiation (PADI) packet.

③ The Access Concentrator, Server,
receives the PADI packet and issues a
PPPoE Active Discovery Offer (PADO)
packet identifying itself and listing the
different services it has to offer.

④ The Host receives the PADO packet and
decides to accept it. In response it sends
out a PPoE Active Discovery Request
(PADR) packet stating that it accepts the
offer and the service it wishes to use.

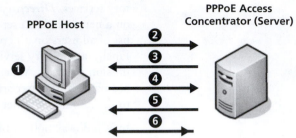

⑤ The Server receives the PADR packet and issues a PPPoE Active Discovery Session-confirmation
(PADS) packet delineating the session identification number and the identification number
of the service the Host requested to use.

⑥ When either the Host or the Server decides to terminate the session, they issue a PPPoE
Active Discovery Termination (PADT) packetto terminate the session.

number can be created and a link established. Figure 10-8 illustrates the following steps
that PPPoE uses to do this:

- **Step 1:** The PPPoE host decides to establish a PPPoE session and enters into the PPPoE
  discovery stage.

- **Step 2:** The host sends out a PPPoE Active Discovery Initiation (PADI) packet. The
  purpose of the PADI packet is to determine if there are any PPPoE servers out there and
  if so what their addresses are.

- **Step 3:** Once a server is located and receives the PADI packet, the server (access concentrator) issues a PPPoE Active Discovery Offer (PADO) packet. The PADO packet identifies
  the server to the host and lists the different services it can offer the host. Once the host
  receives the PADO packet from the server, or access concentrator, this step is complete.

- **Step 4:** The host that received the PADO issues a PPPoE Active Discovery Request
  (PADR) packet. The PADR packet is required for two reasons. First, the host may
  have been given a PADO from more than one server and so it must choose which one
  to use. Two, the host needs to tell the server which of the available services it wishes
  to use. To accomplish this, the host issues a PADR to the server it has chosen to use
  and identifies to that server which service it is requesting. Once the server receives the
  PADR, this step is complete.

- **Step 5:** The server that received the PADR issues a PPPoE Active Discovery Session-
  confirmation (PADS) packet. The server only issues the PADS once a session has been
  set up and given an identifier. Once this is done, the sever issues a PADS packet to the
  host requesting the service telling the host what the session identification number is and
  the identification number of the service the host requested to use.

- **Step 6:** This last step, accomplished by either the server or the host, ends the PPP session by ending the PPPoE session. To end the PPPoE session, a PPPoE Active Discovery
  Termination (PADT) packet must be issued. When the PADT packet is issued by either
  the host or the server, the entire PPPoE session is over. This includes any PPP sessions
  that may have been encapsulated within the PPPoE session.

After the PPPoE session is setup, but before it is terminated, PPPoE uses several protocols to
send data across the connection. A description of how PPPoE functions during a session is as

follows. PPPoE uses PPP's LCP (Link Control Protocol) as previously discussed to establish the Layer 2 communications session. PPPoE also uses the NCP (Network Control Protocols) as previously discussed to encapsulate the Network layer protocol being used in the PPP session. This part of the PPPoE session is called the PPP Session Stage. The PPP Session Stage works just like the normal PPP session described earlier in this lesson.

Remote Desktop Protocol (RDP)

Remote Desktop Protocol (RDP) is a proprietary protocol from Microsoft that is used to create a graphical interface from one computer to another. The latest version of RDP is version 7, which was released with Windows Server 2008 R2 and Windows 7. Currently Microsoft's RDP server component is called *Remote Desktop Services* and their client portion of RDP is called *Remote Desktop Connection*. In former versions of Windows, these were referred to as *Terminal Services* and *Terminal Services Client* respectively.

Some of the features of RDP in current Microsoft operating systems consist of the following:

- 32-bit or lower color support
- 128-bit encryption using the RC4 algorithm
- Audio redirection (This allows audio to be played on the remote computer but the sound is redirected to the connected computer.)
- File system redirection
- Printer redirection (This allows print jobs created on the remote computer to be redirected to a local printer.)
- Port redirection (This allows programs that are opened via a port on the remote computer to be redirected to a port on the local computer.)
- Shared clipboard (This allows shared copied content to be used interchangeably on the remote and local computers.)
- Terminal Services gateway to allow IIS session to be controlled remotely
- Network level authentication
- Support for TLS
- Multiple monitor support

While RDP is a proprietary Microsoft protocol, there have been several non-Microsoft implementations of it. Some of these non-Microsoft implementations are rdesktop, tsclient, and KRDC. Rdesktop is a command-line version of RDP used for Linux/UNIX computers. Tsclient and KRDC are graphical user interfaces built on top of rdesktop.

Virtual Network Computing (VNC)

Virtual Network Computing (VNC) is a program developed in 1999 at the Olivetti Research Laboratory in Cambridge, UK. Since that time, VNC development has moved around a bit. However, since VNC and many of its derivatives are licensed under the GNU GPL license, it is widely available and not a proprietary program.

VNC allows a user to get remote access to a desktop computer much like Microsoft's RDP does. There are however some significant differences. The first and most obvious is that VNC is an open source standard and not proprietary. Another way that VNC is different is that it can work with pretty much any *Graphical User Interface (GUI)* available. This includes Windows, OS/X, and *X11*, which is the underlying system for the various Linux GUIs that are available. This last advantage is even more significant than it first seems because it means that when you are using VNC on one operating system it can connect to VNC running on a computer using either the same operating system or a different one. This is something that the RDP from Microsoft can only do when connecting between specific Windows operating systems.

However, VNC does have one significant limitation. In order for VNC to operate across multiple platforms, it has to be pixel based. A pixel-based program means that the program uses the *x* and *y* coordinates of a specific pixel along with its color to identify it. For a graphic to be seen, all the pixels and their colors need to be accounted for. This results in a pixel map of the screen rather than a true copy of the screen, which means VNC is less efficient than similar programs that are platform specific. This inefficiency comes from the fact that VNC is not able to understand the underlying graphical system of the operating system it is running on, so additional translation has to be done by the operating system to make VNC work. The operating system has to take the pixel map of the remote screen provided by VNC and map it to the actual graphical subsystem that's being used on the local computer. When this translation is completed, any graphics provided by VNC on the local machine are duplicated on the remote machine.

There are three components that make VNC work—the VNC server; VNC client, which is sometimes called the VNC viewer; and the VNC communications protocols. One of the communications protocols is the Remote Framebuffer (RFB) protocol, which is the protocol used to create the pixel map described earlier. Essentially what RFB does is place a rectangle of pixel data at specific *x* and *y* coordinates on the client computer. The second communication protocol used by VNC is an event message protocol that conveys information back and forth between the VNC server and client.

From the end user's point of view, for VNC to work, one computer has to have VNC server on it and another computer connected to the first via a network of some sort needs to have VNC client or viewer on it. If an end user wishes to access the computer with VNC server on it, he or she needs to go to the computer with VNC client on it and send a signal to the VNC server requesting access to the server via VNC. After this is done, the client is able to take remote control of the remote computer running VNC server.

Independent Computing Architecture (ICA)

CERTIFICATION READY
What does ICA stand for? Who developed ICA? What is ICA used for?
5.2

Independent Computing Architecture (ICA) protocol is a proprietary protocol developed by Citrix Systems, Inc. The ICA protocol lays down specific rules for passing data between a client and a server but is not limited to any one specific platform. Some programs that currently use ICA are Citrix WinFrame, Citrix XenApp, and Citrix XenDesktop. Besides Windows platforms, ICA also supports OS/X, various UNIX platforms, and various Linux platforms. The purpose of ICA is to run an application on a server while allowing client computers to access the application remotely.

SSH

SSH or Secure Shell protocol was discussed in Lesson 5. However since this section of Lesson 10 is dealing with remote access it should be brought up again. SSH is a more updated and secure version of TELNET that allows a person to connect to a computer or other networking device over a network connection and issue command line commands to it. It can be used to remotely configure devices or simply remotely control a device via command line commands. Both SSH and TELNET are able to do this. The difference between the two is that TELNET issues the command and/or configuration instructions over the network in the clear. SSH on the other hand makes an effort to encrypt the commands and/or configuration instructions as they are sent across the network connection so that they cannot be easily read if intercepted.

■ Wireless Authentication and Encryption

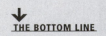

In this section of Lesson 10, we discuss various wireless authentication and encryption techniques. Specifically we discuss WPA, WEP, RADIUS, and TKIP technologies as they relate to wireless LANs.

One of the fastest growing areas of networking technologies is wireless networking. With the growth of wireless networking, security for wireless networking is becoming more and more of an issue. In this section of Lesson 10, we discuss common methods used to secure wireless LANs using authentication and encryption.

Wi-Fi Protected Access (WPA)

Many people think *Wi-Fi Protected Access (WPA)* is a security protocol used in wireless networking; however, in point of fact WPA is actually a specification or a certification and not a protocol at all. WPA was created by the Wi-Fi Alliance as a way to show that networking devices such as network cards and access points met wireless security standards and to replace WEP, which is discussed next. WPA is able to ensure a certain level of security by certifying that every wireless device claiming to be WPA compliant has a certain subset of features and capabilities. Some of the features or capabilities a device has to prove in order to be considered WPA compliant are TKIP encryption and the use of authentication as well as other features.

WPA was originally created as a security placeholding standard that was meant to replace WEP until IEEE 802.11i came out. WPA held most of the same level standards as IEEE 802.11i but not all of them. Once IEEE802.11i came out, the WPA certification was updated to include all the mandatory requirements of IEEE 802.11i and the WPA certification became known as WPA2.

Both WPA and WPA2 also have an Enterprise version of these certifications. As would be expected, the enterprise certification versions are called WPA Enterprise and WPA2 Enterprise. The WiFi Alliance added support for additional types of EAP (Extensible Authentication Protocol) protocols to the WPA certifications in an effort to ensure that all WPA setups used in Enterprise network environments could interoperate with each other. This addition was done in April of 2010 and is now part of the WPA Enterprise certifications.

Wired Equivalent Privacy (WEP)

The idea behind *Wired Equivalent Privacy (WEP)* was to make wireless communications just as secure and private as wired communications, and it was released as part of the original IEEE 802.11 standard. Unfortunately WEP never lived up to expectations. Even follow-up variations of WEP failed to provide the privacy equivalent to that found on a wired network.

WEP is sometimes known as Wireless Encryption Protocol. This is a misunderstanding of what WEP is. While WEP does have some encryption capabilities, those encryption capabilities are not the result of some mythical encryption protocol called WEP so much as the fact that the WEP standard includes the streamed cipher RC4 to insure confidentiality and the 32-CRC (Cyclical Redundancy Check) to insure integrity. In addition to encryption, the WEP standard also includes authentication components. The two authentication methods permitted by WEP are Open System authentication and Shared Key authentication.

Remote Authentication Dial-In User Service (RADIUS)

In the previous lesson, we discussed the use of *RADIUS (Remote Authentication Dial-In User Service)* as an authentication protocol. In this lesson, we discuss RADIUS as it relates to being an authentication protocol in a wireless network. The best way to explain the role of RADIUS in a wireless environment is to go back to the IEEE 802.1x authentication protocol from last lesson. Figure 10-9 offers a refresher on 802.1x.

Figure 10-9

How 802.1X works

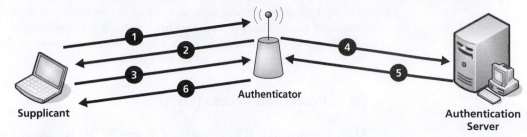

1 Client, also known as the supplicant, wishes to access the WLAN that the access point, also known as the authenticator, controls.

2 Authenticator places the supplicant into unauthorized mode so that only EAP message can be sent to and from supplicant and requests the supplicant's identity and credentials.

3 Supplicant responds back with its identity and credentials.

4 Authenticator forwards the supplicant's identity and credentials to the authentication server.

5 Authentication server verifies the supplicant's identity and credentials and sends a message to the authenticator allowing it to permit the supplicant full access to the WLAN.

6 The authenticator changes the state of the supplicant to authorized so it has full access to the WLAN.

In Figure 10-9 we see an Authentication Server. In a wireless network environment, a RADIUS server often takes this role. As discussed in Lesson 9, RADIUS has a dual role of authenticator and authorizer. As an authenticator, it allows a user onto a wireless network. However, in addition to allowing a user on the network, in its capacity of authorizer, it also has the added ability of controlling where a user can go once they are on the network. It is this last capability of RADIUS that allows it to provide access security on the wireless network. RADIUS's ability as an authorizer makes it a very attractive protocol to use as the Authentication Server in IEEE 802.1x type wireless networks.

Temporal Key Integrity Protocol (TKIP)

Temporal Key Integrity Protocol (TKIP) is a suite of algorithms that are designed to add additional security on top of that provided by WEP. TKIP effectively takes what WEP provides and wraps or encapsulates additional code on top of it. One of the ways TKIP adds strength to WEP is by using stronger encryption keys than WEP does. In addition to this, there are four main things that TKIP does to increase its strength and capability over WEP. TKIP is able to:

- Encrypt each individual packet, rather than the whole message or blocks of the message, using its own unique key rather than one key for all the packets.

- Include the time the packet was sent with the secret key known only to the computer in order to increase the effectiveness of the encryption. In other words, to crack the encryption on a packet, you need to know both the secret key and the time the packet was sent. This is actually where the "Temporal" part of Temporal Key Integrity Protocol comes from.

- Employ a sequence counter, which keeps track of the order in which packets are sent out and therefore the order in which they should be received. If a packet arrives out of sequence, there is a possibility that the packet represents a hacker attempting a replay attack. With the sequence counter in place, any packets that are received out of order are rejected thereby limiting the effectiveness of replay attacks against the system.

- Use a stronger Cyclical Redundancy Check than WEP does. WEP used a 32-CRC system to ensure message integrity. TKIP uses a 64-CRC system to ensure message integrity.

While all of these techniques to ensure the integrity and confidentiality of messages being sent using TKIP are helpful, you should never forget that wireless LANs are still inherently not secure. Organizations like the IEEE and the Wi-Fi Alliance are constantly looking for better, stronger ways to protect wireless LAN communications.

■ Best Practices

THE BOTTOM LINE

In this section of Lesson 10, we discuss various policies and procedures that need to be in place to help maintain a network's security. We also discuss why these policies and procedures are needed.

Webster's dictionary defines ***best practices*** as "an assessment recommending the most appropriate way of handing a certain type of task, based on an observation of the way that several organizations handle that task." Best practices as they relate to network security are discussed in this section of Lesson 10. A successful network administrator will have best practices and policies laid out before an emergency takes place rather than waiting until there is an emergency and then figuring out what to do as they go. When procedures are laid out ahead of time, when an emergency does occur, the response time and how effectively the emergency was handled goes up significantly.

Policies and Procedures

CERTIFICATION READY
What do policies and procedures refer to? What types of policies and procedures should a company have on hand for its network?
5.4

Policies and procedures are two sides of the same coin. ***Policies*** are defined by Webster's dictionary as "a definite course or method of action selected (as by a government, institution, group, or individual) from among alternatives and in the light of given conditions to guide and usually determine present and future decisions." Another way of looking at this is to say that policies are rules and expectations of what is to happen in the general day-to-day operations of a network or organization. ***Procedures*** are defined by Webster's dictionary as "a series of steps followed in a regular definite order." In other words, procedures could be defined as standardized steps, rules, and expectations to be followed when a certain event or occurrence takes place.

These are very similar definitions, but are very different things. Policies are created to be guidelines to be followed during the normal daily operation of a network or company. Procedures do not kick in until a certain event or occurrence takes place. An occurrence or event can be anything from an emergency situation to what to do to keep a network, machine, or the general daily affairs of an organization running smoothly.

CREATING A NETWORK SECURITY POLICY

A ***network security policy*** is a detailed document outlining a large variety of policies related to the security of a company or organization's network. Network security policies should not be used only to keep bad guys out; they are also intended to outline what activities legitimate users of the network are allowed to do. Some of the things covered in a network policy include network access rules, password policies, e-mail usage rules, web browsing rules, and general network usage rules.

Beyond laying out network rules, network security policies can also include information about the architecture of the network as well. This architecture information is there to explain how network security works as well as some of the reasons why the network security was laid out the way it was. There may also be guidelines in a network security policy discussing how network security is to be updated and expanded at a later date.

A network security policy is a very important document to develop for a network. It should not be thrown together quickly but should be developed over time. Also, a network security policy should not be set in concrete. There should be mechanisms built into the network security policy that allow for the policy to be changed over time as new threats and technologies come along. A policy should also allow for changes in how employees work and many other things of this nature. Network security policies should undergo a regular review process so that you can be sure that they still meet the company's needs. If they do not, they should be adjusted until they do.

PASSWORD POLICIES

As you may expect, *password policies* are policies related to passwords and their usage. One of the areas defined in a password policy should be the complexity of a password. You can do this by defining the minimum number of characters a password can contain. Another way to enforce password complexity is to define how many character sets a password should contain. There are four character sets on a keyboard. Those character sets are capital letters, lowercase letters, numbers, and special characters. By stating in your password policy that each password must contain at least eight characters of which at least one should be a capital letter and one a number you are encouraging your end users to use at least eight characters and least three character sets in their passwords, thus making them harder to crack.

Another thing that should be included in a password policy is how often a password must be changed. Many companies require that passwords be changed at least every 30 days. This is to minimize the use hackers could get out of any passwords they managed to crack or steal. For example, if a password is stolen on day 27 of the 30-day period, then the hacker only has use of that password for three days. After those three days, the password is no longer valid.

Password policies should also contain information about why passwords should have a certain level of complexity or a limited use lifetime. This information should be contained in the password policy so that end users understand the reasons behind the rules. When end users understand the reasons behind a policy, they are more likely to comply with that policy. Additionally, there should also be information in a password policy explaining why passwords should be memorized and not placed somewhere where they are easily accessible to other people.

Finally, if you create a password policy, it needs to be both enforceable and enforced. Enforcing a password policy is fairly easy because most network operating systems have a mechanism in place to enforce things like how long a password is valid for, the minimum number of characters a password should contain, and how complex the password should be.

Making a company's password policy enforceable is another question. I once met a network administrator who was so paranoid about how easy it was to crack the passwords of the end users that he started assigning passwords to end users that were randomly generated groups of letters, both cases, numbers, and special characters. Nobody who was given these special "secure" passwords could remember them. As a result everyone wrote down their passwords and placed them somewhere in their work area where they could easily access them, including writing them on sticky notes stuck to their monitors. This resulted in passwords that were even easier to steal and use than if the end users were left to their own devices in creating passwords. While the network administrator had passwords he was sure could not be easily cracked, thus enforcing the complexity policy, everyone stopped following the part of the policy about not writing their passwords down. Eventually management had to step in and force the network administrator to allow end users to create their own passwords again. However, this story does illustrate why password policies need to be enforceable in their entirety.

ACCESS POLICIES

Access policies define two aspects of a network—who is permitted access to the network and what methods are permitted to gain that access. Access policies can also refer to what resources are permitted to which end users and which resources are denied which end users.

Both aspects of network access can be defined in one way. Less is better. In the case of access to the network, you want to set up policies so that only those access methods needed by employees are the ones they are permitted. An example would be remote access. If employees can do all their work from offices, cubicles, or desks within the company, then that is all the access they should be given.

Another issue related to network access is who has access to it. Again, applying the rule that less is better, end users should only be permitted the minimum amount of access needed to do their jobs. If a consultant is hired to do a specific job, her access to the network should be limited to only what she needs to accomplish that specific job. This limiting can be done in a couple of different ways. One, it can be done by limiting her access only to those network resources needed to accomplish what she was hired to do. This gets into the second aspect of access policies mentioned earlier. Limiting access to the network can be accomplished by limiting the consultant to a specific computer that only has access to the resources she needs to do her job.

The best way to sum up what resources the end user has access to, is to follow one very simple rule: all employees should only be given access to those network resources they need to accomplish their jobs. A corollary to this rule is that if an end user's job changes, you do not add his new access permissions to those he already has; you reset his permissions to the minimum he needs to accomplish his new job.

REPORTING PROBLEMS

A policy and procedure that addresses reporting problems is very important. Without a good policy and procedure to do this, it becomes very difficult to keep the network working in optimum condition.

The policy portion of reporting problems should clearly delineate what types of problems need to be reported to whom. It should also clearly define spheres of responsibility in the resolution of different types of problems. Without this being clearly defined, end users become confused about to whom they should report specific types of problems. This results in problems being reported to individuals who do not have the ability to fix them. This means that problems take longer to be resolved and some problems end up being reported multiple times, resulting in confusion about what the problem actually is and who is responsible for resolving it.

On the procedures side of reporting problems, a very clear and easy-to-understand system needs to be in place concerning how problems are reported. This can consist of forms that need to be filled out, specific e-mail addresses to report different types of problems to, or any other system that works for the people responsible for fixing the problem. Many companies and organizations have actually instated whole help desks whose only job is to make sure that the right people get the information about the problems that needs to be resolved. Whatever works for a specific situation, there must be a very clear reporting procedure in place for dealing with problems.

User Training

User training is one of the single most important things you can do to ensure that all the various network policies and procedures are properly understood and implemented by the end users. There should be a training process that new employees go through, and there should also be a process in place for the ongoing training of employees as new policies and procedures are developed or revised.

The best way I can think of to illustrate the importance of user training is the following anecdote. Before the I became a teacher, I worked in the computer industry for about 12 years. While there, the company I worked for created a password policy where one never existed before. The call center where the I worked as the systems administrator was required to follow this new policy. The policy was implemented, but the end users, who never had to worry about passwords before were very unhappy about the policy and actively worked against making the policy successful. Because of this I was, getting frustrated with the whole situation and asked the site manager if I could run a training class explaining why the policy was needed and require all the administrative and supervisory staff to go through the class over the course of a week. The site manager agreed to my request and I created the training class. After the administrators and supervisors had gone through the class, they understood the password policy and exactly why it was needed. Finally, instead of actively working against the policy, the supervisors and administrators actively helped enforce the policy. This resulted in a lot less frustration and things began to move smoothly again. It also earned me a bit more cooperation in other areas from the administrative and supervisory staff because they now had a clearer understanding of what my job was. In fact, the training class was such a hit I was asked to do other training classes on a semi-regular basis about other policy and procedural issues, which I did up until I started teaching full time.

As you can see from this anecdote, training end users in what your network security policies and procedures are and why you have them can reap great dividends for the people tasked with carrying out those policies and procedures. Taking the time to do similar training when the need to change policies and procedures comes along can have similar, if not even greater, benefits.

Patches and Updates

CERTIFICATION READY
What are patches and updates? Why are they important? What are some policies you should have in place regarding updates and patches?
5.4

Patches and updates have become a way of life in the computer industry. Companies make a software product and then they have to create patches and updates for that product when it is found to have bugs or security glitches. This is not just limited to operating systems; this is just as common with application software. It really does matter if the software company is large or small they all do this. However, just because a software patch or update is available does not mean you have to implement it immediately.

In fact, your company or organization should have policies about how and when patches and updates are implemented. The reason for this is that just because a patch or update is available does not mean that it will work as expected. Just a reminder about Service Pack 2 for Windows XP or the infamous Service Pack 6 for Windows NT that people who were around then still have nightmares about, is enough to illustrate this point. It is this proven spotty history of patches and updates that require the establishment of procedures and policies related to them.

TAKE NOTE*

Service Pack 6 for Windows NT trashed any Windows NT operating system that was updated with it. Service Pack 6 did such a good job of trashing the patched operating system that all the data on the affected computer was destroyed and the operating system had to be re-installed from scratch.

Now that we have established that policies and procedures related to updates and patches are needed, we need to look at what they should contain. One thing a patches and updates procedure should contain is a method for testing new updates and patches before implementing them. If a patch is going to totally trash your operating system to the point of destroying your data and requiring a complete re-install from scratch, you want to know this before you start trying to place that patch on your servers.

Another thing that should be covered in an updates and patches procedure is how to roll it out to your production systems. It is generally not advisable to roll out a major patch to every system all at once. You should roll out the patch to some of your systems, let them use the patch or update for a while to see how it works in a production environment before rolling it out to more computers. How you do this and the time interval you place between each phase of the rollout are part of what should be in the updates and patches procedure and policy.

Finally, you should have a procedure in place to rollback an update or patch as well. Sometimes, despite all the testing you can do, a patch or update simply will not work. You need to have a procedure in place to put the systems back to their original state quickly in case this happens. The procedure to put the systems back to their original state is called the rollback plan or procedure. From personal experience, many IT professionals can tell you, the one time you do not have a rollback plan will be the one time you absolutely need it. To avoid putting yourself in that situation, you should always make sure there is a rollback procedure in place before you ever update or patch your first production system.

SKILL SUMMARY

IN THIS LESSON YOU LEARNED:

- What firewalls are.
- How firewalls block unwanted access to a network.
- How NIDS/NIPS devices can be used on a network as well as a computer.
- What some common features of firewalls are.
- The difference between stateful and stateless firewalls.
- What ACLs are.
- What some of the different types of filtering ACLs can do.
- What tunneling is and how it works.
- Some protocols related to tunneling.
- What PPP is and how it relates to other protocols used to create tunnels.
- Different methods of gaining remote control over a desktop or server.
- Some wireless technologies and standards used to secure wireless networks.
- What policies and procedures are.
- Some common policies and procedures that should be used in a network.
- Why user training is important.
- Why patches and updates should not be applied without first testing them.

■ Knowledge Assessment

Fill in the Blank

Complete the following sentences by writing the correct word or words in the blanks provided.

1. The two most common layers that firewalls work on are _____ and _____.

2. A _____ is able to keep track of the connection a particular packet is using and what state that connection is in.

3. _____ is a method used by some firewalls to identify threats based on a database of patterns followed by known attacks.

4. Two forms of filtering used by ACLs are _____ and _____.

5. Two commonly used tunneling protocols are _____ and _____.

6. _____ is a suite of protocols designed to give security to the Internet Protocol.

7. The Microsoft protocol that allows a person to take remote control of a desktop over a network is _____.

8. For PPP to work over an Ethernet network a new stage called the _____ had to be developed.

9. A _____ is an assessment recommending the most appropriate way of handing a certain type of task, based on an observation of the way that several organizations handle that task.

10. A _____ is a series of steps followed in a regular definite order.

Multiple Choice

Circle the letter corresponding to the correct answer.

1. A firewall that does not take into account the state of a connection is called a _____.
   a. VPN firewall
   b. IDS
   c. Stateless firewall
   d. VNC

2. _____ is a protocol designed to provide security to the Internet Protocol.
   a. IPSec
   b. ICA
   c. PPP
   d. SSL VPN

3. Which of the following does RDP stand for?
   a. Remote detection protocol
   b. Rear directed policy
   c. Remote directory protocol
   d. Remote desktop protocol

4. Which of the following protocols use PPP as part of their function? (Choose all that apply.)
   a. VPN
   b. PPTP
   c. L2TP
   d. RDP

5. _____ is a program that requires a client component on one end and a server component on the other to work.
   a. WPA
   b. VNC
   c. WEP
   d. IDS/IPS

6. A policy that defines who has access to a network as well as what they can access is called a/an _____.
   a. Authentication policy
   b. Access policy
   c. Directory services
   d. Password policy

7. An authentication protocol that can be used on both wired and wireless networks is what?
   a. RADIUS
   b. PPP
   c. TKIP
   d. PPTP

8. _____ is a suite of algorithms that added additional security on top of the security provided by WEP.
   a. MS-CHAP
   b. CHAP
   c. TKIP
   d. PKI

9. L2TP stands for what?
   a. Layer 2 Tunneling Protocol
   b. Level 2 Tunneling Protocol
   c. Level 2 Forwarding Protocol
   d. Level 2 Tunnel Processing

10. A firewall that is an actual network device is called what?
    a. Network security firewalls
    b. Signature identification firewalls
    c. Network authentication firewall
    d. Network-based firewalls

Lab Exercises

■ Lab 1

Constructing an ACL Using Windows Firewall

The purpose of this lab is to show the student how to construct an ACL using the Windows 7 Firewall. After completing this lab, the student will have practical knowledge of what an ACL is and how it can be used to protect a computer.

MATERIALS

- A computer running Windows Vista or Windows 7
- Paper
- Pen or pencil

THE LAB

Open the Windows 7 Firewall ACL Dialog Box

1. Click on the Windows 7 **Control Panel**. (This is found under the Start Menu and over to the right.)
2. When the Control Panel opens, it can be in one of two configurations—Category view or Icon view. By default, it will be in Category view. Figure 10-10 shows Category view and Figure 10-11 shows Icon view.

Figure 10-10

Control Panel in Category View

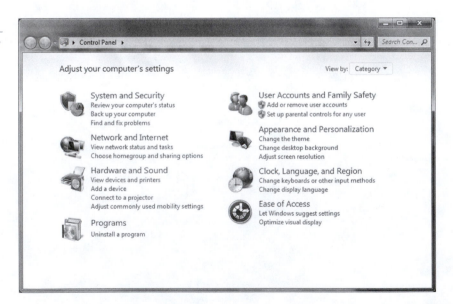

Figure 10-11

Control Panel in Icon View

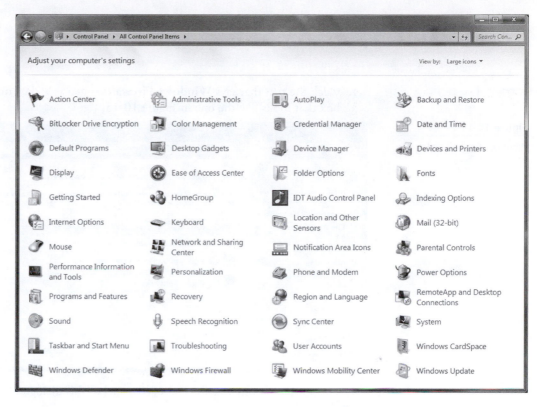

You can switch between the two views by clicking on the link located next to the *View by:* text in the upper right corner of the Control Panel dialog box.

3. From the Category view, when you click on **System and Security**, you should get a dialog box that looks like Figure 10-12.

Figure 10-12

System and Security dialog box

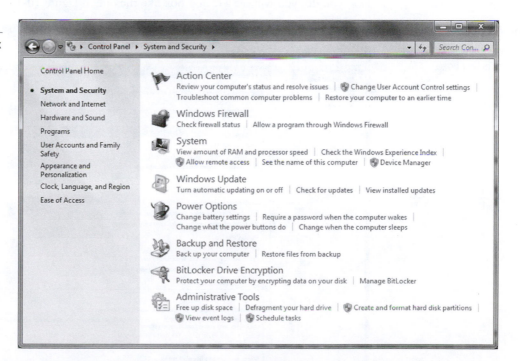

If you do not get a dialog box that looks like Figure 10-12, you clicked on one of the text lines below the text that says System and Security. Close out that dialog box by clicking on the red X in the upper right corner and click on the correct text line.

List all the main categories found under this dialog box.

4. Click the text that says **Windows Firewall**. When you click on this, you will see a dialog box that looks like the one in Figure 10-13.

Figure 10-13

Windows Firewall dialog box

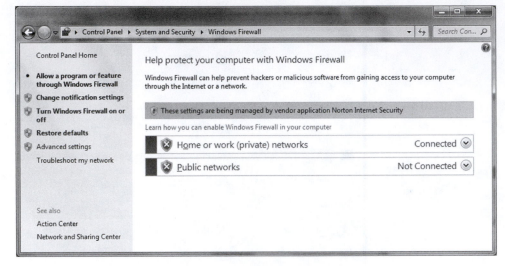

List all the options you see in the left panel of this dialog box.

5. Click on **Advanced Settings** in the left panel of the Windows Firewall dialog box. When you do, you will see a dialog box like the one in Figure 10-14.

Figure 10-14

Windows Firewall Advanced Settings dialog box

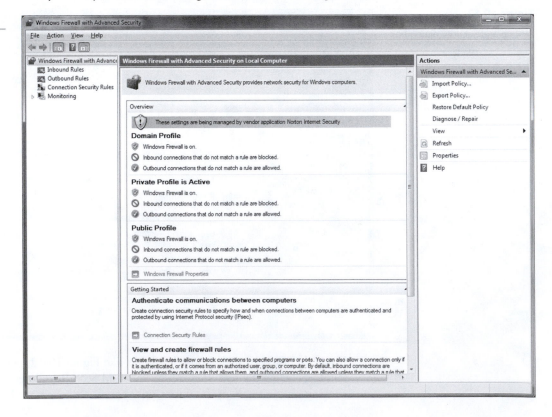

When you open the Advanced Settings Firewall dialog box, you will see a window with three panes in it. The left pane contains a menu of the different options. The middle pane is where you manipulate the menu sections. Finally, the right pane contains the different actions that you can take with each menu selection.

Expand the menu options in the left pane and list all the menu options that are present.

6. Scroll down in the middle pane until you see a link labeled **Windows Firewall Properties**. Click on this link. You should see a dialog box like the one in Figure 10-15.

Figure 10-15

Windows Firewall Properties dialog box

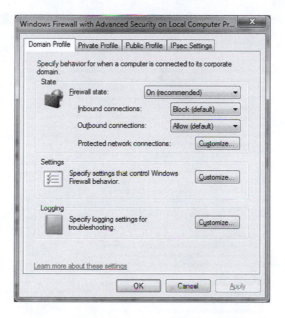

This shows the Windows Firewall options that were available in Windows XP. Obviously you have a lot more options now. List all the tabs you see at the top of this dialog box.

7. Click on each of the tabs. What do you notice about the first three tabs versus the last tab? Why do you think this is the case?

8. Click on the tab labeled **IPSec Settings**. What options do you see? List them.

9. Click the **Customize** button in the first section of the IPSec dialog box. What comes up?

10. Click the **Advanced** radial button in each of the sections of the new dialog box, then click the **Customize** buttons, but always close out of the new dialog boxes by clicking **Cancel**. Look around, what do you see? Describe what you think you are seeing.

11. Return to the *Firewall and Advanced Security Settings* dialog box. That is the dialog box shown in Figure 10-14.

12. Notice that in the left pane you have two icons that look like brick walls. One is labeled *Inbound Rules* and the other is labeled *Outbound Rules*. Click on the **Inbound Rules** icon. When you do, the center and right panels will change as shown in Figure 10-16.

Figure 10-16

Windows Firewall Inbound
Rules dialog box

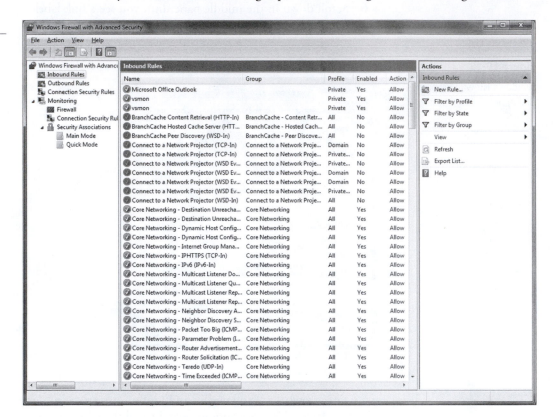

13. Each line of text in the center panel is a Firewall Rule that can apply to inbound network communications. Each rule with an active check mark in it is a rule that has been applied. Each rule with a check mark that is not active is a rule that has not been applied. You can turn rules on or off by clicking the check marks. If the check mark is on, clicking it will turn it off; if the check mark is off, clicking it will turn it on. The list of rules that are turned on becomes your ACL for all inbound network communications.

14. There is a similar set of rules if you click the **Outbound Rules** icon in the left pane. The rules that are turned on there make up the ACL for all outbound network communications.

TAKE NOTE*

The Outbound and Inbound ACLs together is simply referred to as the ACL. By manipulating these two ACLs you can create or customize the ACL on your Windows Firewall. You even have the option of creating customized rules by using the "New Rule" option in the right panel of these two dialog boxes. Depending on whether the Outbound or Inbound panels are open in the middle determines if the "New Rule" is for outbound or inbound network communications.

15. Right-click on one of the rules listed in the middle panel. Now click the Properties option. When you do, you will see a dialog box similar to the one shown in Figure 10-17.

Figure 10-17

Windows Firewall Rule
Dialog Box

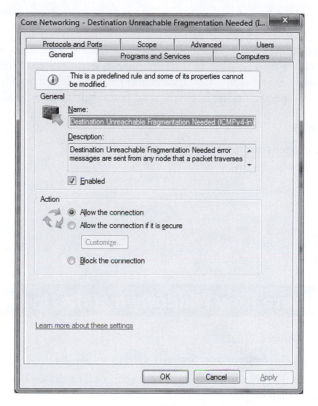

16. You will notice that there are seven tabs across the top of this dialog box. We will look at the General tab first. Two main features of the General tab are the Rule Name and the Rule Description. The Rule Description is very important because it tells you exactly what the rule does. The Rule Description box contains two lines of description, but there are little arrows to the right of the rule. These little arrows allow you to scroll up and down because the descriptions usually take more than two lines.

17. Write down the entire description of the rule you chose. Use the little arrows to view the entire description if needed to write down the whole thing.

TAKE NOTE*

- The Programs and Services tab allows you to choose the computer programs or services to which you want to apply a specific rule.
- The Computers tab allows you to choose to apply or not apply the rule based on a computer's name.
- The Protocols and Ports tab allows you to apply the rule to specific protocols or ports only, assuming the rule relates to a specific protocol or port.
- The Scope tab allows you to restrict the rule based on IP address.
- The Advanced tab allows you to apply the rule based on network interface, assuming you have more than one, and the network profile under which you are operating.
- The Users tab allows you to apply or not apply the rule based on which user is logged on to the computer at any given time.

18. Once you have finished examining all the tabs and the options available in them, you may close the Firewall dialog box and the Control Panel dialog box. However, you may wish to leave the computer running for the next lab.

■ Lab 2

Updates and Patches

As discussed in the lesson, sometimes software updates and patches can cause problems on a computer rather than helping. In this lab, students learn how to set up Windows 7 so that it will not automatically install untested updates and patches. This lab also helps students learn how to determine if a specific update or patch could potentially cause a problem for their computer.

MATERIALS

- A computer running Windows Vista or Windows 7
- Access to the Internet
- A web browser
- Paper
- Pen or pencil

THE LAB

Configure How Windows Installs Updates and Patches

1. Go to Control Panel.
2. Click on the **System and Security** category.
3. Click on the **Windows Update** sub-category. The dialog box you see should look similar to Figure 10-18.

Figure 10-18

Windows Update dialog box

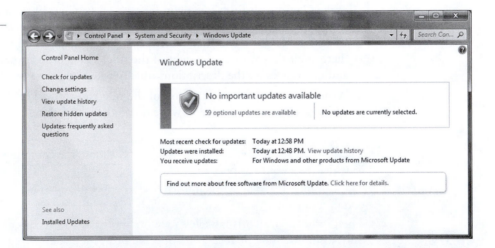

4. Notice that the dialog box gives a summary of how many patches are available from Microsoft. This dialog box also lists how many updates are optional, recommended, and critical. Write down how many of each are shown in your dialog box.

5. If you click on each one of the general groups of updates, you will get a list of what updates are available in each group. You will also be able to select that update to install or not.

6. In the Windows Update dialog box, there are several options on the left side. Write down what the options are.

7. Choose the **Change Settings** option. When you do, you will see a dialog box that looks similar to Figure 10-19.

Figure 10-19

Windows Update Change Settings dialog box

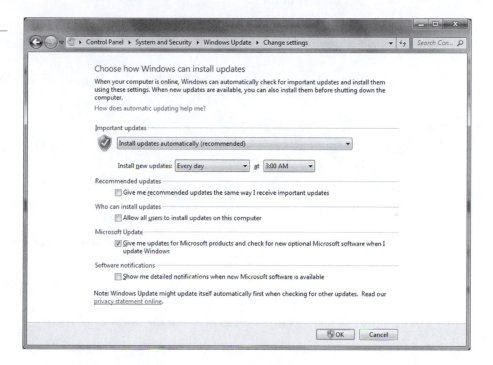

8. The important part of this dialog box for our purposes is the top section of it where it allows you to choose how you want to install updates. By default, Microsoft wants you to let Windows automatically install updates as soon as new ones are available. As discussed in the lesson, this is not always the wisest thing to do. To change how Microsoft installs updates, simply click on the down arrow on the far end of the button. Write down the four options you see there.

9. Which option do you think would be the best option for you to use? Why?

10. Which option do you think would be the worst one to use? Why?

11. Click on the options you want to use and close the dialog box then close the Control Panel. However, leave the computer up for the next step of this lab.

Research Patches to Determine Whether It Is Safe to Install a New Patch

1. Open a web browser and go to Google or some other search engine.
2. Enter **Microsoft Patch News** into the web browser.
3. What are some of the most recent news stories related to Microsoft patches that you saw? List three of them.

4. Are there any critical patches that have recently come out or will be coming out soon?

5. What do the news stories say about them?

6. Were there any recent "problem" patches that you may not want to install on your system?

7. What are three news sources that the stories came from?

8. Would you want to rely on information from only one source? Why or why not?

9. Would you want to rely on information only from Microsoft? Why or why not?

Network Management

EXAM OBJECTIVE MATRIX

TECHNOLOGY SKILL COVERED	EXAM OBJECTIVE	EXAM OBJECTIVE NUMBER
What is Network Management and Why Do We Need It?		
Documentation	**Describe the purpose of configuration management documentation.** • Wire schemes • Network maps • Documentation • Cable management • Asset management • Baselines • Change management	4.5
Network Monitoring	**Given a scenario, use the appropriate network monitoring resource to analyze traffic.** • SNMP • SNMPv2 • SNMPv3 • Syslog • System logs • History logs • General logs • Traffic analysis • Network sniffer	4.4
	Categorize different types of network security appliances and methods. • NESSUS • NMAP	5.6
Network Optimization	**Given a scenario, install and configure routers and switches.** • QoS	2.1

Explain different methods
and rationales for network
performance optimization.

4.6

- Methods:
  - QoS
  - Traffic shaping
  - Load balancing
  - High availability
  - Caching engines
  - Fault tolerance
  - CARP
- Reasons:
  - Latency sensitivity
  - High bandwidth applications
    (VoIP, video applications, unified
    communications)
  - Uptime

KEY TERMS

accounting	history log	redundancy
baseline	jitters	regulations
bit error	latency	reliability
bit rate	latency sensitivity	schematics
caching engine	load testing	speed test
caching server	logical network diagram	storage delay
CARP	media	stress testing
compartmentalization	network diagram	system logs
connectivity monitoring software	network management	throughput tester
connectivity software	network monitoring	traffic shaping
delays	network optimization	transmission
documentation	network video application	uptime
downtime	packet drop probabilities	video application
edutainment	packet shaping	video communications
event logs	performance	video surveillance
Event Viewer	physical network diagram	virtualization
fault tolerance	policy	Voice over Internet Protocol (VoIP)
high availability	procedure	wire management
high bandwidth application	propagation	wiring schematic
	quality of service (QoS)	

Widgets Incorporated has just hired Ray Villalobos as their new network administrator. Unfortunately the previous network administrator was fired with cause and so is not available to answer any questions. Ray has no information about how the network is configured and laid out. What will Ray have to do to find out what he needs to know about the network to do his new job? What can Ray do to make it easier for the next individual who needs to take over the administration of the network?

What Is Network Management and Why Do We Need It?

THE BOTTOM LINE

In the first section of Lesson 11, we discuss what network management is and answer the question of why we need it. We also address the various considerations that need to be thought about when managing a network.

Network management refers to the various actions, procedures, and methods related to monitoring, configuring, maintaining, supporting, and updating a network and its infrastructure. There are a wide variety of tools, both hardware and software, available to help in various activities related to the management of a network. Some of these tools are examined later in this lesson.

Now that we have defined what network management is we need to answer the question of why we need it. The most basic reason is because if we do not, over time the devices related to creating the network will deteriorate. This deterioration can take the form of configurations and software becoming corrupt, devices that stop working, power surges hitting the network, network configurations needing alteration because of changing work needs, and many other things.

The act of watching for, preventing, and adjusting to these types of things is what network management is all about. It is not enough to simply wait for a problem to manifest itself in an obvious manner. For network management to truly be effective, you need to find problems and correct them before they become obvious. This lesson is about different methods, technologies, tools, and procedures for doing just that.

Network Management Considerations

When managing a network, there are quite a few things to take into consideration. Different people find different things important in this process. The truth of the matter is that all of them would be correct; they just have different things they consider priorities depending on their network situation and the purposes for which their network is used. The considerations we examine in this lesson are reliability, configuration, accounting, performance, and security. There is no special significance to the order because all are equally important when it comes to network management, although RCAPS does seem to make a nice acronym.

RELIABILITY

One main consideration when talking about network management is the *reliability* of the network. This refers to how likely it is that the network will function properly. Networks are usually very important to the overall productivity of the company that owns them. If the network does not function properly, then productivity in the company suffers. If productivity suffers, then the company loses money. Given these facts, it becomes very important that the company's network be reliable.

There are several ways to ensure that a network is able to function reliably. One way is to use reliable networking equipment that will not break down. Another way is to have redundant equipment, so that in the rare even that some of your network equipment fails, you have a backup system in place.

However, even with the most reliable equipment available and backups for everything, if no one is actively maintaining the network equipment, it will eventually fail. One of the most important parts of network reliability is making sure that the network is well maintained.

When discussing network reliability, this is where network management comes in. Regular maintenance needs to be carried out on all network equipment. You should not wait until something breaks before everything is checked. Depending on the type of equipment being used, different maintenance activities need to be carried out on a regularly scheduled basis.

You should make sure that your wiring is always neat and well ordered. Everything needs to be labeled correctly and wiring should not be allowed to run all over the place. Very specific wiring paths need to be laid out and adhered to when new cabling is used. The patch panels and switches where cables are plugged in or connected also need to be organized and orderly. When adding new cables, you should use a logical and previously thought out process when connecting up switches and patch panels. Handling and planning for wiring in the manner described is called *wire management*. Good wire management can make a lot of difference when it comes to troubleshooting and resolving network problems quickly.

In the case of routers, someone should always watch over them. If a connection goes down, or a new route has to be followed because of a downed connection, someone should be aware of it immediately and take the proper steps to bring the downed connection, port, or route back up. If such things are left to take care of themselves, sooner or later enough connections and routes will be down and the network will lose the ability to communicate across itself. When that happens, you have such a big problem that everybody will notice and want to know why it was not taken care of before. This is not a question you want to find yourself having to answer. Another important aspect of keeping a watch on the routers is that even though the routers are capable of finding alternate routes if a chosen route goes down; the new alternate route is almost always slower and less efficient than the original one. This means that even though the network is still able to communicate across itself, it is communicating less efficiently. If enough suboptimal routes are being used, the network's overall efficiency will diminish, *and* the company's overall productivity will go down. Sooner or later people will start noticing things like that.

Servers are other networking devices that need to be regularly maintained in order to keep the network running reliably. Depending on the operating systems being used the amount of maintenance varies. In the case of Microsoft operating systems, servers need to be rebooted periodically to maintain their health and reliability. Part of maintaining a reliable network may include having a regular schedule where you reboot your servers every couple of months. Also in order to maintain the reliable operation of your network, servers should be updated or patched in a regular manner. This is important because new bugs and security risks are constantly being found in servers and so regular updates are patches are provided to fix them. If your servers are not regularly patched, eventually there will be so many vulnerabilities and bugs in your servers that they will become easy targets for hackers and have a high likelihood of failing outright. That is not what you would call a reliable network.

A final thing that should be checked on servers is the integrity of the servers' file systems. Over time, files become lost, cross linked, or corrupted. In fact, one of the earliest signs that a hard drive is beginning to fail is an increase in lost clusters, cross links, and corrupted files. If you are doing regular file system checks on your servers, you are likely to catch a failing hard drive before it fails catastrophically. This means that you will be able to recover the data off of a server's hard drive and replace the failing hard drive before the loss becomes so severe that you lose the entire contents of the hard drive, possibly irretrievably.

There are many other things that can be done to ensure the reliability of a network. Some of those things are discussed later. Additionally, you are sure to think of some other ways to help maintain a network that are not discussed here and thereby increase the reliability of any network for which you may be responsible.

CONFIGURATION

Configuration has to do with how the network is laid out and how the equipment is set up. The logical question is "What does this have to do with managing a network?" Surprisingly, it has quite a lot to do with network management. The way a network is laid out and the way the hardware is configured has very large implications for how you go about managing it.

First let us look at basic items such as the topology you use on the network. If you use a ring topology, you need to have equipment and procedures in place that affect what happens if there is a problem. In a ring network, if a single section of the ring goes bad, the whole ring goes down. It takes specialized equipment and procedures to deal with this problem. If on the other hand you are using a star topology, when a single section goes down, it only affects that computer or that section specifically. This makes it much easier to find the problem and resolve it, but it also means that since there is more wiring and equipment involved, problems may happen more often and you need to have procedures in place to resolve them.

The equipment you use and how you configure it also affects how the network is managed. If you have one massive central switch where everything is connected, it becomes easier to create VLANs and such because you only have to configure one large switch rather than numerous smaller switches. This makes network management easier; however, if something happens to the one large switch, the entire network is affected. On the other hand, if you have multiple smaller switches, if something happens to one of those switches, only that portion of the network is affected. Again there are trade-offs, and again those trade-offs affect how you go about managing your network.

Even what you do with servers can affect how the network is managed, and there are more options here than you would initially think. The first decision to make in regards to servers is what operating system you wish to use. You can choose Microsoft solutions, Linux/UNIX solutions, or a combination of both. That decision alone has major consequences for how the network is managed and how you are going to train your support personnel. If you go with Microsoft solutions, things tend to be easier to set up and update, but you will have higher costs and a higher probability of server software problems. There are also greater issues related to security. If you go with the Linux option, your initial cost will be lower, you will likely have less downtime, and security will be better; however, you will have greater difficulty updating your software, you will not have as many software options to begin with, and you will need a much more skilled support staff, which means a better-paid support staff. As you can see, just the operating systems you choose can have a large impact on how you manage a network.

Another question about servers is how many and how large you want them to be. If you decide to go with many lower cost servers, you will be able to get things up and running faster and cheaper, but you will have to add more servers on a regular basis. Also the more servers you have, the more network administrators you will need and the more complex the structure of the network will get over time. On the other hand, you could decide for fewer but larger, more powerful servers. This results in a much bigger startup cost, but only requires a smaller network administrator staff and the overall server structure will be less complex. On the downside, it will cost you more to upgrade and expand your capacity when the time comes.

Finally, you have to decide if you want to use virtualization instead of actual servers. *Virtualization* is where you take one very large and very powerful server and install a program such as VMWare on it. After you have installed VMWare or other virtualization software, you then set up multiple instances of your sever to run on the virtual machine and place all your server functionality on the virtual servers inside the virtualization server rather than on separate hardware boxes. This is how the XP Mode in Windows 7 works and is also how Windows is able to run old DOS programs. Once you decide to go with virtualization, you then have the cost of a very powerful server with lots of RAM and the difficulty of finding people trained to use virtualization on a server. Beyond that, if something were to happen to your virtualization server, your entire network would be down until it is fixed. The upside to virtualization is that one very power server with lots of RAM is likely to cost quite a bit less than 10 or more smaller servers. Another upside is that you can consolidate all your servers down to just a single server box or two. This is basically taking the idea of one or two larger servers mentioned before to its ultimate logical conclusion.

ACCOUNTING

The accounting mentioned here is not doing your books or keeping track of the financial status of your network, instead *accounting* is keeping track of what is being done on your network and by whom as well as how it is performing. In fact, an argument can be made that accounting actually is part of the next two topics we discuss.

The goal of accounting in networking is to keep track of what is going on with your network. Accounting is used to track what resources are being used, who is accessing which resource, who is attempting to access resources they are not supposed to, how various components of the network are performing, and many other things. How this is done is discussed later in this lesson. What is important right now is to realize that these are the kinds of things network accounting is used for.

Depending on what and how many things you are keeping track of with accounting can have a profound impact on how your network is managed. If large numbers of items are being tracked, then more time and resources have to be dedicated to accounting. This may even result in needing to hire personnel whose job is strictly running the network accounting department so to speak.

Another consideration when talking about network accounting are the resources and overhead you want to dedicate to this activity. If you choose to do a lot of accounting on your network, you will need to dedicate more resources to the network and manage it accordingly. The more accounting done on a network, the more physical resources you need on the network to do so. At some point, you reach a place where the return you are getting from your accounting does not justify the resources being dedicated to it. When managing a network, you need to know where this point is given the situation, purpose, and functioning of your network and the company it serves.

PERFORMANCE

Performance has to do with how well the network is functioning and has two components:

- **How to determine how the network is performing:** This component has to do with monitoring the network, and it is where performance overlaps with accounting.
- **How to make the network perform better:** This can be done with new equipment, better procedures, and/or more efficient software.

These two areas of network performance are different but related topics. Both of these areas are discussed in more detail later in this lesson, but greater emphasis is given to monitoring.

In the case of monitoring a network, the first step is to develop a base from which you can determine later network performance. This is called a baseline. Baselines and how they are obtained is discussed later in this lesson. Once you have established a baseline, it will become what you compare all future network monitors against. From a network management point of view, if a current network monitor compares favorably with the baseline, then you can conclude that the network is running optimally. If a future network monitor compares unfavorably with the baseline, then you need to determine why. The other part of performance is seeing what you can do to make the network perform better. If you are successful, then that becomes your new baseline.

There are a number of things that can contribute to making a network perform better. One thing that can be done is to come up with more efficient use of the existing network capacity. This may include developing newer more efficient procedures and policies, or finding and implementing more efficient software. Also simply fixing bugs in existing software can result in a more efficient use of network resources. A good example of this last situation was Service Pack 3 for Windows XP. That service pack on average actually increased a computer's performance by nearly 10 percent. That 10 percent gain in performance all came down to fixing bugs and more efficient coding.

Another way to increase a network's performance is to actually increase the resources available to the network. You can do this by adding additional switches, adding more or faster servers, or bringing more bandwidth physically into the network. Another way to increase the resources available to a network is to upgrade the actual infrastructure of the network. This is not a decision to be taken lightly and will actually end up being quite expensive. The expensive part comes because it will most likely require the replacement of most if not all switches and possibly even the actual wiring of the network. Unfortunately, if a network is in existence long enough, there will come a time when it becomes necessary to physically upgrade the entire setup. Part of network management is to determine when that time comes based on the needs of the company and how the upgrade should be accomplished.

SECURITY

We have already spent a couple of lessons on network security; however, it is important to realize that maintaining the security of a network is also part of managing a network. What security measures need to be taken, what security technologies to use in securing the network, even deciding whether to have a wireless segment are all security-related questions involved in network management. These questions, like all other network management questions, are answered based on the needs of the company and the direction received from the company's upper management. How sensitive your data is and how readily you want your employees and others to have access to that data are all parts of determining what type of security should be built into your network.

■ Documentation

THE BOTTOM LINE

In this section of Lesson 11, we discuss network documentation. We discuss what it is, why it is important, and what types of documentation there are.

Documentation is a very important consideration when talking about network management. With sufficient network documentation, network management becomes much easier and more efficient; this remains true for others who may come in later to manage the network. However, when network documentation is not present or even worse only partially present, network management and support becomes very difficult. This part of Lesson 11 discusses what network documentation is, why it is important, and some different types of network documentation that a company may want to have.

Types of Network Documentation

CERTIFICATION READY
What is network documentation? Why is network documentation needed?
4.5

There are a number of different types of network documentation available. What management considers important and the purpose behind the documentation affects the type of documentation that should be kept. What the network is used for will also have an impact on the type of network documentation needed.

Network documentation comes in two broad categories. The first category is actual records of what you have, how it is configured, and where it is located. This type of documentation also contains records of what has been done to specific network devices and the network in general. The second type of network documentation consists of procedures and policies used to manage and maintain the network.

Both types of documentation are necessary and important to manage a network smoothly. The actual physical records are needed so you know where everything is and what has been done to it. The policies and procedures are needed to make sure that everybody knows what their responsibilities are in managing the network and so that clear lines can be drawn when it comes to reporting network problems. Without clear reporting lines, problems with the network and devices on it become lost and cannot be corrected in a timely manner, resulting in problems that get larger and more difficult to correct over time.

NETWORK MAPS

Network diagrams are very important pieces of documentation for any network. *Network diagrams* show either the physical layout or the logical layout of the network. Put another way, *physical network diagrams* show where everything on the network is physically located. And *logical network diagrams* show how everything works on the network. Figure 11-1 shows a fictional physical network diagram of a section of a call center.

In this figure, you can see the locations of different stations in the call center as well as the station numbers. To enhance your documentation, you can create a spreadsheet that is tied to the station numbers on this diagram. In the spreadsheet, you can include information such as jack number, MAC address, IP address, model of computer located at the location, and even a list of software the computer at the given location is supposed to contain. Using these two pieces of documentation, whenever a problem is reported to network support based on station number, the tech would know exactly where the station is located, what jack number the station is connected to, and all the other pieces of information listed in the spreadsheet. This would help the tech determine what could be causing the reported problems, which would reduce the amount of time it would take to resolve the problems. Figure 11-2 shows a logical network diagram.

Figure 11-2 does not give us any information about the physical layout of a network. Instead it gives us information about how a network works. In this case, it tells us how the firewalls and other security features possessed by this theoretical network work. Looking at this figure, we can tell that the network has two firewalls that form a DMZ; four NIDS; and that the e-mail, DNS, and web servers are located inside the DMZ. We can also see that additional servers, specifically the domain, database, and file server, are located in the internal network. We do not know where any of these servers are located physically. It is entirely possible that all six servers could be in the same room but on different sides of the firewall, but this is not information included in a logical network diagram.

Like the physical network diagram, we can also tie a spreadsheet to a logical network diagram. In the case of the logical network diagram, we could include all kinds of information about the devices shown. We could have configuration information about the servers in the spreadsheet. We may also decide to list what protocols and IP addresses the firewall's ACLs are set to block. We may even decide to include a copy of the actual ACLs being used by the firewall. We can also include the IP addresses of all the devices shown in the diagram. Really, you can include any pieces of information that you decide would be useful to have easily accessible about the devices shown. When your information is so well organized, it becomes much easier to manage the network for which you are responsible.

BASELINES

Baselines are another useful piece of documentation to have when it comes to managing a network. A baseline provides a representative sample of how the network is working at a specific point in time. Essentially, a *baseline* is a snapshot of what is going on in your network. This snapshot is important as a comparison point in the future to determine how the network is working compared to how it worked previously. Doing this type of comparison on a regular basis can help you catch problems in the network before they become severe enough to noticeably affect network performance.

Before you create a baseline, there are some basic questions that you need to answer. The answers to these questions determine what is monitored to create the baseline.

The first question we need to ask is "What is the purpose of our baseline?" or "Why are we creating this baseline and what is its objective?" For example, if we want to create a security baseline, then we need to know what protocols are being used, who is accessing information and what information are they accessing, where do most requests of a specific type originate, as well as other information like this. If we want a performance baseline, we need to know how much bandwidth is being used, what memory resources are being used, what the load on various networking devices is, and other related information. Answering these questions will help us determine the scope of our baseline.

CERTIFICATION READY
What are physical and logical diagrams? What is the difference between the two? Why are both needed?
4.5

CERTIFICATION READY
What is a baseline? Why is it needed?
4.5

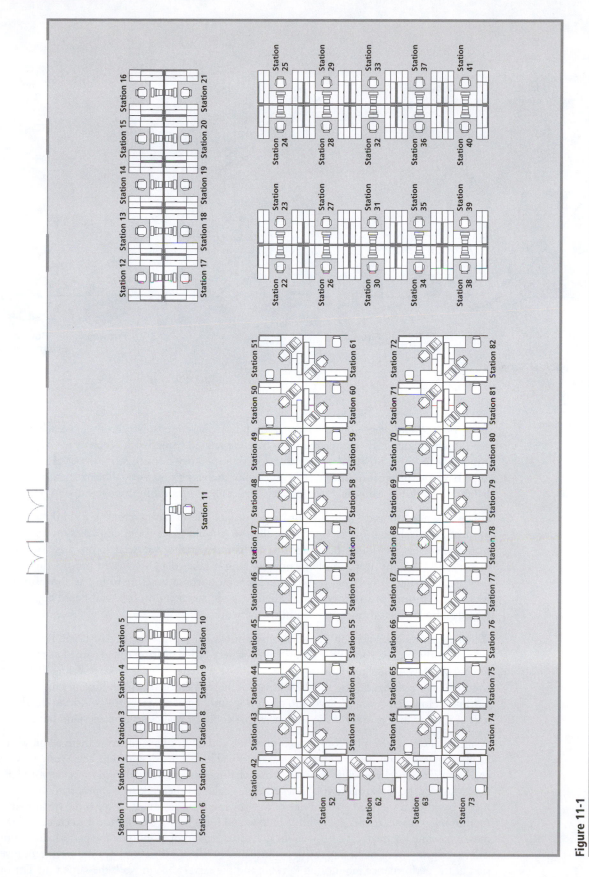

Figure 11-1

Physical network diagram

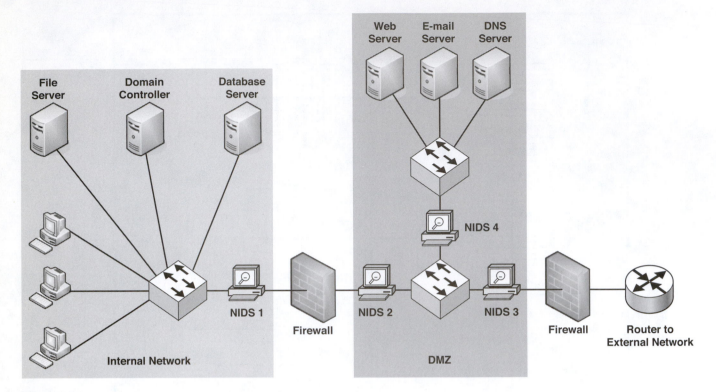

Figure 11-2

Logical network diagram

Once we know what the objective or reason for our baseline is, we can then ask what devices need to be included. If we are creating a baseline related to network security, it really is not important to know how the servers are allocating memory resources. However, if we are creating a baseline for performance testing, suddenly the way the servers allocate memory as well as how much CPU time they use for each process becomes more important.

Finally, we need to ask, "What is our long term goal here?" Are we trying to build a case that we need to purchase more servers? If so, then we should place more emphasis on how much work the servers are doing. If we want to determine whether we need to buy new switches, then we need to put more emphasis on how long it takes the switches to process the frames they are receiving. If our goal is to create a general purpose baseline to use as a measuring stick in the future for network health, then we need to take a more broad-based approach that records a bit of everything going on in the network.

When creating a baseline, you should also take into account the time of day. If you record the baseline at the busiest part of the day, it will look very different from one recorded at the slowest time of the day. A baseline recorded during peak use periods is much more revealing and informative than one recorded during the slowest part of the day, especially when it comes to performance baselines. However, if you are trying to create a security baseline, recording it during the slowest part of the day may actually make anomalies that could be malicious hackers stand out more.

While baselines can be a bit complicated to create, you do not have to create them all on your own. There are a number of software packages available that are designed to help create network baselines. These packages allow you to choose what measurements you wish to use in your baseline. Many of them also allow you to set baseline goals and then take the appropriate measurements based on a specified goal. In one of the labs from this lesson, we look at the performance monitoring software that comes with Windows and learn how we could use it to create a performance baseline for the local computer. In the server version of Windows, the performance software will also allow you to make a network performance baseline. However, both the workstation version of the performance monitoring software and the server version work the same way. The only difference is that the server version has some additional monitoring options that the workstation version does not. Figure 11-3 is a screenshot of Windows 7's Performance Monitoring Software.

Figure 11-3

Windows 7 Performance
Monitoring software

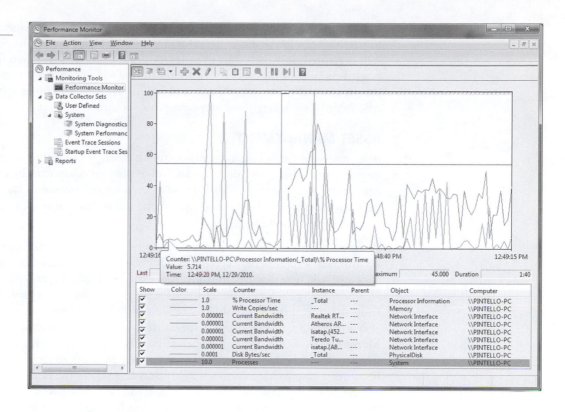

CERTIFICATION READY

What is a wiring
schematic? What is a
wiring schematic used
for?
4.5

WIRING SCHEMATICS

When people think of wiring schematics, they tend to think about those really hard to understand diagrams that explain how a fancy electronic device works. While that is a type of wiring schematic, it is not what we are talking about in networking. In networking, a *wiring schematic* is a diagram of where all the wires in a network are in relation to the physical layout of the facility the network is located in. One way of looking at this is to think of a wiring schematic as a physical diagram of a network that shows where the wires are rather than where the network devices are.

When troubleshooting network wiring problems, these wiring schematics become very important because they show where the wire runs are, as well as which jacks connect to which ports on the patch panels and switches in the switch room. Without a wiring schematic, it becomes necessary to test both ends of every individual wire run to determine where each jack is connected on the patch panel or switch. This is a very tedious and time-consuming process. It is much more efficient to already have this laid out in a wiring schematic. Also, if there is a problem with the actual wire in a wire run, knowing where that wire is located all along its path makes it much easier to find and fix any physical break in the wire should that become necessary.

CABLE MANAGEMENT

Cable management refers to making sure that all the cabling in a network is well organized and documented. This is done be labeling jacks, patch panels, switches, cables, and anything else that will help the people responsible for maintaining the network keep track of the cables. However, labeling everything is not enough. It is also necessary to document all the cabling so that when network support personnel need to find something, they know where to look in order to locate it.

Beyond labeling and documenting, cable management is also about keeping all the cables need in the switch room, along the cable runs, and at the end destinations of the cable runs. Keeping everything need is important because it makes it easier to find specific cables and connections. It does not matter how well things are labeled and how well everything is documented, if the cables are disorganized and strewn all over the place, it is still hard to see where everything is at and to see where specific cables are connected.

In addition to helping keep things organized and neat, cable management also makes it easier to troubleshoot problems. If the cables in a network and the connections in a switch room are well organized, it makes it much easier to locate a problem and then fix it. If things are not labeled properly it becomes very difficult to fine which connection or cable is responsible for the problem. If things are not neat and well organized, it becomes very difficult to trace a specific cable to see where there may be a problem with that cable.

ASSET MANAGEMENT

Asset management is basically an inventory system. When setting up asset management it is important to label every computer and other piece of equipment in a network. Once all the equipment on a network is labeled and entered into an inventory system it becomes much easier to locate a specific piece of equipment and to know when a specific piece of equipment is not where it should be.

If the people managing the network know where every piece of equipment is supposed to be, this has several beneficial effects. One obvious beneficial effect is that it something is stolen or taken without permission it is easily noticed. If a potential thief knows that it will be quickly notices if something is stolen, the thief is less likely to steal something from that location. A less obvious benefit of good asset management is that it makes it very easy for a network support specialist to fine and fix network equipment that is down. Many times when a network device fails, it is noticed by network monitoring equipment first. In a poorly documented network, once a network device is noticed to have failed, it becomes a case of hide and seek to try and fine where the failed device is located. However, if the network is well documented and the network managers know where all their assets are, all that the support specialist has to do is go to the documented location failed device and fix or replace it.

CHANGE MANAGEMENT

Change management has to do with documenting changes on the network. In other words, change management is making sure that anytime anything on the network is changed, updated, added, etc. that changes is added to the appropriate network documentation so that everyone knows the change has taken place and what the change was. This can actually save a lot of time by preventing support personnel from having to "fix" things in the network that were actually planned changes. It also means that when a real problem occurs after a change has been made, the support person tasked with resolving that issue will know what has been changed recently and can adjust his plan to resolve the problem accordingly.

It should go without saying that change management assumes that the network is already well documented. If the network is not well documented then the first step in a good change management plan is go through and create accurate and comprehensive documentation for the network.

Assuming that the network is already well documented, change management involves making sure that any changes done to the network make their way into all the right locations in the network documentation. What this means is that if a computer is replaced then the appropriate notations of this replacement is made in the network documentation. If some software is added to one or more devices on the network then this too is recorded in the existing network documentation. Change management does not stop here though. If the configuration of a router or switch is changed, that change also should be recorded in the network documentation in the appropriate locations.

POLICIES, PROCEDURES, AND CONFIGURATIONS

In the previous lesson, we discussed policies and procedures in a general sense. In this lesson, we discuss policies and procedures as they relate to network management. However, we will start with configurations.

Configurations

Configurations are not how you configure the computers and other devices on your network, rather in this context, *configurations* refer to the record of how the various devices on your network are configured. The easiest way to create configuration records is to make them at the time you initially set them up. This way the configuration is fresh in your mind and you do not have to go back and research and run the risk of missing an important detail. Unfortunately, many times configuration records were not made at setup so the only option is to go back and research the configuration so you can document it.

CERTIFICATION READY
What are configurations? Why are they needed?
4.5

Configurations are important and we need them because they contain a record of how a particular device is configured. If something was to happen to a networking device and it had to be replaced, a copy of the original configuration makes it possible to do so. Otherwise, you have to find out what the configurations of all the other devices were and then figure out how the malfunctioning device fit into the whole setup. You then have to figure out how to configure the replacement device based on that. Undoubtedly you would end up making a number of incorrect configurations before you found one that worked. Even then, you would still have to worry about having missed something you did not know about. All things considered, having a hard copy of the original configuration is a much better option.

Policies and procedures

CERTIFICATION READY
What are policies and procedures? How are they different? Why are they needed?
4.5

As mentioned earlier, the policies and procedures under consideration here are related to network management and not just general network usage and such. *Policies* about network management should concern how the network is documented. They should also be concerned with regular maintenance procedures and contain methods to verify that the specified maintenance procedures have been followed. Network management policies should also deal with how the content of the network is backed up and what should be done in the event of different kinds of failures. Network management policies should also contain provisions for the continuing function of business should natural disasters and such happen and how to recover from them. There should also be network management policies that deal with how the network's capacity can be expanded or upgraded.

Network management *procedures* go hand in hand with network management policies. While network management policies lay out how the network should be maintained and what should happen if failures take place and other such issues, network management *procedures* deal with how to implement those policies. The purpose of network management procedures is to lay out the steps and actions to be taken to make sure that the network policies are met and followed. You really cannot have one without the other, which is why they are discussed together here.

Creating network management policies

When creating network management policies, there are several considerations you need to keep in mind. One consideration is to keep the scope of your network in mind. This means you need to create your management policies in accordance with the size of your network. If you have a small network that only meets the needs of a small business, you need to have management policies that keep that in mind. Large networks require lots of support staff, which requires a clear delineation of duties, and this fact should be addressed in the network management policies you create. If you have a smaller network, then your existing support staff has to cover many different jobs per person. Again, this is a fact that should be addressed in any network management policies you create.

Beyond the size of your network, you also should consider the job your network is there to accomplish. Depending on the purpose of your network, how it is managed will change. If your network is primarily used to access a large central database, then you will need to place more emphasis on database management, support, and maintenance in your network management policies. If yours is more of a general use type network, then provisions for a larger variety of applications and more generalized uses need to be placed in your network management policies.

Finally, when creating network management policies, you should consider how important security is to your network. One trade-off that you need to be aware of when creating network management policies is that the more secure you attempt to make a network, the more difficult it will be for end users to access and use that network. You need to strike a balance between how easy it is for your end users to use a network and how secure that network is. Each layer of security you add to a network is also a potential additional layer of complexity. Like always the decisions you make in this area when creating a network management policy, should be dictated by what your company and its network is expected to do. If your company manufactures and tests new secret military technologies, then the more secure your network the better. If your company makes kazoos for elementary school ensemble groups, a highly secure network is just going to frustrate your end uses.

At the end of this lesson we have a lab that examines various network policies and procedures that are in the public domain and determines what they have in common. We also look at what is different about them. Finally, we also attempt to locate examples of different types of network policies, procedures, configurations, and regulations.

REGULATIONS

CERTIFICATION READY
What are regulations? How are they different from policies?
4.5

Regulations are similar to policies and procedures but different. Whereas policies and procedures are guidelines and rules a company imposes on itself, *regulations* are rules and guidelines imposed on the company by outside agencies and/or organizations. Another thing to consider about regulations is that if they are not followed, your business may not be allowed to do business any more. Whereas if you do not follow your own policies and procedures, the worst to happen may be that your network will not work as efficiently as it should or it may fail, but you could probably correct that. Put another way, if you do not follow your own policies and procedures, you may be out the money necessary to fix it. If you do not follow the proper regulations, you may be out of a job.

Perhaps one of the areas where regulations are the most stringent and closely watched is the medical industry; however, all industries have regulations of some sort that they have to follow, even if they are just labor laws. When starting a new job, or switching career fields, you should find out what regulations apply to your industry and make sure that your company and your network meet those requirements. When making network management policies and procedures, it very important that you know the regulations that apply to your industry and then design your network management policies and procedures to ensure that those regulations are not only being met but are also being exceeded.

Using Network Documentation

CERTIFICATION READY
How do you use network documentation? What is a possible scenario where network documentation would be used?
4.5

There are many ways to use network documentation, and those ways are determined by what type of documentation it is. If the documentation is configuration information, it is used to configure equipment that may be replaced so that new equipment will be able to effectively do the job of the equipment that was replaced. Configuration information can also be used to determine if a device's configuration has been changed. These changes can come about via malicious activity, in which case the configuration documentation may help track it down. Changes can also come about because somebody unknowingly makes changes to a configuration. Configurations can also change because of bugs in device software or because that software became corrupted. Finally, configurations can change simply because equipment is getting old and worn out. In all these situations, configuration documentation can be used to set things right.

Policies and regulations are also forms of network documentation. These types of documentation can be used to make sure that a network meets certain predetermined requirements. They can also be used as guidelines for future expansion and development of a network. Policies and regulations can also be used make sure that a network is maintained at a certain predetermined level of functionality.

Finally, network documentation known as procedures can be used to make sure that a network is maintained properly. Procedures can also be used as a guideline for when things do not work right or when some unexpected problem arises. Procedures can also be used to ensure that a network's support personnel know what to do when specific situations arise. Network documentation can be used in these and many other ways.

Keeping Network Documentation Up to Date

CERTIFICATION READY
Why is it important to keep network documentation up to date?
4.5

Just having good network documentation is not good enough; you must also keep that documentation up to date. If you have network documentation that is very thorough but never update it, it can quickly become worse than having no network documentation.

Having out-of-date documentation is worse than no documentation. At least if you have no network documentation, you know that you do not know what is on your network. However, if you have network documentation that is out of date, you assume that you know what is on your network, but networks always change over time. With out-of-date documentation, when something breaks and you try to use your network documentation to help you fix it, that documentation will most likely make the problem worse. To avoid that unhappy circumstance, keep all of your documentation up to date.

Keeping your documentation up to date can be easy if you have a regular maintenance program where you make adjustments to your network information every time a change is made on your network. This requires a little more work from your support staff, but it can be done and in the long run will pay off handsomely for you. The best way to make sure that your support staff members update their documentation every time a change is made is to include information updates in your network policies and procedures. In this way, you can initially train your staff to do this, and then enforce it if they do not. Since it is a matter of policy that the data be updated, if someone on the staff does not do this, you can reprimand them for not doing so without them being able to retaliate.

Aside from making sure that you or your staff updates the network documentation every time something is changed, you should also perform a regular inventory. While counting things during the inventory process, you should also use the opportunity to compare the reality of your network with what it is documented to be. Where you find differences, you can then investigate the differences and find out why they are there. More often than not it will be simply that somebody forgot to update something or wrote it down wrong when they did. Occasionally, you may find the divergence is caused by hardware or software failure or malicious intent. In those rare occasions, you have the opportunity to correct a small problem before it becomes a big problem. If the divergence was caused by human error or laziness, then you have the opportunity to catch the error before it combines with other errors and becomes a major problem.

Do not always assume that people not doing their jobs, malicious intent, or hardware/software failures caused the errors or divergences. It is a simple fact that over the course of time, things sometimes are simply missed. The whole point of the documentation inventory is to catch those things. If you find other things as well, you are ahead of the game.

■ Network Monitoring

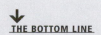
THE BOTTOM LINE

Methods and technologies used to monitor networks are the topic of discussion in this section of Lesson 11. We discuss what network monitoring is and some of the tools that are available to do network monitoring.

Network monitoring is the act of watching a network and determining its current state. Network monitoring can be used to collect any number of statistics that are useful for determining a network's current state. Another aspect of network monitoring is determining what people are doing on the network at any given time. In this case, instead of monitoring the actual functioning of the networking technology, you are monitoring the activities the users are putting the technology to. There are good and valid reasons for doing both kinds of monitoring. However, in this lesson we examine monitoring the actual network rather than the uses a network's end users are putting it to.

Many of the technologies used to create a baseline can also be used to monitor the network's functioning in real time. The main difference is that instead of creating a reference point like a baseline does, network monitoring is more concerned with what is happening now so that you can identify any unusual activity and track down what is causing it. Sometimes the unusual activity really does not indicate anything and sometimes it may be the precursor to a problem that will reveal itself more obviously down the road.

Network monitoring is also useful for determining when it is time to consider upgrading the network. You can upgrade the network by increasing its capacity, updating its equipment, altering the basic infrastructure, or otherwise enhancing it. However, when looking at upgrading a network, there are a few rules that you may want to follow.

One rule to keep in mind is that you generally do not want the normal network load to be greater than 80 percent of its total capacity. If your normal network load is pushing 100 percent of its total capacity, when a peek time comes, there will be no way to accommodate the greater demand on the network. When the greater demand cannot be accommodated, network components begin to fail. In fact, the whole point behind a DoS attack is to stretch a network's demand beyond its capacity and thereby bring it down. You do not want to effectively launch a DoS attack against yourself because the demand on your network exceeds the capacity of the network to accommodate it.

Additionally, you should not wait until you are pushing the limits of your network's capacity before you think about upgrading it. If you do this, you will almost inevitably exceed your network's capacity before you are able upgrade it because you usually cannot simply up and buy new equipment to upgrade your network at will. Such upgrades are almost always very expensive and require approval from higher management before you can even begin to purchase what you need to carry out the upgrades. Getting such approval takes time, and while you are waiting for that approval, the demands on your network will continue to increase. Furthermore, even after you gain approval to spend the money, it takes time to actually order the equipment, have it delivered, and finally, get it installed. It is best to start the process of getting more equipment as soon as you notice your network capacity going over 70 percent or 80 percent on a regular basis even at low usage times during the day. If your company or organization is especially slow about giving approval to spend large amounts of money, start seeking approval when you see your network capacity regularly exceeding 60 percent or 70 percent. If worse come to worst, when the network does eventually crash because demand exceeded its capacity, you can honestly say you tried to get the approval to upgrade the network so this would not happen months ago, but nobody listened to you.

Packet Sniffers

Packet sniffers are one tool that can be used to monitor a network. The primary function of a packet sniffer is to capture data packets and deconstruct them so that you can know what protocols they contain and what their content is. There are several ways that this type of information can be useful for network monitoring.

One way that a packet sniffer can help in monitoring a network is to allow you to see when error packets are being sent. If one workstation or server generates more error packets than any other workstation, then that may be an indication of a problem with that workstation or server. You would then know to go check that workstation or server out for problems.

Another way packet sniffers can help monitor a network is by creating statistics about what types of packets are passing over the network and what ports are being used. For example, if there are an unusually high number of ICMP packets moving across a network, it could indicate an attempt to launch a DoS attack against the network. Alternatively, a packet sniffer could determine that a large number of FTP packets are coming from a specific port. This may indicate that somebody is using network resources to either download or upload many files. Conversely, large numbers of HTTP packets could be coming and going to a specific workstation all day long. This could indicate that somebody is spending more time surfing the web than they are working. Packet sniffers could also be used to see the content of those HTTP packets as well so you can see exactly what the employee spending all his or her time surfing the Internet is looking at when they do. As you can see, there are many ways that a packet sniffer can be used to help monitor a network.

One of the most widely used packet sniffers is a program called Wireshark. You already have had some experience with this program since it was used in Lesson 5. However, there are a few things you need to be aware of when using Wireshark or any other packet sniffer. Figure 11-4 illustrates Wireshark capturing packet information.

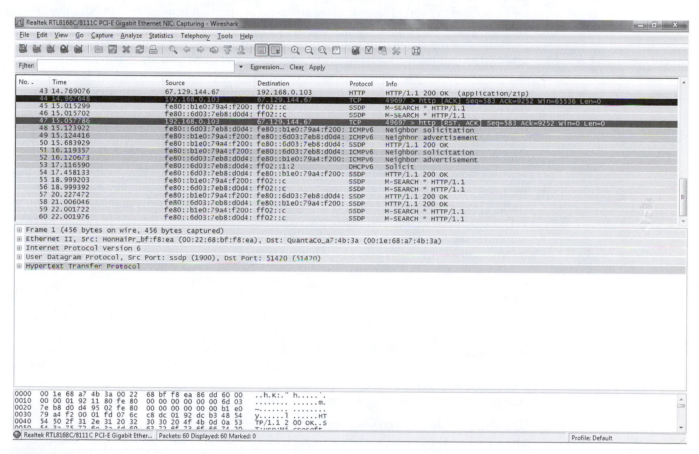

Figure 11-4

Wireshark capturing data packets

One thing to be aware of when using a packet sniffer is that it is considered a felony to use any kind of software to capture and view packets that are moving across a public network. This means that if you go to Starbuck's or some other location and run Wireshark to capture the packets passing over their wireless network, you are committing a felony. This also means that you are also committing a felony if you use Wireshark, or some other packet sniffing technology, on your home computer if your home Internet access is sent over some type of shared media. Generally speaking cable-based home Internet access is of this variety.

On the upside, if you use Wireshark or some other packet sniffing software on a corporate network that you are responsible for monitoring, you have broken no laws. The courts have ruled that corporate networks are private property and the employees that use them should have no reasonable expectation of privacy while on them. This means that as long as you are using a packet sniffer to monitor the activity on your corporate network, you are good.

The use of Wireshark, or some other packet sniffer, in a school environment uses the same rules that apply to a corporate network. In that situation, if your instructor tells you to use Wireshark on your classroom network, it is fine for you to do so. The one catch to this is that the school has to have had all its students and employees sign a network use policy that makes it clear to them that any activity they engage in on the school's network is subject to monitoring. However, if you use Wireshark without your instructor's express permission to do so on a school network; you are once again in violation of federal law and probably school policy too.

One other issue related to using Wireshark has to do with the nature of the connection to the network the computer running Wireshark is using. This also explains why the situations described earlier in this section apply. If the computer running Wireshark is connecting to a network using a wireless NIC, then it is a federal violation if the computer in question is not on an isolated network. However, if the computer in question is using a wired NIC that is connected to a switch, then using Wireshark on that computer is not a violation of federal law, assuming the switch does not connect directly to a public network. The reason for this seemingly weird rule is that wired NICs connected to a switch are only able to see packets that are sent directly to or from a specific computer. This means that Wireshark is only capturing those packets intended for the computer it resides on and so it is not capturing data that other users have a reasonable expectation of being private. However, if the NIC in question is connected to a hub, or is wireless, then all traffic that passes on the related network segment is sent to all the computers on that segment, including the computer running Wireshark. This results in Wireshark capturing all the data passing over the connected network segment. In other words, Wireshark is not only capturing those packets intended for its host computer, it is also capturing packets intended for all the other computers on the network. This means that Wireshark is now capturing data that other users of the network do have a reasonable expectation of being private. When this happens, federal laws about wiretapping come into play, and the user capturing the packets is committing a felony. For more information on this, you can read the United States Code Title 18, Part I. The most relevant chapter is Chapter 119, though other chapters in Part I are also relevant.

SNMP

In Lesson 5 SNMP was looked at from a protocol point of view, here we will look at it from a network management point of view. When SNMP is running on a network, it constantly provides updates on the status of the devices it is running on. SNMP can also be used to interrogate any device it is running on to provide detailed information about the device. This is very useful from a network management and support point of view because it makes it easier to monitor the network and see what is going on with the network and network devices at any given time.

The ability to monitor network devices that SNMP provides is very useful; however, it also creates a security risk for the network running it on the network's devices. If network managers can get all the useful information described in the previous paragraph by using SNMP, so can hackers. Common practice in the industry is to keep SNMP turned off on the network unless there is a specific need to run SNMP. Once that need has passed, SNMP is again turned off.

Two additional version of SNMP have been introduced. These two versions of SNMP are SNMPv2 and SNMPv3. SNMP was first introduced in 1988 with RFCs 1065 – 1067. SNMPv2 was introduced in 1993 with RFCs 1441 – 1452. Finally, SNMPv3 was introduced in 2002 with RFCs 3411-3418.

SNMPv2 added some security capabilities to SNMP as well as a few management enhancements. SNMPv3 primarily enhanced security for SNMP, including some encryption capabilities. That said, SNMP can still be exploited by hackers and so should only be run on a network when it is needed, not at all times.

Connectivity Software

Connectivity software is software that is used to connect to a network or other computer either remotely or locally. For example, a VPN client is considered connectivity software for remotely connecting to a network across the Internet. Alternately, VNC is also considered connectivity software. The difference is that VNC is normally used to connect to a server or other host on a local network instead of remotely across the Internet.

CONNECTIVITY MONITORING SOFTWARE

A variation of connectivity software is *connectivity monitoring software.* This type of software has been designed to monitor network connections. Connectivity monitoring software is very important for network monitoring because it is able to keep track of what computers are connecting to the network, what ports those computers are using, what protocols those computers are using, and what other computers they are connecting to. This type of monitoring allows you to develop a good bird's-eye view of what is happening on a network at any given time. This type of monitoring is also usually able to create a graphical representation of the network connections that are active on the computer or network being monitored.

There are two very good programs available for network connectivity monitoring and both are open source—**The Dude and nmap**—both of which can be obtained from www.filehippo. com. Figure 11-5 shows how a local computer is connected topographically to a network.

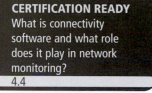

CERTIFICATION READY

What is connectivity software and what role does it play in network monitoring?
4.4

Figure 11-5

nmap Zenmap of a local computer connected to a network

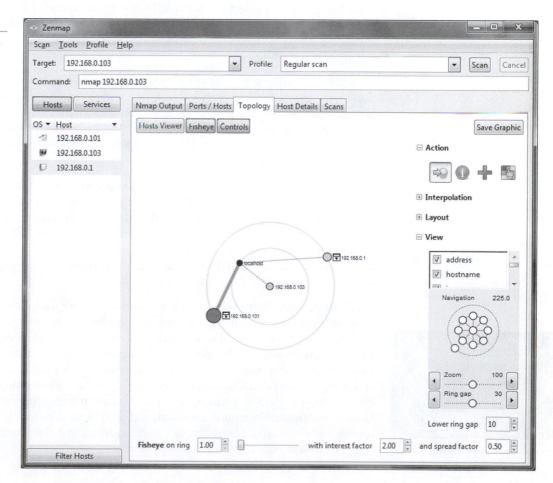

In Figure 11-5, a local computer with the IP address 192.168.0.103 is shown as well as the other network devices it is connected to. In this graphic, the IP address 192.168.0.101 is a wireless NIC on the same computer as the wired NIC with the IP address 192.168.0.103. The wired NIC is the central focus of this topographical network connectivity map. The device with the IP address 192.168.0.1 is the gateway or interface of the router the computer uses to get out to the Internet.

If nmap had been run with the focus being a server, router, or switch in a corporate network, a much larger topographical map would have been created. The Dude is able to do something similar to what nmap does, but the map is a bit different. The Dude is also able to label devices as routers, switches, computers, and so on. As you can see from Figure 11-5, this type of software can be very useful for monitoring the connections being made on a network.

A third program that is good for monitoring a network is Nessus. Nessus is specifically designed to monitor a network for security vulnerabilities. Nessus versions 1 and 2 are open source and can be used by anyone. Nessus 3 is proprietary but is still free for personal and educational use. If you wish to use Nessus in a business network environment, you will have to use the older version 2 or purchase version 3. It should be noted that the company that owns Nessus has updated the older version 2 engine a few times since it has released version 3.

VULNERABILITY TESTING

Network vulnerability testing is the practice of testing a network by looking for ways that a network can be compromised either by accident, circumstances, or deliberate action. Vulnerability testing is a very important part of network management because it bears directly on being able to protect the network from outside threats. The best way to protect a network from outside threats is to identify those threats before somebody from outside the network does. Once vulnerabilities are identified, then steps should be taken to remedy or correct those vulnerabilities.

Vulnerability testing is not limited to simply finding weaknesses in a network and remedying those weaknesses ahead of time. Vulnerability testing can also be used after a network has been compromised as a way to track down and demonstrate how the breach took place in the first place. You want to do this so that you can find a way to fix the vulnerability revealed by the security breach so that the same vulnerability cannot be exploited again either by the same attacker or a different one.

Vulnerability testing is sometimes referred to as penetration testing. However, when vulnerability testing is described as penetration testing it is primarily targeted at determining what types of hacker threats exist for a network. The term vulnerability testing takes into account a wider range of possible threats than just hackers. When vulnerability testing is discussed issues of policy, user habits, environmental factors, and even weather conditions common to where the network is located are taken into account. Penetration testing is primarily concerned with the specific threat of malicious attacks.

While nmap and Nessus were discussed above as network management and connectivity monitoring software, both of these tools can also be used for network vulnerability testing. Both these tools can be used as vulnerability testing tools because they allow the network administrator to identify the specific device a particular packet came from. These software tools can also identify different devices on a network and what kind of traffic is coming from and going to them. This is another useful ability to have when doing vulnerability testing. Finally nmap in particular can be used in conjunction with other tools such as Metasploit to launch specific attacks against a network and then be used to monitor how the network response to the attack. The ability to launch an attack and then monitor how the network responds to it is essential to vulnerability testing.

CERTIFICATION READY
What two network management and connectivity monitoring software tools can also be used for network vulnerability testing?
5.6

Load Testing

Another useful tool for monitoring a network is load testing. **Load testing** is the act of deliberately putting greater than normal demands on a network or the devices in a network to see how they will behave. The purpose of this is to see how far the network or devices can be pushed before they begin to produce errors. This can tell network administrators what the true capacity of their network or the devices in it are rather than making assumptions about that point. Once the capacity of the network or devices has been empirically tested to identify their true "breaking point," that point becomes the point that the network is said to be at 100 percent capacity. Everything else on the network is scaled from this point.

A variation on load testing is stress testing. The goal of **stress testing** is to deliberately load networks or devices beyond the point where they can function properly in order to see what will happen. Stress testing is done so that administrators will know what it looks like when a network or the devices on that network are stressed beyond the breaking point. The way a network or devices can get stressed to this point is usually by malicious intent. When network administrators see the symptoms they have identified as an overstressed network, they will know what it looks like and have a better idea of where to look to stop it.

Throughput Testers

As the name implies, **throughput testers** are programs that are designed to test the actual throughput of a network. If you remember from previous lessons, throughput is the amount of data that can pass through a communications medium in a specific amount of time. The purpose of a throughput-testing software is to determine what the exact throughput is at any given time.

Good examples of a throughput tester that many people may be familiar with are the different **speed tests** that can be found on the Internet. While Internet speed tests are only designed to test the speed of your Internet connection, they are still testing the throughput of your internet provider. A good example of an Internet speed test can be found at www.speedtest.net. This URL has been up for a very long time. In fact this URL has been up since the 1990s, although it has undergone a number of revisions over the years, and so is probably a reliable place to go for testing the throughput of your Internet provider.

The main difference between an Internet speed test and a network throughput tester is that a network throughput tester is testing the throughput of a private network, rather than a public one. Because a private network is the object of a network throughput test, the results reported should be consistent at all times. If they are not, then the inconsistent results could be an indicator of a problem with the network. With an Internet speed test, the result can vary depending on how far you are from the test location, what type of Internet connection you have, which browser you are using, and any number of other variables.

Logs

In networking, logs are data files that are created by different programs to keep a record of what the program has done, what that program has evaluated, or what events related to that program have happened inside the computer. There are literally dozens of logs kept by a computer in the normal course of its daily use. If the computer happens to be a server, then there may be even more logs kept on it. In this section of Lesson 11, we look at a couple classes of logs.

SYSTEM LOGS

System logs are data files that are kept by the operating system or components of the operating system. System logs record information about system changes, device changes, system events, driver changes, and other similar types of information. What system logs record is generally predetermined by the operating system or its components and that is something on which end users are not likely to have much input.

HISTORY LOGS

History logs are an ongoing record of the activity in a specific device or on the network. History logs are generally used as a reference that allows you to go back and examine past activities on the device or network in question. History logs are usually designed to record events for a set amount of time and then they roll over from the top again. In other words, if a history log was set to record events for a week, then every seven days the history log would start recording information at the top again and overwrite the previous week's information as it went. The result is that the history log would have a record of everything it was set to record for a week back from the current point in time.

EVENT LOGS

Event logs are data files that contain information about events that have happened in an operating system, application, or other software components. An event occurs when a software program requires a specific action. If a software program requires that a database be accessed, then accessing the database becomes an event that gets recorded in the event log. If a person wishes to access a specific resource on a network, then the command requesting that specific resource becomes another event. Depending on the software being used and the events that are considered important, event logs can be customized to provide a record of any events a network administrator may want to know about.

EVENT VIEWER

Event Viewer is an application or component that is found on all current versions of Windows that allows you to see all event logs on a local computer. Figure 11-6 shows the Event Viewer found on Windows 7.

Figure 11-6

Windows 7 Event Viewer

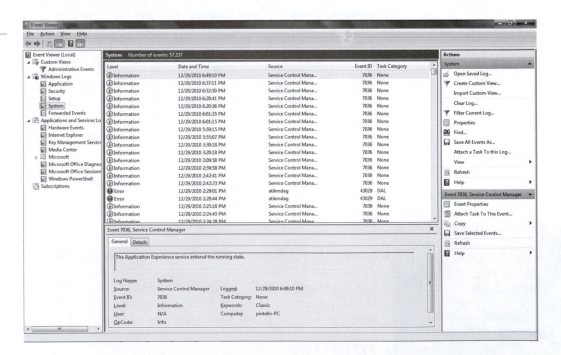

Event Viewer contains three main event logs. These main event logs are the Application Log, the Security Log, and the System Log. Windows 7 has added the Setup Log and the Forwarded Events log to this list. Windows 7 also gives you the option of activating some other logs that earlier versions of Event Viewer did not have.

The Application Log records events that applications have initiated on the local computer. The Security Log records events that have been flagged by either the system or the end users as events that need to be audited for security reasons on the local computer. Finally, the System Log records events that are initiated by the local computer's operating system. More information about Windows Event Viewer is discussed when we use it in one of the labs for this lesson.

■ Network Optimization

THE BOTTOM LINE

In this section of Lesson 11, we look at why network optimization is important as well as how companies decide to go about optimizing their networks. Additionally we also look at some issues and technologies that can have an impact on network optimization. Finally, this section of Lesson 11 also spends some time looking at the technologies that can be used to optimize a network.

CERTIFICATION READY
What is network optimization and why is it needed in networking?
4.6

Network optimization is basically striking a balance between network performance and network cost. How you do that and where that balance exists exactly is determined by what your network's main purpose is and what aspects of your network your company values the most. The following sections of this lesson deal with various aspects of network optimization.

Reasons for Network Optimization

The reasons a company would wish to optimize its network are as diverse as the companies themselves. Different companies place different demands on their networks. What one company may consider a benefit to their network, another company may consider a liability. In this way, the purpose of the network and what the company considers valuable in its network becomes the guiding force behind how much a company is willing to spend, the technologies it is willing to use, and the reasons it chooses to employ network optimization.

To illustrate this point, consider a company where the main purpose of the network is to transfer large amounts of data around between computers (e.g., a movie company that uses lots of computer-generated content). A company like that would need to transfer large amounts of data quickly and efficiently over the network and would place a very high value on being able to transfer multi-gigabyte files quickly between computers on the network. This value would then be the motivating and guiding force behind how much money the company would be willing to spend and what technologies they would want to accomplish this. This company would focus on the high-speed transfer of data across their network and would want to optimize it so that the most efficient use of the available bandwidth was made in order to maximize their actual throughput.

Alternatively, let's consider a company that works with top-secret technologies. That company would be most concerned with security instead of speed of transmission. This type of company would be willing to take a hit in speed performance if it meant the data flowing across their networks was more secure and harder to steal. Again we see that the purpose of the network and the goals of the company impact how much a company is willing to spend and what technologies they are willing to use to optimize their network. This company would focus on the secure transfer of data across their network rather than how fast it was transferred. This company would also be willing to use a lot more of their network's overhead for security purposes such as encryption and authentication, which would slow down the actual throughput of the network more than the previously mentioned movie company would.

While all companies have different reasons for optimizing their networks, there are some issues that a company will always have to consider when they do this. We discuss a few of those considerations next.

LATENCY SENSITIVITY

To understand *latency sensitivity*, the first thing we have to do is define latency. In the network sense, *latency* is the time it takes a packet of data to move from one designated location on the network to another. Often the time a packet takes to go to a specific network location and return is considered the latency value of the network. Latency is an inevitable part of network technologies. There really is nothing that can be done to prevent latency; however, latency can be minimized, which is one of the ways that networks are optimized.

Some of the causes of network latency are propagation, media, transmission, processing, and storage delays. *Propagation* is simply the amount of time it takes a packet to travel to its destination. The absolute fastest a packet can travel is the speed of light.

However, not all media are able to propagate at the speed of light. This is where the second cause of latency comes in. The *media* is what is used to transmit the data packets. Some examples of different media would be copper wire, fiber-optic cable, radio waves, and so on. Different media have maximum propagation rates based on the properties of the media itself. For example, fiber-optic cable is able to propagate faster than copper, and copper is able to propagate faster than sound. Depending on what your media is will change and thereby contribute to or limit latency.

Another contributing factor to network latency is *transmission*, which is a combination of the limitations of the media being used and the size of the data packet being sent. The larger a data packet, the longer it will take to move from one point on the network to the other. Larger packets increase latency because it takes longer for a larger packet to be received and then returned than it does a smaller packet.

Processing time also contributes to latency. Processing is basically what happens every time a packet hits a switch, router, gateway, or other network appliance. What type of network device a packet has to pass through determines how much time is required to process the packet. When a packet hits a networking device, the device has to analyze the packet in order to determine what to do with it. A switch has to deconstruct the packet enough to determine which port to send it to on the switch. A router has to deconstruct a packet enough to determine which path it needs to take to reach its destination and changes its MAC addresses accordingly. *Processing* is taking place every time a packet has to be deconstructed or otherwise evaluated in any way before it is passed on. Furthermore, many devices have to add information into the header of a packet every time it passes through a new device. This may be as simple as removing one tick from the packet's time to live to actually changing MAC addressing, and many other changes. These changes are also part of processing. The more processing the packet has to go though, the longer it will take to reach its destination and therefore the greater that packet's latency.

Finally, not all packets have to go through storage delays, but some do. A *storage delay* is where a packet has to be temporarily stored before it can be passed on. This may be because it has to stay in a buffer or queue while waiting for other packets to be processed, or it could be that an application requires a packet to be stored until the entire message is assembled before passing it on. It could simply mean that a particular device such as an e-mail server has to store messages for a certain amount of time or until a certain number of messages have built up before it can forward them. There are many reasons that a packet may have to be stored before it can be passed on. Whatever the reason for the storage delay, it does contribute to the overall latency of a packet. Also the type of storage medium used can also contribute to storage delays. Hard drives are slower than RAM, static, or flash memory, so packets that have to be stored in hard drives will have a longer latency than the same packet being stored in some other type of storage medium.

Now that we have talked about latency, what it is, and what some of its causes are, we can look at latency sensitivity. Latency sensitivity has to do with how well a program or network device can handle latency. Some devices and/or technologies can only tolerate very low levels of latency before they get out of synchronization with the network and start to fail. Other types of devices and/or technologies are very lenient in regards to latency and can tolerate high levels of latency and still stay synchronized with the network. As a general rule, the faster data can be moved over a network, the less tolerant of latency the components of the network in question are. Put another way, the faster a network technology is, the more sensitive to latency that technology is.

CERTIFICATION READY
What is latency sensitivity? Why does it contribute to the need for network opitimization?
4.6

This is something that is very important to take into consideration when optimizing a network. First off, you need to be sure that you do not combine high latency-sensitive technologies with low latency-sensitive technologies. If you do, inevitably the low-sensitivity devices will bring down the high-sensitivity devices. The type of technology you are using should also be kept in mind when you are tuning your network. If you tune your network to tolerate high levels of latency but the devices on your network can only tolerate low levels of latency, you have built a failure point directly into your network. Be aware of the types of devices you have on your network and optimize it accordingly in the area of latency sensitivity to maintain a smooth-functioning and reliable network.

HIGH BANDWIDTH APPLICATIONS

CERTIFICATION READY
What are high bandwidth applications? What are some examples of high bandwidth applications? What role does a high bandwidth application play in the need to optimize a network?
4.6

High bandwidth applications are those network applications that require a lot of bandwidth to function. In other words, to use them requires network capacity. Some examples of high bandwidth applications are video streaming, videoconferencing, Voice over Internet Protocol (VoIP), and bit torrents. We discuss both VoIP and video applications later in this lesson.

When you are optimizing your network to get the most use out of it, you need to take into account any high bandwidth applications that are used on the network and consider how often those types of applications are being used. If you only do a couple of videoconferences a month using WebEx or some other application, then even though videoconferencing is a high bandwidth application, it is not a major strain on your network resources and is not a very significant consideration when optimizing your network. However, if videoconferencing is a major component of your daily network usage, videoconferencing becomes a very major consideration in network optimization.

One of the best ways to accommodate high bandwidth applications on a network is to set aside bandwidth specifically for those applications. One way to set aside network capacity is to create a VLAN that is specifically intended for a particular high bandwidth application, say VoIP. In this example, you can set things up so that only those devices that use VoIP, such as VoIP telephones, are able to access the VoIP VLAN. Another way to do this is with routers and traffic shapers. However, this topic is discussed in more detail later in this lesson.

Voice over Internet Protocol (VoIP)

Voice over Internet Protocol (VoIP) is a group of protocols and standards that allow voice communications and multimedia sessions over packet-switched networks using the IP protocol. VoIP is considered a high bandwidth application, and so when optimizing a network that uses VoIP, this is something you need to keep in mind.

VoIP is used in several different ways. Internet phone services are actually VoIP applications. Phone services provided by Internet service providers that are not traditional phone companies also use VoIP. Initially VoIP was just for voice communications; however, over time VoIP grew and included some multimedia capabilities to assist in videoconferencing.

Many companies have started using VoIP in their corporate phone systems because using traditional phone systems require two separate networks that need to be maintained and supported. With traditional phone systems, you have a phone switch that has dedicated wiring that connects it to all the phones within a company that is totally independent of the data network. This creates a parallel switching and wiring infrastructure for voice communications. However, if a company switches to VoIP, they are able to run the phone system and the data network over the same infrastructure because VoIP uses the IP protocol just like other TCP/IP based protocols and systems do, which allows companies to eliminate the parallel infrastructure mentioned earlier.

While this is all good, it does result in some challenges with the data network. The biggest challenge is that you now have two different communications networks—one data and the other voice—trying to use the same infrastructure. This places much higher demands on the network, which has the potential of allowing one to bring down the other if steps are not taken to prevent this. This is how it can become an issue for network optimization.

An example of one of these communications networks bringing down the other occurred during the 911 attacks at one organization the author knows about. At that time, the organization had both VoIP and their data communications network running on the same infrastructure, but no attempt was made to keep the two separate. Unfortunately, the organization had many people attempting to access the Internet that day trying to find out what happened. Eventually, so much bandwidth was going to the Internet that the organization's VoIP was being overwhelmed and getting voice calls out or in was problematic and sometimes not even possible. This prompted some changes in how the organization configured their network. They ended up setting aside a part of the total bandwidth of the network just for VoIP communications and isolated that portion from the data network so a similar problem would not happen again. This meant that as far as the data side of the network was concerned, it only had a certain amount of total bandwidth available to it and it could not use the bandwidth set aside for VoIP at all. Of course, the same was also true for VoIP.

This kind of solution to a VoIP problem is a good example of network optimization. In this case, an existing network was optimized to allow both VoIP and regular data communications while ensuring that both had a minimal amount of bandwidth available and that neither was allowed to bring down the other.

Video applications

Network video applications use conventional data communications technologies and networks to carry video over IP. Network video applications can be used in almost limitless ways. However, they primarily fall into just a few categories—surveillance, communications, and edutainment.

The first category of network video applications is surveillance. Network ***video surveillance*** applications use cameras to record what is happening in a specific area and transmit the image to a central server location. These applications are considered network video applications because they transmit their recorded images over a standard LAN connection. Each camera in a setup like this would have its own LAN connection back to the server. There are also network video surveillance systems that can transmit across WAN connections or even the Internet.

Communications is another category of network video applications. Network ***video communications*** applications are used for communications purposes. The most obvious of these is videoconferencing. However, video seminars, remote collaboration, video classrooms, and so on also fit under this category. Applications in this category use video cameras as a component of a communications system. These systems also require that sound be present as well, something video surveillance does not require. Because both video and sound are included in these types of applications, they are considered high bandwidth applications.

The final category is edutainment. ***Edutainment*** applications are intended to entertain and/or educate the people who are using them. Some examples of edutainment would be watching streaming movies or videos, viewing and interacting with multimedia presentations, and playing multimedia games that teach you about a certain topic or for fun. Because animated graphics, videos, and high-quality sound are usually a part of applications that fit into this category, they are gain considered high bandwidth applications.

Any of these different types of network video applications that you are using on your network should be taken into account when optimizing your network. Just like with any other type of network optimization, how many of these applications, which kinds of these applications, and how often these applications are running on your network should all be taken into consideration.

Of these three, video surveillance actually takes the least amount of network bandwidth when used on a regular basis because the video being captured generally has a very low frame rate and does not capture sound. Edutainment applications actually have high bandwidth requirements when used on a regular basis because of all the different types of data being used at the same time. Network video communications applications are somewhere in the middle in their requirements. You should keep all of this in mind when considering how to optimize networks using these types of high bandwidth video applications.

Unified communications

Unified communications is the idea of having multiple communications technologies using the same network and/or interface. Perhaps the best current example of a unified communications device would be a smart phone. These devices are able to use video communications, text communications, and voice communications all on the same platform. To go even further, smart phones are able to use all these different types of communications on the same cellular network.

In the networking world unified communications takes the form of using various types of communications on the same network. Both the previously mentioned VoIP and video communications are examples of this. With the Internet becoming more and more important to our lives, it becomes necessary to be able to leverage all the various communications technologies available with the Internet on the local and enterprise networks.

The biggest drawback and challenge to unified communications is the very large amounts of bandwidth needed to use these various communications forms on the same network. This problem does not manifest itself when only a small number of unified communications devices are using the network. If it did, we would not be able to use these technologies in our homes. This problem manifest itself when hundreds or even thousands of devices are attempting to use these unified communications devices in a single network. This is the situation that corporate networks have to face. Even though a corporate LAN may be able to run at 1000 megabits per second, when there are hundreds or even thousands of devices on that LAN attempting to use unified communications, the available 1000 megabit throughput is used up very quickly. This problem is made even larger when a corporation is attempting to use unified communications over an Enterprise WAN. One of the purposes of network management is to leverage the available bandwidth in a given network so as to optimize that network for the demands that unified communications place on it.

UPTIME

CERTIFICATION READY
What is uptime and how does it contribute to the need for network optimization?
4.6

Uptime is the measure of how long a network and/or the devices on it have been up without having any outages or being shut down. The goal is to achieve 100 percent uptime; however, this is not a realistic expectation. Networks and devices have to shut down for maintenance, upgrades, updates, and many other things. Given this fact, the goal is to have the network and/or devices on a network down for the absolute minimal amount of time possible or to have the least amount of downtime possible. *Downtime* is the amount of time a network and/or network device is not functioning.

Maximizing uptime and minimizing downtime are very important parts of network optimization. Even when you know you will need to have a maintenance window that requires you to bring down the network, you need to minimize the amount of time the network will be down. A maintenance window is a time slot that is prescheduled to do work on a network or component of a network for a specific reason. You do not schedule a maintenance window without a plan stating what you are going to do and why. If you find additional work that needs to be done over the course of a maintenance window, you make note of it and schedule a new maintenance window to take care of it. You do not try to fix it while working on the original objective of the maintenance window. If you find you cannot complete the scheduled work in a maintenance window without first fixing the newly discovered problem, you call a halt to what you are doing, put anything back to its original state that needs to be put back, and schedule a new maintenance window with a new plan. You do things this way because the goal is to keep your downtime very low while keeping your network in a functional state.

You can minimize the downtime required by a maintenance window in several different ways, usually in combination with each other. One, make sure that you first do everything possible related to the maintenance window that does not require bringing down the network. Only after you have done everything you can without bringing down the network do you bring it down to accomplish the scheduled maintenance tasks. Two, make sure that everything you need to do during the downtime is setup and organized ahead of time. Only after you are positive you have everything you will need and have organized it in the most efficient manner to do the job should you actually bring down the network. Many IT departments, where the absolute minimum downtime necessary is given a very high value, will actually rehearse the entire operation before doing it. They will rehearse the operation until everyone can do his or her job flawlessly in the smallest amount of time possible. Only after they have done that, will they actually bring down the network to implement the maintenance window. Even IT departments that do not go to the extreme of rehearsing the operation generally make sure that all involved employees clearly understand their jobs before the network is brought down.

Another aspect of maximizing uptime and minimizing downtime is related to how a network is designed. To optimize a network in this manner, you can design it from the start with a lot of **redundancy** in either the whole network or in critical parts of the network. Redundancy is the ability to have standby components online and running so that if a main component goes down, the redundant component will be able to pick up the load seamlessly. This redundancy allows you to bring down a redundant system and work on it. After you have done this, you can shift the load from the main system over to the redundant system and work on the main system. This lets you update or upgrade a network or a portion of the network without ever bringing it down. Once you are done with whatever you need to do, you can shift back to the main system.

A final area to consider when optimizing a network for maximum uptime is compartmentalization of the network. **Compartmentalization** means the network is designed in such a way that if one section of a network is brought down, the other sections of the network will not be directly affected. In this way, you can minimize downtime by limiting it to a subsection of the network instead of having it affect the entire network.

Methods to Achieve Network Optimization

There are several methods used to achieve network optimization. We discuss a few of those methods—quality of service (QoS), traffic shaping, high availability, caching engines, and fault tolerance—next.

QUALITY OF SERVICE (QOS)

In sales and service, quality of service (QoS) refers to how well the employees did their jobs; however, in networking, **quality of service (QoS)** means something else entirely. In networking, QoS refers to the network mechanisms that allow a network to reserve resources and control how those resources are distributed. QoS allows network administrators to allocate priorities to different applications, users, and general data flow. This permits network administrators to guarantee specific levels of performance in the network's data flow.

QoS tools can be used to minimize:

- **Bit rates:** This means that the network administrator can guarantee that data will not flow over the network below a preset minimum.
- **Delays:** We have already discussed some of the things that contribute to delays or latency on a network. Using QoS tools, network administrators can minimize these delays to a certain extent.
- **Jitters:** Jitters are a specific kind of network delay that results from packets leaving the same source but not arriving at the same destination in the same amount of time. The difference in the amount of time that two packets take to reach the same destination is called sometimes called jitter.
- **Packet drop probablities:** This reduces the chance that a packet will be dropped. It is unavoidable that some packets will be dropped while they are moving across a network. This can happen for any number of reasons. The goal of QoS is to make sure that this happens to the smallest number of packets possible.
- **Bit errors:** These occur when bits in a particular packet or frame, but not the entire packet, are lost. Some QoS tools are designed to catch dropped bits and correct them before they cause the data in a packet to be lost.

CERTIFICATION READY
What is QoS and how does it help in optimizing a network?
4.6 & 2.1

CERTIFICATION READY
What is traffic shaping and how does it help in optimizing a network?
4.6

TRAFFIC SHAPING

Traffic shaping, also known as *packet shaping*, is a tool for network optimization. *Traffic shaping* is similar to QoS except that it controls and prioritizes traffic based on what type of packet is being passed through the network. The purpose of traffic shaping is to guarantee performance, improve latency, and/or increase bandwidth for certain types of packets.

Traffic shaping does not increase the actual bandwidth on the network; instead, it increases the usable bandwidth for certain types of packets by reducing bandwidth for others. By prioritizing packets, traffic shaping is able to ensure that certain types of packets get through the network more quickly than other types. Traffic shaping is able to guarantee performance using similar methods. By giving higher priority to specific types of packets or protocols, traffic shaping is able to guarantee a certain level of performance on the network for those specified types of packets. This also improves latency by giving smaller packets with less latency priority over larger packets with greater latency.

LOAD BALANCING

Load balancing is a network management technique that is intended to minimize the impact of high traffic on network. Load balancing is done by spreading out the traffic on a network evenly among multiple servers, routers, switches etc. In order for load balancing to work, all the devices doing the load balancing must be connected to the network the same way and have access to the same resources. There also needs to be a software component to control the routes data packets on the network takes so that the data traffic can be evenly distributed among the balanced devices.

CARP

CARP stands for Common Address Redundancy Protocol. CARP allows multiple devices in a common pool to use the same IP address. For a group of devices to use CARP they have to be on the same segment of a network. When devices are setup like this, they are called a redundancy group. One of the devices in the redundancy group is designated the master device and all the other devices in the group are designated as backup devices. The master device holds shared IP address and is the device responsible for responding to the IP address on the network. CARP is used in some instances to carry out load balancing.

HIGH AVAILABILITY

CERTIFICATION READY
What is high availability and how does it help in optimizing a network?
4.6

High availability is not a tool so much as a goal or a concept in network optimization. Cisco, which has a high availability campaign, describes it best. According to Cisco, high availability refers to the ability to keep a network up and running reliably with the least amount of downtime. This high availability is achieved by building large amounts of redundancy into network devices and the design of the network itself.

You build high redundancy into network devices by setting up a high level of fault tolerance. This means the device is designed in such a way that it has multiple redundant systems so if something goes wrong, there are backup components to take up the slack. In a high availability network, this same idea is carried over to having multiple backup components in the network as well. If a server, switch, or other device goes down, there is an alternate server, switch, or other device to take up the slack.

Another way to build high availability into a network is to have alternate routes or paths to every major location or segment on the network. This means a network should always have at least two viable but independent paths to each major location or segment on the network. If one path goes down, an alternate path is available to take up the slack. An example of this would be a WAN connection between two sites, such as Atlanta and Orlando. At these two WAN sites, a main connection between the two locations would exist and act as the primary means to communicate between these sites. However, both locations would also have a secondary link between them that is slower and/or only comes up when the main link goes down to reduce cost through an alternate service provider. In the event that something happens to the main link, network operations would automatically fall over to the secondary link, thus preserving the availability of the network.

CACHING ENGINES

Caching engines are actually only one component of an entire network optimization system. The entire system is called a network caching system. Anytime a host asks for content from a web server, off the Internet, or sometimes a database server, the network caching system goes to a caching server to see if a copy of the requested information can be found there before going to the requested source.

This caching system has two main components. It has a caching server and a caching engine. The *caching server* stores a copy of any content that is requested from the content source and holds it for a set amount of time. The *caching engine* determines what content to send to the server and also checks the server for a copy or requested content before going to the original source if a copy of the content is not there.

A network caching system optimizes a network's performance by retrieving data locally without having to go elsewhere to find it. This optimizes performance because it takes less time to retrieve data from a local source than it does from a non-local source. In a network where one or more caching engines are in use, the routers are programmed to route requests from non-local data through the caching engine in case the caching engine already has a local copy of the requested information. If the caching engine does not, it then becomes the caching engine's responsibility to retrieve if from whichever non-local sources it needs to.

Another part of the caching engine's job is to determine what data should be stored locally in a cache server and what data should not be. One way a caching engine is able to do this is by keeping track of what data is commonly asked for and what data is not. Commonly asked for data is stored in the cache server, while data that is not commonly requested is not stored after it is retrieved from the non-local source. Some caching engines are also able to make predictions about what may be asked for next and retrieve that data before it is asked for, which also speeds up a network's performance.

One thing to keep in mind is that caching engines and cache servers are not necessarily different devices. It is quite common for the caching engine and the caching server to be the same device, in which case the whole thing is referred to as a caching engine. Cisco makes a whole line of devices just like this. Figure 11-7 illustrates how a caching engine works.

In Figure 11-7, Computer 3 wants access to some specific content on the Internet so it sends the request to Router 1 which is Computer 3's Internet gateway (step 1). Router 1 sees the packet from Computer 3 and determines that Computer 3 wants to access the Internet. Router 1 redirects that request from the Internet to the caching engine (step 2). The caching engine evaluates the request from Computer 3 to determine what content it is looking for from the Internet. The caching engine then checks the Internet content stored in its caching server to determine if the content Computer 3 is seeking is located there (step 3). If the content that Computer 3 is seeking is found in the caching server, then the caching engine retrieves the content and sends it back to Computer 3 (step 4). If the content Computer 3 is looking for is not found in the caching server, then the caching engine returns the request to Router 1 where the request is then sent out to the Internet in the normal manner (step 5).

FAULT TOLERANCE

Fault tolerance is something that has already been addressed in quite some detail in this section of Lesson 11. In fact, many of the things we have discussed to build redundancy into the network are exactly the same things we would do to build fault tolerance into a network. In terms of networking, fault tolerance is the ability of a network to have a portion of the network fail but to still continue to work at some level of functionality. The level of functionality you want the network to work at is the level of fault tolerance you build into it. In a very real way, you could say that fault tolerance is the reason redundancy is built into a system. In other words, the goal of redundancy is fault tolerance.

Figure 11-7

How a caching engine works

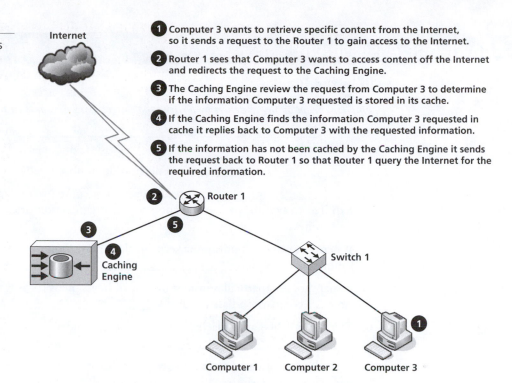

1 Computer 3 wants to retrieve specific content from the Internet, so it sends a request to the Router 1 to gain access to the Internet.

2 Router 1 sees that Computer 3 wants to access content off the Internet and redirects the request to the Caching Engine.

3 The Caching Engine review the request from Computer 3 to determine if the information Computer 3 requested is stored in its cache.

4 If the Caching Engine finds the information Computer 3 requested in cache it replies back to Computer 3 with the requested information.

5 If the information has not been cached by the Caching Engine it sends the request back to Router 1 so that Router 1 query the Internet for the required information.

The level of fault tolerance you build into your network depends on how much money you are willing to spend and how important fault tolerance is to you. If your organization has a high need for fault tolerance, then your organization will spend very large amounts of money to ensure that the network can provide the amount of fault tolerance needed. There is a saying that goes something like this, "If you are willing to spend enough money, then you can make a network that can withstand anything." This is a true statement; you can make a network that can withstand even a nuclear blast if you want to spend the money. The problem is that to withstand that nuclear blast would cost so much that nobody but the military could or would be willing to spend the money to do so.

SKILL SUMMARY

IN THIS LESSON YOU LEARNED:

- What network management is.
- Why network management is important.
- What some considerations are when managing a network.
- What documentation is and why it is needed.
- What baselines are.
- How to create and use baselines.
- The difference between a logical network diagram and a physical network diagram.
- The difference between policies and procedures and regulations.
- What network configurations are and why they are needed.
- The importance of keeping network documentation up to date.
- What is involved in creating network management policies and procedures.
- What network monitoring is and why it is important.
- What some of the different tools used for network monitoring are and how they are used.
- The importance of logs and the Event Viewer tool for viewing logs.
- What network optimization is.
- Reasons for network optimization.
- Some applications that benefit from network optimization.
- Some methods of network optimization.

■ Knowledge Assessment

Fill in the Blank

Complete the following sentences by writing the correct word or words in the blanks provided.

1. _____ and _____ are the two types of network diagrams.

2. A _____ is a description of how a network device or host is set up.

3. _____ are imposed on a company or organization and are required to be followed so the company or organization does not lose its ability to do business.

4. When a network administrator keeps track of how different portions of a network are running it is called _____.

5. A snapshot of a particular instant in time of how a network is functioning that is used later as a comparison base is called a _____.

6. The act of deliberately placing a network system under stress to see how it reacts is called _____.

7. Text files that are used to make a record of different actions or events that take place during the regular operation of a network are called _____.

8. _____ is striking a balance between network performance and network cost.

9. _____ is the act of building backup components and systems into a network so that when a component or system fails the backup component or system can take over.

10. The main goal of building redundancy into a system is _____.

11. A protocol that allows multiple devices in a common pool to use the same IP address is called _____.

12. The process of making sure that all the cabling in a network is properly organized and documented is called _____.

Multiple Choice

Circle the letter corresponding to the correct answer.

1. A diagram that shows the physical location of workstations and other network components is called a _____.
   a. Baseline
   b. Wiring schematics
   c. Logical network diagram
   d. Physical network diagram

2. A diagram that shows how a network functions but does not necessarily show how it looks physically is called a _____.
   a. Physical network diagram
   b. Logical network diagram
   c. Wiring schematics
   d. Configuration

3. What are the three main types of logs found in a computer? (Choose all that apply.)
   a. Authentication log
   b. System log
   c. History log
   d. Event log

4. In Event Viewer, which log is used to record events that are flagged for auditing by either the system or a network administrator.
   a. Application log
   b. Security log
   c. System log
   d. Setup log

5. In Event Viewer, which log is used to record events that are initiated by software applications.
   a. Application log
   b. Security log
   c. System log
   d. Setup log

6. In Event Viewer, which log is used to record actions that are taken by the operating system.
   a. Application log
   b. Security log
   c. System log
   d. Setup log

7. Two applications that are considered high bandwidth applications are _____ and _____. (Choose two.)
   a. VoIP
   b. E-mail
   c. Event logging
   d. Video applications

8. Which of the following is a common network video application category? (Choose all that apply.)
   a. Communications
   b. Web design
   c. Edutainment
   d. Surveillance

9. The network mechanisms that allow a network to reserve resources and control how those resources are distributed is called what?
   a. QoS
   b. Traffic shaping
   c. Load balancing
   d. Fault tolerance

10. The network optimization system that allows a network to save commonly used information from a non-local site on a device that is found locally is called what?
    a. Load balancing
    b. Packet shaping
    c. Caching engines
    d. Latency sensitivity

11. The management technique used to minimize the impact of high network traffic on the network is called what?
    a. Protocol Analyzing
    b. Intrusion Detection
    c. Content Filtering
    d. Load balancing

12. A program that is good for monitoring what is happening on your network is _____. (Choose all that apply.)
    a. NESSUS
    b. NMAP
    c. Civilization V
    d. The Dude

Lab Exercises

■ Lab 1

Using Windows 7 Performance Monitoring Software

The purpose of this lab is to familiarize students with performance monitoring software. When the student has finished this lab, he or she will know how to use performance monitoring software in general and Windows Performance Monitor specifically.

MATERIALS

- A computer running Windows 7
- Paper
- Pen or pencil

THE LAB

Open the Windows 7 Performance Monitor

1. Click on the Windows 7 **Control Panel**. (This is found under the Start Menu and over to the right.)

2. When the Control Panel comes up it may be in one of two configurations. It may be in Category view or Icon view. By default, it will be in Category view. Go ahead and put Control Panel into Large Icon view since that is what we will use from now on. Lesson 10 Lab 1 explains how to do this.

3. Double-click on the icon labeled **Performance Information and Tools**. When the dialog box shown in Figure 11-8 comes up, it shows something called the *Windows Experience Index*.

Figure 11-8

Performance Information and Tools dialog box

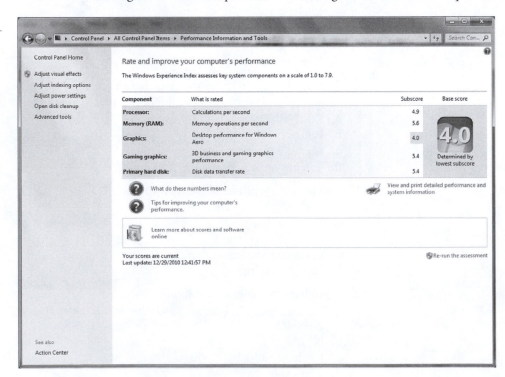

You can score a Windows Experience Index score anywhere between 1.0 to 7.9

Write down the Windows Experience Index Score for the computer you are using.

4. On the left side of the screen shown in Figure 11-8, there is a list of additional options. Click on the **Advanced Tools** option (last on the list). When you do so, the Performance issues dialog box (shown in Figure 11-9) opens.

Figure 11-9

Performance issues dialog box

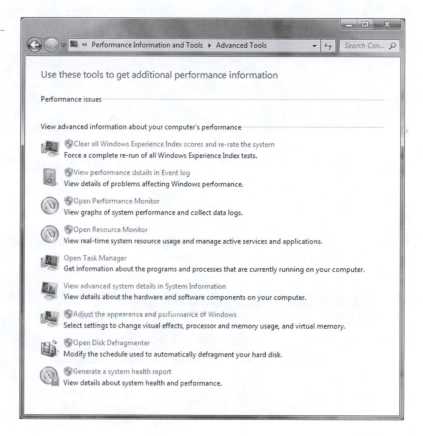

List all the options you see in displayed in this dialog box.

5. Click on the **Open Performance Monitor** option. When you do, The Performance Monitor utility screen shown in Figure 11-10 opens.

Figure 11-10

Windows 7 Performance
Monitor utility

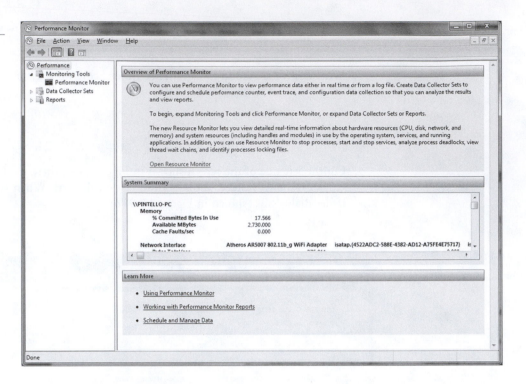

List the options shown in the left panel of the Performance Monitor Screen.

6. Click on the option in the left panel labeled **Performance Monitor**. You should see a dialog box like the one in Figure 11-11.

Figure 11-11

Windows 7 Performance
Monitor actual tool

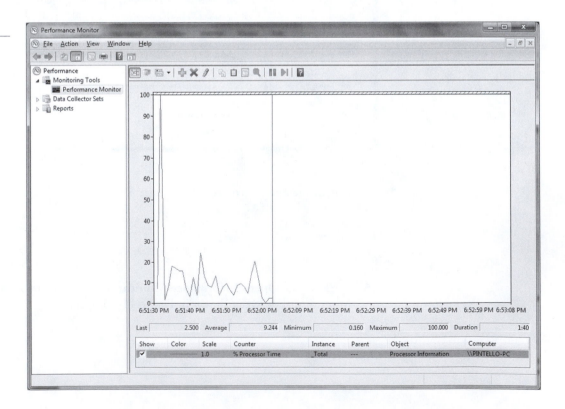

7. The tool that came up in the main right panel when you clicked on this is the actual Performance Monitor Tool. Write down the name of the Counter or Counters that came up by default in this screen. This information is on the bottom of the screen where the legend for the graph is located.

8. Across the top of the Performance Monitor you will see a set of icons that look like those in Figure 11-12. This is the Performance Monitor toolbar. Click on the plus sign.

Figure 11-12

Performance Monitor toolbar

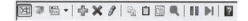

9. Clicking on the plus sign brings up a dialog box similar to the one shown in Figure 11-13.

Figure 11-13

Adding or Removing Counters dialog box

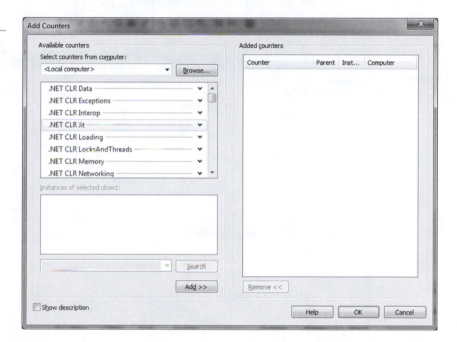

This dialog box allows you to add or remove counters from the graph seen in the main portion of the screen.

10. Each entry in this dialog box is a category for counters related to the title of the category. If you click on the down arrow to the right of the category name, you will see a list of possible counters under that category. If you scroll down, more categories appear. As you can see, there are a number of potential counters to examine.

11. Place a **checkmark** in the *Counter description* check box.

TAKE NOTE*

If you are not sure what a counter does, click on the "Show description" check box in the lower left corner and a "Description" window-pane will open. When you click on a counter, a brief description of the counter will show in the Description window-pane. Some descriptions are better and more detailed than others.

12. Choose three counters under three different Counter Categories and write down what you see in the *Description* pane in the space provided. Be sure to include the name of the Counter.

Counter 1:

Counter 2:

Counter 3:

13. To add a counter to the graph, click the counter you wish to add and then click on the **Add** button on the bottom left center of the Add Counters dialog box. When you do this, you will get a screen that looks like Figure 11-14.

Figure 11-14

Add counters to Performance Monitor

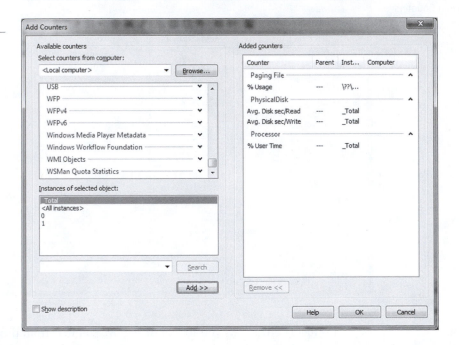

14. Click the **OK** button on the bottom right of the *Add Counters* dialog box. How did the graph on the Performance Monitor Tool screen change?

Why do you think that is?

15. The Windows 7 Professional version of Windows Performance Monitor does not allow you to create a baseline. However the Servers 2008 version does. All you can do with the Windows 7 version of Performance Monitor is save a subset of Counters and make it your default setting or to make customized Counter Sets.

■ **Lab 2**

Using Windows Event Viewer

The purpose of this lab is to make the student familiar with Event Viewer. This lab will help the student learn what Event Viewer is. This lab will also help the student learn what types of information can be found using Event Viewer.

MATERIALS
- A computer running Windows 7
- Paper
- Pen or pencil

THE LAB

Open Windows 7 Event Viewer

1. Go to **Control Panel** in Large Icon view.
2. Double-click the **Administrative Tools** icon. A dialog box similar to the one shown in Figure 11-15 opens.

Figure 11-15

Administrative Tools dialog box

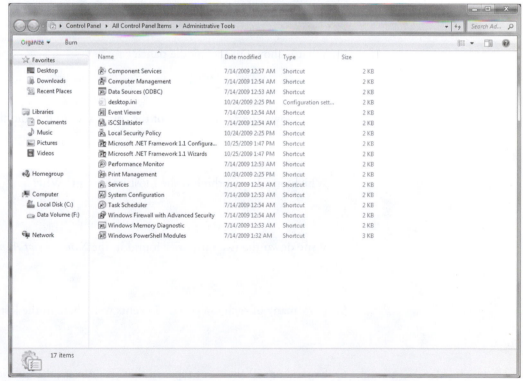

Write down five of the applets that can be found in this dialog box.

3. Double-click on the applet labeled **Event Viewer.** It should be the fourth or fifth applet down the list. When you open the Event Viewer, you should see an application similar to the one shown in Figure 11-16.

Figure 11-16

Event Viewer opening screen

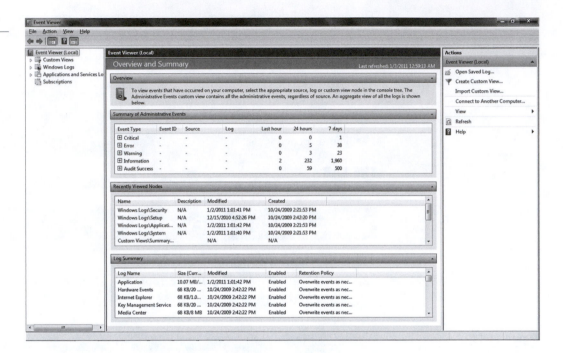

What is shown in the middle panel?

Write down the name of each of the four panes in the middle panel.

Which one do you think is the most important? Why?

4. Write down the five categories found in the *Summary of Administrative Events* pane.

5. How many of each categories of events were there in the last seven days? Write it down.

6. Expand one of the event types so that you can see the individual events recorded.

7. Double-click one of the events. What comes up?

8. Is this useful information? Why or why not?

9. Click the back arrow button in the upper left corner of the Event Viewer window to get back to the last location.

10. Double-click the **Windows Logs folder** in the left panel. These are the Event Viewer Logs discussed in Lesson 11. Write down the names of the different logs listed there.

11. Double-click the **System Log**. When you do, you will see a screen similar to the one shown in Figure 11-17.

Figure 11-17

System Log in Event Viewer detail screen

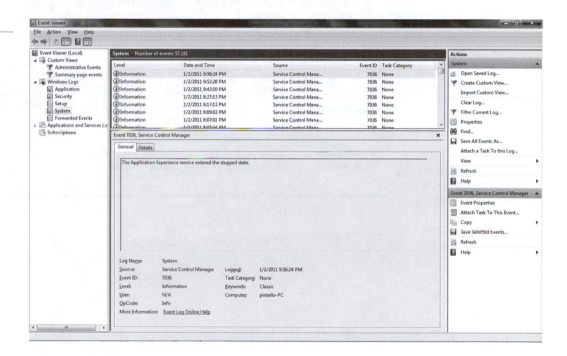

12. There are three types of messages that can be displayed in the System Log. Figure 11-18 shows what an *Informational Message* looks like.

Figure 11-18

Informational Message in Event Viewer

ⓘ Information   1/2/2011 9:43:10 PM   Service Control Manager   7036   None

13. Notice the "i" symbol inside a circle to the left of the message. That symbol is used to designate that a Log Entry is informational in nature. This type of log entry gives you information about what is going on with the operating system but does not contain any information that needs to be acted on. The pane below the log entries contains more details about the message.

Figure 11-19 shows what a *Critical Message* looks like.

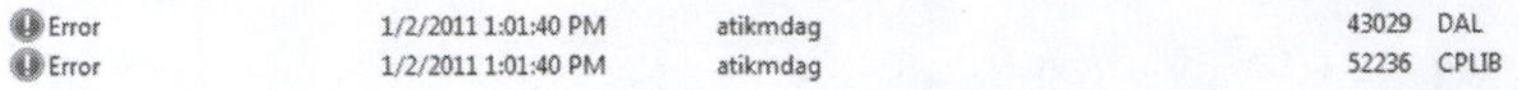

Figure 11-19

Critical Message in Event
Viewer

| Error | 1/2/2011 1:01:40 PM | atikmdag | 43029 DAL |
| Error | 1/2/2011 1:01:40 PM | atikmdag | 52236 CPLIB |

14. Again notice the symbol to the left of the message. The exclamation mark inside a circle is the standard symbol to designate a critical error. This error message describes a real problem with the operating systems and needs to be acted on. When something does not work on a computer, going to the Event Log and reading the Critical Errors can help determine the nature of a the problem and give you good clues about how to resolve the problem.

Figure 11-20 shows what a *Warning Message* looks like.

Figure 11-20

Warning Message in Event
Viewer

| Warning | 1/2/2011 1:23:56 AM | WLAN-AutoConfig | 4001 None |

15. The exclamation point inside a triangle is the designated symbol for a warning message. Log entries of this type report any anomalies experienced by the operating system that do not have a direct impact on whether the operating system is working correctly or not. Messages of this type can be very useful for spotting potential problems that may come up down the road.

TAKE NOTE *

Both the Applications Event Log and the Setup Event Log use the same symbols as the System Event Log. However the Security Event Log uses two different symbols. Figure 11-21 shows both the Audit Success (key) icon and the Audit Failure (lock) icon.

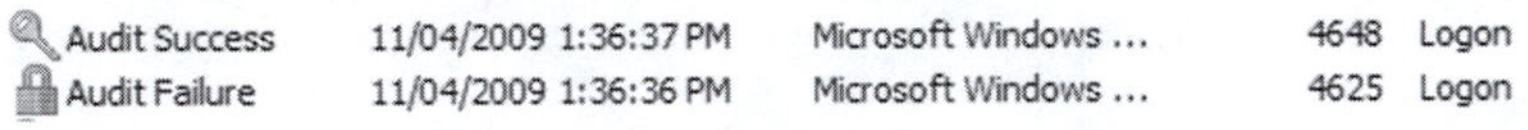

Figure 11-21

Audit Success and Failure
Messages in Event Viewer

| Audit Success | 11/04/2009 1:36:37 PM | Microsoft Windows ... | 4648 Logon |
| Audit Failure | 11/04/2009 1:36:36 PM | Microsoft Windows ... | 4625 Logon |

Network Troubleshooting

EXAM OBJECTIVE MATRIX

TECHNOLOGY SKILL COVERED	EXAM OBJECTIVE	EXAM OBJECTIVE NUMBER
One Size Does *Not* Fit All		

Stages of the Troubleshooting Process	**Given a scenario, implement the following network troubleshooting methodology:**
	• Identify the problem:
	  • Information gathering
	  • Identify symptoms
	  • Question users
	  • Determine if anything has changed
	• Establish a theory of probable cause
	  • Question the obvious
	• Test the theory to determine cause:
	  • Once theory is confirmed determine next steps to resolve problem.
	  • If theory is not confirmed, re-establish new theory or escalate.
	• Establish a plan of action to resolve the problem and identify potential effects
	• Implement the solution or escalate as necessary
	• Verify full system functionality and if applicable implement preventative measures
	• Document findings, actions and outcomes
		1.8

Network Tools and What They Are Used For	**Given a scenario, use appropriate hardware tools to troubleshoot connectivity issues.** • Cable tester • Cable certifier • Crimper • Butt set • Toner probe • Punch down tool • Protocol analyzer • TDR • OTDR • Multimeter • Environmental monitor	4.2

	Given a scenario, use appropriate software tools to troubleshoot connectivity issues. • Protocol analyzer • Throughput testers • Connectivity software • Ping • Tracert/traceroute • Dig • Ipconfig/ifconfig • Nslookup • Arp • Nbstat • Netstat • Route	4.3
Troubleshooting Actions	Given a scenario, troubleshoot common router and switch problems. • Bad cables/improper cable types • Mismatched MTU/MUT black hole • Power failure • Bad modules (SFPs, GBICs)	2.5
	Given a scenario, use appropriate hardware tools to troubleshoot connectivity issues. • Loop back plug	4.2

Common Connectivity Issues	Given a scenario, install and configure routers and switches.
	• Interface configurations
	  • Full duplex
	  • Half duplex
	  • Port speeds
	  • IP addressing
		2.1

	Given a scenario, troubleshoot common wireless problems. • Interference • Signal strength • Configurations • Incompatibilities • Incorrect channel • Latency • Encryption type • Bounce • SSID mismatch • Incorrect switch placement	2.4
	Given a scenario, troubleshoot common router and switch problems. • Switching loop • Bad cables/improper cable types • Port configuration • VLAN assignment • Bad/missing routes	2.5

- Wrong subnet mask
- Wrong gateway
- Duplicate IP address
- Wrong DNS

Given a scenario, troubleshoot common physical connectivity problems.

- Cable problems:
  - Bad connectors
  - Bad wiring
  - Open short
  - Split cables
  - DB loss
  - TXRX reversed
  - Cable placement
  - EMI/Interference
  - Distance
  - Cross-talk

3.6

KEY TERMS

arp	impedance	route
ARP ping	interference	short
arp table	ipconfig	snips
bounce	loopback testing	standards mismatch
butt set	multimeter	switch loop
cable tester	my traceroute (MTR)	temperature monitor
command-line interface (CLI)	nbtstat	test environment
crosstalk	netstat	Time-Domain Reflectometer (TDR)
Domain Information Groper (dig)	Nslookup	toner probe
environmental interference	Optical Time-Domain Reflectometer (OTDR)	trace route testing
ESSID mismatch	ping	traceroute
hostname	ping testing	tracert
ifconfig	punch down tool	voltage event recorder

John Jones works at Wigardium Widgets LLC as a network administrator. The network he is responsible for is beginning to drop packets and freeze up at unexpected times. John does not know what is causing all these problems. What steps does John need to take in order to properly troubleshoot his network?

■ One Size Does *Not* Fit All

↓ THE BOTTOM LINE

We will start Lesson 12 by discussing why there is not one set of solutions that solves all networking and computer problems.

There is a general misconception out there that if you know how to fix one computer or one network you know how to fix them all. That is not actually true. One comment heard from numerous individuals in the computer industry is that many new hires do not know how to troubleshoot computers or networks. This may be because many of the certifications available to Information Technology Professionals revolve around specific brands of technology and not how the technology works in general. So, people who have passed those certification exams know how one specific brand or device works but do not know anything about the larger picture of how the technology works and why, which results in individuals who do not know how to resolve problems that were not covered in their certification classes and exams.

Troubleshooting is as much a matter of knowledge as it is intuition and experience. To do it well, you need to have knowledge, intuition, *and* experience. While the first can come from studying and taking tests, the last two can only come from a great deal of hands on troubleshooting over a long period of time. There is why people who have more experience are paid more.

Part of the point of this book has been to give you an idea about how networking technologies work in general while also preparing you to pass the CompTIA Network+ exam. Fortunately, CompTIA exams in general are not brand specific and so allow quite a bit of leeway when it comes to explaining how networking technologies work in general. This is an attempt to get you away from simply learning facts and to start understanding what you are learning.

There are so many variables involved in computers and networks that one size does *not* fit all when it comes to troubleshooting. Two computers with the exactly the same problem symptoms may require two totally different solutions to resolve. It is entirely possible to have exactly the same equipment with exactly the same software installed with exactly the same problem symptoms to require totally different solutions to resolve. To illustrate this, when I was working in corporate America, there was a time when I was responsible for supporting the computers and networks at three different call centers. Every time there was a problem, I had to stop and think about which call center I was in before I went to resolve the problem. The reason I had to do this was because even though the symptoms and equipment were the same, the solution varied based on which call center I was in. If you talk to individuals in the industry who have had to support computers and networks in multiple locations or even different buildings in the same location, they will tell you they have experienced the same thing. This goes against what you would expect, but it is nonetheless the reality.

By bringing this up here I hope to help you understand why there is no three-step, 12-step, or whatever process that you can use to resolve every computer or network problem you ever come across. If things were that simple, there would not be much of a need for people with expertise in maintaining and supporting networks.

Have you ever tried to use a troubleshooting guide to resolve a computer problem, perhaps like the one that is built into Microsoft Windows? If so, how successful was following that guide at resolving your problem? If you have tried it multiple times, how often was it successful? Your answer to these questions is probably something like "Following the guide did not help me resolve the problem or it only helped me resolve the problem some of the time."

Fortunately there is a solution. Instead of trying to learn a magic process (something that does not exist) that will always resolve the problem, you need to learn how computers and networks work. Once you understand that, when you see a network problem that needs troubleshooting, you can see how the whole system works and get an idea of where the real problem may be. It is not always in the most obvious place. Once you have narrowed down where the problem is, you can start eliminating things that you know are not the problem. This will make the scope of the problem even smaller. Eventually you will get to where the problem really is and you can then resolve it. It other words, learn the reasons why and how things work and it becomes much easier to figure out why they are not working when they should.

Another upside to the approach just described is that while the how of networking and computers changes pretty much every time a new version comes out, the why does not change. Even when new technologies are developed, the why is still the same, it is just that the how has gotten better, faster, or more efficient.

There is some other good news in all of this. Generally speaking, once you have a solution to a specific set of symptoms in a given location, whenever you see those same symptoms in another computer or device in that same location, the solution will likely remain the same. The key words here are "the same location." When you leave that location, you will likely have to develop a totally different solution to the same set of symptoms. This is another one of these realities that does not match up with expectations, but it is still real. Again, any information technology professionals who have worked in multiple locations at the same time will verify that this is how it is.

One other piece of good news is that problems tend to cluster in locations. Once you get a handle on the set of problems common to a specific location, most of the problems you experience there will fit into that set. It seems that every location has 20 to 40 problems that are common to that location. Once you have a handle on the 20 to 40 most common problems in a given location, a significant percentage of the all the problems in a location will come from those 20 to 40 common areas. However be warned, there will always be random problems that pop up from time to time that you have never seen before or have only seen once in a very great while. When that happens, you still have to use the troubleshooting skills mentioned earlier to find the right solution. Also, once in a while a standard solution to a standard set of symptoms does not work. Again, when that happens, you will have to work out a new solution at least for that instance of the problem. The next section goes into more detail about how to apply standard troubleshooting processes.

■ Stages of the Troubleshooting Process

↓ **THE BOTTOM LINE**

In this portion of Lesson 12, we discuss the various stages you should follow in order to effectively troubleshoot a network problem. The stages discussed in this section of Lesson 12 apply to all types of troubleshooting, not just network troubleshooting.

As mentioned before, troubleshooting is not just memorizing some steps that will allow you to resolve all the problems you may encounter in a computer or on a network. Instead, troubleshooting is a process that you have to follow to get down to where the problem is and then work to resolve. While this process does have steps, the steps are very general and designed to lead you to possible solutions rather than give you the answer. To follow these steps, you really need to understand how computers or networks function before they become helpful. The following sections take you through the steps of the troubleshooting process and explain what each is supposed to help you accomplish.

CERTIFICATION READY
What are the nine stages of the troubleshooting process?
1.8

Information Gathering—Identify the Systems and the Problems

CERTIFICATION READY
What do you do during the information gathering stage of the troubleshooting process?
1.8

The first step in any troubleshooting process is to gather information about what is not working. This process can involve the original problem report as well as discussions with the person who initially reported the problem. These first two components of information gathering are very important because they help you narrow down where the problem may be. These two steps will also help narrow things down to the actual system or systems that are having the problem.

Once you have read the original trouble ticket and talked to the individual making the report, you then need to examine the actual system that is having the problem. If possible, you should also get the person who reported the problem to run through what they did when they noticed the problem. Sometimes the problem is as simple as the end user making a mistake. When that is the case, all you have to do is correct what the end user did wrong by showing them the correct way to do things. Other times, there is a genuine problem with the system. Examining the system and asking the end user to show you what happened are very important steps in the process.

One thing you need to be very conscious of when you are talking to end users who have reported problems is how you interact with them. You are there to help the end users better accomplish their jobs. In many ways, they are your customers and you need to treat them accordingly. Many technicians have a problem doing this and seem to have the view that end users are stupid and that things would be so much better if they did not have to deal with end users. Well the bottom line is that if there were no end users, technicians would have no jobs. Those end users guarantee that you the technician actually have a job, so you should treat them accordingly.

Identify the Affected Areas of the Network

CERTIFICATION READY
How do you identify affected areas of the network?
1.8

When troubleshooting a network, if a problem shows up in one area remember that it is usually not actually limited to that one area. More often than not, the problem is larger than the area where the problem was initially reported; it is simply that there has to be one person who notices the problem first and reports it. When a network problem is reported, it is your job as the technician to verify that the problem is either limited to the area reporting it, or to identify other areas that are also impacted. This last part is somewhat simplified because even if one person notices a problem first, a problem that affects more than one area of the network ends up getting reported by multiple people. This is one of the technician's best tools for identifying the areas affected by the network problem. The technician simply has to be able to see how different reported problems are connected and act accordingly.

Determine Whether Anything Has Changed

CERTIFICATION READY
How do you go about determining if anything has changed? Why is it important to do this?
1.8

One of the first questions you should ask when a problem is reported is "Has anything changed?" This question may be simple to answer when you personally made a change or it could be more complicated. Just because a technician has not changed anything locally on a computer or on the network does not mean that nothing was changed. Many times end users install software or patches and updates without letting anybody know they have done so. Alternatively, a different technician in your department may have made a network change that you did not know about. Possibly somebody in a different department such as the WAN engineers may have made changes you do not know about. Whatever the case, when a problem is reported, one of the first things you need to determine is whether anything has changed.

Changes made on the network or on the local computer can be the cause of the problem. It is not very common for a network or a computer that has worked without any problems for a long period of time to simply stop working. This does happen, but usually there is something that causes the abrupt change in reliability of the network or computer in question. Many times that abrupt change can be traced back to some change that someone made. Finding out what changes were made, if any, will very often lead directly to the cause of the problem.

There are several things you can do to determine the answer to the question "What has changed?" One thing you can do is talk to the end user who first reported the problem. It is possible he or she installed some software or patch that may have caused the problem. Sometimes the end user may have deleted or removed some program or hardware component he or she did not think was important, when in reality it was. Possibly the end user copied a file onto the computer from a USB or other external media that had a virus or spyware on it. There are many things an end user could have done that changed the system and resulted in the reported problem.

Keep in mind that it may not have been the end user who changed something that caused the problem. Maybe technicians somewhere made a change to the network that caused the problem. They may have installed a patch to the server that was not fully tested. Maybe they added a piece of equipment to the network that is interfering with the system having the problem. Possibly a router, switch, or server configuration was changed that caused a section of the network to lose connectivity to all or part of the rest of the network. There are many things that could have changed that the end user had nothing to do with; because of this, do not assume that the end user is the cause of the problem.

There are many things you can do to determine if part of the network was changed by somebody other than the end user. One of the first things you can do is talk to any other technicians with whom you may work. They may have done something or know of something someone else did that you do not know about. You can also go and talk to technicians in other departments to determine if something they may have done caused the problem. You can also go back and look at your e-mail to see if any maintenance windows had occurred recently that may have changed something that caused or resulted in the problem you are trying to resolve. You can also go into the switch room where all the network hardware is and see if there is anything in there that is obviously different. Maybe something was disconnected either accidentally or because it had to be disconnected for a maintenance window but was not reconnected. Maybe a power switch is off that should not be. Anything like these things mentioned and others can be the cause of the problem. I have seen situations where each one of the items just mentioned were the cause of a problem reported somewhere else.

Establish the Most Probable Cause

Once you have received a problem report, gathered additional information about the problem, and investigated any network or system changes, the next step is to determine what the most probable cause of the problem may be. After you have looked at all the information you have available, you can then analyze it to spot what you consider the most likely cause of the problem. This most probable cause becomes the starting point of your solution.

Determine if Escalation Is Necessary

CERTIFICATION READY
When is escalation necessary? What factors help determine this?
1.8

Before you begin to create an action plan to resolve what you believe the problem may be, you need to first determine if the problem needs to be escalated. There are several reasons why you may want to escalate a problem. One reason is that you have come to believe that the problem actually exists in a portion of the network you do not have access to. If you do not have access to something, you cannot fix it. In that situation, you need to pass the problem on to someone who does have access to where you think the problem is. You also need to give that person the details of the problem that leads you to believe they are the better person to resolve the issue.

Another reason to escalate a problem is if you do not believe you have the skills and/or know-how to fix the problem. This is often a very hard decision to make because most technicians like to think they can fix anything. It takes a certain amount of character to realize you do not know what is needed to resolve a problem. If you find yourself in this situation, you can escalate the problem and then use it as a learning opportunity. You can do this by asking the person who has the ability to fix the problem to teach you what you need to know so that you can fix the problem next time. If you ask this nicely, most people are more than glad to "take you under their wing" so to speak and teach you what you need to know.

A final reason to escalate a problem is if you have tried a number of solutions and are simply not able to resolve the issue. Just because you cannot fix a problem does not mean you are stupid or cannot do the job. Many times, you have looked at the problem too long and have fixed certain ideas in your mind concerning it and are not able to shift those perceptions. In this case, it may only take a fresh pair of eyes to see an obvious solution that you missed.

Admitting that a problem has stumped you also takes a certain level of character. Just as we do not like to admit we do not know something, we also do not like to admit when something has simply stumped us. While it may be good for your ego to refuse to admit you're stumped, it is better for the organization you work for to do so. Keep in mind that management watches things like this. If management sees that you are willing to ask for help when you need it, they are much more likely to promote you when the time comes. Alternatively, they will be more inclined to keep someone on who knows when to ask for help than they would someone who tries to go it alone if they have to start letting people go.

All that said, be sure that you don't always ask for help every time you have a problem, at least not without trying to fix it yourself first. If you are always asking for help, it begins to appear as if you do not know what you are doing and this may work against you. On the other hand, if you do have to ask for help with every problem that comes along, there is a chance that you really do not know what you are doing. If this is the case, it is entirely possible that you have taken on a job that you are not yet ready to do. If you find yourself in this situation, you need to get yourself some additional training at you own expense before the organization you work for decides to let you go and hire someone who *does* know what they are doing.

If you are not able to escalate the problem or ask somebody else to take a look at it, the next best thing you can do is go do something else that is unrelated to the problem for a while and come back to it later. Many times when you do this, you see things that you simply did not see previously. In this case, the fresh pair of eyes on the problem just happens to be yours. One thing you should never do is let a problem get to the point where you are visibly frustrated or angry. If you feel yourself getting to that point, immediately take a break and regroup.

Create an Action Plan and Solution

CERTIFICATION READY
What is an action plan? How do you go about developing one?
1.8

Escalation questions aside, once you have come up with what you think is the most probable cause of the problem, you need to create an action plan, which is a plan you create to resolve the problem you have identified. The action plan consist of the steps you think you need to take to resolve the problem. Depending on the nature of the problem you are facing, the action plan you develop can be simple and straightforward or very complex. Once you have an action plan, if it is sufficiently complex, you will want to have someone else look at it and to also help you implement it.

Depending on the nature of the problem and where in the network the problem is located, some action plans can be implemented right away. Problems with specific workstations are usually situations when an action plan can be implemented immediately. However, if you determine that the most probable cause is something more critical like a switch, router, server, or similar device, it may become necessary to schedule a maintenance window to resolve the problem. Maintenance windows are scheduled when it is necessary to bring down a critical piece of equipment that the rest of the network needs to function properly. Also if an action plan calls for many devices such as workstations to be affected or brought down, that too may require a maintenance window.

Generally speaking, if you determine that a specific device, even a critical device, that is not working is the problem, then very seldom is a maintenance window required to resolve the issue. In this situation, the problem is a device that is not working at all. When this happens, replacing or switching out the device does not impact the rest of the network. However, when you go to bring the device back up, there could be some disruption of the network. Then a maintenance window is needed.

IDENTIFY POTENTIAL EFFECTS

Never implement an action plan without first identifying any potential effects the action plan can have on the network. This is very important because even small changes can have large effects elsewhere in the network. Another reason you will want to identify potential effects of an action plan is so that you can identify other equipment and users that will be affected by implementing that plan. Once you have done this, you need to notify all users affected by the proposed action plan so that they will know what to affect.

Identifying potential effects of the action plan also helps you decide whether a maintenance window is needed to implement the plan. If the potential effects of a proposed action plan are sufficiently far reaching or affect a sufficient number of end users, it is a good idea to call or schedule a maintenance window just to be safe.

Identifying potential effects of an action plan also allows you to identify things that could potentially go wrong. By identifying those problems ahead of time, you can develop contingency plans to use if those problems develop. Identifying potential effects also helps you identify a problem if it occurs quickly because if you have thought of the possibility of a problem, when you see something that looks like it you will know what it is.

A final reason you will want to identify potential effects ahead of time is so that you can develop a rollback plan. A rollback plan should be developed so that you may put the system back to its original state if something goes really wrong. It is better to fall back to a network configuration that at least partially works, than to find yourself in a situation where the proposed solution actually makes things worse. If you see that your solution is making the problem worse rather than fixing it, then do not press forward with the solution. Instead, roll back the network to its original state and then go back to the drawing board to see why your action plan did not resolve the problem.

There are a lot of reasons that an action plan may not work. You may have incorrectly identified the problem or your solution may be incorrect. It could also mean that you correctly identified the problem, but that the problem you solved actually exposed another or a worse problem that now has to be resolved. In this situation, you will have to have two action plans: one that solves the original problem and another action plan to resolve the new problem.

A final reason an action plan may not work is because you resolved the original problem, but you missed an adverse potential effect when you were trying to identify all the potential effects of your action plan. This is quite often the case. Networks and computers are very complex systems involving many variables. With so many variables being affected by any action plan you come up with, eventually you are going to miss an important one. When this happens, implement your rollback plan and go back to the drawing board. Even large companies in the Information Technology Industry run into this problem once in a while. Why do you think you occasionally come across a software patch that ends up causing more problems than it fixes?

Implement and Test the Solution

CERTIFICATION READY
Why is it important to test a solution before you implement it?
1.8

Once you have developed an action plan and identified potential effects you need to implement it. However, if the plan is a complex one or involves major changes to equipment, then it would probably be best to set up a test environment first. A *test environment* can be a special lab scenario that you set up to resemble the real environment, or it can be a small portion of the network to be changed. Either way, running the action plan in a test environment can help you identify any unintended results of the action plan before it has been implemented.

Once the initial testing of the plan has been completed, you can implement the plan, which simply means going forward with the action plan as you laid it out. If the action plan is small or only affects a small number of computers, it is not always necessary to test it before implementing it.

Identify the Results and Effects of the Solution

Once the plan is implemented, you should not simply assume that everything is set. Instead you should test the solution as best you can and watch it a while to see if any unexpected problems arise from the solution. This is what it means to identify the results and effects of the solution.

In effect you test the action plan twice— once before implementing it and then again after you have implemented it. You should always test an implemented action plan after implementing it to verify that it truly has resolved the problem it was initially created to resolve and to ensure that no unintended effects resulted from the solution or action plan you implemented.

Document the Solution and the Entire Process

CERTIFICATION READY
Why is it important to document the entire solution process?
1.8

As with all areas of networking, you should have documentation of the entire process you went through once you have resolved a problem. There are several reasons for this documentation. One, it gives you a record of everything you did and will serve as a guide should the problem come up again. Documenting the entire process also lets you keep a record of things that did not work as well as things that did. By knowing the effects of a wrong solution, if similar effects show up later, you have a place to start. Finally, documenting the entire process provides a reference place for any future technicians who may take over your job after you are promoted or choose to work elsewhere. Also, if anyone questions what you did perhaps in an attempt to discredit you in some way, you can always go back and show them the documentation and thereby blunt their criticism of you.

A final reason, and perhaps the best reason, to document the entire troubleshooting process is because you can go back and analyze the whole thing once the problem is resolved. When you go back and analyze the cause and the solution of a specific problem, you can sometimes see a way to prevent the same problem from happening again. Implementing the extra solution you come up with will usually require a new action plan, testing, implementation, and so on, but when it is all done, you will end up with a more robust, fault tolerant network.

DOCUMENTING PROBLEM REPORTING

The first step in any troubleshooting process is reporting the process. This is the start of the documentation trail you need to create for every problem you resolve on the network. A well-designed reporting form can also be a very strong asset when you begin to resolve the problem.

There are several things that should be included on the report form whether it's paper or online. One, it should have a place for the name of the person reporting the problem so that you can find them when you need to gather more information.

Second, there should be a place for the name and location of the problem device being reported. In order for the person to provide this information, the device should be clearly labeled with both its name and its location and end users should be trained to give that information. This is especially important if you have a large number of workstations and the problem being reported is related to one of them.

Next, the form should have a large area for the end user reporting the problem to write out a description of what the problem is. If the end user has more room to detail a description of the problem, they will often give more details than if they have a very limited area to describe the problem. The more details you have about the problem, the easier it becomes to diagnose the problem.

The form should also have a clear tracking number. This is especially important if escalation becomes necessary because it will make things easier when it comes to tracking how the problem is being handled and by whom.

Another thing the form should have is a place for the technician responding to the problem to put his or her name or identification number. This is very important if the problem has to be revisited at some later date. If you have a way to identify the technician who was originally responsible for resolving the problem, if any questions about the system come up later, you will know who to talk to. Additionally, if the problem should come back or another problem arises on the same system, you will be able to talk to the person who originally resolved the issue. This allows you to find out if there is anything that you need to know about the system in question before you have to tackle it yourself.

Finally there should be plenty of room on the form for the technician working to resolve the problem to take notes. This makes it much easier to reconstruct what happened after the problem has been resolved in order to make a more detailed after-action report should such a report be necessary. This can also serve as a reference point if the problem is escalated to other technicians. They will be able to read the notes of previous technicians to find out what they did to resolve the problem and not have to repeat those actions themselves. Also knowing what has not worked, can help point the escalating technician in a direction the previous technician had not thought about. Notes from previous technicians can also help the escalating technician form an action plan that takes previous actions into account.

DOCUMENTING THE TROUBLESHOOTING PROCESS

Documenting the troubleshooting process simply refers to the practice of recording all the major steps a technician went through to resolve a problem. This includes both the successful actions as well as those actions that were not successful. By recording failed actions as well as successful ones, a lot can be learned about how to resolve an issue, not the least of which being what *not* to try next time.

Aside from the actual steps a technician took, good documentation should also include why the tech tried different things. This gives a window into the thought processes that went on in resolving the problem. By knowing the thought processes going on, a more experienced technician can later look them over and help the employee who resolved the problem refine their skills. Also being able to see the thought process behind different actions can also help you or someone going over the work behind you determine if you are on the right track to resolving the issue if the issue has to be escalated.

DOCUMENTING THE SOLUTION

Once a solution to the problem has been found, the solution should be documented so that should the same problem arise again, a working solution will already be on record. It is also a good idea to record why a solution worked. This can give insights into resolving other related or unrelated problems later.

Bringing the Steps of the Troubleshooting Process Together

CERTIFICATION READY
How would you go about bringing the steps of the troubleshooting process together in a specific situation or scenario?
1.8

Following is a scenario of how the various steps of the troubleshooting process can be brought together. An end user suddenly loses connectivity to the corporate network, so she reports the problem to tech support. Tech support assigns you to resolve the issue.

The first thing you need to do is talk to the individual reporting the problem. Ask her to tell you what happened in her own words. She tells you she was looking up data on an approved website when suddenly she lost connectivity to the network. While talking to her, you also try to find out if she installed anything on her computer before the problem happened. She reports to you that she did not. Finally, while there you look around on her computer for any obvious configuration problems. You also decide to check her network setup and notice that it is still set to DHCP like it is supposed to be. You tell her you need to check a couple of things to try and solve the problem and leave to return to your desk.

Back at your desk you try and figure out what happened, and you notice that a few other end users are beginning to report the same problem. Looking at all the computers reporting problems you notice that they are all on the same segment of the network. Because everything is happening on the same network segment, you go talk to the WAN engineer to see if anything had changed at the switch. He tells you that nothing had been changed and all the switches are working fine. You leave the WAN engineer feeling more perplexed than ever.

When you get back to your desk you notice that even more computers on that affected segment have lost connectivity. Going to several of the people reporting problems you discover that all of them are configured correctly and are using DHCP to get their network addresses as they should. This causes you to wonder if the DHCP server is working properly. To find out, you go to several of the affected end users and use the command line tool ipconfig to see what IP addresses they are using. When you do this, you notice that all the computers are reporting an IP address of 169.254.X.X. You remember from your Network+ class that IP addresses that start with 169.254 are IP address that have been automatically assigned by Microsoft Windows when DHCP or a static addressing is not available. This leads you to conclude that the most probable cause of the lost connectivity is that the DHCP server that is responsible for the affected network segment is completely down.

Depending on where you work, at this point you would most likely escalate the problem up to the network administration staff and let them resolve the issue. However, we will assume for this scenario that you are responsible for both network support and network administration. Is should be noted that in smaller networks and companies, there is a good chance that the same person would be responsible for both at a given site.

You go and check the DHCP server and find that it is indeed down. When you look at it hoping it had come unplugged or something simple like that, you find that its operating system has been corrupted. What are you going to do? It is going to take you at least a few hours to reinstall the operating system and reconfigure it to do its job, assuming there is not a hardware problem that caused the operating system to become corrupted in the first place. In the mean time, you have more and more people out on the floor losing their network connectivity, which means they are unable to do their jobs. You need an action plan.

After thinking about it, you realize that if you give everybody in the affected segment a static IP address in the proper range, they will be able to get back on the network with no problem and continue to do their jobs. You also realize that there are actually only about 30 computers on the affected segment. You decide to go out on the floor and manually assign static IP addresses to the affected end users. This will buy you time to fix the DHCP server while the end users are still able to do their jobs. This is an example where a seemingly small problem ends up leading you to an even larger one. Once you have implemented your action plan to bring all the affected end users back up on the network, you verify that everyone is really able to get to the network. Once you have verified that everyone is on the network you go to see what is wrong with the DHCP server.

Once you have gotten a good look at the DHCP server, you find out that the hard drive is bad. Fortunately you have a spare hard drive and are able to replace the bad one with the new one. Now you have to install Windows Server and configure it to be a DHCP server for a specific segment of the network. Once you have done all this, you then test the new DHCP server and verify that everything is working fine. Now you have to shift everybody on the segment back to DHCP. You decide that the best way to do this is in a brief maintenance window that you schedule for an hour before work starts the next day.

When the scheduled maintenance windows arrives, you go in and set all the computers on the affected segment back to DHCP and then test them to see if they are working. Verifying that they are, you go to document the whole troubleshooting process using notes that you made along the way.

Once you have resolved all the problems related to this incident, you decide to go back and review the documentation. Upon doing so, you realize that having only one DHCP server per segment is a weakness in your network. You also realize that the company cannot afford to buy a second server for every segment. This means that the easiest way to fix the problem is not possible. However, after thinking about it for a while you realize that you can double up the various DHCP servers so that they are able to cover two segments—their original segment and one more. You decide that a good redundancy scheme is to set up the VLANs so that each VLAN allows access to the DHCP server for that VLAN and a DHCP server for an adjacent VLAN. With this scheme in place, in the future when one DHCP server goes down, the other one can take up the slack while you fix the failed one. Looks like you are going to have to talk to the WAN engineer again, and schedule a few more maintenance windows. Another action plan is in the works.

■ Network Tools and What They Are Used For

THE BOTTOM LINE

In this section of Lesson 12, we examine various tools that can be used to troubleshoot or repair a network. We first discuss various command-line tools to troubleshoot networks. We then discuss some physical tools that are also used to troubleshoot networks.

When it comes to troubleshooting networks, the more tools you have in your toolkit to work with the better. Many networking tools are actually included in Windows or Linux distributions; although, many people do not even know about them, mainly because they are command-line based tools. We discuss some of these tools first.

Beyond command-line tools, there are also other software tools like Wireshark and Windows Performance Monitor, which we have discussed in previous lessons. Aside from software tools, there are also a number of hardware tools. Hardware tools are physical devices that are used for troubleshooting and fixing networks. A few of these types of network tools are also discussed.

Command-Line Interface Network Tools

CERTIFICATION READY
What are some command-line tools that are available for network troubleshooting?
4.3

Command-line interface (CLI) network tools are some of the least-known and least-utilized tools in a network administrator's or support specialist's toolbox. They are available on every computer and can offer very valuable information when you are trying to troubleshoot a local computer problem or a network problem. One such tool was mentioned in the troubleshooting scenario earlier. That tool was ipconfig. We discuss that particular CLI networking tool a little later in this lesson.

CLI tools are some of the most underutilized networking tools available because they require the person using them to go to a command line to access them. When people hear that a tool is a command-line tool they automatically assume two things. One they assume it is hard to use. Two they assume it is very difficult to understand whatever output the tool gives back. Both assumptions are wrong.

To use a CLI tool, all you usually have to do is type the command into a CLI. This consists of a single word or abbreviation. If you want more precise or detailed information, there are a handful of parameters you can add to the end of the command to expand or refine its output. To find out about a CLI tool's parameters or how it works, type the command followed by a question mark and you can get all the information you ever wanted about the CLI tool in question. The idea that the CLI tool's output is hard to understand is also incorrect. Most CLI tools organize their output so that the results they display are pretty much self-explanatory via labels.

CLI tools are useful because pretty much all operating systems have them built in already, they are usually small programs that do not take a lot of processing power to use, and they are designed to give limited information. This means each CLI tool is designed to report back specific information. The advantage of this is that the data you get back from a CLI tool is not hidden in a large volume of extraneous data. The data you get back is targeted to a very small subset of data, which means that when you get a report from a CLI tool, you do not have to wade through a huge amount of extraneous data just to find what you really need. Instead, you use a specific CLI tool that reports the specific data you want and nothing more. Table 12-1 lists the CLI tools discussed in this section and the platforms on which they are used.

Table 12-1

CLI Tools and their platforms

CLI Tool	Platform
Ipconfig	DOS/Windows
Ifconfig	Linux/UNIX
Ping	DOS/Windows & Linux/UNIX
Traceroute	Linux/UNIX
Tracert	DOS/Windows
My traceroute (MTR)	Linux/UNIX
Pathping	DOS/Windows
Arping	Linux/UNIX
Arp	DOS/Windows & Linux/UNIX
NSlookup	DOS/Windows & Linux/UNIX
Hostname	DOS/Windows & Linux/UNIX
Domain Information Groper (Dig)	Linux/UNIX
Route	DOS/Windows & Linux/UNIX
Nbtstat	DOS/Windows
Netstat	DOS/Windows & Linux/UNIX

IPCONFIG

Ipconfig is a command-line tool that is found in all current versions of Microsoft Windows. The primary use of ipconfig is to display the IP address, subnet mask, and default gateway of each adapter on which the computer is run. Figure 12-1 shows the output of the ipconfig command.

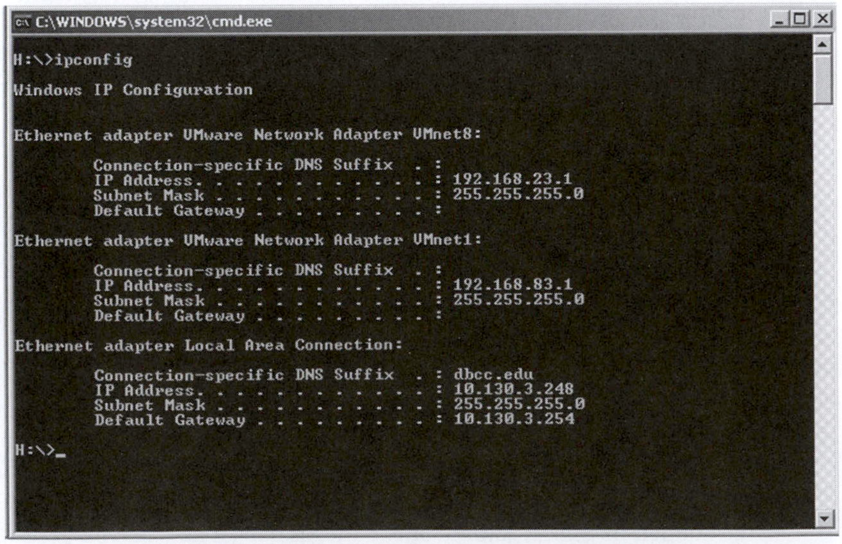

Figure 12-1

Ipconfig command

```
C:\WINDOWS\system32\cmd.exe

H:\>ipconfig

Windows IP Configuration

Ethernet adapter VMware Network Adapter VMnet8:

        Connection-specific DNS Suffix  . :
        IP Address. . . . . . . . . . . . : 192.168.23.1
        Subnet Mask . . . . . . . . . . . : 255.255.255.0
        Default Gateway . . . . . . . . . :

Ethernet adapter VMware Network Adapter VMnet1:

        Connection-specific DNS Suffix  . :
        IP Address. . . . . . . . . . . . : 192.168.83.1
        Subnet Mask . . . . . . . . . . . : 255.255.255.0
        Default Gateway . . . . . . . . . :

Ethernet adapter Local Area Connection:

        Connection-specific DNS Suffix  . : dbcc.edu
        IP Address. . . . . . . . . . . . : 10.130.3.248
        Subnet Mask . . . . . . . . . . . : 255.255.255.0
        Default Gateway . . . . . . . . . : 10.130.3.254

H:\>_
```

In Figure 12-1, you can see that there is one local adapter and a couple of VMware adapters configured on this computer. The local adapter has an IP address of 10.130.3.248, a subnet mask of 255.255.255.0, and a default gateway of 10.130.3.254. While the screenshot shown in Figure 12-1 is from Windows XP, if the same command was issued in Windows Vista or Windows 7, you would also get information about the IPv6 IP address.

Ipconfig also comes with some additional functionality. If you use the command ipconfig /all, you receive more detailed information about the adapters on the computer, including the device's MAC address. Figure 12-2 shows the result when you use the ipconfig /all command.

Figure 12-2

Ipconfig /all command

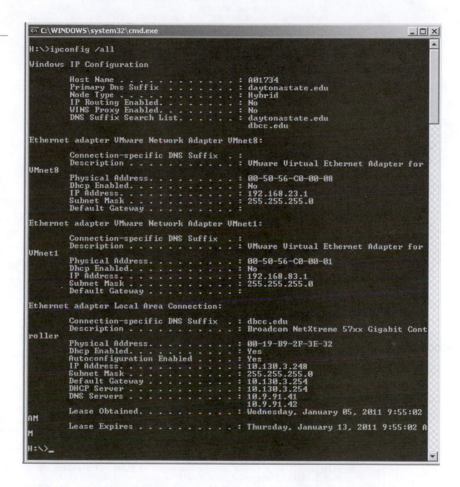

There are several other parameters besides the /all parameter that you can use with ipconfig. Probably the three most common are

- **/?**: Helps you with how to properly use the ipconfig command.
- **/release**: Valid for all Windows-based CLI tools. This parameter allows you to end a DHCP IP lease early.
- **/renew**: Used to manually renew a DHCP IP lease.

There are other parameters available with the ipconfig command: /flushdns, /registerdns, /displaydns, /showclassid, and /setclassid. For additional information about these parameters, or more information about ipconfig, you can use the ipconfig /? command.

IFCONFIG

Ifconfig stands for Interface Configuration and is the Linux/UNIX equivalent to ipconfig. Ifconfig can give you the same information that ipconfig does when used without any parameters. However ifconfig has a lot more parameters than ipconfig does. Figure 12-3 shows the output of the ifconfig command in a Linux/Unix terminal window. You can see that the ifconfig output looks a bit different from ipconfig, but the basic information is still clearly there.

Figure 12-3

Ifconfig command (Linux/UNIX)

```
pintello@pintello-virtual-machine ~ $ ifconfig
eth0      Link encap:Ethernet  HWaddr 00:0c:29:97:da:36
          inet addr:192.168.23.129  Bcast:192.168.23.255  Mask:255.255.255.0
          inet6 addr: fe80::20c:29ff:fe97:da36/64 Scope:Link
          UP BROADCAST RUNNING MULTICAST  MTU:1500  Metric:1
          RX packets:923 errors:0 dropped:0 overruns:0 frame:0
          TX packets:884 errors:0 dropped:0 overruns:0 carrier:0
          collisions:0 txqueuelen:1000
          RX bytes:635910 (635.9 KB)  TX bytes:91371 (91.3 KB)
          Interrupt:19 Base address:0x2000

lo        Link encap:Local Loopback
          inet addr:127.0.0.1  Mask:255.0.0.0
          inet6 addr: ::1/128 Scope:Host
          UP LOOPBACK RUNNING  MTU:16436  Metric:1
          RX packets:52 errors:0 dropped:0 overruns:0 frame:0
          TX packets:52 errors:0 dropped:0 overruns:0 carrier:0
          collisions:0 txqueuelen:0
          RX bytes:4528 (4.5 KB)  TX bytes:4528 (4.5 KB)

pintello@pintello-virtual-machine ~ $ █
```

To learn about command-line commands and tools in DOS/Windows use the /? parameter. To learn about command-line commands and tools in Linux/UNIX use the man command. The man command stands for manual page. To use the manual page, all you have to do is type man followed by the command or CLI tool you want to know about. For example, to learn about the ifconfig command you would type "man ifconfig" at the prompt. Figure 12-4 shows the first page shown when "man ifconfig" is typed at the command prompt.

Figure 12-4

Man ifconfig command (Linux/UNIX)

```
IFCONFIG(8)                  Linux Programmer's Manual                  IFCONFIG(8)

NAME
       ifconfig - configure a network interface

SYNOPSIS
       ifconfig [-v] [-a] [-s] [interface]
       ifconfig [-v] interface [aftype] options | address ...

DESCRIPTION
       Ifconfig is used  to  configure the kernel-resident network interfaces. It is
       used at boot time to set up interfaces as necessary. After that, it is  usually
       only needed when debugging or when system tuning is needed.

       If  no arguments are given, ifconfig displays the status of the currently active
       interfaces.  If a single interface argument is given, it displays the status  of
       the given interface only; if a single -a argument is given, it displays the sta-
       tus of all interfaces, even those that are down.  Otherwise,  it  configures  an
       interface.

Address Families
       If  the  first  argument after the interface name is recognized as the name of a
       supported address family, that address family is used for decoding and  display-
       ing  all  protocol addresses.  Currently supported address families include inet
       (TCP/IP, default), inet6 (IPv6), ax25 (AMPR Packet Radio), ddp (Appletalk  Phase
       2), ipx (Novell IPX) and netrom (AMPR Packet radio).

OPTIONS
       -a      display all interfaces which are currently available, even if down

       -s      display a short list (like netstat -i)

       -v      be more verbose for some error conditions

       interface
               The  name  of the interface. This is usually a driver name followed by a
               unit number, for example eth0 for the first Ethernet interface. If  your
               kernel  supports  alias  interfaces, you can specify them with eth0:0 for
               the first alias of eth0. You can use them to assign a second address.  To
               delete  an  alias  interface use  ifconfig eth0:0 down. Note: for every
               scope (i.e. same net with address/netmask combination)  all  aliases  are
               deleted, if you delete the first (primary).

       up      This  flag causes the interface to be activated.  It is implicitly speci-
               fied if an address is assigned to the interface.
Manual page ifconfig(8) line 1
```

If you do not have a version of Linux available to you, you can get a copy of the Linux Manual pages for all Linux commands at http://linuxmanpages.com/. When you go to this URL, enter the command you want to look up in the "Search for:" box and then hit the <Enter> key or the "Get Man Page" button.

Aside from giving information about the configuration of a network interface, the ifconfig command can also be used to actually configure or manipulate a specific interface on a computer. This gives the ifconfig command a bit larger scope and capability than the ipconfig command. As a general rule, Linux/UNIX CLI commands and tools all have more capacity than the DOS/Windows equivalents.

Both ifconfig and ipconfig are used to determine the configuration of the NICs available on a computer. These tools can also be used to reset DHCP configurations as well.

PING

Ping is a little program that is designed to determine if a specific IP address is reachable on the network. By pinging various IP addresses you can test your network and possibly determine where a loss of connectivity may be occurring. We discuss how to do this testing later in the lesson. Ping is used the same way in both Linux/UNIX and DOS/Windows environments. Figure 12-5 shows what the ping program's output is in the DOS/Windows environment. The screenshot in Figure 12-5 also shows the parameters that can be used with ping. Figure 12-6 shows the ping command in a Linux/UNIX environment.

Figure 12-5

Ping command (DOS/Windows)

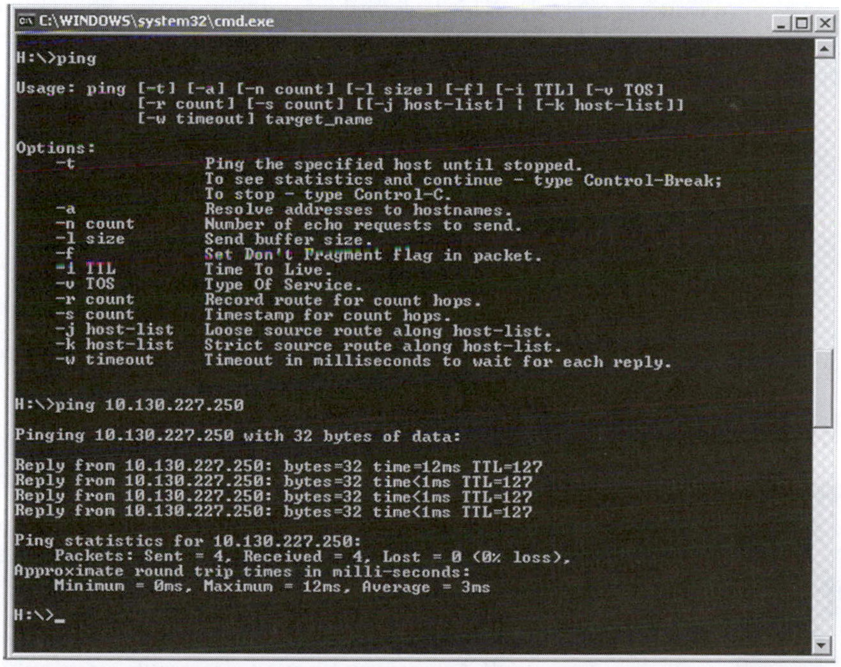

The main difference between the DOS/Windows ping and the Linux/UNIX ping is that the DOS/Windows ping will only show you four responses while the Linux/UNIX ping will keep showing responses until you break the loop. There are a number of parameters available with the Linux/UNIX ping just like with the DOS/Windows version. To find out more about the Linux/UNIX ping parameters you will need to do a "man" page look up for ping.

CERTIFICATION READY
What is ping? How does it work? What is it used for?
4.3

Figure 12-6

Ping command (Linux/UNIX)

```
pintello@pintello-virtual-machine ~ $ ping 10.130.227.250
PING 10.130.227.250 (10.130.227.250) 56(84) bytes of data.
64 bytes from 10.130.227.250: icmp_req=1 ttl=128 time=2.44 ms
64 bytes from 10.130.227.250: icmp_req=2 ttl=128 time=0.808 ms
64 bytes from 10.130.227.250: icmp_req=3 ttl=128 time=0.746 ms
64 bytes from 10.130.227.250: icmp_req=4 ttl=128 time=0.764 ms
64 bytes from 10.130.227.250: icmp_req=5 ttl=128 time=0.787 ms
64 bytes from 10.130.227.250: icmp_req=6 ttl=128 time=0.759 ms
64 bytes from 10.130.227.250: icmp_req=7 ttl=128 time=0.708 ms
64 bytes from 10.130.227.250: icmp_req=8 ttl=128 time=0.769 ms
64 bytes from 10.130.227.250: icmp_req=9 ttl=128 time=0.695 ms
64 bytes from 10.130.227.250: icmp_req=10 ttl=128 time=0.759 ms
64 bytes from 10.130.227.250: icmp_req=11 ttl=128 time=0.833 ms
64 bytes from 10.130.227.250: icmp_req=12 ttl=128 time=0.757 ms
64 bytes from 10.130.227.250: icmp_req=13 ttl=128 time=0.777 ms
64 bytes from 10.130.227.250: icmp_req=14 ttl=128 time=0.758 ms
64 bytes from 10.130.227.250: icmp_req=15 ttl=128 time=0.761 ms
64 bytes from 10.130.227.250: icmp_req=16 ttl=128 time=0.769 ms
64 bytes from 10.130.227.250: icmp_req=17 ttl=128 time=0.759 ms
64 bytes from 10.130.227.250: icmp_req=18 ttl=128 time=0.816 ms
^C
--- 10.130.227.250 ping statistics ---
18 packets transmitted, 18 received, 0% packet loss, time 17025ms
rtt min/avg/max/mdev = 0.695/0.859/2.446/0.387 ms
pintello@pintello-virtual-machine ~ $
```

The screenshot in Figure 12-6 also reveals how ping works. Ping uses the ICMP protocol and issues an "echo request" packet to the IP address you are attempting to ping. Once the IP address receives the "echo request" packet, it responds back with an "echo reply" packet. The ping command measures the amount of time it takes for a round-trip and reports that back in the output. Also, if any message besides an "echo reply" comes back, ping reports what that message is. If ping fails to receive an "echo reply" message within a reasonable amount of time, it reports that the IP address pinged is unreachable.

Ping is a very useful tool for determining whether the network device you are on directly is working correctly and whether other networking devices elsewhere on the network are working correctly. A bit later in this lesson, we discuss how ping can be used to run tests on a network device.

TRACEROUTE

Traceroute is a Linux/UNIX CLI tool that reports back each stop a packet makes on its way to a destination; this is called a packet's route. The destination for which you wish to find the route to is identified by the destination's IP address. Figure 12-7 shows the output of the traceroute tool.

Figure 12-7

Traceroute (Linux/UNIX)

```
pintello@pintello-virtual-machine ~ $ traceroute 10.130.227.250
traceroute to 10.130.227.250 (10.130.227.250), 30 hops max, 60 byte packets
 1  192.168.23.2 (192.168.23.2)  0.494 ms  0.105 ms  0.085 ms
 2  10.130.227.250 (10.130.227.250)  2.236 ms  2.039 ms  2.006 ms
pintello@pintello-virtual-machine ~ $
```

CERTIFICATION READY
What does traceroute do? What is the equivalent command in the Windows command-line environment?
4.3

In Figure 12-7, the destination IP is 10.130.227.250. To arrive at the designated destination, it took the packet two hops. In other words, the packet had to make two stops before it was able to reach 10.130.227.250. To learn about all the parameters available with traceroute, you need to reference its man page.

Like ping, traceroute uses the protocol ICMP to acquire the results it reports. The difference is in how the ICMP protocol is used. Traceroute starts out by setting the time to live (TTL) field in an IP packet to 1. When the packet moves out one hop, its TTL expires and the device with the expired TTL responds back with a "TTL expired" message using ICMP. The information contained in the "TTL expired" ICMP packet is then used by traceroute to display the results for the first hop. Traceroute then sets the TTL of the next packet it sends out to 2 and repeats the process. However this time, it will be the second device that reports back with a "TTL expired" ICMP message. In this way, traceroute keeps building up information for each hop until it receives a "destination unreachable" message or the TTL exceeds 30. The "destination unreachable" message means that there are not more hops after the last hop. If traceroute does not receive a "destination unreachable" message, it will keep sending out IP packets until the TTL of the IP packet exceeds 30. At that point, traceroute stops reporting back.

If you wish to traceroute a destination in excess of 30 hops, you can alter the maximum number of TTL that can be set using traceroute parameters. You can learn more about traceroute's parameters from its man page.

TRACERT

Tracert is the DOS/Windows equivalent to traceroute. Tracert works the same way that traceroute does, however, as you can see in Figure 12-8, it does not have as many parameters as traceroute. The tracert in Figure 12-8 is to the destination IP address 10.130.227.250 just like with the screenshot for traceroute (Figure 12-7).

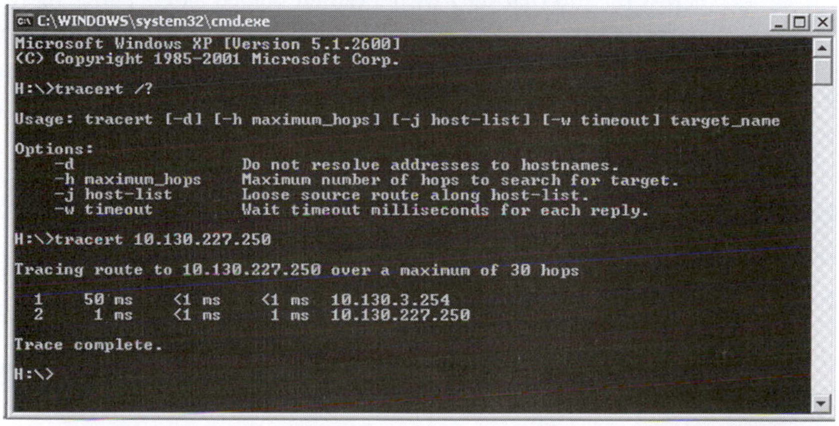

Figure 12-8

Tracert (DOS/Windows)

```
C:\WINDOWS\system32\cmd.exe

Microsoft Windows XP [Version 5.1.2600]
<C> Copyright 1985-2001 Microsoft Corp.

H:\>tracert /?

Usage: tracert [-d] [-h maximum_hops] [-j host-list] [-w timeout] target_name

Options:
    -d                 Do not resolve addresses to hostnames.
    -h maximum_hops    Maximum number of hops to search for target.
    -j host-list       Loose source route along host-list.
    -w timeout         Wait timeout milliseconds for each reply.

H:\>tracert 10.130.227.250

Tracing route to 10.130.227.250 over a maximum of 30 hops

  1     50 ms    <1 ms    <1 ms  10.130.3.254
  2      1 ms    <1 ms     1 ms  10.130.227.250

Trace complete.

H:\>
```

Traceroute or tracert, depending on which environment you are in, is an especially useful tool for finding out why you cannot access a specific device across a network. Using traceroute you can see how far down a network a packet is able to get towards a specific IP address before it can go no further. This in turn can give you a good clue where a network device such as a router may be down. If a packet can successfully get to a specific router and then cannot go any further, then this is a good indication that either the next router down the line is down or something is wrong with the connection between the router you can reach and the one you cannot reach.

Both traceroute and tracert are very useful tools for determining why you are not able to connect to a network device elsewhere on the network. These tools also can be used to help locate devices on the network that are not working correctly. Finally, these two tools can also be used to create a rough logical map of where all the devices on a network are located.

MY TRACEROUTE (MTR)

My traceroute (MTR) is a Linux/UNIX command-line tool that combines the capabilities and functionality of traceroute and ping. Figure 12-9 illustrates the results from issuing the mtr command.

```
                              My traceroute [v0.75]
pintello-virtual-machine (0.0.0.0)                    Fri Jan  7 10:25:05 2011
Keys:  Help   Display mode   Restart statistics   Order of fields   quit
                                     Packets                Pings
   Host                        Loss%   Snt   Last   Avg  Best  Wrst StDev
   1. 192.168.23.2              0.0%    46    0.3   0.3   0.2   0.4   0.0
   2. 10.130.227.250            0.0%    45    0.8   0.9   0.8   1.2   0.1
```

CERTIFICATION READY
What is MTR? What is it used for? What Windows command-line tool is equivalent?
4.3

As you can see from the results shown in Figure 12-9, both ping and traceroute information is shown. The traceroute portion of the output is derived the same way traceroute derives it. The information shown for the ping portion of the mtr tool is derived from the traceroute results and do not require a separate ICMP packet like ping uses. There are only a few parameters that can be used with mtr and they can be found in the man page for mtr.

One of the reasons there are only a few parameters for mtr is because mtr has a small menu that can be used with it. If you look back at Figure 12-9, you will notice that there are names across the top that start with a capital bolded letter. Those are the menus you can select to get more information about the IP address you entered. These menu options are **H**elp, **D**isplay mode, **R**estart statistics, **O**rder of fields, and **q**uit.

Mtr is a very good tool for combining the information from traceroute with ping. However, this tool is only available on Linux/UNIX computers.

PATHPING

Pathping is similar to the Linux tool mtr. This tool does not have the helpful menu that mtr has, but it does combine the functionality of the ping and tracert commands. The basic command for this tool is pathping. There are also several parameters that can be used with pathping. Figure 12-10 is a screenshot of the pathping help command. Figure 12-11 is the result of running the command pathping yahoo.com –q 10.

Figure 12-10

Pathping help screen (Windows)

```
C:\Windows\system32\cmd.exe                                        _ □ X

Microsoft Windows [Version 6.1.7600]
Copyright (c) 2009 Microsoft Corporation.  All rights reserved.

C:\Users\pintello>pathping

Usage: pathping [-g host-list] [-h maximum_hops] [-i address] [-n]
                [-p period] [-q num_queries] [-w timeout]
                [-4] [-6] target_name

Options:
    -g host-list     Loose source route along host-list.
    -h maximum_hops  Maximum number of hops to search for target.
    -i address       Use the specified source address.
    -n               Do not resolve addresses to hostnames.
    -p period        Wait period milliseconds between pings.
    -q num_queries   Number of queries per hop.
    -w timeout       Wait timeout milliseconds for each reply.
    -4               Force using IPv4.
    -6               Force using IPv6.
```

As you can see from Figure 12-11, pathping gives you the same routing information as tracert, while also being able to give you the same statistics information as ping.

ARP PING

An *ARP ping* is a ping command using the ARP protocol to issue an "arp request" rather than the ICMP protocol to issue an "echo request." This can only be done in the Linux/UNIX environment. The command to do an ARP ping is arping. The main advantage of

Figure 12-11

Pathping yahoo.com –q 10

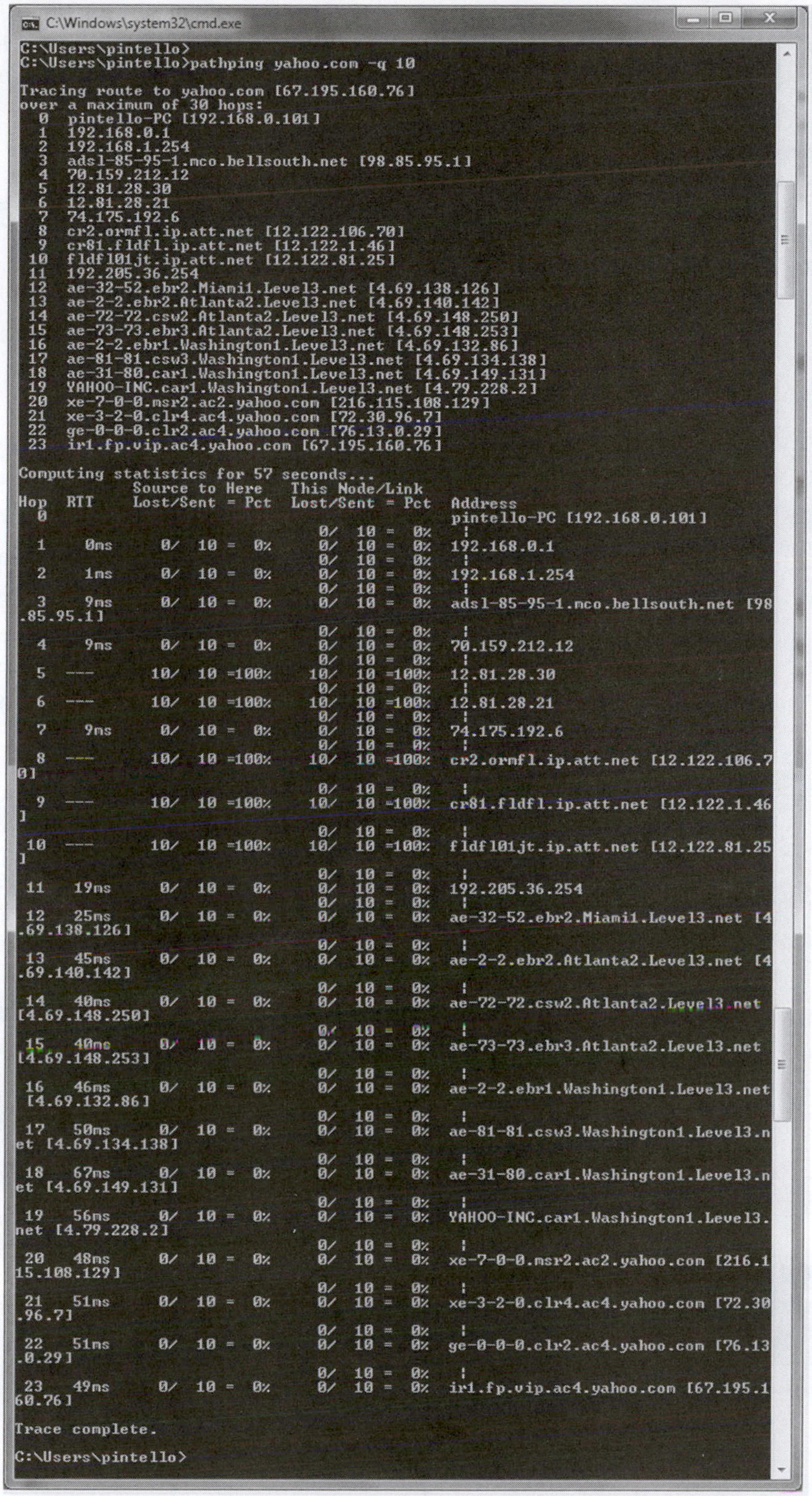

```
C:\Users\pintello>
C:\Users\pintello>pathping yahoo.com -q 10

Tracing route to yahoo.com [67.195.160.76]
over a maximum of 30 hops:
  0  pintello-PC [192.168.0.101]
  1  192.168.0.1
  2  192.168.1.254
  3  adsl-85-95-1.mco.bellsouth.net [98.85.95.1]
  4  70.159.212.12
  5  12.81.28.30
  6  12.81.28.21
  7  74.175.192.6
  8  cr2.ormfl.ip.att.net [12.122.106.70]
  9  cr81.fldfl.ip.att.net [12.122.1.46]
 10  fldfl01jt.ip.att.net [12.122.81.25]
 11  192.205.36.254
 12  ae-32-52.ebr2.Miami1.Level3.net [4.69.138.126]
 13  ae-2-2.ebr2.Atlanta2.Level3.net [4.69.140.142]
 14  ae-72-72.csw2.Atlanta2.Level3.net [4.69.148.250]
 15  ae-73-73.ebr3.Atlanta2.Level3.net [4.69.148.253]
 16  ae-2-2.ebr1.Washington1.Level3.net [4.69.132.86]
 17  ae-81-81.csw3.Washington1.Level3.net [4.69.134.138]
 18  ae-31-80.car1.Washington1.Level3.net [4.69.149.131]
 19  YAHOO-INC.car1.Washington1.Level3.net [4.79.228.2]
 20  xe-7-0-0.msr2.ac2.yahoo.com [216.115.108.129]
 21  xe-3-2-0.clr4.ac4.yahoo.com [72.30.96.7]
 22  ge-0-0-0.clr2.ac4.yahoo.com [76.13.0.29]
 23  ir1.fp.vip.ac4.yahoo.com [67.195.160.76]

Computing statistics for 57 seconds...
            Source to Here   This Node/Link
Hop  RTT    Lost/Sent = Pct  Lost/Sent = Pct  Address
  0                                           pintello-PC [192.168.0.101]
                                0/  10 =  0%   |
  1    0ms     0/  10 =  0%     0/  10 =  0%  192.168.0.1
                                0/  10 =  0%   |
  2    1ms     0/  10 =  0%     0/  10 =  0%  192.168.1.254
                                0/  10 =  0%   |
  3    9ms     0/  10 =  0%     0/  10 =  0%  adsl-85-95-1.mco.bellsouth.net [98
.85.95.1]
                                0/  10 =  0%   |
  4    9ms     0/  10 =  0%     0/  10 =  0%  70.159.212.12
                                0/  10 =  0%   |
  5  ---      10/  10 =100%    10/  10 =100%  12.81.28.30
                                0/  10 =  0%   |
  6  ---      10/  10 =100%    10/  10 =100%  12.81.28.21
                                0/  10 =  0%   |
  7    9ms     0/  10 =  0%     0/  10 =  0%  74.175.192.6
                                0/  10 =  0%   |
  8  ---      10/  10 =100%    10/  10 =100%  cr2.ormfl.ip.att.net [12.122.106.7
0]
                                0/  10 =  0%   |
  9  ---      10/  10 =100%    10/  10 =100%  cr81.fldfl.ip.att.net [12.122.1.46
]
                                0/  10 =  0%   |
 10  ---      10/  10 =100%    10/  10 =100%  fldfl01jt.ip.att.net [12.122.81.25
]
                                0/  10 =  0%   |
 11   19ms     0/  10 =  0%     0/  10 =  0%  192.205.36.254
                                0/  10 =  0%   |
 12   25ms     0/  10 =  0%     0/  10 =  0%  ae-32-52.ebr2.Miami1.Level3.net [4
.69.138.126]
                                0/  10 =  0%   |
 13   45ms     0/  10 =  0%     0/  10 =  0%  ae-2-2.ebr2.Atlanta2.Level3.net [4
.69.140.142]
                                0/  10 =  0%   |
 14   40ms     0/  10 =  0%     0/  10 =  0%  ae-72-72.csw2.Atlanta2.Level3.net
[4.69.148.250]
                                0/  10 =  0%   |
 15   40ms     0/  10 =  0%     0/  10 =  0%  ae-73-73.ebr3.Atlanta2.Level3.net
[4.69.148.253]
                                0/  10 =  0%   |
 16   46ms     0/  10 =  0%     0/  10 =  0%  ae-2-2.ebr1.Washington1.Level3.net
 [4.69.132.86]
                                0/  10 =  0%   |
 17   50ms     0/  10 =  0%     0/  10 =  0%  ae-81-81.csw3.Washington1.Level3.n
et [4.69.134.138]
                                0/  10 =  0%   |
 18   67ms     0/  10 =  0%     0/  10 =  0%  ae-31-80.car1.Washington1.Level3.n
et [4.69.149.131]
                                0/  10 =  0%   |
 19   56ms     0/  10 =  0%     0/  10 =  0%  YAHOO-INC.car1.Washington1.Level3.
net [4.79.228.2]
                                0/  10 =  0%   |
 20   48ms     0/  10 =  0%     0/  10 =  0%  xe-7-0-0.msr2.ac2.yahoo.com [216.1
15.108.129]
                                0/  10 =  0%   |
 21   51ms     0/  10 =  0%     0/  10 =  0%  xe-3-2-0.clr4.ac4.yahoo.com [72.30
.96.7]
                                0/  10 =  0%   |
 22   51ms     0/  10 =  0%     0/  10 =  0%  ge-0-0-0.clr2.ac4.yahoo.com [76.13
.0.29]
                                0/  10 =  0%   |
 23   49ms     0/  10 =  0%     0/  10 =  0%  ir1.fp.vip.ac4.yahoo.com [67.195.1
60.76]

Trace complete.

C:\Users\pintello>
```

CERTIFICATION READY
What is arping? Is there an equivalent tool available for the Windows command line?
4.3

arping over ping is that network devices are required to respond to an arp request even if they are behind a firewall that blocks ICMP echo request packets. This tool is useful if you really need to ping a target computer when an in-place firewall prevents you from doing so using the standard ping tool.

ARP

The *arp* tool is used to display the arp table of a computer. The *arp table* is a table that is kept by all network devices and contains the IP address and MAC address of all the other network devices with which it has been in contact. Aside from displaying arp tables, arp can also be used to manipulate arp tables by adding or removing MAC addresses. Hackers sometimes use this last functionality for quite a few nefarious purposes.

Figure 12-12

Arp (Linux/UNIX)

```
pintello@pintello-virtual-machine ~ $ arp
Address           HWtype  HWaddress           Flags Mask       Iface
192.168.23.2      ether   00:50:56:ea:9c:05   C                eth0
192.168.23.254    ether   00:50:56:e9:97:50   C                eth0
pintello@pintello-virtual-machine ~ $
```

Figure 12-12 shows the result of using the arp command in a Linux/UNIX environment. The result of using the arp command in a DOS/Windows environment is much the same.

Arp can be used to view a local computer's arp tables to see if they are even able to see local computers based on MAC addresses. Arp is also a good tool for manipulating a system's arp table either by adding MAC addresses to it, or removing MAC addresses from it.

NSLOOKUP

Nslookup is a CLI tool that is used to look up DNS servers. If you have a domain name, you can find out what the servers are for that domain. Nslookup also displays the IP address of the DNS server on the network being used to run nslookup. Figure 12-13 shows the output of nslookup in a DOS/Windows environment for the yahoo.com domain name.

Figure 12-13

Nslookup yahoo.com (DOS/Windows)

```
C:\WINDOWS\system32\cmd.exe

H:\>nslookup yahoo.com
Server:  dc-1.gc._msdcs.daytonastate.edu
Address:  10.9.91.41

Non-authoritative answer:
Name:    yahoo.com
Addresses:  67.195.160.76, 69.147.125.65, 72.30.2.43, 98.137.149.56
         209.191.122.70

H:\>
```

CERTIFICATION READY
What does nslookup do? What is it used for?
4.3

The output from nslookup in a Linux/UNIX environment is essentially the same. The only difference is that the Linux/UNIX version separates out the IP addresses of the targeted domain name in a nice table rather than just a comma-delimited list. Nslookup is a good tool to use in order to find out the IP address is of a specific DNS name.

HOSTNAME

Hostname is a CLI tool that is used to either display or change the DNS hostname of the local machine. Figure 12-14 shows the output of the "hostname" command in a Linux/UNIX environment. The output in a DOS/Windows environment is almost identical.

Figure 12-14

Hostname command (Linux/UNIX)

```
pintello@pintello-virtual-machine ~ $ hostname
pintello-virtual-machine
pintello@pintello-virtual-machine ~ $
```

If you do not know a system's hostname, this tool is a quick command line way to find out. It is also an easy way to change a hostname; although that is not a recommended action to take because it could cause unforeseen problems with the system.

DOMAIN INFORMATION GROPER (DIG)

Domain Information Groper (dig) is used to query DNS servers to gain information about them. In this way, it is similar to nslookup. However, unlike nslookup, dig can provide much more detailed information. Dig is also only available in Linux/UNIX environments. Figure 12-15 shows a screenshot of the dig output when two DSN server IP addresses were entered as parameters.

Figure 12-15

Dig tool (Linux/UNIX)

```
pintello@pintello-virtual-machine ~ $ dig 10.9.91.41

; <<>> DiG 9.7.1-P2 <<>> 10.9.91.41
;; global options: +cmd
;; Got answer:
;; ->>HEADER<<- opcode: QUERY, status: NXDOMAIN, id: 3660
;; flags: qr rd ra; QUERY: 1, ANSWER: 0, AUTHORITY: 1, ADDITIONAL: 0

;; QUESTION SECTION:
;10.9.91.41.                     IN      A

;; AUTHORITY SECTION:
.                       5       IN      SOA     a.root-servers.net. nstld.verisign-grs.com
. 2011010700 1800 900 604800 86400

;; Query time: 2 msec
;; SERVER: 192.168.23.2#53(192.168.23.2)
;; WHEN: Fri Jan  7 10:26:18 2011
;; MSG SIZE  rcvd: 103
pintello@pintello-virtual-machine ~ $ dig 10.9.91.42

; <<>> DiG 9.7.1-P2 <<>> 10.9.91.42
;; global options: +cmd
;; Got answer:
;; ->>HEADER<<- opcode: QUERY, status: NXDOMAIN, id: 62415
;; flags: qr rd ra; QUERY: 1, ANSWER: 0, AUTHORITY: 1, ADDITIONAL: 0

;; QUESTION SECTION:
;10.9.91.42.                     IN      A

;; AUTHORITY SECTION:
.                       5       IN      SOA     a.root-servers.net. nstld.verisign-grs.com
. 2011010700 1800 900 604800 86400

;; Query time: 2 msec
;; SERVER: 192.168.23.2#53(192.168.23.2)
;; WHEN: Fri Jan  7 10:26:29 2011
;; MSG SIZE  rcvd: 103

pintello@pintello-virtual-machine ~ $ 
```

CERTIFICATION READY
What is dig? What operating system is it available in? How is dig similar to nslookup? How is dig different from nslookup?
4.3

Dig is most often used to troubleshoot DNS problems and there are a number of parameters that can be used with it. To get more information on dig, you can look at the dig man page. This tool is useful for getting more detailed DNS information about a local computer than what nslookup can provide.

ROUTE

Just going by the name, you would assume that the route command was similar to the traceroute command, however it is not. The traceroute command is used to determine the number and IP addresses of the hops a packet takes to reach a specific destination. The ***route*** command is used to view and/or manipulate the routing table located on the targeted device, either by adding or removing static routes. Specifically the route command is intended to set up static routes to specific network locations from the local interface. This command works the same way in both the Linux/UNIX and DOS/Windows environments. Figure 12-16 shows the routing table for a computer using the route command in a DOS/Windows environment.

Figure 12-16

Route (DOS/Windows)

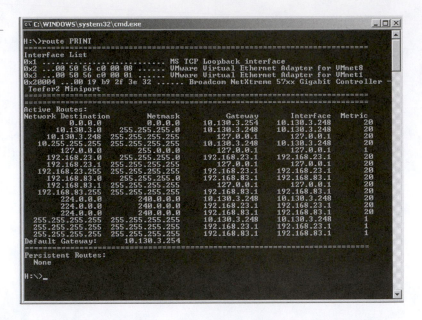

The Linux/UNIX output would be similar to what is seen in Figure 12-16. The main differences between the two environments are the layout of the output and parameters used to accomplish specific tasks. The tool is useful for reading the routing tables on a local computer as well as adding or removing additional routes to the local routing table.

CERTIFICATION READY
What does the route command do?
4.3

NBTSTAT

Nbtstat is used to obtain information about a local machine and the devices it is connected to, based on NetBIOS names. Figure 12-17 shows the result of the nbtstat command in a DOS/Windows environment.

Figure 12-17

Nbtstat (DOS/Windows)

```
H:\>nbtstat -A 10.130.227.250

VMware Network Adapter VMnet8:
Node IpAddress: [192.168.23.1] Scope Id: []

    Host not found.

VMware Network Adapter VMnet1:
Node IpAddress: [192.168.83.1] Scope Id: []

    Host not found.

Local Area Connection:
Node IpAddress: [10.130.3.248] Scope Id: []

        NetBIOS Remote Machine Name Table

    Name              Type         Status
    ---------------------------------------------
    INSTRUCTOR1    <00>  UNIQUE   Registered
    WORKGROUP      <00>  GROUP    Registered
    INSTRUCTOR1    <20>  UNIQUE   Registered
    WORKGROUP      <1E>  GROUP    Registered
    ConfigServer   <1C>  GROUP    Registered
    instructor1    <2D>  UNIQUE   Registered
    WORKGROUP      <1D>  UNIQUE   Registered
    .._MSBROWSE_.<01>  GROUP    Registered
    GhostCast      <1C>  GROUP    Registered
    gg             <2C>  UNIQUE   Registered

    MAC Address = 00-03-47-73-5D-FB

H:\>
```

NetBIOS names are based on older Novell and Windows systems and are not used by Linux. For this reason, there is not an nbtstat command for Linux. Nbtstat is good for determining the NetBIOS name for specific Windows computers and connections. As Novell and Windows no longer use NetBIOS names for creating network IDs, nbtstat is no longer in common usage. However, if you encounter older Novell networks, it may come in handy to be familiar with nbtstat.

CERTIFICATION READY

What is nbtstat? What information does nbtstat provide? Is there an equivalent tool for Linux?

4.3

NETSTAT

Netstat is a command-line tool that is used to display information about network connections, routing tables, interface statistics, masquerade connections, and multicast memberships. Depending on what parameters you use, you can get quite a bit of information about a computer using the netstat tool. This tool is also one of those CLI tools that works in both the Linux/UNIX and the DOS/Windows environment, making it even more useful. To show the diversity of netstat, take a look at Figures 12-18 and 19. Figure 12-18 shows a screenshot of netstat in the Linux/UNIX environment and all the active protocols and sockets on a local computer. Figure 12-19 is a screenshot of netstat in a DOS/Windows environment.

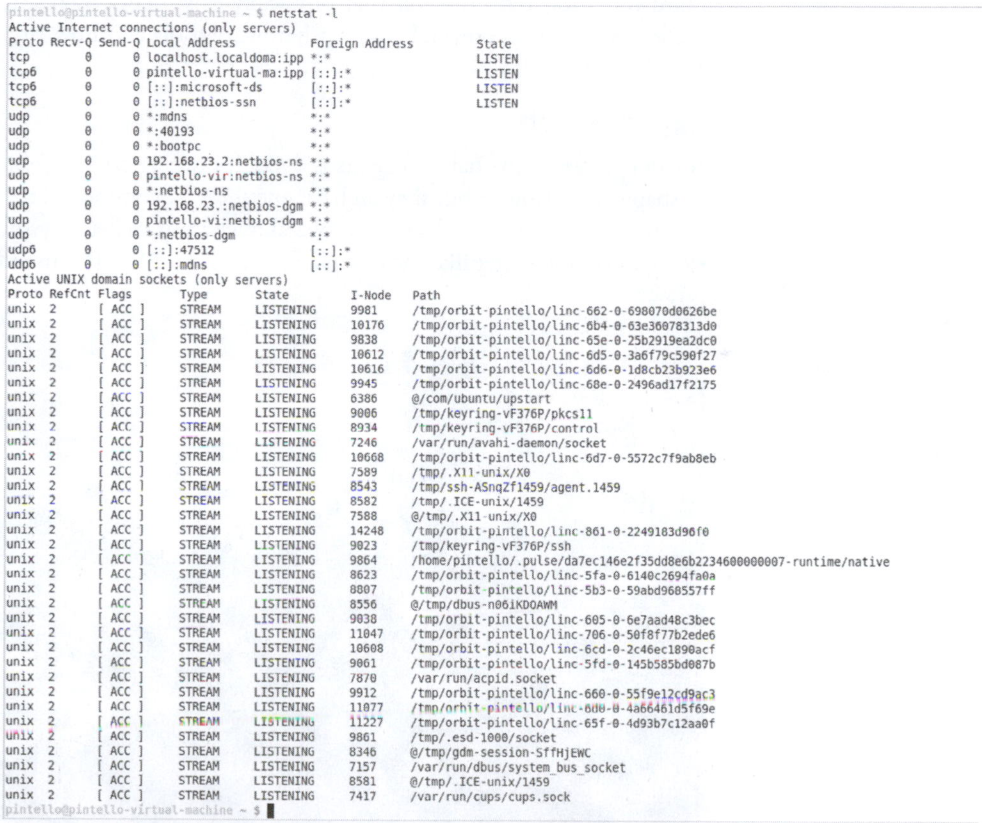

Figure 12-18

Netstat (Linux/UNIX) showing all the active protocols and sockets on a local computer

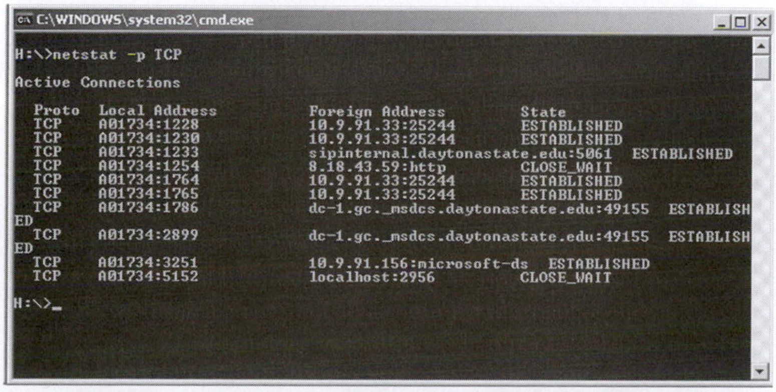

Figure 12-19

Netstat (DOS/Windows) showing all the open TCP ports on a local computer

CERTIFICATION READY

What is netstat? How is it used? What information does netstat provide?

4.3

The Figure 12-19 netstat screenshot is from a DOS/Windows environment and shows all the open TCP ports on the local computer. As you can see from these two figures, netstat is a good tool for identifying open ports and active protocols on a local computer.

CONNECTIVITY SOFTWARE

Connectivity software is a broad category of software that refers to programs that are used to connect computers or other types of electronic devices to another computer or a network. Most connectivity software is usually specifically designed for the device it is being used to connect and is hardware dependent. Connectivity software also usually comes with a test component to verify that the device is connected to a computer or network and to help determine the problem if a device is not connecting like it should.

Hardware Tools

Hardware tools refer to tools that physically exist as opposed software programs. In this section, we examine several types of hardware tools and how they can be used to troubleshoot and fix a network.

CABLE TESTER

A *cable tester*, as the name suggests is a tool for testing cables. Cable testers come in a wide variety of shapes and designs, but they all have one thing in common. They are devices that are intended to test the connectivity of various cables as a whole as well as any subcomponents within them. For example, a cable tester like the one pictured in Figure 12-20 is used to test twisted-pair cabling.

Figure 12-20

Twisted-pair cable tester

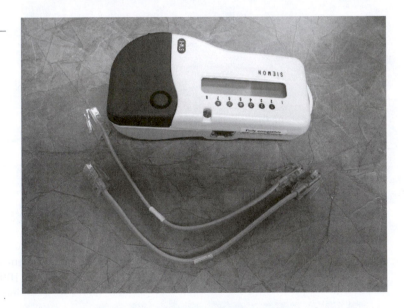

This cable tester is able to test all the pairs in a twisted-pair wire. It is designed to be compact and portable. This cable tester is designed specifically for testing patch cabling in twisted-pair networks. In comparison, the cable tester shown in Figure 12-21 is more diverse and can be used for testing a wide variety of cables.

Figure 12-21

Cable tester designed to test a large variety of cable wires

This cable tester is much more diverse than the one in Figure 12-20 and is designed to test pretty much any copper cable that may be used on a personal computer. This cable tester can also get power from either batteries or an external converter. There are other cable testers that are designed to test fiber-optic cables.

All cable testers are designed to run some specific test. Most are designed to test for continuity. They test to make sure that there is a continuous connection from one end of a cable to the other on each wire that makes up the cable. Most cable testers are also made to test whether the wire on one end, matches up with the correct wire on the other end. The way the wires match up on one end as compared to the other end depends on what kind of cable is being tested and what the appropriate specifications are for that cable.

If a cable does not match the specifications it is designed to match and the two ends of a wire do not go where they are supposed to go, bad things can happen. At best, if the cable ends to not match specifications, the cable will not be able to carry data. At worst, it is possible that the cable or more likely the device connected to the cable can be destroyed because the ends do not match up. In this last scenario, if a wire that is intended to carry power connects to a pin on the device that is intended to carry data, the data portion of the device could be fried.

Cable testers can be used to verify that the cables being used on a network are good. If a tested cable turns out to be bad, then you can replace it with a cable that you can verify as good before you use it.

PROTOCOL ANALYZER

We have already looked at one type of protocol analyzer—Wireshark, which was software based. Now we will look at a hardware-based protocol analyzer. This type of protocol analyzer works just like the software one does in that it captures and analyzes packets as they pass across a network. The difference is that a hardware-based protocol analyzer does not require a full computer to be connected to the network in order for it to function. A hardware-based protocol analyzer is an entirely self-contained system that has all the software it needs built into it. To use this type of protocol analyzer, simply connect it to an available data jack and turn it on. From there, it will begin to analyze the packets that flow by the jack to which it is connected. A hardware protocol analyzer also automatically runs specific tests on the network and the protocols on it to see how they are working. Finally, there are also predefined tests that you can run on a hardware-based protocol analyzer that are chosen by selecting them from a menu or by pushing a button.

Hardware protocol analyzers are useful because they can test a network to see if different segments on that network meet the specifications needed to run different types of data networks. For example, you have a network that was originally created to run 100 mbps Ethernet. However, when you built the network, you actually used Cat 6 cabling because that was what was most readily available. Now you want to see if you can upgrade your equipment to gigabit Ethernet. You can use a hardware protocol analyzer to verify that the network is able to support gigabit Ethernet. If you find it is not able to support gigabit Ethernet, then you have to consider if it is worth rewiring your network to support gigabit Ethernet. However, if you find that it will support gigabit Ethernet, you can proceed to buy the new equipment accordingly.

While there was a time when protocol analyzers were large bulky devices with their own screens and all, they have gotten much smaller. Today most protocol analyzers are smaller devices that can fit in your hand and connect to a computer on one side via a USB port and the network on the other side via an RJ-45 or other type cable.

CERTIFIERS

A cable certifier is a device used to certify that the cables in a network configuration meet the required physical specifications. Remember that protocol analyzers test a network for use with a specific protocol. A certifier on the other hand, is designed to verify that the cable in question meets the physical functional requirements. Some of the things that certifiers can verify are the physical properties of the cable, the signal carrying properties of a cable, the length of a cable, where connections are made within a system, and many other physical properties. The certifier shown in Figure 12-22 is able to certify both copper and fiber-optic cables.

CERTIFICATION READY
What is a cable tester?
What is it used for?
4.2

CERTIFICATION READY
What are cable certifiers?
How do they differ from cable testers?
4.2

Figure 12-22

Cable certifier

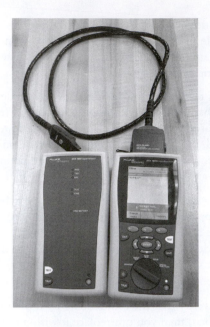

TIME-DOMAIN REFLECTOMETER (TDR)

The main use for *Time-Domain Reflectometers (TDRs)* is to test cables that are in place. A TDR is not only sonar for copper cables and other connections. When you connect a TDR to a metal cable it will send an electrical pulse down the wire. The response back tells the TDR if there is a fault in the wiring somewhere and exactly how far down the cable the fault is located if there is one. TDRs can also be used in metal circuit boards and can tell where faults may be in the circuit board. Some cable certifiers like the one shown in Figure 12-22 have TDR capabilities built into them. Figure 12-23 shows a TDR.

Figure 12-23

Time-Domain Reflectometer (TDR)

CERTIFICATION READY
What are TDRs and
OTDRs? How are they
related? How are they
different?
4.2

OPTICAL TIME-DOMAIN REFLECTOMETER (OTDR)

An *Optical Time-Domain Reflectometer (OTDR)* is basically a TDR for fiber-optic cables. It works the same way as a TDR, except that it is designed for fiber-optic cable instead of copper cables. The cable certifier shown in Figure 12-22 also has OTDR capabilities.

MULTIMETER

A *multimeter* is a device that is designed to take several types of measurements, which is why it is called a multimeter. Most multimeters are able to measure voltage, amperage, resistance, and continuity. Many multimeters also are able to test other types of measurements as well such as temperature. Figure 12-24 shows a basic multimeter that also has the ability to measure temperature.

Figure 12-24

Multimeter

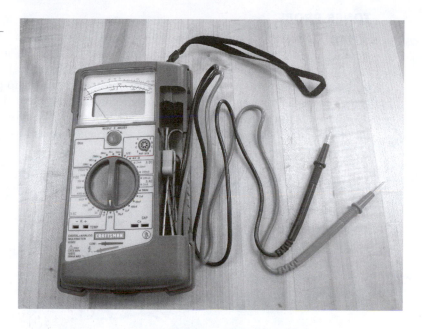

One thing you can do with a multimeter is troubleshoot the power supply in a network device. This is important because many times when motherboards or other components go bad, it can be traced back to a bad power supply. If you replaced the component that went bad, but did not replace the power supply that was the cause of the component going bad, then you will have another bad component. By testing the power supply with a multimeter whenever a major component, such as a motherboard goes out, you can prevent the loss of the replacement component by determining that the power supply was the cause of that component's failure.

THROUGHPUT TESTERS

A throughput tester is usually a device or software program that is used to test how fast data is actually passing through a network connection. Throughput testers can be hardware devices or software programs, but they both serve the same function, which is to test the throughput of a network connection.

Hardware throughput testers are used when network wiring is first run in a site where network wiring is being run. Throughput testing is usually one of the functions of a cable certifying device and is used to prove that the installation meets the requirements to match up to the specific standard the site is intended to conform to.

Software throughput testers are more often used after a network is in place. The reason software throughput testers are used to verify that a network connection is still running at the speed it is supposed to after time. Another reason to run a software throughput tester is to verify that a network is still operating at the expected levels after additions or changes have been made to it.

There are a number of software throughput testers found online. One such software throughput tester is found at www.speedtest.net. This website can be used to test how fast your home Internet connection is or even how fast the internet connection at work runs, provided the test has not been blocked by the company.

Software throughput testers use different methods to test the throughput of a connection. The best way to find out what method is being used to test the connection is to read any documentation that may be on the website of the throughput tester you are using. Two common methods are to use Ping request to test the connection and to time how long it takes to download and/or upload a file of known length. Both methods can tell what the throughput of a network connection is, but there are also other methods available as well.

TONER PROBE

A *toner probe* is a tool that is used to find the end of a long run of a specific cable. Generally speaking, a tone generator is connected to one end of the long run and turned on. The technician then goes into the switch room where the various cable runs terminate and waves the wand of the toner probe over the different terminations until she is able to pick up the tone that is generated by the tone generator. This lets the technician know that the cable she is picking up the tone on is the termination point in the switch or patch panel for the cable she is trying to find the end of. Figure 12-25 is a picture of a tone generator and its accompanying wand.

Figure 12-25

Toner Probe and Tone Generator

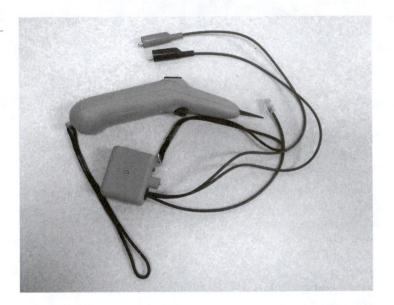

CERTIFICATION READY
What is a toner probe?
What is it used for?
4.2

This device is used to troubleshoot a network by finding where different cables from the floor or elsewhere within the company terminate in the switch room. This is especially important because many times a jack on the floor will not match up to the location on the switch or patch panel it is supposed to. When this happens, it becomes necessary to determine the true point on the patch panel or switch at which a cable terminates.

BUTT SET

Butt sets, also called lineman phones, are devices used in telephone communications that allow a technician to connect the butt set to any phone connection and use that connection like a regular phone, or to test the connection to make sure it is working. These devices often look like miniature phone handsets with alligator clips hanging off them. These alligator clips are used to connect to the existing phone line.

PUNCH DOWN TOOL

A *punch down tool*, or punchdown tool, is intended to terminate wires on a 110 block or a 66 block. These are the connections that are generally found on the back of patch panels where the cables going out to the wall jacks are connected. This tool is also generally used to terminate the wires into an RJ-45 jack as well. Figure 12-26 shows what a punch down tool looks like.

Figure 12-26

Punch down tool

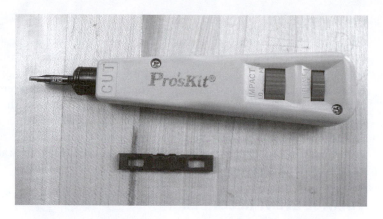

CABLE STRIPPER

Cable strippers come in all shapes and sizes. However, they all have the same function; they are used to strip the insulation off of a cable for various purposes. The shape and size of a cable stripper is greatly dependent on the type of cable it is designed to strip. As you can see from Figure 12-27, there are many varieties of cable strippers available, each specialized for stripping a certain type of cable.

Figure 12-27

Multiple cable strippers

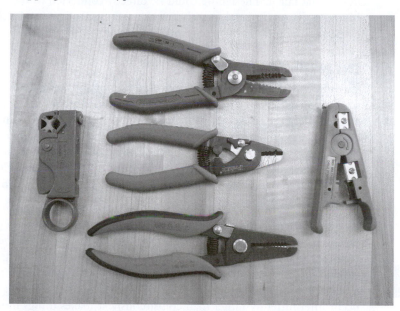

SNIPS

Snips, also known as wire cutters and telecommunications scissors, are handheld devices that are intended to cut wire, wire ties, and other similar things. Figure 12-28 is a picture of kind of wire cutter, or snips, known as telecommunications scissors. These are very versatile and can also serve reliably as a cable stripper.

Figure 12-28

Telecommunications scissors

CRIMPER

Crimpers are devices used to attach connectors to the end of a cable. In the lab in Lesson 3 a RJ-45 crimper was used to attach the RJ-45 connectors on the UTP cables created in that lab. Other types of cables require crimpers of different designs. Even many fiber optic connectors use crimpers to attach fiber optic connectors to the ends of fiber optic cables. If a crimper is designed for a specific cable or connector type, that cable or connector type are the only type of cable or connector typr that specific crimper can be used used with. Occasionally it is possible to find crimpers which have multiple removable dies that come with them. In this situation the crimper can be used on all the cable and connector types it has a removable dies for.

VOLTAGE EVENT RECORDER

A *voltage event recorder* is a device that is designed to monitor electrical circuits and look for problems in the electricity coming though the circuit. Voltage event recorders can detect and report a number of electrical conditions—power sags, power swells, transient power events, outages, and spikes or other variations in the power system. The ability to detect these types of events is important because when a network problem happens during one of these events, if you know about it, you will be more able to diagnose what went wrong with the network device that failed. The failure could be directly connected to the voltage event recorded. However, if you do not know about the event, you cannot make the connection between the event and the problem you are troubleshooting.

ENVIRONMENTAL MONITOR

Environmental monitors are devices used to monitor the area in a building where equipment sensitive may be located. The types of conditions these monitors look for are conditions that are detrimental to the equipment located in the room being monitored. It is common to have environmental monitors in switch rooms, server rooms and other such locations. Items such as fire alarms and smoke alarms are the first types of environmental monitors we may think about. However, there are environmental conditions other than fire and smoke that may be detrimental to computer equipment. Two such detrimental environmental conditions are temperature and humidity.

Temperature monitors are important because when electronic devices rise above a certain temperature they begin to act unreliably. The interesting thing about temperature and electronics is that before a device gets hot enough to quit functioning all together, it first begins to send incorrect signals. This can result in electronic equipment that behaves in strange and unexpected ways and gives intermittent errors instead of constant errors. When problems occur intermittently rather than continuously, it makes things much more difficult to troubleshoot. One way to avoid this is to use temperature monitors in your electronic and networking devices. If the temperature in a device begins to rise above a certain level, you need to find some way to cool it down before the problems start.

Room temperature monitors are a type of temperature monitor that is useful for networks. The hotter a room is, the more difficult it is for electronic equipment to cool itself. In a warmer room, electronic equipment cannot cool as fast or as much and the problem mentioned earlier about heat will become a reality. If a room begins to warm up above a certain level and the alarm on your room temperature monitor goes off, then you can take steps to cool that room and determine why the room is so much warmer than normal. Without room temperature monitors in place, you may not know the room is warming up until problems begin to manifest on the network.

Related to temperature monitors are *humidity monitors*. Humidity monitors keep track of the amount of humidity in the air inside a monitored room. This is important the same way that temperature is important. The more humid the air becomes, the less that air can dissipate heat. For this reason, when a room with electronic equipment becomes humid, it is more difficult for the equipment in that room to dissipate heat into the air and the equipment begins to run hotter. This leads right back to the problem of electronic networking equipment behaving erratically when components are too hot. If the humidity monitors in a room begin to go off, steps need to be taken to reduce the humidity in the affect room. Also, if a room that has not had a past history of being humid starts to become so, you need to discover why and take steps to correct the problem.

■ Troubleshooting Actions

 THE BOTTOM LINE   In this last section of Lesson 12, we discuss different actions—both basic and advanced—that should be taken when troubleshooting.

While there are no one-size-fits-all solutions in troubleshooting, there are certain actions you can take in troubleshooting to narrow down the scope of the problem you are attempting to resolve. In the remainder of this lesson, we examine what actions you can take to help narrow down a troubleshooting problem.

Basic Troubleshooting Actions

CERTIFICATION READY
Given certain situations, what actions should you take? What tools are available to use when specific situations come up?
4.2

There are two levels of action you can take when you find yourself in a troubleshooting situation. The first level includes basic actions. These actions are easy to do and do not require any special equipment.

CHECK FOR PHYSICAL PROBLEMS

The first basic check should be for physical problems, which includes things like cables not being connected or plugged in, power switches being turned off, cables being cut or broken, jacks being pulled out, non-boot disks being in boot drives, and other such problems. Ironically enough, physical problems like the ones listed account for a large percentage of all the problems you may come across. Given that large percentage, it is always a good idea to make a check for physical problems first.

LOOPBACK TESTING

In *loopback testing*, a specially designed connector is attached to a physical port that allows a signal to be sent back to the device that initially sent the signal. This tests the port to make sure that it is physically functional. Loopback testing can be done on any type of port and is an important step in troubleshooting because it allows you to verify the functionality of the port itself. If the port does not work, then you have already found a large clue as to what the problem is.

Although we said that basic testing does not require any special tools, loopback testing is something of an exception to this. Some devices require a special loopback connector to do this test. However, many devices, including almost all modern NICs, actually can have a loopback test run on them without the need of the specialized loopback connector.

Figure 12-29 shows the wiring of a RJ-45 loopback connector. Notice that the send pin is connected to the receive pin, (pin 1 to pin 3) and that the receive pin is connected to the send pin (pin 2 to pin 6).

Figure 12-29

RJ-45 loopback connector

PING TESTING

Ping testing is a series of tests that you can do using the ping command discussed previously. In ping testing, the first IP you should ping is 127.0.0.1—the loopback IP. You ping the loopback IP to verify that the equipment is physically functional, the TCP/IP protocol is installed and running on the computer, and the computer is able to find the NIC. If a loopback ping does not work, there may be something physically wrong with the NIC or the TCP/IP protocol suite may not be working.

The next IP you should ping is the IP of the computer you are testing, which allows you to verify that the drivers are working properly and that the NIC knows what its IP should be. If this test does not work, it indicates that there may be problem with the driver for the NIC.

Next you should ping the gateway to which the computer is connected, which lets you verify that the computer can communicate with a device somewhere else on the same segment as the computer you are testing. This test also verifies that the computer you are testing can send and receive packets outside of the NIC. If this test does not work, it could indicate a problem somewhere on the local segment, which may be an indication that the switch or the router containing the gateway is down.

Next you should ping a device beyond the gateway. You run this test to verify that devices on the other side of the gateway can be successfully reached. If this fails, it could indicate that there is something wrong with the router containing the gateway or possibly that a configuration somewhere on the network is incorrect.

Finally, you need to ping the IP of the DNS server to verify that the DNS server is up and running. If this test fails, it could indicate that the DNS IP you have on your computer is incorrect or that the DNS server is down. To verify whether the problem is the DNS server or something else, you can ping the IP address of a known website. If you can ping the IP address of a known website but cannot ping the DNS server, then the problem is the DNS server.

TRACE ROUTE TESTING

Trace route testing is a variation on ping testing. If you are unable to ping a device beyond the gateway, you can determine where the actual problem is by performing a traceroute on an IP address that you know for a fact is beyond the local network, which will give you a list of good IP addresses. This also tells you where the IP addresses stop working. By knowing this, you can identify where the problem is. If a traceroute reaches a specific router and then goes no further, the problem is on the other side of the last good IP address. This gives you a very good location to start from when trying to determine why the network is not working.

Advanced Troubleshooting Actions

If the basic actions that have been discussed so far do not help you determine where a network problem is, then you need to take some more advanced actions to test the network. Alternatively, if the basic tests do give you a good idea about where to start looking for the problem, then you may need to take some of the more advanced troubleshooting actions to narrow the possibilities down. The next few sections of Lesson 12 will be about some of those more advanced troubleshooting action you can take to test a network.

CABLE TESTING

If your initial testing indicates that there is something wrong with the cabling, but does not give enough specifics, you can run a cable test. A cable test requires that you use a cable tester as discussed earlier. This would primarily test patch cables and other types of cables. If you wish to test longer cable runs, a different type of testing is required.

There are several types of problems that can be revealed using cable testing. You can verify the pin out of the cable. Sometimes when a patch cable is bought or created, some of the wires in the cable may be connected to the wrong pin or pins. If this is the case, then the network device using the cable will not be able to communicate to the network. If ping shows that the loopback test and the NIC IP test work, but the other tests do not, that could indicate a cable problem like the one just described.

Another problem that a cable test may reveal is if the wrong type of cable is being used. Sometimes, when a person hooks up a new computer to the network, he will pick a cable from a pile of patch cables to connect the computer to the local jack. That pile of patch cables may contain patch cables of more than one type. If the person selecting the patch cable does not verify that he is choosing a straight-through cable, for example, he may pick up a crossover cable instead. When that happens, the computer will not be able to connect to the network. Cable testing allows you to catch this mistake.

Bad cables

A very basic type of problem you may run into when testing cables is bad cables. Simply put, bad cables are cables that do not carry the signal in the way they are intended to. This can be caused by several things.

One common cause of bad cables is rodents or other animals chewing on them. When this happens, the cable often loses its insulation covering and sometimes can be bitten in half. When a cable looses it insulation or is bitten in half the cable can no longer be used to carry signals. Once an animal gets a hold of a cable, the only real solution is to replace the cable.

Another situation that may cause a cable to go bad is simply wear and tear on the cable if it is exposed. Like in the case of the animal, cables that become bad through wear and tear also need to be replaced. Power surges though a cable can also result in the cable becoming bad. Again, the way to fix this is to replace it.

Aside from the causes mentioned, environmental factors can also cause a cable to go bad. Some of these environmental factors are humidity, heat, water, and even constant direct sunlight. When running cables initially it is a good idea to be aware of the type of environment the cable will have to survive in and purchase cables that have been designed for that specific environment. While this may cost more in the short term, in the long term you will end up saving quite a bit of money. It is almost always cheaper to run the correct type of cable in the first place than it is to replace cables that are already in place.

Improper cable types

Improper cable types can be something as simple as having coaxial cable when UTP cable is needed or single-mode fiber optic when multi-mode fiber optic is needed. However, with good planning this type of situation can be avoided.

A more difficult situation where improper cable is used is when the wrong type or specification of a specific cable is used. A good example of this is the coaxial cable used in cable television. Many times the cable used to carry the signal from one cable provider may not work in the case of a different cable provider. In this situation it becomes necessary to run a different type of cable when changing cable providers.

Another situation is where a specific type of cable was run originally to meet the needs of a company's network requirements that can no longer do so because of changing technology. An example of this type of situation would a company that ran CAT 3 cable in the early or mid 90s for their 10 megabit network, but now want to upgrade their network to 1 gigabit. In this situation, it is not possible to use the existing cables to meet the needs of the company. In this situation it is necessary to replace the entire cable infrastructure to meet the company's new requirements. This is one of the reasons why it is considered good building methodology to purchase the most advanced cables available even if the cable you purchase is way beyond the needs of your current network requirements. Sooner or later the company will want to upgrade to whatever the newest technology is and when that happens you and your company will be very glad you went with the higher end cable.

PROTOCOL ANALYZING

Protocol analyzing is the act of running a protocol analyzer on the network. You do this to verify that the network is able to pass certain protocols such as gigabit Ethernet or if it has to be rewired before you can run it.

Running a protocol analyzer on the network can also give you a picture of what is going on with your network. For example, if the network seems to be running too slow, you can run a protocol analyzer to look for suspicious network activity. A protocol analyzer can reveal if a particular computer is pushing out packets at a constant rate and therefore slowing down the network by congesting it. The computer throwing out the packets could have a bad NIC, or it could have some type of malware on it causing it to behave in this way. Either way, by running a protocol analyzer on the network, you will be able to see this type of suspicious activity.

TIME-DOMAIN REFLECTOMETER (TDR)

If you feel you have a cabling problem on your network, but you have tested all your patch cables, then it may be time to pull out the TDR. This device is used to test longer copper cable runs to verify that there are not breaks in the network cable. If there is a break in the network cable, the TDR will be able to spot it and tell you the approximate location of the break. You then have the option of physically splicing the break, running a replacement cable, or activating a cable you ran when you built the network but did not utilize because you wanted to use it for a reserve, depending on the situation you are in. Optical TDRs serve a similar function for fiber-optic cables.

Running extra cables as a reserve is a very good practice to get into when you are initially wiring a network. The idea behind running a couple of reserve cables to every location on the network is to have backup cables in case one goes bad. It is very difficult to run a single cable if the walls and jacks are already in place. It is much easier to run a few extra cables to each general location in a network to use as an in-place reserve should the extra cables be needed to take up the slack for a bad cable or if the network location needs to be expanded unexpectedly.

SWITCH AND ROUTER CONFIGURATION TESTING

Sometimes the problems on a network are not physical problems like the ones we have already mentioned. Sometimes the problem is in the configuration of the routers and/or switches on a network.

In the case of switches, a particular port on a switch may be configured for VLAN 3 when the computer connected to that port needs to be in VLAN 4. In that case, you can either move the cable or reconfigure the VLAN. Also, sometimes network engineers find it necessary to reconfigure the switches and the VLANs because the needs of the network have changed. Whenever a major reconfiguration of this type takes place, there is a good chance that something will get missed and a computer that could access the network before will no longer be able to. In those instances, you need to go back and reevaluate or test the new configuration to determine why a certain computer or group of computers were missed and to correct the network accordingly.

All of this is also true of routers. Occasionally a router somewhere on the network may go down and access is cut off to that part of the network. When this happens, it sometimes becomes necessary to reconfigure one or more routers to bypass the failed router. Another reason the routers on a network may need reconfiguring is when a new section is added to the network or two previously unconnected networks are now being connected. Like with switches, when a reconfiguration takes place, there is always a chance that the person doing the reconfiguring may make a mistake. They may lead to a wrong interface, IP address, subnet mask, network ID, or some other such mistake. When this happens, a portion of the network becomes unavailable. To determine the problem, the network engineers have to test the router configurations to see where the error was made.

Mismatched MTU

MTU stands for maximum transmission unit and is the maximum size packet that a specific protocol is able to accommodate when transmitting on a network. Different protocols have different MTU sizes they will accept. A mismatched MTU can mean one of two things. It could mean that the MTU being sent by a computer is greater than the protocol being used to handle the MTU is able to support. Alternatively, it can mean that one side of a network connection is expecting an MTU of one size, but is receiving an MTU of a different size.

When a problem similar to either of the ones just mentioned occurs, the devices communicating with each other are forced to change the size of the MTU they are using to accommodate the setting on the other end of the connection. This can result in lots of extra processing going on inside the transmitting and receiving devices. This slows down the device's ability to handle in coming traffic and can even in some cases result in the sender or receiver loosing the ability to transmit data. When configuring connectivity devices such as routers, switches, or NICs you should take the effort to ensure that all devices on the network are expecting MTUs of the same size. Fortunately many if not most modern devices automatically regulate MTU size thus ensuring that all MTUs on the network are the same.

MTU black hole

An MTU black hole occurs when a device on a network transmits a packet that is larger than the possible MTU size of the protocol carrying the packet. When this happens, the packet is normally broken up into smaller packets and they are able to still be received successfully. However, on occasion the IP packet that exceeds the MTU of the IP protocol also has a flag that does not allow the packet to be broken up into smaller packets. In this situation the destination of the packet is designated as unreachable. An MTU black hole is a router or other device that has been set to such as

CERTIFICATION READY
What is meant by the term mismatched MTU? What is an MTU black hole?
2.5

small MTU that all the packets received by that router are rejected as too big. One way to resolve this issue is to re-configure the router or other device with a larger MTU.

Bad modules

Many modern routers and switches have modular expansion cards just like computer do. With these modular expansion cards, additional capabilities can be added to the router or switch receiving the expansion card. However, on occasion those expansion cards can be bad because of power surges, heat, humidity, or simply because they wore out. Should this happen it becomes necessary to replace the bad card or cards with a new one.

SFPs. SFP stands for small form factor pluggable module and is sometimes referred to as a Mini-GBIC. SFPs are transceivers that are used in routers and switches to support a large variety of media technologies. These transceivers usually come in the form of a single port connection and are hot-swappable.

GBICs. GBIC stands for gigabit interface controller. GBICs have a larger form factor than SFPs, but are otherwiseused in the same manner. Like SFPs, GBICs are pluggable and hot swappable.

Power failure

Power failure is an obvious switch or router problem that is surprisingly common. Power failures can because by natural disasters, problems with the electric company, or even by squirrels stepping on the wrong parts of a transformer sitting on a power pole. Because routers and switches like other computing devices require software to be running in memory before it can be used. However, if power fails, then the memory is not refreshed resulting in the loss of the ability of the router or switch to continue to do its job. With this limitation in mind, many companies have some form of backup power available for their switches and routers. This usually takes on a two-stage solution. An UPS, uninterruptible power supply is connected to the router or switch that is able to keep it up for a limited amount of time. While the UPS is keeping the switch or router up the company's standalone generator kicks on and provides the power requirements for the building until the main power can be brought back on.

However, such elaborate scenarios as just described are not the only power failures you have to worry about. Another power failure that is actually more common is the power failure that occurs when a router or switch is accidentally turned off or unplugged. When a router or switch stops functioning for no apparent reason, it is always a good idea to first check to see if it has been turned off or unplugged before beginning more elaborate troubleshooting measures. It is surprising how often something as simple as turning the router back on or plugging it back in will resolve the issue of a non-functioning router or switch.

■ Common Connectivity Issues

THE BOTTOM LINE

We examine common connectivity issues in this section of Lesson 12. First, we take a look at common physical issues related to connectivity, next we discuss logical connectivity issues. Finally, we examine common connectivity issues found in wireless networks.

Connectivity issues have to do with a network computer or device being unable to communicate or connect to the rest of the network. These connectivity issues come in two types— physical and logical issues. We examine both types of connectivity issues in this lesson. Keep in mind that no matter whether a connectivity issue is physical or logical in nature, there are several common causes that account for a significant percentage of connectivity issues. We inspect some of these common issues in this section of Lesson 12.

Physical Issues

Physical issues mean something is physically wrong with the network. This could be related to the length of cable runs, proximity of cables to each other, electromagnetic interference, or any number of other issues.

DB loss

DB loss stands for decibel loss and refers to the signal over a connection becoming weaker or even disappearing. There are many things that can cause db loss. Anytime something happens that results in the signal being sent across the connection becoming weaker or disappearing, db loss has occurred. As such physical issues such as bad connections, bad wires, cross talk, attenuation, even collisions can result in db loss. All of these situations and more are discussed below.

BAD CONNECTORS

One physical issue is bad connectors. When connectors are bad, you may get an intermittent problem or no signal at all. When a connector goes bad it is necessary to replace it with a good one.

BAD WIRING

Bad wiring is similar to bad cabling we discussed above and will result in intermittent signal problems or no signal at all. When wiring goes bad, full replacement is usually the best solution.

SPLIT CABLES

Split cables occur when one or more wires in the cable are separated from the other wires in the cable and can no longer carry a signal. When this happens the cable needs to be replaced.

Another type of split cable occurs when two different connectors are run off the same cable but using different wires in the cable. Many times older network configuration will allow splitting off more than one connector from a single cable, however, when it comes time to upgrade the system, split cables can result in the signal not getting where it needs to go. When this happens, the cables that have been split off to carry two different signals often have to be replaced by two separate cables to do the same job.

TXRX REVERSED

TXRX stands for transmit signal and receive signal. When TXRX are reversed this means that the transmit wire is connected to the receive wire on the other end of the cable and the receive wires is connected to the transmit wire on the opposite end. If you are attempting to create a crossover cable as discussed in Lesson 3 this is good and expected. However, if you are simply attempting to connect two devices up to a network this can cause a problem. If the cable is a short patch cable then the cable with the crossed transmit and receive wires needs to be replaced. If the cable with the crossed transmit and receive wires is part of a longer cable, then the current connector needs to be taken off and a new connector placed on the crossed end with the correct wires going to the correct pin locations.

CABLE PLACEMENT

Cable placement is important because you do not want to run a cable in area where there is electromagnetic interference to disrupt the signal. In order to avoid this, cables should not be placed near electric motors, run alongside wires carrying large amounts of power, or across florescent lights. All of these things can disrupt the signal in a copper cable through EM.

CROSSTALK

One physical issue that you may encounter in a network beyond physical problems with the cables is *crosstalk*. This is where the signal in one wire interferes with the signal in another wire. When this happens, the signals in both wires are impacted and both are weakened. The result of this is that a signal is not able to travel as far down the wire as it should or the packets being sent down the wire could be corrupted and possibly lose their content.

CERTIFICATION READY
What is crosstalk and how would you go about diagnosing it?
3.6

A good way to think about crosstalk is to think about AM radio stations—when you are moving out of range of one radio station and moving into range of another radio station that uses the same channel, you can kind of hear what is being said on both radio stations but not clearly. That is a form of crosstalk. In computers, crosstalk occurs when two wires are too close together or are not shielded well. However, the result is the same. Just like with the two radio stations, you will not be able to clearly hear the information that is passing down the two wires. We discuss two types of crosstalk—nearing crosstalk and near end crosstalk.

Nearing crosstalk

Nearing crosstalk is more commonly called alien crosstalk (AXT). This type of crosstalk occurs when two or more data cables are brought too close together. When this happens, the signal in one cable bleeds over into the other cable resulting in the signal of both cables being corrupted. Alien crosstalk can also occur when a data cable is brought too close to a cable belonging to a power circuit or ballast in a florescent light. These two items as well as other types of items give off large amounts of electromagnetic interference (EMI) or noise. Excessive EMI can result in the signal on a data cable being washed out to the point that the receiving network device is not able to understand the contents of the packet.

The best way to deal with this type of crosstalk is to be careful where you run data cables. Avoid placing them alongside wires carrying power for the facility. You should also avoid draping the data cables across florescent lights, especially their ballast. Finally you want to avoid placing your data cables too close to any other source of EMI as well, such as fan motors or similar items.

Near end crosstalk

Near end crosstalk (NEXT) occurs when the signal of one cable is heard on another cable. This type of crosstalk is not only corrupting the signal; it is actually overriding the other signal. The most likely cause of this type of crosstalk is a poorly constructed patch cable. Near end crosstalk can occur when an RJ-45 connector ends up with two wires forced into the same contact. This usually manifests itself on a cable tester as two signals being seen on the same pin.

ATTENUATION

Attenuation, as previously discussed, is the gradual weakening of a data signal over time and distance. All forms of network media have attenuation. However, the amount of attenuation over a set time and/or distance depends on the media being used. Fiber-optic cables have the lowest attenuation rates, while Wi-Fi and other types of wireless media have the highest.

In copper cables, this problem usually shows up as a progressive loss of more and more packets as you get beyond the range of data that the cable can reliably carry. In Wi-Fi environments, attenuation usually manifests itself as lower and lower throughput data rates and a progressively weaker signal.

Attenuation becomes a problem with networks when there are devices located at the very end of the network media's range or even slightly beyond. Attenuation shows up as lost signals, weak signals, dropped packets, lower data rates, a greater susceptibility to electromagnetic interference, and other similar symptoms. One thing to keep in mind about attenuation and EMI: the greater the EMI, the greater the attenuation. If EMI is sufficiently bad, it can even reduce the signal range of the media.

The way to work around the impact of EMI on network attenuation is to use network media that are less vulnerable to EMI. Fiber-optic cable is virtually immune to EMI. Shielded copper cable is the next least affected by EMI. Unshielded copper cable is third least affected by EMI. Finally WiFi and other wireless networking technologies are the most affected by EMI. This also means that the impact of what EMI is present is directly proportional to the media being used.

If you find yourself in a situation where attenuation is becoming an issue, there are a couple of things you can do about it. One, you can make shorter or more direct cable runs.

CERTIFICATION READY
What causes attenuation? What steps can be taken when attenuation is an issue?
3.6

Alternatively you can boost or repeat the signal once attenuation gets to the point that it is on the verge of interfering with the signal. Keep in mind that this can only be done a few times before repeating the signal loses its effectiveness. Finally you can set up an additional Intermediate Distribution Frame (IDF) to connect the computers in the area of the network where attenuation is beginning to adversely affect data signals. An IDF is a switch room that is designed to be a central collection point for a network beyond the point where the network originated. IDFs contain their own switches and are generally connected to the Main Distribution Frame (MDF) by fiber or some other type of high-capacity media. An MDF is the point of origin for an entire local network. An MDF is generally located at the point where any outside data signals come into a building to be distributed to other network devices within the building. A large LAN has one MDF and as many IDFs as needed to make sure that clear clean signals are able to reach every part of the LAN.

Distance

Distance and attenuation are related issues. Attenuation becomes noticeable and can affect network performance when the distance a signal has to travel is further than the recommended length of a cable for a specific specification. When a cable exceeds the recommended length, attenuation and other problems related to signal loss become more pronounced. If a cable needs to be longer than the recommended length, you need to change to a different standard that allows for a longer cable length or you need to place a device in between that can increase the strength of a signal such as a switch or a repeater.

COLLISIONS

Collisions are a regular part of Ethernet networks. When two different devices attempt to transmit at the same time over the shared media, a collision is inevitable. Ethernet, as we discussed in previous lessons is designed to take this into account and compensate for it. The problem occurs where there are too many collisions, which usually shows itself in the form of a very low throughput rate, many lost packets, or a noticeable slowing down of the network. There are several reasons that too many collisions can occur.

You may have too many collisions because you have too many devices on the same network segment. The solution to this is to break the large segment up into smaller segments using a switch or a bridge.

You could have too many collisions on a network because you have one end user using too much bandwidth on the segment and the other devices on the segment are having a hard time getting their packets moving across the network. A single end user can take up too much bandwidth doing several different things, such as downloading very large files such as videos or MP3s, watching a lot of streaming video, or playing multiplayer games on the company network. To pinpoint which end user and to find out what they are doing, it may be necessary to use a protocol analyzer to see where most of the packets are coming from and what those packets contain. Once you have identified the guilty end user, you can take steps to limit that person's bandwidth usage and thereby curtail whatever activity required so much bandwidth.

Another reason a large number of collisions can appear on a network is because of a faulty network device. You may have a bad network device that is constantly broadcasting signals over the network. This is called a broadcast storm. To locate what device is making the network storm, a protocol analyzer would again come in handy. Once you have located the device causing the broadcast storm, you can then take whatever steps you need to fix whatever problem there is with the device.

Not all broadcast storms are caused by faulty equipment. Viruses and other malicious software can also cause broadcast storms with the same result. Before you jump on that end user using too much bandwidth, you need to verify that the end user really is using the bandwidth. It may actually be some malicious software that has been snuck onto his or her computer causing the problem and the end user is unaware of it.

SHORTS

Shorts can occur when wires carrying electrical signals or power physically touch each other after having their insulation worn off at the point where they make contact. The result is a signal that shorts out at that point and is not able to go any further. This problem often shows up as a lost connection. When a short takes place, the only viable option is to either reinsulate the wires or run new wires.

Shorts can also take place when a wire is cut. If a wire is cut, it can no longer carry an electrical signal. There are really only two solutions to this problem. You can either reconnect the two parts of the cut wire by splicing them, or you can run a new wire.

TDRs are good devices for locating both kinds of shorts on a network. If you are using fiber-optic cable, then you would use an OTDR.

OPEN IMPEDANCE MISMATCH (ECHO)

Impedance refers to a data cable's electrical resistance. An impedance mismatch is where the resistance placed on the cable does not match the resistance of the cable. When this happens, the signal on the cable can be reflected back, which can result in collisions and other signal problems. If the reflection or echo is not too bad, it may just affect the attenuation of the network and still allow signals to get through. However, signal reflection can be so bad that it takes out any signal it is reflected back onto.

One way to minimize impedance mismatch on a network is to place a terminator on either end of the network cable. A terminator is basically a resister that is placed at the end of a network cable. The resister acts to absorb an excess electromagnetic signal, thereby preventing impedance mismatch and reflection.

INTERFERENCE

We have discussed various types of interference that network devices can cause in each other, but interference does not have to just come from other network devices. Any device that contains an electrical motor can cause interference on a network. Even a fan sitting too close to a network device or computer can cause electromagnetic interference (EMI).

Interference that is caused by something external to the network is called *environmental interference*. Environmental interference can be caused by something like the fan just discussed or by close proximity to high-tension power lines, large transformers, or generators. Close proximity to a powerful radio broadcast antenna can result in enough environmental interference to even interfere with the broadcast over an unshielded twisted-pair network. Too many electrical devices pulling power from the same electrical circuit can also cause environmental interference. This is one reason that houses and offices have multiple circuits to meet all the electrical demands placed on them. Environmental interference can be caused by anything outside of the network that creates strong electromagnetic fields.

The best way to avoid environmental interference is to make sure that you do not place any network cabling or network devices near sources of strong electromagnetic fields. If you find a device that is generating a strong enough electromagnetic field near a networking device, you should move either the network device, or the device creating the strong electromagnetic field, depending on which is more practical.

One the biggest causes of environmental interference you may encounter in the workplace is actually cell phones and similar devices. A way to see this is to have your cell phone near a computer with speakers on and then have somebody call you on it. When they do, you will hear a crackling or a popping from the computer speakers. That crackling or popping sound is caused by the electromagnetic interference caused by the power spike created when the cell phone receives the call. Small personal fans in the workplace have also been known to create a certain amount of electromagnetic interference.

Logical Issues

Logical connectivity issues are the other type of connectivity issue we will look at. Logical connectivity issues usually have something to do with a configuration being wrong or incorrect somewhere on the network. The configuration issue can be on a local computer, switch, router, server, or some other network connectivity device. The main logical connectivity issues we examine here are incorrect IP addresses, incorrect VLANs, wrong subnet mask, wrong gateway, wrong DNS address, port speed, or a port duplex mismatch.

INCORRECT IP ADDRESS

Incorrect IP addresses can have a couple of different results depending on how incorrect the IP address is. If the IP address is simply a duplicate IP address on the network, then you will receive an error to the effect that there is an IP conflict on the network. This problem, whatever its cause, usually manifests itself in the form of an IP conflict error message. When you receive the IP conflict error, it means that there is another computer on the network with the same IP address as the computer that just showed the IP conflict error. When this happens, you can look around for another computer that displays the same error. Once you find that computer, you need to change the IP address on one of the affected computers. One of the ways that this error can come about is if one computer is set to DHCP and another computer is set to static IP. This situation can be resolved by changing both computers to DHCP, or by modifying the DHCP server to leave an exception for the IP that is static. By making the static IP an exception, DHCP will not attempt to assign that IP address to another computer. In the case of duplicate IP addresses, the affected computer can often still get on the network; it will consistently display the IP conflict error message.

When the incorrect IP address is so incorrect that it is not even in the same logical network as the rest of the computers in same physical segment of the network, the computer with the incorrect IP address simply will not be able to get on the network at all. When this happens, you need to go in and change the IP address to one that is in the same logical network as all the other computers in the same physical segment. Alternatively, you can set the affected computer to use DHCP. If the computer is already using DHCP, you need to check the configuration of the DHCP server for the affected segment to be sure that it is only attempting to issue IP addresses in the correct range.

INCORRECT VLAN

If a computer is connected to an incorrect VLAN, several things can happen. If the network is segregated based on VLANs, then a computer connected to an incorrect VLAN will not be able to access those resources to which it needs access. Depending on how the VLANs are configured, a computer in the wrong VLAN could lose contact with needed resources. If connected to the wrong VLAN, a computer could also lose access to the Internet. Perhaps in certain situations, a computer could gain access to resources and information to which it is not supposed to have access. In some ways given the right circumstances, a computer gaining access to resources it should not have access to could be worse than not having access to resources to which it does need access. Making sure everything is connected to the right VLAN is a very important function of a network administrator or support specialist.

An incorrect VLAN can be either a physical issue or a logical issue. If you remember from Lesson 6, VLANs are often grouped based on port locations on a switch. If the patch cable from a wall jack is connected to the wrong port on a switch, it could be connected to an incorrect VLAN. In this situation, once you have located the error, all you have to do is move the patch cable to the correct port and the affected computer is back in the correct VLAN.

However, it is also possible that a computer being connected to an incorrect VLAN can be a logical problem. This is a logical problem if the switch is configured incorrectly. If your plan calls for specific ports to be part of a certain VLAN, but when you go to configure the switch you put one or more ports in the wrong VLAN, then the computer connected to those ports will be in the wrong VLAN. When this happens, you need to do a couple of things. First, you need to verify that the patch cables are connected to the ports they are supposed to be connected to. Once you have verified the patch cables are where they are supposed to be, then you need to look at the switch's configuration. Once you have located the problem in the switch's configuration, you can then correct the configuration and everything will be back in the correct VLAN.

WRONG SUBNET MASK

As you remember from Lesson 4, the subnet mask tells the computer what portion of an IP address is network and what portion is host. If you have the wrong subnet mask in a computer, the computer will identify the network the computer is part of incorrectly. When this happens, the end user will not be able to access the network they are attempting to access, and more often than not, no network at all. The way to resolve this is to change the computer's configuration so that it contains the correct subnet mask. If you are using DHCP, then the subnet mask is coming from the DHCP server just like all other IP configuration is. If you are running DHCP and the subnet mask is wrong, then the configuration of the DHCP server needs to be changed to send out the correct subnet mask.

WRONG GATEWAY

The gateway is basically where the computer goes if it does not know where a particular IP address is located. Usually the gateway is the IP address of the router that controls access to the larger network for a particular switch or network segment. If you have the wrong gateway in a computer, you will not be able to access any computers or other resources outside of what is accessible by the switch or segment you are currently on. In real terms, this often means that you can access your local network but you cannot access the Internet or any other network outside of the local network. When you come across this problem in your daily support activities, you simply need to change the gateway IP address to the correct gateway address and the problem will be solved. However, because gateway IP addresses are assigned by the DCHP server just like other IP configuration information, if you see a computer that does not have the correct gateway information, but is set to DHCP, then you will again need to check the configuration of the DHCP server to verify that it is sending out the correct gateway IP address.

WRONG DNS ADDRESS

DNS addresses are the IP address of the DNS server or servers that translates URLs for the local computer to IP addresses for access outside the local network. Put another way, without a DNS server, you would not be able to use the Internet or access any locations outside of the local computer unless you happen to know what the IP address is. Given this fact, if a person seems to be able to get on the local network, but cannot access the Internet, you may want to verify that they have the correct DNS addresses saved in their TCP/IP configuration. If they do not, you will need to change their DNS address to the correct one. If you do not know the correct DNS IP addresses, you can go to a computer on the same segment that can get on the Internet and run an "ipconfig /all" from its command line. This will tell you what the DNS IP addresses are. You can write those down and then go back to the computer with the problem and change its DNS IP address settings to the same DNS IP address that works for the other computer.

DNS IP addresses are one of those things that DHCP servers are supposed to configure automatically. Therefore, if you see a computer with the wrong DNS address using DHCP, you may want to verify the configuration of the DHCP server. Both the nslookup tool and the dig tool may be helpful in diagnosing problems related to DNS.

PORT CONFIGURATION ISSUES

Port Configuration issues are those situations where the ports on a router or switch are configured incorrectly. When this happens, it prevents data on the network from getting to the destination it is intended to get to. The next two sections of this Lesson deal with different issues where the ports on a router or switch are configured incorrectly.

CERTIFICATION READY
What types of router and switch configurations might cause you to encounter connectivity issues?
2.1

A different type of port configuration issue can take place when software is being configured to run on a network device. Anytime a program, process, or protocol runs on a network, it is assigned a network port address to use. If a program, process, or protocol is assigned one port address but attempts to use a different port address then another type of port configuration issue called an address port configuration issue has occurred. In order to fix a problem of this nature, it is necessary to change the configuration of the program, process, or protocol so that it can use the correct port address. Alternatively, the network device that the protocol, process, or program is using needs to have its configuration changed to allow for the new port address.

PORT SPEED

Port speed is another one of those things that is both physical and logical. Port speed is physical because it is the rate at which a port is sending out data. Port speed is logical because it is something that is generally configured within the router or switch. Port speed can be wrong if you have a 100 mbps NIC connected to a gigabit port. The 100 mbps NIC will not be able to read the data coming out of the much faster port. When something like this happens, you need to either move the connection to a slower port, or change the configuration of the switch or router to send data out at a slower rate. Fortunately this is not something that you will likely run into because most routers and switches are designed to sense the speed of the NIC connected to them and adjust their speed accordingly.

The one place where port speed may become an issue is when configuring serial interfaces on routers. In that situation, you need to be sure that you set the serial interface to a speed that the serial connection can handle. If you do not configure the serial interface correctly, the two ends of the serial connection may not be able to communicate with each other.

PORT DUPLEX MISMATCH

Port duplex mismatches are one of those things that you are not likely to ever see because most of the devices you come across are able to sense what the duplex being used is and adjust themselves accordingly. Port duplex mismatch is where the port on the switch or the router is set to either half-duplex or full-duplex while the NIC or other connecting device is set to the other. In this case, either the NIC will adjust itself, the switch or router will adjust itself, or you will have to go in and manually adjust one or the other. It is generally easier to adjust the NIC because there is a setting under the NIC's properties dialog box that will allow speed and duplex to be adjusted. It will usually be under the advanced tab and may be labeled something like Speed and Duplex. Figure 12-30 shows the Advanced Tab of a NIC's Properties Dialog Box with the Speed & Duplex setting highlighted.

Figure 12-30

Speed & Duplex options in a NIC's Properties dialog box

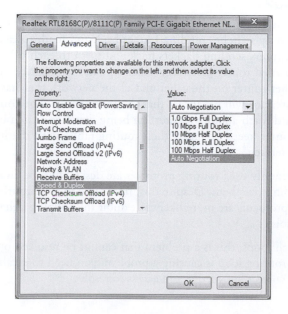

Figure 12-30 also shows all the Speed and Duplex settings that are possible for this particular NIC. Notice that the default setting of the NIC is "Auto Negotiate." This is because most NICs are designed to determine port speed and duplex setting automatically. NICs and other network devices should be left to determine port speed and duplex setting automatically unless there is a compelling reason to change it for a particular network or device.

Issues That Should Be Escalated

As mentioned previously in this lesson, there are some problems that you simply cannot fix yourself. Either you do not have the prerequisite knowledge or you do not have the necessary access, or both. When you come across those types of problems, they need to be escalated or redirected to the person who has the necessary knowledge and/or access to resolve the problem. In this section of Lesson 12, we discuss some problems that usually fall into the need-to-be-escalated category, such as switch loops, routing loops, route problems, proxy arp servers, and broadcast storms.

SWITCH LOOP

A *switch loop* is where two or more switches keep sending frames back and forth to each other and nowhere else. When a switch loop occurs, the end users are unable to access anything on the network and their requests keep timing out. When this happens, it usually means that a switch went down or a switch's configuration has been corrupted. As you remember from Lesson 6, the Spanning Tree Protocol is designed to prevent switch loops from taking place. However, sometimes a switch breaks or something else will happen that prevents the spanning tree from doing its job.

When you suspect a switch loop is going on, you should escalate that up to the department that deals with switch and router configurations and support, usually the WAN engineering department. In smaller companies, there may not be a separate department that deals with switches and routers. However, even if there is not a department, there will be someone either on staff or who can be called in to resolve issues related to switches and routers. This is the person this type of problem should be escalated to. When you suspect a problem of this nature, you should not try to fix it unless you have the proper training and access to do so.

ROUTING LOOP

A routing loop is another one of those problems that should be escalated. Where switch loops are caused by switches sending frames back and forth to each other, routing loops are caused by routers sending packets back and forth to each other. Routing loops can be caused by a downed router interface, which updates its neighbor routers of the outage. However another router on the other end of the network that has not gotten the report of the downed interface will broadcast that the router is up. The routers in the network broadcasting back and forth about the interface being down and then being up again results in a loop as each router keeps updating their routing tables with the incorrect information on the downed interface.

The most commonly used routing protocols are designed to be aware of routing loops and to take steps to minimize them. Despite this, from time to time routing loops may form. Vector-based routing protocols are more likely to exhibit this looping behavior than link state–based routing protocols.

Like with switch loops, this is a problem that cannot be resolved by looking at a computer. If you think a routing loop is causing a problem, you need to escalate that problem to somebody with the correct knowledge and access to resolve it.

X REF

These types of protocols were discussed in Lesson 5. You can reread the section of that lesson about routing protocols if you want more information.

ROUTE PROBLEMS

Route problems are not loops in a router's routing table, but they are problems with the router's routing table. Routing loops are a specific type of routing table problem where each router's routing table keeps getting updated back and forth about a downed interface. Any other problem with a router's routing table, hardware, configuration, and so on falls under the category of routing problems.

If you suspect the cause of a problem you are attempting to resolve is related to a router, it should be escalated to somebody who has the knowledge and access to resolve it. In most cases problems related to switch loops, router loops, and other router and switch problems should be escalated either to the WAN engineering department or the individual in the company with a comparable title.

PROXY ARP

We discussed proxy servers in Lessons 6 and 10.

A proxy ARP server is just another type of proxy gateway. In the case of a proxy ARP server, it is a server intended to answer ARP queries from other computers on the network that are not on the same segment. A proxy ARP server is essentially an ARP query redirector. It takes an ARP query from one place on the network and forwards it to another place on the network using its own MAC address instead of the MAC address of the device making the query. In a way, it acts as a NAT server for MAC addresses.

A proxy ARP server is essentially a MAC gateway. As such, any problem with a proxy ARP server should always be escalated to someone with the appropriate knowledge and access to resolve the problem. Depending on the organization of the company you are working for, the appropriate escalation direction would either be to WAN engineering or network administration.

BROADCAST STORMS

Broadcast storms are caused when packets keep getting broadcasted from one network device to another. Any device connected to a network can cause broadcast storms. Sometimes they are caused by faulty hardware and sometimes they may be caused by malicious software.

A problem with broadcast storms can sometimes be resolved by a network support technician and sometimes need to be escalated. Once you know what is causing the broadcast storm, then you can determine whether the broadcast storm can be resolved by the tech or should be escalated. If a NIC in a workstation is causing the broadcast storm, then the network support tech would be expected to replace the NIC and thus resolve the issue. If a server is causing the broadcast storm, then the network administrator would be expected to resolve the issue. If a router or some other type of network device, not a server or workstation, is causing the broadcast storm, then the WAN engineer would be expected to resolve the problem.

A broadcast storm caused by malicious software usually requires a team effort to resolve. The WAN engineer may be forced to shut down key network devices or gateways in order to contain the broadcast storm and possibly reconfigure firewalls to stop any malicious packets from coming into the network. Network administrators may have to shut down or disconnect a server from the network if the malicious software causing the storm is coming from a specific server. Meanwhile, the network support specialist may need to go to each workstation on the network and erase any malicious software to ensure that the broadcast storm will not start up somewhere else.

There was a company back in the late 90s that experienced exactly what was just described. The Melissa virus had hit the company and infected pretty much every computer the company owned, servers and workstations. Every time someone opened e-mail the virus would propagate to every computer on the network. This resulted in a broadcast storm that brought the network to a halt.

To resolve this problem, the entire IT staff in all departments had to work together to fix it. The WAN engineers of the company were forced to shut down all outside links to the network. They did this to prevent any more e-mails or other packets from outside the company getting into the corporate network to re-infect computers. The WAN engineers also had to reconfigure the firewalls to block any packets from outside the company that carried the virus. After the WAN engineers disconnected all outside links, the network administrators had to disconnect the e-mail servers and all the other servers from the network to halt the spread of the virus between the servers. Once they did that they used a program to remove the malicious software from all the servers and to immunize the servers against further infection. While the network administrators were doing that, the IT analysts, aka network support specialists, had to go to every non-server computer in the company and clean them of the virus and immunize them from further infection using the same program the network administrators used on the severs. It took the entire day to clean every computer in the company, even with eight or nine people working on it. After the network administrators were finished with the servers, they were able to bring them back up, and the WAN engineers then brought up the outside links. Once that was done, the network administrators spent the rest of the day helping the IT analysts clean and immunize the company's non-server computers.

Following the troubleshooting steps mentioned earlier in this lesson, the IT staff got together after everything was resolved to determine what happened. After that meeting, both the WAN engineers and the network administrators took steps to harden their equipment against similar attacks. The IT analysts were also tasked with going to every end user in the company and explaining to them what happened and what they could do to help the IT staff next time something like this happened.

A few months later, another virus was released on the Internet called the I LOVE YOU virus. The I LOVE YOU virus behaved very similarly to the Melissa virus with the same results on infected networks. Because of the training the IT analysts did with company employees and the preventative measures taken by the WAN engineers and network administrators, the I LOVE YOU virus did not infect a single computer in the company. The employees remembered what they were taught by the IT analysts and recognized e-mails infected by the I LOVE YOU virus for what they were and deleted them without opening them and then reported them to the IT staff.

By analyzing what happened during a troubleshooting incident and taking preemptive actions to stop something similar from happening in the future, a second disaster was averted at one company. Unfortunately a lot of other companies that had been hit by the Melissa virus did not follow through with the troubleshooting steps outlined in this lesson. Those companies ended up getting hit again by a similar situation, which was on an even bigger scale than the Melissa virus.

Wireless Issues

CERTIFICATION READY
What are some wireless issues that may occur on a network? What steps can be taken to mitigate specific wireless issues that may come up?
2.4

Just like there are different issues related to connectivity with copper or other cables, there are also issues with wireless connectivity. Some issues are similar to those you would encounter with wired networks, and some are unique to wireless networks. Also there are issues related to wireless networks that are the same as wired networks except they manifest themselves in different ways. We discuss some of these issues—interference, incorrect channel, incorrect, encryption, incorrect frequency, ESSID mismatch, standards mismatch (802.11 a/b/g/n), distance, bounce, and incorrect antenna placement in this section of Lesson 12.

INTERFERENCE

In wired networks, *interference* is caused by strong electromagnetic fields that interfere with the electric impulses used to send signal across a copper wire. In wireless networks, you can have the same problem. The difference is that instead of interfering with electric impulses in a copper wire, the electromagnetic fields interfere with the radio frequency (RF) waves that are used to carry data from one wireless device to another. Because RF waves are a lower frequency than other types of signals used to send data across a network, it is actually easier to interfere with wireless networks than wired networks. In a wired network, the object causing the interference has to be pretty close to the copper wires it is interfering with to disrupt the signal. However, in wireless networks, the object sending out the electromagnetic interference (EMI) actually does not have to be very close to the wireless devices to disrupt the RF signals being used to send data.

While interference in a wireless network is more common and much easier to accomplish than in a wired network, the result is the same. Data signals lose their strength, signals get attenuated more quickly, packets get dropped more often, and less data can be carried over the media the further from the source it is. These problems are very similar to those found when wired networks are interfered with; they are just more pronounced when wireless networks are involved.

One major difference in how you deal with interference in a wired network and a wireless network is how you go about avoiding the interference. In a wired network, when you find an object that is interfering with a signal on a wire or a group of wires, you can move the wires away from the interference and the problem is solved. Things do not work that way with wireless signals. You cannot physically move an RF wave like you can a CAT 6 wire. In a wireless network, you have to physically move the object causing the interference out of the range of the wireless network. If the object causing the interference cannot be moved, you have to use a different medium of communications than wireless networking.

The best way to avoid problems with interference and wireless networks is to check for them ahead of time. Before you decide to build a wireless network, verify that there is not enough EMI in the area to affect the wireless network. If there is, then you need to either find some way to shield from it or use some other medium than wireless for your communications network. Your boss will not be happy with you if you purchase a lot of wireless network equipment only to find out that the high tension power lines right outside the window causes too much interference to actually use that wireless networking equipment.

Bleed

Bleed is a specific kind of interference that has to do with the signal on one channel of the wireless network being picked up by another channel on the wireless network. The best way to picture bleed is to think of AM radio. Sometimes when you listen to an AM radio station you can also hear another AM radio station. That is bleed. The signal from one AM station is bleeding into another AM station. The result is that you can hear parts of both stations, but you cannot hear either station clearly. In wireless networking, you can have the same problem. If you have a couple of different wireless access points (WAPs) in a network, then each WAP needs to have a different channel. If the channels being used by the WAPs are close together, then the signal from one WAP will bleed over into the signal of the other WAP, which results in data from both WAPs being garbled and lost.

In order to avoid this problem, you need to make sure that the channels on the different WAPs are far enough apart that one does not bleed into the other. Depending on which wireless standard you are using, you will have different channels available to you. When setting up WAPs in close proximity, you need to verify that the frequency range for the channel used by each WAP does not overlap the frequency range of any other WAPs that are nearby. If the different frequencies do overlap, you will get bleeding from one channel to the other. Also, because the different wireless standards only have a limited number of channels available to them, you will need to make sure that two WAPs using the same channel do not overlap each other's range. Figure 12-31 illustrates how this would work.

Figure 12-31

Wireless networks with overlapping ranges but not overlapping channels

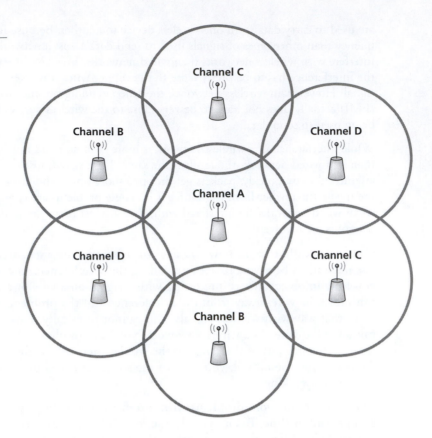

As you can see in Figure 12-31, there are four different channels (A, B, C, and D) available to the wireless network. The WAPs are arranged so that full coverage for the network is available. However, because only four channels are available, each WAP had to be assigned a channel that did not touch the range of another WAP with the same channel. If two WAPs with the same channel overlap each other's range, then bleed would occur where the channels overlapped. Fortunately there is a theorem called the four-color theorem, which states that if you have four colors available to denote different contiguous regions on a map, no two regions of the same color will have borders that are adjacent to each other. The same principle applies here. However, instead of four colors, we have four channels. With four channels available, it is possible to arrange the network so that no two ranges with the same channel assigned to them will be adjacent to, or overlap, each other's range.

Another issue related to bleed is the fact that the wireless signal can be heard or picked up outside of the building where the network is located. In this instance, the bleed is not so much a form of interference as it is a security issue. Because wireless signals use radio frequencies, a person with a laptop computer and a wireless NIC sitting in the parking lot of a company using wireless networking may actually be able to pick up the wireless signal of the network. With the correct hacking tools installed on the laptop, it is not very difficult for a person with malicious intent to hack into the corporate network and gain access to resources you may not want them to have access to via that wireless link.

There are a couple of ways to counter this type of bleed. One option is to use special "paint" coatings on the inside walls of the building with the wireless network. Paint-type coatings that can be used to reflect the wireless signals back into the building so they are not available to be picked up on the outside of the building. Another way to counter this type of bleed is to use encryption and other security tools to make your wireless network more secure. However, you need to keep in mind that if one person can figure out how to secure a wireless signal, another person can figure out how to circumvent that protection.

Environmental factors

Environmental factors are another form of interference. As alluded to in the previous section, environmental factors are objects within the environment of the network that cause interference. These can be the previously mentioned high-tension power lines, or these factors may be other things. Any source of strong electromagnetic fields can be a cause of environmental interference. Some examples would be a power generator near the wireless network, motors for strong fans, high-tension power lines, strong broadcast signals from powerful antenna such as from a TV station, x-ray machines, or many other things.

In some cases, you can move the source of electromagnetic interference so that it is not close enough to interfere with the wireless network; sometimes it is not possible to move them. If it is not possible to move the source of electromagnetic interference, you will have to use media other than wireless for network communications.

Environmental interference is something it is always best to check for before building a wireless network. If you do not, you run the risk of building a network with less range or less reliability than you were planning on. The result of using a wireless network in a high interference area is more dropped packets, less range, and more corrupted data.

CERTIFICATION READY

How can environmental factors affect wireless communications? What can be done about environmental factors?

2.4

INCORRECT CHANNEL

Earlier we discussed the fact that when access points have overlapping ranges, they need to have different channels so that one channel does not bleed over into the other. When one access point has the same channel as an overlapping range, it can be said that one of the access points has an incorrect channel. However, in this case incorrect channel is the channel to which the network device connected to the wireless network is set. When different access points use different channels, then the devices connected to a specific access point need to be set to the same channel as the intended access point. When the network device is set to the wrong channel, it is not able to access the network it is intended to access. Instead, it will access a different network or no network at all. To resolve this problem you need to set the channel on the network device to be the same as the access point that gives it access to the network it is attempting to access.

INCORRECT ENCRYPTION

Incorrect encryption can mean a couple of different things. For the purposes of this lesson, incorrect encryption is using the wrong encryption algorithm when attempting to decipher a message being sent across a wireless network. When configuring a wireless interface, if you choose to use encryption, you are asked which algorithm you wish to use. WPA and WEP are examples of some encryption algorithms that can be chosen. If you choose one encryption algorithm when you set up a wireless NIC but a different algorithm is used by the WAP, then you have an incorrect encryption set up on your NIC. To resolve this situation, you need to go back to the wireless NIC configuration and change the encryption algorithm to the same one being used by the WAP.

Alternatively, incorrect encryption could be short for incorrect encryption key. When you get this error, it means you are not using the correct password or passphrase as the key to decrypt the message. You need to find out what the correct password or passphrase is and use that to decrypt the data coming across the network.

INCORRECT FREQUENCY

Each wireless standard has a certain range of frequencies available to it to break into channels. While there are standard frequency ranges for each channel, it is possible to manually choose the frequency ranges that are to be used by specific channels. If you choose to use customized frequency ranges for each channel, then you run the risk of not setting all the channels used on the wireless network to the same frequency ranges. When this happens, you have a device set to the incorrect frequency. The easiest way to avoid this is to simply use the default channels and then verify that you have set your NICs to the correct channel. However, you may have certain circumstances where you need to use customized channels. In this situation, it is best to make sure all wireless devices use the same ranges. If a device is unable to connect to the network, you may have forgotten to set up a particular device to the correct frequency range for the channel you are using.

ESSID MISMATCH

Wireless devices on a network use ESSIDs to identify them to other devices connected to the same WAP. If a wireless device on the network does not have the correct ESSID set up in its configuration (***ESSID mismatch***), it will not be able to communicate to the WAP. To resolve this, make sure the ESSID in the network device is set to the same ESSID as the WAP. If you do not know what the correct ESSID is, you need to find a network administrator or whoever has that information to get the correct ESSID.

STANDARDS MISMATCH (802.11 A/B/G/N)

There are four common wireless standards currently available for wireless networks. Those standards are the 802.11a, 802.11b, 802.11g, and 802.11n standards. A ***standards mismatch*** is when all the devices on a network do not use the same standard for communication. Some standards mismatches are worse than others. For example, if my WAP is set to *g* but my wireless NIC is set to *n*, there is no big problem because the wireless *n* NIC can read the wireless *g* signal. However, if my access point is set to *a*, but my NIC is set to *g*, I have a problem because *g* cannot read the *a* signal.

Here is a brief rundown of which standards can read which other standards:

- **N devices:** Can read all the other devices.
- **G devices:** Can read G and B devices.
- **A devices:** Can only read themselves, and can be read by N devices.
- **B devices:** Can only read other B devices, and can be read by G or N devices.

CERTIFICATION READY
What is a standards mismatch? Why can this be a problem for wireless networks?
2.4

DISTANCE

Depending on the wireless standard being used, a wireless network can have a range anywhere from 30 feet with Bluetooth to up to 300 feet with 802.11n. You need to keep these limitations in mind when setting up a wireless network. The further away from the center of the wireless range, the lower the data rate for the wireless network. Devices that are close to the periphery of the range will only receive signals erratically. You should also keep in mind that the more interference in the environment, the shorter the actual range of the wireless network becomes.

To overcome this problem, it may be necessary to move the WAP around to find the best location to give your facility maximum coverage. Alternatively, you may find it necessary to boost the wireless signal. A wireless signal can have its range extended by adding one or more wireless routers between the access point and the periphery of the wireless network. Before setting up a wireless network, you need to run a test to determine just what ranges to expect from a wireless network and then position WAPs accordingly.

Latency

We have discussed latency in previous lessons. In this lesson we will discuss it in relationship to wireless networks and troubleshooting. As stated in Lesson 3, one of the causes of latency is the amount of processing that has to be done on a signal as it is passed from one device to another in a network. With wireless networking this is especially true. For a wireless network to ensure that data is sent to the correct destination and arrives at the correct destination multiple addresses are used and different types of identification values are used. Some examples of this would be SSIDs, BSSIDs, ESSIDs, etc. All of this adds more processing requirements to a wireless networks that wired networks do not have. This results in greater latency in a wireless network. The best way to minimize this latency in a wireless network is to minimize the processing that is going on. This means you need to make sure that unneeded processes and services are not running on the wireless network. Another way to minimize this latency is to not run torrents over a wireless network.

Finally, making sure that a wireless signal is as clean and stable as possible is important for reducing latency on a wireless network. One way to keep a wireless network signal clean and stable is to minimize the amount of high powered electrical and electronic devices that are running in the vicinity of your wireless network. Anything that sends out a signal can cause the wireless signal to become unstable. This includes cell phones, simply running powerful electric motors, or even microwave ovens near your wireless devices. Another way to prevent instability in a wireless connection is to make sure that your receiving devices are not too far from your transmitting devices. This goes back to Wireless Access Point placement. If your wireless access point is too far from your wireless receiving device, then all the factors that have just been mentioned as adding instability into a wireless connection is multiplied.

BOUNCE

Bounce refers to the fact that certain surfaces and materials can reflect and split radio signals. The bouncing that wireless signals do can limit the range of a wireless network. Bounce also has the potential to physically disrupt a signal that is sent out from a WAP or NIC. Repositioning a NIC or WAP is probably the best way to minimize the effects of bounce on a wireless network. If this does not work or is not feasible, you may need to reposition furniture or other surfaces that may be contributing to bounce. Ultimately you may have to simply accept that bounce is disrupting your signals and add more access points to the wireless network to work around those obstacles.

INCORRECT SWITCH PLACEMENT

The topic of incorrect switch placement was discussed in Lesson 7. The main point to remember about this topic is that you want a wireless switch placed in a central location so that all the devices that need to connect to it are close to it and not far away. One other consideration for switch placement is that switches should not be placed in a location that is near a source of EMI. The greater the EMI in the area the shorter the range over which a wireless switch can connect.

INCORRECT ANTENNA PLACEMENT

Antenna placement has to do with how the antenna of a wireless device is placed to receive the wireless signal. One thing to keep in mind about antenna placement is the further an antenna is away from the wireless device it is serving, the more disrupted the signal will be because it has to follow a longer wire. In many modern wireless devices, this is not an issue because the antennas are placed inside the devices themselves. However, occasionally you may run across a wireless device that uses an antenna connected to it via a wire. When this is the case, remember to keep the antenna as close to the wireless device as possible to reduce the amount of time the signal stays on the wire.

SKILL SUMMARY

IN THIS LESSON YOU LEARNED:

- That there is not one set of answers that solve all troubleshooting problems.
- The importance of documenting what you do while troubleshooting.
- The different stages of the troubleshooting process.
- How to identify symptoms and problems.
- How to determine what area of a network a problem affects.
- How to establish the most probably cause of a problem.
- How to determine if escalation is needed.
- How to create an action plan and identify potential effects of that action plan.
- How to test and implement a solution.
- How to identify the results of a solution.

- About both Windows and Linux command-line tools that are useful for troubleshooting a network.
- About some hardware tools that are useful for network troubleshooting.
- About some basic actions to take while troubleshooting.
- About some advanced actions you can take while troubleshooting.
- What some common physical connectivity issues you may encounter in networks are.
- What some common logical connectivity issues you may encounter in networks are.
- About some issues that should normally be escalated.
- What some common wireless issues you may encounter are.

■ Knowledge Assessment

Fill in the Blank

Complete the following sentences by writing the correct word or words in the blanks provided.

1. The _____ step is the stage in troubleshooting where you talk to the person reporting the problem in order to gain more information about the problem so that you can resolve it.

2. The _____ step is the stage in troubleshooting where you determine what area or areas of the network are affected by the reported problem.

3. The _____ step is the stage in troubleshooting where you ask about any upgrades or changes that have been made on the network.

4. The _____ step is the stage in troubleshooting where you look at all the evidence you have gathered and decide what the most likely cause of the reported problem is.

5. The _____ step is the stage in troubleshooting where you decide if the problem is something that you can resolve or if it is something that needs to be handed off to someone who is better trained and/or has better access to resolve it.

6. The _____ step is the stage in troubleshooting where you develop a possible solution for the problem and a way to carry out the solution.

7. Once you have completed the step mentioned in question 6, you need to _____ so that if something does not work you will be able to figure out why.

8. The _____ step is the stage in troubleshooting where you carry out your plan and test the results.

9. The _____ step is the stage in troubleshooting where you identify anything that may have changed in the network due to your solution.

10. The _____ step is the stage in troubleshooting where you write down what you did and the reasoning that led you to the solution you chose.

Multiple Choice

Circle the letter corresponding to the correct answer.

1. Which of the following is a Windows CLI tool that can be used to determine what the IP address, subnet mask, gateway, and other addressing information is for the NICs in the local computer?
   a. ifconfig
   b. ipconfig
   c. nslookup
   d. ping

2. Which of the following is a Linux CLI tool used to gain information about DNS servers?
   a. DIG
   b. nbtstat
   c. MTR
   d. snips

3. A CLI tool found in both Linux and Windows that can be used to find out information about ports and protocol usage on a computer is called what?
   a. route
   b. ifconfig
   c. hostname
   d. netstat

4. A CLI tool that can be used in both Windows and Linux that is used to determine if a specific IP address is reachable is called what?
   a. traceroute
   b. arp
   c. ping
   d. route

5. A networking tool that can be used to determine voltage, amperage, continuity, and other measurements is called what?
   a. Protocol analyzer
   b. Tone probe
   c. Multimeter
   d. Butt set

6. When signals on two parallel wires interfere with each other it is called what?
   a. Short
   b. Collisions
   c. Open impedance mismatch
   d. Crosstalk

7. When a signal weakens over time and distance it is called what?
   a. Attenuation
   b. Interference
   c. Nearing crosstalk
   d. Short

8. If a workstation can get on the local network but cannot locate any URLs on the Internet, then the most likely problem is what?
   a. Port speed
   b. Wrong DNS address
   c. Wrong subnet mask
   d. Port duplex mismatch

9. If two switches keep sending the same data frame back and forth to each other but not to any other switches, the most likely problem is what?
   a. Switch loop
   b. Routing loop
   c. Proxy ARP
   d. Broadcast storm

10. When a device keeps sending out packets to all the other devices on a network, what is taking place?
   a. Wrong subnet mask
   b. Wrong gateway
   c. Routing loop
   d. Broadcast storm

11. When a signal is weakened or lost over a network connection it is sometimes referred to as what?
   a. DB Loss
   b. Routing Loop
   c. Loopback
   d. Broadcast storm

12. _____ and _____ are expansion cards that can be used in routers or switches. (Choose two.)
   a. MPLS
   b. SFP
   c. GBIC
   d. TIFF

Lab Exercises

■ **Lab 1**

Doing a Ping Test

The purpose of this lab is to familiarize the student with running a ping test. This lab will also help the student correctly interpret the results of a ping test that they have run.

MATERIALS

- A computer running Windows
- Paper
- Pen or pencil

THE LAB

Run Ipconfig

1. Click the **Start** button.

2. Type **cmd** in the Run box or the Search box depending on which version of Windows you are using.

3. When the CLI windows comes up type **ipconfig /all** then hit the <**Enter**> key on your keyboard. (Note: There should be a space between ipconfig and the /.) The result should be similar to Figure 12-32.

Figure 12-32

Ipconfig /all command

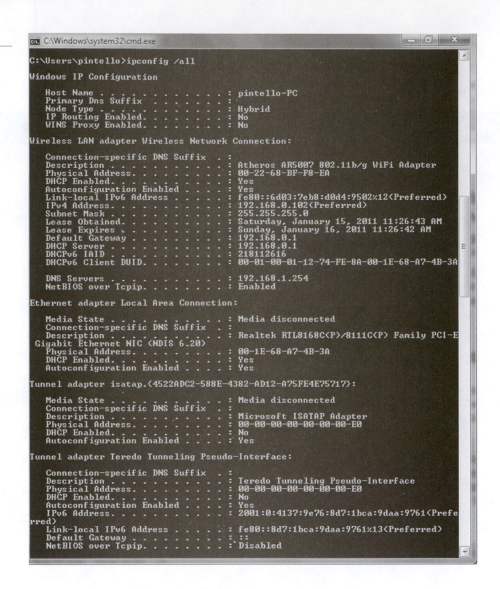

The screenshot shown in Figure 12-32 is taken from Windows 7. If you are running Windows XP your screen will look more like the one shown in Figure 12-2 from earlier in this lesson.

4. Write down the IP address of the local computer.

5. Write down the subnet mask of the local computer.

6. Write down the IP address of the default gateway of the local computer.

7. Write down the IP address of the local DNS server.

Conduct the Ping Test

1. In the Command box type **ping /?** and hit the **<Enter>** key. What are some of the options available for the ping command? Write down six of them and what they do.

2. Type the command **ping 127.0.0.1** and hit the **<Enter>** key. You should get a screen that looks like Figure 12-33.

Figure 12-33

Ping 127.0.0.1 command results

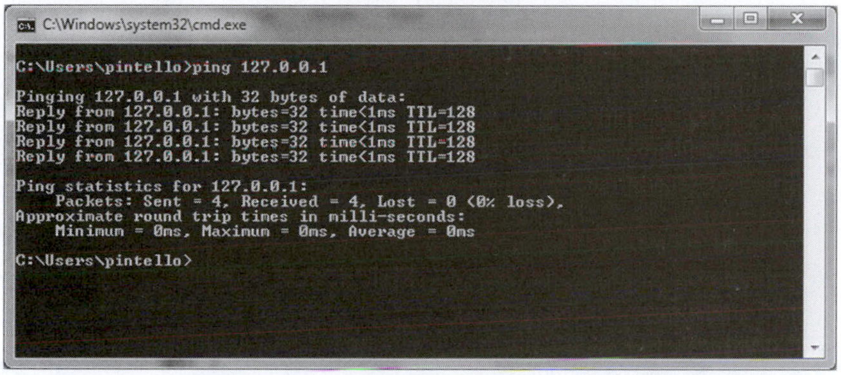

What is significant about the IP address 127.0.0.1?

What does being able to ping the IP address 127.0.0.1 tell us about the local computer?

What would it mean if we could not ping the IP address 127.0.0.1.

3. Ping the IP address of your local computer, which you recorded in step 4 of Lab 1. Were you able to ping your local IP address successfully?

What does being able to ping your local IP address tell us about the local computer?

What would it mean if we could not ping the IP address of the local computer?

4. Ping the IP address of your local computer's gateway that you recorded in step 6 of Lab 1.
   Were you able to ping the IP address of your local gateway successfully?

   What does being able to ping the IP address of the local gateway tell us about the local network?

   What would it mean if we could not ping the IP address of the local gateway?

5. Ping the IP address of your local DNS server that you recorded in step 7 of Lab 1.
   Were you able to ping the IP address of your local DSN server successfully?

   What does being able to ping the IP address of the local DNS server tell us about the local network?

   What would it mean if we could not ping the IP address of the local DNS server?

Lab 2

Using Tracert

The purpose of this lab is to teach the student how to use the tracert Windows CLI command. This lab also teaches the students how to interpret the information they get back from the tracert command and how they can use that information in troubleshooting a network.

MATERIALS

- A computer running Windows
- Paper
- Pen or pencil

THE LAB

Use the Tracert Command

1. Open a command-line window like you did in Lab 1.
2. Type the command **tracert /?** and hit the **<Enter>** key on the keyboard.
   Write down all the options available with tracert and what they do.

3. Do a tracert on the URL yahoo.com. The command you should use is **tracert yahoo. com** and then press the **<Enter>** key. You should get a screen that looks similar to the one shown in Figure 12-34.

Figure 12-34

Tracert yahoo.com command results

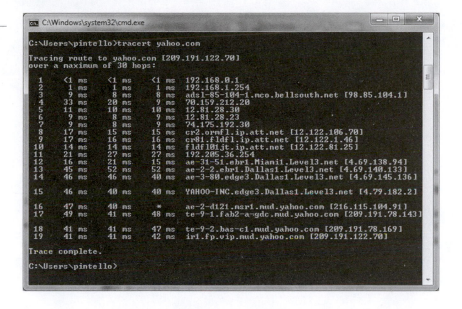

4. Write down the IP address of yahoo.com that was used for the trace route. (Note: There are a number of IPs that Yahoo owns so answers here will vary.)

5. Were you able to get to yahoo.com?

6. If you were not able to get to yahoo.com, why do you think that was?

7. Could a firewall have stopped you?

If you think a firewall stopped you, what do you think the IP address of that firewall is based on where the trace route stopped?

If you do not think a firewall stopped you, what does the last IP address appearing in the trace route list tell you?

TAKE NOTE *

Although your results will look similar to Figure 12-34, they will not be the same; so you cannot use Figure 12-34 to answer the questions.

476 | Lesson 12

8. If you were able to do a trace route all the way to yahoo.com, how many hops did it take?

9. List the name and IP address of a few of the servers you passed through on your way to yahoo.com.

10. As a troubleshooting tool, what types of things do you think you can learn by using the tracert command?

Exam Objective	Exam Objective Number	Lesson Number
Networking Concepts		

Compare the layers of the OSI and TCP/IP models.
• OSI model:
  • Layer 1 – Physical
  • Layer 2 – Data link
  • Layer 3 – Network
  • Layer 4 – Transport
  • Layer 5 – Session
  • Layer 6 – Presentation
  • Layer 7 – Application
• TCP/IP model:
  • Network Interface Layer
  • Internet Layer
  • Transport Layer
  • Application Layer
    • (Also described as: Link Layer, Internet Layer, Transport Layer, Application Layer)
	1.1	2

Classify how applications, devices, and protocols relate to the OSI model layers. • MAC address • IP address • EUI-64 • Frames • Packets • Switch • Router • Multilayer switch • Hub • Encryption devices • Cable • NIC • Bridge	1.2	2, 4, 6

Explain the purpose and properties of IP addressing.
• Classes of addresses
  • A, B, C, and D
  • Public vs. Private
• Classless (CIDR)
• IPv4 vs. IPv6 (formatting)
	1.3	4, 5

Exam Objective	Exam Objective Number	Lesson Number
• MAC address format • Subnetting • Multicast vs. unicast vs. broadcast • APIPA		

Explain the purpose and properties of routing and switching.
• EIGRP
• OSPF
• RIP
• Link state vs. distance vector vs. hybrid
• Static vs. dynamic
• Routing metrics
  • Hop counts
  • MTU, bandwidth
  • Costs
  • Latency
• Next hop
• Spanning-Tree Protocol
• VLAN (802.1q)
• Port mirroring
• Broadcast domain vs. collision domain
• IGP vs. EGP
• Routing tables
• Convergence (steady state)
	1.4	4, 5, 6

Identify common TCP and UDP default ports. • SMTP – 25 • HTTP – 80 • HTTPS – 443 • FTP – 20, 21 • TELNET – 23 • IMAP – 143 • RDP – 3389 • SSH – 22 • DNS – 53 • DHCP – 67, 68	1.5	5
Explain the function of common networking protocols. • TCP • FTP • UDP • TCP/IP suite • DHCP • TFTP • DNS • HTTPS • HTTP • ARP • SIP (VoIP) • RTP (VoIP) • SSH	1.6	5

Exam Objective	Exam Objective Number	Lesson Number
• POP3 • NTP • IMAP4 • Telnet • SMTP • SNMP2/3 • ICMP • IGMP • TLS		
Summarize DNS concepts and its components. • DNS servers • DNS records (A, MX, AAAA, CNAME, PTR) • Dynamic DNS	1.7	6

Given a scenario, implement the following network troubleshooting methodology.
• Identify the problem:
  • Information gathering
  • Identify symptoms
  • Question users
  • Determine if anything has changed
• Establish a theory of probable cause
  • Question the obvious
• Test the theory to determine cause:
  • Once theory is confirmed determine next steps to resolve problem.
  • If theory is not confirmed, re-establish new theory or escalate.
• Establish a plan of action to resolve the problem and identify potential effects.
• Implement the solution or escalate as necessary.
• Verify full system functionality and if applicable implement preventative measures.
• Document findings, actions and outcomes.
	1.8	12

Identify virtual network components. • Virtual switches • Virtual desktops • Virtual servers • Virtual PBX • Onsite vs. offsite • Network as a Service (NaaS)	1.9	6
Network Installation and Configuration		
Given a scenario, install and configure routers and switches. • Routing tables • NAT • PAT • VLAN (trunking) • Managed vs. unmanaged	2.1	4, 5, 6, 10, 11, 12

Exam Objective	Exam Objective Number	Lesson Number

• Interface configurations
  • Full duplex
  • Half duplex
  • Port speeds
  • IP addressing
  • MAC filtering
• PoE
• Traffic filtering
• Diagnostics
• VTP configuration
• QoS
• Port mirroring		

Given a scenario, install and configure a wireless network. • WAP placement • Antenna types • Interference • Frequencies • Channels • Wireless standards • SSID (enable/disable) • Compatibility (802.11 a/b/g/n)	2.2	3, 6, 7
Explain the purpose and properties of DHCP. • Static vs. dynamic IP addressing. • Reservations • Scopes • Leases • Options (DNS servers, suffixes)	2.3	4, 6
Given a scenario, troubleshoot common wireless problems. • Interference • Signal strength • Configurations • Incompatibilities • Incorrect channel • Latency • Encryption type • Bounce • SSID mismatch • Incorrect switch placement	2.4	12
Given a scenario, troubleshoot common router and switch problems. • Switching loop • Bad cables/improper cable types • Port configuration • VLAN assignment • Mismatched MTU/MUT black hole • Power failure • Bad/missing routes • Bad modules (SFPs, GBICs)	2.5	12

Exam Objective	Exam Objective Number	Lesson Number
• Wrong subnet mask • Wrong gateway • Duplicate IP address • Wrong DNS		
Given a set of requirements, plan and implement a basic SOHO network. • List of requirements • Cable length • Device types/requirements • Environment limitations • Equipment limitations • Compatibility requirements	2.6	7

Network Media and Topologies

Exam Objective	Exam Objective Number	Lesson Number

Categorize standard media types and associated properties.
• Fiber:
  • Multimode
  • Singlemode
• Copper:
  • UTP
  • STP
  • CAT3
  • CAT5
  • CAT5e
  • CAT6
  • CAT6a
  • Coaxial
  • Crossover
  • T1 Crossover
  • Straight-through
• Plenum vs. non-plenum
• Media converters:
  • Singlemode fiber to Ethernet
  • Multimode fiber to Ethernet
  • Fiber to Coaxial
  • Singlemode to multimode fiber
• Distance limitations and speed limitations
• Broadband over powerline
	3.1	3, 6

Categorize standard connector types based on network media.
• Fiber:
  • ST
  • SC
  • LC
  • MTRJ
• Copper:
  • RJ-45
  • RJ-11
  • BNC
	3.2	3

Exam Objective	Exam Objective Number	Lesson Number
• F-connector • DB-9 (RS-232) • Patch panel • 110 block (T568A, T568B)		
Compare and contrast different wireless standards. • 802.11 a/b/g/n standards • Distance • Speed • Latency • Frequency • Channels • MIMO • Channel bonding	3.3	3, 6
Categorize WAN technology types and properties. • Types: • T1/E1 • T3/E3 • DS3 • OCx • SONET • SDH • DWDM • Satellite • ISDN • Cable • DSL • Cellular • WiMAX • LTE • HSPA+ • Fiber • Dialup • PON • Frame relay • ATMs • Properties • Circuit switch • Packet switch • Speed • Transmission media • Distance	3.4	8
Describe different network topologies. • MPLS • Point-to-point • Point-to-multipoint • Ring • Star • Mesh	3.5	1, 8

Exam Objective	Exam Objective Number	Lesson Number
• Bus • Peer-to-peer • Client-server • Hybrid		

Given a scenario, troubleshoot common physical connectivity problems.
• Cable problems:
  • Bad connectors
  • Bad wiring
  • Open, short
  • Split cables
  • DB loss
  • TXRX reversed
  • Cable placement
  • EMI/Interference
  • Distance
  • Cross-talk
	3.6	3, 12

Compare and contrast different LAN technologies.
• Types:
  • Ethernet
  • 10BaseT
  • 100BaseT
  • 1000BaseT
  • 100BaseTX
  • 100BaseFX
  • 1000BaseX
  • 10GBaseSR
  • 10GBaseLR
  • 10GBaseER
  • 10GBaseSW
  • 10GBaseLW
  • 10GBaseEW
  • 10GBaseT
• Properties:
  • CSMA/CD
  • CSMA/CA
  • Broadcast
  • Collision
  • Bonding
  • Speed
  • Distance
	3.7	7

Identify components of wiring distribution. • IDF • MDF • Demarc • Demarc extension • Smart jack • CSU/DSU	3.8	3, 6

Exam Objective	Exam Objective Number	Lesson Number
Network Management		
Explain the purpose and features of various network appliances. • Load balancer • Proxy server • Content filter • VPN concentrator	4.1	6, 10
Given a scenario, use appropriate hardware tools to troubleshoot connectivity issues. • Cable tester • Cable certifier • Crimper • Butt set • Toner probe • Punch down tool • Protocol analyzer • Loop back plug • TDR • OTDR • Multimeter • Environmental monitor	4.2	12
Given a scenario, use appropriate software tools to troubleshoot connectivity issues. • Protocol analyzer • Throughput testers • Connectivity software • Ping • Tracert/traceroute • Dig • Ipconfig/ifconfig • Nslookup • Arp • Nbstat • Netstat • Route	4.3	5, 12
Given a scenario, use the appropriate network monitoring resource to analyze traffic. • SNMP • SNMPv2 • SNMPv3 • Syslog • System logs • History logs • General logs • Traffic analysis • Network sniffer	4.4	9, 11

Exam Objective	Exam Objective Number	Lesson Number
Describe the purpose of configuration management documentation. • Wire schemes • Network maps • Documentation • Cable management • Asset management • Baselines • Change management	4.5	11

Explain different methods and rationales for network performance optimization.
• Methods:
  • QoS
  • Traffic shaping
  • Load balancing
  • High availability
  • Caching engines
  • Fault tolerance
  • CARP
• Reasons:
  • Latency sensitivity
  • High bandwidth applications (VoIP, video applications, unified communications)
  • Uptime
	4.6	11

Network Security

Exam Objective	Exam Objective Number	Lesson Number

Given a scenario, implement appropriate wireless security measures.
• Encryption protocols:
  • WEP
  • WPA
  • WPA2
  • WPA Enterprise
• MAC address filtering
• Device placement
• Signal strength
	5.1	7, 10

Explain the methods of network access security.
• ACL:
  • MAC filtering
  • IP filtering
  • Port filtering
• Tunneling and encryption:
  • SSL VPN
  • VPN
  • L2TP
  • PPTP
  • IPSec
  • ISAKMP
	5.2	8, 10

Exam Objective	Exam Objective Number	Lesson Number

• TLS
• TLS1.2
• Site-to-site and client-to-site
• Remote access:
  • RAS
  • RDP
  • PPPoE
  • PPP
  • ICA
  • SSH		

Explain methods of user authentication. • PKI • Kerberos • AAA (RADIUS, TACACS+) • Network access control (802.1x, posture assessment) • CHAP • MS-CHAP • EAP • Two-factor authentication • Multifactor authentication • Single sign-on	5.3	9

Explain common threats, vulnerabilities, and mitigation techniques.
• Wireless:
  • War driving
  • War chalking
  • WEP cracking
  • WPA cracking
  • Evil twin
  • Rogue access point
• Attacks:
  • DoS
  • DDos
  • Man-in-the-middle attacks
  • Social engineering
  • Virus
  • Worms
  • Buffer overflow
  • Packet sniffing
  • FTP bounce
  • Smurf
• Mitigation techniques:
  • Training and awareness
  • Patch management
  • Policies and procedures
  • Incident response
	5.4	9, 10

Exam Objective	Exam Objective Number	Lesson Number

Given a scenario, install and configure a basic firewall.
• Types:
  • Software and hardware firewalls
• Port security
• Stateful inspection vs. packet filtering
• Firewall rules:
  • Block/allow
  • Implicit deny
  • ACL
• NAT/PAT
• DMZ
	5.5	4, 6, 10

Categorize different types of network security appliances and methods.
• IDS and IPS:
  • Behavior based
  • Signature based
  • Network based
  • Host based
• Vulnerability scanners:
  • NESSUS
  • NMAP
• Methods:
  • Honey pots
  • Honey nets
	5.6	6, 10, 11

Appendix B
Network+ Protocols

Acronym	Full Name
APIPA	Automatic Private Internet Protocol Addressing
ARP	Address Resolution Protocol
BGP	Border Gateway Protocol
BOOTP	Boot Strap Protocol
CHAP	Challenge-Handshake Authentication Protocol
DHCP	Dynamic Host Configuration Protocol
DNS	Domain Name Service
EAP	Extensible Authentication Protocol
EIGRP	Enhanced Interior Gateway Routing Protocol
FCP	Fibre Channel Protocol
FTP	File Transfer Protocol
HTTP	Hypertext Transfer Protocol
HTTPS	Hypertext Transfer Protocol Secure
ICA	Independent Computing Architecture
ICMP	Internet Control Message Protocol
IGMP	Internet Group Management Protocol
IGRP	Interior Gateway Routing Protocol
IMAP	Internet Message Access Protocol
IP	Internet Protocol
IPSec	Internet Protocol Security
IPv4	Internet Protocol version 4
IPv6	Internet Protocol version 6
IPX	Internetwork Packet Exchange
IS-IS	Intermediate System to Intermediate System
Kerberos	Kerberos
L2TP	Layer 2 Tunneling Protocol
LDAP	Lightweight Directory Access Protocol
MS-CHAP	Microsoft Challenge-Handshake Authentication Protocol

Acronym	Full Name
NTP	Network Time Protocol
OSPF	Open Shortest Path First
PPP	Point-to-Point Protocol
PPPoE	Point-to-Point Protocol over Ethernet
PPTP	Point-to-Point Tunneling Protocol
PoE	Power over Ethernet
POP3	Post Office Protocol version 3
RADIUS	Remote Authentication Dial-In User Service
RDP	Remote Desktop Protocol
RIP	Routing Information Protocol
RTP	Real-Time Transport Protocol
SCP	Secure Copy Protocol
SDH	Synchronous Digital Hierarchy
SFTP	Secure File Transfer Protocol/SSH File Transfer Protocol
SIP	Session Initiation Protocol
SMTP	Simple Mail Transport Protocol
SNAP	Subnetwork Access Protocol
SNMP	Simple Network Management Protocol
SONET	Synchronous Optical Network
SSH	Secure Shell
SSL	Secure Sockets Layer
STP	Spanning Tree Protocol
TACACS+	Terminal Access Controller Access-Control System Plus
TCP	Transmission Control Protocol
Telnet	Terminal Network
TFTP	Trivial File Transfer Protocol
TKIP	Temporal Key Integrity Protocol
TLS	Transport Layer Security
UDP	User Datagram Protocol
VoIP	Voice over Internet Protocol

Glossary

100-pair cable A telephony cable that combines 100 twisted pairs of wires inside one large, insulated sheath.

110 block A newer type of wiring distribution point used in telephone and network installations.

25-pair cable A telephony cable that consists of 25 twisted pairs of wires inside one common insulating sheath.

60-bit Extended Unique Identifier (EUI-60) A variation on the standard MAC address in which the host extension is 36-bits long rather than 24-bits long, allowing for more host addresses for each manufacturer's organizationally unique identifier (OUI). The EUI-60 format has now been deprecated by the IEEE in favor of EUI-64.

64-bit Extended Unique Identifier (EUI-64) A variation on the standard 48-bit MAC address format in which the host extension is 40-bits long, allowing for more host addresses per OUI. EUI-64 is especially important because IPv6 uses a modified form of this format to create unique interface identifiers out of MAC addresses.

66 block A legacy type of wiring distribution point used in telephone and network installations and patch panels.

802.11x
A standard used to secure wireless LANs that follow the various 802.11 standards.

A

AAA (authentication, authorization, accounting) A network security term that refers to the following:
- *Authentication,* or any process by which an entity's identity is verified
- *Authorization,* or any process used to verify that an entity has permission to perform some activity or has access to some resource
- *Accounting,* or the ability to track various events on a network

Access Control List (ACL) A list of rules or policies programmed into a router or other device to control what can gain access to a network. When used in servers ACLs are used to control what resources are available to specific users or devices. When used in routers and firewalls, ACLs are used to define what protocols are allowed in a network and what content various protocol packets are allowed to bring into the network.

access policies Rules that define who is permitted access to the network, what methods are permitted to gain that access, and which resources users are permitted to access.

accounting The ability to track various events on a network.

ACL See *Access Control List (ACL).*

active hub A type of network connection device that repeats all incoming signals from one connected computer and transmits them out to all of the other connected computers. To function properly, an active hub must be connected directly to a power source.

Address Resolution Protocol (ARP) A protocol used to determine a network host's address. ARP can also refer to a command line tool that is used to display and/or manipulate the ARP table on a network computer.

ad hoc wireless network A network composed of only independent wireless computers in which each device participates in forwarding packets.

ADSL See *asymmetric digital subscriber line (ADSL).*

algorithm A mathematical formula that is applied to a data packet or packet header so that the information contained in the packet or header can be encrypted, compressed, checked for errors, or manipulated in some other fashion.

anomaly-based detection One technique that an *intrusion detection system (IDS)/intrusion protection system (IPS)* uses to detect a network intrusion. Using this method the IDS/IPS reviews *baseline* activity for any anomalies and then deals with any threat it finds according to how the IDS/IPS is programmed.

APIPA See *Automatic Private Internet Protocol Addressing (APIPA).*

Application layer The top layer of the OSI Model. This layer is the closest to the end user. It synchronizes software applications and end-user processes.

application layer firewall A type of network protection device that works with protocols and services located on the Application layer of the TCP/IP protocol stack. Administrators can use Application layer firewalls to block TELNET, DNS, FTP, HTTP, and any other protocols or services located on the Application layer. Such firewalls are also sometimes known as proxy servers.

arp A command line tool used to display and manage the contents of a computer's Address Resolution Protocol (ARP) table.

ARP See *Address Resolution Protocol (ARP).*

ARP ping A *ping* command that uses the *Address Resolution Protocol (ARP)* to issue an "arp request" rather than the Internet Control Message Protocol (ICMP) to issue an "echo request."

arp table A table, generated by the Address Resolution Protocol (ARP), stored in the memory of a network device, which contains the IP addresses and MAC addresses of other network devices on the local subnet with which it has been in contact.

asymmetric digital subscriber line (ADSL) One of the most common forms of high-speed DSL found today that provides a different data throughput for upstream communications than it does for downstream communications.

asymmetric loading A load-balancing methodology that involves varying throughput to a network's devices or segments based on the speed and capacity of the items receiving the data. As a result, some devices will get a heavier workload than others.

asynchronous time division multiplexing A signal multiplexing technique that uses time slots to split a communications signal into different channels. Unlike standard time division multiplexing, the asynchronous variant only splits the signal into the number of channels being used in any given time slot, rather than into all channels, regardless of whether they are in use or not.

Asynchronous Transfer Mode (ATM) A switching technique for telecom networks that uses asynchronous time-division multiplexing to break up communications into small frame-like segments or cells.

attackers People (hackers) who threaten to get something from or do something to end users that the end users don't want them to get or do.

attenuation The gradual weakening of a data signal over time and distance.

authentication The ability to ensure that the data came from a valid source or from where it claims to have come from.

Authentication Header (AH) A security protocol that is part of the IPsec suite. AH provides packet integrity and origin authentication, but it cannot provide encryption.

authorization The ability to verify that an entity has permission to perform some activity or has access to certain resources.

Automatic Private Internet Protocol Addressing (APIPA) A Microsoft Windows feature that acts as a failover in case a problem occurs when trying to connect to an IP address range.

B

bandwidth In networking, a measurement of data transfer capacity, typically measured in multiples of bits per second. Another way of looking at this is to say that bandwidth is the theoretical maximum of how much data a specific cable or other medium can carry.

bandwidth shaper A software or hardware-based network management technology that enables administrators to optimize how a network uses its available bandwidth by managing and/or controlling network utilization.

bandwidth shaping A process that involves managing and/or controlling network usage in order to optimize how a network uses its available bandwidth. Also known as *traffic shaping*.

baseband cable A type of cable that can carry only one signal one way at a time.

baseline A useful piece of documentation that provides a representative sample of how the network is working at a specific point in time.

best practices An assessment recommending the most appropriate method for performing a certain task based on observations of and experience with that task.

binary A system of numerical notation using only 2 digits (1 and 0).

bit error A type of signaling fault that occurs when one or more bits in a particular packet or frame, but not the entire packet, are lost.

bit rate The preset minimum below which the network administrator can guarantee that data will not flow.

bit The basic unit of information storage; a single binary digit that is either 0 or 1. The term bits is also used to describe the encapsulation component when data reaches the Physical layer of the OSI Model.

BNC connector A common type of connector that must be used with *Thin Ethernet (Thinnet) cables to attach stations to a network*.

bonding A technique used to increase network throughput by using two or more *network interface cards (NICs)*, channels, or connections—instead of just one—to push data through.

botnet A group of computers that have been compromised by a single attacker or a group of attackers, giving them a certain level of control over those computers.

bounce The act of reflecting or splitting radio signals off certain surfaces and materials.

bridge A device intended to break up networks into smaller sections. A bridge is similar to a switch, except with fewer ports. Because bridges work on the Data Link layer of the OSI Model, they manage data traffic rather than simply rebroadcast to neighboring network segments.

broadband A type of communications technology that can carry multiple signals simultaneously. See *baseband*.

broadband cable A cable that is able to carry multiple signals simultaneously.

broadcast A method of communication in which one computer sends packets to all available computers on the network. See *multicast and unicast*.

broadcast networking A type of communications network that uses broadcast transmissions to send data across a local network. Ethernet uses this type of networking.

buffering A technology that allows a faster network device to process a request from a slower network device quickly and store it in a region of memory, called a buffer, designed to hold data temporarily while it's being moved from one place to another.

bus network topology A topology in which all computers on the network are tied together by one main cable, called a backbone.

butt set A device used in telephone communications that allows a technician to connect to any phone connection and use that connection like a regular phone, or to test the connection to make sure that it's working.

C

cable tester An electronic device used to verify connections in a network cable.

caching A technology in which a specific memory location is set aside on a network device on which frequently requested information is stored.

caching engine A component of a network optimization system that determines what content to send to the server. It also checks the caching server for a copy of requested content before going to the original source if a copy is not there.

caching server A network server that stores a local copy of content requested from another source (such as an Internet server) and retains it for a specified amount of time.

Carrier Sense Multiple Access with Collision Avoidance (CSMA/CA) A *contention-based access method* used by Ethernet to access wireless networks.

Carrier Sense Multiple Access with Collision Detection (CSMA/CD) The primary *contention-based access method* that Ethernet uses to access wired networks.

cell Small, uniformly-sized packets that Asynchronous Transfer Mode (ATM) and other WAN technologies use to carry data across a network.

certificate A digital document that accompanies a public key to certify the origins of the public key and its validity.

certificate authority A trusted server that issues digital certificates to end users.

Challenge-Handshake Authentication Protocol (CHAP) An authentication method used by *Point-to-Point Protocol (PPP)* to verify the identity of a client after a connection has been successfully established.

channel A specific subrange of radio frequencies that has been set aside within the larger 2.4 GHz range.

channel bonding A data transmission technique that uses two or more channels—instead of just one—to push data through a connection at a higher transfer rate.

Channel Service Unit/Data Service Unit (CSU/DSU) A device used to convert a digital signal from one frame format to another.

CHAP See *Challenge-Handshake Authentication Protocol (CHAP)*.

checksum The process of running an algorithm and comparing it to the stored result.

CIDR See *classless inter-domain routing (CIDR)*.

cipher In cryptography, a mathematical formula or algorithm that encrypts the clear text or plaintext of a message in a data packet or packet header.

circuit switching A communications technology that establishes a dedicated communications channel for the duration of a given transmission.

classful IP addressing A method of determining what portion of an IP address is network ID and what portion of an IP address is used to denote host. This method went out of general use around 1993 but is still in use in some routers and other devices today.

classless inter-domain routing (CIDR) A standard notation that came about as a form of shorthand to indicate what portion of a given IP address is to be used for network ID and what part is to used for host ID.

classless IP addressing A method of determining what portion of an IP address is host and what portion is network that is based solely on the subnet mask.

client/server network One of two major types of LANs in which management of the network is concentrated into one main computer called a server or domain controller. See also *peer-to-peer network*.

coaxial cable A cable containing a center conductor made of copper that is enclosed by a plastic jacket.

collision An event in which two different data frames from two different computers interfere with each other because they were released onto the network at the same time.

collision domain The physical section of a network where the various devices connected to it run the risk of having their signals collide with each other because all the devices present use a shared media.

command-line interface (CLI) A character-based computer interface that requires the user to type text commands into a computer or terminal using a specific syntax to execute programs or perform tasks.

compartmentalization The organization of a network into divisions, designed in such a way that if one section of a network is brought down, the other sections of the network will not be directly affected.

compression A method for compacting data by removing redundant information, so that systems can send more data along the network in a given amount of time without making any changes to the hardware.

connectionless protocol A network communications protocol that does not ask for verification that a data packet has successfully reached its destination.

connection-oriented protocol A type of network communications protocol that asks for verification that a packet has successfully reached its destination before sending another packet out.

connectivity monitoring software A type of software designed to monitor network connections.

connectivity software Any type of software that enables a computer to connect to a network or another computer, either remotely or locally.

content filtering A service that looks at the actual content of the data coming into the device and evaluates it against a predefined set of guidelines about what is allowed through.

contention-based access method A method of accessing a network in which the different nodes on the network segment compete to see which node can send out its packet first.

convergence The time it takes a router to send an update of its routing table to all routers directly connected to it.

crossover cable A cable that connects two devices of the same type. A TIA/EIA 568A (straight-through) cable is used at one end and a TIA/EIA 568B (crossover) cable is used on the other end.

crosstalk An event in which the signal in one wire interferes with the signal in another wire.

CSMA/CA See *carrier sense multiple access with collision avoidance (CSMA/CA)*.

CSMA/CD See *carrier sense multiple access with collision detection (CSMA/CD)*.

CSU/DSU See *Channel Service Unit/Data Service Unit (CSU/DSU)*.

customer premise equipment (CPE) Telecommunications equipment that the customer is responsible for providing when leasing a WAN connection. Some examples would be the CSU/DSU for T-1 and Frame Relay connections and the Network Termination equipment for ISDN connections.

D

data The information that a computer program, software application, or networking device operates on. In the top three levels of the OSI Model (Application, Presentation, and Session layers), the encapsulation unit is referred to as *data*. In all other OSI levels, the encapsulation unit goes by other names. See *bits, frame, packet,* and *segment*.

Data Link layer The second layer of the OSI Model, concerned with protocols and transferring data *frames* between network nodes. This layer is divided into two sub layers: the *Logical Link Control (LLC) sublayer* and the *Media Access Control (MAC) sublayer*.

de-encapsulation The reverse process of *encapsulation*.

definition A unique pattern that identifies a threat such as malicious software or a network attack. Various network and system defense software programs use definitions to detect and identify the virus or attack in order to counter the threat.

delays Events, conditions, and limits in a network that contribute to the slow delivery of data, called latency.

demarc Short for demarcation point, the last point of responsibility for a WAN service provider within a local network infrastructure.

demarc extension The length of copper or fiber cable that begins after the demarc point but still does not reach all the way up to the MDF. Demarc extensions are most often found when the external service enters a building somewhere other than the MDF.

demarcation point The point in which the *Public Switched Telephone Network (PSTN)* service provider comes into a local home or business. Also called demarc for short.

Demilitarized Zone (DMZ) The area created between two firewalls, which functions as a buffer between internal and external networks.

Denial of Service (DoS) attack An attempt by hackers to make a target IP address unavailable to its intended users by launching continuous ping requests from numerous computers so frequently that the target computer's network capacity is overloaded and brought down.

Dense Wavelength Division Multiplexing (DWDM) A type of multiplexing that uses wavelength to place more data on a cable rather than time segments.

DHCP See *Dynamic Host Configuration Protocol (DHCP)*.

DHCP options Specific fields in the DHCP Message packet that carry configuration parameters and control information.

dial-up One of the oldest wide area network communication technologies available that uses a device called a *modem* to connect a computer via a *plain old telephone service (POTS)*.

dig See *Domain Information Groper (dig)*.

digital certificate See *certificate*.

Digital Signal (DS) An alternative term sometimes used to refer to T-connections. The DS is usually followed by a number indicating which T-Connection technology it is the same as.

digital subscriber line (DSL) A type of data communications technology that uses the *Public Switched Telephone Network (PSTN)*, except that it transfers data in digital and at a higher frequency than voice communications do.

Directory Service A locally-run database service that contains information about network users and resources, typically used to control access to those resources.

distance How far data has to travel to get from one point on a network to another.

distance vector routing protocol The simplest type of routing protocol that simply informs its neighbors of its routing table.

documentation Paper or digital records of what devices and cables you have on your network, how the network is configured, where it is located, and policies and procedures used to manage and maintain the network.

Domain Information Groper (dig) A command-line tool used to query DNS servers to gain information about them.

DoS (denial of service) See *denial of service (DoS)*.

downtime The amount of time a network and/or network device is not functioning.

DS See *Digital Signal (DS)*.

DSL See *digital subscriber line (DSL)*.

DWDM *See Dense Wavelength Division Multiplexing (DWDM)*.

dual firewall configuration A network defense mechanism that consists of two separate firewalls, one providing protection to the internal network and one providing protection from the outer network. The area between the firewalls is called a demilitarized zone, or DMZ.

dumpster diving A type of attack in which intruders search through trash looking for personal information that they can use to steal identities or gain access to protected computer systems.

duplex True two-way communicationsbetween two devices that can transmit or receive at the same time.

Dynamic Host Configuration Protocol (DHCP) A protocol developed to allow IP addresses to be assigned dynamically without requiring constant input from the network administrator.

dynamic IP addressing A method of assigning a different IP address each time a user logs in. See also *static IP addressing*.

dynamic routing A type of routing that occurs when a protocol dynamically creates its own routing tables and keeps them updated.

E

E1 A line that can carry a total throughput of 2.048mbps and has 31 channels of 64kbps. and is the European counterpart to T1 lines in the United States.

E3 A line can carry a total throughput of 34.386mbps and has 512 channels of 64kbps. and is the European counterpart to T-3 lines in the United States.

e-Directory The directory services environment created by Novell for use on Linux and other operating systems.

EAP See *Extensible Authentication Protocol (EAP)*.

edutainment Software applications intended to both entertain and educate the people who use them.

electromagnetic interference (EMI) *Noise* that can result in the signal on a data

cable being washed out to the point that the receiving network device cannot understand the packet's contents.

Encapsulating Security Payload (ESP) A security protocol that is part of the IPsec suite. ESP provides packet integrity, origin authentication, and data encryption.

encapsulation The process of taking data from a previous layer of the OSI Model and carrying it forward into the next layer.

encryption A process that allows either the header or the entire data packet to be encoded using a predetermined algorithm in such a way that if an eavesdropper on the network can intercept the data as it's transmitted, he still can't understand it without knowing how to decode it.

Enterprise network A WAN used to connect together offices or buildings in widely dispersed areas to keep all facilities and employees of a company connected to each other.

environmental interference Interference caused by something external to the network.

ESSID mismatch A problem that occurs when the incorrect Extended Service Set Identifier (ESSID) is set up in a wireless device's configuration.

Ethernet One of the oldest and the most widely used LAN technologies in use today that defines numerous wiring and frame header standards.

Ethernet bonding A method of combining the bandwidth from two or more Ethernet links, to push data through a connection at a higher rate.

Ethernet DIX The most widely used Ethernet frame type that can be used directly by the Internet Protocol (IP). Also known as *Ethernet II*.

Ethernet II The most widely used Ethernet frame type that can be used directly by the Internet Protocol (IP). Also known as *Ethernet DIX*.

Ethernet SNAP A revision of the Ethnernet_802.2 Logical Link Control standard that allows a larger number of protocols to run on the network. (SNAP stands for Subnetwork Access Protocol.)

Ethernet_802.2 A revision of Ethernet_802.3 in which an identifier number is included to enable the frame header to work with the Data Link layer of the OSI Model.

Ethernet_802.3 A version of Ethernet, developed by Novell, that doesn't include a Layer 2 Data Link identifier. As a result, it can work only with Novell's IPX packets. See *Novell Ethernet*.

event logs Data files that a system uses to record errors, warning, and informational messages generated by operating system components or applications.

event viewer An application or component found on all current versions of Windows that centralizes all event logs on a local computer.

Evolved High Speed Packet Access (HSPA+) A newer version of HSPA that gives greater downlink and uplink speeds than HSPA.

Extended Unique Identifier (EUI) A variation on the standard 48-bit MAC address in which the host extension portion of the address is allowed to be longer than the conventional 24-bits. The two most common versions of EUI are EUI-60 and EUI-64.

Extensible Authentication Protocol (EAP) An authentication protocol primarily used in wireless communications, although it can also be used with *Point-to-Point Protocol (PPP)* connections.

F

fault tolerance A network's ability to have a portion of itself fail but to still continue to work at some level of functionality.

feeder cable A 25-pair or 100-pair cable that supplies signals to many connected pairs.

File Transfer Protocol (FTP) A protocol used to transfer files across the Internet.

filtering A data manipulation technique that firewalls use to protect a network from malicious attacks by preventing data packets that meet certain criteria from entering into the system or network.

firewall A networking device designed to prevent a hacker or other security threats from entering the network or—barring that—limit the ability of threats to spread through the network using intrusion detection software generally into the firewall device.

fractional T1 A T1 connection that is divided up into 24 channels of 64kbps each.

fraggle attack A type of Denial of Service attack that is similar to a Smurf attack, except that it uses UDP echo replies instead of ICMP replies.

frame What a data *packet* becomes known as when it reaches the Data Link layer

of the OSI Model. See also *bits, data,* and *segment*.

Frame Relay A WAN service designed to connect two points that require only intermittent communication.

frame synchronization A method that a specific frame type or protocol uses to delineate, or define, to the computer the beginning and end of any given frame.

frequency The number of oscillations a signal completes in a specific amount of time, usually measured in hertz.

FTP See *File Transfer Protocol (FTP)*.

full-duplex A category of communication in which both devices can send and receive communication at the same time.

G

gateway proxy server A type of proxy server that passes requests and replies in an unmodified form.

geostationary orbit (GSO) A fixed position above the Earth for seeing the largest area on the planet at one time, located 35,786 kilometers up and along the Earth's equator. This orbit is also sometimes called Geosynchronous orbit (GEO).

geosynchronous orbit (GEO) See *Geostationary orbit (GSO)*.

Graphical User Interface (GUI) A mechanism by which humans interact with a computer using graphics, icons, and windows instead of simple text characters.

gigabits per second (gbps) A data transmission speed of billions of *bits* per second.

H

half-duplex A category of communication in which a device can either send communication or receive communication, but cannot do both at the same time.

hardware firewall A special purpose device that acts as a router with a large number of access control lists (ACLs) built into it, designed to recognize activities that can be interpreted as attacks on the network and counter them.

hardware loopback Not a wiring standard, but a way to redirect data flow so that a computer is tricked into seeing its own output as input.

header A series of data fields added by a protocol at a given OSI model layer to data received from a protocol at the layer above. These data fields contain information that describes what the corresponding layer at the destination system should do with the data.

HDSL See *high-bit-rate digital subscriber line (HDSL)*.

hexadecimal A base 16 numbering system that replaces every four bits with the numerals 0–9 or alphabetic letters A–F. The result is a string of numbers and letters that are much easier for a human to read. See also *binary*.

high availability A goal or concept in network optimization that refers to the ability to keep a network up and running reliably with the least amount of downtime possible.

high bandwidth application A network application that requires a lot of *bandwidth* to function.

high-bit-rate digital subscriber line (HDSL) A type of DSL developed to use twisted-pair copper lines and to carry both voice and data.

High Speed Packet Access (HSPA) HSPA is one of the most widely deployed mobile broadband implementations worldwide.

history log Data files that contain an ongoing record of the activity in a specific device or on the network.

holder The owner of a public key.

hop An interim router on the path between a source end system and a destination end system on an IP network.

host-based firewall A software package that runs on a computer platform and evaluates packets that arrive on the host to determine whether they are malicious.

Host-Based Intrusion Detection System (HIDS) Software firewalls installed on a host computer.

Host-Based Intrusion Prevention System (HIPS) A host-based intrusion detection system (HIDS) that also has the ability to prevent an intrusion or take action against a detected intrusion.

hostname A command-line tool used to display the DNS hostname of the local machine.

host-to-host communications A type of communication session in which one host, such as a workstation, connects to another host. An example of this type of communication is a private chat session.

HSPA See *High Speed Packet Access*.

HSPA+ See *Evolved High Speed Packet Access*.

HTTP See *Hyper-Text Transfer Protocol (HTTP)*.

HTTPS See *Hyper-Text Transfer Protocol Secure (HTTPS)*.

hub A device similar to a *repeater* that works as though it were the bus of a larger network.

hybrid routing protocol An Application layer protocol used to transport Hyper-Text Markup Language (HTML) documents, otherwise known as web pages, over the Internet.

hybrid network topology A hybrid or combination of several network topologies.

Hypertext Transfer Protocol (HTTP) A protocol used to transfer web pages across a network, most commonly the Internet.

Hypertext Transfer Protocol Secure (HTTPS) A technology that, combined with an SSL/TLS protocol, can secure a connection on the Internet or some other unsecure network to ensure that the hyper-text data being transferred over that connection is also secured.

I

identity theft The act of presenting yourself as someone you are not in order to steal in one way or another from the person you are presenting yourself to be.

IDF See *intermediate distribution frame (IDF)*.

IDS See *intrusion detection system (IDS)*.

ifconfig A command-line tool that is the Linux/UNIX equivalent to *ipconfig*.

impedance The electric resistance of a data cable.

infrastructure wireless network A type of wireless network that uses a *wireless access point (WAP)* to control access and is often connected to a larger wired network.

Integrated Services Digital Network (ISDN) A set of standards designed to carry voice, video, data, and other services in a digital format over the *Public Switched Telephone Network (PSTN)*.

Integrated Services Digital Network-Basic Rate Interface (ISDN-BRI) An entry-level version of ISDN, and the most commonly used version, which is able to achieve both upstream and downstream data rates by bonding two 64 kbps channels, called B channels, together for data transmission and a third smaller channel of 16 kbps, called the D channel, for control information.

Integrated Services Digital Network-Primary Rate Interface (ISDN-PRI) A version of ISDN similar to ISDN-BRI except that instead of just two B channels bonded together, it has 23 (in North America) or 30 (in Europe). Additionally, the D channel for ISDN-PRI has a throughput of 64 kbps instead of 16 kbps.

intelligent hub A multiport repeater that has additional features, such as diagnostic and management capabilities.

interference A problem that occurs when strong electromagnetic fields interfere with the electrical impulses used to send signal across a copper wire.

intermediate distribution frame (IDF) A wiring point located in an equipment or telecommunications room and connected to the *main distribution frame (MDF)* by a backbone cable.

Internet A hardware and software infrastructure composed of cables, routers, switches, servers, and other technologies used to make a public worldwide communications system consisting of millions of interconnected private, public, academic, business, and government networks linked by a broad range of technologies.

Internet Key Exchange (IKE) A protocol in the IPSec suite that handles the negotiation of protocols and algorithms and to generate encryption and authentication keys.

Internet layer A layer that occupies more or less the same area on the TCP/IP Model as the *Network layer* does on the OSI Model, and performs pretty much the same job. The Internet layer also performs many of the functions of the *Logical Link Control (LLC)* sublayer of the OSI Model's *Data Link layer*.

Internet Protocol (IP) The primary end-to-end protocol in the TCP/IP suite, providing connectionless service at the network layer. IP is responsible for some of the most critical functions on a TCP/IP network, including addressing, subnetting, and routing.

Internet Protocol Security (IPSec) A suite of protocols designed to provide security options to IP.

Internet service provider (ISP) A company that provides access to the entire Internet.

Internet layer A layer of the TCP/IP Model that routes packets between hosts and across networks.

intrusion detection system (IDS) A passive system that monitors network activity and notifies the network administrator so that he can take steps to stop any suspect activity found on the monitored network.

intrusion protection system (IPS) An active system that monitors network activity and takes steps to stop any questionable activity without involving the network administrator.

ipconfig A command-line tool found in all current versions of Microsoft Windows that is used to display network configuration values.

IPS See *intrusion protection system (IPS)*.

IPSec See *Internet Protocol Security (IPSec)*.

IPv4 One of two main versions of IP that is the oldest and most widely used. The logical addresses used in IPv4 are 32 bits long and are generally expressed in 8-bit digital format.

IPv6 An updated version of IP that is the least widely adopted.

ISDN See *Integrated Services Digital Network (ISDN)*.

J

jitters The difference in the amount of time that two packets take to reach the same destination due to network delays.

K

Kerberos A protocol commonly used to authenticate clients over an unsecured network, most commonly LANs.

kilobits per second (kbps) A data transmission speed of thousands of *bits* per second.

L

L2TP See *Layer 2 Tunneling Protocol (L2TP)*.

last mile The telecommunications link from the customer's demarc point to the first remote switching facility. This telecommunications link can be much less than a mile in urban areas and much more than a mile in rural areas.

latched A type of cable connector that uses a mechanism to hold the connector securely attached to its mate to prevent it from falling out.

latency The time it takes a data packet to move from one designated network location to another.

latency sensitivity A measurement of how well a program or network device can handle *latency*.

Layer 2 Forwarding (L2F) A tunneling protocol developed by Cisco Systems that encapsulates the PPP data generated by virtual private networks for safe transmission over the Internet.

Layer 2 Tunneling Protocol (L2TP) A protocol, designed as an extension of the *Point-to-Point Protocol (PPP)*, that allows PPP to establish a Layer 2 (Data Link layer) connection so that the endpoints can reside on two different devices as long as they are connected by a packet-switched network.

leased line A dedicated digital communications link, such as a T-1, permanently set up between two points, providing the subscriber with a constant level of bandwidth at all times.

light-emitting diode (LED) An electronic device that allows electricity to flow only one way through a circuit and produces light.

Lightweight Directory Access Protocol (LDAP) An application protocol that is the basis for various directory services environments, such as Microsoft's Active Directory and Novell's e-Directory.

link aggregation A *bonding* method in which multiple network cables and ports are used to increase link speed.

Link Control Protocol (LCP) A component of PPP that enables it to establish and configure a data-link layer connection between two systems.

link state routing protocol A major protocol type used by routers to construct their routing tables. Each router constructs a map of all routers on a network and updates those routers with its entire network map.

LLC sublayer See *Logical Link Control (LLC) sublayer.*

load balancer A device used to balance network traffic so that no network sections are overloaded.

load testing A testing methodology that consists of deliberately putting greater than normal demands on a network or the devices on a network to see how they will perform.

local access The ability to gain entry to a computer via a LAN.

local area network (LAN) One of two major categories of data networks. A LAN is limited to a local area. See *wide area network (WAN).*

local connector (LC) A fiber-optic connector that uses a ceramic insert similar to standard-sized fiber-optic connectors.

local loop The loop that encompasses the customer's *demarcation point* and the customer's central office.

logical address A network address used as a kind of placeholder as data is moved across different computers and logically assigned depending on the Network layer protocol in use.

Logical Link Control (LLC) sublayer A sublayer of the OSI Model's *Data Link layer* that in some ways resulted in the creation of the IEEE 802.2 standard.

logical network diagram A diagram that shows how everything works on the network.

logical topology The arrangement of network devices and how they talk to one another. See also *physical topology.*

Long Term Evolution (LTE) A result of the 3rd Generation Partnership Project (also known as 3GPP) that is intended to be a replacement for 3G cellular networking.

Long Term Evolution Advanced (LTE Advanced) An updated version of the LTE standard that fully implements all parts of the 4G standard, making it a "true" 4G unlike its predecessor LTE.

loopback testing A testing methodology that uses a specially designed connector or command to feed data back in through the same port that transmitted it, to make sure that the port is physically functional.

Low Earth orbit (LEO) A type of satellite orbit commonly used for handheld satellite communications and generally considered to be any orbit between 160 kilometers and 2,000 kilometers.

M

MAC address The physical binary address that every network device is given when it is created by its manufacturer. See *physical address.*

MAC address filtering A technology in which only a preprogrammed *MAC address* is allowed access to a specific *wireless access point (WAP).*

MAC sublayer See *Media Access Control (MAC) sublayer.*

macro A type of scripted software subroutine that executes a predetermined series of actions on a selected document or part of a document.

macro virus A type of virus that attaches itself to the documents produced by common software applications in the form of a macro created in the macro language of the affected application document.

main distribution frame (MDF) A wiring point generally used as a reference

point for network and telephone lines. Internal lines are connected to one side; lines for external communications companies connect to the other side.

malicious software A broad category of software programs that includes any application that an attacker can use against a company or an individual.

man-in-the-middle attack A type of cyberattack in which a person positions him- or herself between two other people and eavesdrops digitally on them.

mechanical transfer registered jack (MT-RJ or MTRJ) A type of small form factor (SFF) fiber optic connector.

media Whatever carries communications physically across a network, such as copper wires, radio signals, or fiber optic cables.

Media Access Control (MAC) sublayer A sublayer of the OSI Model's *Data Link layer* that provides access control to the media.

media access unit (MAU) A device used to attach multiple network stations in a token-ring network. Sometimes called a token-ring hub, ring hub, or multistation access unit (MAU).

media converter A device used to convert one type of media to another type, such as converting coaxial to twisted pair or fiber to copper, thus allowing different types of technologies on the same network.

Medium Earth orbit (MEO) A type of orbit between 2,000 and 34,780 kilometers, primarily used for GPS networks.

megabits per second (mbps) A data transmission speed of millions of *bits* per second.

mesh network topology A topology commonly used in a WAN environment in which every computer or building is connected directly to every other computer or building in the network.

message switching A data communications technology in which whole messages are routed to their destinations one hop at a time.

metrics Measurements used by a routing protocol to determine the best routes available to it.

metropolitan area network (MAN) A type of network that generally spans a city or large campus and is between the size of a LAN and a WAN.

MDF See *main distribution frame (MDF).*

Microsoft Challenge-Handshake Authentication Protocol (MS-CHAP) An authentication method similar to standard CHAP and designed to work closely with Microsoft operating systems, specifically the authentication protocols and capabilities built into various Windows operating systems.

modem A device used to modulate (change) an analog signal so that it can encode digital information, or to demodulate the encoded signal so that it can be decoded back into something a computer can read. The term is short for modulator/demodulator.

Molniya orbit A type of orbit between 200 and 1,000 kilometers, designed to cover locations in far northern regions of the Earth.

MS-CHAP See *Microsoft Challenge-Handshake Authentication Protocol (MS-CHAP)*.

mtr See *my traceroute (MTR)*.

multicast A method of communication in which a computer sends packets to multiple computers at one time, but not to all computers on the network. See *broadcast* and *unicast*.

Multilink trunking (MLT) A form of bonding which makes it possible to bind two or more ports together on certain switches to allow for fault tolerance or greater throughput between switches or between a switch and a router. Also known as port bonding.

multimeter A device designed to take several types of measurements, such as voltage, amperage, resistance, and continuity.

multimode fiber (MMF) A type of fiber-optic cable that uses light to communicate a signal and is most often used for shorter-distance applications.

multiprotocol label switching (MPLS) A relatively new standard designed to speed up data transmission across a larger network by attaching labels to frames based on their destination rather than their source so that multiple frames going to the same destination can be grouped together.

my traceroute (MTR) A Linux/UNIX command-line tool that combines the capabilities and functionality of *traceroute* and *ping*.

N

nbtstat A command-line tool used to obtain information about a local machine and the devices it is connected to, based on NetBIOS names.

netstat A command-line tool used to display information about network connections, routing tables, interface statistics, masquerade connections, and multicast memberships.

Network Access Control (NAC) An overall approach to computer security that limits what a host, client, or device can do on a proprietary network.

Network Address Translation (NAT) A technology used to stretch out the limited number of IP addresses available to *IPv4*.

Network as a Service (NaaS) The idea that network services should be sold on a general access basis independent of hardware platform and infrastructure rather than based on a specific company or organization's infrastructure.

network-based firewall A type of firewall residing on the network that prevents a threat from actually entering the network it's protecting.

Network Control Protocol (NCP) A component of PPP that enables it to establish and configure different protocols functioning at the network layer of the OSI reference model.

network diagram An important piece of documentation that shows either the physical layout of a network or its logical layout.

Network Fault Tolerance (NFT) A bonding technique that providesnetwork redundancy.

network interface card (NIC) A basic component that connects a computer to a network. NICs can be found in expansion cards or built directly into a computer's motherboard. NICs are also sometimes called Network Interface Controllers.

network interface controller (NIC) See *network interface card (NIC)*.

Network Interface Device (NID) See *smart jack*.

Network Interface layer The last layer of the TCP/IP Model that does much of the job of the *Media Access Control (MAC) sublayer* of the Data Link layer and the *Physical layer* of the OSI Model.

network intrusion detection system (NIDS) Network software designed to look for evidence of threats and report it. Similar to an *intrusion detection system (IDS)* except that it works for the entire network rather than a single host.

network intrusion prevention system (NIPS) Network software designed to look for evidence of threats, report it, and act to stop the threat. Similar to an *intrusion protection system (IPS)*. NIPSs work on the entire network instead of a single device.

Network layer The layer in the OSI Model responsible for moving data *packets* from one end of the network to the other.

network layer firewall A type of network protection device that functions on the network layer of the OSI model and primarily targets packet communications.

network management A collective term for various actions, procedures, and methods related to monitoring, configuring, maintaining, supporting, and updating a network and its infrastructure.

network monitoring The act of observing a network's activity and determining its current state.

network optimization The process of striking a balance between network performance and network cost.

network security policy A detailed document outlining a large variety of guidelines related to the security of a company or organization's network.

network termination An ISDN device that converts the 4-wire subscriber line to the conventional 2-wire service entering most homes.

network topology The logical or physical layout of a network.

network video application A program or service thatuses conventional data communications technologies and networks to carry video over IP.

network-to-host communications A type of communication that occurs when a router on one network communicates with a host, or workstation on another network. An example of this type of communication is remote access.

network-to-network communications A type of communication that occurs when a router on one network communicates with a router on a different network.

next hop The IP or other protocol address of the next stop along the path to the desired destination.

NIC See *network interface card (NIC)*.

noise Anything that interferes with the transmission of information in a given environment, such as *radio frequency interference (RFI)* or *electromagnetic interference (EMI)*.

Novell Ethernet Another name for the *Ethernet_802.3* frame type, which can run only with Novell's IPX packets.

nslookup A command-line tool used to look up DNS servers.

O

OC-x An optic carrier level in which the X is the actual multiple of the base level called OC-1. This measurement is used in reference to SONET networks.

offloading A load-balancing methodology in which packets containing specific protocols, such as Secure Sockets Layer (SSL) or TCP, are sent to one server while other packets are sent to another.

optical time-domain reflectometer (OTDR) An electronic instrument used to test fiber-optic cables. See also *time-domain reflectometer (TDR)*.

OSI Model A reference framework designed to explain how different networking technologies work together and interact.

OTDR See *optical time-domain reflectometer (ODTR)*.

P

packet What a data *segment* becomes when it reaches the Network layer of the OSI Model. See also *bits, data,* and *frame*.

packet analyzer An application designed to capture network packets and break them apart to analyze and interpret them. These applications are also sometimes referred to as packet sniffers.

packet drop probabilities The chance that a packet will be dropped while it is moving across a network.

packet filter Another term for a Network layer firewall that targets packet traffic.

packet shaping The specific practice of limiting packet types, sources, or content as the means to do *bandwidth shaping*.

packet sniffer A program designed to capture network packets and break them apart to analyze them.

packet switching A network communications technology that opens up connections only long enough for a small data packet to move from one network segment to another.

partial mesh network topology A topology that has all the same advantages as a full mesh topology where redundancy is concerned, but requires fewer connections and therefore costs less.

passive hub A type of cabling nexus—rarely if ever used in networking today—that splits one connection into two or more connections, much as a splitter would. Passive hubs do not need a power source and do not repeat signals. Therefore, they cannot extend the reach of a network.

Passive Optical Network (PON) A point-to-multipoint fiber optics network.

password policies A collection of standardized criteria that make a password acceptable for network use.

patch cable Any cable with a connector on both ends that is used to connect a network device to another network device, to a wall jack, or to a patch panel.

patch panel A rack or wall-mounted structure that houses cable connections.

peer-to-peer network One of two major types of LANs in which each computer in the network acts independent of all the other computers, but can share data and resources such as printers with all computers in the network. See also *client/server network*.

performance In networking, an analysis of how well the network is currently functioning and what can be done to make it function better.

phishing A type of cyberattack that uses various means to trick people into revealing passwords, account numbers, Social Security numbers, and various other sensitive pieces of information.

physical address The binary address that every network device is given when it is created by its manufacturer. See *MAC address*.

Physical layer The bottom level of the OSI Model that deals with all aspects of physically moving data from one computer to the next. This layer covers the network's cables and equipment.

physical network diagram A document that shows where everything on the network is physically located.

physical security An essential practice to protect against unwarranted physical access to a computer or network.

physical topology A network's physical design, including the devices, location of devices, and installation of cables.

ping A program used to determine whether a specific IP address can be reached on the network.

ping testing A testing methodology in which you use the ping command to test the full range of functionality for a specific network connection.

PKI See *public key infrastructure (PKI)*.

plain old telephone service (POTS) The standard land-line telephone service that almost every household in America has access to.

plaintext An unencrypted communication packet, message, or password.

plenum The space between the ceiling of one story and the floor of the next.

plenum-rated cable A cable in which the insulating material that can be run in the plenum is composed of materials that do not release deadly gases when burned.

PoE See *Power over Ethernet (PoE)*.

point-to-multipoint topology A variation of the *point-to-point topology* commonly used in both LANs and WANs. In this type of topology, one device is connected to several other devices.

Point-to-Point Protocol (PPP) A Data Link layer protocol that helps ensure that packets arrive at their destination in sequence without having to find their own routes to the destination.

Point-to-Point Protocol over Ethernet (PPPoE) A protocol that allows PPP to be used in an Ethernet environment.

point-to-point topology A topology commonly used in a WAN environment in which one computer is directly connected to one other computer or device.

Point-to-Point Tunneling Protocol (PPTP) A tunneling protocol developed by Microsoft for use with virtual private networks (VPNs).

policy A component of network management that concerns how the network is documented.

PON See *Passive Optical Network (PON)*.

port A feature of the Transport layer protocols used to determine which upper-layer protocols, services, or processes each data segment is intended for. This is also sometimes called the port address.

port address A unique address inside the computer that is associated with a specific protocol, service, or application.

Port Address Translation (PAT) A technology that *Network Address Translation (NAT)* uses to keep track of which device asks for which piece of information.

port authentication A security methodology in which a device limits access to a specific port to certain MAC addresses.

port bonding A form of bonding which makes it possible to bind two or more ports together on certain switches to allow for fault tolerance or greater throughput between switches or between a switch and a router. Also known as Multilink trunking (MLT).

port mirroring A technique in which a switch sends a copy of the frames from one or more ports on a switch to another port on the same switch.

port scanner A software program designed to search a host or a network server for port addresses that are open but not being used.

port security A function of Cisco switches that is designed to counter the ability of attackers to share a switch port with the legitimate user to gain access to network resources.

port-based authentication See *Port Authentication*.

POTS See *plain old telephone service (POTS)*.

Power over Ethernet (PoE) The protocol used to safely transfer power over Ethernet cabling.

PPP See *Point-to-Point Protocol (PPP)*.

PPPoE See *Point-to-Point Protocol over Ethernet (PPPoE)*.

PPTP See *Point-to-Point Tunneling Protocol (PPTP)*.

Presentation layer The layer in the OSI Model concerned with how *data* is presented to the network.

priority activation is the act of sending data packets to a specific device or segment of a network based on their priority thus ensures that data from more important sources are sent to their destination first.

private branch exchange (PBX) A telephone exchange or switch that serves a private business or office rather than one a phone company owns.

private IP address An IP address that cannot be used on the Internet.

private network A network that is not intended to connect directly to the Internet, but uses an intermediary such as *Network Address Translation (NAT)* to allow access to the Internet.

procedure A component of network management that lays out how the network should be maintained, what should happen should failure or other such issues occur, and how to implement established policies.

propagation The amount of time required for a packet to travel to its destination.

protocol A predefined and widely accepted set of rules used to describe exactly how

a specific task is to work in a network environment.

protocol stack All the protocols from a *protocol suite* currently used to carry out specific functions of network communications within the computer.

protocol suite A group of networking protocols designed to work together to carry out all functions needed for data to be communicated across a network.

PSTN See *Public Switched Telephone Network (PSTN)*.

public IP address An IP address that can be used on the Internet. Public IP addresses must be registered with the Network Information Center. See *private IP address*.

Public Key Infrastructure (PKI) A set of people, policies, software, and equipment needed to handle digital certificates for various applications.

public network A network that is intended to have direct access to the Internet.

Public Switched Telephone Network (PSTN) The entire world-wide telephone network.

punch down tool A hand tool designed to terminate wires on a 110 block or a 66 block.

Q

quality of service (QoS) The mechanisms that allow a network to reserve resources and control how those resources are distributed.

R

radio frequency interference (RFI) Strong radio signals that can interrupt transmission through copper cables.

RADIUS See *Remote Authentication Dial-In User Service (RADIUS)*.

RAIN See *Redundant Array of Independent Nodes (RAIN)*.

RAS See *Remote Access Services (RAS)*.

RDP See *Remote Desktop Protocol (RDP)*.

Recommended Standard 232 (RS-232) The cable standard used for serial data cables connecting data-terminal equipment and data-communications equipment.

redundancy A fault tolerance technique in which a network has standby components online and running, so that if a main component ails, the redundant component can pick up the load seamlessly.

Redundant Array of Independent Nodes (RAIN) A *bonding* technology that protects data stored at the file-system

level by providing redundancy across network nodes much like RAID does across hard disk.

registered jack (RJ) A standardized connector for joining telecommunications or data equipment to a service provider using twisted pair cables.

regulations Rules and guidelines imposed on the company by outside agencies and/or organizations.

reliability A term referring to likelihood thata network will function properly over a given time period.

remote access The ability to gain entry to a computer via a WAN connection.

Remote Authentication Dial-In User Service (RADIUS) A service that provides a method of centralized *AAA (authentication, authorization, accounting)* between a computer and a managed network.

Remote Access Services (RAS) A group of technologies used to facilitate remote access to a computer network.

remote access VPN The most widely known type of VPN, used to connect remote users to a corporate network via a public network, usually the Internet.

Remote Desktop Connection The client program for Microsoft's proprietary Remote Desktop Protocol (RDP).

Remote Desktop Protocol (RDP) A proprietary protocol from Microsoft used to create a graphical interface from one computer to another.

Remote Desktop Service The server program for Microsoft's proprietary Remote Desktop Protocol (RDP).

Remote Shell (RSH) A small computer program used to issue line commands remotely across a network.

repeater A device that repeats a signal it receives in order to rebroadcast it, thus extending the range of a particular cable run.

Request for Comment (RFC) Documents by which all networking standards and protocols are defined.

reverse proxy server A type of proxy server that acts as a front end for a private network's Internet requests and returns the resulting data to clients without identifying its source.

ring topology A networking topology that uses a ring-shaped backbone cable to connect all the computers together. Each node is connected to two other nodes.

rogue access point An unauthorized wireless access point that an attacker has added to a network to facilitate illicit access.

rollover cable A cable used to connect a host computer to a router's console port.

route A command used to view and/or manipulate the routing table on the targeted device by adding or removing static routes.

routed protocol A type of protocol that routers and other network devices can use over a network.

router A networking device that moves packets across a network.

routing protocol A type of protocol used by routers to compile routing tables that *routed protocols* move around the network.

routing table Small databases that routers and other networked devices refer to, to determine which route to take to get to a specific network location.

RS-232 See *Recommended Standard-232 (RS-232)*.

RSH See *Remote Shell (RSH)*.

S

satellite communications A variation on microwave communications in which a ground station communicates to one or more orbiting satellites, and then the satellites communicate to a different ground station or to another orbiting satellite.

scanning services The ability of a firewall to scan packets and protocols for specific threats.

schematics A type of diagram that uses graphic symbols rather than realistic pictures to depict the elements of a computer or network system.

SCP See *Secure Copy Protocol (SCP)*.

SDSL See *symmetric digital subscriber line (SDSL)*.

Secure Copy Protocol (SCP) An SSH extension that encrypts and transports data across network connections.

Secure File Transfer Protocol (SFTP) A means of providing access, transfer, and management of files over secure network communication sessions. Sometimes called SSH File Transfer Protocol (SFTP).

Secure Shell (SSH) A protocol that acts to authenticate the user attempting to gain access to a system via encrypted passwords.

Secure Sockets Layer (SSL) A networking protocol that, in conjunction with other protocols, provides security for Internet-based communications.

Secure Sockets Layer VPN (SSL VPN) A specific implementation of a *virtual private network (VPN)* that allows secure VPN sessions to be set up from within a browser. (SSL stands for Secure Sockets Layer.)

segment What *data* is called after it enters the Transport layer of the OSI Model. See also *bits, frame,* and *packet*.

serial A type of data communication in which a system sends one bit after another out onto the wire or fiber of a network and is interpreted by a network card or other type of interface on the other end. The receiving device reads each 1 or 0 separately and then combines them with others to form data.

server-side compression A feature of PPP that conserves bandwidth by compressing a data stream before transmitting it.

service set identifier (SSID) The network name for a particular *wireless access point (WAP)*.

Session layer The layer in the OSI Model that's responsible for managing the dialog between networked devices.

SFTP See *Secure File Transfer Protocol (SFTP)*.

shielded twisted pair (STP) A type of twisted-pair cable that is shielded by a metallic foil.

short A problem that occurs when wires carrying electrical signals or power physically touch each other after having their insulation worn off at the point where they make contact.

signature Unique patterns of threats, whether viruses or network attacks, that uniquely identify them.

signature-based detection A method in which an *intrusion detection system (IDS)/ intrusion protection system (IPS)* compares incoming activity to a signature database of known attacks. When an activity matches a *signature,* the IDS/IPS responds based on how it's programmed to deal with the malicious activity.

signature identification A process that many firewalls, IDSes, and antivirus programs use to identify threats.

Simple Network Management Protocol version 3 (SNMPv3) A set of protocols developed in the early 1980s and used to manage and monitor complex network systems.

simplex A category of communication in which a device can either broadcast or receive but cannot do both.

single firewall configuration A simple securityconfiguration that uses only one firewall to protect the network.

single-mode fiber (SMF) A very high-speed, long-distance media that consists of a single strand—sometimes two strands—of glass fiber that carries the signals.

site-to-site VPN A type of virtual private networking that connects different company-owned sites to each other via a public network such as the Internet without using dedicated leased lines such as a T-1.

small form factor (SFF) connector A fiber-optic connector that allows more fiber-optic terminations in the same amount of space than its standard-sized counterparts.

Small Office Home Office (SOHO) A special category of small LANs used for home offices or small business offices that only contains a small number of networked devices that are well-integrated with the other network devices in the home or office in which it is set up.

smart jack A special network interface owned by the service provider that joins the service provider's network and the internal network of the customer.

smurf attack A type of Denial of Service attack in which the target server or network is flooded with Internet Control Message Protocol (ICMP) replies.

SNAT See *Source Network Address Translation (SNAT)*.

snips A handheld tool used to cut wire, wire ties, and similar type things.

SNMPv3 See Simple Network Management Protocol version 3 (SNMPv3).

social engineering The manipulation of a person into revealing important information.

SOHO See *Small Office Home Office (SOHO)*.

SONET See *Synchronous Optical Network (SONET)*.

Source Network Address Translation (SNAT) A specific type of NAT in which the router/switch, in charge of the NAT process for the network, changes the source IP address of the request going out of the local network.

Spanning Tree Protocol (STP) The protocol used when multiple switches are employed in the same network.

speed The measure of how much data can move through a network in a given amount of time.

speed test A type of application that is designed to test the amount of data passing through a network in a specific amount of time.

spyware A type of malicious software that is secretly installed on a person's computer to spy on a computer system's user and obtain information that the user would not normally allow to be known without the user being aware that the information is being taken.

square connector (SC) Another name for a *subscriber connector (SC)*.

SSH See *Secure Shell (SSH)*.

SSH File Transfer Protocol (SFTP) See *Secure File Transfer Protocol (SFTP)*.

SSID See *service set identifier (SSID)*.

standards mismatch An event that occurs when all devices on a network do not use the same standard for communication.

star network topology The most commonly used networking topology nowadays, consisting of one central switch, hub, or computer to which all other nodes are connected.

stateful filtering A type of filtering in which the firewall needs to know the state of each connection to be able to filter packets properly.

stateful firewall A type of network protection device stateful packet inspection to filter communications.

stateful inspection A form of packet filtering that is based on a packet's state which includes as IP address, port number, sequence number, what session it is part of, and packet type. Also called stateful packet inspection.

stateful packet inspection See *stateful inspection*.

stateful protocol analysis A technique in which the *intrusion detection system (IDS)/ intrusion protection system (IPS)* analyzes each packet for any settings or flags in its header that do not belong there.

stateless filtering A type of filtering in which each packet is treated as though it were a separate entity, regardless of which session it is a part of or the state of that session. Stateless filtering is faster than *stateful filtering*.

stateless packet inspection A type of packet inspection that treats each packet as if it were a separate entity without regard to session or state.

static IP addressing The oldest way to assign IP addresses in which a network administrator manually assigns all of them. Each user uses the same IP address every time he or she logs in. See *dynamic IP addressing*.

static routing Routing that occurs when routing tables are manually changed or updated as new routes are needed on a network or old routes change.

storage delay A condition in which a packet has to be temporarily stored before it can be transmitted.

straight-through cable A cable used to connect a host to a switch or hub, or a router to a switch or hub.

straight tip (ST) connector A fiber-optic connector that uses a BNC-style attachment mechanism similar to Thinnet that makes connections and disconnections fairly frustration free.

stress testing A testing method in which administrators deliberately load networks or devices beyond the point where they can function properly, to see what will happen.

subnetting The process of taking a given IP address range and breaking it up into smaller pieces so that the range can be used on more than one network.

subscriber connector (SC) A fiber-optic connector that uses a mechanism to hold the connector in securely that prevents it from falling out. Also known as a *square connector (SC)*.

supernetting The process of combining several IP ranges into one larger network.

switch A device used to connect multiple networking devices, usually computers, to form a *local area network (LAN)*.

switch loop A condition in which two or more switches keep sending frames back and forth to each othe and nowhere else on the network.

symmetric digital subscriber line (SDSL) A type of DSL technology that offers the same data rates for both downstream and upstream communications.

Synchronous Digital Hierarchy (SDH) A multiplexing protocol that transfers multiple digital bit streams, also called channels, over fiber-optic cables using either lasers or LEDs. SDH is similar to the SONET technology used United States and Canada.

Synchronous Optical Network (SONET) A standardized multiplexing protocol used to transfer multiple digital bit streams, also called *channels,* over fiber-optic cables.

System Intrusion Detection Software (SIDS) See *Host-Based Intrusion Detection Software (HIDS)*.

System Intrusion Prevention Software (SIPS) See *Host-Based Intrusion Prevention Software (HIPS)*.

system logs Data files maintained by the operating system or components of the operating system that record information about system changes, device changes, system events, driver changes, and other similar types of information.

T

T1 A telecommunication technology that can carry a total of 1,544mbps and has 24 channels of 64kbps. The European equivalent to this technology is E1.

T3 A telecommunication technology that can carry a total of 44.736mbps and has 672 channels of 64kbps. The European equivalent to this technology is E3.

T-Lines A group of technologies that uses digital multiplexing to create a number of smaller 64 kbps channels which administrators can combine or separate as needed.

TCP port A code number assigned to network user sessions or applications when using the TCP protocol to identify the transaction.

TCP/IP Model A networking reference framework based on the TCP/IP Protocol Suite and offered as an alternative to the OSI Model.

TCP/IP Protocol Suite The most commonly used group of protocols designed to work together to carry out all functions needed for data to be communicated across a network.

TDR See *time-domain reflectometer (TDR)*.

Telnet A terminal-emulation tool used to enter commands into another computer or other device remotely across a network.

TELNET (TEerminaL NETwork) A terminal emulation program that provides bidirectional interactive command line access to either a remote or local host.

temperature monitor A device that monitors the temperature of an electric device to avoid having it rise above certain temperatures that render electronic devices unreliable.

Temporal Key Integrity Protocol (TKIP) A suite of algorithms designed to add security on top of what *wired equivalent privacy (WEP)* provides.

terabits per second (tbps) A data transmission speed of trillions of *bits* per second.

Terminal Access Controller Access Control System Plus (TACACS+) A Cisco proprietary protocol used for routers, network access services, and similar devices.

Terminal Services A server component in Windows that is now referred to as Remote Desktop Services.

terminal equipment A telephone, computer, or other device connected to a network.

Terminal Services Client The equivalent of remote desktop connection (RDC) in earlier versions of windows.

test environment A special lab scenario set up to resemble the real environment.

Thin Ethernet (Thinnet) A thin coaxial cable, also known as 10Base-2, that is basically the same as thick coaxial cable except that it measures about a quarter inch in diameter.

throughput The amount of actual data being carried at any given time during a connection.

throughput tester A program or device that is designed to test the amount of data passing through a network in a specific amount of time. See speed test or speed tester.

time division multiplexing A signal multiplexing technique that uses time slots to break a communications signal into a set number of channels.

Time-Domain Reflectometer (TDR) An electronic instrument used to test in-place non-fiber cables for faults.

TKIP See *Temporal Key Integrity Protocol (TKIP)*.

toner probe A tool used to find the end of a long run of cable.

trace route testing A variation on ping testing that displays the name or IP address at which a network connection stops functioning.

traceroute A Linux/UNIX command-line tool that reports back each stop a packet makes on its way to a destination.

tracert Microsoft Windows version of *traceroute*.

traffic shaping A technique for network optimization in which traffic is prioritized based on what type of packet is passing through the network. Also known as *bandwidth shaping*.

translation The ability to take data transmitted by one type of computer and change it so that another type of computer can understand it.

transmission The act of sending data across a network connection.

Transport layer The layer of the OSI Model that is concerned with taking data from higher layers and breaking it down into smaller pieces, called *segments,* that can be sent along to lower layers for actual transmission.

transport mode An operational mode of IPSec in which only the payload or the data in a packet is encrypted.

Trojan horse A malicious program that actively masquerades as a legitimate program that belongs on your computer.

trunking Virtual LAN (VLAN) multiplexing, in which data from multiple VLANs are carried across a single cable or other network link.

tunnel mode An operational mode of IPSec that encrypts the entire packet and then surrounds it with a new IP packet containing a new IP header.

tunneling The process of establishing a connection through a public network that looks like a point-to-point connection to the devices on either end of it, but in reality is not.

U

UDP port A connectionless counterpart of *TCP port.* UDP stands for User Datagram Protocol.

unicast A method of communication in which a computer sends a packet to only one computer at a time. See *broadcast* and *multicast.*

universal serial bus (USB) A default built-in serial bus for most motherboards. It provides moderate transmission speed between peripherals and computers.

unshielded twisted pair (UTP) A twisted-pair cable without outer shielding.

uptime The measure of how long a network and/or its devices have been functioning without any outages or shutdowns.

USB See *universal serial bus (USB).*

User Account Control (UAC) A feature of Windows Vista and Windows 7 that requires confirmation and sometimes administrative passwords to allow certain actions to be taken, even when the person attempting the actions has administrative rights.

V

V.44 A compression standard that attempts to work around the speed limitations for dial-up by compressing data by a factor of 6.

very-high-bit-rate digital subscriber line (VDSL) A version of DSL that can provide very high data-transfer rates. Sometimes seen as VHDSL.

video application A type of application that uses conventional data communication technologies and networks to carry video over IP.

video communications Network communications applications which are used to communicate using video transmissions.

video surveillance A network application which uses cameras to record what is happening in a specific area and transmit the image to a central server location.

virtual circuit switching A technology that combines the efficiency of circuit switching with the flexibility allowed by packet switching.

Virtual Desktop A virtual operating system set up in a virtual environment that allows end users to run software programs.

virtual dial-up A term originally used by Cisco do describe virtual private networks.

virtual LAN (VLAN) A logical subgroup on a *local area network (LAN) created via software inside a switch instead of physical cables. VLANs work in Layer 2 (Data Link layer) of the OSI Model and enable you to break up a much larger network into smaller networks.*

Virtual Network Computing (VNC) An open-source standard that gives users remote access to a desktop computer, much like Microsoft's *Remote Desktop Protocol (RDP).*

Virtual PBX A PBX (private branch exchange) switch that has been virtualized on a network.

virtual private network (VPN) A technology used to establish a connection from a client computer outside a local network to an enterprise LAN using the Internet or other public network. VPN is commonly used by corporations to allow their users to gain remote access to their corporate servers.

Virtual Server Either a server program that has been designed to create and support virtual networks or a server operating system that has been set up in a virtual environment to support some function that a real server would do in a physical network environment.

Virtual Switch A software construct in a virtual environment that is designed to carry out the same function on a virtual network that a physical switch would carry out on a physical network.

virtualization The process by which an operating system and/or network is converted into a software construct that runs inside a host environment independent of the hardware platform being used to support it.

virus A type of malicious software that modifies the code of existing programs in an attempt to cause harm, reproduce itself, and/or to escape detection.

VLAN See *virtual LAN (VLAN)*.

VNC See *virtual network computing (VNC)*.

Voice over Internet Protocol (VoIP) A group of protocols and standards that allow voice communication and multimedia sessions over packet-switched networks using IP.

voltage event recorder A device designed to monitor electrical circuits and look for problems in the electricity coming through the circuit.

VPN See *virtual private network (VPN)*.

VPN concentrator A device created by Cisco that is designed to concentrate multiple *virtual private network (VPN) connections into a single device*.

W

WAN See *wide area network (WAN)*.

WAP See *wireless access point (WAP)*.

Web VPN A specific implementation of virtual private networking that allows secure VPN sessions to be set up from within a browser.

WEP See *Wired Equivalent Privacy (WEP)*.

wide area network (WAN) One of two major categories of data networks. A WAN is very large and can stretch across large geographical areas. See *local area network (LAN)*.

Wi-Fi Protected Access (WPA) A specification or certification that ensures a certain level of security for every wireless device that claims to be WPA.

WiMAX See *Worldwide Interoperability for Microwave Access (WiMAX)*.

wire management Handling network wiring in a neat and well-ordered manner.

Wired Equivalent Privacy (WEP) A deprecated security algorithm for IEEE 802.11 to make wireless communications just as secure and private as wired communications.

wiring schematics A diagram showing where all wires in a network are in relation to the physical layout of the facility the network is located in. This diagram shows the location of the network's cables, not the devices.

wireless access point (WAP) A device that combines the roles of a *switch* and a *router* in smaller wireless networks.

Generally, WAPs are connected to larger networks and allow access to them via wireless media.

World Wide Web (WWW) A service that runs on top of the Internet's infrastructure that allows people to use special client software called a *browser* to view the content of different Internet sites in a more visually appealing manner.

Worldwide Interoperability for Microwave Access (WiMAX) WiMAX is a wireless communications standard that uses microwaves as the communications media of choice.

worm A malicious program that is placed on a computer and then activated.

WPA See *Wi-Fi Protected Access (WPA)*.

X

X11 A part of the underlying components used by the various Linux GUIs, such as GNOME. Other underlying components include X-Windows, and X-Server.

X.25 A technology developed in the 1970s as a means to use packet-switched communications in a WAN environment.

Z

zone-based firewall A type of router firewall based on interface groups instead of on individual interfaces, unlike other firewalls.